3/15

CHICAGO PUBLIC LIBRARY

R05008 81265

D1802042

CHICAGO PUBLIC LIBRARY
PORTAGE-CRAGIN BRANCH
5108 W. BELMONT AVE.   606

Polish Freedom Fighters on American Soil

*Polish Veterans in America
from the Revolutionary War to 1939*

Polish Freedom Fighters on American Soil

*Polish Veterans in America
from the Revolutionary War to 1939*

Teofil Lachowicz

*Translated from the Polish
by Albert Juszczak*

Two Harbors Press
Minneapolis, MN

Copyright © 2011 by Teofil Lachowicz.

Two Harbors Press
212 3rd Avenue North, Suite 290
Minneapolis, MN 55401
612.455.2293
www.TwoHarborsPress.com

All rights reserved. No part of this publication may be reproduced, stored in a retrieval system, or transmitted, in any form or by any means, electronic, mechanical, photocopying, recording, or otherwise, without the prior written permission of the author.

All photos except as indicated otherwise are owned by the Polish Army Veterans Association of America, Inc. (P.A.V.A.).

ISBN-13: 978-1-936198-31-3
ISBN-10: 1-936198-31-2

Originally published as *Weterani polscy w Ameryce do 1939 roku*, by RYTM Press, Warsaw, 2000. Copyright © 2000 Teofil Lachowicz

Translated from the original Polish by Albert Juszczak

Funding for this publication was generously provided by The Polish National Alliance of the U.S. of N.A. and by The Polish Army Veterans Association of America, Inc.

Cover Design and Typeset by Melanie Shellito
Printed in the United States of America

R05008 81265

Table of Contents

Author's Preface to the American Edition vii
Introduction ix

Part I. Polish Veterans in America in the 18th and 19th Centuries 1

**I. The Confederates of Bar, Participants in the
Kościuszko Insurrection and the Napoleonic Wars** 3
The Confederates of Bar in the American Revolution 3
Veterans of the Kościuszko Insurrection 5
Participants in the Napoleonic Wars 6

**II. The November Insurrectionists and the Participants
in the Spring of Nations** 9
Veterans of the November Uprising 9
The Polish Committee in New York 11
At War with the Seminole Indians 18
On Behalf of Canada and Freedom 19
The Society of Poles in America 19
The Veterans of the November Uprising in California 20
In Battles for Texas Independence and in the War with Mexico 24
The Democratic Society of Polish Exiles 26
The Veterans of the November Uprising in the Musical Life of America ... 32
Participants in the Spring of Nations 35

III. Polish Veterans in the American Civil War (1861–1865) 39
On the Side of the Union 39
In the Armies of the Confederacy 45
In Support of the January Uprising 48

IV. January Uprising Participants on American Soil **51**
Through Mexico to the United States 52
The Catholic Clergy 53
Co-Creators of the Most Important Polish American Organizations 55

**Part II. The Contribution of the Polish Emigration in America
to the Regaining of Independence by Poland after World War I** **71**

I. The Polish Emigration in America Prior to World War I **73**
Political Orientations in the First Years of the War 75
On the Way to the Polish Legions 75
Volunteers in the Puławski Legion 79
The Schooling of Military Cadres and Mobilization
Preparations Among the Falcons of America 80
Mobilization of Poles for the American Army 81
Recruitment to the Polish Army in France 82
In the Blue Army in France, 1918–1919 85
On the Way to Poland 89
Battles Over the Borders of the Polish State 89
The Demobilization of Volunteers 90
At War With the Bolsheviks 92
The Female Volunteers from America 94

Part III. The Polish Army Veterans Association of America 1921–1939 .... **113**

I. The Genesis of the Association **115**
The Return to the United States 116
The Former Soldiers of the Blue Army Begin to Organize 119
The First Organizational Groups 121
The Polish Army Veterans Association 123
Further Associations, Clubs and Societies 125
The Beginnings of Coalition Efforts 126
The Founding Convention of the Polish Army Veterans
Association of America 128
The By-Laws and Territorial Development of PAVA 131
General Assemblies of the Polish Army Veterans Association of America 135

Table of Contents

Membership in the Polish Army Veterans Association 136
The National Executive Board of the Polish Army Veterans
Association of America 137
The Districts of the Polish Army Veterans Association of America 138
The Posts of the Polish Army Veterans Association of America 145
Independent Posts 148

**II. Auxiliary Organizations of the Polish Army Veterans
Association of America 153**
The Auxiliary Corps of the Polish Army Veterans Association of America 153
The Alliance of Friends of Polish Army Veterans 157
The Sons and Daughters of Polish Army Veterans 158

III. Organizational Symbolism 163
The Emblem of the Polish Army Veterans Association of America 163
Organizational Decorations of the Polish Army Veterans
Association of America 163
PAVA Member Uniforms 165
The Emblem and Insignia of the Auxiliary Corps 166
The Uniform of the Auxiliary Corps 166
The Uniform of the Sons and Daughters of Polish Army Veterans 166
Insignia of the Alliance of Friends of Polish Army Veterans of America 167

**IV. Social and Cultural Activity of the Polish Army Veterans
Association of America 169**
Mutual Aid 169
War Invalids 169
The Unemployed 183
Veteran Shelters 190
PAVA Efforts to Secure American Veteran Privileges 195
Help in Obtaining U.S. Citizenship 196
Other Forms of Mutual Aid 201
Funerals of PAVA Members 204
Custody of the Graves 206
Culture and Education in PAVA Organizational Life 206
Movies 211

Radio Programs 213
Exhibitions 214
Book and Press Readership 216
Theater 218
Lectures 219
Veteran Orchestras and Schools of Polish Dance 219
Celebrations and Patriotic Manifestations 221

V. PAVA Business Activity 231
How PAVA Posts Conducted Their Business 231
The Independent Economic Activity of PAVA Members 234
The Veterans' Workshop 237
The Information Office 238
PAVA Assets and Finances 238

VI. PAVA's Cooperation With the Socio-Political Émigré Milieu 241
The Role of the Roman Catholic Church in PAVA's Life 241
PAVA and Other Polish-American Organizations 248
The Veterans and the Polish Falcons of America 253
The Polish National Alliance on Behalf of the Veterans 255
Cooperation with the Polish Roman Catholic Union of America 257
Collaboration with the Polish Women's Alliance of America 260
PAVA Contacts with the Alliance of Poles in America and
Other Organizations 261
Cooperation of PAVA with Veteran Organizations in the
United States and Canada 262
Cooperation with Veteran Organizations of Polish Provenance 263
PAVA Collaboration with American Veterans 270
Collaboration with Canadian Veteran Organizations 273

VII. Fighting Anti-Polish Propaganda and Communist Infiltration 277

VIII. PAVA In Poland's Social and Political Life 287
PAVA Business Activities in Poland 289
Agribusiness and the Veteran Shelter in Kuligi 289
The Failure of the Resettlement Operation 291

Contacts with the Highest Authorities in Poland 298
PAVA in the Face of Political Events in Poland 306
PAVA's Relationship to Polish Foreign Policy 318
PAVA Contacts with the Polish Army 323
PAVA Post Nr. 130 in Bydgoszcz 336
Cooperation with Veteran Organizations in Poland 347
Contact with the Union of Hallerians 347
Controversies Concerning the Association of Veterans
of the Former Polish Army in France 354
PAVA and the Federation of Polish Associations
of Defenders of the Fatherland 361
PAVA Contacts with Other Veteran Organizations in Poland 364

Conclusion 369

Addenda 393

Addendum 1.   A List of Polish Insurrectionists (November 1830
Uprising Participants) Who Remained in the USA 395
Addendum 2.   Farewell Address of General Bolesław Roja to Soldiers
Returning to America, April 29, 1920 399
Addendum 3.   The Members of PAVA National Executive Boards,
1921–1940 400
Addendum 4.   PAVA Districts, 1921–1939 401
Addendum 5.   PAVA Posts in the Years 1921–1939 408
Addendum 6.   A Listing of the Number of PAVA Posts in Individual
States in the USA and Canada in 1939 413
Addendum 7.   The Development of Auxiliary Corps Posts Alongside PAVA
in the Years 1928–1940 414
Addendum 8.   PAVA Auxiliary Corps Posts in the Years 1925–1940 415
Addendum 9.   PAVA Auxiliary Corps Governing Boards in the
Years 1928–1940 419
Addendum 10. A Register of Membership in the Friends of the Polish Army
Veterans Alliance Circles at PAVA Posts (May 1940) 420
Addendum 11. Excerpts from the PAVA "Union Regulation" of 1934 421
Addendum 12. Financial Aid of the Polish Roman Catholic Union of
America for Polish Army Veterans, 1921–1937 423

Addendum 13. Military Settlers—Volunteers from America on the Eastern Borderlands in 1932 424
Addendum 14. Address of Prime Minister Wincenty Witos to the Polish Emigration in America, September 22, 1923 425
Addendum 15. Greetings of the President of the Polish Republic 427

Bibliography **429**
I. Archival Sources 429
    Archives in Poland 429
    Archives in the United States of North America 429
II. Printed Sources 431
III. Memoirs and Reminiscences 432
IV. The Press 432
V. Studies 433

Index **437**

Author's Preface
to the American Edition

This book is appearing in English for several reasons. The most important is the opportunity it gives the English-speaking reader to learn little known facts about the history of the Polish ethnic group in the United States of America, and especially about the immigration of Polish soldiers, who made a multi-faceted contribution to the development of this enormous country, from the very beginning of the United States. This concerned economic life, military matters, science and culture. In many instances these were contributions of the highest order.

Polish veterans' organizations, active still today in the United States (mainly concentrating veterans of the Polish Armed Forces from World War II) are slowly dying out due to natural causes. It is an inexorable process and that is why the Polish Army Veterans Association of America (the oldest organization of this type outside Poland, founded in 1921 by Polish veterans from World War I), desiring to leave a lasting imprint, decided to have this book published in English, in order to emphasize that this association is also an American organization, and its members, as American citizens, made their contribution to the building of the highly developed American society. This book is a special monument in their honor.

In today's times—when the inter-governmental relations between Poland and the United States are diametrically different from those which existed before the fall of the communist system in East-Central Europe in 1990—this book takes on a totally different dimension. After 1989 Poland became an independent democratic republic, a state which after fifty years of communist rule could finally decide its own fate. In 1999 Poland became a member of NATO and by this token also a military ally of the United States. In 2004 Poland was accepted as a member of the European Union. Thanks to these positive changes the situation of the Polish state is systematically gaining strength on many levels, its economic and political position is improving; as a result Poland's influence in the international arena is growing as well.

The ties between the United States and Poland are becoming stronger. It has become apparent that in the current global geopolitical situation the United States also needs Poland, evidence of which is the presence of Polish troops in Afghanistan and Iraq. Poland on the other hand needs the support of the United States against the threat from Russia, which wants to restore its former sphere of influence in East-Central Europe. The close cooperation, and the deep trust—essential for the desired results in matters of national defense and other spheres of mutual cooperation—which Poland and the United States have toward each other, would not be possible at the existing high level were it not for the large presence of Americans of Polish descent in America, conscious of their American nationality and their Polish roots, and their long history of proven devotion to the cause of freedom and to America. This book documents the measure of that devotion.

Last but definitely not least, I want to acknowledge those persons and organizations without whose support this book in English would not have been possible. I am cordially grateful to Mr. Wincenty Knapczyk (National Commander of the Polish Army Veterans Association of America)for undertaking the initiative to publish this book in English and for his indefatigable efforts to secure the funds for this purpose. I also want to thank the Polish National Alliance of the United States of North America, headed by Mr. Frank Spula, for financing the publication.

Teofil Lachowicz
New York
2010

Introduction

The United States of America from the beginning of its existence became a promised land for immigrants from around the world. Fleeing economic poverty, religious and political persecution, they found a safe haven in the land of Washington. The New World gave immigrants the freedom they so earnestly sought, and great opportunities to exercise their energies and spirit of enterprise. Among the systematically increasing number of immigrants who came to the United States by various routes, Poles were to be found as well. They were first and foremost former soldiers—participants in the Polish pro-nationalist, pro-independence uprisings of the 18th and 19th centuries—from the Confederates of Bar to the January (1863) insurrectionists. The latter had serious influence on the patriotic upbringing of the young generation of Polish immigrants in America at the end of the 19th and beginning of the 20th centuries. During World War I this fostered the enlistment of more than twenty thousand volunteers in the ranks of Polish military formations, mainly the Polish Army in France. After returning from the war they constituted the largest group of former Polish soldiers to have ever landed on American shores. Their lives, as those of their predecessors from the 18th and 19th centuries, are relatively little known, which results, among others, from lack of a thorough study on the subject. This book is an attempt to fill that void.

There is no one definition of the concept of the veteran. According to the *Encyklopedia powszechna [Universal Encyclopedia]* published by PWN [Polish Scientific Publishers, Warszawa, Poland] there are two definitions of this word. The first is: "in ancient Rome soldiers discharged from the army after having completed their active duty, upon settling near the place of encampment of their legion, played a large role in the economy and Romanization of the province." According to the second: "old, retired soldiers, participants in former wars, insurrections; distinguished and aged activists."

In Poland, in describing someone as a veteran, the second definition is generally applied, but in the United States that name is applied to young people who (having been soldiers) participated in a military campaign. That is how it was in the past and *of Historical Documents and Materials.]* New York, Chicago, 1957 served as the fundamental source for the chapter on the Polish-American community's military participation, as also, Artur L. Waldo's *Sokolstwo. Przednia straż narodu [Polish Falcons of America. The Vanguard of the Nation],* vol. 4, Pittsburgh 1974 and J. Sierociński's *Armia Polska we Francji [The Polish Army in France]* Warsaw 1929. Of postwar publications printed in Poland, the following deserve mention: Witold H. Trawiński's memoirs, *Odyseja Polskiej Armii Błękitnej [The Odyssey of the Polish Blue Army]* Wrocław 1989, and Jacek Praga's study *To dla Ciebie Polsko [For You, Poland]* Warsaw 1998, in which the author cites many new facts about the repatriation of American-born volunteers from the demobilized Polish army from Poland to the United States. The studies of Henryk Wielecki *Pod znakiem srebrnego i złotego orła. Polsko-amerykańskie tradycje wojskowe od XVIII do XX wieku [Under the Silver and Gold Eagle. Polish-American Military Traditions From the 18th to the 20th Century]* Warsaw, 1998 and Dariusz Radziwiłłowicz's *Błękitna Armia. W 80 rocznicę utworzenia [The Blue Army. On the 80th Anniversary of its Founding]* Warsaw, 1997, do not add much that is new to already known facts.

Of American authors who partially undertook the subject described here, Donald E. Pienkos deserves mention. In his work *One Hundred Years Young: A History of the Polish Falcons of America, 1887–1987,* New York, 1987, he presented the hundred year history of Polish Falcons of America together with the military participation of this organization in the years 1912–1919; Stanley R. Pliska in an extensive article in *The Polish Review* titled "The Polish American Army 1917–1921" (vol. IX, No. 3/1965) gave an outline of the history of over 20,000 volunteers in America, who became soldiers of the Polish Army in France.

Of other published sources, primarily the press organs of the Polish Army Veterans Association of America *(The Veteran)* and of the Polish Falcons of America *(Sokół Polski)* and also occasional souvenir journals published by these organizations, were used. These publications printed many memoirs from the period of preparations for military action and recruitment from the years 1917–1919, and also wartime memoirs.

Of archival documents, materials found in the P.A.V.A. archives in New York were used.

In subsequent chapters of Part Two, the process that created the Polish veterans movement in the United States and Canada after the conclusion of World War I is described, from which in 1921 emerged the Polish Army Veterans Association of America—a universal, apolitical organization open for membership to former Polish soldiers from various military formations. In further chapters of the study

Introduction

The United States of America from the beginning of its existence became a promised land for immigrants from around the world. Fleeing economic poverty, religious and political persecution, they found a safe haven in the land of Washington. The New World gave immigrants the freedom they so earnestly sought, and great opportunities to exercise their energies and spirit of enterprise. Among the systematically increasing number of immigrants who came to the United States by various routes, Poles were to be found as well. They were first and foremost former soldiers—participants in the Polish pro-nationalist, pro-independence uprisings of the 18th and 19th centuries—from the Confederates of Bar to the January (1863) insurrectionists. The latter had serious influence on the patriotic upbringing of the young generation of Polish immigrants in America at the end of the 19th and beginning of the 20th centuries. During World War I this fostered the enlistment of more than twenty thousand volunteers in the ranks of Polish military formations, mainly the Polish Army in France. After returning from the war they constituted the largest group of former Polish soldiers to have ever landed on American shores. Their lives, as those of their predecessors from the 18th and 19th centuries, are relatively little known, which results, among others, from lack of a thorough study on the subject. This book is an attempt to fill that void.

There is no one definition of the concept of the veteran. According to the *Encyklopedia powszechna [Universal Encyclopedia]* published by PWN [Polish Scientific Publishers, Warszawa, Poland] there are two definitions of this word. The first is: "in ancient Rome soldiers discharged from the army after having completed their active duty, upon settling near the place of encampment of their legion, played a large role in the economy and Romanization of the province." According to the second: "old, retired soldiers, participants in former wars, insurrections; distinguished and aged activists."

In Poland, in describing someone as a veteran, the second definition is generally applied, but in the United States that name is applied to young people who (having been soldiers) participated in a military campaign. That is how it was in the past and that is the way it is now. It is also applied to participants in the 1990 war with Iraq and the latest conflict with Yugoslavia. The subject of this monograph is the fate of former Polish soldiers who lived in the United States, and for this reason the second criterion has been applied.

Existing books about Polish veterans in the United States are more like vignettes and mainly concern particular persons or veteran groups that had arrived in the United States by various routes in the 18th and 19th century. Tadeusz Kościuszko and Kazimierz Pułaski have been given the most attention in other works, for this reason these two heroes and their achievements on American soil have been given less attention herein, and greater attention has been afforded less well known Poles, who also participated in the war for the independence of this country.

The subject scope of the first part of this work encompasses the fate of specific Polish veteran groups (Confederates of Bar, participants in the Kościuszko Insurrection, in the Napoleonic wars, in the Spring of Nations, and in the January Uprising), who in the 18th and 19th centuries found themselves on American soil of their own volition, or who were transported by force to the United States and neighboring countries, among others to Mexico and Canada. This primarily concerns the veterans of the Napoleonic wars, who as prisoners of war were forcibly drafted into the British Army and later fought with American units on the Canadian American border in the years 1812–1815, and also soldiers of the November Uprising, forcibly deported by the Austrians to the United States in the years 1834–1837. We have also presented here the story of former insurrectionists who voluntarily arrived from England and France, and of participants in the European Spring of Nations.

In the latter chapters of the first part of this book the participation of Polish veterans in the American Civil War of 1861–1865 has been shown, as well as their role in the organizing of the Polish community in the United States and in the education of the younger generation.

In the first part of this study we have also discussed the participation of Poles in the American Civil War of 1861–1865; their role in organizing the Polish community and their influence on the education of the young Polish generation in the United States in the second half of the 19th century.

The first part is based on already existing publications, of which the most useful were the works of Mieczyslaw Haiman, *Ślady polskie w Ameryce [Polish Traces in America],* Chicago, 1938; *Z przeszłości polskiej w Ameryce [From the Polish Past in America],* Buffalo, New York 1927; *Historia udziału Polaków w amerykańskiej wojnie domowej [The History of Polish Participation in the American Civil War]* Chicago 1928; Juliusz Szygowski's *Powstanie polskie w r. 1863 i Stany Zjednoczone*

[The Polish 1863 Uprising and the United States] Paris, 1962; Karol Wachtel's *Polonia w Ameryce [The Polish Ameican Community in America],* Philadelphia, 1944; Artur L. Waldo's *Sokolstwo. Przednia straż narodu [Polish Falcons of America. The Vanguard of the Nation],* volumes 1-3, Pittsburgh 1956–1972; Wacław Kruszka *Historia polska w Ameryce [Polish History in America],* volumes 1-2, Milwaukee, 1937.

Caution is required in using the works of Reverend W. Kruszka and A. L. Waldo, because both authors due to lack of appropriate sources often give free rein to their imagination, which is particularly noticeable in the first volume of the work of the Reverend Kruszka. Nonetheless, their books contain valuable fragments of original sources, which they often cite extensively.

Among the most important works written in Poland are those of the following historians: Jan Pachoński *Polacy na Antylach i w Morzu Karaibskim [Poles in the Antilles and the Caribbean]* Kraków, 1979; Florian Stasik's *Przyczynek do dziejów emigracji politycznej w Stanach Zjednoczonych A.P. po powstaniu listopadowym (1831–1936),* "Problemy Polonii Zagranicznej," *[A Contribution to the History of the Political Immigration to the United States of America after the November Uprising (1831–1936),* "Problems of the Polish Community Abroad." Volume 5, Warsaw, 1966–1967 and *Polska emigracja polityczna w Stanach Zjednoczonych Ameryki 1831–1864 [The Polish Political Immigration in the United States of America, 1831–1864]* Warsaw, 1973; Bogdan Grzeloński's *Polacy w wojnach amerykańskich 1775–1783, 1861–1865 [Poles in the American Wars of 1775–1783, 1861–1865],* Warsaw 1973 (co-author Izabella Rusinowa), *Ameryka w pamiętnikach Polaków. Antologia [America in Polish Memoirs. An Anthology.]* Warsaw, 1975; *Polacy w Stanach Zjednoczonych Ameryki 1776–1865 [Poles in the United States of America, 1776–1865]* Warsaw, 1976; *Do New Yorku, Chicago i San Francisco. Szkice do biografii polsko-amerykańskich [To New York, Chicago and San Francisco. Sketches for Polish-American Biographies.]* Warsaw, 1983.

Polski Słownik Biograficzny [The Polish Biographical Dictionary] also proved very useful in preparing the first part of this study.

The second part gives a general outline of Polish-American military participation during World War One and the wartime lot of over 20,000 volunteers fighting in Polish military formations in Europe, who after Poland won independence in the main returned to America. Their postwar destinies in the United States, Canada and Poland and the activity of the Polish American Veterans Association, the organization founded by them in May 1921 in America, constitute an essential part of this study.

Czyn zbrojny Wychodźstwa polskiego w Ameryce. Zbiór dokumentów i materiałów historycznych [The Military Participation of Polish Émigrés in America. A Collection of Historical Documents and Materials.] New York, Chicago, 1957 served as the fundamental source for the chapter on the Polish-American community's military participation, as also, Artur L. Waldo's *Sokolstwo. Przednia straż narodu [Polish Falcons of America. The Vanguard of the Nation]*, vol. 4, Pittsburgh 1974 and J. Sierociński's *Armia Polska we Francji [The Polish Army in France]* Warsaw 1929. Of postwar publications printed in Poland, the following deserve mention: Witold H. Trawiński's memoirs, *Odyseja Polskiej Armii Błękitnej [The Odyssey of the Polish Blue Army]* Wrocław 1989, and Jacek Praga's study *To dla Ciebie Polsko [For You, Poland]* Warsaw 1998, in which the author cites many new facts about the repatriation of American-born volunteers from the demobilized Polish army from Poland to the United States. The studies of Henryk Wielecki *Pod znakiem srebrnego i złotego orła. Polsko-amerykańskie tradycje wojskowe od XVIII do XX wieku [Under the Silver and Gold Eagle. Polish-American Military Traditions From the 18th to the 20th Century]* Warsaw, 1998 and Dariusz Radziwiłłowicz's *Błękitna Armia. W 80 rocznicę utworzenia [The Blue Army. On the 80th Anniversary of its Founding]* Warsaw, 1997, do not add much that is new to already known facts.

Of American authors who partially undertook the subject described here, Donald E. Pienkos deserves mention. In his work *One Hundred Years Young: A History of the Polish Falcons of America, 1887–1987,* New York, 1987, he presented the hundred year history of Polish Falcons of America together with the military participation of this organization in the years 1912–1919; Stanley R. Pliska in an extensive article in *The Polish Review* titled "The Polish American Army 1917–1921" (vol. IX, No. 3/1965) gave an outline of the history of over 20,000 volunteers in America, who became soldiers of the Polish Army in France.

Of other published sources, primarily the press organs of the Polish Army Veterans Association of America *(The Veteran)* and of the Polish Falcons of America *(Sokół Polski)* and also occasional souvenir journals published by these organizations, were used. These publications printed many memoirs from the period of preparations for military action and recruitment from the years 1917–1919, and also wartime memoirs.

Of archival documents, materials found in the P.A.V.A. archives in New York were used.

In subsequent chapters of Part Two, the process that created the Polish veterans movement in the United States and Canada after the conclusion of World War I is described, from which in 1921 emerged the Polish Army Veterans Association of America—a universal, apolitical organization open for membership to former Polish soldiers from various military formations. In further chapters of the study the wide multi-directional activity of P.A.V.A. in the United States, Canada and Poland is detailed up to the commencement of World War II in September 1939. Special attention was paid to mutual aid, cultural and educational activities, and to the aspiration to maintain the apolitical character of the organization, as well as the generous work on behalf of the independent Polish state.

What emerges is a picture of a numerically small Association, which in less than 20 years gained the reputation of one of the most respected Polish American organizations, taking the lead among the most patriotic elements of the Polish immigration.

The rich materials of the P.A.V.A. archives in New York, and the archives of P.A.V.A. District 6 which are located in the Central Archives of the Polish-American Community in Orchard Lake, Michigan were used in writing the story of the Polish Army Veterans Association of America in the years 1921–1939 (an essential part of this study—Part II, chapters 2–5). Also useful were materials from the collection at the Józef Piłsudski Institute in New York, for instance the materials of Aleksander Dubiński, as well as the collection of General Izydor Modelski from the Hoover Institution at Stanford University.

Of archives in Poland, materials located in the New Documents Archive in Warsaw (I. J. Paderewski's archive, files of Polish diplomatic posts in the United States) and in the Library of the Zakład Narodowy im. Ossolińskich in Wrocław, for instance the manuscripts of Wacław Gąsiorowski, were utilized.

Of printed materials P.A.V.A.'s press organ *Weteran (The Veteran)* proved to be an essential, extremely valuable resource, as did souvenir journals published by the National Executive Board of P.A.V.A. and its individual districts and posts, and also by the Auxiliary Corps which operates alongside P.A.V.A.

Jan Wójcik's and Mieczysław Kierkło's (both of them World War II veterans) study *Z dziejów żołnierza-emigranta. Historia "Haller Post" w New Britain [A History of the Immigrant-Soldier. A History of the "Haller Post" in New Britain]* New Britain, 1991 deserves special mention. It is the only existing history of an individual P.A.V.A. post which has been so thoroughly researched.

Of other works two Master's theses proved useful. Both were written in 1988 at the Catholic University of Lublin, *Wątki religijne w działalności Stowarzyszenia Weteranów Armii Polskiej w latach 1939–1945 [Religious Motifs in the Activity of the Polish Army Veterans Association in the Years 1939–1945]* by Rev. Jerzy Samsel, and *Działalność duchowieństwa w Stowarzyszeniu Weteranów Armii Polskiej w Ameryce w latach 1921–1939 [The Activity of the Clergy in the Polish Army Veterans Association of America in the Years 1921–1939]* by Rev. Zbigniew Choromański.

Marek Jabłonowski's study *Polityczne aspekty ruchu byłych wojskowych w Polsce 1918–1939 [Political Aspects of the Former Servicemen's Movement in Poland 1918–1939]* Warsaw 1989 also proved helpful.

In this monograph, the story of P.A.V.A. was concluded at the outbreak of World War II. At that time new assignments emerged for Polish veterans, which in a fundamental way diverged from those that were accomplished in the period from 1921 to 1939. The Second World War opened new chapters in the life of P.A.V.A., which demands a separate, precise study. What also speaks for this is the fact that in World War II P.A.V.A. actively worked with the Polish Armed Forces in the West, whose soldiers joined this organization after the war. That young, dynamic veteran element sustained the life of this organization for the next several decades and steadfastly supports it to this day.

This book is based on a doctoral dissertation prepared at the Institute of History at the Higher School of Pedagogy in Zielona Góra (currently the University of Zielona Góra) under the direction of Habilitated Professor Marian Eckert, whom I wish to thank for all his advice and invaluable suggestions during its writing. I am grateful to the National Executive Board of the Polish Army Veterans Association of America, with headquarters in New York for employing me as the P.A.V.A. archivist and giving me access to computer equipment, which was of great help in writing this book. I also want to thank Dorota Zając and Kazimierz Rasiej for help in editing the text and Eugeniusz Witt—the P.A.V.A. Adjutant General—for valuable advice and reflections connected with the story of the Polish Army Veterans Association of America.

Separate thanks are due to the Reverend Dr. Roman Nir, the director of the Central Polish American Archives at Orchard Lake, Michigan—for enabling my stay at the institution directed by him and for the help rendered during my archival research there.

I would also like to direct words of gratitude to the Board of the Polish Army Veterans Association of America Foundation, as well as to Danuta and Hieronim Wyszyński and Janina and Czesław Jakubik, private sponsors who financed the publication of the Polish edition of this study.

The Author

A List of States and Their Abbreviations as Used in the Text of This Book

Alabama (AL)
Arizona (AZ)
Arkansas (AR)
California (CA)
Colorado (CO)
Connecticut (CT)
Delaware (DE)
District of Columbia (DC)
Florida (FL)
Georgia (GA)
Idaho (ID)
Illinois (IL)
Indiana (IN)
Iowa (IA)
Kansas (KS)
Kentucky (KY)
Louisiana (LA)
Maine (ME)
Maryland (MD)
Massachusetts (MA)
Michigan (MI)
Minnesota (MN)
Mississippi (MS)
Missouri (MO)
Montana (MT)
Nebraska (NE)
Nevada (NV)
New Hampshire (NH)
New Jersey (NJ)
New Mexico (NM)
New York (NY)
North Carolina (NC)
North Dakota (ND)
Ohio (OH)

Oklahoma (OK)
Oregon (OR)
Pennsylvania (PA)
Rhode Island (RI)
South Carolina (SC)
South Dakota (SD)
Tennessee (TN)
Texas (TX)
Utah (UT)
Vermont (VT)
Virginia (VA)
Washington, D.C. (DC)
West Virginia (WV)
Wisconsin (WI)
Wyoming (WY)

PART I

Polish Veterans in America In the 18th and 19th Centuries

I.
THE CONFEDERATES OF BAR; PARTICIPANTS IN THE KOŚCIUSZKO INSURRECTION AND THE NAPOLEONIC WARS

Polish veteran traditions in America reach back to the second half of the 18th century. At that time a group of Poles, freshly arrived from the territories of the Polish Republic as well as Americans of Polish descent living here for several generations, took part in the war for American independence.

One ought to remember that the first Poles came to the American continent already in 1608. These specialists in the production of glass, tar and charcoal were co-creators of the Jamestown Colony in Virginia. They were pioneers of American industry, and also of democracy, because they successfully organized the first political strike there, demanding voting rights equal to those of the British colonists.

In the next decades further groups of Poles sailed to the continent. They were settlers and also various adventurers and seekers of easy fortune. The climax came in the first half of the 18th century. According to Polish American historian Mieczysław Haiman, at the moment of the outbreak of the war for independence this group numbered about 120 persons.[1]

The Confederates of Bar in the American Revolution

In the American Revolution there was a significant group of several Polish volunteers who arrived here while battles between the colonists and the British Army regulars were already in progress. Among them were veterans of the Bar Confederacy: Colonel Kazimierz Pułaski, Maurycy Beniowski, Captain Kotkowski, Maciej Rogowski and Jan Zieliński, who came to America with the intention of participating on the side of the colonists in the on-going war. General Tadeusz Kościuszko should be added to

---

1   Mieczysław Haiman, *Polacy w walce o niepodległość Ameryki. Szkice historyczne*, *[Poles in the War for America's Independence. Historical Sketches]* Chicago 1931, p. 67.

this group, although he was not a Bar confederate.[2]

The Polish volunteers were among the soldiers who distinguished themselves. Tadeusz Kościuszko became famous as an outstanding specialist in the building of fortifications. He fortified Saratoga and West Point.

Kazimierz Pułaski, called the father of the American cavalry, died as a result of a fatal wound received during a cavalry charge at the Battle of Savannah on October 9, 1779.

Both generals have permanently entered the history of the United States, which has found its reflection in many Polish and American publications. Numerous cities, schools, bridges and military units have been designated with their names; monuments have been built and great parades have been organized in dedication to them.

Among Polish volunteers who participated in the American Revolution six died in battle or as a result of wounds: Kazimierz Pułaski, de Botzen, Colonel Michał Kowacz, Kraszewski, Terlecki and Captain Jan Zieliński.[3]

Poles were also to be found in the French expeditionary corps, the so-called Lauzun Legion, which from 1780 supported George Washington's armies. Among others Captain Jerzy Kwiryn Mieszkowski, Michał Grabowski and Jerzy Uzdowski served in it.

Polish veterans of the war for independence of the United States, after the conclusion of the victorious war with England, did not establish any organizational structures, and only kept in loose social contact. Some of them returned to Europe, for instance T. Kościuszko, Captain Kotkowski, Karol Litomski, Jerzy Kwiryn Mieszkowski, Michał Grabowski and Jerzy Uzdowski.

Karol Litomski, after returning to Poland in 1794, participated in the Kościusko Insurrection. During the Napoleonic wars he served in the Second Regiment of the Polish Lancers. In 1805 he participated in the battle of Austerlitz, where he was wounded. For several years he fought in Spain. In 1812 he participated in Napoleon's expedition to Moscow, took part in the battle of Borodino and was a witness to the burning of Moscow. In 1813 he fought at the Battle of Leipzig. After Napoleon's defeat he stayed in the West, where he became a successful businessman. In 1831 he returned for a short time to Poland to participate in the uprising against Russia. This was his fourth war with Russia. After the defeat of the November Uprising he left his country forever, and joined the ranks of the immigrants. He supposedly emigrated to Brazil with the help of friends, where he spent the last years of his bountiful life.[4]

---

2   B. Grzeloński, I. Rusinowa, *Polacy w wojnach amerykańskich 1775–1783, 1861–1865 [Poles in American Wars 1775–1783, 1861–1865]* Warszawa 1973, pp. 82-116.

3   Ibid. pp. 14-51.

4   Ibid.

Veterans of the Kościuszko Insurrection

It is impossible to even approximate the number of former participants in the Kościuszko Insurrection, whom fate, after the defeat of the insurrection, cast across the ocean. There are no doubts about two names, Tadeusz Kościuszko and his adjutant from the time of the insurrection, Julian Ursyn Niemcewicz. The hero of the American Revolutionary War came here again in 1797 accompanied by his former adjutant, whom he persuaded to make this trip when the latter visited him in St. Petersburg in December of 1796.

Kościuszko and Niemcewicz docked at the port in Philadelphia on August 18, 1797. When the news spread in town, enthusiastic crowds went out to meet the Polish General, whose distinguished contributions were well remembered here. The horses were unhitched from the coach and replaced by enthusiastic people who, with joyous shouts, pulled the coach to the house where he was to live.

The second sojourn of Kościuszko in America lasted not quite one year. He left the United States in secret, and this time for ever, on May 5, 1798 heading to France with a clandestine mission entrusted to him by Thomas Jefferson.[5]

Kościuszko informed his former adjutant about his projected departure only several hours before the ship weighed anchor. Niemcewicz remained alone, but already then, thanks to Kościuszko, he knew many outstanding Americans. Thanks to his extraordinary personality and knowledge of several foreign languages, he made new friends and acquaintances, among whom were Thomas Jefferson (from 1802 President of the United States), John Adams (President of the United States in the years 1798–1802), Albert Gallatin (Secretary of the Treasury), and many generals of the American army. He also got to know George Washington at whose personal invitation he was a guest in his residence from June 2 to 14, 1798. This later bore fruit in the form of one of the first biographies of the President of the United States, *Krótka wiadomość o życiu i sprawach generała Washingtona [A Brief Account of the Life and Affairs of General Washington]* published in Warsaw in the *Pisma [Works]* of Niemcewicz, which were published in the years 1803–1805.

Thanks to money lent to him by Jefferson he visited eleven states of the young country, after which he settled down in Elizabeth, New Jersey, where he earned a living through so-called menial tasks. In 1800 he married a rich American widow, thanks to whom he did not have any financial problems for the rest of his life. Leading a peaceful, regulated mode of living, he could write extensively and travel; among others he undertook a fascinating several-week-long journey to Niagara Falls. The scrupulous journals which he kept at this time are currently an invaluable source of United States history.

---

5   B. Grzeloński, *Polacy w Stanach Zjednoczonych Ameryki 1776–1865 [Poles in the United States of America 1776–1865]* Warsaw 1976, p. 99.

After two years Niemcewicz returned to his native country in order to regulate estate matters after his father's death, and to settle publishing issues. He returned to America in 1804. He left the United States for ever in 1807 at news of the occupation of Polish territory by Napoleon's armies. After arriving in Poland he became active in the political life of the Duchy of Warsaw and after its fall, of the Polish Kingdom created in 1815. He participated in the November 1831 Uprising, and after it's defeat he chose to emigrate. Fortunately, he did not have to battle financial problems, like so many of his co-exiles, because his faithful wife, with whom he maintained steady contact by mail, sent him funds from America up to her death in 1833. In her testament she left him an annual pension of $6,000.[6]

Participants in the Napoleonic Wars
Polish veterans of the Napoleonic wars began arriving in the United States in 1803. They were mainly officers of the Polish legions, which had been ordered by Napoleon Bonaparte to participate in quelling the uprising of the black population of Santo Domingo. After the defeat of the expedition, individual garrisons of Polish-French detachments that were defending themselves against the surrounding insurrectionists surrendered to the British, whose flotilla was blockading the shipment of supplies from France.

Polish soldiers taken prisoner by the British were treated in various ways. Only those were recognized as officers who could show evidence of having an officer's diploma. Those whose diplomas did not arrive in time from the War Department or who lost them during military activity were treated as privates. The officers, after paying a fee, could sail for the United States and from there to France, but only after signing a special declaration that they would not fight against Great Britain. Only a very few took advantage of this opportunity, because the vast majority, after having been stripped of their possessions by the British at the moment of imprisonment, lacked the financial means. Among the lucky ones who were able to save their money and pay for the journey to the United States were: General Kazimierz Małachowski, Captain F. Żymirski, Captain J. Tyssot, F. J. Bogusławski, Lieutenant I. Iwaszkiewicz, Second Lieutenant S. Czekajski, I. Karpiński, M. Kowalski, K. J. Narwoyn, J. Wójcikiewicz, J. R. Jurkiewicz, T. Urbański, M. Oyrzanowski, K. Emerych, and F. Truskolaski. Almost all of them, after a brief stay in the United States, sailed for France. S. Czekajski found a job in a goldsmith shop in Philadelphia and decided to remain in that city for good.[7]

---

6   Ibid., pp. 104-105.
7   J. Pachoński, *Polacy na Antylach i Morzu Karaibskim [Poles in the Antilles and the Caribbean]* Kraków: 1979, 190-197.

Of the Polish prisoners who were in British captivity, not only in the Caribbean, but earlier in Italy and Spain (veterans of the Kościuszko Insurrection were also among them) the worst lot befell the rank and file, the junior officers and those who were not recognized as officers. They were quartered in old ships that had been beached. That is how they were treated on the shores of England, Wales and Scotland. In the Caribbean these wrecks stood anchored near the shore, and were not guarded because the British believed that the sharks did a splendid job as sentries. Stanisław Schnuer-Pepłowski, a historian of the Polish legions in Santo Domingo, wrote about the conditions which existed on these ship prisons:

"The British treated their war prisoners worse than their cattle. They were kept in strict confinement on pontoons, where, due to lack of air, and because of humidity and dirt, smallpox, scurvy and a multitude of skin diseases were rampant. They were fed stinking food. Many soldiers preferred death by hunger than this horrible food. Even at night these unfortunates had their peace disturbed by the frolics of rats and billions of bugs nesting in the half rotted ships."[8]

No wonder that after some time the prisoners accepted the repeated English offer to join their ranks, because that was practically the only opportunity to escape the horrendous conditions. Mieczysław Haiman estimates the number of Poles incorporated into British ranks at about 600 and lists approximately 529 names, which he prepared on the basis of official English sources from the London War Office, which preserved the register of the De Watteville Regiment. It was prepared before the regiment reached Canada in the summer of 1813. Almost all the drafted Poles served in this regiment.

The Polish prisoners (incorporated into the British detachments, where the minimum hitch was seven years) participated in the years 1813–1850 in the so-called second war for independence of the United States, which took place mainly near the Canadian border. During that conflict many of them deserted to the side of the American army. Deserters who were caught were at first sentenced to lifelong service in the British detachments. Later, they were punished by death, for instance on October 23, 1813 private J. Danielkowicz was shot in Kingston.

In the summer of 1814 the Poles incorporated into the De Watteville Regiment (the name of the Regiment came from the last name of its commander-owner) participated among others in the fruitless two-month siege of the American Fort Erie. At that time, one of the British officers noticed that the Poles had the ability to take care of themselves under difficult conditions. He wrote "... and so when our boys [i.e. the British] had nothing better than portions of salted meat baked on the ends

---

8 *Opowieści historyczne [Historical Narratives]* Lwów: 1894, p. 226

of their ramrods, those [i.e., the Poles] as practical botanists sent out one soldier to gather a sack full of wild herbs, which together with a little bit of flour changed their portions into a kettle of excellent soup."[9]

After the conclusion of the war, which turned out unfavorably for the British, some of the Poles settled for good in Canada, because they were given land by decision of the British government. Military colonies on the St. Francis River in the province of Québec, and on the Rideau River in Ontario were designated as their place of settlement.[10]

The group of Polish veterans (former participants in the Napoleonic wars, whom fate cast on American soil) included also Wawrzyniec [Lawrence] Gębicki, a Chevalier of the French Legion of Honor, who had been wounded in the battle of Waterloo in 1815 and had been taken into British captivity there. In England he was fortunate to find employment in the Silversmith company, which specialized in the production of knives. After having learned this craft he sailed for America in 1824. In New York he found employment at the Gotman knife factory. After several years he became a partner in the firm and in 1832 (after the death of the owner and a legal settlement with the widow and heirs) he took over the company. From that time, he became a great support for fellow Poles coming to America after the defeat of the November Uprising (of 1830). Gębicki assisted them financially, bought clothes and food and helped them find employment. He founded a shelter and a Polish school for the children of veterans. He died on November 20, 1853.[11]

---

9   M. Haiman, *Ślady polskie w Ameryce [Polish Traces in America]* Chicago 1938, p. 50. W. Dunlop, *Recollections of the American War 1812–1814,* Toronto 1906, p. 74.

10 M. Haiman, op. cit, pp. 51-52.

11 W. Kruszka, *Historia polska w Ameryce [Polish History in America]* vol. I, Milwaukee, pp. 272-273.

II.
THE NOVEMBER INSURRECTIONISTS AND THE PARTICIPANTS IN THE SPRING OF NATIONS

Veterans of the November Uprising
The next sizable group of former Polish soldiers appeared in America in the years 1832–1834. These were veterans of the November Uprising, who by various routes, and after many adventures, made it to the land of Washington.

According to the contemporary American press the first was Major Józef Hordyński of the 10th Regiment of Lithuanian Uhlans. The *New York Whig* of November 23, 1831 wrote about his insurrectionist activities. He had fought in Lithuania in the Corps of General Ignacy Giełgud, with whom (fleeing before the overwhelming Russian forces) he crossed the Prussian border, where he was imprisoned at Piława. After a successful escape, he was able to board an American sail ship, the "Eliza Ann" at the local port, which transported him to Boston. The natives of Boston accepted him with unusual cordiality. He received a large sum of money from one of them. The local press took up a collection to assist the Polish patriot. After not quite one year in the United States Hordyński wrote, in English, a history of the November Uprising: *History of the Polish Revolution and the Events of the Campaign*. He dedicated this work of almost 500 printed pages to the American nation.[1] The book met with tremendous interest and its printing of 5,000 copies quickly sold out. Favorable critical reviews, which appeared in the Boston press were instrumental in the success of Hordyński's book on the American market. The author himself did not see the publication of his work, because he returned to France in the summer of 1832. Later, with Colonel Józef Zaliwski, he participated in an ill-fated expedition to Poland, with the goal of inciting an uprising. During his not quite one year's sojourn in the United States Major Hordyński kept a diary, which

---

1 "Historia gruntów polskich w stanie Illinois" ["A History of Polish Lands in the State of Illinois"] in: M. Haiman, *Z przeszłości polskiej w Ameryce [From the Polish Past in America]* Buffalo and New York 1927, pp. 189-216.

he began writing on September 22, 1831 on board the American ship while he was sailing for America. This diary ends on May 11, 1832.[2]

The next veteran who arrived in America was Dr. Paul F. Eve, a military surgeon. The only American who participated in the November Uprising, he was a Chevalier of the highest Polish Order of Virtuti Militari. The *New York Whig* on January 6, 1832 printed his article about the cholera epidemic brought to Europe by the Russian soldiers of Field Marshal Ivan Paskevich, which dampened the Polish independence initiative.[3]

In the middle of 1832, the Polish Democratic Society in Paris with Joachim Lelewel at its head, turned to the president of the United States with a request to allow the settlement in America of approximately 3,000 to 4,000 Polish exiles and assure them transportation across the Atlantic. A memorandum on this matter was handed to the President by Dr. Samuel Gordon Howe, who for some time had been imprisoned by Prussian authorities for organizing help for interned Polish insurrectionists, unfortunately without results. Nonetheless, successive Polish veterans arrived in America. Some even with their families. In November 1832 the New York newspaper *New York American* wrote about the sizable number of them in the city and about the great poverty in which they lived. Many of them, after pawning the last valuables brought from Poland, lived from day to day. Others, in order to get small sums of money, sold unnecessary parts of their wardrobe. According to the newspaper this group allegedly included a relative of General Kazimierz Pułaski.[4]

The largest group of veterans of the Polish Insurrection was deported overseas by the Austrian government, which in this manner got rid of an inconvenient ballast—the interned participants of the Polish independence movement, who had all been placed in prison at Brno in Moravia. After the Russians declared amnesty on November 1, 1831 for participants of the November Uprising, the Austrians tried to persuade the Poles to return to their native regions. Many who came from the territory of the Polish Kingdom decided to take this step. The Czar's amnesty did not include Poles who had joined the uprising but came from the so-called seized lands, that is, the former Eastern borderlands of the Republic of Poland, which Russia had grabbed as a result of the partitions of Poland. This group of insurrectionists

---

[2] Jerzy Lerski, ed., *Amerykański dziennik mjr. Hordyńskiego [The American Diary of Major Hordyński]* Paris: 1955. in: B. Grzeloński, *Ameryka w pamiętnikach Polaków. Antologia. [America in the Memoirs of Poles. An Anthology]* Warsaw: 1975, pp. 54-71.

[3] M. Haiman, "Dr. Paul Fitzsimmons Eve. Uczestnik Powstania Listopadowego" in: *Polacy wśród pionierów Ameryki* ["Dr. Paul Fitzsimmons Eve. Participant in the November Uprising" in: *Poles Among the American Pioneers*] pp. 217-222.

[4] Ibid.

categorically refused to return since they had absolutely no illusions about what would happen to them.⁵

The Austrians gave the Poles a choice: to be handed over to the Russians or to leave for the United States of America at Austrian expense. Not wanting to find themselves in Siberia, the Poles chose the other option. They walked on foot and under guard from Brno to Trieste which is on the Adriatic Sea. There they were loaded onto Austrian ships on which they undertook the difficult winter passage to America.

The Polish Committee in New York

On March 28, 1834 two Austrian frigates, the "Gueriera" and the "Hebe" docked in New York with 234 former Polish insurgents,⁶ which became a great sensation in the city. Huge crowds of curious onlookers gathered at the port wanting to see with their own eyes those who had given armed resistance to Russian power, fighting for their freedom.

While still on board the frigate "Hebe" on April 1, 1834 before debarking, The Poles elected a committee, which took the name The Polish Committee in New York. Its members included: Captain Ludwik Bańczakiewicz—President, Reverend Ludwik Jeżykowicz—Treasurer, and members: Marcin Rosienkiewicz, Jan Rychlicki, Lieutenant Józef Kossowski, Second Lieutenant Jan Hiż, Feliks Gwinczewski. Soon Lt. Wojciech Konarzewski joined them as secretary.⁷

The Polish Committee in New York was the first known organizational formation which Polish veterans created on American soil. It was the first Polish organization founded in the United States of America.

The committee sent a delegation to the mayor of New York. Second Lt. Julian Juźwikiewicz mentioned this in his memoirs. "The three members of our committee who were sent to the president of the City of New York with a question as to what awaits us in this country, brought back the following news that not only Poles, but every person coming to this country has a right to the freedoms common to all the inhabitants, and the livelihood lies in all the industries and parts of this country, which are open to everyone. Such a cold declaration by the president did not augur much good for the Polish nobility, who had been taught to live only by the work of their peasants."⁸

---

5   F. Stasik, "Przycznek do dziejów polskiej emigracji politycznej w Stanach Zjednoczonych A.P. po powstaniu listopadowym (1831–1836)" in: *Problemy Polonii Zagranicznej* ["Contributions to the History of the Polish Political Emigration to the United States of North America (1831–1836)" in: *Issues of the Polish Community Abroad*] vol. V, Warsaw: 1966–67, p. 32

6   Ibid, p. 35.

7   J. Juźwikiewicz, "Polacy w Ameryce, czyli Pamiętniki 15-to miesięcznego pobytu" ["Poles in America, or Memoirs of a 15 Month Sojourn"] Paris: 1836 in: M. Haiman, *Ślady polskie w Ameryce [Polish Traces in America]* Chicago: 1938, pp. 100-101, 126-128.

8   Ibid., p. 102.

Before leaving the ships on April 2, 1834 everyone received $40 from the Austrians. Thanks to this they had funds for the first few weeks. All of them also taxed themselves toward the support of the Polish committee which, in order to raise its prestige, took up offices in a better hotel. At the same time, the residents of New York founded a civic committee with former Senator Albert Gallatin at its head. He organized events, the income of which was designated to support the Polish patriots. At first, this aid was the only source of support for the former insurrectionists, who realized that they had to depend on themselves alone, for their future. Their situation (as was true of most immigrants, whom fate cast onto American soil) was not easy. The Polish exiles (as they called themselves) before the outbreak of the uprising were in the main educated and often prosperous individuals. But they did not know English. They also were not used to physical labor. Upon leaving Poland they lost everything: their estates, their positions, their social standing and their families.

The Polish Committee in New York had great luck. Dr. Charles Kraitzir appeared before it. He was a Hungarian physician who had participated in the November Uprising as a volunteer. After the uprising he shared the fate of the Polish emigrants. In Paris he was a member of the Polish Democratic Society. He came to America in 1833. He proposed that help for the Polish insurrectionists be sought in Washington. On his initiative, the Polish committee, utilizing the very favorable attitude of the American community toward the Poles, sent a memorandum to the Congress of the United States on April 9, 1834 requesting that the Polish veterans be granted land under favorable conditions substantiating this as follows. "Almost all the rank and file and officers of junior grades were farmers. Most of them lived in the countryside, understand agriculture and want to work in the same vein. Some of the younger ones were students when the uprising began and turned out to be the greatest patriots, which is evidenced by the history of the Polish war... if the Constitution of the United States permits settlers to be granted the privileges of American citizenship, this would be the strongest stimulus for them so they could try to become useful to their new country."

It was decided to send a delegation of the committee (L. Bańczakiewicz, M. Rosienkiewicz, and Dr. Ch. Kraitzir) to Washington in order to seek support from the highest authorities.

The several day stay of the delegation in the capital proved successful. Congress and the Senate acted favorably on the presented memorandum. On May 12, 1834 the Senate passed the following resolution; "A Bill Granting Lands to Certain Polish Exiles."

The bill granted 640 acres of land in the states of Illinois and Wisconsin to 235 former revolutionaries. The Poles were to pay $1.25 per acre after 10 years from the day of settlement on their designated plot.[9]

This was a great success for the Polish committee, because barely 6 weeks had passed since the Poles had landed on American soil!

Major Ludwik Chłopicki (a relative of General Józef Chłopicki) and Jan Prechal, sent in the name of the Committee to the State of Illinois spent the next three years searching for and surveying the land on which the Polish exiles might settle. Their efforts often ended in conflict with local authorities and other settlers.

The Polish veterans were in no condition to make use of the bounty afforded them by the bill passed with them in mind by the Congress of the United States. Lack of money proved to be a major obstacle. They had no way of paying for the distant journey to the state of Illinois; they were unable to acquire agricultural tools and seeds and to get the necessary supply of food for the most difficult initial period.

Attempts to change the bill and introduce amendments allowing the Poles to get loans for settlement ended in failure. The executive decisions to this bill started to complicate themselves and drag out without any prospects for a quick conclusion.

As the interest and generosity of the American population began to wane, the specter of poverty and fear for the future became an inseparable companion of the Polish exiles. They were also oppressed by a great longing for their native country and their families.

The mounting financial difficulties also unfavorably influenced the activity of the Polish Committee. Second Lt. J. Juźwikiewicz mentioned this: "Kraytsir gave salutary advice, but unfortunately as no where and at no time, so also here there was no agreement among our people—they started forming opposing parties, and persecuting one another."[10]

As a result, several months later the Polish Committee in New York ceased to exist. Its members scattered in various directions, looking for employment. Some maintained steady contact trying, despite the distance, to continue activity begun in New York. Among other activities they prepared and signed letters which were sent to American relief committees and to the Senate and Congress in Washington. In these letters they used various names for the organizational body that they represented: The National Committee of Poles in the United States of

---

9   M. Haiman, *Polish Traces in America*, Chicago: 1938, pp. 102-104; "Historia gruntów polskich w stanie Illinois in: *Z przeszłości polskiej w Ameryce*" ["A History of Polish Lands in the State of Illinois" in: *From the Polish Past in America*] Buffalo: 1927, pp. 180-216.

10 J. Juźwikiewicz, "Polacy w Ameryce, czyli Pamiętnik 15to Miesięcznego pobytu" ["Poles in America or a Memoir of a 15 Month Sojourn"] Paris, 1836, in: M. Haiman, *Ślady polskie w Ameryce [Polish Traces in America]* Chicago: 1938, p. 104.

North America (letter of December 23, 1834 Albert Gallatin),[11] The Committee of Polish Exiles (memorandum to the Senate and Congress in February 1840).[12] Nonetheless these letters were always signed by the same three people: Marcin Rosinkiewicz, Feliks Gwinczewski and Dr. Charles Kraitzir. The former President of the Polish Committee in New York, Ludwik Bańczakiewicz, died of yellow fever about 1840.[13]

Before that happened, however, the veterans (impatient with waiting for changes in the bill which would have allowed them to get the loans for settlement), gradually started leaving New York looking for ways to earn a living until such time as they would he able to settle on the lands promised to them. Their destinies varied.

The story of the group of veterans, who in the first months of 1835 arrived in New Orleans, turned out to be tragic. About 20 of them decided to go to Mexico, hoping for a positive change of fortune. Without money, food supplies, or a guide, they started out in the direction of Texas. The rambling group was attacked by Indians. The Poles, armed with rifles, put up a stiff resistance as a result of which the attackers backed off with large losses. Two Poles were killed, the rest were more or less gravely wounded. Due to loss of blood, lack of medical help, thirst and hunger only one veteran from the group survived. He was able to return to New Orleans and tell the story of the tragedy.[14]

Another small group of veterans after leaving New York made it to Buffalo, where they settled for good. The daily newspaper *Western Star* mentioned them in an article of July 23, 1834: "two of these brave but unfortunate Polish exiles, Jan Hiż [a former member of the Polish Committee in New York—T. L.] and Grzegorz Sadłowski, officers of the Polish army came to our city and want to find jobs."[15]

A year later another local newspaper the *Daily Commercial Advertiser* wrote about two Poles who settled in Buffalo. They were Major Mogilski and Antoni Węgierski, also an officer of the Polish army, who earned a living in this city by teaching French.[16]

The largest group of Polish revolutionaries who left New York went to the northwest, hoping that they would soon be able to settle on the government lands promised to them in the state of Illinois.

---

11 Ibid., ppp. 140-141.
12 W. Kruszka, *Historia polska w Ameryce [Polish History in America]* Vol. I, Pittsburgh, pp. 266-267.
13 Ibid., p. 127.
14 M. Haiman, *"Z przeszłości polskiej w Ameryce" [From the Polish Past in America]* Buffalo and New York: 1927, pp. 180-216.
15 W. Kruszka, *Historia polska w Ameryce [Polish History in the United States]* vol. II, Pittsburgh: 1978, p.102.
16 Ibid.

Penniless, they had to travel on foot hiring themselves out for work in settlements and towns along the way. However, the huge expanse was thinly settled by people of European extraction and the wooded terrains were inhabited by Indians. Some of the veterans (unable to cope with the further journey) decided to return to New York. The Paris-based *Polish Emigration Weekly* wrote of their adventures. It published an article dated November 30, 1834 based on letters received from America: "Reading the freshly received letters from America one's heart cracks at the thought of our brothers in that country: there is nothing more sad than the picture of the indifference of the inhabitants of the deep provinces toward the unfortunate, homeless Polish wanderers. They know neither the family background, nor the misfortunes of the Poles, and at inns along the roads, at the site of their bedraggled appearance, doors are closed in the faces of the wanderers, tormented with hunger, and strife. ... the wild natives show the most compassion to the Poles, seeing their afflicted faces. They bring them aid and invite them to their family fires. We have come to understand here what the so-called wild man is, and the degree of inertia to which self-interest leads, of desire for profit, that ideal of perfection of the civilized American. They don't care that as mostly military men or school-age youth, we need time to learn some kind of trade... we are worse than the Negroes, under whom we often work in domestic service situations. We are placed under their supervision because they know the native language."

Some during this wandering, unable to cope with the difficulties and being at the very ends of their tethers, took their own life. Such a case was published in the *Chronicle of the Polish Emigration* (Paris, February 20, 1835), citing an anonymous letter which came from New York, dated December 29, 1834: "I had written to you in my first letter above the thirty who went on foot to the promised land, that is to the colonies, among whom was Rostkowski. This man at his advanced age made that trip on foot from Philadelphia all the way to the province of Ohio, and outside the village of Columbus he slit his own throat with his shaving razor, out of desperation and due to want."[17]

Unfortunately, legal complications which arose regarding the lands granted to the Polish veterans due to settlement there by other colonists, caused the deterioration of the situation of the Poles who were unable to get there in time. When some of them finally arrived it became apparent that those lands had already been settled by other people.

One of those who finally made it from New York after a journey that lasted two years and three months was Wincenty Dziewanowski, a Major of the Polish Armed Forces during the November Uprising. In his diary, under the date August 4, 1836

---

17 M. Haiman, *Ślady polskie w Ameryce. Szkice historyczne. [Polish Traces in America. Historical Sketches.]* Chicago:1938, p. 151.

he wrote: "Kent, the land promised to the Poles, all of which I toured. Very beautiful, but many inhabitants."[18]

The Poles were disenchanted by this state of affairs. Without the funds to seek redress of their rights in court, they took up permanent settlements in small groups in St. Louis, Louisville, Cincinnati, West Troy, Lowell, Boston and other localities, earning their livelihood, mainly by physical labor.[19] One of them, officer Jan Rychlicki—a former member of the Polish Committee in New York—settled in St. Louis, where for many years he worked as an engineer in the federal surveying office. He gained significant social status and general respect. He died on December 22, 1898 at the age of 91.[20]

Major Ludwik Chłopicki, who had participated in the staking out of plots for the Polish veterans in the State of Illinois, was unable to help them. He settled in the town of Peoria. Later, he moved for good to the settlement of El Paso, where to the end of his days he ran a hotel. He was valued in the area as "a person of great culture, educated, and every inch the gentleman."[21]

Veterans living in New York, in order to stay alive, were forced to take the most menial jobs, working in the city and surrounding areas. One of the former insurrectionists wrote about this in a letter to a friend living in France: "aside from deepest desperation I feel like laughing when I recall Olszański, who keeps being pushed around now by the servants in the house, now by the Negroes. This one tells him to shine shoes, that one tells him to empty the urinals. Or when I see old Morawski removing rubble in a wheelbarrow out onto the street and then when I see the kids peeing in his wheelbarrow, or Komar carrying a huge pipe across town and behind him several hundred boys shouting Pole! Pole!

"Purowski handled the meanest jobs in the house and the stables and fat Fakutowicz, digging a ditch for the city's mayor out in the suburbs got bogged down so badly in the muck that they barely pulled him out with ropes. I got a place in a tannery at first. I kept working there even after boils formed on my hands. That's minor, but today, when I was told to climb up on the roof to lay roof tiles and fell to the ground I felt so bad that I just chucked everything and now I am like a madman without room and board, and if it were not for the thought that I might still somehow be useful to my country then I might even try ending this miserable life. In this town

---

18 W. Kruszka, *Polish History in America*, vol. II, Pittsburgh: 1978, p. 108.
19 M. Haiman, *Ślady polskie w Ameryce [Polish Traces in America]* Chicago 1938, pp. 102-104; *Historia gruntów polskich w stanie Illinois [The Story of Polish Lands in the State of Illinois]* in: M. Haiman, *Z przeszłości polskiej w Ameryce [From the Polish Past in America]* Buffalo 1927, pp. 189-216.
20 M. Haiman, *Ślady polskie w Ameryce*, p.127.
21 *Zapomniany grób Chłopickiego [Chłopicki's Forgotten Grave]* in: *The Veteran* April 1932, p. 7

several of us are in a similar situation. We suffer equally. When we meet the first question is "have you eaten today?" We cry over each other's lot—so this is the constant picture of our poverty, please give it heed, I ask this of you."[22]

Antoni Gerard was one of the veterans who settled permanently in New York. He was an engineer from Kalisz who came to America with his wife in 1832, two years before the Austrian frigates brought several hundred Polish veteran exiles to this port. His wife deserves recognition (unfortunately, her name is not known). Being an educated person she taught foreign languages and gave music lessons. She looked after Polish veterans who held her in tremendous respect and esteem. "A person of higher education and great honesty, a good Polish woman, the best of mothers, who was universally respected" would be written about her years later.[23]

Marcin Rosienkiewicz, a former member of the Polish Committee in New York, hastened with another kind of assistance to his fellow countrymen. A former professor of the famous Lyceum in Krzemieniec he settled in Philadelphia, where he founded a school of English language for his fellow veteran colleagues. With Polish exiles in mind, he wrote and published in 1834 the first Polish book in America *Rozmowy dla ułatwienia nauki języka angielskiego (Conversations for facilitating the study of the English language.)* He died in Cincinnati in 1847.[24]

Some of the veterans, after arriving in America, tried at all costs to earn and save money to be able to pay for the return trip by boat to France. One of them was the already frequently cited second Lt. Julian Juźwikiewicz, who attained his goal on June 25, 1835 after 15 months of heavy physical labor. Shortly before his departure, he wrote in his memoir: "This freedom and independence are only like borrowed clothes for me, that neither adorn nor warm. Nothing can sweeten the longing I feel for my country. Poland continuously occupies my mind, and the ends of Europe never fade from before my eyes—I therefore made all effort to earn the funds to pay for the passage to France—where I imagine there must be a concentrated Polish immigration, which being a living protest against the harm done to my native country has its political existence there ... in which there lives some sort of hope of restoring the Fatherland."[25]

22　F. Stasik, "Przyczynek do dziejów polskiej emigracji politycznej w Stanach Zjednoczonych A.P. po powstaniu listopadowym (1831–1836)" ["Contribution to the History of the Polish Political Emigration to the United States of N.A. after the November Uprising (1831–1836)"] in: *Problemy Polonii Zagranicznej [Issues of the Polish Community Abroad]* vol. V, Warszawa 1966–1967, p. 41

23　M. Haiman *Polish Traces in America*, Chicago: 1938, p. 142.

24　M. Haiman, *Stulecie polskiej książki w Ameryce [The Centennial of the Polish Book in America]* in: *Dziennik Zjednoczenia [The Union Journal]* Chicago, January 6, 1933.

25　J. Juźwikiewicz, *Polacy w Ameryce, czyli Pamiętnik 15to Miesięcznego pobytu, [The Poles in America, or the Memoir of My 15 Month Sojourn]* Paris: 1836 in: M. Haiman, *Polish Traces in America*, Chicago: 1938, p. 118.

Lt. Bertold Wierciński was also one of the few veterans who decided to return to Europe. After returning from America he participated in the Sicilian campaign of Ludwik Mierosławski. He died in France in 1868.[26]

The 234 veterans of the November Uprising who were deported to America by the Austrians in 1834 were not the last. On July 31, 1834, the Austrian corvette "Lipsia" brought to New York sixteen former Polish insurrectionists deported from Austria.[27] In August of the same year the American merchant ship "Cherokee" brought to Boston twelve Polish veterans. In November 1834 thirty Poles also sailed into Boston from England. As political refugees they had earlier stayed in Switzerland. Subsequent Polish veterans came to America, singly or in small groups. For instance in 1835 twelve members of the Polish People's Group arrived from Portsmouth, England, where they had been active. These were insurrectionists who had been incarcerated in Prussian dungeons. In May 1835 another group of thirty-nine deported former insurrectionists debarked from the deck of the Austrian corvette "Adria." In the middle of April 1837, the Austrian brig "Talizman" brought to the United States the last group of veterans of the November Uprising, who had been expelled from Kraków.[28]

Florian Stasik, a student of this subject, estimates that 530 participants of the November Uprising had arrived in the United States by 1838. This represented about 6 percent of the total number of émigrés who were forced to leave Polish territories.[29]

At War with the Seminole Indians

Mieczysław Haiman's research indicates that a certain small number of exiles from Poland participated on the American side in the second Seminole war of 1835–1842.

The Seminoles are an Indian tribe inhabiting what is today the State of Florida. In 1819 the United States bought Florida from Spain, but the new owners were unable to foster proper relations with the native inhabitants of those lands. There were constant skirmishes. In 1834 President Jackson decided to resettle this tribe by force to a designated territory west of the Mississippi River. The Seminoles took up arms in defense of their native land. The difficult terrain was in their favor (the famous Florida swamps) as was the climate, which is hard on the white man. They did not give in to American troops armed with modern weapons until 1842. There was also a small group of Poles in the ranks of the victors. Poverty had forced them

---

26 Ibid, p. 128.
27 F. Stasik, *Polska emigracja polityczna w Stanach Zjednoczonych Ameryki 1831–1864 [The Polish Political Emigration to the United States 1831–1864]* Warsaw: 1973, p. 107.
28 Ibid., p. 108.
29 Ibid., p. 126.

to join the American army. Mieczysław Haiman estimates their number at around twenty to twenty-five. Four Polish names are visible among the 1,468 names on the published list of those who died in that war: Stefan Augustynowicz, Kazimierz Bryl, Andrzej Burdzicki and Jakub Filipowski.[30]

On Behalf of Canada's Freedom

The tragedy of Gustaw Szulc, a 30-year-old Polish officer of the November Uprising, came to be widely publicized in 1838. With a group of about 170 volunteers he participated in an expedition that was to assist the anti-British freedom movement in Canada. After landing on the Canadian side of the St. Lawrence River with his group between the 12th and 16th of November the brave volunteers fought in a pitched battle against overwhelming British forces. The promised help never arrived. After inflicting great loss on the attacking British units Szulc's group succumbed after running out of ammunition, and under heavy artillery fire. Szulc was captured by the British, who designated him a mutineer and sentenced him to death by hanging. The Polish fighter "For our freedom and yours" was executed on December 8, 1838 at Fort Henry in Kingston.[31]

The Society of Poles in America

Because of the scattering of Polish veterans across the vast expanse of the United States the Committee of Polish Exiles, which had represented their interests, was disbanded in 1840.

The group of about 70 veterans who remained in New York was joined by 16 former insurrectionists who arrived in July 1834 on the Austrian corvette "Lipsia."[32] The new arrivals also, as the New York press informed, honestly earned their bread by heavy physical labor. A group of activists emerged from among them (headed by Henryk Kałussowski). This group, at a meeting of March 20, 1842 at 235 Division St in New York City founded the Society of Poles in America whose goal it was to maintain collegial contact and render mutual aid.[33]

More ought to be said about Henryk Kałussowski, outstanding émigré activist, poor nobleman from the Żmudź region in Lithuania, participant in the November Uprising in Lithuania, member of the uprising's governing body there, chevalier of Poland's highest military honor, Virtuti Militari, for his participation in the battles

---

30 Polacy w wojnie z Seminolami [Poles in the Seminole Wars] in: M. Haiman, Ślady polskie w Ameryce. Szkice historyczne [Polish Traces in America. Historical Sketches] Chicago: 1938, pp. 155-159.
31 W. Kruszka, Historia polska w Ameryce, [Polish History in America] vol. I, Milwaukee: 1937, pp. 291-297.
32 F. Stasik, Polska emigracja polityczna w Stanach Zjednoczonych Ameryki 1831–1864 [The Polish Political Emigration to the United States 1831–1864] Warszawa: 1973, p. 107.
33 Czyn zbrojny wychodźctwa polskiego w Ameryce [War Efforts of the Polish Emigration in America] New York – Chicago: 1957, p. 17.

of Raygrod, Połąga and Kurszanty. While an émigré in France he tried to prepare the uprising organizationally on Polish territories. In 1833 he went to Galicia, where within the framework of émigré plans for the uprising, in advance of the expedition of Józef Zaliwski, he participated in forming the secret Galician "Węglarstwo" in Żółkiew Province. After the unsuccessful Zaliwski expedition he was fortunate to escape to Belgium, where he was active in Polish émigré circles, working with Joachim Lelewel.

In the years 1837–1838 he was the co-founder of the first Polish printing press in Brussels, where émigré publications of democratic ideology were printed. Thanks to its own bookstore the press distributed them to many Polish communities throughout Western Europe. Financial difficulties forced H. Kałussowski to fold the press and the bookstore, and with his wife, whom he married in Belgium, he departed for England. From there left for the United States. In New York he at first made his living by teaching foreign languages, of which it is said he knew fourteen, several of them fluently. In 1842 he was one of the co-founders of the Society of Poles in America.[34]

The lack of sources makes it impossible to recreate a detailed history of the Society. We do know, however, that in commemoration of the fourteenth anniversary of the commencement of the November Uprising, it organized in New York the first ever Polish national holiday in America. Veterans and other guests came from Boston, Baltimore, Utica, Philadelphia and the Niagara area. Many American, Scandinavian, Italian and even German organizations participated in this event. Henryk Kałussowski was the main speaker, who (pointing to the Polish flag) said: "Rest, our dear native flag, on free though foreign soil, since yours is still in chains! You will not be here long, we will shortly carry you across the foaming billows of the ocean, to plant you by the Vistula, the Niemen, the Dnieper and the Dźwina Rivers."[35]

Those were prophetic words, but the Poles living in the United States had to wait a long time before they were fulfilled.

The Veterans of the November Uprising in California

Various veterans made it to California by different routes. The first known Polish veteran who undertook this difficult task in 1843 was the adjutant of General Wincenty Krasiński, Major Stanisław Pągowski, a Chevalier of the Order of Virtuti Militari. He had formerly sojourned in France, Tunisia, Turkey, England and Australia from where he undertook the journey to California. But he did not stay there long either.

---

34 *Polski Słownik Biograficzny [The Polish Biographic Dictionary]* Warszawa-Kraków 1964–1965, vol. XI, pp. 505-507.

35 *Czyn zbrojny wychodźctwa polskiego w Ameryce [War Efforts of the Polish Emigration in America]* New York-Chicago 1957, p. 19.

The country where he decided to settle for good was Chile. When in 1863 news came from Europe about the outbreak of a Polish uprising against Russia, Stanisław Pągowski decided on the long journey to his native land. In 1864, after reaching the embattled country, he was arrested by the Russians and sentenced to 15 years hard labor. He was able to escape this punishment and go free. He died on the way back to Chile.[36]

Aleksander Zakrzewski was another insurrectionist who made it to the sunny land of California and settled in San Francisco. He is known today as the author of one of the oldest maps of the city, which he drew in 1849. This map is currently stored in the archives of Oregon City, which in the times current to Zakrzewski was the site of the only federal land office in the West.[37]

Dr. Feliks Wierzbicki was also known in California. A participant in the battles of Grochów and Ostrołęka, he came to the United States by way of Austrian prisons for internees.

In 1834 he arrived in Illinois, hoping to get a piece of the land promised by the Congress of the United States. When nothing came of this, he became a hired hand on local farms. Thanks to the help and benevolent care of an American family he received a high school education, and next took up medical studies. His first book, *The Ideal Man—A Philosophical Treatise Between Two Friends Upon the Beautiful, the Good, and the True as Manifested in Actual Life* appeared in Boston in 1841. His next book, which had nothing to do with medicine, was the publication of the essentials of Polish, French and German grammar.

In 1845, to commemorate the 15th anniversary of the commencement of the November Uprising (November 29, 1830), he published several articles on Polish subjects in *American Whig Review*, and was one of the speakers at a commemorative symposium in New York.

After finishing his studies in 1846 Wierzbicki began practicing medicine in Providence, Rhode Island. Soon however, he abandoned this work, because after the outbreak of the American Mexican war he decided to enlist as a military doctor in the detachments, which were to be transported by sea from the East Coast to California, which was in the throes of an anti-Mexican rebellion. After a year and a half long sea voyage along the coast of South America, the ship "Loo Choo" with Wierzbicki and five other Poles on board (probably also veterans of the November

---

36 M. Haiman. *Początki imigracji polskiej w Kalifornii, in: Ślady polskie w Ameryce. Szkice historyczne [The Beginnings of Polish Immigration in California in: Polish Traces in America. Historical Sketches]* Chicago 1938, pp. 211-212, 395-396; *Rocznik Towarzystwa Historyczno-Literackiego w Paryżu [Annual of the Historico-Literary Society in Paris]* Paris 1867.

37 Ibid., pp. 218-219

Uprising) arrived in San Francisco in March of 1847. After a month, at his own request, he was released from military service, because instead of a position in the medical corps of the American army, he had been directed to oversee the building of military barracks. After his release, having a lot of free time, he spent the first year delightedly getting to know the vast terrains of California, which resulted in a guidebook: *California as it is, and as it may be; or a Guide to the Gold Region,* San Francisco 1849. The book became a bestseller, because it appeared at the onset of the Gold Rush, which broke out in the spring of 1848. Wierzbicki's publication contained much valuable, genuine information for gold prospectors. It gave an exact description of the entrance to the Port of San Francisco, described the location of gold bearing territories and living conditions there; it listed several practical gold ore prospecting methods for amateurs, and also gave the author's thoughts on the future of California. He maintained that the future of this beautiful country did not belong to gold, but to agriculture, because of its fertile land and excellent climate. His forecast proved extraordinarily accurate.

Dr. Wierzbicki's guide was the first book in English that was printed west of the Rocky Mountains. The first printing was quickly exhausted and it soon appeared in an expanded second edition. This book was so popular that the California press reprinted whole chapters from it. But its author did not make a fortune on these publications, and he also did not make any money on gold. He settled in San Francisco, he returned to his medical practice with great success, remaining true to the methods of hydrotherapy that he fostered. He had a rich practice, because the massive influx of gold prospectors caused epidemic outbreaks of various infectious diseases such as spotted fever; and numerous cases of gunshot and slash wounds were the order of the day.

Besides his medical practice Dr. Wierzbicki made an essential contribution to the formation of the first association of doctors in California, The Medical Society in San Francisco. Moreover, he contributed to the medical journal, the *California Journal of Medicine,* in which among others he published his *Essays on the History of Medicine.* He died on December 26, 1860. His grave is currently located at the prestigious San Francisco National Cemetery. In 1996 the monument standing on his grave was renovated thanks to the Polish Veterans of World War II-SPK Post 49 in San Francisco.[38]

Unfortunately neither the history nor the names of the little group of five Poles, who came to California together with Dr. Wierzbicki, are known. Other veterans of

---

38 A. M. Salski, *Polacy w Kalifornii* in: *Głos* [*The Poles in California* in: *The Voice*] New York, Vol. XVI, Nr. 2, February 1, 1999, pp. 16-17

the November Uprising arrived after them in later years. They included: Szreder, a soldier of the Second Regiment of Mounted Sharpshooters, who died on the job at one of the gold mines; Wincenty Lutnicki, 2nd Lt. of the Second Uhlan Regiment, who worked as a jeweler at Sutter Creek and died there in 1880; Jan Strentzel, a doctor of medicine, a former Polish army doctor. He settled in Alhambra, California where he manufactured fruit wines; Franciszek Wojciechowski, a former soldier of the Sandomierz Rifle Regiment; who became famous in the San Francisco area as an excellent breeder of thoroughbreds. Aleksander Bednawski was forcibly drafted into the Russian army for his participation in the November Uprising and sent to the Caucasus from where he escaped and after a long journey ended up in California.[39]

Also of note is another Polish insurrectionist, Korwin Piotrowski. He was born in 1814 in Kamieniec Podolski. He was an officer of the Fourth and Seventh Uhlan Regiments. Among other places he fought at Dąb Wielki and Ostrołęka. He came to America in 1840 and settled in California around 1850. He worked there as a farmer and a gold prospector, thanks to which he was able to buy a sizable tract of land in the area of San Francisco, by the Sacramento River. He was a founder of the Polish Society in California. He was known in the circle by his ribald humor, and many pranks, which he pulled on his countrymen. Helena Modrzejewska described his hilarious antics in her memoir. The description of his milk and vodka cure, or the droll faces he made when he winked feigning innocence, and a moment later would yell: "Man, you see what's going on and you don't thunder!" Sometimes while sleeping in his cottage he would fall off his bed and try to find it in the dark waking his roommates with shouts of: "Tartars, you barbarians, you bloodthirsty pagans!" These descriptions are among the most comical in the memoir. Henryk Sienkiewicz, who as a guest of Helena Modrzejewska was a witness to many pranks pulled by Piotrowski, used him as a model for the character of Zagłoba in *The Trilogy*.[40]

Piotrowski's longtime companion, Captain Franciszek Wojciechowski, became Sienkiewicz's model for the character of Podbipięta in *With Fire and Sword*. As Modrzejewska recalls, Captain Franciszek, as everybody called him, just like Podbipięta, "was very tall, very skinny and withdrawn."[41]

Helena Modrzejewska enumerated two more Poles from among her California friends: Kazimierz Bielawski and Bednawski. The first of them worked for the U.S. land office in San Francisco for 45 years. In 1865 he published the *Topographical*

---

39 Ibid., p. 225
40 Ibid, p. 229
41 *Memories and Impressions of Helena Modjeska*, New York 1910, p. 313

and Railroad Map of the Central Part of California and Nevada, which he prepared.[42] In Modrzejewska's opinion Bielawski was a radical Republican, a dyed-in-the-wool antimonarchist and opponent of the Church. The second of them, Bednawski, after the fall of the November Uprising, was drafted into the Russian Army and sent to the Caucusus from where he escaped and after many adventures made it to France, where for many years he served in the French army. After emigrating to California he received a French government pension for his service under the French flag.

Modrzejewska, reminiscing about her friends wrote about them: "they always differed in their opinions and had very heated debates, but when it came to action, they went hand-in-hand. They were all true embodiments of honor and great Polish patriots."[43]

The Polish emigrants, who made their way to California were mostly young, educated people. They had well-paid professions. It is worth noting that they maintained rather close contact with each other, which distinguished them from the remaining groups that lived in other parts of the United States. Despite the distance from their native country they were interested in its fate. The total number of insurrectionists who settled in California is estimated at around 30 persons.[44]

In Battles for Texas Independence and in the War with Mexico

At the beginning of the 19th century Texas was a vast, but thinly populated and economically backward province that belonged to Mexico which was under Spanish rule. An anti-Spanish revolution broke out in Mexico in 1810, and ended with Mexican independence in 1821. The Mexican authorities permitted U.S. citizens to settle in Texas. The Mexicans counted on rapid civilizational development and the economic boom that would be connected with it. The influx of American settlers proved so large that after less than two decades the proportion of Mexicans to Americans was 1 to 4. The Americans settling in Texas brought their own labor force along in the form of slaves. This was against Mexican law which forbade slavery. That led to conflicts on this issue. The Americans, feeling their numeric superiority, respected Mexican laws less and less. As a result the Mexican authorities decided to halt the influx of American settlers. This led to a revolt of American settlers already living there, their refusal to obey the Mexican government and the declaration of the independence of Texas. The Mexican government had no intention of tolerating a separatist rebellion in its own country and sent a punitive military expedition under the command of General Antonio Lopez de Santa Anna. The Mexican forces included several thousand infantry, cavalry

---

42 *Ameryka w pamiętnikach Polaków: Antologia. [America in Polish Memoirs. An Anthology]* Selection and commentary by Bogdan Grzeloński, Warszawa, 1975, p. 9

43 Ibid., p. 313

44 F. Stasik. *Polska emigracja polityczna w Stanach Zjednoczonych Ameryki 1831–1864 [The Polish Political Immigration in the United States of America 1831–1864]* Warszawa, 1973, p. 252

detachments and batteries of artillery. The American settlers, spread out over a vast area, were not prepared for an armed conflict with Army regulars. The first significant resistance to the Mexican army was given by 184 American Texans at the Spanish mission church of the Alamo. Their resistance, after a heroic defense, was quelled with much bloodshed on March 6, 1836. Only one defender made it our alive, the rest were killed. Two weeks later the Mexican army launched an assault against Fort Goliad, the capital of the American separatists, and captured it. The defense was directed by Colonel of the Army James W. Fannin (a West Point graduate, class of 1819). There were also Poles, four artillery officers, among the defenders. They were the brothers Adolf and Franciszek Petrussewicz, Napoleon Dębicki and Jan Kornicki—all veterans of the November Uprising of 1830–31. Franciszek H. Petrussewicz was gravely wounded while directing the artillery in defence of the fort, and died on March 19, 1836 as a result of his wound. About four hundred defenders, together with commanding officer Col. J. W. Fannin, were taken prisoner. On orders of Gen. Antonio Lopez de Santa Anna they were all shot on March 27, 1836, including Col. James W. Fannin, even though he was wounded. Three Polish officers were also victims of this crime: Napoleon Dębicki, Jan Kornicki and Adolf Petrussewicz.[45] There is a monument on the mass grave of the victims, with the inscribed names of all the murdered defenders of Fr. Goliad.

A month later General Antonio Lopez de Santa Anna, who was responsible for that crime, was defeated by American forces on April 21, 1836 at the battle of San Jacinto and was captured there. Thanks to this victory Texas won its independence and almost ten years later, in 1845, it became the 28th state of the United States of America. The official annexation of Texas by the United States caused a war between Mexico and the USA, which was fought on land and sea in the years 1846–1848. The war was fought over a vast territory stretching from California and Texas all the way to areas south of Mexico City and the shores of both the oceans. As a result of this war Mexico lost half of its territory to the United States.

Fifty Polish veterans of the November Uprising, who enlisted in the American Army, participated in this war. Captain Karol Radzimiński, Captain Napoleon Kościałkowski and Sergeant Ignacy Szumowski distinguished themselves most in battle.[46] The war, which was provoked by the United States, had an aggressive character. Mexico was defending its territorial integrity against a much stronger opponent. Some American soldiers felt that they were fighting on the wrong side. Their inner conflict was deepened by the fact that they were witness to the desecration of

---

45 Herbert Davenport, "The Men of Goliad" in: *The Southwestern Historical Quarterly* vol. XLVIII, No. 1, July 1939, pp. 33-36

46 W. Kruszka. *Historia polska w Ameryce [Polish History in America]* Milwaukee 1937, p. 291

Mexican Catholic churches by American armies composed in the main of Protestant soldiers. For many, these occurrences were incompatible with moral principle. About 250 U.S. soldiers (mainly Irishmen) went over to the Mexican side, where they organized the St. Patrick's Battalion. During the battles some of the soldiers from this Battalion became American prisoners. They were identified as traitors and shot. Of the Poles who fought on the Mexican side those who distinguished themselves included Konstanty Tarnawa-Malczewski (who earned the rank of General), Lt. Antoni Jabłoński and the physician Seweryn Gałęzowski.[47]

After the conclusion of the war Karol Radzimiński, who had served in the American army, worked on the commission that was marking the new border between Mexico and the United States. After arriving in the United States he finished an engineering degree and worked in Richmond, Virginia. Radzimiński worked on the border survey for many years. During the first three years he measured its entire length. He prepared a special report on his journey for the federal authorities. It became a very valuable government document. In the course of further surveying work he died in a skirmish with the Indians on September 18, 1858.[48]

Lt. Władysław Sokalski was also in the group of former insurrectionists who arrived in the United States in 1834. He joined the Army as a private and was stationed for a long time at the Watervliet Arsenal. There he married Jane Leonard of Troy, New York, an American girl. Their son George Sokalski was the first American of Polish descent to graduate from the military Academy at West Point, on May 6, 1861.[49]

The Democratic Society of Polish Exiles

The group of Polish veterans living in New York showed great political and organizational vigor. In 1852 they founded a new organization, the Democratic Society of Polish Exiles (DSPE).

It appears from the minutes of the Society that in 1853 four of its members (Bogacki, Adolf Rarz, Gruenbaum, Krzesłowski) left New York and headed for California.[50] In 1854 DSPE in New York had over 200 members. Its main activists were: H. Kałussowski, Z. Karczewski, F. Kiczman, F. K. Kępiński, A. Małuski, Ludwik Spaczek. This was the apex of its development. Not without reason, because at that time the Russian Turkish war

---

[47] J. Wróbel. *Meksyk pamięta rok 1848* in: "Kalejdoskop Tygodnia" (dodatek kulturalny *Dziennika Związkowego*) [*Mexico Remembers the Year 1848* in: "Weekly Caleidoscope" (cultural supplement to *The Alliance Daily*)] Chicago October 16, 1998; p. 4, 17

[48] K. Wahtl. *Polonia w Ameryce [The Polish-American Community in America]* Philadelphia 1944, p. 54

[49] "A Civil War Centennial Tribute to Lieutenant Colonel George O. Sokalski," Troy, New York 1964, p. 1

[50] M. Haiman. *Początki imigracji polskiej w Kalifornii* in: *Ślady polskie w Ameryce.Szkice historyczne* [*The Beginnings of Polish Immigration in California* in: *Polish Traces in America. Historical Sketches*] Chicago 1938, p. 224

was raging, which generated substantial hopes among the Polish émigrés. Members of the Society tried to mold American public opinion against Russia. Awaiting news of the outbreak of an uprising in Poland, they were getting ready to leave and planned an adventurous expedition through America and Siberia in order to threaten Russia from that side, which at that time was fighting in the Crimea.

The activity of the Society started to decrease after 1854, although it was active until 1860.[51]

Some of the veterans of the November Uprising, who came to live in America, stopped their political activity and tried to find their place in American society. Thanks to their gifts, determination and hard work, with time they were able to rise above mediocrity. Henryk Głowacki became an outstanding lawyer in the State of New York, Ludwik Bańczakiewicz and several others taught in American schools, others worked as chemists.

Paweł Sobolewski, the youngest of the group of former insurrectionists sent by Austria to America in 1834, was 18 when he disembarked at New York. In 1842 he began publishing an illustrated magazine in New York: *Poland—Historical, Literary, Monumental and Picturesque*. It was the first Polish periodical in America. The artist-engraver Eustachy Wyszyński helped Sobolewski in his work. He also was a former insurrectionist, one of those who tried to walk from New York to Illinois (Wyszyński made it to Pittsburgh).[52] Thanks to this undertaking Paweł Sobolewski has been named the father of Polish American journalism. He finished law and practiced as a lawyer in the state of Illinois. On his initiative an impressive celebration of the 200th anniversary of the Relief of Vienna was organized in Chicago in 1883. At the request of Sobolewski and other veterans from the years 1830–1831, 1846, 1848 and 1863–1864 the famous actress Helena Modrzejewska together with her husband K. Bodzenta-Chłapowski took part in the event. For this occasion Paweł Sobolewski published a brochure in English, dedicated to King John III Sobieski of Poland. He is known to this day as the author of the work *Polish Poets and Poetry*, Chicago 1884. It is a collection of translations into English of verse by Polish poets from Mikołaj Rey to the times contemporary to the author.[53]

Another former insurrectionist, Józef Truskolaski, had the good fortune of having James Fenimore Cooper, the author of the *Last of the Mohicans* as his patron. Thanks to his help he was able to complete an engineering degree.

---

51 M. Haiman. *Historia udziału Polaków w amerykańskiej wojnie domowej [The History of Polish Participation in the American Civil War]* Chicago 1928, pp. 10-11

52 M. Haiman. *Ślady polskie w Ameryce. Szkice historyczne [Polish Traces in America. Historical Sketches]* Chicago 1938, p, 147

53 H. Archacki, "Paweł Sobolewski w hołdzie Sobieskiemu" in: *Dziennik Związkowy* ["Paweł Sobolewski in Homage to Sobieski" in: *The Alliance Daily*], Chicago July 25, 1983

Some of the Poles were able to quickly adjust to American conditions and thanks to their enterprising efforts were, with time, able to amass considerable fortunes. One of them was Karol Plinta who lived in New York.[54]

Kazimierz Stanisław Gzowski made the greatest career in a truly American style. He was an officer in the Corps of Engineers during the November Uprising. After arriving in the United States he quickly learned English and finished law. He soon abandoned this profession and began working as an engineer building railroad lines and water canals in Pennsylvania. In 1842 he resettled to Canada, where the British government put him in charge of the building of roads, bridges ports and canals.

"While holding the office of Superintendent of Public Works for the western part of the Province of Ontario he built the first hard-surface roads in the country. He also became reknown as a waterways engineer; he supervised the deepening of the St. Lawrence River and built several harbors on this important waterway; he also expanded the Port of Montreal. His construction and organization gifts gained him recognition in the eyes of his Canadian superiors, who appointed him chief engineer for the St. Laurent and Atlantic Railroad, and later on its General Director. In 1857 he founded his own prosperous firm, Gzowski and Company, which produced railroad rails. The rank of this enterprise is well illustrated by the fact that it received a government order for the construction of the Grand Trunk Railway—a great railway line on the route Toronto—Guelph—Sarnia. Thanks to this order Kazimierz Gzowski became one of the wealthiest residents of Toronto. Nonetheless his greatest specialization was building bridges. He tore down wooden bridges and replaced them with stone and steel ones. His most outstanding creation was the famous International Bridge spanning the Niagara River, which connects the Canadian town of Fort Erie with the American city of Buffalo—an important industrial and port center. In planning and building this bridge Gzowski had to solve many serious and complicated technical issues caused by the depth of the Niagara River and the swiftness of its current. International Bridge was a significant engineering feat for those times, which brought the Polish engineer world-wide acclaim. Thanks to this construction he is counted among the most outstanding engineers of the 19th century.

"From 1884 Kazimierz Gzowski, on behalf of the government of the Province of Ontario, organized a national park around Niagara Falls and also created the infrastructure for today's Canadian city of Niagara Falls. Gzowski's contributions for this region are recounted by a memorial plaque that stands in the center of this internationally known national park.

---

54 M. Haiman. *Polish Traces in America*. Chicago 1938, p. 145

"Kazimierz E. Gzowski was a great social activist. He was an inspector of the Royal Military Academy, co-founded the Riflemen's Association, was a colonel in the civic militia. He was the president of the Canadian Society of Engineers. He founded a lending bank in Toronto, a symphony orchestra and a riding club. He was a member of the Senate of the local university. He was a widely respected citizen. His contributions to Canada are memorialized by streets, squares and parks named after him, and by memorial plaques, also by a special postage stamp with his likeness and a monument in Toronto which stands on the shore of Lake Ontario."[55]

As of today, the activity of Kazimierz Gzowski is the best documented in scholarly literature of any of his compatriots in America.[56]

Józef Sędzimir was another Polish engineer who worked in the United States in the second half of the 19th century. He took part in the November Uprising of 1830–1831 as a young 2nd Lieutenant. After its defeat he emigrated to France where he became associated with the Polish Democratic Society. He traveled to England in search of work, and he married there in 1841, but soon thereafter became a widower. It is difficult to determine exactly when he emigrated to America. After arriving in United Sates he settled in Amityville on Long Island in the State of New York. There he married the sister of his first wife. In April, 1857 the respected periodical *Scientific American* published a long article discussing Józef Sędzimir's plan to construct a tunnel that would connect Manhattan with Brooklyn. The plan called for laying enormous metal segments on the bottom of the East River, which after being sealed tight would form an underwater tunnel. Two lane roads were to be laid in its interior for horse-drawn vehicles and walkways for pedestrians. The tunnel was to be lit by a row of gas lamps. The plan never materialized, however.[57] Several years later construction began on the Brooklyn Bridge over the place where the tunnel was to have been laid.

Józef Sędzimir patented only one of his inventions in the United States. It was a modernized wind turbine of simple design, simple enough that any farmer or mechanic could construct it.

While living in America J. Sędzimir maintained contact with his family which remained behind in the Polish territories that were under Russian occupation. His

---

55 *Polski Słownik Biograficzny [Polish Biographical Dictionary]* vol. IX, pp. 209-211; H. Mąka "Sir Gzowski przewidział" ["Sir Gzowski Foresaw It"] in: *Forum Polonijne [Forum of the Polish Community Abroad]* Warszawa, January 2005, pp. 20-21

56 W. Turek. *Sir Casimir S. Gzowski. A Biographical Sketch* Toronto 1957; L. Kos-Rabcewicz-Zubkowski, W. E. Greesing, *Sir Gzowski* translated by J. Radzicki, Warszawa 1984; A. Wołodkowicz *Polish Contributions to Art and Science in Canada* Montreal 1969; W. Michałowski *Najemnicy wolności [Mercenaries of Freedom]* Białystok 1991

family received the last letter from him in August 1881, in which among other things he wrote: "By the time you receive this letter I am no longer among the living, I have taken my own life, because it has become disgusting to me—I lost my wife, whom I loved dearly—therefore I lost the object, the goal of life; I am too old to look for a new purpose—fate has dragged me around for too long for me to live any more and prolong this state. I am unable to take my loneliness and orphan state any more."[58]

Many veterans of the November Uprising scattered across the vast territories of their new homeland, melting into its social structures. Their progeny, mainly due to the fault of their fathers, quickly became Americanized and only their strange sounding and difficult to pronounce last names indicated their Polish heritage.

It is astonishing that this group of Polish émigrés, several hundred strong, mainly of aristocratic background and reasonably well-educated, did not try to instill knowledge of the Polish language in their children, not to speak of organizing a Polish school, for instance. The reason for this was that they were so widely scatterered across the entire United States. But the greatest reason of all was a lack of Polish women and the belief that knowledge of their native language was without value in American society. The daughter of one of these insurrectionists, Maria Dziewanowska-Walbridge, who was 83 years old in 1934, wrote in a letter to the Reverend Wacław Kruszka: "My mother [who was not Polish—T. L.] wanted my father to teach us Polish. But my father, who at that time was the only Pole in our entire area, thought that the Polish language is useless and that we would never have occasion to use it."[59]

With time, some began to realize the mistake they had made in the upbringing of their offspring. In the main, however, it was too late. The *Album Pamiątkowy Osady Polskiej w Buffalo [The Souvenir Journal of the Polish Settlement in Buffalo]* published in 1906 wrote about one of those veterans and the conflicts that were later experienced for this reason: "At supper Mr. Jacquard introduced his Anglo-American wife to us and their two sons. Neither of them spoke Polish. At parting Mr. Jacquard said as follows: "It no doubt surprises you gentlemen that I am concealing my Polish surname. I find it hard, but I meted out this deserved punishment to myself. It would have been better had I died in the uprising than to have lived this long and thought only of myself, having forgotten the obligations incumbent upon me as a Pole, to bring my sons up in the Polish tradition. Not wanting future generations to throw the stone of condemnation at me, I decided to cross myself out of the list of living Poles. When I finally saw the light I tried to rescue my sons, but it was already too late.

---

58   S. Łotysz. "Pierwszy z Sędzimirów w Ameryce" ["The First of the Sędzimirs in America"] in: *Nowy Dziennik [Polish Daily News]* New York June 21–22, 2003, p. 39

59   W. Kruszka, *Historia polska w Ameryce, [Polish History in America]* vol. I, Pittsburgh 1978, p. 324

"I am a desperado together with those who acted like I did, having lost faith in everything. Believe me, we had never supposed that aside from us, other Poles would come here, that we should have lived differently, so that future generations would not disdain us. It was our duty to become pioneers of Polishness, but we betrayed the cause, thinking only of ourselves. Therefore it is better gentlemen that you not learn my true name, and those of others like me. Because first we grew to doubt the future of our nation and forgot about it. So therefore let everyone forget about us, because we did not live up to expectations and turned out to be dwarfs."[60]

Among veterans of the November Uprising who came to the United States on their own, aside from the best-known Henryk Kałussowski, Henryk Dmochowski also deserves mention. After the defeat of the uprising and Poland, he emigrated to France, where he associated himself with Colonel Zaliwski. Together with him in the years 1833–1834 he tried to incite an insurrectionist movement in Galicia and in the Polish Kingdom. After being arrested, he languished in prison until 1841, where he started to sculpt. After regaining his freedom he left for Paris and began studying in the Sculpture Department of the École des Beaux Arts. There in the years 1846–1847 at the side François Rude he worked on Napoleon's sarcophagus at the Palais des Invalides. In 1852 he left for the United States, where he made many medallions and busts of American personalities, among them George Washington, Benjamin Franklin and Thomas Jefferson. Among the most important works that Dmochowski created in America are the marble busts of Tadeusz Kościuszko and Kazimierz Pułaski. Both sculptures were purchased by the
Congress of the United States and placed in the Capitol in Washington. In 1861 he returned to the lands of the former Polish Republic and settled in Vilnius. There he opened a sculptor's studio. He quickly associated himself with a conspiratorial movement. After the outbreak of the January (1863) Uprising he became a commissioner of the insurrectionist national government. He died in 1863 in a battle with Russian troops.[61]

Adam Gurowski was also one of those November insurrectionists who came independently to the United States from Europe. He was the most controversial figure of the Polish political immigration to America in the 19th century. In his youth he was a conspirator and participant in insurrectionist battles in 1831, for which he received the Order of Virtuti Militari. While an émigré in France in 1834 he broke off completely with the Polish Democratic Society, and with Poland, because he lost

---

60 Ibid., pp. 105-106
61 M. Haiman, *Polish Past in America 1808–1865*. Chicago 1939, p. 92; T. Walendowski "Posąg zwrócony ku rzece" in: *Przegląd Polski* ["The Statue Facing the River"] Chicago 1939, p. 92 in: *[The Polish Review]* New York, August 17, 2001, pp. 10-11

faith in the possibility of the existence of a sovereign Polish state! In his publications he popularized the theories of so-called panSlavism and declared himself completely on the side of cooperation with Russia. Thanks to this he received amnesty from the Russian authorities and returned to Warsaw. Despite successive Russophile publications in which among others he proposed a complete Russification of the Polish nation (!) he did not gain the confidence of the Russians. Even his sister's marriage to Baron Frideric, the Adjutant-General of Tsar Nicolas I, did not help. Gurowski, surrounded by the contempt of his countrymen, decided in 1844 to leave the Polish Kingdom. After a year's sojourn in Western Europe, where he continued to popularize the idea of panSlavism, he decided to go to the United States. In Boston and New York he became famous for his extreme abolitionist viewpoints, propagating in his writings, mainly in *The New York Tribune,* the abolition of slavery. He devoted a book, *Slavery in History*, to this issue. It appeared in 1860, just before the outbreak of the Civil War. He remained true to his panSlavic ideas to the end of his life and called himself a Russo-Slavist. He included his ideas in a book, *Russia as it is*, published in 1854.[62]

Veterans of the November Uprising in the Musical Life of America
Most of the veterans of the November Uprising, especially the officers who came from Europe to America, were well educated. Many of them had musical talent, which they developed to varying degrees of success in America. Aleksander Janta-Połczyński (a Polish World War II veteran) extensively documented their achievements in a valuable study titled *A History of Nineteenth Century American-Polish Music* (New York, 1982).[63] Over a period of fifteen years of laborious research work he made an astonishing discovery, or better said, he drew out from the shadows of oblivion more than twenty Polish composers (including one woman) who wrote music in the United States in the first half of the 19th century, and who were not mentioned in American music encyclopedias. In this group are included: Anna M. Abłamowicz, Edward B. Bohuszewicz, Julian Fontana, T. Gaszyński, Leon Rawicz-Gawroński, Feliks Janiewicz, Edward Janowski, Józef Kossowski, Teofil Tomasz Klonowski, Adam Kurek, Edward Kański, Nuna J. Lepowski, B. R. Lignowski, Markowski, Leon Rembieliński, Marcin Rosienkiewicz, Edward Sobolewski, K. Soloski, A. Sowiński, Feliks Tadeusz Strawiński, Zawistowski, Maksymilian Zuboff (a/k/a Mackiewicz). In the main they were Polish veterans of the November Uprising

---

62 *Ameryka w pamiętnikach Polaków. Antologia [America in Polish Memoirs. An Anthology]* selection and commentary by Bogdan Grzeloński, Warszawa 1975, pp. 126-140.

63 A. Janta. *A History of Nineteenth Century Ameican-Polish Music/ with annotated Bibliography and Illustrations* New York: The Kosciuszko Foundation, 1982

of 1830–31 who after arriving in the United States developed their talents as best they could, gave piano lessons for various instruments, popularized in American society the best known Polish musical compositions, composed their own and published them. Thanks to this they left permanent traces of their activities for posterity. The most distinguished of these veterans were: Julian Fontana, Adam Kurek and Edward B. Bohuszewicz.

Julian Fontana was undoubtedly the chief composer in this group. He was a close friend of Frederic Chopin whom he knew from the early days when they both attended the music conservatory in Warszawa under the directorship of Józef Elsner. Unlike Chopin, Julian Fontana did participate in the anti-Russian November Uprising of 1830–1831, where he rose in the ranks to 2nd lieutenant of the artillery. After the defeat of the Uprising he emigrated to Paris where in 1832 he met his friend F. Chopin and became his most trusted confidant. Julian Fontana took care of a lot of matters for Chopin: he managed his money, organized his travels, rented his apartments for him, etc. He was also the corrector of some of the compositions that Chopin was preparing for publication. Chopin dedicated the two Polonaises Op. 40, No. 1 (in A major) and No. 2 (in C minor) to Fontana. They also made plans for an artistic trip to America, but Chopin's family dissuaded him from this idea and the genial composer never got to see the land of Washington. On the other hand Fontana went to America at the beginning of the 1840s mainly to promote his friend's music. Being an outstanding virtuoso pianist he concertized in many American cities, mainly playing Chopin's compositions. These were the first interpretations of Chopin's music on American soil. Julian Fontana also concertized with the violinist Camillo Sivori, a student of Paganini.[64] While traveling around America he composed music and wrote short articles for the Parisian press. In 1848 he took a short trip to Europe. During his American voyages he kept up a lively correspondence with Chopin, up to the latter's death in 1849. He also went to Cuba, where he met his future wife Calle Dalcour. Their wedding took place in the Roman-Catholic cathedral in New York on September 9, 1850, after which they left for Paris. There in 1853 a son was born to them, whose godfather was Poland's most celebrated poet Adam Mickewicz. After his wife's untimely death in 1855 Julian Fontana again went to America. In New York he obtained his American citizenship and returned to Paris. Two years later, in 1857 Fontana made his last trip to the American continent; he visited Cuba and New York. In 1858 together with his five year old son he returned to Paris. He was the author of numerous piano compositions, published in many countries, including the United States. In several of his compositions he placed musical motifs connected with his American voyages, for instance *La Havanne, Fantasy*

---

64 A. Janta, op. cit. "The American Chapter of the Life of Julian Fontana" pp. 22-36

with American and Spanish Motifs, and *Recollections from the Island of Cuba.*[65] He also prepared compositions of his friend Chopin for posthumous publication. As an American citizen he made trips to Polish territories under Prussian and Austrian occupation in the years 1858–1860. He never got to visit his native regions which were under Russian occupation. Toward the end of his life, living in Paris, he faced an ever more difficult financial situation; he became depressed, which led to a nervous breakdown and suicide; he died of gas poisoning on the night of December 23/24, 1869. He was buried at the cemetery of Montmartre in Paris.[66]

Adam Kurek was the most active Polish composer in the United States in the first half of the 19th century. He was a veteran of the November Uprising and came to America from France in 1833.He settled in Boston where he composed many pieces for orchestra, for instance the "Seventh Company National Grand March" (1840), "Twelve Admired Quick Steps to the Memory of Lost Poland" (1842), "Gov. Morton's Grand March" (1843), "Kurek's Grand March" (1843). The premiere performances of Adam Kurek's compositions were mostly given by the Boston Brigade Band. On the program books printed for these occasions, next to the name of the composer there was always the note: "Polish Exile."

Another Polish musician, a former Polish soldier, Edward B. Bohuszewicz, also lived in Boston for several years. He sailed to New York from Trieste in July 1834 on board the Austrian corvette "Lipsia" with a group of November Uprising insurgents who had been forcibly deported overseas by the Austrians. He was a native of Podolia, that is, the southeastern territories of the former Polish Commonwealth. In America he at first lived in Boston, Massachusetts where he gave piano and violin lessons. His good musical background, young age and faultless manners brought him many fiends and sizeable popularity. In 1837 he moved to Providence, Rhode Island, where he became organist at the Westminster Unitarian Church. In time he became the president of the local Beethoven Society which was evidence of his significant position in the cultural life of the community. He composed marches, waltzes, mazurkas and polkas. Many of them were published in Boston and Providence. One of his works, the waltz "The Aquila," he dedicated to his friend Dr. Feliks Wierzbicki of New York (also a veteran of the 1830–31 Uprising) with whom he corresponded to the end of his life.

He died in Septmber 1848 at the age of barely 38. His death was deeply felt by the residents of Providence. He was buried at the local Swan Point Cemetery. A monument (by architect Thomas A. Tefft) was placed on his grave with the following inscription:

---

65 Ibid.

66 Andrzej Biernat and Sławomir Górzyński, eds. *Polacy pochowani na cmentarzu Montmartre oraz Saint-Vincent i Batignolles w Paryżu;* praca zbiorowa [*Poles buried at the cemeteries of Montmartre, Saint-Vincent and Batignolles in Paris*; a group work] Warszawa 1999

Edward B. Bohuszewicz
Born at Podolia in Poland, 1813
Died at Providence Sep. 18, 1848
From the Country Where He Was Born in Affluence
He Found With Us a Home
And With Manly Fortitude, Made the accomplishments of His Youth
Not Only a Source of Independence
But of Generous Aid to His Countrymen.
Gentle, Just and Vigorous,
He Won the Love of Many and the Respect of All.

This Stone is a Tribute to His Memory
From the Community Who Mourn For Him as an Adopted Son.[67]

Participants in the Spring of Nations

When in the early spring of 1848 news reached America about the outbreak of a revolution in Paris, which had been initiated by the Spring of Nations, some of the political émigrés decided to return to Europe. One of them was Henryk Kałussowski, who by way of Paris made it to Wielkopolska, which was caught up in the ferment of the independence movement. He concentrated on political activity. He tried without effect to represent the Polish cause before a universal German parliament in Frankfurt. After the fall of the uprising in Wielkopolska he was arrested by the Prussian authorities. He was released from prison thanks to the intervention of the United States ambassador in Berlin, because prior to arriving in Europe, he had already obtained U.S. citizenship. After returning to America in 1850 he settled in Washington, where he began working in the statistical department of the Land Office and was promoted several times. He successfully completed his medical studies, receiving the degree of Doctor of Medicine. He did not stop his political activity on behalf of the Polish cause.[68]

After the events connected with the Spring of Nations, a significant group of its participants sailed for the United States. They came from many countries. There were, of course, Poles among them. Aside from the already mentioned Henryk Kałussowski they were participants in the earlier Kraków uprising of 1846 (Jan Tyssowski),[69] of the uprising in Wielkopolska (Józef Karge, Andrzej Józiakiewicz, Stanisław Młotkowski) of the Hungarian Uprising (Albin Franciszek Schoepf,

---

67   Ibid., pp. 41-43
68   *Polski Słownik Biograficzny [Polish Biographical Dictionary]* Kraków-Warszawa-Wrocław 1964–1965, entry: Kałussowski Korwin Henryk, vol. XI, p. 505
69   N. M. Rutkowska, *John Tyssowski*, Chicago, 1943

Antoni Leszczyński, Captain Lessen), soldiers of Giuseppe Garibaldi in Italy (Ludwik Żychliński). Some of them had almost all of the above mentioned campaigns behind them, for instance Konstanty Błędowski. One of the veteran groups of the Hungarian uprising (Poles and Hungarians) founded in 1850 a colony called Hungary in the Richmond Virginia area of Henrico County.[70]

Captain Lessen, who hailed from the Kalisz region in Poland, settled in distant California.

Antoni Leszczyński fought in Hungary in the years 1848–49 as a soldier in the Polish Legion. He came to America with his wife. He settled in Detroit, where he was one of the first to establish Polish American organizations. Among others, he founded the brotherhood of St. Stanislaus Kostka and the Brotherhood of the Holy Rosary. During meetings of the organizations in his home he taught Polish history and narrated his war time experiences in the Polish Legion in Hungary. He would show his listeners his most precious souvenir of that time, his service card from the Polish Legion with a seal showing the white eagle and the caption: "Headquarters of the Polish Legion." He brought up five sons as Polish patriots living in the United States. This is confirmed by the fact that they were among the most active members of the Polish Falcons of America which was being organized in Detroit. One of them, Piotr Leszczyński, was able to convince the city's authorities to open a Polish section in the public library. In the years 1907–1912 thanks to his efforts, the Polish American community in Detroit built a grand Polish Home, which became the center of Polish American life.[71]

Jakub Gordon can also be placed among the veterans of this period. He was not a participant of armed battles, but a political prisoner. In 1844 he was arrested by the authorities for his connection to the movement of the Reverend Piotr Ściegienny. He was condemned to long military service deep in Russia. On his way to Siberia he escaped and made his way to Galicia and from there to France. In 1848 he returned to Galicia from where he tried to make his way to Wielkopolska which was in the throes of an uprising. At the crossing of the border into the Russian occupied zone he fell into Russian hands. Accused of desertion from the Russian army and of conspiratorial activity he was sent to do military service into the penal battalions in Siberia, from where in 1855 he was able to flee once again, and made it to Germany. From there he went to the United States, where he stayed for five years, visited many states and obtained American citizenship. In 1860 he returned to France, from where in 1866 he

---

70 M. Haiman. *Historia udziału Polaków w amerykańskiej wojnie domowej [The History of Polish Participation in the American Civil War]* Chicago, 1928, pp. 30-31

71 A. L. Waldo. *Sokolstwo. Przednia straż narodu. [Polish Falcons of America. The Vanguard of the Nation.]* vol. II, Pittsburgh 1972, pp. 73-74

went to Galicia, where he took up journalism. He published the bi-weekly "Reforma" in Sanok, and "Zagroda. Tygodnik dla Ludu" in Kraków. From 1872 on, he lived in Lwów. Due to sharp criticism he stopped writing and abandoned journalism. He worked as an archivist in the National Division. He published ten books, mostly memoirs; among them: *Moskwa, Pamiętnik Polaka z Korony;obywatela Stanów Zjednoczonych; Przechadzki po Ameryce; Podróż do NowegoOrelanu.* *[Moscow; Memoir of a Pole from the Polish Crown Lands, a United States Citizen; Walks Across America; Journey to New Orleans]*. He died in 1895.[72] About 300 to 500 Poles, who had participated in battles during the Spring of Nations period, came to America.[73]

---

72 Ameryka w pamiętnikach Polaków. Antologia. *[America in Polish Memoirs. An Anthology]* Selection and commentary by B. Grzeloński. Warsaw 1975, pp. 97-98

73 F. Stasik. *Polska emigracja polityczna w Stanach Zjednoczonych Ameryki 1831–1864. [The Polish Political Emigration in the United States of America 1831–1864.]* Warszawa 1973, p. 208

III.
POLISH VETERANS IN THE AMERICAN CIVIL WAR (1861–1865)

Some of the Polish veterans who arrived in the United States in the years 1834–1864 participated in the American Civil War, fighting on both sides of the barricades. Nonetheless, the decided majority of them due to their opposition to slavery declared themselves on the side of the Union. It is very difficult to determine the exact number of Poles who participated in the war. There are serious differences on this issue among historians, for instance Mieczysław Haiman estimates their number at 5,000, Bogdan Grzeloński at 2,500, while Marian Kukiel ventures 500.[1]

The fact is that many of them earned their officer's stripes, and some even very high ones. Three Poles were generals in the Union Army (Włodzimierz Krzyżanowski, Józef Karge and Albin F. Schoepf), two were colonels, five were Majors and sixty were Captains. Both Krzyżanowski and Karge came from Wielkopolska, but only Karge was a veteran of the Wielkopolska Uprising in 1848. The following fought in the Armies of the South: Kasper Tochman (a Major of the Polish Armed Forces in 1831) who was a Brigadier for a short time; Walerian Sulakowski, Ignacy Szymański and Hipolit Oladowski (veterans of the November Uprising) were Lt. Colonels.[2]

On the Side of the Union

Captain Konstanty Błędowski was one of those who fought in Union regiments. He had participated in the uprising of 1848 in Wielkopolska, in the Hungarian Uprising, and as one of Garibaldi's soldiers in Italy. On May 10, 1861 he was gravely wounded while overpowering the Jackson confederate encampment near St. Louis. He died of

---

[1] F. Stasik. *The Polish Political Emigration in the United States of America 1831–1864.]* Warszawa 1973, p. 256; M. Haiman, *Historia udziału Polaków w amerykańskiej wojnie domowej [History of the Polish Participation in the American Civil War]* Chicago 1928, pp. 31-33; B. Grzeloński, *Polacy w Stanach Zjednoczonych Ameryki 1776–1865 [Poles in the United States of America 1776–1865]* Warsaw 1976, p. 142.

[2] F. Stasik, op. cit., pp. 261-262

his injuries on May 25, 1861. He was one of the first officers to die in the American Civil War.[3]

Captain Aleksander Bielawski, adjutant of Major General John A. McLernand, died in the routing of the Confederates out of their camp in Belmont, Missouri on November 7, 1861. This is what the General wrote about him in one of his reports: "...Captain Aleksander Bielawski, one of my adjutants... having dismounted off his horse, which had already been wounded several times, was felled by a bullet while he marched forward with the flag of his adopted country in his hand, calling on the soldiers marching behind him to follow him. His bravery was matched by his loyalty as a soldier and patriot. He died and the starry standard became his shroud. Hail to his memory!"[4]

Captain Stanisław Młotkowski, residing in Philadelphia, (a veteran of the Spring of Nations on Polish lands in 1848) at news of the outbreak of the Civil War declared himself on the side of the Union and organized an independent light artillery battery. In the Fall of 1861 Captain Młotkowski was nominated the commander of an artillery company in the regular army and assigned to the defense of Fort Delaware, built on Pea Patch Island on the Delaware River near Wilmington. This fort guarded the entrance to Philadelphia from the south. At Fort Delaware Captain Młotkowski had the following commanders: Captain Gibson, Major Burton, Colonel Perkins and Colonel Buchanan. From April 25, 1863 to the end of the war his commanding officer was a native countryman from Poland, Bigadier General Albin F. Schoepf.[5]

"The composer Adam Kurek, a veteran of the November Uprising mentioned earlier, also declared himself for the Union. He traveled indefatigably from town to town with an orchestra that he himself founded, supporting with its engagements recruitment to the Union army."[6]

Captain Józef Głoskowski, a former member of the Democratic Society of Polish Exiles in New York, was a respected pioneer of the signal corps in the American Army. His signaling ability allowed Union detachments to avoid danger many times. This service required great intelligence and courage. The signal man had to be stationed on forward positions, to track the enemy and inform his detachments about the enemy's movements by the use of small flags. Thanks to this he saved the army of General Burnside from being outflanked at the Battle of Antietam, Maryland on September 17, 1862. He also distinguished himself on December 13, 1862 at the

---

3   M. Haiman. *Historia udziału Polaków w amerykańskiej wojnie domowej* [*The History of Polish Participation in the American Civil War*] Chicago 1928, pp. 95-96

4   Ibid., p. 98

5   "Polacy komenderowali największą fortecą "Delaware" ["Poles Commanded the Largest Fortress, Fort Delaware"] in: *Weteran [The Veteran]* New York: October 1961, p. 14

6   A. Janta, op. Cit., p. 58

Battle of Fredericksburg, Virginia, which was lost by the Union, where he directed the artillery fire. He was constantly threatened by enemy fire, because he was a perfectly visible target. In April 1864 Captain J. Głoskowski left the Union ranks. He died on December 7, 1886 in the Polish settlement of Radom in the southern part of the State of Illinois.[7]

Captain Ludwik Żychliński joined the Union Army immediately after arriving in the United States in 1861. He was a veteran of the Spring of Nations, and fought for Garibaldi during the battles in Italy. Together with other Poles he participated in various battles against the Confederates, among others in the state of Missouri and Virginia. In the Fall of 1862 in the area of Washington, D.C. he had a personal meeting with President Abraham Lincoln, of which he wrote in his memoirs: "I went in a delegation with several Poles to see the President, who was accommodated in a spacious tent in the camp, in order to greet him and assure him that the spirits of Kościuszko and Pułaski alone were responsible for our joining the ranks of the United States, in order to fight on the battle fields for lofty ideas, to defend freedom and the threatened Republic, whom our heroes one hundred years before had helped to establish with their blood and had lent their pure, noble hands to this enterprise. On this occasion General Hooker presented me to the President, praising the courage of the Poles in battle, their diligence in fulfilling duties in service and their ardent, sincere love of freedom.

"The President also shook my hand and declared that every Pole already has bravery in his blood and is a good soldier, and that the United States feels deep empathy for Poland, and will never deny its sons hospitality and a livelihood. He also asked us how many Poles there were in the Army, and spoke with praise of Rozenkranc, Krzyżanowski and many other Poles whom he knew personally, and then, with greater cordiality than most Americans, he bid us goodbye, saying: "Until we see each other again, and after the war too, because we will not forget to reward those who helped us fight the enemy that wants to keep slavery in the Republic and strives to keep the Union divided, which is voluntarily united into a strong state and a mutually supportive whole."[8]

President Lincoln's compassion for Poland did not prevent him from conducting a friendly policy toward czarist Russia, which was in line with the contemporary American *raison d'etat*. At that time there was no Polish cause in American politics, just as the Polish state did not exist either. Poles fighting on the side of the Union were gladly accommodated as good soldiers, but nothing beyond that.

---

7   Ibid., pp. 104-107
8   M. Haiman *Historia udziału Polaków w amerykańskiej wojnie domowej* [*The History of Polish Participation in the American Civil War*] Chicago 1928, pp. 84-85

Colonel Józef Smoliński was an unusually colorful figure among the Poles who participated in the Civil War. A Chevalier of the Order of Virtuti Militari for his conduct at the Battle of Olszynka Grochowska, after the fall of the November (1830–1831) uprising he emigrated to France where he signed up for service in the colonial armies in Algeria. After concluding his enlistment he left for Canada. In 1854 at news of the outbreak of the Russian Turkish war and the formation of a Polish Legion in Turkey, he immediately left for Istanbul. He earned the rank of colonel in the Crimean war. After its conclusion, he settled down in Istanbul, where he started a brewery, which was soon confiscated by the Turkish authorities. So he departed for America, this time to the United States, where in Washington, D.C. he became an official in the Department of the Treasury. After the outbreak of the Civil War he received a colonel's commission and permission to form a cavalry regiment but he was unable to fulfill this task. After news of the outbreak of the January uprising he left America and went to Poland. But he only got as far as Ołomuniec, where he was detained by the Austrian authorities. Thanks to the intervention of the American ambassador in Vienna he was freed and returned to America, where he became associated with the Irish independence movement, which strove to free Ireland from British shackles. He participated with members of this movement in two unsuccessful expeditions (1866 and 1870) against Canada, which was in British hands. In 1869 he published in New York a two volume work: *Infantry Tactics for the Exercise and Manoeuvres of Troops*.[9]

Albin Franciszek Schoepf, from Kraków, an artillery officer of the Austrian Army, attained the rank of General. As often happens with known positive historical figures there is a dispute concerning him between Poles and Hungarians, because his mother was Polish and his father was Hungarian. The upbringing his parents gave him was effective enough that after the outbreak of the Hungarian uprising Shoepf resigned from service in the Austrian Army and joined the Polish Legion. After the fall of the uprising he fled to Turkey from where in 1851 he emigrated to the United States. After the outbreak of the Civil War he joined the Union Army as a volunteer, where he was commissioned general in the army of General George Thomas in the State of Kentucky. He participated in the victorious battle of Mill Springs on January 19, 1862. He commanded a brigade in the Army of the Ohio. Several months later, at the Battle of Perryville, he was already in charge of a division. In the last period of the war he was the commander of Fort Delaware.[10]

---

9   Ibid., pp. 110-112
10 H. Wielecki, *Pod znakiem srebrnego i złotego orła. Polsko-amerykańskie tradycje wojskowe od XVIII do XX wieku.* [*Under the Sign of the Silver and Gold Eagle. Polish-American Military Tradition from the 18th to the 20th century*] Warszawa 1998, pp. 40-41.

The greatest career in the armies of the Union was made by Józef Karge, a participant of the Wielkopolska Uprising of 1848. He came to America in 1851. Being a linguist (he completed his studies at the University of Wrocław and the famous Collège de France in Paris) he founded two foreign language schools in New York City and Danbury, Connecticut, where he was recognized as an excellent teacher.

After the outbreak of the Civil War, as a declared opponent of slavery, he volunteered for military duty. As a former officer of the Prussian and Polish cavalry he received a nomination for lieutenant colonel in February 1862 with the First Cavalry Regiment of the State of New Jersey, which had its baptism by fire on June 1, 1862 during a difficult crossing of the mountains in the area of Strasburg. During this skirmish with the Confederates, an artillery shell exploded under Karge's horse. Horse and rider were blown into the air by the power of the explosion. The horse was torn to bits, but the rider fell to the ground, just spattered with the blood of his mount.[11]

At the head of his regiment in the Battle of Barnett's Ford on August 7, 1862, he was instrumental in saving the army of the State of Virginia from annihilation by the armies of General Jackson. By the same token, he saved Washington, D.C. from capture by the Confederates. In the next Battle of Brandy Station on August 20 he again conducted himself very bravely: "When the Second New York Mounted Regiment scattered and masses of enemy cavalry fell on Karge, who stood on the right flank, the brave Pole, have shouted an order to attack, was the first to rush at the Confederates. Having used up all of his bullets on them, he threw his pistol at the head of the closest Confederate and taking out his sword fell on the enemy throng. The soldiers standing closest to him, heartened by the excellent example of their commander, rushed after him. But the rest again, just as at Harrisonburg, scattered. Once again Karge tried to gather his dispersed people for an attack and by himself, together with his adjutants, plunged into a group of the enemy. By this act, he saved the regiment, because thanks to the delay Bayard's detachments were able to rush to the aid of the hard-pressed soldiers. But Karge paid with a serious wound to the leg, thanks to which he spent the next three months in a hospital.[12]

After recuperating, Karge returned to active duty at the beginning of October 1862. He received an order to capture the town of Warrenton. Thanks to a strategem his cavalrymen captured this town together with a huge amount of material. 1,600 prisoners were captured. But the town itself presented a horrifying view, which the deeply moved Karge wrote about in his official report: "Every house in town was filled with the wounded and sick and even the streets were filled with reconvalescents

---

11   Ibid, pp. 67-8
12   Ibid, p. 69

... The conditions in the hospitals were horrible. The sick were dying on the bare ground, having a skimpy blanket as their entire bedding, and a straw filled pillow under the head. In certain houses, the sick and wounded were simply rotting in their own excrement, and there was no one to help them ... Up to 50 people died daily from lack of attention, food and medicine."[13]

Several weeks later Karge again distinguished himself in the Battle of Aldie. In December 1862 illness and festering wounds forced him to interrupt his military service. He returned to duty in June 1863, when the Department of War in Washington proposed that he organize the Second Cavalry Regiment of the State of New Jersey. Governor J. Parker gave him command of the entire cavalry of the state conferring on him the rank of colonel. After the defeat of the Army of the South at Gettysburg (July 13, 1863) Karge was sent with his cavalry to mop up small Confederate detachments that were engaged in guerilla warfare in the south-western states. Over a period of eighteen months Colonel Karge organized seven big expeditions in the states of Mississippi, Tennessee, Kentucky, Arkansas and Louisiana, and fought tens of battles and skirmishes, gaining big recognition from his superiors. One of them, General Gierson, wrote to Undersecretary of War E. M. Stanton with a request to confer the rank of Brigadier General on Karge, motivating this with the observation that during the war Colonel Karge had often successfully led a division. This request was acted on positively and by a decision of Congress of March 13, 1865 J. Karge "in recognition of his bravery and invaluable service during war" was accorded the rank of Brigadier General in time of war.

After the conclusion of hostilities he remained in the army for another three years at his own request, where after verification in the rank of lieutenant he was made commander of the Army Reserves in the State of Nevada, on the so-called frontier, which at that time teemed with Indians.

After discharge from the army in 1868 he returned to teaching. Two years later, in 1870, he received a proposal to assume the position of Professor of Foreign Languages and Literatures at Princeton University, He worked there up to his death in 1892.[14]

Adam Gurowski was a widely publicized figure during the American Civil War. He was called a monster by Poles in America because of his slogans about panSlavism under Russia's leadership, which rendered the existence of a Polish state impossible. Those views were in harmony with the Union's pro-Russian policy at that time. He was a great proponent of the abolition of slavery. At the beginning of

---

13 Ibid, p. 70
14 W. A. Wojciechowski. "W obronie całości Unii i demokracji. Udział generała Józefa Kargego w wojnie domowej" ["In the Defense of the Entirety of the Union and Democracy. The Contribution of General Józef Karge in the Civil War"] in: *Weteran [The Veteran]* October 1962, p. 7

the war he worked at the Department of State in Washington, D.C. as a German press reviewer. He propagated abolitionist ideas in the newspapers, at club meetings and at public gatherings. Though he was handicapped (he had lost an eye) he wanted to form a regiment made up of African Americans. When the capital was threatened by Confederate divisions he enlisted in the Union army, for which he received personal thanks from President Abraham Lincoln.[15]

In the Armies of the Confederacy

Tadeusz A. Strawiński was the first American of Polish descent who on January 27, 1861 sacrificed his young life for the Confederacy. He was noted in official documents as the first victim of the Civil War. He came from Charleston, South Carolina, where he was born in 1843. His father, Tadeusz Strawiński, Sr., was a political émigré, a former participant in the 1830–1831 Uprising. The Charleston *Mercury* of January 28, 1861 informed as follows about the death of the young T. A. Strawiński: "Tadeusz A. Strawiński, age 18, died Saturday evening in the Naval Hospital due to a chance revolver bullet. This promising young man was on guard duty in the Columbia artillery encampment at Fort Moultrie, where the sad accident occurred. He was a noble young man, who barely within a week after registering for his freshman year at South Carolina College, abandoned his studies and together with his brave father hurried to enlist at the call of the State. When he was being carried on a stretcher to the hospital, he said to those who were walking with him: 'Friends, how sorry I am that you will be storming Fort Sumter without me!' During his suffering he constantly bemoaned the fact that he would not be present at the storming of the fort. To the end he was calm and resigned to his fate. He died devoutly, with the Lord's Prayer on his lips. The gentle influence of his mother sweetened his last moments. His father accepted the heavy blow like a soldier and gave his son up to God. The sympathy of the entire city is with the bereaved family."[16]

Kasper Tochman, already mentioned earlier, was the most well known Pole fighting on the side of the Confederacy. He was a Major in the Polish Army during the 1831 campaign, and a Chevalier of the Order of Virtuti Militari. His declaration on the side of the Confederates caused a great sensation in Polish circles both in America and in Europe, because he was a known figure there. Tochman wanted to organize a Polish Brigade, which he was to command in the rank of Brigadier General, which he was guaranteed by the Department of War. In a matter of six weeks

---

15 *Ameryka w pamiętnikach Polaków. Antologia [America in Polish Memoirs. An Anthology]* selection and commentary by B. Grzeloński, Warszawa 1975, p. 128

16 M. Haiman *Historia udziału Polaków w amerykańskiej wojnie domowej. Antologia [The History of Polish Participation in the American Civil War. An Anthology]* Chicago 1928, pp. 40-41

he organized at his own expense one regiment, commanded by Colonel Walerian Sulakowski. He ran out of funds to form a second regiment. His efforts undertaken in Richmond, Virginia (the capital of the Confederacy) were not successful, and the plan to create a Polish brigade was unequivocally torpedoed by intrigues. After this failure Tochman resigned from military service. Although he never commanded on the battlefield in the rank of General, in official confederate documents he was titled a Brigadier General. After the conclusion of the Civil War, the Governor of the State of Virginia appointed him a state agent to attract immigrants to the depopulated and war-ravaged state. In the course of this work he founded a Polish settlement, Nowa Polska [New Poland] in Spotsylvania, which, however, due to its great distance from major roadways, ultimately was disbanded.[17]

Another veteran of the November Uprising, Colonel Walerian Sulakowski, also distinguished himself in the Confederate Army. In the first phase of the war he commanded the first regiment of the Polish Brigade, formed by General Kasper Tochman. This unit, later renamed the 14th Louisiana Infantry Regiment, participated in battles in Virginia. Colonel Sulakowski was nominated, on October 3, 1861, commander of the 7th Brigade, which was composed of the 10th and 14th Louisiana Infantry Regiments. In 1862, as part of General McLernand's army, he participated in battles in Texas and Louisiana, where he distinguished himself as an outstanding engineer, a specialist in the construction of military fortifications. Among others he fortified the main port in Texas—Galveston and the Sabine Strait which connects a lake of the same name with the Gulf of Mexico, as well as the environs of Valesco and Quintana.

Seeing how the confederate forces were continually shrinking in the ongoing war, he proposed a plan to bring to America over thirty thousand former Polish insurrectionists, who were aimlessly wandering around various countries of Europe. He had in mind to form a Polish Legion, a Polish Corps out of them. After many attempts he succeeded in interesting the Confederacy's military authorities in this project, from whom he received a double masted ship, the "Dodge," with a load of cotton worth close to $80,000. Sulakowski wanted to break through the naval blockade of the Union's warships and make it to Cuba, where he was to buy a steamboat for the sold cotton, with which he would have been able to bring the former Polish insurrectionists from Europe. The plan did not succeed because the "Dodge" was unable to overcome the naval blockade. After being detained it was forced to sail to New Orleans, where Union forces confiscated the ship and its cargo. Sulakowski by ways known only to himself succeeded in making it to Mexico, where all further traces of him were lost.[18]

---

17   Ibid. pp. 119-130
18   Ibid., pp. 131-140

Colonel Ignacy Szymański was also a November 1831 insurgent, who after arriving in America settled in the state of Louisiana, where he became the owner of a plantation. After the outbreak of the Civil War he enlisted in the Confederate army where, in the rank of Colonel he commanded the Chalmette Infantry Regiment. In 1862 he participated in the hopeless defense of New Orleans. On April 5 he became a prisoner of war, but was released as part of a prisoner exchange. He did not return to front line duty. To the end of the wear he served as an army inspector for the exchange of prisoners in the Trans-Mississippi department.[19]

Hipolit Oladowski was a Lt. Colonel of the artillery on the Confederate side. He also had participated in the November Uprising. During the four years of the Civil War he served as chief armorer of General Bragg's army. On May 8, 1862 he was appointed chief armorer of the entire Army of the Mississippi, the so-called Army of the West. To the end of the war he had oversight of all armories and arsenals on the enormous terrain of the western states of the Confederacy. It was a very difficult and responsible task. Only the chief armorer of General Lee's army (the Army of the East) held a similar position. Oladowski demanded a lot from himself and his subordinates. He was tactful, which is evidenced by his letter of August 11, 1862, sent to Major W. R. Hunt, commander of one of the arsenals: "I personally do not have a moment's rest; I am totally, body, mind and soul dedicated to the task of preparing such a great amount of arms and ammunition. You in your position can help me a lot and gain the gratitude of your fatherland, which is in need. You probably haven't yet had time to take care of or acknowledge the receipt of my letter of the 3rd of this month and perhaps I am too hurriedly imposing myself on you; but the gathering of arms and ammunition for 60,000 infantry, 5,000 cavalry and one hundred field cannon is not an easy thing, and my soldier's nature incites me to act without rest, until I am certain that I have the needed supplies.

"In my opinion, this war demands that one never rest, never postpone anything, but work from morning to evening and into the night, if something has to be done today. It is better, much better to die of exhaustion in a righteous and worthy cause, than to give up or permit oneself to be conquered. I think that our victory depends only on our energy and self-sacrifice. I therefore want us to work diligently and all together. I believe in Providence, but I also believe that God helps those who help themselves.

"And so, my Dear Sir, please send me as soon as circumstances allow, ammunition for small arms, as well as equipment and outfittings."[20]

---

19 Ibid., pp. 145-146
20 Ibid., pp. 141-145

In Support of the January Uprising

The War of Secession in the United States coincided with the outbreak of the January (1863) Uprising in Poland.

While a lopsided struggle unfolded on Polish lands between the Polish guerillas and the overwhelming Russian forces, the revolutionary National Government in Warsaw, through its emissary in Paris, on February 12, 1864 appointed Henryk Kałussowski its official representative in the United States. He was a veteran of the November 1830 Uprising and well known in Polish émigré circles. Thus Kałussowski became the first official Polish diplomatic envoy in the United States.[21]

Unfortunately, due to President Lincoln's pro-Russian policy, Kałussowski was ignored by the administration.[22]

At the news of the outbreak of the Uprising in Poland Poles living in the United States began to organize relief committees in New York, Cincinnati, Chicago, St. Louis, Washington, D.C., Albany, Philadelphia, Leavenworth City and San Francisco. Efforts were initiated to collect funds for the Polish uprising, which was not easy during the on-going Civil War. Henryk Kałussowski directed the action. On behalf of the National Government in Warsaw he was also the general collector of the *Podatek Ofiary Narodowej* (Tax for National Sacrifice) in the United States.

Many Poles participating in the American Civil War wanted to return to Europe to take part in the Uprising. Unfortunately, stern regulations of the American Army did not permit it. Only several were successful in this effort. One of them was Ludwik Żychliński, who recalled many years later: "Many Poles wanted to go to the Uprising, but having learned the consequences of leaving the army during an on-going war, they remained in the ranks and only several of us, after much running around, were able to depart from America in April 1863."[23]

Żychliński under the pretext of needing to heal his wounds in European sanatoriums received an official army discharge, after which he left using a false passport and traveled through Germany to Warsaw. The Uprising authorities appointed him commander of armed forces in Warszawa and Rawa Counties. There he headed a detachment, and was involved in many skirmishes with the Russian army up to the moment when he was taken prisoner. For his participation in the Uprising he was sent to the trans-Baikal region of Siberia, from where after many years he returned to his native Wielkopolska. In 1882 he

---

21 K. Murzynowski. "Henryk Korwin-Kałussowski (1806–1894)" in: *Problem Polonii Zagranicznej [Issues of the Polish Community Abroad* vol. IV, Warszawa 1964–1965, p. 126

22 J. Szygowski *Powstanie polskie w roku 1863 i Stany Zjednoczone [The Polish Uprising of 1863 and the United States]* Paris, 1962, p. 19

23 M. Haiman. *Historia udziału Polaków w amerykańskiej wojnie domowej [A History of Polish Participation in the American Civil War]* Chicao 1928, p. 92

published his memoirs in Poznań: *Przygody Wielkopolanina w Azji i Ameryce [Adventures of a Native Wielkopolian in Asia and America].*

After the outbreak of the January Uprising, veterans of the 1830–31 and 1848 campaigns living in New York, while collecting funds to help their native country, realized they had an obstacle in not having their own publication. Thanks to their initiative the first Polish newspaper in America *Echo z Polski [Echo from Poland]* began appearing on June 1, 1863. Under the editorship of Roman J. Jaworowski it focused on the issue of the uprising in Poland, propagandized on its behalf and sought help for fighting countrymen. This paper informed for instance that on July 5, 1863 in Pythagoras Hall in New York Poles of Jewish heritage held a Ball, the profit from which was designated for the uprising.

Unfortunately, as a result of this and many other events barely $16,000 was collected.[24] If we compare this result with the sum of one million dollars which was the amount that New York spent on a welcoming banquet for the Russian flotilla that paid a visit to New York harbor, we then have the most telling evidence as to which side of the Polish-Russian conflict contemporary American policy was on.

Henryk Kałussowski, bitter about the failure of the fundraising for the uprising in Poland, wrote to Józef Ignacy Kraszewski: "The times of cordial American sympathy have passed. The fashion for adoring liberal Moscow and its Czar has spread from the dailies to the populace. Touring authors, such as Mssrs. Bayard and Taylor, who were cordially shaken by the hand by Girchakov, the Russian Foreign Minister, went from town to town and city to city arguing that the Polish uprising was a matter of fanaticism and of the Czartoryski political party. So thereafter the Russian flotilla appeared and the Russians starting spreading the gold around that our exiles had been mining in Siberia ... then there were magnificent festivities and the cordial coming together of the Protestants with the Schismatics."[25]

The American authorities, at the demand of the Russians, ended up handing over to the Russians those Poles who had deserted the Russian army and had joined the Union army. One of them was a Milewski, in whose defense Poles and Czechs living in New York organized a joint and unfortunately unsuccessful demonstration on September 8, 1864.

No wonder that *Głos Wolny [The Free Voice]* of London warned Polish refugees heading for America, in these words: "The Federals did not stop at celebrating and

---

24 Ibid., p. 153
25 B. Grzeloński, *Polacy w Stanach Zjednoczonych Ameryki 1776–1865* [*Poles in the United States of America 1776–1865*] p. 137; W. Kruszka. *Historia polska w Ameryce* [*Polish History in America*] vol. I, Milwaukee, p. 467

rubbing noses with the Muscovites, but went so far as to break international law and infringe on the sanctity of shelter for the persecuted, handing into Russian hands Milewski and several other Poles, who had left the service of the fatherland's enemy and joined the ranks of the Federals with the mistaken notion that these are fighting for the rights and freedom of those who seek shelter from the despots chasing them."[26]

The fall of the January Uprising depressed the Poles living in the United States. Various committees that had been organizing aid dissolved. Instead of a committee, in September 1864 the so-called Fraternal Aid for Those Arriving from the Field of Battle was formed, with political refugees in mind.[27] Henryk Kałussowski was actively involved in its work.Generally speaking, however, the political activity of the Polish refugees was diminishing. This phenomenon did not by-pass the Polish American community in New York, of which the most obvious symptom was the folding in April 1865 (after almost two years of existence) of the paper *Echo from Poland*.[28]

---

26 Ibid., pp. 467-468
27 K. Murzynowska. *Henryk Korwin-Kałussowski (1806–1894)* in: *Problemy Polonii Zagranicznej [Issues of the Polish Community Abroad]* vol. IV, Warszawa 1964–1965, p. 127
28 W. Kruszka, op. cit., pp. 476-478

IV.
January Uprising Participants on American Soil

Participants in the tragic January Uprising began arriving in America toward the end of 1863. Several months later numerous groups had arrived. The London-based Polish émigré *Głos Wolny [Free Voice]* wrote on July 31, 1864: "...the departure of fresh refugees to American camps is happening en masse."[1] In later years only individuals would emigrate.

It is impossible today to even estimate the number of former January insurrectionists who immigrated to the United States. Nonetheless one ought to approach the information from *The Free Voice* with a sizeable grain of salt, because there is lack of proof that "crowds" of former January insurrectionists had arrived in the United States. Maybe those people concealed who they really were, because they were aware of cases of Poles being handed over to the Russians.

It seems certain that there were no group arrivals. Among the people who came to the United States were: Stanisław Artwiński, Stefan Cieszewski, Henryk Dołęga-Lewandowski, Erazm J. Jerzmanowski, Błażej Korzeniowski, Engineer W. Kosiński, Major Józef Krzemieniecki, Marcin Kwiatkowski, Piotr Leszczyński, Julian Lipiński, Dr. Mieczysław Mackiewicz, Major Mikołaj Michalski, J. Morozowicz, Wincenty Pietrowicz, Jan Rychlicki, Hilary Skwierzyński, Jan Smoliński, Wincenty Smołczyński, Franciszek Śmietanka, Edward Wilkoszewski, Piotr Wodzicki and Major Antoni Zaręba.[2]

Some of the former January insurrectionists took part in the American Civil War, joining the ranks on both of the fighting sides, mainly however on the Confederate side. The latter, in contrast to the Union forces, were decidedly more popular. The Poles new the sympathies toward Russia shown by the highest authorities of the Union.

---

1 Ibid., p. 439
2 A. L. Waldo. *Sokolstwo. Przednia Straż Narodu* [*The Falcons. Vanguard of the Nation*] vol. III, Pittsburgh, p. 164; *Dziennik Związkowy* {*The Alliance Daily]* Chicago, Nr. 304 vol. XL, December 27, 1947; *Weteran [The Veteran]*, March 1931, p. 20; D. E. Pienkos, *PNA A Centennial History of the Polish National Alliance of the United States of North America* New York, 1984

Through Mexico to the United States

A small group of veterans of the January Uprising made it to the United States through Mexico, where in the years 1865–1867 they fought as soldiers of the Mexican Legion that was formed by Austria in 1864 to support Ferdinand Hapsburg (Ferdinand Maximilian Joseph, Archduke of Austria), who was appointed the Emperor of Mexico. Insurrectionists held in Austrian prisons and military fortresses were given a choice: enlisting in the Mexican Legion, where they would receive high pay and in the future large land grants in Mexico, or getting handed over to the Russians, where the gallows or deportation to Siberia awaited them. Pinned against the wall they chose service in the Mexican Legion. Their number is estimated at 2,000 to 4,000.

In January 1865 the Legion was sent to fight against the armies of Benito Juarez. Tens of Poles died in battle. Many were shot for trying to desert, and many of them went over to the side of the Mexican insurrectionists.

There were also Poles in Juarez's ranks who had been released from the army after the conclusion of the American Civil War. Finding themselves out on the street, they were easy marks for Juarez's emissaries. It was significant that in Mexico they were to fight with one of Poland's occupying powers (Austria).

The Mexican Legion was disbanded after Juarez's victory and the execution of Maximilian in 1867. The soldiers of this legion ended up variously. A part returned to Polish lands and settled mainly in Galicia, mostly in Lwów. Some remained for good in Mexico, mostly those who were supporters of Juarez. A few decided to go to the United States, where the bloody Civil War had recently ended.

Unfortunately, it is impossible to establish the facts. It is only known that during the war in Mexico, and also after its conclusion, wounded Polish soldiers were transported to New Orleans, and 60 of them died.

A part of Juarez's Polish adherents also resettled in the United States. And also in this instance we do not know their number. Mieczyław Haiman, a well known scholar of the Polish American community, was able to establish only four names. Antoni Grocholski—a January Uprising participant, after being wounded in the battle of Tesoca, was transported to New Orleans where he died in the hospital there. Edward Płachecki, also a January insurrectionist, came from Warsaw, fought in Marian Langiewicz's detachment and died of yellow fever in New Orleans (according to another version he died in St. Louis) in 1867. Jan Sobieski fought on the side of the Union. After the conclusion of the American Civil War he enlisted in Juarez's army in Mexico, where he allegedly rose to the rank of Lt. Colonel. He returned to the United States and settled in Minnesota. He was elected a delegate to the state's constitutional convention. He died on November 12, 1927 in Los Angeles. August Zieliński was born in Lubycza near Lwów and was a Captain in the Austrian Army. After the outbreak of the January Insurrection he left the Austrian army and crossed the Russian border in order to fight against the Russian forces. Wounded in battle he was imprisoned by the Russians, but was able to escape. After many adventures, thanks to the help of friends, he made it to Mexico and joined Juarez's army. After the victorious conclusion of the war he moved to the United States and settled in New Orleans, where he taught music and also engaged himself in painting and literature. In 1896 he moved to Baltimore. To the end of his life he edited and published a periodical, *Przyjaciel Domu [Friend of the Home]*. He died of a heart attack on Christmas Eve 1904.[3]

A few Poles remained in Mexico, for instance Makuszewski, Sierpiński, Sorokosz, Wiśniewski, Norbert Topolnicki, Chlewski.

One of the participants in the Mexican war, a member of Marian Langiewicz's detachment, Terkowski (first name unknown), after the disbanding of the Mexican Legion left Mexico and settled for good in Cuba.[4]

The Catholic Clergy

Reverend Kruszka writes about another group of former participants in the January Uprising who arrived in the United States: "It should be known that after the November Uprising Piotr Semenenko and Hieronim Kajsiewicz, both 1831 insurrectionists, together with Jański, founded the Congregation of the Resurrection in 1863 in Paris. This Congregation, founded by former November Uprising insurrectionists, was later joined by participants in the January 1863 Uprising, both lay and religious. Some took monastic vows, and these were Resurrectionists in full title; others did not take vows, but just kept the Resurrectionist rule, and these were called tertiaries. Priests who had participated in the uprising, and therefore had to go into exile abroad, also joined the congregation as tertiaries. These were sent to Polish missions in Texas and Michigan.

"But there were also numerous priests—insurrectionists, such as Reverend Adolf Bakanowski, Wincenty Barzyński, Szymon Wieczorek, Jan Wołkowski and others, who took the monastic vows of the Congregation of the Resurrection and became fully titled Resurrectionists, and were later sent to Texas and Michigan. There were also lay insurrectionists, such as Feliks Żwiardowski, who became a priest in Texas only after joining the Resurrectionists."[5]

Reverend Adolf Bakanowski, a former army chaplain in the January Uprising,

---

3 J. Białynia Chołodecki. *Polacy w Legionach Meksykańskich 1864–1867* [*Poles in the Mexican Legions 1864–1867*] in: PAVA National Executive Board Archives in New York, file: *Polacy w Legionie Meksykańskim* [*Poles in the Mexican Legion*] 1864–1867

4 Ibid.

5 A. L. Waldo. *Sokolstwo. Przednia Straż Narodu* [*Falcons Falcons of America. Vanguard of the Nation*] Pittsburgh 1972, pp. 481-481

arrived in the Polish settlement of Panna Maria, Texas in 1866. Its residents had not had a priest for three years. Thanks to his organizational abilities he achieved significant successes in just a few years together with the faithful. He wrote about it in his memoirs: "I called all the farmers to a meeting, at which we decided on the maintenance tax, the fee for weddings, funerals, etc. and at the same time we discussed the upkeep of the church and the building of a rectory and a school. Everything was decided harmoniously and the work began right away. The people are obedient, devout, loved us so much that without my permission no one, for instance, held any parties at his place. Every party with music had to be preceded by my permission, with the setting of a time limit, usually until midnight, which was conscientiously adhered to. After the passage of three years the Poles built for us a beautiful two story house which was designated for the school and our apartment."[6]

A school for Polish children was also organized in that building, the first of its kind on the American continent. Father Adolf Bakanowski found good use for his military experience, gained in the January Uprising, because he had to defend the church and his Polish parishioners with gun in hand, against the aggression of the local Americans, mostly former confederates, who tried to treat the Poles the way they used to treat the Blacks: "On the road, at home and even in church we had no peace from the Americans. One of them wanted to gallop into the sacristy on his horse and shoot the church up ... they shot at a Pole on the road and wounded him in the leg, and later wounded a woman with a knife... Seeing such sad cases, in order to scare away robbers, as also in defense against snakes and wild animals, I bought myself a revolver, which always accompanied me in my journeys together with my rosary. It usually hung in its holster by my saddle, so that everybody who did not believe in God, would respect my revolver—the American deity—from afar."[7]

Father Bakanowski was ordered to Chicago by Church authorities in 1870, from where after three years he returned to Europe. The reflections on his stay in America are noted in his memoirs, which were published in Lwów in 1913.[8]

Rev. Józef Juszkiewicz also belonged to the group pf former January Uprising participants. He had been deported to Siberia, and in 1869 became the first Polish pastor in Chicago at St. Stanislaus Kostka Parish.[9]

Another former January insurrectionist was the Rev. Józef Dąbrowski, who after

---

6   *Ameryka w pamiętnikach Polaków. Antologia. [America in the Memoirs of Poles. An Anthology]* selection and commentary by B. Grzeloński. Warszawa 1975, p. 154

7   Rev. A. Bakanowski *Pobyt w Texas [Sojourn in Texas]* in: W. Kruszka, *Historia polska w Ameryce [Polish History in America]* Milwaukee 1937, pp. 489-490

8   A. Bakanowski. *Moje wspomnienia 1840–1863–1913 [My Memoirs 1840–1863–1913]* published and with commentary by Rev. Tadeusz Olejniczak, Lwów 1913

9   W. Kruszka. *Historia polska w Ameryce [Polish History in America]* Milwaukee 1937, p. 580

years of wandering all over Western Europe as a refugee took holy orders. He did his theological studies in Rome and was ordained a priest there on August 1, 1869. He arrived in America in 1870. He directed the Polonia parish in Wisconsin, near the town of Poland Corner. He was a great promoter of Polish Catholic education on American soil. Due to a lack of teachers he imported the Felician Sisters from Kraków, who with time became a true support for Polish schooling, and their achievements in this field were enormous.

The Reverend Dąbrowski also became famous for organizing, despite many difficulties, a seminary in Detroit in 1887, which was to educate Polish priests. The need for them kept growing as the wave of emigrants from Polish territories continued to swell. In his efforts he had to overcome the resistance of the American Roman Catholic Church hierarchy, dominated by Irish clergy, who at all costs did not want to allow the development of a Church and education that would be Polish in character.

Due to a lack of highly qualified professors for the seminary that he had founded, Rev. Dąbrowski imported Polish educators, both secular and religious, from Kraków and Rome. The many years of labor to organize and maintain the seminary undermined Rev. Dąbrowski's health, and he died of a heart attack on February 15, 1902.[10]

In 1909 the seminary he founded was moved to a 100 acre property that was purchased for this purpose. It had several buildings that formerly housed the Military Academy at Orchard Lake near Detroit. It is still functioning there today as a well known Polish American center.

Co-Creators of the Most Important Polish American Organizations

Veterans of the January Uprising laid the foundations for organizations that proved to be the largest in the Polish American community: The Polish Roman Catholic Union of America and the Polish National Alliance.

The first was founded in 1873. Rev. Wincenty Barzyński was one of its founders. After coming to America he at first directed the Polish mission in San Antonio, Texas. Next he was directed to Chicago, to St. Stanislaus Kostka Parish, where he worked to the end of his life. Due to the policy of the Irish clergy, which was hampering the founding of new Polish parishes, this parish grew to incredible proportions—it counted 35,000 faithful, who did not want to belong to non-Polish parishes. Almost 4,000 children attended the parish school which he established!

When Rev. Barzyński was appointed Provincial of the Congregation of the Resurrection he began organizing Polish parishes, building churches, schools and orphanages. In 1890 in Chicago he founded the College of St. Stanislaus Kostka. He

---

10 K. Wachtl. *Polonia w Ameryce [The Polish Community in America]* Philadelphia 1994, pp. 138-139

also founded various organizations and societies: "Organizacja Patriotyczna Polska pod Opieką Królowej Korony Polskiej [The Polish Patriotic Organization under the Protection of the Queen of the Polish Crown], Liga Polska [The Polish League] and Zjednoczenie Polskie Rzymsko-Katolickie [Polish Roman Catholic Union of America] which set its main purpose as the defense of the Polish immigration against loss of the Catholic faith and Polishness. He also began publishing the *Dziennik Chicagowski [Chicago Daily]* which after some time grew to be the largest daily paper published outside Poland.[11]

Agaton Giller was the initiator of the founding of the Związek Narodowy Polski [Polish National Alliance]. He was a member of the National Government of the Uprising. While an émigré in Switzerland he kept in close touch through correspondence with many fellow countrymen in America (mainly with Henryk Kałussowski) and thanks to this was well informed of the circumstances prevailing in the Polish American community of that time. Perceiving the danger of total loss of Polishness by Polish immigrants in the American environment, he called, in a letter-memorandum titled "Organizacja Polaków w Ameryce" ["The Organization of Poles in America"] published in Chicago in 1879, for harmonious cooperation and creation of one great, joint organization. Here is how he justified its creation: "Thus the Organization—is not only able to maintain Polishness for the masses of Polish presence in America, not only can it educate it and form it into an element that is useful for the Polish Cause on the territories of the American Republic, with whose power and influence Europe must reckon, but it can also train and return to the Fatherland many of those who had left it voluntarily or under duress."[12]

Many Poles in Philadelphia accepted this idea. Thanks to their efforts and determination the first convention of Polish associations and societies took place in Chicago on September 20, 1880. These were organizations that at that time were active in many American cities, mainly in the North Eastern part of the country. The Polish National Alliance was founded, which (being a liberal-democratic organization that has,over the span of its more than 100 years of activity, competed with the Polish Roman Catholic Union of America) did an enormous amount of work in maintaining Polishness among Poles living in the United States.

From its very beginnings the Polish National Alliance owed a lot to another veteran of wars for independence, the already frequently mentioned Henryk Kałussowski, who for the next several years was one of the most active members of this organization.

This most outstanding Polish political activist in America was greatly valued by the government. He worked as a medical doctor. He also fulfilled important

---

11 Ibid., pp. 66-67
12 K. Wachtl. *Polonia w Ameryce [The Polish Community in America]* Philadelphia 1944, p. 169

functions that he was commissioned for by the U.S. government, among others he translated into Russian the document for the purchase of Alaska, which the United States bought from Russia in 1867. He was appointed director of the Department of Business and Industry in the State Department.[13]

Henryk Kałussowski amassed an enormous collection of archival and museum objects connected with the Great (Polish) Emigration and the Polish emigration to America. Toward the end of his life he decided to donate these collections to Polish institutions and organizations with which he was connected. Part of his rich library and some of his museum pieces he offered to the Society of Friends of the Sciences in Poznań, while the archival files of the Polish Democratic Society from the time of the Great Emigration he gave to the Polish Museum in Rapperswil, Switzerland. The remainder of his valuable collections became the basis of the library and archives of the Polish National Alliance in America.[14]

Edward Odrowąż (1840–1889) also belonged to the first rank of activists in the Polish National Alliance. He came from an aristocratic family and had participated in the January Uprising. He came to the United States from Paris in 1875 and settled in New York. In 1800 he participated in preparatory work for the first PNA Convention in Chicago, where he was elected the first secretary of that organization. He held that post until 1881. In the years 1881–1882 he founded and edited the weekly *Zgoda* in New York—the press organ of the PNA. By decision of the Third Convention of the PNA the offices of the weekly were relocated to Chicago. Ignacy Wendziński (1828–1901) hailing from Bydgoszcz, became the new editor of *Zgoda*. He was a teacher, a participant in the Spring of Nations and in the January Uprising. He came to the United States in 1870. He worked as a teacher in the newly formed Polish schools and as a journalist in the periodicals: *Orzeł Biały, Gazeta Polska,* and *Przyjaciel Ludu*. He was the editor-in-chief of *Zgoda* from 1882 to 1886.[15]

Another January Uprising insurrectionist, Hilary Skwierzyński, organized the first Group of the Polish National Alliance in Philadelphia.[16]

Among January Uprising veterans who found themselves in the United States the greatest career belonged to Erazm Józef Jerzmanowski. He had fought under Marian Langiewicz in the Uprising. After the defeat of the Uprising he crossed over into Galicia from where, after being interned, he went to France where he finished

---

13 *Polski Słownik Biograficzny [Polish Biographical Dictionary]* vol. XI Kraków-Warszaw-Wrocław 1964–1965; entry: Kałussowski, Korwin Henryk, p. 506

14 Ibid., vol. II, pp. 505-507

15 D. E. Pienkos, *PNA: A Centennial History of the Polish National Alliance of the United States of North America* New York 1984, p. 403

16 "Śp. Hilary Skwierczyński—powstaniec z roku 1863" ["The Late Hilary Skwierzyński—insurgent of 1863"] in: *Weteran [The Veteran]* April 1935, p. 10

engineering studies. During the Franco-Prussian War in 1871 he participated in the defense of Paris. In 1873 he left for the United States, where he promoted the use of gas for lighting. He founded the Gas Light Company in New York, Chicago and Baltimore and built gas factories in which he had sizeable shares of stock. He had factories in Indianapolis, IN, Brooklyn, Troy, Albany, Yonkers and Utica in New York, in Memphis, TN, Lafayette, IN and Longansport. "For 23 years, to 1896, he was one of the most outstanding leaders of the highly developed gas industry in the United States, became a multi-millionaire and gained the recognition of industrial and professional spheres, as well as positive opinions in the American and Polish-American press."[17] He participated actively in the life of the Polish American community. He headed the Central Charitable Committee (Komitet Centralny Dobroczynności), and on behalf of the Polish National Alliance he was President of the Polish League in America (Liga Polska w Ameryce). Thanks to him an Immigrant Aid Office for Poles was opened in New York. He financially supported Polish parochial schools and supported a Polish library in New York. He personally funded the construction of a Catholic church—St. Anthony of Padua—in Jersey City, New Jersey. He was a major financial backer of a new Polish catholic church in Manhattan on Seventh Street. In recognition of his merits Pope Leon XIII in 1889 bestoewed on him the Order of the Golden Spur. That was the first time in history that a lay person residing in the United States received this high Papal award.

In 1890 Jerzmanowski became a member of the Board of Directors of the Polish National Museum in Rappersvil, Switzerland. This museum gathered documents and historical mementos connected with the Polish national uprisings. Jerzmanowski donated a sizeable amount of money to the museum, paid very generous annual dues, assisted in the solicitation of dues in the United States, and sent the museum gifts of works of art, valuable autographs and numismatic items that he himself purchased.[18] He took frequent trips to Galicia under Austrian occupation.

In 1896 he settled in Galicia for good. He bought a landed estate in Prokocim near Kraków. He financially supported many social initiatives. Among these "…ought to be mentioned the financing of the Wawel stained glass windows by Mehoffer, a subvention for the Land Bank in Poznań, The Mianowski Fund, and an orphanage named after Jerzmanowski's parents in Warszawa, the Gimnazium (High School) in Cieszyn, schools in Biała, The Mutual Aid Society for Participants in the 1863 Uprising, The Academic House, The Association of Women Teachers and Summer

---

17 J. Hulewicz "Erazm Józef Jerzmanowski" in *Polski Słownik Biograficzny* [*The Polish Biographical Dictionary*] Vol. XI, Wrocław 1965, pp. 178-180

18 J. Kajdański, "Polak, który oświetlił Amerykę," in: *Gwiazda Polarna*, Stevens Point, WI, Nr. 6, Year/Vol. 100, March 14, 2009, p. 119

Camps in Kraków, The Polish Theater, The Marcinkowski Scientific Society and the Society for Public Reading Rooms in Poznań."[19]

In his Last Will and Testament he left the Academy of Sciences in Kraków the sum of 1,200,000 Austrian Kroner to create an award for Polish science within the National Foundation of Erazm and Anna Jerzmanowski. The first to receive this award in 1915 were Henryk Sienkiewicz and Ignacy J. Paderewski. He died in Prokocim on February 7, 1915.

Former participants in the January uprising, who found themselves in America, never were able to organize themselves into a separate veterans group, although some of them were later active in various Polish American organizations, which were organized in the subsequent decades, after the arrival of the great wave of emigrants who came to America looking for work. Wincenty Smołczyński ought to be enumerated first of all among them as also Stefan Cieszewski—local activists of the Polish National Alliance and the Polish Falcons of America.

Veterans of the 1863 uprising living in the United States were very sympathetic toward the Polish Falcons, a sports organization of a paramilitary character, which was founded by former January 1863 insurrectionists in Lwów in 1867 under Austrian occupation. Its ideas came to America together with the immigrants.

In the independent land of America this organization, aside from its very popular sports activities, also engaged itself without any constraint in patriotic and educational work among Polish youth. Veterans of the January Uprising played an extremely important role in this work. As direct participants of Poland's wars for independence they had a decisive influence on the shaping of independence minded attitudes among the young generations of Poles who were living far from Poland. Their popularity among the youth of the Falcons organization is confirmed by the fact that they were always invited for various ceremonies, sports events and organizational meetings, where they were treated with great respect and honor, and their speeches were met with great enthusiasm. That is how it was for instance during the eighth Polish Falcons of America convention in Detroit in 1907 where veteran Wincenty Smołczyński spoke as follows to the many gathered Falcons: "Poland has not yet perished and will not perish, if you will continue to move along the path that has been shown you by our Falcon ideology and by the founders of the Falcons. Today all of Poland awaits help from you, as previously from the valiant heroes of the uprising of 1863... today in my old age I would not be able to fight with arms in hand, as previously I did in the defense of Poland. My only hope lies in you, my dear brothers and colleagues. What we began—

---

19 J. Hulewicz "Erazm Józef Jerzmanowski" in *Polski Słownik Biograficzny* [*The Polish Biographical Dictionary*] Vol. XI, Wrocław 1965, pp. 178-180

you'll finish. Poland must be free! The gray-haired insurrectionist was given a lengthy standing ovation to shouts of Live Long!"[20]

Many other veterans of the January insurrection participated in the Detroit convention. Among those marching in the great Falcons parade, which passed through the streets of the city, were: Franciszek Kujawa from Wyandotte, Jan Skowroński of Newark, Wincenty Smołczyński, Jakub Pyszara, Kajetan Mroczkowski, Józef Pniewski of Detroit, Feliks Maciejewski of Buffalo, Józef Pochrzyn of Pittsburgh, and Tomasz Laski of Philadelphia.[21]

Wincenty Smołczyński began pioneering research on the history of the Polish-American community in Detroit. The fruit of his labors was the 242 page book *Historia osady i parafij polskich w Detroit, MI [The History of the Polish Settelement and Parishes in Detroit, MI]* Buffalo 1907.

Smołczyński was one of the most valuable members of the Polish Falcons of America. At every possible occasion he recruited new members to his beloved organization. NO wonder that his person became widely known in Falcons circles and also in other Polish American organizations. In September 1914 in Buffalo during one of the largest Falcons conventions, which had 5,000 participants, Wincenty Smołczyński gave his famous address in which he clearly defined the goals of his activity among Polish American youth in America: "The Falcons grew out of us the insurrectionists as the seed of the new Polish Army, remember this. ... I am the living voice of all those insurrectionists who died on the field of battle, when all of Poland appoints you our successors and avengers. It is your task to educate the Polish community to be brave and valiant and first of all physically and mentally strong, so they will be ready to fight for Poland's right to liberty, and so they will have the strength to secure that right. On you, colleagues, falls in the duty to return Poland its independence, a duty passed on to you by the veterans of the last Polish uprising against the Russians in the years 1863–1864. The fate of Poland will be as you make it!"[22]

These words were immediately titled Smołczyński's Testament and they served as the guidelines for further patriotic and educational work among the young members of the Falcons, who at this time were chafing at the bit to fight for the independence of their nation. The mood was heightened by the fact that a huge armed conflict had broken out in Europe in which the occupiers of Poland were facing off.

---

20 A. L. Waldo. *Sokolstwo. Przednia Straż Narodu* [*The Polish Falcons of America. The Vanguard of the Nation*] Vol. III Pittsburgh 1972, p. 107

21 Ibid., p. 97

22 Ibid., vol. I, Pittsburgh 1956, p. 451

Title page of the Waltz "The Aquila" which Edward B. Bohuszewicz dedicated to Dr. Feliks Wierzbicki of New York (Boston, MA 1845)

Grave of Edward B. Bohuszewicz at Swan Point Cemetery In Providence, Rhode Island, as it was in 1943

A piano arrangement by Julian Fontana published in Philadelphia, PA about 1837–1839. This publication appeared with the following note: *This melody was written some twenty years ago, in Commemoration of the celebrated* [Polish] *Constitution of 1791. The very mention of this date being accounted a crime under the Russian Government, this song could not be sung but out of the towns, in groves and woods, where the patriotic youth used to go chiefly in the Spring in order to give vent to their feelings, by singing this and other patriotic songs.*

The Grave of Feliks P. Wierzbicki—National Cemetery, Presidio of San Francisco, plot 58 nr. 2 Section 05.

Monument on the mass grave of the murdered prisoners in Goliad, Texas

The monument to the fallen and murdered defenders of Ft. Goliad with the names of the victims, including the Polish officer Franciszek Petrussewicz

Paweł Sobolewski

Sir Casimir Gzowski
(1813–1898)

Henryk Dmochowski

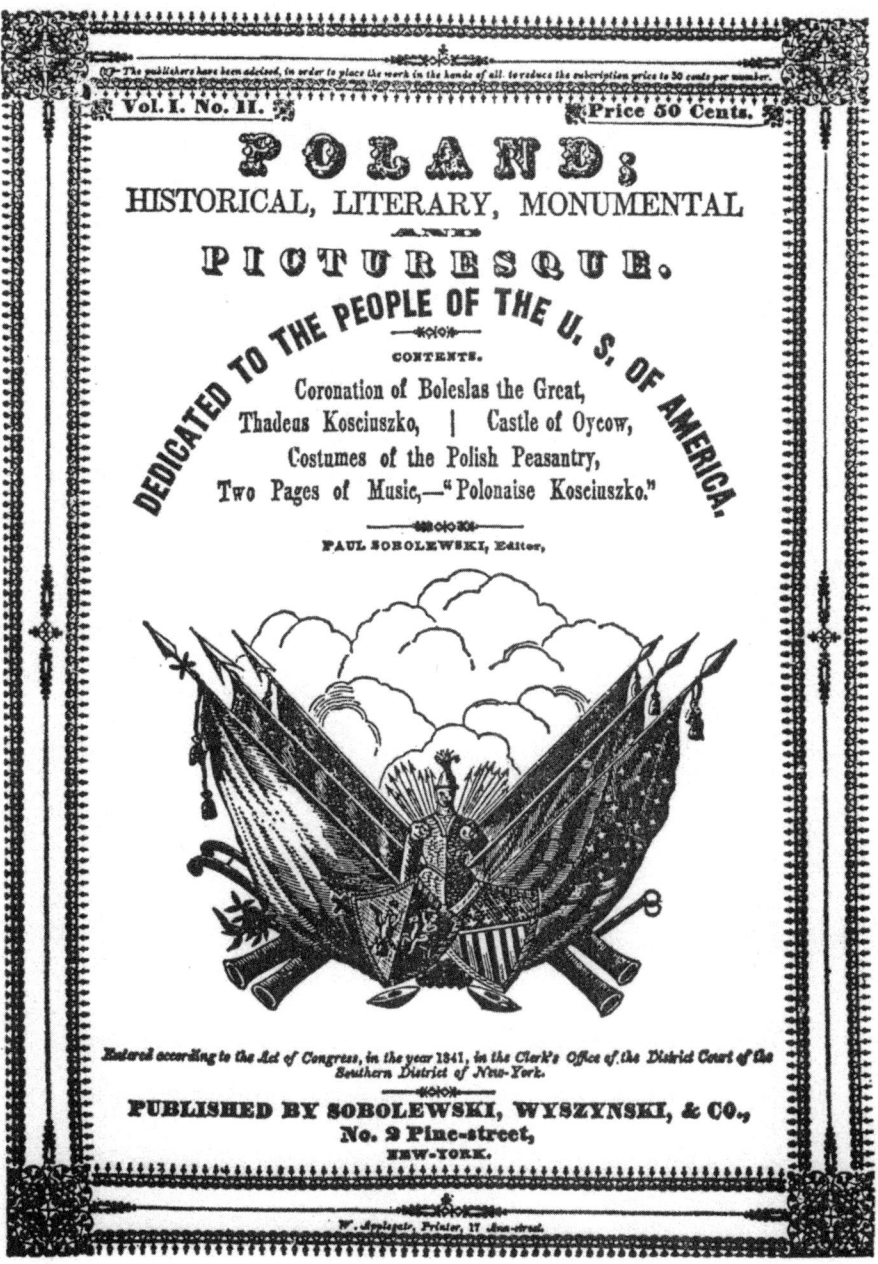

Reproduction of the front cover of Sobolewski's magazine—the first Polish periodical published in America

Sculpture of General Casimir Pulaski,
by sculptor H. Dmochowski, commissioned
by the United States Congress

Henryk Kałussowski
(painted by Ryszard Morawski)

General Włodzimierz Krzyżanowski
(painted by Ryszard Morawski)

General Józef Karge
(painted by Ryszard Morawski)

Colonel Walerian Sulakowski
(painted by Ryszard Morawski)

Ludwik Żychliński
(painted by Ryszard Morawski)

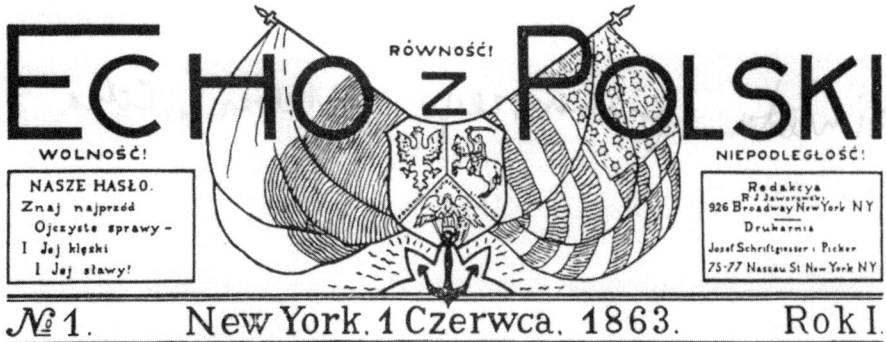

The masthead of the first issue of *Echo from Poland,* the first periodical published in Polish in America

Reverend Józef Dąbrowski

Reverend Wincenty Barzyński
(1839–1899)

Erazm Józef Jerzmanowski

Wincenty Smołczyński
(photograph made in 1923)

PART II

The Contribution of
the Polish Emigration
in America to the Regaining
of Independence by Poland
After World War I

I.
The Polish Emigration in America Prior to World War I

At the outbreak of World War I the Polish American community in the United States numbered about 3 million people, also counting the third generation of immigrants.[1] Its roots were in the so-called folk emigration, which saw its peak at the turn of the 19th century. At that time the largest congregations of ethnic Polish population in the United States were in the territories stretching from the East Coast to the Great Lakes and the Canadian border, mainly in such states as New York, New Jersey, Connecticut, Massachusetts, Maryland, Virginia, Pennsylvania, Ohio, Indiana, Illinois, Michigan, Minnesota and Wisconsin. The greatest number of Polish parishes were formed in those areas. The Polish community's life was centered around them. Polish churches were built, societies and associations were formed, mostly of a religious or mutual aid character. In time some of them grew into huge, wealthy organizations, whose activity stretched across many states, such as the Związek Narodowy Polski (Polish National Alliance), Zjednoczenie Polskie Rzymsko-Katolickie (The Polish Roman Catholic Union of America), Związek Polek w Ameryce (The Polish Women's Alliance) and the Związek Sokolstwa Polskiego (Polish Falcons of America). These and many other organizations had in their By-Laws as one of their most important goals—activity on behalf of regaining Polish independence. Some societies, such as "Ochotnicy Pułaskiego" (Pulaski's Volunteers), "Towarzystwo Rycerzy Polskich pod opieką Św. Michała Archanioła," (The Society of Polish Knights Under the Protection of St. Michael the Archangel), "Towarzystwo Gwardii Kościuszki" (The Kosciuszko Guards Society), "Towarzystwo Wolnych Polskich Krakusów" (The Society of Free Polish Cracovians), due to nostalgia for the Polish army implemented "historical" uniforms for their membership, which were often grotesque, and elements of military drill. Their activity was generally limited to participation in parades and

---

1 A. Pilch. "Emigracja z ziem polskich do Stanów Zjednoczonych od lat pięćdziesiątych XIX w. do roku 1918" ["Emigration from Polish Lands to the United States from the 1850s to 1918"] in: *Przeszłość i wpołczesność* [*The Past and the Present*] Wrocław-Warszawa-Kraków-Gdańsk-Łódź 1988, p. 40

the celebration of Polish national holidays.[2] But this also was significant, because their sight gladdened the eyes and intensified yearning for a real Polish army and an independent homeland.

A Polish-American demonstration with over 100,000 participants, which took place in May 1910 in Washington at the unveiling of the monuments to Tadeusz Kościuszko and Kazimierz Pulaski, was expressive proof of how great these longings were. At the Polish national Congress that was held on this occasion representatives of the Polish emigration in the United States unanimously passed the following resolution. "We Poles have the right to an independent national existence, and believe it our holy duty to work to obtain the political independence of our nation."[3]

This was a breakthrough moment for the activity of many Polish American organizations, among which the Falcons were most eager to act. Unfortunately, at this time they were divided into two rival groups: Związek Sokołów w Chicago (The Falcons Alliance in Chicago—connected with the Polish National Alliance), and Związek Sokołów Wolnych (The Society of Free Falcons)—with its headquarters in New York. A positive consequence of this split was that the two fraternal organizations competed in the development of their ranks. Thanks to this, the number of Falcon nests began to grow rapidly. For instance in 1909, before the split, the Falcons had 140 nests and 4,692 members and three years later the movement already numbered 344 nests and 11,551 members. Of this amount, the Falcons Alliance in Chicago had 248 nests and 8,353 members and the New York—based Society of Free Falcons had 98 nests and 3,198 members.[4]

Fortunately, these organizations came to an understanding in 1912, and at a special meeting in Pittsburgh on December 15 and 16, they united. From that moment the president of the unified Falcons organization, The Polish Falcons of America, was Dr. Teofil Starzyński of Pittsburgh. He was the first Pole to obtain the degree of Doctor of Medicine in the state of Pennsylvania.

On his initiative a militarization of the troops began, that is training of a military character was introduced, which included drill, use of weapons, the science of commanding, and maneuvers with larger detachments. The undertaking of this type of activities popularized the Falcons even more among Polish American youths, who saw in the battle formations a foretaste of the Polish army.

---

2   *Czyn zbrojny wychodźstwa polskiego w Ameryce* [*The War Effort of the Polish Emigration in America*] New York-Chicago 1957, pp. 38-41
3   Ibid. p. 58
4   *Pamiętnik Zjazdu Dwudziestego i Zlotu Szesnastego Sokolstwa Polskiego w Ameryce w dniach 7-12 lipca 1933 roku* [*Souvenir of the Twentieth Convention and the Sixteenth Jamboree of the Polish Falcons of America July 7–12, 1933*] Chicago 1933, p. 17

Political Orientations in the First Years of the War

The outbreak of World War I caused a polarization in the attitudes of the Polish American community (frequently called the Polonia). The Komitet Obrony Narodowej (National Defense Committee) was organized, which pinned its hopes on the Austro-Hungarian Empire, and considered the legions being formed in Galicia at the initiative of Józef Piłsudski to be the true Polish armed forces. The adherents of this orientation were popularly called konists (from KON, the abbreviation for Komitet Obrony Narodowej). They considered Russia to be Poland's greatest enemy. A second orientation of an anti-German and anti-Austrian character declared itself on the side of England and France in the ongoing armed conflict, that is, with countries that were closer to the ideals of freedom and democracy. In consequence, they also had to agree to support of one of the occupiers of Polish territory (Russia), which was a war ally of England and France. The Wydział Narodowy Polskiego Centralnego Komitetu Ratunkowego (The National Department of the Central Polish Aid Committee) was a representative of this orientation. The largest Polish American organizations were part of this committee, such as the Polish National Alliance, the Polish Roman Catholic Union of America, The Polish Women's Alliance of America and the Polish Falcons of America.[5]

After the outbreak of war in 1914 the generosity and self-sacrifice of the Polish American community (Polonia) grew enormously on behalf of its native land, across whose territories heavy battles were being fought by the armies of those who up to then had been the occupiers of Poland. Collecting funds on behalf of Poland was not enough for Polish American youth. They were attracted to armed action. The Falcons, of course, were in the vanguard on this issue, but the leaders of this organization tried to control the ebullient moods prevailing in the ranks, maintaining that there could be no full engagement in the ongoing conflict until there was a clear declaration from the countries of the Entente concerning Polish independence.

On the Way to the Polish Legions

Not all the members wanted to go along with this posture of the Falcons leadership. Some at the news of the formation of the Polish legions at the side of the Austro-Hungarian army decided to leave the Falcon ranks and go to Galicia, under the command of Józef Piłsudski. Witold S. Rylski, the former commander of the Falcons, headed this group of hotheads. On September 1, 1914, together with 18 people, he left Detroit determined to reach Poland. This was a very

---

5   These divisions proved to be quite permanent. They held for the duration of the war, and during the years of Polish independence (1919–1939) they effectively poisoned mutual relations between the Polish American community and the government of the Second Polish Republic, especially after 1926.

difficult task, because Europe was already engulfed in the conflagration of war.[6] A couple of weeks later similar groups of volunteers left from Newark (15 Falcons) Philadelphia (9 Falcons) Amsterdam, New York (3 Falcons) and Detroit (3 Falcons). Not all the names of those who departed are known, because many of them left America secretly.

The National Defense Committee inspired the departure of volunteers for the Legions together with the Alliance of Polish Youth, which cooperated with the Committee on this action from the organizational and financial side.

"The Congers farm outside New York City was the site of military preparedness for volunteers. The first name (of this camp) was Polska Szkoła Wojskowa (Polish Military School). Later the name Konary was adopted, to commemorate the battle Piłsudki's Legions fought at the town of Konary, where the 3rd battalion of the 1st Brigade fought under a flag donated by the Women's Committee of Chicago (Ms. Paradzińska, president). There were also Poles from America in this battalion.

"This camp was maintained by KON, with which the Polish Youth Alliance of America cooperated. Citizen Jeziorański, a former Russian army officer, was the commander and main instructor. In all probability over 100 volunteers left this camp for the Legions. Citizen Jeziorański left with the last group after the camp was shut down in July 1916.

"In Chicago the Polish Youth Alliance conducted military courses on Ashland Avenue and 16th Street and re-training in the Legion style. These courses were conducted by a former captain of the Austrian army, citizen Gepert."[7]

Fate did not treat the departing groups equally. The last two were interned by the British in Ireland for the duration of the war, because they were unable to evade the English blockade on the Atlantic.[8] All passengers of detained ships were meticulously inspected. If they came from Germany or Austro-Hungary they were detained and placed in internee camps. Polish volunteers heading for the Legions mostly had fake Russian passports, thanks to which they were able to make it to Norway, from there to Copenhagen, where they went to the Austrian consulate to get documents for the trip across Germany. After crossing the Austro-Hungarian border some of them were arrested and incorporated into the Austrian army from where they had to escape to the Legions.

---

6   AZG SWAP [PAVA NEB Archives]; AO, file: Agnieszka Wisła, letter of Leopold Krzyżak of June 15, 1940

7   Piłsudski Institute of America; archives of individuals: Aleksander Dubiński, "Ochotnicy z Ameryki do Legionów Piłsudskiego" ["Volunteers from America for Piłsudski's Legions 1914–1918"]

8   M. Zawadzki. "W niewoli u Anglików" ["Imprisoned by the English"] in: A. L. Waldo *Czyn zbrojny Polonii Stanów Zjednoczonych w nowelkach, gawędach i opowiadaniach wojskowych* [*The War Effort of the Polish American Community in the United States in short stories, yarns and army tales*] Chicago 1938, pp. 73-81

In the winter of 1914/15 the Falcons leadership tried to interest the administration in Washington in the issue of Polish independence. An appropriate memorandum reached U.S. President Woodrow Wilson, who on February 19, 1915 received a Falcons delegation in the White House, under the leadership of its president, Dr. Teofil Starzyński. "The audience lasted over half an hour. The President expressed himself very graciously about the whole matter and promised that if the United States were to participate in the peace congress, then the delegate of the United States will support the Polish cause as much as possible," president Starzyński wrote in his report.[9]

President Wilson, who represented the United States' neutral position with regard to the European war, nonetheless clearly supported the Polish independence movement. But that was to occur in the undefined future, and in the meantime the ranks of the Falcons were eager to fight. News was impatiently awaited from those Falcons who had left in the Fall of 1914 for the Legions.

The Falcons' official press organ, *Sokół Polski (Polish Falcon)* on March 18, 1945 printed the first news about those who had reached their goal, citing a fragment of a letter from W. S. Rylski, which had been mailed to the Falcons headquarters in Pittsburgh: "I presented myself to Piłsudski, who greeted me cordially although with some reserve. He did not quite fully trust us because we belonged to the Falcons, because the Falcons here had betrayed their slogan and their calling. Being under the leadership of the National Democratic Party, which had a pro-Russian policy, they stood aside. Only a small number of (local) Falcons joined the Legions."

Two weeks later a second letter arrived from Rylski (published in the *Dziennik Polski (Polish Daily News)* in Detroit in which, just as passionately as he had offered encouragement before, he now discouraged departure for the Polish Legions: "I adjure you by the blood of these Polish legionnaires, to arm yourselves with patience and wait! Currently you cannot get through to us, but remember, that Polish Falcon groups and individuals from other organizations in America have a great task to fulfill before them, even after armistice, and you should not light-heartedly play with your hot, noble blood. Not many of us will remain in good health or alive. You will then be the heart of the future army in free Poland."[10] This dramatic letter of the former head of the Falcons held back other Falcons members, who had been eager to follow in his footsteps.

---

9 *Czyn zbrojny wychodźstwa polskiego w Ameryce* [*The War Effort of the Polish Emigration in America*] New York-Chicago 1957, p. 155

10 A. L. Waldo. *Sokolstwo, Przednia Straż Narodu* [*The Polish Falcons of America,The Vanguard of the Nation*] vol. IV, pp. 263-265

Those volunteers from America who did reach the Legions later fought against the Russian army. The first volunteer from America, Witold S. Rylski, having finished Austrian military school, advanced quickly and after some time became the commander of the 6th Infantry Regiment of the Legions. Ostrowski, from Chicago, headed a company of the 4th Infantry Regiment. Another Chicago volunteer, Aleksander Dubiński, a former artillery man in the 1st Field Artillery Regiment of the 1st Brigade of the Legions, mentioned in his story (without giving full names) that the following volunteers served in the Legions: Abramajtis, Baranowski, Dr. Bochenek, Dr. Bogacki, Cichowski, Cikorski, Aleksander Dębski, Dobrowolski (later a delegate to the Polish Parliament), Drzewnicki, Dymidas, Figler, Głuchowski (later the Polish consul to Brazil), Kasicki, Kopeć, Kuc, Liszko, Majcher, Małochleb, Mitochor, Młynarski, the Nitecki

brothers, Ostrowski, Rawski, Rupiński, Sitek, Sochacki, Szaniawski, Szorynos, Tomaszewski, Wąsowicz, Wójcik and one female volunteer, Dodatko.[11]

"The American volunteers in the Legions did not form any special battle unit. After enlistment they were assigned to various detachments and types of arms. Some were sent to Cadet school, several to the Austrian school in Vienna. Others again were transported to do secret organizational work in the Polska Organizacja Wojskowa (Polish Military Organization: PMO). Some of those in the PMO simply hid the fact that they were volunteers from America. Few knew each other, and only by chance found out that this one, or that one in the Legions, or this or that PMO member, is from Chicago, Pittsburgh, Detroit, Milwaukee or New York. These people suffered the same fate as their other comrades in arms from Poland.

After the disbanding of the Legions a large percentage of natives of Małopolska were shunted into the Austrian army and sent to the Italian front. Others were sent to the Marmaros-Szyngiet prisoner of war camp and to prisons. Several "Królewiaks" did time behind barbed wire fences in German camps or in prisons. Others continued the work of the PMO."[12]

Today it is difficult to ascertain the exact number of volunteers from America who served in the Polish Legions and in the PMO. The already mentioned Aleksander Dubiński estimated the number at about 300 persons, though after some years, together with another volunteer Władysław Maźnicki, he gave a list of approximately 54 names.[13]

---

11 Piłsudski Institute in America, archives of individuals: Aleksander Dubiński, folder I, Aleksander Dubiński "Ochotnicy z Ameryki w Legionach Piłsudskiego 1914–1918" ["Volunteers from America in Piłsudksi's Legions 1914–1918]

12 Ibid

13 *Weteran [The Veteran]* New York September 1967, p.4

Volunteers in the Puławski Legion

Another group of Falcons from America departed Chicago at the end of November, beginning of December 1914, aiming to reach the Puławski Legion, which was formed in August 1914 by Witold Gorczyński, and which was to fight at the side of the Russian army. In this group were: Gabriel Pawłowski, Adam Trygar, Leon Sułkowski. Lorenz Rakowski of Hammond, Indiana joined them. They made it to Puławy in January by a circuitous route (through Norway and Finland), where the Polish unit was being formed. Their first telegrams to the leadership of the Polish Falcons of America were full of enthusiasm and called virtually all Falcons to come. But the Falcons leadership did not allow that to happen, because they were waiting for political decisions from Russia concerning the recognition of Poland's independence. But they waited in vain. In May 1915 the Russians nullified the separateness of the Puławski Legion, also changing its name to "Druzhina Opolcheniya" and after a few months they sent this unit to the front to fight the Germans. Leon Sułkowski died at the front on September 8, 1915. Adam Trygar, wounded five times in the legs in 1917, was sent to a Moscow hospital, from where he made his way to the Polish Corps of Colonel Lucjan Żeligowski. He fought with the Bolsheviks and was captured, but fled in 1919. Lorenz Rakowski lost a leg at the battle of Nury on August 20, 1915. He was treated in Moscow, and after the Russian Revolution he traveled through Murmansk to the Polish Army in France, with which he arrived in Poland in 1919, and settled for good in Kraków. Gabriel Pawłowski fought the Germans until 1917, later joined the Polish Corps in Kuban' and Odessa, where together with General Żeligowski's 4th Division he made it to Poland in June 1919. In May 1920 he returned to America.[14]

The fate of the first volunteers indicated to the Polish Falcons of America leadership that it was too early to undertake military action. Nonetheless, the prolonged wait for the right moment for such an action favored political attacks by members of the National Defense Committee (KON). The aggressors used all available means. Characterizations of the "moscophiles" and "austrian agents" type were publicized quite often, and were the most mild of the lot. These mutually harmful allegations and accompanying invectives only served to enflame passions that were already running hot, and deepened divisions. Nonetheless it is a fact that in this confrontation, the proponents of the anti-German orientation had the decided upper hand.

---

14 A. L. Waldo *Sokolstwo. Przednia Straż Narodu* [*The Polish Falcons of America. Vanguard of the Nation*] vol. IV, Pittsburgh 1974, pp. 273-277

The Schooling of Military Cadres and Mobilization Preparations Among the Polish Falcons of America

The neutrality of the United States in the ongoing war was not favorable to a decision by the Falcons to begin open military preparations. That is why political feelers were extended to neighboring Canada which (as part of the British Empire) participated in the war against the Germans and the Austro-Hungarians. The greatest problem in the Falcon ranks was the lack of an officers' cadre. The breakthrough came with the decision of the Canadian military authorities at the end of 1916 to form a Polish officers' school in Canada. On January 1, 1970 twenty three Falcons secretly arrived from the United States at the officers' school in Toronto. Among them were: Lucjan Adamczak, Wojciech Albrycht, Lucjan Chwałkowski, Andrzej Małkowski (the creator of Polish scouting) and Józef Sierociński.[15] This was the group of the so-called First Officers' Course in Canada.

While this course was in progress, news came from Washington that U.S. President Woodrow Wilson, in a speech given to the Senate on January 22, 1917, declared that "...there should be a united, independent and autonomous Poland."[16] This leader of a great nation, which at that time was the deciding factor in the war, was the first to clearly and distinctly voice the Polish nation's right to an independent state. After this declaration, which echoed widely across the world, the Polish American community (Polonia) intensified its efforts on behalf of military action. On March 19, 1917, a cadet school was opened in Cambridge Springs, Pennsylvania, which was directed by Franciszek Dziób, the leader of the Polish Falcons of America. The American authorities looked through their fingers at the Polish goings-on.

Ignacy Jan Paderewski, the famous pianist and great patriot, at the Special General Convention of the Falcons in Pittsburgh, held on April 1–4, 1917, ventured the idea of creating a 100,000 strong Polish Kościuszko Army alongside the American Army. But American authorities rejected this project. Soon thereafter, the United States on April 17, 1917 declared war against Germany. From this moment Falcons military activity in America and Canada came out into the open. At the end of May 1917, the cadet school in Cambridge Springs, Pennsylvania began schooling under the instructorship of the five most talented graduates of the First Officers' Course in Toronto, among them, W. Albrycht and J. Sierociński. Over a period of several months, 389 students were trained in Cambridge Springs of which the majority left for Camp Borden in Canada in order to finish their officer course. The patriotism of the Falcons who were studying at Cambridge Springs is well substantiated by the fact that each

---

15 Ibid., p. 313
16 Speech of the President of the United States before the Senate on January 22, 1917. 64th Congress, 2nd Session. Document Nr. 685. Washington, D.C. Congressional Records 1917.

of the course participants had to pay their own way to the training camp, located in central Pennsylvania, buy their own uniform, and pay for the costs of room and board at the Camp. The three-month course cost about $150, and this was at a time when a worker in a steel factory earned three dollars a day. Moreover, the decision to go for the three month training course in Cambridge Springs was connected with loss of employment. The number: 389 course graduates, is eloquent testimony that for the Falcon youth the financial factor did not play the most important role.[17]

Mobilization of Poles for the American Army

Nonetheless the Falcon youth were still unable to join the ranks of the Polish Army. When the United States, after declaring war on Germany, announced volunteer enlistment into its armed forces, crowds of young Poles arrived at the recruiting stations (from April to September 1917). In this way they wanted to gain the opportunity of getting involved in armed confrontation with the Germans. At one recruiting station alone, at the headquarters of the Polish Roman Catholic Union of America in Chicago, more than 1,600 Polish volunteers signed up for the American Army.[18]

This is how Józef Sierociński recalls the recruitment days to the American army: "According to statistics in the first three months alone, more than 38,000 Polish volunteers joined the American army; this was the flower of the Polish Falcons and of seriously minded Polish youth. In certain cities the percentage of Polish volunteers was just incredible: for instance in South Bend, Indiana out of a hundred volunteers who enlisted in the American army. 94 were Poles. For this, the president of the local Civic Committee, Mr. Ignacy Werwiński, received the personal thanks of the president of the United States."[19]

Several months later tragic news came from France regarding Polish volunteers who died on the battlefield fighting in the detachments of General John Joseph Pershing. From the moment these detachments arrived at the front on November 5,1917, until the end of hostilities on November 10, 1918 the losses, just among soldiers from Chicago, were as follows: 40 dead, 17 dead of wounds, 33 who died of other reasons, 84 critically wounded, 45 with lesser wounds and 6 who were either taken prisoner or lost. All told 225. Thirty-six of them were Poles.[20]

According to Karol Wachtl, the first American soldier who died in the First World War was a Pole, P. Wojtalewicz of Chicago, from St. Albert's parish. His remains

---

17 S. R. Pliska. "The Polish-American Army 1917–1921" in: *The Polish Review*, New York: Polish Institute of Arts and Sciences in America, vol. X, No. 3/1965, pp. 46-59
18 M. Haiman. *Zjednoczenie Polskie Rzymsko-Katolickie w Ameryce. 1873–1948 [The Polish Roman Catholic Union of America. 1873–1948]* Chicago 1948, pp. 309-310
19 J. Sierociński. *Armia Polska we Francji [The Polish Army in France]* Warszawa 1929, p. 81
20 K. Wachtl. *Polonia w Ameryce [The Polish American Community in America]* Philadelphia 1944, p. 302

were laid to rest at the local cemetery. Also, the first American soldier to be decorated in France with the Grand Cross of Valor was an American of Polish descent, John Kuroski of Milwaukee, WI, as "Stars and Stripes," (Nr. 25/1917) informed, which also placed his photograph on the cover. The information is sketchy. There is a lack of scholarly research on the subject.

Recruitment to the Polish Army in France

The recruitment of over 40,000 Polish Americans to the American army was a serious obstacle to the formation of a Polish army. Such a significant outflow of young people of enlistment age did not, however, halt activities aiming to form Polish Armed Forces at the side of the Entente countries. The impulse for these preparations was the news that French president Raymond Poincaré by a decree of June 4, 1917, permitted the formation of an autonomous Polish army under French command. This was, at last, what the leadership of the Falcons had been hoping for from the very beginning of the war.

In August 1917 a Polish military mission from France arrived in the United States led by Lt. Wacław Gąsiorowski (the well-known historical novelist) and Prince Stanisław Poniatowski, to gain the support of the Polish American community for the idea of forming a Polish army in France. It was crowned with complete success, because the Wydział Narodowy Polskiego Centralnego Komitetu Ratunkowego (National Department of the Polish Central Relief Committee) at its meeting of September 21, 1917 in Chicago decided to begin recruitment for this army. The Chicago-based *Dziennik Związkowy [Alliance Daily]* in an article titled "To Arms"datelined September 24, wrote: "Our dreams have finally come true. The National Division, which represents nine tenths if not more of our émigré community, at its last plenary session passed a resolution under Maestro Paderewski to most vigorously support the attempts to form a Polish army in France, and to call our community to arms."

Nonetheless, before actual recruitment could begin, the agreement of the American government was required. It was obtained on October 6, 1917. On this basis, Polish Americans from the United States could be recruited to the ranks of the Polish army in France, who were not of enlistment age (18–30 years of age) and were not American citizens or did not have resident status (the equivalent of today's "green card.")

Recruitment centers, under the leadership of the military commission (Tadeusz Heliński, Teofil Starzyński, Aleksander Znamięcki) created under the National Department began work according to plans prepared by Franciszek Dziób. The centers were opened in the largest Polish American communities in the United States and Canada from October 1917 to February 1919. There were 47 of them and 38,018 volunteers reported to these centers.[21] The recruiting commissions rejected those who were recruitable to the United States Army, who had large families, or who were invalids or sick, because even those reported to the centers. There were numerous cases where Polish American youth that was of recruitable age for the U.S. Army used various tricks to get into the Polish ranks. They frequently used false names, or else crossed the American Canadian border illegally and in thus made their way to the military camp on Lake Ontario at Niagara-on-the-Lake, which had been made available by the Canadian authorities for the exclusive use of Polish volunteers. The Canadian side provided for the indispensable officer and junior officer cadre in this camp, providing all necessary provisions and supplies, as well as armaments for the students of the officer and junior officer school that was active there. The Canadian cadre was supported by Polish officers who were graduates of the officers school in Toronto and Camp Borden. The cost of maintaining the camp was covered by France. The camp commander for the entire period that the camp was open was the Canadian Colonel A. D. Le Pan.

Two temporary camps had to be organized due to the massive wave of volunteers in November 1917 and the subsequenct overfilling of the camp at Niagara-on-the-Lake. One of them was situated at St. Jones near Montréal in the Canadian province of Québec, and the second at the American Fort Niagara, which lay opposite Niagara-on-the-Lake.[22] The goal was to keep the Polish volunteers coming from the United States and Canada together, and to give them military training based on the Canadian model before their departure for France. These activities were closely coordinated with the continuing recruitment efforts in Polish communities.

Recruitment officers, appointed as managers of recruitment centers, organized supporting Civic Committees and Ladies Committees which were composed of the most influential and respected persons in the given community. Their task was to support the recruitment effort and to support the reporting volunteers, that is, to make sure that they had warm clothes and food for the journey, and also to organize festive farewells for them. Their departure for the training camp at Niagara-on-the-Lake in Canada was transformed into a great national holiday in each local Polish American community (Polonia). The few young people who were not eager to join the Polish army were boycotted in their own community.

The widely publicized recruitment effort to the Polish army in France was in great measure supported by the local Polish Catholic clergy headed by Bishop Paweł

---

21 Jednodniówka na Zjazd Byłych Oficerów i Pracowników Rekrutacyjnych [*Souvenir Journal for the Convention of Former Officers and Recruitment Staff*] Cleveland, February 19–20, 1938, p. 14

22 T. Trawiński. *Odyseja Polskiej Błękitnej Armii* [*The Odyssey of the Polish Blue Army*] Wrocław 1989, pp. 159-167

Rhode. The Polish clergy encouraged enlistment in the ranks of the forming Polish army from their church pulpits and one of the priests, Reverend Lucjan Bójnowski, as a recruitment officer, managed Recruitment Center Nr. 41 in New Britain, Connecticut.

Of the 38,000 volunteers who registered at the Recruitment Centers in the United States and Canada, the military commissions qualified 22,395 men for training at the camp in Niagara on the Lake in Canada. The others were rejected for various reasons, mainly due to discovered health defects, as also because they had families, or were too young or too old.

In the course of training at Niagara on the Lake it came to light that some of the volunteers were not fit to be soldiers for psycho-physical reasons, others were subject to American legislation and had to be directed to the American Army, and there were cases of desertion. Two flu epidemics, in 1918 and 1919, brought the death of two Canadian and 41 Polish soldiers. Their graves at the local cemetery are carefully maintained to this day.

At final count 20,720 Polish soldiers were trained and sent to France from the camp at Niagara on the Lake during a period of almost 18 months, i.e. from October 1917 to March 1919.[23]

A group of 42 nurses from the Polish White Cross, organized by Helena Paderewska, also have to be counted among the group of volunteers from America who hastened to the Polish army in France, as well as a group of 20 girls, the so-called Gray Samaritans, who were eager to join the action.[24]

But not everyone supported this enormous endeavor. The KONists, that is, the adherents of the pro-Austrian-German orientation, tried by all possible means to obstruct the creation of a Polish army at the side of the Entente. When in April 1917, in Pittsburgh I. J. Paderewski ventured the idea of creating a 100,000 man Kościuszko Army by the Polish American community, the KON (Komitet Obrony Narodowej: National Defense Committee) published a response condemning this venture, and belittling the person of Paderewski: "... we are against the creation of independent detachments or armies regarded as if they were the reincarnation of Roosevelt's Roughriders or of Kosciuszko's army, this is an unfortunate and comical idea of an artist who does not at all understand the principles of statehood."[25]

---

23 A. D. LePan. "Polish Army Camp" in: *Niagara Historical Society* Nr. 35, Niagara 1923, pp. 48-60
24 T. Lachowicz. "Ciche bohaterki" ["Quiet Heroines"] in: *Przegląd Polski* [*Polish Review*] New York February 23, 1995, pp. 1, 15
25 ZG SWAP [PAVA National Executive Board] Archives, AR, File: Rekrutacja w Ameryce do Armii Polskiej we Francji, "Komitet Obrony Narodowej w Ameryce, Odezwa" (document niedatowany) [Recruitment in America for the Polish Army in France, "National Defense Committee in America, Response" (undated document)]

Half a year later, the KON leadership, with similar consistency, opposed the action to recruit for the Polish army in France. This posture, which did not take into consideration the current mood of the Polish American community, caused an internal division within the organization, and a crossing over of a part of its adherents to the support of the recruitment action. In addition, the KON leadership, on June 14, 1918 was summoned before the American authorities in Washington, where they were told that due to their germanophilic activity they must immediately dissolve their organization, or else pass a resolution supporting the recruitment to the Polish army in France, or they would be immediately imprisoned. In practice, this meant the end of anti-recruitment propaganda by the KON as of October, 1917.[26]

In the Blue Army in France, 1918–1919

In December of 1917, after completing their training at the Canadian camp at Niagara-on-the-Lake, the volunteers were sent by train to New York, where they boarded ships bound for France.

Date of Departure	Name of Port	Name of Ship
Dec. 16, 1917	New York	"Niagara"
Dec. 29, 1917	New York	"Tourraine"
Jan. 10, 1918	New York	"Rochambeau"
Jan. 18, 1918	Halifax, NS	"Dvinsk"
Feb. 11, 1918	New York	"Tsar"
Feb. 19, 1918	New York	"Tsaritsa"
Feb. 22, 1918	New York	"Rochambeau"
March 8, 1918	New York	"Chicago"
April 1, 1918	New York	"Niagara"
April 16, 1918	New York	"Rochambeau"
April 30, 1918	New York	"Chicago"
April 30, 1918	New York	"Niagara"
May 7, 1918	New York	"Rochambeau"
May 15, 1918	New York	"Roma"
May 23, 1918	New York	"Chicago"
June 11, 1918	New York	"Espagne"
June 15, 1918	New York	"Lorraine"
June 29, 1918	New York	"Chicago"
July 5, 1918	New York	"Rochambeau"

---

26   *Czyn zbrojny wychodźstwa polskiego w Ameryce [The War Effort of the Polish Emigration in America]* New York-Chicago, pp. 574-575; J. Sierociński, *Armia Polska we Francji [The Polish Army in France]* Warszawa 1929, p. 108

From July 5, 1918 to January 1919 all the transports were serviced by the French Line on the ships "Rochambeau" and "Tourraine."[27]

Not all volunteers for the Polish Army in France were able to avail themselves of such an organized form of recruitment and transport. The road to the Polish army was practically closed for those volunteers who were American citizens and were of draft age, but not for all of them. Dr. Aleksander Pietrzykowski was one of those who knew how to handle the problem. He was already in the camp at Niagara on the Lake. At the demand of the American authorities he had to return to Chicago, where he was from. Unabashed by this he got himself a passport and left for France as a tourist. Upon arrival at his destination he immediately enlisted in the Polish Army, where he busied himself training the medical corps.[28]

The systematic flow of volunteers from America rescued the idea of forming a Polish army on French soil. Due to poor recruitment results in France itself, there was growing concern about the viability of the project. Unexpectedly the American volunteers became the heart of the Polish Army in France. Their arrival was widely publicized and became an encouragement for Poles scattered all over the world to join the ranks of the Blue Army, which was how this formation came to be known because of the color of its uniforms. With time volunteers from Holland joined, as well as Polish prisoners from the German army, who were recruited in the prisoner of war camps in France and England, Polish prisoners from the Austrian army, who came in droves from Italy, Poles from Russian brigades, which up to the 1917 Revolution fought as auxiliary corps in France and Greece, Poles from Brazil and other South American countries and a small numbers of Poles from Australia and China.

The arrival of the American volunteers hastened the formation of the Polish Army in France. At the beginning of January 1918 the 1st Regiment of Polish Riflemen was formed, and then two more. Also, detachments of cavalry, air force, artillery and support services were created. The junior officer cadre in the 1st Regiment of Polish Riflemen was in the main composed of officers who arrived from America— graduates of the officer schools in Toronto, Camp Borden and Niagara on the Lake. Of the 72 officers in the regiment, 48 came from America, and 70 percent of the rank and file came from America as well.[29]

American volunteers also had the absolute majority when it came to chaplains in the Blue Army. Of the overall number of 23 chaplains, 19 came from the United

---

27 *Weteran [The Veteran]* January 1936, p. 11
28 A. L. Waldo. *Sokolstwo. Przednia Straż Narodu [Polish Falcons of America. The Vanguard of the Nation]* vol. V Pittsburgh 1984, pp. 286-7
29 J. Wróbel. "Z ziemi amerykańskiej do Polski" ["From American Soil to Poland"] in: *Przegląd Polski [Polish Review]* New York January 23, 1998 pp. 1,15

States and Canada.[30]

In the military camps in France the "Americans" (as they were popularly called) brought up in the spirit of freedom and citizens rights, often came into conflict with the French officers, who tried to treat them like mercenaries from the Foreign Legion, and also with the officers who came from the Russian auxiliary corps. The volunteers decidedly defended simple human and national dignity. They emphasized at every step, that they were Polish soldiers in the Polish army, who need to be treated with full respect because of the motives which guided them to enter the ranks of the Polish Army and whom it was unconscionable to hit in the face or flog. Their stance was confirmed by their effective mutiny in February 1918, when the French demanded the removal of the little Polish Eagles with the motto "Armia Polska" from their helmets, which they had brought with them from the camp at Niagara on the Lake. The French officers could not comprehend that at a time of war someone would dare to start a military mutiny over such an insignificant matter; but seeing the determined posture of the "Americans" they relented.[31]

In June 1918 the Polish Army found itself under the political authority of the Polish National Committee in Paris at whose head stood Roman Dmowski. That same month the 1st Regiment of Polish Riflemen saw its baptism by fire at the front in the neighborhood of Reims. During the night of July10/11, 1918 Lt. Lucjan Chwałkowski became the first officer from America to become a casualty of war. His death caused a great stir in the Polish American community (Polonia), because he was well known in Falcons circles. From that moment all news coming from France that informed of subsequent battles fought in July and August 1918 by detachments of the Blue Army at St. Hilaire, were read with pride and fear. The losses were considerable:106 killed, died of wounds or lost without news of whereabouts. Among them 75 came from the United States.[32]

The 1st Regiment of Polish Riflemen was removed from the front after these battles. The soldiers were awarded many French military decorations and singled out with laudatory operational orders.

By the end of September 1918 General Józef Haller (the former commander of the 2nd Brigade of the Polish Legions who had arrived from Russia; he was a legendary commander in battles with the three forces occupying Poland) was nominated the Commander of the Polish Army in France. From that moment he

---

30 *Czyn zbrojny wychodźstwa polskiego w Ameryce* [*The War Effort of the Polish Emigration in America*] New York-Chicago 1957 p. 522

31 A. L. Waldo. *Sokolstwo. Przednia Straż Narodu* [*Polish Falcons of America. The Vanguard of the Nation*] vol. IV Pittsburgh 1974, pp. 417-419

32 *Czyn zbrojny wychodźstwa polskiego w Ameryce* [*The War Effort of the Polish Emigration in America*] New York-Chicago 1957, pp. 608-621.

was recognized by the member nations of the Entente as the Commnander in Chief of the Polish Armed Forces, and the soldiers he led became known as "Hallerians" (Hallerczycy). On November 11, 1918 Germany capitulated. Soon diplomatic tussles began in Paris over the shape of the borders of the Polish state.

Roman Dmowski wrote to Jan Smulski, in a letter of October 12, 1920, about the role which Polonia played up to that moment: "...Poland would not have gained in this war what it now has if millions of Poles did not live in the United States, and were it not for your cooperation.

"Your material help made it possible for the National Committee in Paris to develop its work, especially in its very difficult beginnings, when it had virtually no funds. Your recruitment of volunteers to the Polish Army in France made it possible to create this Army, and thanks to its existence we were acknowledged as allies and given access to the peace conference; finally your strong support of the demands of the Polish Delegation at the conference was highly influential in getting the President of the United States to side with us, together with the entire American delegation. Your contribution to the Fatherland at a great historical moment will never be forgotten and every conscientious historian in the future, speaking of Poland's resurrection, will have to emphasize the role which the Polish emigration in America played and the contributions made by the National Department (Wydział Narodowy) in Chicago."[33]

At the conclusion of armed hostilities in France the soldiers of the American army began returning to the United States. Many of the Poles serving in it expressed the desire to join the ranks of the Polish Army. When demobilization began, the American and Canadian military authorities did not create any obstacles. In some instances some of the Poles in the American Army returned to America and only there signed up for the Polish Army in France. One of them was Wacław Czupajło, a "Falcon" from Nest Nr. 515 in Jersey City, NJ, who after returning from France and resting in his family's home for a week, went to the Polish Army recruitment center in New York on November 31, 1918. He made it back to France via the camp at Niagara on the Lake, on January 15, 1919. After arriving with the Blue Army in Poland he was assigned to the 7th Kosciuszko Squadron—an air force unit manned by American pilots. After demobilization in March 1920 he returned to America.[34]

---

33 *Czyn zbrojny wychodźstwa polskiego w Ameryce* [*The War Effort of the Polish Emigration in America*] New York-Chicago 1957, p. 793

34 AZG SWAP [PAVA National Executive Board–NEB-Archives] signature A-XXX/12, file: *Krzyż Niepodległości* "Wniosek o nadanie Krzyża Niepodległości dla Wacława Czupajło" [*Cross of Independence* "Motion to Confer the Cross of Independence on Wacław Czupajło"]

The current state of research does not make it possible to ascertain the number of Poles who, after the end of the war in France, crossed over from the Canadian and America detachments stationed there, to the Polish Blue Army.

On the Way to Poland

The World War I was concluded on the Western front in November 1918, but the Polish Army in France had to wait for another six months to return to Poland, where armed conflict continued over the shape of the boundaries of the independent state. The army kept increasing up to the Spring of 1919. By April, that is, just before departure to Poland, it had 80,000 soldiers. If one adds to that the two Polish divisions in Russia (the 4th Division of General Lucjan Żeligowski in the Ukraine and the 5th Siberian Division of Colonel Walerian Czuma) which were organizationally subordinated to the Polish Army in France, then we can speak of a 100,000 man Blue Army.

In the Spring of 1919 the Polish Army in France was transported by railroad through Germany to Poland, and its commander General Józef Haller, after arriving at the Polish border, sent a telegram to Józef Piłsudski, in which he subordinated himself to the Head of State and to his orders, by the same token dashing the hopes of many National Democrats in Poland for removal of Piłsudski from power.

Battles Over the Borders of the Polish State

The detachments of the Blue Army, almost as soon as they had arrived in Poland, were dispatched to the southern front to fight the Ukrainian armies. Lt. Stanisław Woronowski, graduate of the so-called second class of the officer's course in Toronto in 1917, died in a bravura attack at Beresteczko.[35] Lt. Konstanty Godziszewski, a "Falcon" from Nest Nr. 79 in Detroit, also died in battle with the Ukrainians.[36]

After defeating the Ukrainian Army the Blue Army units in the first days of June 1919 came into hostile contact in Volhynia with Bolshevik detachments that were arriving from the East. After the capture of Równe and Dubno the front was established on the rivers Słucz and Horyń. There the units that had arrived from France received an order dated September 1, 1919 to integrate the Blue Army with the Polish Armed Forces. The volunteers from America, after the reorganization, found themselves by and large in the 13th Division of Borderland Riflemen, mostly in the 43rd, 44th and 45th infantry regiments. In those formations, for more than half a year, they repulsed the constant

---

35 W. Trawiński. "W obronie honoru żołnierskiego," ["In Defense of a Soldier's Honor"] in: *Weteran* [*The Veteran*] Chicago, Nr. 85, April 1928, p. 17

36 "Cześć poległym bohaterom" ["Hail to the Fallen Heroes" in: *Pamiętnik Gniazda 79-go S.P. w Ameryce i Legionu Weteranów Armii Polskiej z okazji odsłonięcia tablicy pamiątkowej dla uczczenia poległych członków Gniazda 79-go, 12 maja 1935 Detroit* [*Souvenir Program of Polish Falcons of America Nest Nr. 79 and the Legion of Veterans of the Polish Army on the Occasion of the Unveiling of the Memorial Plaque to Honor the Fallen Members of Nest Nr. 79, May 12, 1938 Detroit*]

attacks of the Bolsheviks along battle front. They staged frequent, bold forays into the terrains occupied by the enemy; for instance at Romanów, Czudnów, and Ostropol. During these battles, among others, Lt. Jakub Dąbrowski (a "Falcon" from Nest 79 S.P. in Detroit) was killed, and lies buried in the cemetery at Włodzimierz in Volhynia.[37]

Up to May 1920 sixteen volunteers from America, known by name, died in battle or of wounds on Polish territory (these were soldiers in the Blue Army who had American citizenship): Makary Kulkowski—buried on the field of battle on June 28, 1919; Jan Lenart, buried on the field of battle in November 1919; Stanisław Pawlik, buried in Lwów August 23, 1919; Michał Kaba, buried in Kraków on January 14, 1920; Ludwik Skulski, buried at Stanisławów February 18, 1920; Józef Lędzian, buried at Chelinów January 15, 1920; Michał Kłos, buried in Stanisławów February 12, 1920; Aleksander Zbrzeźniak, buried in Stanisławów February 12, 1920; Paweł Kuliński, buried in Stanisławów February 24, 1920; Jan Wilkowski, buried in Przemyśl on May 15, 1920; Franciszek Rygielski, buried in Zamość on April 22, 1920; Henryk Głowacki, buried in Warszawa on September 9, 1919; Stanisław Kawecki, buried on January 4, 1920; Leon Machinkowski, buried at the Powązki Cemetery in Warszawa; Harvey J. Horoschak, buried at the Powązki Cemetery in Warszawa; John M. Urbanski, buried at the Powązki Cemetery in Warszawa.[38]

Some of the American volunteers, for instance those serving in the 48th regiment, participated in defending the Polish borders in Upper Silesia, from where in February 1920 they were shifted over to the northern front, where they took control of the Gdańsk seacoast from the Germans. It had been ceded to Poland on the basis of the Paris Peace Conference in 1919. Many former American "Falcons," being soldiers of the Polish Army, entered Toruń, Tczew and Puck, where on February 19, 1920 General Józef Haller concluded the famous marriage of Poland with the sea.

The Demobilization of Volunteers

The demobilization of the volunteers began in the Autumn of 1919, when the senior-most enlistees were discharged. The demobilized soldiers were grouped in Skierniewice, where they were to await departure for the United States. In March 1920 (one month before the Kiev expedition) a second demobilization order was announced, this time of younger enlistees. This order encompassed more than 12,000 soldiers from the United States and Canada. In connection with the demobilization the Commander in Chief, Józef Piłsudski, issued a farewell order to the soldiers leaving for America, in which he wrote:

---

37 Ibid.
38 "Polegli w Polsce ochotnicy z Ameryki" ["Volunteers from America Buried in Poland"] in: *Weteran* [*The Veteran*] July 1931, p. 19

"Dedicated to labor in the enormous workplaces of the United States, surrounded by an abundant flourishing of life, by the splendor of outstanding conditions, and by the incalculable opportunities which America offers, when the first call came, at the first summons of Poland, you abandoned all profitable views of the future and joined the Polish ranks.

"What was the voice that caused you, unmindful of personal discomfort, security and abundant advantage, to choose hard military service, far from your family hearths, what was the command that caused you, although with your blood, manliness, courage and life you could have served that magnificent part of the world, the one that can offer you a good livelihood, to come serve a country which in comparison to America is a poor country, touched by the destiny of thousands of sufferings and needs?

"That voice, that irresistible command, was the noble love of the Fatherland, unmuted in your hearts by any distance, any separation. It was the holiest feeling of love for your Fatherland which ordered you to choose the Polish ranks. That feeling of love of the Fatherland, present and highest in every Pole, ordered you to break through all difficulties and come here, to fight for the freedom of this land, which brought you forth, as it did your fathers and grandfathers. Once again you showed the world, led by the example of all your knightly forebears, that there is no distance, there is no time, there is no place in this enormous world, where the voice of the fatherland could not reach the heart of Poles, calling them to battle.

"By battle and toil, suffering and blood you renewed the ties which bind you to Poland. Having returned to your homes and former professions, spread among your countrymen everywhere that love which guided you during the heavy years of the war so that, as in this period to you, in each succeeding one the voice of the Fatherland will be able to reach your children and grandchildren across all oceans and distances, calling its sons to action.

Piłsudski, m.p.[39]

---

[39] *Ilustrowany Kurier Codzienny* [*The Illustrated Daily Courier*] Kraków, Nr. 79, March 20, 1920, p. 1

His farewell address, rendered in a very cordial tone, was unable to stifle the enormous bitterness toward the demobilization order. It was a shock for many volunteers from America. They could not understand why they had to leave the ranks of the Army at a time when war was still raging.

They asked bitterly why this was done. After all, they were volunteers who had come all the way from far off America, and not draftees. In America they had been preparing for many years in the ranks of the Falcons to fight for Poland's freedom; and now, when they could fulfill this task, fulfill their dreams and the dreams of their ancestors, that right was being taken away from them.

This is how General Władysław Jung remembered the state of emotion of the American volunteers: "...the typical volunteer, when he heard the order, had the look of a hurt child on his face. For the first time since leaving American soil he had tears in his eyes. This soldier, who had faced death in battle as if he were facing his daily work with a pipe clenched in his teeth, cried at not being allowed to fight and die for his Fatherland.

"One had to witness how gunners kissed their dearest comrades in arms at the farewell—their horses. One had to hear the neighing of the horses, saying goodbye to their cordial friends—the soldiers. They left with heartache that they were not given the ability to finish what they had so gloriously begun. Let me emphasize here however, that despite the order hundreds of them still remained in the ranks, those adopted sons of America, who without concern for how their trip beyond the sea would turn out, wanted to complete their filial obligation to the Motherland.

"That is the 'morale' of the volunteer from America. With such a soldier you could cross the entire world. A nation that has soldiers with such heart has not the slightest reason for fear of any kind. When now, so many years later, I recall those old campaigners of the Blue Army, I get tempted to stand at the head of such soldiers and lead them to glory.[40]

At War with the Bolsheviks

The volunteers who were not demobilized as well as those who remained in the ranks despite the orders, found themselves in the Kiev campaign a month later. There they came in contact on several occasions with American pilots of the 7th Kosciuszko Squadron, commanded by Major Cedric Fauntleroy. In the course of battles with the cavalry of Semyon Budyonny during the retreat, the pilots of this squadron supported the 13th Infantry Division, which received the moniker "Iron

---

40 W. Jung "Duch patriotyczny Polonii amerykańskiej w Armii gen. Józefa Hallera" ["The Patriotic Spirit of the Polish American Community in General Józef Haller's Army"] in: *Weteran [The Veteran]* New York July 1939, pp. 2-3

Brigade" for courage shown in battle. In beating back the massive attacks of the overwhelming forces of the Bolshevik cavalry, this Division never allowed itself to be torn apart, and inflicted painful losses. The battles of Koziatyn, Żywotów, Medówka, Dziunkowo, Napadówka, Klitno, Ostróg, Butowce, Koszelówka, Horynka, Podkamień, Popowce, Wiśniowiec, Cebrów, Nuszce, Swaczew, Krasno, on the peripheries of Lwów, at Biłka Szlachecka, Zadwórz, Kurowice and the battle of Komarów near Zamość map out the path of conflict of the volunteers from America. Many of them died in battle, and their nameless graves are scattered across the vast expanses of the eastern Polish lands from Zamość and Lwów all the way to the Dnieper River. Due to a lack of data it is impossible to give the complete list of casualties. Only some of the names can be cited, available from fragmentary sources, for instance Lt. Witold Trawiński, the former commander of the 10th Company of the 43rd Regiment of the Borderlands Riflemen, on remembering his comrades in arms from the second class of the officers' training course in Toronto, enumerated those who had died in battles with the Bolsheviks: Lt. Col. Jan Bartmański (former head of the Polish Falcons of America, bestially murdered after being taken prisoner at Czarny Ostrów); Lt. Józef Michniewicz (a "Falcon" from Nest Nr. 79 in Detroit, hacked to death with sabers while manning his machine gun during the repulsion of a charge by Budyonny's cavalry at the village of Rozkopane in the area of Pohrebyszcze near Kiev), Lt. Paweł Niemiec (killed at the village of Rzadkówka in the area of Zwiahlo); Lt. Sebastian Szembarski (died in a skirmish with Budyonny's cavalry at Żywotów); Lt. L. Urban (died at the Bolshevik front); Lt. Jan Urbaniak (died in a foray into Równe); Lt. Walenty Walaszczyk (died in a counter-attack near the village of Iwanówka in the Zwiahlo region by the Słucz River). To these losses one also ought to add cadet Wincenty Rusiłowski (a "Falcon" from Nest Nr. 79 in Detroit) and Lt. Czesław Pawłowicz, who died of typhoid fever at the front in Volhynia.[41]

In July 1920 the Bolshevik armies crossed the Bug River and started to approach Poland's capital, Warszawa. The demobilized American volunteers who were encamped at Skierniewice and in Grupa near Grudziądz, and were waiting for the next ship that was to take them back to the United States, at the news of the mortal danger again faced by the Fatherland, left the camps and once again joined the ranks of the volunteer army being formed by their former commander, General Józef Haller. They once again went into battle under his orders and died in the areas surrounding Warszawa (for instance Lt. Ignacy Król from the first class of

---

41 W. Trawiński. "W obronie honoru żołnierskiego" ["In Defense of A Soldier's Honor"] in: *Weteran* [*The Veteran*] Chicago, Nr. 85, April 1928, pp. 16-17

the officers' training course in Toronto in 1917) and they pursued the enemy in the victorious counter-offensive which began under the leadership of the Commander in Chief, Józef Piłsudski, in mid-August 1920.

The Bolshevik forces were defeated by October and pushed far to the East. On the southern front the 13th Infantry Division, after repelling the attacks of Budyonny's Cavalry army at Zamość, went on the offensive, breaking through successive enemy lines of resistance, among others at Wakijów and Werbkowice. Detachments of the Division captured Łuck and Równe. In battles at Iwaszówka, Katerynówka and Kuki, The Poles annihilated the 56th and 57th Regiments of the Bolshevik infantry. That is where the volunteers from America learned that Armistice had been signed on October 18, 1920.

The Female Volunteers from America
One ought to mention the lot of the women volunteers who found themselves in Poland in the period under discussion. They were nurses in the Polish White Cross and in the so-called Gray Samaritans.

The first of these groups, after arriving in France, numbered 42 nurses, but due to financial difficulties (this organization was being financed by Helena Paderewska) eighteen of them had to be sent back to America and twelve were assigned to the American Red Cross, while the remaining twelve continued to serve in the Polish White Cross. The paramedics from both groups were sent to Poland in the Spring of 1919, where they worked in Helena Paderewska's hospital in Warszawa on Dzielna Street. Two of them (Helena Gaczorowa and Agnieszka Wisła) were assigned to supplying medical stations at the front. Helena Gaczorowa, after her first trip to the Ukrainian front lines, caught typhoid fever and died. Agnieszka Wisła made the rounds of the front lines until February 1920. For instance she spent Christmas Eve 1919 at the battle front medical station at Berezyna.[42]

After the war ended the female nurses returned to America with the last large transport on the SS "President Grant" in February 1921.

Twenty Gray Samaritans arrived in Poland in the summer of 1919 and were assigned to work with the American Relief Administration directed by Herbert Hoover, who later became President of the United States. Hoover's mission provided food supplies for the hungry Polish civilian population, and secretly transported war materiel for the fighting Polish army.[43]

---

[42] *Czyn Zbrojny Wychodźstwa Polskiego w Ameryce* [*The War Effort of the Polish Emigration in America*] New York-Chicago 1957, p. 549

[43] Z. L. Stańczyk, "Herbert Hoover a wojna polsko-bolszewicka" ["Herbert Hoover and the Polish-Bolshevik War"] in: *Przegląd Polski* [*The Polish Review*] New York, August 28, 1997, pp. 5, 11

The Gray Samaritans distributed clothes and food for the poorest, first of all the children (especially the orphans). The greatest amount of aid was directed to the Eastern voievodships (counties) which were the most devastated by the battles fought there with the Bolsheviks. As soon as the Polish forces occupied a territory, the Gray Samaritans immediately showed up in their wake, coming with ready aid for the suffering population and forming an organizational network through which further aid was sent. After the conclusion of the war they worked at eastern border points where they organized basic aid for the Poles returning from within Russia, who were in awful physical shape.

They arrived by the thousands. Some on wagons, others in freight cars in which they often traveled for many months. They presented a deplorable view: in rags, filthy, starving and sick, and some half-insane after horrific experiences in the Soviet Union. Many did not make it to independent Poland. On average, for every two thousand repatriates crossing the Polish border in these groups, there were about 700 corpses, victims of the spreading typhoid fever. In addition, the view of horribly frostbitten hands and feet, especially of children, awoke fear in the eyes of the Samaritans, even though they had already seen quite a lot. Field kitchens were quickly organized, thanks to which, by cautiously rationing food, the starving people were brought back to life.

The vermin-covered rags were burnt in big heaps, and their owners were given new, warm clothing, after which they were all directed to quarantine centers, where the sick were isolated.

Unfortunately, there were incidents when the starved people, in desperation, threw themselves with sticks in their hands at the groups of Samaritans and food committee members, threatening to stone them if they didn't immediately receive food or clothes, which at that very moment were not in stock. Sometimes the girls could gain control of the situation only with the greatest effort, and only the arrival of new supplies calmed the nerves of the stressed out populace.

After undergoing the required quarantine the repatriates returned to their old settlements, where they often found just the ruins of their burned homes, and fields overgrown with weeds. They had to begin life in their freed homeland by living, half-starved, in make-shift dugouts. And again the Samaritans came to their aid, supplying food and clothes, and even seeds for planting.[44]

After this enormous task in the years 1921–1922 the Samaritans began organizing schools and orphanages for village children. They provided these outposts with

---

44 T. Lachowicz. "Ciche bohaterki" ["The Quiet Heroines"] in: *Weteran [The Veteran]* New York, Nr. 973, March 2002, pp. 5-9

books, notebooks and writing instruments, often giving their own last dime for this purpose. It was the last assignment that they were given to fulfill in free, but very ruined Poland. The Gray Samaritans, after honorably completing their mission, returned to the United States where they utilized the experience gained in Poland for work in American hospitals, orphanages and homeless shelters.[45]

In the years 1917–1918 the generosity of Polonia on behalf of independence-related activity reached its zenith. Aside from the most valuable sacrifice, the volunteers, serious funds were collected for the support of this cause. From August 16, 1918 to September 30, 1919 $4.5 million dollars was collected.[46] Just one organization, the Polish Women's Alliance of America, handed over the sum of $109,587, aside from $73,139 which had been contributed in the years 1910–1919 for other Polish social goals.[47]

The Polish American community through the Polish Central Relief Committee, the National Department and the National Polish Department, gave Poland $5,939,419.34 from October 12, 1914 to December 31, 1920.[48] No other immigrant group in America had ever managed such a feat. It was without precedent in the history of the United States. In this way the Polish American community realized its and its ancestors' dreams and longings. The dreams of an independent Poland were becoming a reality.

---

45 R. Tarczyński "Polskie szare samarytanki" ["The Polish Gray Samaritans"] in: *Weteran [The Veteran]* New York, February 1933, p. 11; T. Lachowicz "Ciche bohaterki" ["The Quiet Heroines"] in: *Przeglad Polski [The Polish Review]* New York, February 23, 1995, pp. 1, 15

46 "Sprawozdanie skarbnika Wydziału Narodowego, N. L. Piotrowskiego, za okres od 16 sierpnia 1918 do 30 września 1919" ["Report of N. L. Piotrowski, Treasurer of the National Department, for the Period from August 16, 1918 to September 30, 1919"] in: *Czyn Zbrojny Wychodźstwa Polskiego w Ameryce [The War Effort of the Polish Emigration in America]* New York – Chicago 1957, pp. 647-648

47 M. Mirecka-Loryś, "Udział Związku Polek w Ameryce w organizowaniu czynu zbrojnego amerykańskiej Polonii" ["The Share of the Polish Women's Alliance in America in Organizing the War Effort of the Polish American Community"] in: *Dziennik Związkowy [Alliance Daily]* Chicago October 30, 1998, p. 3

48 *Szczegółowy wykaz ofiar zebranych przez Wydział Narodowy Polski; Sprawozdanie finansowe Skarbnika Wydziału Narodowego Polskiego za czas od 1go grudnia 1919 do 31go grudnia 1920 [A Detailed List of the Contributions Collected by the National Polish Department; A Financial Report of the Treasurer of the Polish National Department for the Period December 1, 1919 to December 31, 1920]* Chicago 1921, p. 68

The Polish Military Society
in Kensington, PA, founded
March 21, 1903

Dr. Teofil Starzyński, the first
President of the Polish Falcons
of America

Jan Bartmański, organizer of fighter units of the Polish Falcons of America

Witold S. Rylski, instructor for Polish Falcons of America (1913)

Falcons in the 1st Officers' Course in Canada (Toronto, January 1917)

Recruitment Center
No. 2 in Chicago, IL
(October 1917)

Administration of the oath to volunteers from Chicago, IL who are about to leave for the Polish Army in France, October 1917

A farewell for volunteers in Monessen, PA, who are leaving for training camp in Niagara on the Lake in Canada, October 15, 1917

A farewell for volunteers leaving for the Polish Army in France, November 1917

A farewell for volunteers from Falcons Nest # 336 in Jackson, MI, who are departing for the Polish Army in France

A group of soldiers from the First Regiment of Polish Fusilliers in France, with Lieutenant Chodźko in the lead. They had come to the USA in 1918 for promotional reasons. Each one of them has been wounded at the front in a battle with the Germans.

The last group of volunteers from New Britain, CT. Seated: Rev. Lucjan Bójnowski; February 3, 1919

Training at the camp in Niagara on the Lake, Canada, 1917

A baseball game at the training camp in Niagara on the Lake in Canada, 1918

Trained Polish volunteers depart for France. Niagara on the Lake, Deecmber 1917

The graves of Polish volunteers at the cemetery in Niagara on the Lake, Canada, as they are today

Female participants in the course for medics of the Polish White Cross in New York, August 1918

The Gray Samaritans at a course in New York, 1918

Elizabeth Ascher—protectress and custodian of the Polish graves at Niagara on the Lake, Ontario, Canada

Lieutenant Lucjan Chwałkowski—the first volunteer from America to die at the front in France, July 11, 1918

Mr. and Mrs. Hofman (volunteers from America) in the Polish Army in France, 1918

General Józef Haller takes an oath as the Commander in Chief of the Polish Army in France, October 6, 1918

Artur L. Waldo, volunteer from America, at the grave of a fallen comrade, Ukraine, 1920

Corporal Komorowski, volunteer from America, died in battle with the Bolsheviks on the outskirts of Warsaw in 1920

Lieutenant Jan Pela, a volunteer from Detroit, MI, recipient of the highest Polish military order, the Virtuti Militari

Rev. Major Jan J. Dekowski, volunteer from America, chaplain of the Polish Army in France; photo from 1920

Gustaw Pieprzny, volunteer from America, recipient of the Virtuti Militari order

The certificate for the Virtuti Militari order of American volunteer Lucjan Adamczak

General Józef Haller with demobilized soldiers returning to America, 1920

A diploma for the Volunteers from America Cross with the signature of Józef Piłsudski—the Head of State and Commander in Chief

PART III

THE POLISH ARMY VETERANS ASSOCIATION OF AMERICA
1921–1939

I.
The Genesis of the Association

After fulfilling their soldierly duty on behalf of Poland and being demobilized from the ranks of the army most of the volunteers decided to return to the United States. Nonetheless, because of the continuing war, that could not happen quickly. The demobilized volunteers, concentrated in camps at Skierniewice and Grupa near Grudziądz were practically left to their own devices. The *Urzędowe Sprawozdanie z czynności i wydatków Wydziału Narodowego Polskiego w Ameryce z okazji powrotu i demobilizacji Armii Polskiej we Francji za okres od kwietnia do sierpnia 1920 roku [Official Report of the Activities and Expenses of the Polish National Department in America on the Occasion of the Return and Demobilization of the Polish Army in France for the Period of April to August 1920]* tells us about the method of resolving the problem of transporting them to America.:

"Due to a lack of ships, soldiers of the Polish Army in France, who in May 1919 were relieved of further military duty, did not have the occasion to return to America for a long time. The first detachment of demobilized soldiers, comprised of almost 1,000 people, was housed in quarters at the camp in Skierniewice for almost half a year, waiting for departure.

"Finally the Polish Government turned to the Government of the United States through its embassy in Washington requesting that the Polish soldiers recruited in America from Gdańsk be transported back to the United States in American government ships. The American Department of Defense did not have the authority on its own to undertake this task. Authorization from the Congress of the United States was needed to use American ships for such a purpose. So Congressman Jan C. Kleczka of Milwaukee, WI introduced a Bill in the House of Representatives authorizing the Secretary of Defense, Baker, to use American military transport ships standing at anchor in Antwerp to carry the Polish soldiers from Gdańsk to America. A similar Bill was introduced in the Senate by Senator James Wolcott Wadsworth, Jr. of New York. The Bill passed at the beginning of April 1920 and the transport ship "Antigone" immediately left Antwerp for Gdańsk."[1]

---

1 AAN, sign. 2273/67-77, Ambasada RP w Waszyngtonie [Polish Embassy in Washington]

The Return to the United States

The departure of the first group of demobilized volunteers happened very quickly, at the beginning of April 1920. The Polish Head of State, Józef Piłsudski, personally bid farewell to the departing soldiers in the camp at Skierniewice, of which J. A. Żebrowski wrote in his memoir: "The first transport left Skierniewice, near Warszawa. That first transport was taken leave of by the Head of the Polish State— Józef Piłsudski. I had the privilege and honor to be chosen to reply to the farewell address of the head of the government at that time."[2]

The Commander of the General Seacoast District, Lt. General Bolesław Roja, prior to the departure of the third transport in May 1920, issued a special address dated April 29, 1920 (see addendum 2).

The first transports of the "Americans" leaving by train from Skierniewice and Pomiechówek were directed to Gdańsk, where they embarked on the SS "Antigone." This ship, with 1,166 soldiers on board, arrived in New York on April 18. The Polish soldiers were not disembarked at the Port of New York, however, but in nearby Hoboken, New Jersey.

Before this happened there was a feverish flurry of negotiations between the Polish and American authorities as to who was going to foot the bill for transporting the former soldiers from Poland to the United States. The Polish American Polish National Department joined the negotiations in the person of president Jan F. Smulski. The already quoted document of this department, the "Official Report…" gives the result of these talks: "Congressman Kleczko and the Polish Minister Plenipotentiary, Prince Kazimierz Lubomirski, obtained the agreement of the Department of Defense to permit Camp Dix in New Jersey to be used as temporary quarters for the returning soldiers.

"After returning from Poland president Jan. F. Smulski struck a deal with the Polish Embassy on financial matters. The Embassy, in the name of the Polish Government, agreed to cover the cost of maintaining these soldiers at Camp Dix, to pay their rail transport from Camp Dix to their place of residence, and to pay out a bonus of $10 to each soldier, and $20 to each officer. The Polish National Department, on the other hand, gave each soldier a $15 bonus and each officer $30. Thus together each soldier was to get a railroad ticket home and $25 and the officers a ticket and $50, which was enough for the first necessary expenses, after which each soldier was on his own.

"As a result of talks and agreements the American Red Cross offered snacks on the day the ship arrived at Hoboken, and then when the soldiers were departing home by train, Red Cross canteen units gave the soldiers food at the various

---

2   J. A. Żebrowski, "S.W.A.P. w Ameryce" ["P.A.V.A. in America"] in: *Weteran [The Veteran]* October 1962, p. 9

stations, while the Knights of Columbus and the Y.M.C.A. supplied them with cigarettes and sweets.

"Upon arrival at Camp Dix every soldier had to go through a gasoline bath, after which he received a clean set of underwear and a pair of socks from American Army provisions. The Polish Government paid for this and for the food at Camp Dix. Simultaneously with the bath the soldiers' uniforms were dry-cleaned. Military blankets were also cleaned, packed in cases and shipped back to Poland together with the tin canteens and dinnerware."[3]

After the first transports from Gdańsk had arrived it became clear that the soldiers' uniforms were in terrible shape. Many were literally falling apart. This was the result of many steam disinfections in the Polish camps before departure under the supervision of Polish and American sanitary commissions. This was yet another immediate problem that the Polish National Department in America had to quickly resolve: "Because in many localities the Civic Committees and local Societies were unable to give civilian clothes to the soldiers who arrived on the first three transport ships, without which they would have been unable to look for work, therefore the National Department decided to clothe the soldiers immediately upon their arrival in Camp Dix. It made an agreement with a wholesale garment warehouse in New York to supply piles of clothes at $12 per suit. Beginning with the third transport ship ("The Pocahontas") which arrived in Hoboken on June 16, 1920, every soldier who so desired received a jacket, vest, pants, shirt and tie. The soldiers taking the civilian clothes also got $5 from the Department, while those who do not take the clothes got $15 in cash, as before.

"In addition, the Department gives every soldier with worn-out shoes a pair of good, repaired military shoes from the supplies of the American Army in Camp Dix, for which the Polish National Department pays the military authorities."[4]

There was one more surprise for the Polish soldiers undergoing a quarantine at Camp Dix. They were invited to join the American Army: "American Army officers try to persuade the new arrivals to join the U.S. Army (they know that Poles make good soldiers). They offer a 30 day furlough and present the advantages of military service, during which the soldier can attend camp schools and become proficient in English and various trades. No wonder that quite a few let themselves be enticed. About 7 percent of the new arrivals decide to do this, but supplying the soldiers with civilian clothes reduced the number of volunteers for further military service."[5]

---

3 AAN, Ambasada RP w Waszyngtonie, [New Documents Archive in Warszawa, The Polish Embassy in Washington] op. cit
4 Ibid.
5 Ibid.

The expenses sustained by the Polish and Polish American sides to cover the cost of the return of the American volunteers from Poland to the United States, were substantial. Between April and August 1920 the Polish Embassy in the United States expended $310,000 for this purpose, while the Polish National Department at this same time contributed $192,700 to the same goal.[6]

Between April 1920 and February 1921 eight big transport ships returned from Poland to the United States with over 12,500 demobilized soldiers. Here is a list of these transports (with the name of the ship first, its arrival date, and the number of passengers last):

1. SS "Antigone," April 18, 1920; 1,166 soldiers
2. SS "Pocahontas," May 2, 1920; 1,708
3. SS "Princess Matoica," May 27, 1920; 1,716
4. SS "Pocahontas," June 16, 1920; 1,314
5. SS "Mercury," June 29, 1920; 1,866
6. SS "Princess Matoica," July 21, 1920; 2,099
7. SS "Pocahontas," August 12, 1920; 1,255
8. SS "President Grant," February 16, 1921; 1,285 soldiers and 24 wives.[7]

To this list ought to be added 137 sick soldiers who arrived on the SS "Rochambeau."

On January 20, 1921, prior to the departure of the last big transport from Poland (composed mostly of participants in the battles for Warszawa in August 1920 and the battles of the 13th Infantry Division on the southern front) General Józef Haller visited the camp at Grupa near Grudziądz. The "Blue General" spoke to the gathered soldiers: "You are leaving for America, to the country from which, at the call of your conscience and heart, you crossed the ocean to fight on the fields of France and Poland, the Poland that whole centuries of your grandfathers and fathers died and suffered for.

"I know that you fulfilled your soldierly duty well. Now you must fulfill one more obligation, which I demand of you. Being in America remember first of all to always and everywhere speak well of Poland, represent our culture and faith there, as befits former Polish soldiers. Knowing you, as your leader, I know that you will fulfill this obligation on American soil, as true-born Poles.

"I know that you experienced a lot of heartache here, you were often treated badly by certain people, but you must forget that, because you were soldiers of your

---

6   Ibid.
7   *Czyn Zbrojny Wychodźstwa Polskiego w Ameryce* [*The Armed Effort of the Polish Emigration in America*] New York – Chicago 1957, p. 789

own will. Poland gave you nothing because it is a country ravaged by war. You take with you to America scars, wounds, ruined health, but remember everywhere and at all times, that he is a soldier who must suffer for all."[8]

A witness of this event, Józef Chojnacki, further recalled: "Then the general turned to those who in August of last year were part of the transport which was leaving Grupa on its way to America just before the defense of Warszawa. At that time the General had come to Grupa and in response to his appeal several hundred of those who were demobilized and were to leave for Gdańsk in two days re-enlisted in the army. After words of thanks addressed to them, of whom he knew more than a dozen personally, the general now said to them: 'You already had one foot in America, and yet at my appeal you joined the ranks again. That is why I consider you the very first who deserve awards.'

"After he finished the general sat down and we walked up to him, receiving from his hand crosses especially minted and intended for us, which we wear on our breasts today, and on which the following words are visible: *To its soldiers from America, Liberated Poland.*"[9]

From April 18, 1920 to February 16, 1921 12,546 volunteers returned. Later Polish volunteers from America still kept coming to the United States in smaller groups up to 1923. Taking everyone into consideration, about 14,000 soldiers returned to America.[10]

The Former Soldiers of the Blue Army Begin to Organize

Ideas for creating an organization that would gather former soldiers of the Polish army, who had been volunteers from America, cropped up already in Poland, during the stay of demobilized volunteers in the camps at Skierniewice and at Grupa near Grudziądz. The soldiers, waiting for transport to the USA, created visions of the future organization, thanks to which they would be able to cultivate soldierly traditions while living scattered across the vast expanses of the United States. It was characteristic that plans for such an organization were being developed independently by all the volunteer groups who passed through the above-mentioned camps. The ideas for this organization were also discussed on board the ships in which the men were going home.

Nonetheless first place is deserved to the group of oldest volunteers, who were the first to be demobilized from the ranks of the Polish army at the end of 1919 and were grouped in the camp at Skierniewice. These veterans arrived in America on April 18, 1920 on the SS "Antigone." One of these volunteers, Jan A. Żebrowski,

---

8 J. Chojnacki "Jak nas żegnał generał Józef Haller" ["How General Józef Haller Bid Us Farewell"] in: *Weteran [The Veteran]* March 1940, p. 2

9 Ibid.

10 *Czyn Zbrojny Wychodźstwa Polskiego w Ameryce* [*The War Effort of the Polish Emigration in America*] New York – Chicago 1957, pp. 787-793

recalled years later: "The oldest volunteers were demobilized first in Poland. A group of them gathered in the beautiful camp in Skierniewice, near Warszawa. There was plenty of time for thought, so we discussed everything, and first of all we talked about our future collegial organization after returning to our home turf.

"In Skierniewice there were several or more colleagues from Buffalo, Chicago, Milwaukee, Pittsburgh, Youngstown, Erie, Cleveland and even St. Louis and other localities. It was there that an "organizational committee" was formed which I had the privilege of heading. The matter was discussed down to the minutest detail."[11]

The circumstances under which the first post of Polish veterans in America was formed, was described in the December 1920 issue of *The Veteran*: "During the voyage of the first transport ship this issue, that is, the founding of the organization, was discussed many times. There we also made tentative arrangements for the souvenir flag which we received from Polish women of the capital city of Warszawa in the presence of the Head of State, Józef Piłsudski, who came to say goodbye to the first transport going back across the ocean.

"Taking advantage of the opportunity of being together on board the ship, we got the addresses of colleagues from individual localities and promised that we would make an appropriate announcement in cooperation with other settlements. A more precise agreement as to the mode of operation happened on the train which took us from Camp Dix to Buffalo. The following colleagues were included in the committee: Jan A. Żebrowski, Bronisław Kaniasty and Władysław Kowalski.

"A few days after arrival we got together to discuss the matter of organizing a post, at the same time we awaited news from Chicago and other cities. We decided to wait a little while yet, checking Polish American papers in the hope that we would find something about the beginning of an organizational effort.

"Not having read anything like that, and wanting to fulfill our promise, on May 3, 1920 we published our first announcement in the Polish press to our colleagues, the veterans of the Polish Army.

"The effect was minimal, because only two colleagues from Milwaukee and New York contacted us for information.

Simultaneously with the appeal to all veterans colleagues we published another for our colleagues in Buffalo, NY, asking them to come to a meeting at the Polish Home on May 6, 1920. Barely four people showed up, so an organizing committee was formed which was to convene the next meeting. At the next meeting on May 12, 1920 a post was organized."[12]

---

11 *Weteran [The Veteran]* June 1951, p. 17
12 "Placówka 1 w Buffalo" ["Post # 1 in Buffalo"] in: *Weteran [The Veteran]* Cleveland, Nr. 3, December 1921, p. 14

The First Organizational Groups

The post founded on the initiative of J. A. Żebrowski in Buffalo (the later Post Nr. 1 of PAVA) took the name Związek Weteranów Wojsk Polskich (The Union of Polish Army Veterans).[13] By June 1920 it had 68 members. A month later there were already 237 members enrolled.

The second center in America where veterans of the Blue Army started organizing themselves the earliest was Chicago. The first post there was founded in Town of Lake, on May 15, 1920 on the initiative of the following Blue Army veterans: J. Drętkiewicz, Lisiecki, Lech and Walczak, with the help of the local Civic Committee. It took the name Stowarzyszenie Weteranów Polskich Armii gen. Hallera (Association of Veterans of Gen. Haller's Polish Armies). It later became PAVA Post Nr. 2.[14] These three sources are contradicted by information published in the August 1932 issue of *The Veteran*, where on page 11, under the title "The History of Post Nr. 2 in Chicago," the following is mentioned: "Post Nr. 2 was organized on June 20, 1920 in Chicago, IL. The founders of our post are colleagues: Jan Drętkiewicz, Jan Wutkowski, Franciszek Lesicki, Wawrzyniec Petecki, Roman Madejewski and Władysław Kościołowski."

The Posts in Buffalo and Chicago were the first documented veteran posts established in the United States by former soldiers of the Blue Army after their return to America.

In May 1920 a veteran post called Polscy Weterani z Wojny Wszechświatowej (Polish Veterans of the World War) was founded in New Britain, CT. Its initiator was the indefatigable social activist and outstanding administrator, Rev. Lucjan Bójnowski. He deposited $300 in the new association's account and paid for six months of membership dues for each of the veterans. This former recruiting officer from the years 1917–1919 thought with great concern about those who had fought on the battle fronts for Poland's independence. With them in mind, the local Civic Committee, inspired by Reverend Bójnowski, created the "St. Hedwig's Fund for Polish Invalids." By the time the former volunteers returned from Poland the local Polonia had collected over $22,000 for this fund. Thanks to this every returning veteran, not just the invalids, received a grant of $50 which in those days was substantial help.[15]

---

13 "Jednodniówka Weteranów Armii Polskiej" ["Souvenir Journal of Polish Army Veterans"] Chicago, May 1920, p. 50

14 "Powstanie i rozwój Stowarzyszenia Weteranów Armii Polskiej w Ameryce" [The Founding and Development of the Polish Army Veterans Assocation of America"] in: *Sprawozdanie z kampanii prowadzonej przez Stowarzyszenie Weteranów Armii Polskiej w Ameryce za zebraniam funduszu na osadnictwo na Kresach wschodnich i na zabezpieczenie bytu inwalidom* [*Report on the Campaign of the Polish American Veterans Association of America to Collect a Fund for Settlement on the Eastern Borderlands and to Secure the Welfare of Invalids*] Chicago, May 1920, p. 50

15 J. Wójcik "Haller Post 111. Diamentowy Jubilat" ["Haller Post 111. Diamond Jubilee"] in: *75 lat Placówki Nr. 111* [*75 Years of Post Nr. 111*] New Britain 1995, p. 7 (a souvenir journal).

It ought to be noted that thanks to the provident care and strong hand of Father Bójnowski the Polonia in New Britain was the only Polish American center that was properly prepared for the return of its soldiers from war, in line with the assurances that had been given during recruitment for the Polish Army in France.

Unfortunately, the exact date of the founding of the veterans association in New Britain is not known. The first minutes of a meeting of the post is dated June 10, 1920.[16]

After the third transport arrived from Poland, the Club of General Haller's Veterans was formed in Detroit in July 1920 at the initiative of Szczepan Sidor, Marian Jackowicz and Jan Żbikowski. The first meeting of the club was held on July 16, 1920. At that time a set of By-Laws prepared by Jan Przyprawa was approved. Its main stated goal was organizing mutual aid among the veterans. In a short time many members of the club who were in need received concrete help from their colleagues. In several cases help was rendered to former Polish soldiers who were not members of the club. When the dramatic news arrived of the Bolshevik invasion of Poland, threatening Poland with loss of its newly gained independence, the club members collected $150 for the Polish Red Cross.[17]

On July 25, 1920 sixteen local Polish veterans in Passaic, NJ formed the Polish Army Veterans Association. At the founders meeting the following Board was elected: Henryk Zając (President), Jan Walenciak (Vice President), Józef Nogacki (Secretary), Stanisław Marczak (Treasurer) and Władysław Joniec, S. Marciszewski, A. Rzeszutek and L. Jackulak—Auditing Committee.[18]

Former soldiers of the Blue Army living in Milwaukee, Wisconsin founded a similar society of the same name on July 30, 1920. At the initiative of Bronisław Spott the Polish Army Veterans Association was founded there, whose aim was to serve the Polish cause and to organize mutual aid. The first Board was composed of: Antoni Leszczyński (President), Zygmunt Woldański (Vice President), Bronisław Spott (Recording Adjutant), Florian Imilkowski (Financial Adjutant), Franciszek Zaczek (Treasurer) and the so-called Council members: Antoni Raczkowski, Michał Kapela, Antoni Rupiński, Mieczysław Lewandowski and Antoni Prostka.

Activity commenced with a fundraiser for the Polish Red Cross. In short order $1,061 was collected for this purpose.[19]

---

16 J. Wójcik, M. Kierkło *Z dziejów żołnierza emigranta* [*A History of the Emigrant Soldier*] New Britain 1991, p. 7
17 *The Veteran* June 1929, p. 88
18 PAVA National Executive Board (NEB) Archives. Collection: PAVA Posts, box: Post 36 in Passaic; "Protokół z posiedzenia organizacyjnego odbytego w dniu 25 lipca 1920 roku" ["Minutes of the Organizational Meeting Held on July 25, 1920"] in: PAVA Post 36 Minute Book. 1920–1931, p. 1
19 *The Veteran* June 1971, p. 53

This association joined the growing Polish Army Veterans Union in Chicago on November 5, 1920, where it was designated Post Nr. 3.[20]

The Gen. Józef Haller Society of Polish Army Veterans was established in Chicopee, MA in August 1920. The first Board was composed of: Wincenty Smołczyński (a veteran of the 1863 Uprising)—Honorary President; Franciszek Wajda—President; Jan Kołodziej—Vice President; Wincenty Stec—Recording Secretary; Klemens Partyka—Marshall (?), Rev. Wawrzyniec Cyman—Chaplain. The purpose of the society was to render aid to needy colleagues and veteran's widows and orphans. Veterans of the Polish Army or the American Army could belong to the society, because "...they fought for one and the same cause."[21]

On the other hand the veterans of Youngstown, Ohio founded the Polish American World War Veterans Association on August 20, 1920 which boasted nineteen members. This association was directed by a Board composed of: Adam Wolanin—President; Franciszek Woźniak—Secretary; Wacław Czubakowski—Treasurer.[22]

The Polish Army Veterans Association

In the spring of 1920 about 400 wounded and war invalids who could weather the ocean voyage returned to Chicago from Poland. This step was decided upon because there was frequently lack of space and medicine in the Polish hospitals. These veterans needed constant care during the ocean crossing and also after arrival in Chicago. Those without families were in the most difficult situation of all. Mainly with them in mind, in the first days of August 1920 Rev. J. Rozmus (former Polish Army chaplain), Major Dr. A. Pietrzykowski and Captain Dr. Franciszek Lenart published an appeal in local papers to all former volunteer veterans to come on August 12th to a mass meeting at the Polish Women's Alliance Building. This appeal met with a strong response: 500 veterans came. During this meeting the Związek Weteranów Armii Polskiej (Polish Army Veterans Association) was formed and its officers were elected: Dr. A. Pietrzykowski—President; Dr. F. Lenart—Vice Presdient; S. Z. Stachowicz—Secretary; Szczepan Obrzut—Treasurer (several weeks later S. Obrzut resigned and Michał Rudnicki became the treasurer). Together with the officers 34 veterans signed on as members of the organization; they named their group Post Nr. 1. It soon had a membership of 200 veterans, who taxed themselves on behalf of their

---

20 "Krótka historia Placówki 3 SWAP w Milwaukee, Wis." ["A Short History of PAVA Post Nr. 3 in Milwaukee, Wis.,"] in: *Weteran [The Veteran]* May 1941, p. 83

21 "Życiorys Tow. Weteranów Armii Polskiej im. Generała Hallera, Plac. 168, w Chicopee, Mass." ["A biography of the General Józef Haller Polish Army Veterans Society, Post 168 in Chicopee, Mass."] in: *Weteran [The Veteran]* May 1941, p. 82;

22 PAVA NEB Archives: PAVA Posts, Album pamiątkowy Placówki 4 SWAP w Youngstown, OH [Souvenir Album of PAVA Post # 4 in Youngstown, OH]

disabled comrades, in some instances even up to one third of their earnings, thanks to which it was possible to rent a home at Racine and Milwaukee Avenues for invalids who were single.[23]

At that meeting a resolution was approved by unanimous vote that Polish veterans ought to affiliate into one organization in Chicago, and later throughout the entire country, after prior consultation with colleagues from other Polish American communities.

Guided by this resolution the executive board of the Polish Army Veterans Association, with the help of the Polish American press, published an appeal throughout the United States to all former veterans—volunteers, that they should organize themselves into posts in their communities. The authors of the appeal started to get a stream of letters from existing clubs, associations and societies. The lively correspondence evinced the need to call a nationwide convention of delegates in the near future, of already existing veterans alliances in order to form a common organization.[24]

At its second meeting the Polish Army Veterans Association (PAVA) in Chicago formed a committee (Dr. A. Pietrzykowski, S. Z. Stachowicz, W. Krawczewski, A. Legieć, A. Karaś) to draft a so-called Constitution, i.e. By-Laws, on the basis of which new posts were to be established and the whole organization was to function. After three successive meetings of this post at which the draft prepared by the committee was read and amended, it was approved as a document binding on further organizational activity.

Thanks to the efforts of the executive board the veterans secured permanent access to the local press, of which "Dziennik Narodowy" ["National Daily"] turned out to be the most favorable, printing a whole page of the *Polish Army Veterans Association Section* once a week, which contained current information about the progress of PAVA's organizational work and where various issues that came up in the communities of the former soldiers were discussed. These materials were also sent out to Polish American newspapers that appeared in other Polish American centers.

This method of communicating soon bore fruit in the form of tangible effects. By the end of 1920 the Chicago-based ZWAP (PAVA) had already congregated 17 Posts under its wings. There were seven of them in the Polish American "fortress" as Chicago was called then, and two in New York. The remainder were scattered in other cities. Each new post received the next number in the series, thanks to which one can trace the succession and place of their formation:

---

23 "Historia 5-tej Placówki Macierzystej SWAP" ["The History of the 5th Mother Post of the PAVA"] in: *Placówka Macierzysta Nr. 5 SWAP w Ameryce. 70-ecie, 1920–1990* [*Mother Post Nr, 5 of the PAVA. 70th Anniversary, 1920–1990*] Chicago 1990, p. 3 (souvenir brochure)

24 S. Z. Stachowicz "Początki naszej organizacji" ["The Beginnings of Our Organization"] in: *Weteran [The Veteran]* May 1951, p. 59

Post Nr. 2 in the neighborhood of St. Hedwig's Parish, Chicago
Post Nr. 3 in Cicero, IL
Post Nr. 4 in the Brighton Park area of Chicago
Post Nr. 5 in the neighborhood of St. Adalbert's and St. Ann's parishes in Chicago
Post Nr. 6 in the St. Casimir's parish neighborhood, Chicago
Post Nr. 7 in South Bend, IN
Post Nr. 8 in Gary, IN
Post Nr. 9 in Boston, MA
Posts Nr. 10 and 11 in New York[25]
Post Nr. 12 in St. Louis, MO
Post Nr. 13 in Monnesen, PA
Post Nr. 14 in West Pullman, IL
Post Nr. 15 in Cohoes, NY
Post Nr. 17 in the Bridgeport area of Chicago, IL

These Posts together had about 600 members, who taxed themselves voluntarily for the purposes of the organization (35 cents per month) of which 20 cents went for the needs of the given Post, 5 cents for the American Red Cross, 5 cents for the Polish Red Cross and 5 cents for their own periodical which was to be published in the future.[26]

Further Associations, Clubs and Societies

Independently of the Chicago center, autonomous veterans organizations were formed in other cities. In August 1920 a veterans' post was formed in Cambridge, Mass., established by former soldiers who had returned from Poland in the first transport. The membership of the governing body of this post (unfortunately we don't know its name at that time) was: S. Stefanowicz—President; Wiktor Pryszmont—Vice President; Konstanty Jankowski—Financial Secretary; S. Samodziewicz—Treasurer.[27]

Cleveland saw the formation of its second Polish Veterans Club on October 3, 1920. Its organizers were: F. W. Gruszka, W. Sitko, S. Staniszewski, W. Kulczycki, T. Ząbkowski, J. Wata, B. Sadowski, P. Olkowski, J. Warszawski and Osiecki. At the beginning of its existence, even though this club needed help itself, it sent its first funds ($239.41) to Poland for the Polish Red Cross, and after some time another $240 for invalids and soldiers' orphans.[28]

---

25   The existence of these Posts in New York has not been corroborated by any other source material [author's note]
26   "Jednodniówka Weteranów Armii Polskiej" ["Souvenir Journal of the Polish Army Veterans"] Chicago, May 1921, pp. 50-52
27   "Z działalności Plac. 37 SWAP w Boston, Mass." "Activity of PAVA Post 37 in Boston, Mass." in: *Weteran [The Veteran]* June 1971, p. 66
28

On October 10, 1920 a veterans post was established in Jersey City, NJ (unfortunately, its name is unknown). Its organizers were: Jan Maciejewski, Jan Głowacki, Franciszek Romanowski, Antoni i August Cieplikowie. Their aim was to help former Polish soldiers financially and in finding jobs.[29]

The next group in the state of New Jersey was the Post in Elizabeth, which was established on December 12, 1920. Its name and the name of its members are unknown.[30]

On the other hand the names of the group of veterans who registered the Polish Army Veterans Club in Cleveland on February 2, 1921, are known. The official surviving incorporation document carries the following names: W. J. Gruszka, Stanisław J. Dzielak, P. Olkowski, W. Karolczak, J. M. Staniszewski, J. Woroniec, H. Firley.[31]

Further associations known to us came about in March 1921. On March 4 the Haller Society was established in New York. It had fourteen members. The first executive board was composed of: W. Stanicki—President; Myszak—Vice President; Stanisław Węglarski—Recording Secretary. Meetings were organized once a month at the Immigration House of the Polish National Alliance in Manhattan (the current headquarters of the Piłsudski Institute)[32]

The Polish Veterans Club was established in Utica, NY on March 6, 1921, with the following executive body: J. Gomuła –President; Karwacki—Secretary; A. Dombrowski—Treasurer.[33] Both Polish Army and American Army veterans belonged to this club. For the next nine years they held joint commemorative meetings, parades, balls, picnics, etc.[34]

The Beginnings of Coalition Efforts

By the spring of 1921 the situation of the Polish veterans groups in the United States began to slowly polarize. The centers in Chicago, Buffalo and Cleveland stood out especially. The dynamic development of Chicago's Polish Army Veterans Association and its aspirations to subordinate to itself all other veterans clubs and societies was being observed with great reserve by the already organized veterans in Buffalo and Cleveland. They accused the Chicago association of being too dependent on the

---

29 B. Łyczak. "Historia Placówki 51 SWAP" ["The History of PAVA Post 51"] in: *Weteran [The Veteran]* June 1929, p. 86

30 *Weteran [The Veteran]* June 1928, p. 23

31 PAVA NEB, collection: PAVA Posts, box: PAVA Post 6, file: Correspondence

32 T. Zieliński "Krótka historia nowojorskiej Placówki No. 21 SWAP" ["A Short History of PAVA New York Post No. 21"] in: *Weteran [The Veteran]* June 1929, p. 65

33 *60ta rocznica istnienia Stow. Weteranów Armii Polskiej, Placówka Nr. 105* [*The 60th Anniversary of the Polish Army Veterans Association, Post Nr. 105*] (Souvenir journal) Utica 1971, p. 7

34 "Krótka historia Placówki 105 SWAP w Utica, NY" ["A Short History of PAVA Post 105 in Utica, NY"] in: *Pamiętnik XI Walnego Zjazdu SWAP w Utica, 30, 31 maja—1 czerwca 1952* [Souvenir Journal of the XI PAVA National General Assembly in Utica, May 30,31–June 1, 1952]

National Department, which according to the opinion of veterans from Buffalo and Cleveland: "did not account for a million dollars collected for veterans relief."[35]

The PAVA in Chicago accused its colleagues in Buffalo, Erie and Cleveland of being KON (National Defense Committee) sympathizers. During the war that committee, being in favor of a pro-Austrian orientation and of Józef Piłsudski's Legions, had unsuccessfully attempted to oppose in America the idea of cooperation with the nations of the Entente. Its opposition was especially strongly visible in its attempts to block recruitment acticity for the Polish Army in France in the years 1917–1918.

Despite the animosity it was obvious that there was a pressing need to create one organization for the former soldiers of the Blue Army, so that by combined effort help could be given as soon as possible to the unemployed and homeless colleagues, especially the war invalids, who because of wide-spread unemployment had the least chance of finding steady work. For these reasons the veterans in Buffalo and Cleveland (Jan Z. Żebrowski and Walenty Karolczak) proposed to Post Nr. 1 of the Polish Army Veterans Association in Chicago to organize a conference of all local veterans' organizations. PAVA accepted the proposal and on the name day of the two Polish leaders: Józef Piłsudski and Józef Haller, March 19, 1921, joint talks were held in Cleveland. At the conference held in the local "Falcons" headquarters, that is the building of the Polish Falcons of America, Chicago was represented by S. Z. Stachowicz (mandate of the Polish Army Veterans Association), Buffalo by J. A. Żebrowski (mandate of the Polish Armed Forces Veterans Association) and Erie by W. Kulczycki (mandate of the Veterans Post). Karolczak, F. W. Gruszka and Firley played host and represented the Cleveland veterans. The conference brought positive results. One of its participants, S. Z. Stachowicz, recalled: "At this conference the colleagues from Cleveland, Buffalo and Erie realized that "the devil isn't as horrible as he's been painted" that is, that the Chicago veterans are not tied to anybody's apron strings. And conversely, Chicago found out that their colleagues from Cleveland, Buffalo and Erie are no KON sympathisers, but just as good volunteer veterans as the ones from Chicago.

"It was decided that for the sake of economy the national convention should take place in a transportation hub. This place is the city of Cleveland. There is a strong Civic Committee here (an agency of the National Department) which supports the veterans, which will guarantee the conventioneers room, hospitality, a banquet, etc. It was decided that the Convention would take place on May 28, 29 and 30 in Cleveland, in the Polish National Home (headquarters of Polish National Alliance Group 6)"[36]

J. A. Żebrowski enumerated other important particulars of this conference:

---
35 S. Z. Stachowicz, "Początki naszej organizacji" ["The Beginnings of Our Organization"] in: *Weteran [The Veteran]* May 1951, p. 59

36 S. Z. Stachowicz, op. cit. p. 60

"At this meeting we decided to call an Organizational Congress of all our veteran groupings which were already organized. The Congress was planned for the end of May 1921 at the local Falcons' building on Broadway Street.

"I was to prepare the By-Laws for our Veteran Organization; Stanisław Stachowicz, because he had all the addresses, took care of sending out letters to the already existing veteran associations, and Walenty Karolczak was to prepare everything else for the coming Organizational Congress to be held in Cleveland, Ohio."[37]

After that conference announcements were mailed to all known veteran associations informing them about the coming congress. Before that came to pass, new veteran associations were founded. On April 10, 1921 a veteran post was organized in Pittsburgh, PA.[38] On May 5, 1921 the veterans in Bridgeport, CT organized themselves.[39] On that same day a post was founded in Hammond, Indiana. At its first meeting the following governing body was elected: W. Paluch—Commander; J. Pikor—Vice Commander; J. Świerszcz—Financial and Recording Secretary; J. Grochowski—Treasurer, and J. Sumara and S. Jarosz—Finance Committee Members.[40]

Three days later, on May 8, 1921 the Haller Club Nr.2 was established in Detroit. Its organizers were: A. Durda, A. Drabicki, Sebastian Międlar, J, Rup, S. Ruszel and S. Rzucidło.[41]

At approximately the same time the General Haller Club of Polish Army Veterans 1917–1921 was organized in Philadelphia.[42]

A post was established on the last day of that same month in Newark, NJ in an old building on New York Avenue. Its first governing board was also constituted there, consisting of: Jan Kalinowski—Commander; Stefan Nieużytek—Vice Commander; Wincenty Gałuszka—Financial Secretary; Józef Ślubowski—Treasurer; Józef Niebylski—Recording Secretary.[43]

The Founding Convention of the Polish Army Veterans Association in America

In accordance with the directives of the March conference in Cleveland, the first General Assembly of Polish Army Veterans living in the United States took place in

---

37 J. A. Żebrowski "SW.A.P. w Ameryce" ["PAVA in America"] in: *Weteran [The Veteran]* October 1962, p. 10
38 *Weteran [The Veteran]* June 1929, p. 43
39 *Weteran [The Veteran]* June 1921, p. 63
40 "Krótki zarys Placówki 40-tej" ["A Short Sketch of Post Nr. 40"] in: *Jubileusz Placówki 40-tej SWAP [PAVA Post 40 Jubilee]* Hammond, IN 1996, p. 11
41 *Weteran [The Veteran]* June 1971, p. 74
42 "Zarys historii Plac. 12 SWAP i K.P.P. w Filadelfiii, PA" ["An Outline of the History of PAVA and 'W.A.C.' in Philadelphia, PA"] in: *Weteran [The Veteran]* June 1971, p. 57
43 "Z historii Plac. 25 SWAP Newark, NJ" ["A History of PAVA Post 25 Newark NJ"] in: *Weteran [The Veteran]* May 1951, p. 19

that city from May 28 to 30, 1921. Thirty eight delegates participated. Among them, with the approval of the Convention's presiding officers, was the military attaché of the Polish Embassy, Major Kazimierz Mach, who was invited as a guest and granted full delegate rights. The list of delegates of this historic convention, and the centers they represented, is as follows:

> Washington, DC—Major K. Mach
> Pittsburgh, PA—Dr. T. Starzyński, Pingielski, Zawada
> Chicago, IL—S. Z. Stachowicz, Cz. Żuławski, Małek, Rudnicki, Samborski, Hawrylewicz, Poźniak, Drętkiewicz
> Milawukee, WI—Karaś
> Cleveland, OH—L. Adamczak (Chevalier of the Order of Virtuti Militari), W. Karolczak, F. W. Gruszka, Firley, Sadowski, J. Kruszyński, Staniszewski and M. Kowalski (Chevalier of the Order of Virtuti Militari)
> Erie, PA—W. Kulczycki, A. Joniec
> Boston, MA—Stefański
> Buffalo, NY—J. A. Żebrowski, J. Kazanowski, Kubala, Hulak, Czachowski, Rev. Łukasik
> Youngstown, OH—Wolanin
> Monessen, PA—Wojciechowski
> Toledo, OH—Kania and J. Matecki (Chevalier of the Order of Virtuti Militari)
> Elyria, OH—Sobótka (a delegate representing Polish veterans from the American Army)
> New York City—Misiak
> Philadelphia, PA—Kuszewski, Targowski, Grabowski[44]

During the Convention's sometimes very heated deliberations, the delegates decided to create one common organization which on a motion by Józef Kazanowski of Buffalo was named the Stowarzyszenie Weteranów Armii Polskiej w Ameryce (SWAP)—the Polish Army Veterans Association of America (PAVA).

The most important document approved at the convention was the PAVA Constitution (By-Laws) which regulated the entirety of issues connected with the functioning of the association, and also described its main goals and tasks. At the initiative of Major Kazimierz Mach the name of the organization was reserved in the text of the By-Laws, in order to enable all former soldiers of the Polish Army who had fought for Poland's freedom, to enter its ranks. By this simple means PAVA avoided the antagonisms that effectively divided the veterans of various military formations in Poland.

---

44 "Historyczny protokół" ["Minutes of a Historic Meeting"] in: *Weteran [The Veteran]* May 1951, p. 19

During the elections the delegates showed greatest trust toward Dr. Teofil Starzyński of Pittsburgh, the President of the Polish Falcons of America, greatly distinguished for his work on behalf of Polonia's military efforts in the years 1910–1919. The convention unanimously elected him the President of PAVA. This trust also had its source in the fact that the decided majority of veterans participating in the convention were former "Falcons" serving under Starzyński's command.

Also elected as officers were: Lucjan Adamczak of Cleveland—1st Vice President; Czesław Żuławski of Chicago—2nd Vice President; Stanisław Z. Stachowicz of Chicago—Secretary General; J. Kruszyński of Cleveland—Assistant Secretary General; J. Firlej of Cleveland—Treasurer; Rev. Łukasik of Buffalo—Chaplain, and members of the Board of Directors: A. Joniec of Erie, J. Matecki of Toledo; J. A. Żebrowski of Buffalo; F. W. Gruszka, W. Kulczycki and M. Kowalski of Cleveland and also J. Dybowski of Detroit.

During the voting on the site for the headquarters of the National Executive Board 24 delegates were in favor of Cleveland, and 14 were for Chicago. S. Z. Stachowicz, who had been elected Secretary General and lived in Chicago, was to move with his family to Cleveland. The organization committed itself to paying for the costs of the relocation.

The new Board was to call for the next general assembly in one year in Chicago, and was to begin efforts to publish its own periodical.

During the convention there was a closed-door session (limited to the delegates alone) dedicated to the funds collected during the war by the Polish National Department, which were to have been used to insure war invalids and to safeguard the families of volunteers who died in battle or were wounded. Department representative Vice President Teodor Heliński who had arrived from Chicago, tried to clarify this touchy subject. Here is how S. Z. Stachowicz remembered those moments: "Teodor Heliński, Vice President of the Department, arrived. He was sharply attacked over that million. The attack was unmerited. Heliński, almost with tears in his eyes, asked: 'Please choose people, let them come to the offices of the Department, let them audit our books. You will find out that the Department did not deprive the Veterans of even one penny.' That won over both feelings and minds. The convention chose three people to review the books of the Department: Roman Hanasz, Czesław Żuławski and S. Z. Stachowicz."[45]

After the convention the commission audited the account books of the Polish National Department. It turned out that the "Veteran Funds" had not been misappropriated, but had been used to promote the Polish cause during the war

---

45 S. Z. Stachowicz. "Początki naszej organizacji," ["The Beginnings of Our Organization"] in: *Weteran [The Veteran]* May 1951, p. 61

and after its conclusion, which in the face of the anti-Polish propaganda at that time by German and Jewish circles, especially in the United States, had enormous significance. This sort of action was undertaken because it was believed (according to S. Z. Stachowicz) that the veterans and invalids would not be returning to America, because they might all be staying in Poland.

After the conclusion of the closed-door session, by decision of the convention Head of State Józef Piłsudski and General Józef Haller were made honorary Presidents of PAVA, while the American Pilot Cedric E. Fauntleroy, the former commander of the 7th Squadron, The Kościuszko, which assisted the Poles in their battles with the Bolsheviks in 1919–1921, was made an honorary PAVA member.

The Convention sent telegrams to Head of State Józef Piłsudski, General Józef Haller and U.S. President Warren G. Harding. On a motion by Teofil Starzyński a telegram was also sent to Wojciech Korfanty, who at that time was directing the 3rd Silesian Uprising.

The Cleveland Convention was a total success. The essential foundation for building a unified veteran organization of former Polish army soldiers living in the United States was created. The choice of Dr. Teofil Starzyński as PAVA President, an outstanding organizer and patriot, with an excellent understanding of the soul of the émigré soldier, gave full guarantee for the success of the undertaking.

It also became apparent in Cleveland, how very necessary were meetings between former colleagues from time of war, who had been scattered across the enormous expanses of America. It was again possible to shake the hand of an old comrade, retell war adventures, share the experiences of civilian life, or toss back a shot in good, old company. "There were some who were still having a good time in Cleveland one week after the convention concluded," recalled S. Z. Stachowicz.[46]

The By-laws and Territorial Development of PAVA

The most important document regulating the life of PAVA was the bylaws adopted at the founding convention under the name "Constitution and Regulations of the Polish Army Veterans Association of America."

Unfortunately, the original of the document approved at that time has not survived. The first printed text of the "Constitution and Regulations of PAVA" comes from 1925 and contains amendments that were approved at the second PAVA General Assembly in Chicago in 1922 and at the third convention in Detroit in 1925. These amendments were published in the convention reports, thanks to which we can quite faithfully reproduce the basic text of the primary document, which was adopted at the convention in Cleveland in 1921.

---

46 Ibid. p. 60

The text of the "Constitution and Regulations of PAVA" was composed of four parts: I—"The Association"; II—"The Districts"; III—"The Posts"; and IV—"General Rules."

On the basis of the analysis of later amendments it can be stated that the first part contained the following articles:

- Name, headquarters, logo
- Tasks and goals
- Principles
- Funds and means
- The Make-up of the National Executive Board of PAVA of America
- General and Special Assemblies
- The members of the Association
- The members of the National Executive Board of the Association
- The President of the Association, his rights and duties
- The Vice Presidents, their rights and duties
- The Secretary General, his rights and duties
- The Treasurer, his rights and duties
- The Standard-Bearer, the assistant Standard Bearers, their rights and duties
- Directors of the National Board, their rights and duties
- The agenda of meetings of the National Executive Board of PAVA
- PAVA members, their duties and obligations
- The Referendum
- The continuity of the organization
- The Text of the Oath of PAVA officers
- The second part contained the following articles:
- The essential function of the Post, its name, location and logo
- The goals, tasks and principles of a Post
- Funds and means
- The governing board of a Post, its tenure, rights and duties
- The Post President, his rights and duties
- The Vice President, his rights and duties
- The Post Financial Secretary, his rights and duties
- The Post Treasurer, his rights and duties
- The Recording Secretary, his rights and duties
- The Standard Bearer and assistant Standard Bearers, their rights and duties
- The Management Council, its rights and duties
- The legality of resolutions and the right to pass resolutions

- The agenda of Post meetings
- The rights and duties of Association members and fees to the Executive Board
- The member's oath
- Continuity of the Post.

The third part is composed of only one article: "The Behavior of PAVA members in America." This part also mentions the issue of an arbitration type Peer Court, but without any detailed description of the procedure of its functioning. In point 3 of this article it is merely stated that "The regulations concerning an arbitral Peer Court are in the possession of the office of the National Executive Board and Posts may obtain a copy upon request."[47]

The bylaws approved at the founding convention of PAVA in May 1921 were later amended many times. The development of organizational life made it necessary to adjust the internal regulations to the constantly changing reality. Some specific regulations proved to be untenable, while there was a lack of reference in the PAVA By-Laws to various issues that were cropping up. All amendments to its text were introduced by successive general assemblies, because only those congresses have the right to do so. The most important changes were introduced in the years 1922–1939. They concerned the following issues:

- The Second PAVA General Assembly in Chicago in 1922 introduced a new section to the PAVA By-Laws: "The Districts." It was also approved that "Polish female nurses also have the right to belong to PAVA in America." This issue took the form of Article Nr. XXI—"The Female Nurses." A new article, Nr. XIV "The Editor of *The Veteran* his rights and duties" was introduced. A paragraph was added stating that "A Funeral fund shall be established by PAVA."

- The Third General Assembly in Detroit in 1925 introduced the next article into the PAVA By-Laws, Article Nr. XXII "The Auxiliary Corps in PAVA;" two paragraphs regulating the functioning of PAVA districts were amended. The amended paragraph 4 stated: "PAVA districts are established where the Posts so determine and with the knowledge and approval of the National Executive Board," while paragraph 5 read: "Districts do not have the right to tax members of Posts that are part of a District. The Posts have a free hand to create funds needed to organize a District."[48]

---

47 PAVA NEB Archives, signature Gr. III/vol. I, "Konstytutcja i regulaminy Stowarzyszenia Weteranów Armii Polskiej w Ameryce" ["The By-laws and Regulations of the Polish Army Veterans Association of America"] 1925, p. 38
48 Ibid., p. 22

- The Fourth General Assembly in Buffalo in 1928 carried out several amendments of specific points in the text and clarified others. For instance, it was approved that November 11 would be a PAVA holiday (up to then it was May 3).[49] Moreover, a new article was introduced: "the Mother Post" which sounded as below: "As approved at the Fourth Convention Post number five in Chicago, Illinois has been named the Mother Post of the Polish Army Veterans Association of America." Thus this post was honored for the role it played in August 1920, when it called on all former soldiers of the Polish army to organize into veteran posts, associations and unions.

- The Fifth General Assembly in Pittsburgh in 1931 changed the content of the article "Continuity of the Organization" which spoke of the conditions which must be fulfilled in order to dissolve PAVA. The existing text: "the Polish Army Veterans Association of America cannot be dissolved, so long as even one Post belonging to it remains. Should even that one cease to exist, then the entire estate of the Association will be passed on to the Fund for Invalids in Poland," was changed to: "the Polish Army Veterans Association of America cannot be dissolved so long as even one Post belonging to it remains. When the final Post ceases to exist, then the entire remaining estate of the Association will pass on to the fund for widows and orphans of veterans, members of PAVA in America."[50]

- The Sixth PAVA General Assembly in Newark, NJ in 1934 changed the names of the titles of the main officers of PAVA. "President of the Executive Board" was changed to "Commander in Chief," "Vice Presidents" to "1st and 2nd Vice Commander," "Secretary General" to "Adjutant General" "Treasurer" to "Treasury Officer" Also a new article was introduced: "Detachments of the Sons and Daughters of Polish Army Veterans."[51]

- The Seventh PAVA General Assembly was held in Rochester, NY in 1937, in addition to numerous amendments of many paragraphs, it introduced

---

49 PAVA NEB Archives, sign. Gr. III/vol. 1, "Konstytucja i Regulaminy Stowarzyszenia Weteranów Armii Polskiej w Ameryce" ["By-Laws and Regulations of the Polish Army Veterans Association of America"] 1934, p. 24

50 PAVA NEB Archives, signature GR III/ vol. 1 "Poprawki przyjęte do Konstytucji SWAP na Walnym Zjeździe, odbytym w mieście Pittsburgh'u w 1931 roku." ["Amendments to the PAVA By-Laws approved at the General Assembly held in the city of Pittsburgh in 1931."]

51 "Protokół VI Walnego Zjazdu SWAP w Ameryce, odbytego w dniach od 26 do 30 maja 1934 roku w Polskim Domu Narodowym, pn. 42 Beacon St., Newark, NJ" ["Minutes of the VIth General Assembly of PAVA in America, held May 26 to 30, 1934 in the Polish National Home, at 42 Beacon St., Newark, NJ"] in: Weteran [The Veteran] Nr. 158, July-August 1934, pp. 11-32; PAVA NEB Archives, PAVA By-Laws and Regulations, 1934, pp. 5, 24

an entirely new "Marching Regulations" and a "Funeral Ritual for PAVA Members."[52]

General Assemblies of the Polish Army Veterans Association in America

The highest authority in the Polish Army Veterans Association of America was the General Assembly of Delegates.

Ex Officio delegates to the General Assembly were: the President (PAVA Commander), the Vice Presidents (Assistant Commanders), the secretary general (the Adjutant General), the Treasurer (The Treasury Officer), the editor of *The Veteran*, the Chief Medical Officer, the Madame President and Madame General Secretary of the PAVA Auxiliary Corps.

The members of the Board of Directors of PAVA, District Commanders and all Chevaliers of the Order of Virtuti Militari who were members of PAVA also had the right to be delegates to the General Assembly.

Every PAVA post had the right to send one delegate to the PAVA General Assembly for every 25 members it had. The largest posts had the greatest number of delegates and they played a significant role in the life of the association. A requirement was instituted as of 1934 that all delegates from posts had to be active members of PAVA for at least three years.

The General Assembly of PAVA Delegates was to approve reports of the Board, elect and nominate a new National Executive Board for the period between General Assemblies, approve changes and amendments to the PAVA By-Laws, appoint honorary members, and select the site of the next convention.[53]

The first two PAVA general assemblies took place in succeeding years. The next assemblies took place every three years. Here is their full list for the years 1921–1939:

I PAVA General Assembly	Cleveland, May 28–30, 1921
II PAVA General Assembly	Chicago, May 28–30, 1922
III PAVA General Assembly	Detroit, May 29, 30 to June 1, 1925
IV PAVA General Assembly	Buffalo, May 26–30, 1928
V PAVA General Assembly	Pittsburgh, May 29–31, 1931
VI PAVA General Assembly	Newark, May 26–30, 1934
VII PAVA General Assembly	Rochester, May 29, 30 to June 1, 1937

---

52 PAVA NEB Archives, sign. Gr. III/vol. 1, "Zmiany i poprawki do Konstytucji uchwalone na VII Walnym Zjeździe SWAP w Rochester, NY 1937" ["Changes and amendments to the By-Laws approved at the 7th PAVA General Assembly in Rochester, NY 1937"]

53 PAVA NEB Archives, sign. Gr. III/vol. 1, "Konstytucje i Regulaminy SWAP z 1925 i 1940 roku" ["PAVA By-Laws and Regulations from 1925 and 1940"]

Every general assembly, whose dates coincided with the Memorial Day holiday, was a great event in the life of the organization. Representatives of the largest Polish American organizations, of the clergy, of Polish diplomatic posts, of state and federal authorities honored it with their presence, which greatly raised the prestige of this veteran association.

In the years 1922–1939, that is in the period when the veterans were full of energy and greatly active in life, there were real battles among the largest veteran centers for the right to organize the next convention. It was a rivalry to host one's war comrades in the best possible style, and at the same time to present the city and local Polonia from their best aspects.

Membership in the Polish Army Veterans Association

According to the "PAVA By-Laws" of 1925 members of the Polish Army Veterans Association in America were divided into active and honorary members. "Any former member of the Polish Army, honorably discharged and belonging to one of the posts of the Association can be an **active member** of PAVA. **Honorary members** are specially nominated by the General Assemblies of the Association in recognition of exceptional contributions to the Polish cause or work for PAVA."[54]

But there were cases that did not fit the PAVA By-Laws, as when veterans from the American army of Polish descent were admitted to the association. That caused protest in the ranks and that is why at PAVA's Fourth General Assembly in Buffalo a prohibition was voted through. Only those had the rights of full membership who had been accepted prior to the IV PAVA Convention. From that time on veterans of Polish descent who had served in the Aemrican army could only be accepted into the PAVA Auxiliary Corps.

Who could become a member of PAVA was also made more precise: "Anyone can be a member of the Polish Army Veterans Association of America, regardless of the military formation in which he served, who fought for the freedom and independence of Poland from 1914 to November 11, 1920 and was honorably discharged from the Polish Army."[55]

An additional rule was introduced regarding PAVA membership at the Sixth General Assembly of PAVA held in Newark, NJ in 1934: "Polish women, who served in the ranks of the Polish Army, served at the front, in a supporting role, or as nurses,

---

54 "Konstytucja i Regulaminy Stowarzyszenia Weteranów Armii Polskiej w Ameryce 1925 roku" ["The By-Laws and Regulations of the Polish Army Veterans Association of America of 1925"], p. 8

55 PAVA NEB Archives, sign. Gr. II/vol. 4, "Protokół IV Walnego Zjazdu SWAP odbytego w dniach 26 do 30 maja, roku 1928 w Buffalo, NY" ["The Minutes of the IVth General Assembly of PAVA held from May 26 to 30, 1928 in Buffalo, NY"] p. 20

have the right to active membership in P.A.V.A. of America."[56]

Those were the last changes and amendments in the PAVA By-Laws prior to September 1939.

The National Executive Board of the Polish Army Veterans Association of America

The highest authority in the organization between PAVA general assemblies were the meetings of PAVA's National Executive Board, composed of the PAVA Main Council (president, two vice presidents, secretary general, treasurer and the editor of *The Veteran*) and the Privy Council (nine directors, the chief chaplain and the chief physician)—which functioned as an advisory body.

The highest executive authority was the PAVA Main Council.

The so-called PAVA National Executive Board was composed of: the president (represented PAVA externally to American and Polish authorities); the secretary general (administered the organization's offices); the treasurer (responsible for the organization's finances).[57]

This structure of the National Executive Board survived until 1931. At that time, at the General Assembly in Pittsburgh, the following amendment to the PAVA By-Laws was approved: "The National Executive Board of the Polish Army Veterans Association is composed of a president, two vice presidents, a secretary general, treasurer, editor in chief, physician, chaplain, four local directors and one from the East and all District presidents who are automatically vice presidents of the Association in their District."[58]

The so-called local directors mentioned in the aforesaid amendment lived closest to the headquarters of the National Executive Board. At that time it was located in Detroit, Michigan. The director "from the East" on the other hand, was to be the representative of PAVA districts from the East Coast of the USA.

This amendment was caused by the limited financial capabilities of those districts that lay far from the headquarters, which due to the continuing economic depression were unable to cover long trips for officials who were part of the National Executive Board. There is a list of the PAVA National Executive Boards for the years 1921–1940 in Addendum 3.

---

56 "Konstytucja i Regulaminy Stowarzyszenia Weteranów Armii Polskiej w Ameryce" ["By-laws and Regulations of the Polish Army Veterans Association of America"] New York, 1934, p. 9

57 "Konstytucja i Regulaminy Stowarzyszenia Weteranów Armii Polskiej w Ameryce" ["The By-laws and Regulations of the Polish Army Veterans Association of America"] New York 1934, p. 9

58 Ibid., pp. 8-15

The Districts of the Polish Army Veterans Association of America

The idea behind the creation of districts was to make the functioning of the organization—spread out over the enormous expanses of the United States and Canada—more efficient. The districts would greatly help the National Executive Board to run the administration, which with the increasing number of posts had become a very time consuming task. Given this situation already the First PAVA Convention in Cleveland in 1921 directed the PAVA National Executive Board to begin the task of organizing the districts.

Soon after the convention the secretary general, Stanisław Z. Stachowicz, according to information on hand about where the concentrations of former Polish Army soldiers were located, divided a map of the territory of the United States into the planned districts. The PAVA Vice President, Lucjan Adamczak, was to bring the plan to fruition. By decision of the PAVA National Executive Board he was to visit the largest veteran concentrations and organize posts (if such did not yet exist there) and PAVA districts.[59]

During his tour in August and September 1921 Adamczak visited Polish veteran groups in the following states: Pennsylvania, Maryland, Delaware, New Jersey, New York, Connecticut, Massachusetts, Michigan and Ohio. Here is a fragment of his itinerary, which partially survived:

"August 21—Camden, NJ; August 22—Philadelphia, PA; August 23—Baltimore, MD; August 24—Wilmington, DE; August 25—Reading, PA; August 26—Perth Amboy, NJ; August 27—Passaic, NJ; August 28—Newark, NJ; August 29—organizing the District in Newark NJ; August 30—meeting in Jersey City, NJ; August 31—meeting in Paterson, NJ; September 1—meeting in New York, NY; September 2—meeting in Trenton, NJ; September 3—meeting in Bridgeport, CT; September 4—meeting in New Haven, CT; September 5—meeting in New Britain, CT; September 6—meeting in Meriden, CT; September 7—New London, CT; September 8—organizing the New England District in Cambridge, MA; September 9—meeting in Chicopee, MA; September 10—meeting in Cambridge, MA; September 10—meeting in Boston, MA."[60]

From the surviving minutes of the meeting held in Newark, NJ on August 29, 1921 it is apparent that at Adamczak's initiative delegates from posts in Newark, Elizabeth, Jersey City and Bayonne established PAVA District V with headquarters

---

59 PAVA NEB Archives, sign. Gr. VII/ vol. 1, "Protokół z posiedzenia Zarządu SWAP odbytego dnia 7.VII. 1921 roku" ["Minutes of a Meeting of the PAVA National Executive Board held on July 7, 1921"] p. 9

60 Central Archives of the Polish American Community in Orchard Lake, MI, collection: PAVA District VI archives, Folder: "Protokoły Placówki 7 SWAP od 20 VII 1921 do 28 IX 1921" ["Minutes of PAVA Post 7 from July 20, 1921 to September 28, 1921"]

in Newark, with the following governing body: President Kalinowski, Newark; Vice President Romanowski, Jersey City; Recording Secretary Malecki, Elizabeth; Financial Secretary Kiczek, Elizabeth; Treasurer W. Galuszka, Newark; Auditors: Maciejewski, Jersey City; Niemiec, Elizabeth; organizer—Gorzelnik, Elizabeth. After the swearing in of the officers Gorzelnik presented to Adamczak the very difficult current situation of the veterans, who would have a hard time paying dues to their posts, the district and the National Executive Board.[61]

In consequence of his extremely intense and busy itinerary Adamczak organized eight new posts and five districts: II, III, IV, V and VI.[62]

By October 1921 PAVA already had eight districts:

Nr. I in Chicago,
Nr. II in Philadelphia,
Nr. III in Pittsburgh,
Nr. IV in Nanticoke (a suburb of Wilkes Barre, PA)
Nr. V in Newark,
Nr. VI in Boston,
Nr. VII in Cleveland,
Nr. VIII in Schenectady.[63]

The districts, organized from the top down (with the exception of District I in Chicago, which was the continuation of the former District of the Polish Army Veterans Union) did not have appropriate legal organizational guidelines, under which they could function. "Regulations for Districts of the Polish Army Veterans Association of America" were adopted at the plenary session of the PAVA National Executive Board in Cleveland on November 6, 1921. It had been drafted by the Organizing Committee composed of: Lucjan Adamczak, Stanisław Z. Stachowicz, W. Karolczak.

The Regulations also stated that: "A District shall be composed of several Posts located near to each other, and assigned to the District by the PAVA National Executive Board. ... The Districts are subordinated to the absolute control and directives of the PAVA National Executive Board...Posts assigned to a District tax their members an additional 5 cents per month for the needs of the District .... Posts belonging to a given District are obliged to carry out absolutely all directives of the District."[64]

---

61 PAVA NEB, sign. Gr. VIII/ vol. 26
62 PAVA NEB, sign. Gr. VII/vol. "Protokół z posiedzenia Zarządu SWAP odbytego dnia 9 października 1921 roku" ["Minutes of the meeting of the PAVA National Executive Board held on October 9, 1921"] p. 18
63 "Sprawozdanie Sekretarza Jeneralnego z dnia 9 października 1921 roku" ["Report of the Secretary General of October 9, 1921"] in: *Weteran [The Veteran]* November 1921, Nr. 2, p. 5
64 PAVA NEB, sign. Gr. VI/1, "Regulamin Okręgów Stowarzyszenia Weteranów Armii Polskiej w Ameryce." ["Regulations of the Districts of the Polish Army Veterans Association of America."]

In line with these regulations the NEB assigned existing posts to the following districts:

PAVA District I. Chicago, IL, President Roman Hanasz
PAVA Post Nr.2, Chicago, IL, J. Kostrubala
PAVA Post Nr. 5, Chicago, IL, Secretary J. Ćwik
PAVA Post Nr. 9, Chicago, IL, Secretary A, Kaczmarz
PAVA Post Nr. 10, Cicero, IL, Secretary S. Ładniak
PAVA Post Nr. 13, South Bend, IN, Secretary J. Juszczak
PAVA Post Nr. 14, Chicago, IL, Secretary A. Szara
PAVA Post Nr. 15, Gary, IN, Secretary F. Bilski
PAVA Post Nr. 20, Chicago, IL, Secretary S. Gadowski
PAVA Post Nr. 28, Kensington, IL, Secretary Fr. Jendrejaszek
PAVA Post Nr. 39, Chicago, IL, Secretary J. Jenkner
PAVA Post Nr. 40, Hammond, IN, Secretary J. Świercz
PAVA Post Nr. 41, Peru, IL, Secretary A. Turczyn
PAVA Post Nr. 56, Chicago, IL, Secretary M. Perzga
(In sum 13 posts)

PAVA District II. Philadelphia, PA, President S. Wojciechowski
PAVA Post Nr. 12, Philadelphia, PA, Secretary S. Jastrzębski
PAVA Post Nr. 21, Camden, NJ, Secretary A. Pawlak
PAVA Post Nr. 48, Wilmington, DE Secretary J. Sobczak
PAVA Post Nr. 49, Baltimore, MD, President Dr. K. Siwiński
PAVA Post Nr. 55, Reading, PA, Secretary A. Wołek
PAVA Post Nr. 65, Manayunk, PA, Secretary L. Puścizna
(In sum 6 posts)

PAVA District III. Pittsburgh, PA, President A. Pingielski
PAVA Post Nr. 16, Pittsburgh, PA, Secretary J. Jóźwiak
PAVA Post Nr. 19, Monessen, PA, Secretary F. Kosieniak
PAVA Post Nr. 30, Johnston, PA, Secretary B. Kloc
PAVA Post Nr. 38, New Castle, PA, Secretary Bonk
PAVA Post Nr. 45, Weirton, WV, Secretary M. Baca
PAVA Post Nr. 47, Washington, PA, Secretary K. Gardocki
PAVA Post Nr. 60, Ambridge, PA, Secretary F. Tuwalski
PAVA Post Nr. 61, Braddock-Wilmerding, PA, Secretary J. Zbrzeżny
(In sum 8 posts)

PAVA District IV, Nanticoke, PA, President A. Florkowski
PAVA Post Nr. 31, Nanticoke, PA, Secretary F. P. Rokosz
PAVA Post Nr. 32, Wilkes Barre, PA, Secretary B. Leśniewski
PAVA Post Nr. 44, Hazleton, PA, Secretary F. Bradowski
PAVA Post Nr.63, Mocanaqua, PA, Secretary W. Czerwonka
(In sum 4 posts)

PAVA District V, Newark, NJ President J. Kalinowski
PAVA Post Nr. 25, Newark, NJ, Secretary J. M. Niebylski
PAVA Post Nr. 36, Passaic, NJ Secretary J. Walenciak
PAVA Post Nr. 43, Port Chester, NY, Secretary J. Sudoł
PAVA Post Nr. 51, Jersey City, NJ Secretary F. Romanowski
PAVA Post Nr. 57, Elizabeth, NJ, Secretary J. Nowak
(In sum 5 posts). Posts to be organized: Trenton and Bayonne, NJ

PAVA District VI, Boston, MA, President E. Kamieński
PAVA Post Nr. 11, Holyoke, MA, President A. Czarnota
PAVA Post Nr. 23, Adams, MA, Secretary S. Czaja
PAVA Post Nr. 24, Bridgeport, CT, Secretary J. Kondracik
PAVA Post Nr. 37, Cambridge, MA, Secretary H. Jankowski
PAVA Post Nr. 53, West Lynn, MA, Secretary J. Kalapiński
PAVA Post Nr. 54, Salem, MA, Secretary A. Gesek
PAVA Post Nr. 62, Indian Orchard, MA, Secretary W. Nowakowski
PAVA Post Nr. 64, New Bedford, MA, Secretary P. Feruś
(In sum 8 posts). Posts to be organized: Lowel, MA, Meriden, CT, Norwich, CT.

PAVA District VII, Cleveland, OH, President A. Krakowiak
PAVA Post Nr. 4, Youngstown, OH, Secretary A. Sajkiewicz
PAVA Post Nr. 6, Cleveland, OH, Secretary S. Staniszewski
PAVA Post Nr. 7, Detroit, MI, Secretary J. Rychlicki
PAVA Post Nr. 17, Erie, PA, President A. Joniec
PAVA Post Nr. 22, Toledo, OH, Secretary J. S. Skalski
PAVA Post Nr. 34, Ironwood, MI, K. Szymczyk
(In sum 6 posts). Posts to be organized: Johnson, MI, Oil City, PA, Akron, OH

PAVA District VIII, Schenectady, NY, President A. P. Osielski
PAVA Post Nr. 18, Schenectady, NY, Secretary M. Żytkowski
PAVA Post Nr. 27, Rochester, NY, Secretary J. Mazur
PAVA Post Nr. 35, Amsterdam, NY, Secretary J. Mazurek
PAVA Post Nr. 46, Binghamton, NY, Secretary W. A. Tenerowicz

PAVA Post Nr. 50, Cohoes, NY, Secretary S. Ząbek
PAVA Post Nr. 1, Buffalo, NY, Secretary J. A. Żebrowski
PAVA Post Nr. 58, Hamilton, ONT, Canada, Secretary S. Biały
PAVA Post Nr. 59, Herkimer, NY, Secretary J. Kowlaski
(In sum 8 posts). Posts to be organized: Lackawanna, NY; Niagara Falls, NY; Utica, NY.

PAVA District IX
(In planning stages) it was to be situated in Milwaukee, WI. It was to be composed of posts that were to be organized in Milwaukee and also in St. Paul MN and Minneapolis, MN.

PAVA District X
(In planning stages) it was to be situated in St. Louis, MO. The posts that were to be part of it were to be organized in St. Louis, MO; East St. Louis, IL; St. Joseph, MO; Topeka, KS; Kansas City, KS; Omaha, NE; and Springfield, IL.[65]

PAVA Vice President Lucjan Adamczyk was supposed to organize Districts IX and X. But nothing came of this project, because it became quickly apparent that the districts, organized with a lot of hard work, in practice (with small exceptions) did not act according to the guidelines laid down by the National Executive Board of PAVA. Secretary General Stanisław Z. Stachowicz wrote about this in his report, which covered the period from June 1, 1921 to May 28, 1922: "Right after the convention the secretary general divided the territory of the United States into Districts. There were to be 12 such districts in the Association. In November the National Executive Board approved a special set of regulations for the Districts, but neither the Districts nor the Posts adhered to these regulations. Some Districts existed on paper alone, others began giving the National Executive Board orders and demands, and when something was asked of them, they did not do it."[66]

There were several factors that influenced the failure of the effort to create districts. First of all, the effort was made too soon, because the association was just in its formatory stages. The newly organized posts were still very weak both in terms of organization and finances. Most of their members were in financial straits, and the burden of an additional tax to maintain the district seemed out of proportion to the necessity for creating yet another organizational structure. The instability of the posts also did not help this effort, because the members were forced to leave for other cities in search of employment.

---

65 Ibid.
66 PAVA NEB Archives, sign. Gr. VII/1, "Książka protokołów ZG SWAP 1921–1925" ["The Minute Book of the PAVA NEB 1921–1925"] in: *Weteran [The Veteran]* Nr. 18, August 1922, p. 12

In many cases entire posts had to be dissolved.

Nor was the creation of the districts helped by the fact that the effort was made from the top, by the National Executive Board, which had the exclusive right to decide where the PAVA districts were to be located and which posts were to belong to them. This method was reminiscent of a military drill, where the leadership gives the orders and the soldiers carry them out in full. The "Regulations for PAVA Districts" affirmed this. The phrase "absolute control" was frequently repeated in them, as well as "blind fulfillment of all directives," etc. This was a very important and simultaneously extremely delicate psychological aspect, because these phrases brought a natural reaction of protest from the rank and file members of PAVA. After all, this association was an organization of colleagues, in which the members also wanted to have something to say and some kind of ability to be in on the decision-making.

The leadership of the organization found out that without strong posts in the field it was not possible to organize the districts by fiat. The future showed that only District I in Chicago was able to continue its activity throughout the entire period of the association's existence. Of the remaining ones, formed in 1921, only District V in Newark, NJ remained active, and functioned until April 1922, and also District VI in Boston, MA, which was active to June 1922.[67]

At the PAVA 2nd General Assembly in Chicago in May 1922 a motion was passed that read: "… to dissolve Districts in areas where they prove to be unneeded, and leave them only where they show real vitality and where the Posts want it."[68]

Soon after the convention, as a result of the resolution, only District I in Chicago remained. It had functioned the best of all up to that point and had posted solid gains in organizing help for its disabled and unemployed colleagues.

The next attempt at creating districts was undertaken by the PAVA National Executive Board in the Spring of 1922. It prepared a huge fund drive for a Settlement and Invalid Fund. Thanks to enormous work on the part of PAVA Vice President Lucjan Adamczak, twelve "Fund Drive" districts were organized in the United States, composed of veterans and top representatives of the local Polish American communities. These districts, of a rather civic than veteran character, worked with outstanding results from March to August 1922 in the following regions:

District I—Chicago, IL and surrounding areas
District II—Philadelphia, PA and surrounding areas
District III—Pittsburgh, PA and surrounding areas

---

67 PAVA NEB Archives, sign. Gr. VIII/vol. 26, 27 "Okręgi SWAP. 1921–1940" ["PAVA Districts. 1921–1940"]
68 PAVA NEB Archives, sign. Gr. II/vol. 2, "Protokół z II Walnego Zjazdu SWAP, odbytego w Chicago, IL, w dniach 28–30 maja 1922" ["Minutes of the PAVA 2nd General Assembly, held in Chicago, IL May 28–30 1922"] p. 7

District IV—Wilkes Barre, PA and surrounding areas
District V—Newark, NJ, New York and surrounding areas
District VI—Boston, MA and surrounding areas
District VII—Cleveland, OH and surrounding areas
District VIII—Schenectady, NY and surrounding areas
District IX—Buffalo, NY and surrounding areas
District X—St. Louis, MO and surrounding areas
District XI—Milwaukee, WI and surrounding areas
District XII—Detroit, MI and surrounding areas.[69]

The Fund Drive districts were organized according to the plan that was in force at the time the districts were being organized in 1921. The National Executive Board made efforts to transform the fund drive districts with their civic character into veteran PAVA districts after the conclusion of the fund drive. But the plan did not work, because the districts dissolved after the campaign's conclusion, and the veterans who participated in them did not make any effort to transform those structures into PAVA districts.[70]

From the 2nd to the 3rd PAVA General Assembly (May 1922 to May 1925) only PAVA District I in Chicago was active together with the posts subordinated to it in Illinois and Indiana.

Further districts began forming only after the 3rd General Assembly (Detroit, MI, 1925) where two essential changes were made to the PAVA By-Laws (thus acknowledging the postulates voiced by the posts) which stated that: "Districts shall be formed where Posts desire them and with the knowledge and approval of the National Executive Board. Districts do not have the right to tax members of Posts that are part of a District. The Posts have a free hand to establish funds in order to organize a District."[71]

In the end, from 1925 to 1939, eleven new districts were organized. The most (five) were established in the years 1933–1935, that is, just after the Great Depression ended in America.

In comparison to the former (leadership-initiated) efforts in the years 1921–

---

69 PAVA NEB Archives, "Sprawozdanie z Kampanii prowadzonej przez Stowarzyszenie Weteranów Armii Polskiej w Ameryce za zebraniem funduszu na osadnictwo na Kresach wschodnich i zabezpieczenie bytu inwalidom" ["Report from the Campaign Directed by the Polish Army Veterans Association of America to Create a Fund for Settlement on the Eastern Borderlands and to Secure the Livelihood of Invalids"] Cleveland 1922, p. 67

70 F. J. Waluś, "Przed trzydziestu laty" ["Thirty Years Ago"] in: *Weteran [The Veteran]* May 1953, p. 10

71 PAVA NEB Archives, sign. Gr. III/vol. 1 "Konstytucja i Regulaminy Stowarzyszenia Weteranów Armii Polskiej w Ameryce." ["The By-Laws and Regulations of the Polish Army Veterans Association of America."] 1925, p. 22

1922, which came from the PAVA National Executive Board, this time the process of creating districts was from the bottom up, taking into consideration the interests of the psots and their members, which gave evident results.

In 1939 twelve districts were functioning within the PAVA's organizational structure.

(For a list of PAVA districts, the posts belonging to them and the list of District Presidents see Addendum Nr. 4). Every district was made up of many posts located near each other.

Executive Boards guided the work of the districts, and were elected for one year during the annual district convention. Every district executive board consisted of a commander, two vice commanders, an adjutant, a secretary and a treasurer. The districts were under the absolute control and directives the the PAVA National Executive Board.[72]

The Posts of the Polish Army Veterans Association of America

The post was the basic organizational cell of the Polish Army Veterans Association of America, having its own number assigned to it by the PAVA National Executive Board, and the name of the locality in which it functioned. The full name of a post would be, for example, Post Nr. 1 in Buffalo of the Polish Army Veterans Association of America.

All honorably discharged veterans of the Polish Armed Forces could be members of every PAVA post, regardless of the military formation in which they served.

The general meeting of the post decided in each case about accepting a new member.[73]

It was decided to give wider access to membership, for instance to former members of the Polish Legions, who because of wounds and poor health were unable to fight in the ranks of the revived Polish Army after 1918. Consequently, time frames were established (from 1914 to November 10, 1920) at the 4th General Assembly of PAVA in Buffalo in 1928, which were accepted as the period of the Polish soldier's fight for independence.

Each PAVA post had its executive board, which was elected for one year by a general assembly of the post. The post's executive board was composed of a president (as of 1934—commander), two vice presidents (vice commanders), two secretaries (adjutants)—financial and recording—and a treasurer.

The number of PAVA posts in the years 1921–1939 wavered, but generally in an upward trend. Their number decreased in the first years of activity and during the Great Depression, which occurred in the years 1929–1932. This was caused by

---

72 "Konstytucja i Regulaminy Stowarzyszenia Weteranów Armii Polskiej w Ameryce." ["The By-Laws and Regulations of the Polish Army Veterans Association of America."] 1934, New York City, p. 25

73 "Konstytucja i Regulaminy Stowarzyszenia Weteranów Armii Polskiej w Ameryce." ["The By-Laws and Regulations of the Polish Army Veterans Association of America."] 1925, pp. 22-37

problems with finding employment by many post members, who were forced to wander all over the country in search of work. In many cases this phenomenon was so widespread that many posts had to be dissolved.

Unfortunately, due to lack of data it is impossible to give a year by year statistical presentation of this occurrence. We have to limit ourselves to information concerning the years when PAVA general assemblies took place:

Year	Number of Posts	Number of Members
1921	66	1,746
1922	78	2,820
1925	68	1,304
1928	98	2,058
1931	86	2,402
1934	108	3,168
1937	127	4,334
1939	141	4,450

Source: T. Lachowicz. Prepared on the basis of PAVA NEB collections

It is clear from the above table that from 1934 on, that is after the end of the Great Depression, there was a strong increase in the number of PAVA posts. The number of members in the organization increased. This was connected with the systematic progress toward economic stability and the personal prosperity of the majority of the veterans. This had an obvious influence on the wealth of the individual posts, which was an added incentive that attracted veterans that had not yet joined the association.

In the period under discussion the number of PAVA posts was very unstable, because new ones were being established, but others ceased to exist. Some disappeared for ever, others renewed their activity after some time.

At first the serial number of a dissolved post was passed on by the PAVA National Executive Board to a newly organized post. When a once dissolved post was reactivated after some time it received a new serial number. In 1923 the newly formed post in Trenton, NJ received Nr. 81, which had belonged previously to the PAVA post in Wallingford, CT, which had been dissolved. When the latter was reactivated in October 1934 it received a new serial number, 103. The same happened with Post Nr 86 in Scranton, PA (later Post 117); with Post Nr. 58 in Hamilton, Canada (later Post Nr. 163).[74] Posts with serial number 79 had the worst luck.

---

[74] PAVA NEB Archives, "Sprawozdanie urzędników zarządu SWAP i K.P. na 7-my Walny Zjazd SWAP w mieście Rochester, NY, za czas 1934 roku do 1937 roku" ["Report of the officers of the PAVA National Executive Board and the A.C. for the 7th PAVA General Assembly in Rochester, NY for the period 1934 to 1937"] p. 14

In 1922 that was the number carried by the PAVA post in Union City, CT. After it ceased to exist this number was assigned to the newly established PAVA post in Chicopee, MA, which was founded in 1923 and ceased to exist in 1924. In the years 1925–1926 the PAVA post in Glen Cove, Long Island, NY had the number 79.[75]

This numbering method brought protests because it became evident that some of the reactivated posts were emotionally attached to their old number, which was simultaneously a distinguishing mark in the veteran community.

Due to increasing pressure, the PAVA National Executive Board decided not to reassign old numbers of former posts to newly created posts, so that the latter could get their number back should they renew their activity.

With veterans in mind who lived in small towns, scattered individually or in small groups of two or three (which did not give them the opportunity to form an individual post) and who very much wanted to belong to PAVA, the National Executive Board in 1932 established a so-called Floating Post, which received the number 100 in the organization.[76] In 1934 it had 42 veterans as members, in 1937—56 members, and in 1940—64 members strewn all over America, from Florida to California.[77]

In the years 1921–1940 the Polish Army Veterans Association had a total of 173 posts (with various periods of duration) in three countries: 164 in the USA, 6 in Canada and 1 in Poland (PAVA Post Nr. 130 in Bydgoszcz).[78] (For the list of PAVA posts active in the years 1921–1939 see addenda 5 and 6).

The greatest concentration of posts was on the East Coast and in the Great Lakes region, both on the American and the Canadian side, which were the same areas where, in the period 1917–1919, the greatest recruitment effort took place for the Polish Army in France.

Some PAVA posts assumed the names of known Polish historical figures, contemporary military leaders, and also colleagues-leaders who had died at the front fighting for Poland's independence. In one instance it was the name of a city and a military unit:

The General Józef Haller PAVA Post Nr. 5 in Chicago, IL
The "Lwów" PAVA Post Nr. 7 in Detroit, MI

---

[75] PAVA NEB Archives, collection: "Placówki SWAP, Akta Placówki 79." ["PAVA Posts, Post 79 Files"]
[76] *Weteran [The Veteran]* Detroit, October 1932, p. 89
[77] "Sprawozdanie urzędników zarządu SWAP i K.P. na 7-my Walny Zjazd SWAP i K.P. w mieście Rochester, NY, za czas 1934 roku do 1937 roku" ["Report of the officers of the PAVA National Executive Board and the A.C. on the 7th PAVA and A.C. General Assembly in Rochester, NY for the period 1934 to 1937"], p. 15; "Sprawozdanie urzędników zarządu SWAP na IX Walny Zjazd SWAP w mieście New Britain, CT, za czas od 1940 roku do 1946 roku" ["Report of the officers of the PAVA National Executive Board and the A.C. for the 9th PAVA General Assembly in the city of New Britain, CT for the period 1940 to 1946."] p. 12
[78] *Weteran [The Veteran]* Detroit, December 1932, p. 15

The Tadeusz Kościuszko PAVA Post Nr. 10 in Cicero, IL
The Lucjan Chwałkowski PAVA Post Nr. 12 in Philadelphia, PA
The Tadeusz Kościsuzko PAVA Post Nr. 14 in Chicago, IL
The Lucjan Moros PAVA Post Nr. 61 in Braddock, PA
The 1st Regiment of Polish Riflemen PAVA Post Nr. 90 in Chicago, IL
The General Józef Haller PAVA Post Nr. 93 in Southington, CT
The Józef Piłsudski PAVA Post Nr. 102 in Greenpoint, Brooklyn, NY
The General Józef Haller PAVA Post Nr. 107 in Terryville, CT
The General Józef Haller PAVA Post Nr. 110 in Torrington, CT
The General Józef Haller PAVA Post Nr. 111 in New Britain, CT
The General Lucjan Żeligowski PAVA Post Nr. 116 in Wallington, NJ
The Józef Piłsudski PAVA Post Nr. 118 in Elizabeth, NJ
The I. J. Paderewski PAVA Post Nr. 123 in Maspeth, Queens, NY
The General Józef Haller PAVA Post Nr. 156 in Bristol, CT
The General Józef Haller PAVA Post Nr. 168 in Chicopee, MA
The Józef Piłsudski PAVA Post Nr. 171 in Thompsonville, CT

Source: T. Lachowicz. Based on the collections of the PAVA NEB Archives

Independent Posts

In the years 1921–1939, aside from Polish Army Veterans Association of America posts, other Polish veteran associations were also active. In the main these were clubs and associations established by former Polish soldiers in the years 1920–1922 after their return to the United States. The vast majority of the veteran groups that formed at that time became a part of PAVA, but not all. Some of them, for various reasons, held onto their independence. On the whole prestige and financial matters played a decisive role.

First of all they did not want to share their modest funds, part of which in case they joined PAVA, would have had to be given to the National Executive Board. Additional costs would have had to be incurred to maintain the district. In case of retaining independence all the funds remained in the club's account and were at its sole disposal.

The issue of prestige was just as fundamental, where human ambition played a significant role. Somebody who was the president of a small club or association often felt this to be a rung up on the social ladder. In joining PAVA, "Mr. President" was forced to carry out the directives coming from "higher up," that is from the National Executive Board, which was at odds with an ambition to lead others.

Nonetheless with the passage of time it became ever more evident that in acting alone not much could be accomplished. When it was noticed that PAVA, despite criticism from the side of the independents, was doing better and better, was becoming an organization that others were taking notice of (American authorities included) that it was capable of taking care of many matters that were troubling veterans, and give them concrete, quantifiable help—slowly the attitude toward the organization began to change, which in many instances ended with joining its ranks.

What acted in favor of PAVA was the natural tendency of the members of the independent posts to be in one collegial veteran family. The frequent applications of independent posts to join PAVA are evidence of this. That is what happened with the **Independent Polish World War Veterans Gen. J. Haller Post** in New Britain, CT.[79]

Among the independent posts active in the years 1921–1939, there was the Polish Army Veterans Association in Philadelphia, PA (organized in 1922). It joined PAVA on August 16, 1925 as Post Nr. 12. A post with the same number had been active in Philadelphia in the years 1921–1922. After re-joining PAVA the veterans of that city got their old number back.[80] The **Hallerians Club Nr. 2 in Detroit, MI** established on May 8, 1921. As of 1922 it had a new name—**The Józef Piłsudski Hallerian Colony** (This group joined PAVA in 1925 as Post Nr. 78.[81] The Yonkers, NY post (organized on June 19, 1921) joined PAVA in February 1926 as Post Nr. 84.[82] **The Polish Veterans From the World War** (an organization formed in New Britain, CT in May 1921) as of 1922 was known as **The Independent Post of Polish Veterans of the World War.** It joined PAVA in December 1929, where it was registered in January 1930 as Post Nr. 111.[83] **The Polish Veterans Club in Utica, NY**: it was already active in 1926, and joined PAVA in March 1928.[84] **The Society of Polish and American Veterans of the World War** in New Bedford, MA was established in 1923. Bronisław Buczyński, in a letter of March 7, 1931 to the PAVA National Executive Board in Detroit, wrote about the circumstances of its formation: "I myself belonged to the post that existed in New Bedford, but after two years only six of us were left. An opportunity arose and Dr. Wróblewski visited us so we gave him a stadning room only reception with the participation of American Army veterans of Polish descent and after this manifestation we organized a new association called the Society of Polish and American Veterans of the World War. There are 62 of us, and there is a

---

79   I. Wójcik, M. Kierkło, *Z dziejów żołnierza emigranta [A History of the Emigrant Soldier]* New Britain, 1991, p. 9
80   "Szkic historyczny Placówki Nr. 12 we Filadelfii'["A Historical Sketch of Post Nr. 12 in Philadelphia"] in *Weteran [The Veteran]*, February 1926, p. 22
81   "Jednodniówka wydana nakładem Kolonii Hallerczyków im. Józefa Piłsudskiego w Detroit" [Souvenir Journal Published by the Józef Piłsudski Hallerian Colony in Detroit"] March 19, 1922
82   "Krótki szkic historii Placówki 84 w Yonkers, NY" ["A Short Sketch of the History of Post Nr. 84 in Yonkers, NY"] in: *Weteran [The Veteran]* May 1937, p. 25
83   PAVA NEB Archives, Collection: PAVA Posts, file: Post Nr. 111 in New Britain. 1928–1931
84   PAVA NEB Archives, Collection: PAVA Posts, file: Post 105 in Utica, NY. 1928–1934

total of about 300 [veterans] in New Bedford, so they should all be signing up, yet they don't want to."[85] From the By-Laws of this society (adopted October 8, 1923) it is apparent that its main goal was to give mutual aid to Polish and American veterans in New Bedford, MA. Among the outstanding activists there were: Józef Marnik, Jan Irzyk, A. Dombal, P. Feruś, L. Peltz, P. Koczara, Jan Bodzioch, S. Rymszewicz, F. J. Waluś and Bronisław Buczyński.[86] **The Polish Army Veterans Club in Fort William, Ontario, Canada.** Founded in January 1931 it had 48 former soldiers of the Polish Army on its rolls. Most of them had joined the ranks of the Polish Army on Polish territory in the years 1918–1920. There were also several Hallerians who had enlisted in the Blue Army in France. None of the members of this club had been recruited to the Polish Army on U.S. and Canadian territory in the years 1917–1919. All of them arrived in Canada only after 1926. Józef Kocoń was the president of this club. The purpose of this club was material and moral mutual aid, keeping up Polish heritage by organizing celebrations of national anniversaries, meetings, lectures, amateur theatrical productions, social affairs, etc. One of the main goals was also to counteract the anti-Polish propaganda being spread in Canada by the Ukrainian emigration. In February 1931 the veterans of the club made contact with the PAVA National Executive Board in New York in order to organize a PAVA post in Fort William. However, due to widespread unemployment and the inability to pay membership dues the plan fell through.[87]

The Veterans Club in Bayonne, NJ joined PAVA in January 1926, where it was registered in February 1926 as Post Nr. 85.[88]

The Legion of Polish Army Veterans in Detroit, MI. It was founded on September 22, 1934 in the building of the Polish Falcons of America Nest 79 by nineteen of its members. In 1935 the Legion already had 41 veterans. It was directed by an executive board with the following roster of officers: L. Igras—commander; J. Kwiatkowski—1st vice commander, J. Maguder—2nd vice commander, S. Baliński—financial adjutant, S. Majtyka—recording adjutant, W. Szczepański—treasury officer.[89]

---

85 PAVA NEB Archives, sign. Gr. X/ vol. 3, Independent Posts.
86 Ibid.
87 PABA NEB Archives, sign. Gr. X/ vol. 1a, Letter of the Polish Army Veterans Club in Fort William to the PAVA National Executive Board of February 22, 1931.
88 PAVA NEB Archives, sign. Gr. X/vol. 3, Independent Posts
89 "Krótki raport Legionu Weteranów Armii Polskiej" ["A Short Report of the Legion of Polish Army Veterans"] in: *Pamiętnik Gniazda 79-go S.P. w Ameryce i Legionu Weteranów Armii Polskiej z okazji odsłonięcia tablicy pamiątkowej dla uczczenia poległych członków Gniazda 79-go. 12 maja 1935 w Detroit, MI*. [*Souvenir Journal of the Polish Falcons of America Nest 79 and the Legion of Polish Army Veterans on the Occasion of the Unveiling of a Memorial Plaque to Honor Fallen Members of Nest 79. May 12, 1935 in Detroit, MI*]

The General Józef Haller Polish Army Veterans Society in Chicopee, MA. It was organized in August 1920. It did not join PAVA until 1939, where it was registered as PAVA Post Nr. 168. Before joining PAVA it had accumulated sizeable assets. From 1936 it had its own building, where the life of the local Polonia was concentrated. Moreover this society could boast that from the funds that it had accumulated during the period of its activity, it was able to pay out $1,050 to its members and their families for funeral expenses, $3,125 for aid in time of sickness, $2,100 for patriotic purposes, $900 for charitable goals, $500 as relief for widows and orphans, $100 to cover hospital expenses for its veteran colleagues and $600 for annual Christmas parties for children.[90]

The development of organizational life caused certain PAVA posts and independent posts to cooperate more closely. That was what happened in the state of Connecticut, where in Southington in 1927, at a convention of delegates representing PAVA Post Nr. 73 in Meriden (the initiator of the convention), PAVA Post Nr. 93 in Southington and independent posts in New Britain and Terryville, it was decided in 1927 to form an **independent District I of the Polish Army Veterans Association.** This district, despite using the name PAVA, did not belong to the organizational structures of the Polish Army Veterans Association of America. That situation remained until 1929, when due to the efforts of PAVA Post Nr. 73 in Meriden the independent District I was finally incorporated into the proper PAVA structures and was registered as District IV.

Shortly thereafter the independent posts in Terryville, Torrington and New Britain also joined PAVA, where as new organizational units they received the numbers 107, 110 and 111.[91]

---

[90] "Życiorys Tow. Weteranów Armii Polskiej im, Gen. Józefa Hallera, Plac. 168 w Chicopee, MA" ["A Sketch of the General Józef Haller Polish Army Veterans Society, Post 168 in Chicopee, MA"] in: *Weteran [The Veteran]* May 1941, p. 82

[91] PAVA NEB Archives, sign. Gr. VIII/ vol. 20, PAVA Districts

II.
AUXILIARY ORGANIZATIONS OF THE POLISH ARMY VETERANS ASSOCIATION OF AMERICA

The Auxiliary Corps of the Polish Army Veterans Association of America

Its beginnings go back to 1922. At that time a group of Polish women from Chicago, at the initiative of Agnieszka Wisła (a former nurse of the Polish White Cross, who had tours of duty behind her in the Polish Army in France and in Poland) formed an ad hoc group called The Committee to Help Veterans. It was a spontaneous initiative, whose goal was to help those veterans who found themselves in the most difficult conditions, that is war invalids, the sick, the homeless and the unemployed. This committee was included: Agnieszka Wisła, H. Bogucka, Z. Różańska, Z. Jaworska, L. Kasperek, M. Obarska, L. Paluszek and J. Wolf.[1]

Other cities also followed Chicago's example, where Polish women founded various circles and committees for the same purpose, and all acted on their own. This fragmentation was not conducive to greater success. It was not until **May 1925 that at the III General Assembly in Detroit, MI a unified organization, the PAVA Auxiliary Corps, was created** in order to consolidate efforts on behalf of invalids and sick veterans under one leadership.

The name and idea for the creation of trhe Auxiliary Corps was born in Milwaukee, Wisconsin, where prior to the opening of the 3rd PAVA General Assembly, the local PAVA Post Nr. 3 organized an Auxiliary Corps composed of 39 male and female members. After the General Assemby it received the Number 1 in recognition of its activity.

The *Auxiliary Corps Regulations* also came about in Milwaukee. It later served as the basis for the *Auxiliary Corps By-Laws.* On the basis of a resolution of the PAVA 3rd General Assembly the By-Laws project was completed by Agnieszka

---

1   PAVA NEB Archives, sign. Gr. XXXIII, Auxiliary Corps, File: Agnieszka Wisła

Wisła, Dr. Franciszek Lenart and Stanisław Krygowski. All were from Chicago, where the PAVA headquarters moved after the General Assembly. That is also where the Auxiliary Corps By-Laws were ratified and sent out to all PAVA posts with a request for organizing auxiliary corps. They were to be composed of friends and sympathizers of the veterans—both men and women—especially those who at one time had helped in recruitment for the Polish Army in France. By a decision of the 3rd PAVA General Assembly Poles who were soldiers in the Americna army could join the Auxiliary Corps, who at that time were barred from joining PAVA's ranks.[2]

The main purposes of the Auxiliary Corps were:

"1. To gather into the Corps all the workers from the time when the Polish Army was being formed, and current friends and sympathizers of the veterans.

"2. To uphold and pass on to posterity the only tradition in the history of the world, of the creation by the Polish emigration of a Polish Army, in order to fight for the lost [national] independence.

"3. Material and moral aid for disabled veterans of the Polish Army, for the sick and their families that are in need, without regard to whether or not they belong to the Polish Army Veterans Association.

"4. To uphold the Polish image in America, to maintain the Polish language, Polish culture and traditions, by means of commemorative symposiums, meetings, festivities and similar activities.

"5. To get the emigration closer to American society and to acquaint them with Polish culture."[3]

The Auxiliary Corps was to be guided by three principles in its activity:

"1. The PAVA Auxiliary Corps in America will be—just like the Veterans Association—an apolitical organization of Polish ethnicity; it will fight all attempts to undermine the credibility and good name of the Polish Republic, the Polish Army and the American Republic.

"2. Outside the organization, the Corps members, as individuals, shall fulfill their civic and religious obligations according to their own conscience and attitudes.

"3. There is no place in the Auxiliary Corps for individuals believing in Communist principles."[4]

According to the *PAVA Auxiliary Corps Regulations* the Auxiliary Corps was divided into Districts (coinciding with the PAVA Districts) and posts. The Auxiliary

---

2 PAVA NEB Archives, sign. Gr. II/ vol. 3, *Protokół z III Walnego Zzjazdu SWAP* [*Minutes of the 3rd PAVA General Assembly*]

3 *Regulamin Korpusu Pomocniczego Stowarzyszenia Weteranów Armii Polskiej w Ameryce, 1925 roku* [*Regulations of the Polish Army Veterans Association of America Auxiliary Corps of 1925*, p. 1

4 Ibid.

Corps general assemblies were to take place parallel to the PAVA general assemblies, at the same time and at the same place. At these conventions the female delegates each time elected an Auxiliary Corps Executive Board, which was to guide the organization through its term, which lasted three years. The official organ of the Auxiliary Corps was *The Veteran*—the PAVA media organ in America."[5]

From 1925 the Auxiliary Corps operated with a National Executive Board, because one had not been elected at the PAVA General Assembly in Detroit, Michigan, because that was still the beginning phase of organizing the auxiliary corps. At the same time it became evident that it was mostly women who wanted to join the new organization, and with time only and exlusively they joined. The Boardless state lasted for three years.

The first National Executive Board of the Auxiliary Corps was elected at the 4th PAVA General Assembly in Buffalo, New York in May 1928. It had two members: the President (Agnieszka Wisła) and the secretary (Józefa Rzewska).

At that time the Auxiliary Corps had fifteen posts, with 536 male and female members. The men—who were few in number—soon left of their own accord.

In May 1928 a complete list of the posts of the Auxiliary Corps—in the order of their founding and thus of the serial number that they received on that basis (a different number than that of the PAVA post at whose side the Auxiliary Corps was functioning)—was as follows:

    Auxiliary Corps Post Nr. 1 in Milwaukee, WI, founded in 1925, 91 members
    Auxiliary Corps Post Nr. 2 in Chicago, IL, founded on October 6, 1926, 116 members
    Auxiliary Corps Post Nr. 3 in Newark, NJ founded on November 18, 1926, 12 members
    Auxiliary Corps Post Nr. 4 in Jersey City, NJ, founded on November 18, 1926, 25 members
    Auxiliary Corps Post Nr. 5 in Detroit, MI, founded on January 8, 1927, 37 members
    Auxuiliary Corps Post Nr. 6 in Bayonne, NJ, founded on April 12, 1927, 22 members
    Auxiliary Corps Post Nr. 7 in Erie, PAN, founded on March 27, 1927, 26 members
    Auxiliary Corps Post Nr. 8 in Passaic, NJ, founded on November 28, 1927, 17 members

---

5   Ibid., p. 6

Auxiliary Corps Post Nr. 9 in Yonkers, NY, founded on December 8, 1927, 12 members
Auxiliary Corps Post Nr. 10 in Braddock, PA, founded on March 6, 1928, 11 members
Auxiliary Corps Post Nr. 11 in Buffalo, NY, founded on April 5, 1928, 56 members
Auxiliary Corps Post Nr. 12 in Monessen, PA, founded on April 20, 1928, 2 members
Auxiliary Corps Post Nr. 13 in Niagara Falls, NY, founded on May 12, 1928, 15 members
Auxiliary Corps Post Nr. 14 in Chicago, IL, founded on May 14, 1928, 78 members
Auxiliary Corps Post Nr. 15 in Cicero, IL, founded on May 16, 1928, 70 members.[6]

At the 5th PAVA General Assembly in Pittsburgh, PA in 1931, the Auxiliary Corps received a large measure of autonomy within the PAVA. From that moment it had the right to its own financial management. Moreover it chose its own Board independently. It was united with PAVA by ideology alone.[7]

The granting of such extensive autonomy to the Auxiliary Corps, especially in the area of finances, soon caused many misunderstandings and conflicts. It became apparent that in many cases the granting of financial aid to the disabled, the sick and unemployed veterans depended on the "mood" of the president of the given Auxiliary Corps post.

No wonder that at the next, 6th PAVA General Assembly in Newark, NJ in 1934 the Corps' financial autonomy was voided. The independence of the Auxiliary Corps' Executive Board was also nullified. From that moment on it was to work closely with the PAVA National Executive Board. All its activites had to be approved by the PAVA National Executive Board. By this means the Auxiliary Corps was really reduced to the role of an auxiliary formation within the PAVA.[8]

The number of PAVA Auxiliary Corps grew systematically over the following years. By 1940 there were 113 of them (Please see addenda 7, 8 and 9).

---

6   T. Lachowicz, "Jak powstał Korpus Pomocniczy przy Stowarzyszeniu Weteranów Armii Polskiej w Ameryce" ["How the Auxiliary Corps by the Polish Army Veterans Association of America was Created"] in: *Weteran [The Veteran]*, Nr. 882, May 1995, pp. 4-5

7   "Po Zjeździe w Pittsburghu" ["After the Pittsburgh Convention"] in: *Weteran [The Veteran]*, June 1931, p. 17

8   "Protokół III Zjazdu Korpusów Pomocniczych SWAP w Ameryce. Newark, NJ od 26 do 31 maja 1934 roku" ["The Minutes of the 3rd Convention of PAVA Auxiliary Corps of America. Newark, NJ from May 26 to 31, 1934"] in: *Weteran [The Veteran]* October 1934, pp. 12-15

The Alliance of Friends of Polish Army Veterans

This was an auxiliary organization created in 1931 by the Polish Army Veterans Association of America during the period of the Great Depression in the United States. At that time PAVA was desperately looking for additional sources and means of enlarging its shrinking I. J. Paderewski Invalids Fund, from which subsidies were payed out to war veterans and the rapidly increasing number of unemployed veterans. The Związek Przyjaciół Weteranów Armii Polskiej (ZPWAP) (Alliance of Friends of Polish Army Veterans (AFPAV), as the name itself indicates, was to gather all those who had heretofore in various ways helped the veteran organization. Its units were to be created next to the individual PAVA posts, nonetheless all the candidates for the alliance were to be approved each time by the organization's National Executive Board.

The AFPAV sections operated with varying effectiveness alongside many PAVA posts in the years 1931–1933. During the Great Depression the AFPAV's activity finally terminated.

The idea to reactive it was taken up at the 7th PAVA General Assembly in Rochester, NY in 1937. On the basis of a special resolution the *Regulation of the Alliance of Polish Army Veterans of America* was drafted. It stated that among the main tasks of the AFPAV were:

"—To support PAVA efforts to bring aid to invalid, sick and abandoned veterans and the orphans of deceased veterans.

"—To organize various social affairs on behalf of the Invalids Fund, the profits from which are to be transferred to the main PAVA invalid account through the intermediary of the Post.

"—To repel anti-U.S. and anti-Poland propaganda.

"—To encourage young people to study the Polish language and Polish history."

In the matter of membership the *Regulations* stated: "Every Pole of good character can be a member of AFPAV, who has a spotless national past, as also a foreigner, who is a sincere friend of Poland and PAVA." At the same time it was noted that: "The AFPAV organization, just like PAVA, is apolitical, and does not engage itself in any political movement."

AFPAV members could organize into circles alongside a given PAVA post. The Alliance could have its delegate during a PAVA post meeting, on the other hand each circle had the right to send a delegate to meetings of the district and the PAVA General Assembly, where he could take the floor in an advisory capacity exclusively in matters of that organization.

The Alliance of Friends of Polish Army Veterans did not have a structure on the district and central level. There were executive boards of the AFPAV circles at the PAVA post level only.

After the General Assembly in Rochester, NY in 1937 the first circles to be formed were alongside PAVA Post Nr. 119 in Hartford, CT, PAVA Post Nr. 24 in Bridgeport, CT and PAVA Post Nr. 97 in Grand Rapids, Michigan. By January 1939 there were eight circles; they had a total of 194 members.[9] In May 1940 there were already twenty circles with a total of 484 members (please see addendum 10).

The Sons and Daughters of Polish Army Veterans

The issue of organizing veterans' children in a separate organization was brought up at several of the first PAVA general assemblies, but no decisions were made at that time, due to the very young age of the veteran youth. It was not until the 5th PAVA General Assembly in Pittsburgh, PA in 1931 that it was decided that the PAVA posts (those that wanted to) could form an organization for young people under the name Sons and Daughters of Polish Army Veterans. But at that time the regulations of this organization had not yet been prepared. This issue was left entirely up to the individual PAVA posts.

The first Sons and Daughters of Polish Army Veterans chapter was organized at PAVA Post Nr. 16 in Pittsburgh, PA in 1932. At first only sons of veterans joined, who together with their fathers participated in various jubilee celebrations and trips organized by the post. Later girls also joined the chapter. By May 1938 this chapter counted 23 boys and 21 girls, who were supervised by the Chaperoning Committee. Its members were: Kowalewski (presiding), K. Dąbek, F. Bubacz, S. Gołembiewski, M. Tusiak from that post and the following ladies from the Auxiliary Corps: Z. Woźniak, H. Klara and Z. Orpikowska.[10]

The need to organize more chapters of Sons and Daughters of Polish Army Veterans was discussed at the next, 6th PAVA General Assembly in Newark, NJ in 1934. An appropriate *Regulation* was introduced into the PAVA By-Laws, on the basis of which the organization of veteran youth was to function. It is stated in this document that the aim of this organization is:

"a) cultivation of the Polish language, of the traditions of the Polish soldier and the Polish Army Veteran in America among children of veterans of the Polish Army

"b) encouragement of the more gifted children (of members) to further study by giving them appropriate scholarships

"c) preparing successors to further work on the national and veteran level."[11]

---

9 "Związek Przyjaciół Weteranów Armii Polskiej" ["The Alliance of Friends of Polish Army Veterans"] in: *Weteran [The Veteran]* February 1939, p. 14
10 *Weteran [The Veteran]*, May 1938, p. 11
11 *Konstytucja i Regulaminy Stowarzyszenia Weteranów Armii Polskiej w Ameryce* [*By-Laws and Regulations of the Polish Army Veterans Asociation of America*] New York, 1934, p. 42

These aims were to be achieved by:
"a) organizing lectures, trips and stage performances
"b) supporting Polish émigré schools
"c) organizing summer camps operated by Polish organizations
"d) encouraging recitation, public speaking and singing
"e) encouragement of membership in Polish organizations"[12]

The *Regulations* also explain who can belong to the organization of veterans' children: "Every son and daughter of a Polish Army Veteran, after their 6th birthday, regardless of whether or not the father is a PAVA member, can be a member of the chapter.

"Orphans of volunteer soldiers from the World War and the Polish-Bolshevik War have the same rights."

The Chaperone Committee was to take care of organizational matters within PAVA until the young people attained the age of sixteen. The Committee was to be composed of three veterans from the given post, three ladies from the Auxiliary Corps (where there was no Auxiliary Corps, three additional veterans) and the PAVA post commander. Upon attaining sixteen years of age the young people were free to elect their own governing body, which was to work in close cooperation with the Chaperone Committee.[13]

Despite the existence of the *Regulations* the next chapter of the Sons and Daughter of Polish Army Veterans was not organized until April 30, 1937. At that time veteran youth were organized at the PAVA Post Nr. 5 in Chicago, IL. The chapter of 35 girls and boys was quickly provided with regulation uniforms. Veterans A. Trygar and B. Piecuch taught the children the rudiments of military drill. By May of 1938 this chapter already had 85 members.[14]

A chapter of the Sons and Daughter of Polish Army Veterans was organized in the Fall of 1937 at PAVA Post Nr. 21 in New York City. There was a Polish language supplementary school for all the members of this chapter directed by Marian Nowakowski. Another veteran, Czesław Sołczyk, held national and folk dance courses for them. A wind orchestra was also organized, whose conductor was Rev. Ziemiak, assistant to Rev. Feliks Burant, the Chaplain of PAVA District II. This orchestra, with about 40 boys and girls, was very popular throughout the New York metropolitan region's Polish American community (Polonia), by which it was gladly invited to all sorts of festivities.[15]

---

12   Ibid., p. 43
13   Ibid., pp. 43-44
14   *Weteran [The Veteran]* May 1938, p. 11
15   *Weteran [The Veteran]* March 1938, p. 15

The PAVA National Executive Board tried to mobilize other posts to create similar youth chapters. An appeal printed in the Febraury 1938 issue of *The Veteran* declared:

"We are not creating these chapters as competition for other youth organizations. Quite to the contrary, we expect that, under the care and guidance of the genuine, selfless and patriotic fathers, veterans of the Polish Army, a powerful reserve of youthful energy will be created, which will reinforce other Polish youth organizations—that next émigré generation.

"We will first of all instill in this, our youth, respect for tradition and true merit, the need for selfless service to the community and maintenance of a Pole's honor at the highest level. We will thus obtain ranks of co-workers and later successors for our ranks."[16]

But the results were meager. In May 1938 a chapter of the Sons and Daughters of PAVA was organized in Newark, NJ (numbering more than 50 girls and boys, but it was active for only a very short time) and the next new chapter was not established until December, when the young people were organized at PAVA Post Nr. 111 in New Britain, CT. An orchestra was formed there, a drum and bugle corps, for which the post procured musical instruments and attractive uniforms.[17]

A similar orchestra, at a cost of more than $2,500, was formed at PAVA Post Nr. 12 in Philadelphia, PA.[18]

The youg people especially liked this form of activity, they became known in the town and surrounding areas, took part in various festivities, of which they liked the parades in town the best of all, because they could also present themselves there to an American audience as well.

In May 1940 these were the chapters of the Sons and Daughters of Polish Army Veterans at individual PAVA posts:

Post Nr. 21 in New York City, 25 members
Post Nr. 39 in Chicago, IL, 20 members
Post Nr. 41 in Pittsburgh, PA, 20 members
Post Nr. 61 in Wilmerding, PA, 17 members
Post Nr. 111 in New Britain, CT, 68 members.
(Total 150 members)[19]

---

16 *Weteran [The Veteran]* February 1938, p. 12
17 J. Wójcik, M. Kierkło, *Z dziejów żołnierza-emigranta. Historia "Haller Post" w New Britain [A History of the Soldier Emigrant. The History of the Haller Post in New Britain]* New Britain 1991, p. 21
18 *Pamiętnik VIII Walnego Zjazdu SWAP. [Souvenir Journal of the 8th PAVA General Assembly]* Philadelphia, 1940, p. 36
19 PAVA NEB Archives, sign. A-II/9, *Sprawozdanie urzędników Zarządu SWAP i K.P. na 8-my Walny Zjazd SWAP w Ameryce w mieście Philadelphia, PA za czas od 1937 roku do 1940 roku [Report of the Officers of the National Executive Board of PAVA and the A.C. at the 8th PAVA General Assembly in America in the City of Philadelphia, PA for the period 1937 to 1940]* p. 20

As the nearest future would show, the hopes of the veterans that their children would be that next generation to take over the entire PAVA organization, proved fruitless. For, despite great efforts of their patriotically minded parents, the young people fell under the spell of the process of Americanization, gradually distancing themselves from the Polish environment. To the young, mainly born and educated in America, the forms of activity offered by PAVA were not very attractive. The young people were taking advantage of the great opportunities for development which the American society afforded them, and they wanted to utilize them in full.

This explains the fact that the chapters of the Sons and Daughters of the Polish Army Veterans were organized only at several PAVA posts, and after activity barely lasting several years, by which time the young children had attained adulthood, the chapters were dissolved.

III.
Organizational Symbolism

The Emblem of the Polish Army Veterans Association of America

At its 1st General Assembly in Cleveland, Ohio in 1921 the Polish Army Veterans Association adopted as its emblem the Souvenir Cross that had been designated by the Polish government for volunteers from America. The image of a Polish crowned eagle rests in the middle of the white cross. The arms of the cross bear the sign: "To Their Soldiers from America Liberated Poland." Between the arms of the cross, in the background, are the names: "Szampania, Lwów, Wołyń, Pomorze."

This emblem was used universally in organizational life. It was visible on flags, decorations, seals, documents and on the masthead of *The Veteran*. Thanks to this it was popularized and became an authentic identifying mark of the association.

Organizational Decorations of the Polish Army Veterans Association of America

The first organizational decoration of the Polish Army Veterans Association of America was a medal established in 1927, commemorating the tenth anniversary of the recruitment efforts for the Polish Army in France.

The front of this medal carries the bust of a soldier of the Blue Army, in a four-cornered cap, holding a rifle in his hands. Around the perimeter of the medal are the words: "Stowarzyszenie Weteranów Armii Polskiej w Ameryce" ["Polish Army Veterans Association of America"].

On the back in the center there are two heraldic shields. The one on the right side with an American flag, the one on the left with the characteristic "Haller" eagle. Above the shields the following dates are visible: "1917–1927"; beneath the shields there are two laurel branches. Around the permiter of the back of the medal the following words are inscribed: "W Dziesiątą Rocznicę Rekrutacji Do Armii Polskiej We Francji." ("On the Tenth Anniversary of Recruitment for the Polish Army in France").

Another PAVA organizational decoration was the Cross of Merit of the Polish Army from America. It was established in 1932 to honor persons who distinguished themselves during the formation of military detachments by the Polish American community during the First World War.

This decoration has the form of a four armed, eight-cornered cross, made of white oxidized metal. On its face in the center of the cross there is a shield with the image of a Blue Army soldier armed with a rifle ready to attack. On the reverse there is a flag with the Polish eagle. This is the replica of a well known promotional poster by Tadeusz Benda made during the period of recruitment to the Polish Army in France, which took place in America in the years 1917–1919. The lower arm of the cross contains a miniature of the PAVA emblem, the Souvenir Cross for volunteers from America. On the reverse side are the words: "Za Zasługi Dla Polski Przy Organizowaniu Zbrojnego Czynu Wychodźstwa w Latach 1916-17-18 / W Piętnastolecie Armii Polskiej Z Ameryki / Stowarzyszenie Weteranów Armii Polskiej w Ameryce." ("For Contributions to Poland During the Organization of Military Effort By the Emigration in the Years 1916-17-18 / On the Fifteenth Anniversary of the Polish Army from America / The Polish Army Veterans Association of America") The cross was worn on a light blue ribbon.

The next PAVA organizational decoration from the years 1921–1939 was the Polish Army Veterans Association Medal, instituted March 1, 1936 to commemorate the fifteenth anniversary of PAVA's founding. PAVA members who had been active members of the organization continuously for the past fifteen years could receive it.

The front of the medal shows the figure of a Blue Army soldier supporting a fainted comrade. Around the perimeter of the front of the medal are the words: "Fifteen Years On the Watch."

The back of the medal shows the PAVA emblem around which, along the perimeter, run the words: "Polish Army Veterans Association of America."

The medal was worn on a scarlet ribbon with two vertical blue stripes.[1]

The highest PAVA organizational decoration was the Gold Cross of Merit. Up to 1939 the only recipients of this medal were: the regiments constituting the 13th Infantry Division (43rd, 44th, 45th and 50th regiments); Ignacy Mościcki, President of Poland; Marshall Edward Śmigły-Rydz; Dr. Teofil Starzyński; and Ignacy Jan Paderewski.[2]

The PAVA organizational decorations chapter was composed of the chief officers of the association, that is, the President, the Secretary General and the Treasurer.

---

1 "Jubileuszowy Medal Stow. A.P." ["Jubilee Medal of the Polish Army Veterans Association"] in:*Weteran [The Veteran]* July 1963, p. 13

2 *Weteran [The Veteran]* February 1939, p. 20

The decoration "Hallerian Swords" was extremely popular and highly prized by PAVA members. It was instituted in 1924 as an organizational decoration of the Association of Hallerians—a fellow veteran organization active in Poland. The chapter for this decoration was also in Poland, and its first president was Rev. Dr. Jan Więckowski, the former army chaplain of the Polish Army in France. Only the PAVA National Executive Board in America had the right to submit requests to the Association of Hallerians for granting "Hallerian Swords" to its members and also to other individuals living in the United States who had distinguished themselves in efforts on behalf of Poland's independence during the First World War.[3]

PAVA Member Uniforms

During the first years of the existence of the Polish Army Veterans Association of America its members used the uniforms they had brought from Poland as their organizational uniform. The PAVA leadership paid special attention to respect for the uniform, which is affirmed by the note in the PAVA By-Laws of 1925: "Since the uniform, so long as members of the Association have one, is a pleasant souvenir of the soldier's battles and hardships on behalf of the Independence and Sovereignty of the Fatherland, therefore it is not right to use this uniform for purposes which do not comport with the honor of the Polish soldier, such as: for purposes of agitation, for party or business matters; it is prohibited to go to bars in it, to get drunk in it, etc. Members who abuse the uniform of the Polish soldier, as well as the principles of the By-Laws, will be placed before the collegial arbitration court.[4]

With the passage of years the old uniforms wore out completely, especially since they were the only change of clothes their owners had. This was especially true of invalids who lived alone, and of the unemployed.

For these reasons the PAVA National Executive Board standardized uniform regulations, in order to stop arbitrariness in the acquisition of new organizational dress. A *Uniform Regulation* was adopted at the General Assembly in Newark, NJ in 1934, which described what a new uniform of a PAVA member ought to look like. (Please see addendum 10).

There were many gaps in these regulations, which were sedulously taken advantage of by PAVA members. It then became apparent how deeply attached the veterans were to their uniforms. They had to throw away the torn cloth, but they kept the original buttons, stripes denoting rank, and first of all sew-ons with the Polish

---

3   T. Lachowicz, "Geneza odznaki 'Miecze Hallerowskie' " ["Genesis of the Decoration 'Hallerian Swords' "] in: *Weteran [The Veteran]* October 1996, pp. 23-24

4   *Konstytucja i Regulaminy Stowarzyszenia Weteranów Armii Polskiej w Ameryce. 1925 [The By-Laws and Regulations of the Polish Army Veterans Association of America. 1925]* p. 38

Eagle, which they had once worn on their shoulder straps. Now they sewed these elements onto their new organizational uniforms, and the PAVA authorities did not oppose this "transgression."

The introduction of the *Uniform Regulation* had a positive influence on the general appearance of PAVA members, which was especially evident during parades and other festivities. Homogeneous uniforms and appearance according to the principles of military drill pleased the eye, which meant a lot in the American reality. No wonder that the local press would frequently note that in this respect the Polish veterans decidedly distinguished themselves from other veterans groups.

The Emblem and Insignia of the Auxiliary Corps

The Auxiliary Corps took the emblem and insignia of PAVA as the model for its emblem and insignia: the Cross of Polish Soldiers from America, but with changed wording on the arms of the cross. On the vertical arm the inscription reads: "Pol. Am. Vet. Ass'n. In Am.", while on the horizontal arm are the words: "Auxiliary Corps." This is the only writing on it.

The Uniform of the Auxiliary Corps

Decisions concerning the uniform of the female members of PAVA's Auxiliary Corps were made at the Auxiliary Corps General Assembly held in Rochester, NY in 1937. At that time the following note was introduced to the *Auxiliary Corps Regulations:* "The female members of the Auxiliary Corps are required to wear the following: a white dress, a blue cape with an amaranth lining and an "overseas" cap."[5]

In this instance the model was the uniform of a similar women's formation, "The American Legion Auxiliary," active alongside the American Legion—an organization of veterans of the American Army.

The Uniform of the Sons and Daughters of Polish Army Veterans

PAVA's youth organization did not have its own emblem and insignia. The regulation prescribed the following uniform for the members of this formation: "Boys: navy blue pants, blue shirt (French blue), a four-cornered cap (French blue); sweater for the winter (French blue); Girls: white dress, cape (French blue), caps (of the Auxiliary Corps)."[6]

---

5 "Protokół z 4-go Zjazdu Walnego Korpusów Pomocniczych przy SWAP w Ameryce, odbytego w Rochester, NY, w dniach od 29 maja do 2 czerwca 1937 roku" ["Minutes of the 4th General Assembly of the PAVA Auxiliary Corps of America, held at Rochester, NY, from May 29 to June 2, 1937"] in: *Weteran [The Veteran]* September 1937, p. 20

6 *Konstytucja i Regulaminy Stowarzyszenia Weteranów Armii Polskiej w Ameryce* [*By-Laws and Regulations of the Polish Army Veterans Association of America*] New York 1934, p. 44

Insignia of the Alliance of Friends of Polish Army Veterans of America

The Alliance of Friends of Polish Army Veterans of America did not have its own emblem. Its members did not have a special uniform. But this formation had its own insignia, which was a likeness of the PAVA insignia.[7]

The process of creating PAVA organizational structures and its auxiliary organizations lasted continuously from 1921 to 1939. It was extremely helpful that many of the PAVA activists at that time had previously been officers of the Polish Falcons in America, for instance Dr. Teofil Starzyński and Franciszek Dziób. Their experience in the Falcons and in military service were exceedingly useful and helpful in the creation of the veteran organization, whose character was closely connected with Falcon and military tradition. The PAVA organizational structures formulated by these and other activists proved themselves to be lasting and efficient. The most compelling testimony to the quality and effectiveness of the organizational solutions applied in the years 1921–1939 is that the majority of them are still functioning in PAVA in the twenty-first century.

---

[7] Regulamin Związku Przyjaciół Weteranów Armii Polskiej w Ameryce [Regulations of the Alliance of Friends of Polish Army Veterans of America] p. 5

IV.
Social and Cultural Activity of the Polish Army Veterans Association of America

Mutual Aid

One of the most important reasons that former soldiers of the Polish Army organized themselves after their return to the United States was the noble, comradely gesture of bearing aid to colleagues from the army who found themselves in difficult material and living conditions. To these belonged war invalids, the sick, the unemployed and the homeless. The issue of organizing help for them existed from the very beginning of the first veteran societies and clubs. Later it totally dominated the activity of the Polish Army Veterans Association of America.

War Invalids

War invalids found themselves in the most difficult situation of all after their return to America. Despite earlier assurances by Polish American organzations, they were left to their own devices. During the post-war economic depression they had the least chance of finding work. There were cases of Polish soldiers falling down dead of starvation on the streets of American cities. They were identified by their military identification cards and by the decorations hanging from the tattered rags of their military uniform. These people—forgotten and abandoned by everyone—were buried in municipal cemeteries at the cost of the city, next to perverts and criminals.

The Polish Army Veterans Association, founded in 1921, did now want to accept this situation. It set the organizing of mutual aid as it main aim. It became apparent, however, that the scope of the help that ought to be given was so enormous that it absolutely transcended the modest capabilities of the newly formed association. In this situation the veterans turned with a passionate appeal, among others, to Polish women, believing in their compassion for people down on their luck. And they were not disappointed. The women of Chicago were the quickest to react. Under the leadership of Agnieszka Wisła a Committee for Aid to Veterans was organized in the summer of 1922. Similar committees were also established in other large Polish American communities. In 1925 the PAVA Auxiliary Corps was born from these organizations. It made enormous contributions in organizing help for war invalids, and the sick, unemployed and homeless former Polish soldiers. This work demanded tremendous self-sacrifice and selfless effort. This is what Agnieszka Wisła said years later about those pioneering times: "Those who had no family or friends had to be helped. Employment had to be found for them—which you couldn't even buy. We gave them tickets so they could at least have one square meal in a restaurant, for which we paid having received a discount from our fellow countrymen. Those who were falling down in the streets of exhaustion had to be helped, placed in hospitals, or in shelters at a lower price that we had to plead for. Let me cite one such example: a unconscious veteran was found out in the street, the police called for a military hospital ambulance, but when they found out that he was a Polish Army veteran they threw him out, and they sent the bill several times, for the ambulance and the three day stay in the hospital, to my address, because I was the president then. I wrote to them that we don't have that kind of money, but that didn't help, so I wrote back that if America cannot help a man like that, then I don't want to know an America like that, and that finally helped. For others, who died in the street, funeral directors had to be pleaded with for a cheap coffin and service, and patriotic priests had to be asked for church services and a grave in the cemetery, in order to give a former Polish Army veteran a decent burial."[1]

Nonetheless this type of activity had the character of ad hoc help in emergencies. So some sort of permanent system of continual care for invalids had to be created.

PAVA began working on such a system from its very first General Assembly. A "Plan of Aid for Polish Army Veterans in America" was drafted. It aimed at giving war invalids permanent or ad hoc financial aid. In accordance with this plan the invalids were to distribute and sell *The Veteran*—the PAVA press organ—and the calendar "Hallerczyk" ["The Hallerian"]. The invalids received these periodicals at the cost of the printing, and whatever they earned on top of that they could keep for themselves.

In order to fulfill the plan for financial relief for war invalids, money had to be obtained. Hopes were especially pinned on the generosity of the local Polish American community. Ignacy Jan Paderewski gave the initial impulse, by donating $5,500 for this purpose in August 1921. Together with his check he also passed on his suggestions on how to utilize the money: "I believe that the entire sum ought to be divided into two parts, of which the larger ought to be used for immediate

---

[1] T. Lachowicz, "Jak powstał Korpus Pomocniczy przy Stowarzyszeniu Weteranów Armii Polskiej w Ameryce" ["How the Auxiliary Corps of the Polish Army Veterans Association in America Came About"] in: *Weteran [The Veteran]* May 1995, pp. 4-5

relief for the sick, the disabled and the unemployed, and the second half ought to be a permanent capital fund from which the interest ought to be paid out to widows, orphans and those veterans who are permanently disabled. And thus: in this particular case, of the $5,500 sent by me I would like $3,000 to be used as grants-in-aid for those in most immediate need, and $2,500 set aside for the capital fund, which no doubt will grow, because it must, to a significant size."[2]

Following Ignacy Paderewski the largest Polish American organizations hastened with financial aid for the disabled veteran, giving significant sums for this purpose: The National Department—$10,000; Polish National Alliance—$10,000 and the Polish Women's Alliance $1,000.[3] In this case I. J. Paderewski proved to be a real "locomotive" that mobilized and pulled others into concrete philanthropic actions on behalf of war invalids.

Many priests and their parishioners joined the large donors with their modest sums, as did business people, and the workers at Polis diplomatic posts, for instance the employees of the Polish Consulate General in Chicago collected $23.50 for this purpose in January 1922.[4]

Thanks to these donations PAVA was able to help those most in need with $25 or $10 per month, depending on the severity of the invalid's disability. These were not great sums, they only allowed the invalid to scrape by. In order to get such aid the invalid had to present his military service documents, documents confirming his war-time injuries attested to by a military or civil doctor with a note as to inability to be gainfully employed. A further requirement was confirmation by a local pastor, or a civic committee, or a Polish American organization. The final opinion about granting the aid was rendered by the chief PAVA physician, and the decision to grant to relief was made by the organization's governing board. By introducing these requirements the PAVA authorities hoped to have the funds, gathered with great effort, get to those who truly were the most in need because, unfortunately, there were efforts to swindle the money by alcoholics, or even persons with the flu.[5]

Polish invalids were sent to hospitals or sanatoriums only in extereme, life-threatening cases. The expense of their treatment and maintenance was then paid by the American federal government or charitable organizations, and that meant that

---

[2] PAVA NEB Archives, AO, File: Ignacy Jan Paderewski

[3] *Sprawozdanie z kampanii prowadzonej przez Stowarzyszenie Weteranów Armii Polskiej w Ameryce za zebraniem funduszu na osadnictwo na Kresach Wschodnich i na zabezpieczenie bytu inwalidom* [*Report from the Campaign of the Polish Army Veterans Association to Raise Funds for Settlement on the Eastern Borderlands and to Secure the Welfare of Invalids*] Cleveland 1922, p. 9

[4] PAVA NEB, sign. A-XVIII/8

[5] PVA NEB, sign. A-VI/1 *Plan niesienia pomocy inwalidom Armii Polskiej przebywającym w Ameryce* [*The Plan to Render Aid to Polish Army Invalids Living in America*]

the hospitals or sanatoriums had to make long-term and difficult attempts to recover their costs. That is why the stay of Polish veterans in American health care centers was shortened to a minimum, and in many instances they were simply refused treatment. Then the intervention of PAVA representatives proved indispensable. In many instances, especially when the patient was a PAVA member, the association paid part of the expense. Moroever the patient himself, if he was single, received a $10 monthly subsidy from PAVA. There were cases when after the conclusion of the hospital stay the veterans had nothing to wear out onto the street, because their rags had been burned. In such cases PAVA purchased clothes for the person. Often additional money had to be designated for reconvalescents for the purchase of necessary medicines or prostheses.

In case of the death of veterans who were single a dignified funeral had to be procured and the expenses paid for it. When the deceased was a PAVA member the association paid $100 toward partial coverage of funeral costs.

These expenses caused a systematic shrinking of the donated funds which could in no way be made up by the modest membership fees. Obtaining money for the invalid fund was the absolute number one priority of PAVA activity.

The Polish government unexpectedly came to the aid of PAVA veterans. Several months after the 1st PAVA General Assembly in Cleveland, Ohio in 1921 news arrived from Poland that the Polish government, appreciative of the help volunteers from America gave in the regaining of independence, decided to grant them land, for which war invalids and those who had distinguished themselves had priority. This was a great and most pleasant surprise for Polish veterans in America. Over four thousand veterans applied for the land grants.

This was a huge job for the PAVA National Executive Board, because the departure of such a large number of people required enormous organizational and financial effort. Serious funds (about $200,000) had to be secured in a short time to cover the costs of the voyage, agricultural training for the future settlers and credits for starting up a farm, because the Polish authorities offered the veterans land alone.

In thinking of the most seriously disabled veterans, the PAVA governing board turned to the Polish government with a separate request to designate a larger plot of land on which the association could establish a model farm and sanatorium for invalids who were unable to work.

Preparations were in progress over the next several months for a large fundraising campaign to support the resettlement of veterans and to secure the existence of the war invalids. In the Spring of 1922, despite the difficult post-war times, as the result of a campaign excellently organized by PAVA Vice President Lucjan Adamczak, more than $107,000 was collected for veteran resettlement and invalid support.[6] For PAVA this was a huge financial success, even though only slightly more than half the planned amount was collected. The Polish Roman Catholic Union was one of the top donors with a grant of $3,161.25.[7] Thanks to the Polish American community's "awakening" and its generosity to the veterans the existence of the invalids was secured for a longer period of time.

In the meantime news arrived from Poland that, unfortunately, the Polish government did not grant the request of PAVA for a larger tract of land on which a model farm and invalid sanatorium could be organized. The refusal was justified on the grounds that the Parliament's bill concerning granting of land to military settlers did not foresee such a possibility. So the PAVA National Executive Board sent a delegation to Poland which in December 1922 purchased a former German estate called Kuligi near Brodnica in Pomerania for $15,000, where the hope was to establish a visionary veteran farm which would simultaneously serve as a shelter for war invalids. But this endeavor ended in failure and PAVA, in maintaining this shelter in the years 1923–1929, suffered large expenses which did not bring the desired results.

Meanwhile the war invalids—PAVA members who remained in the United States—remained under the continual care of the association. Their number fluctuated constantly. Some of them were able to fund jobs and become independent, others were too sick or impractical. In addition new invalids and sick appeared, who fell ill due to wounds sustained some time before at the front, or due to gas poisoning in battle, or who had serious catarrhal conditions. Tuberculosis was rampant in this latter group.

In the years 1921–1924 PAVA had 56 invalids under its care, including those who had been sent to Poland. From August 1, 1921 to February 29, 1924 they received $10,021.55 in aid. $1,210.44 was spent for one-time grants. In addition the invalids were given loans for treatments, maintenance, and their own work shops in the sum of $3,050. In this period twenty invalids died. Their funeral expenses amounted to $1,712.50. The sum total of all the expenses was $15,994.49.[8]

The veterans who were alone had the most difficult situation among the disabled, and they needed help the most. The PAVA Auxiliary Corps played an exceptional role in this task. It was directed with great devotion by Agnieszka Wisła who (in writing in *The Veteran* about the work of this formation for the year 1926) gave an example of what had been accomplished in that period in Chicago: "So far we found fifteen abandoned former soldiers. We found them in shelters, municipal hospitals

---

6 Ibid., p. 68
7 M. Haiman *Zjednoczenie Polskie Rzymsko-Katolickie w Ameryce. 1873–1948* [*The Polish Roman Catholic Union of America. 1873–1948*] Chicago 1948, p. 556
8 *Weteran [The Veteran]* April 1924, p. 6

and in private homes, where they had to rely on the winds of fate. Based on their needs and our capabilities, we try to help as best we can, so that they can experience the warmth of feeling of their own community....

"One invalid, after getting artificial legs, is trying to earn his own living. Another, after successful surgery on both his legs, feels rather well and is working. We are helping yet another with his leg treatments, which unconscionable doctors were ready to amputate.

"The most frequent are cases of tuberculosis, so we visit these patients often, carrying them words of comfort, and also underwear and needed clothing.

"We are currently trying to help a mother who remains in deplorable circumstances after the death of her son.

"We have also tried to locate the graves of the deceased, which—when we do find them—have to be renovated, because they were neglected and crumbling. We erected plaques with inscriptions, and in the summer flowers grace the graves of our homeless-wanderer soldiers.

"So let our community—which is basically good—remember that these poorest of the poor should not be forgotten and from time to time at least a bit of heart should be shown to them."[9]

In April 1926 Ignacy Jan Paderweski again aided the war invalids in a big way. He donated the proceeds of his biggest concert in Chicago for this cause. The enormous hall was filled to the brim during this concert and four veterans stood on stage holding Polish and American flags. The net profit amounted to $8,300. The Master rounded this sum out with his personal funds and gave the veterans a $10,000 check. This took place on April 26, 1926 and initiated a new fund within PAVA named the "Ignacy Jan Paderewski Invalid Fund."[10]

Thanks to donations and fund drives this fund grew in the years 1926–1928 to $13,967.65. For instance, the Polish National Alliance donated $5,000 in 1928.

During this same period $3,788.32 was paid out in regular subsidies for invalids and the sick, thanks to which the "founding" capital donated by Paderewski was not depleted.[11]

From 1929, at the beginning of the great economic crisis, the condition of the Invalid Fund began to rapidly deteriorate. Due to the insolvency of certain banks $5,552.05 was frozen. Fortunately the funds had been placed in many different banks, thanks to which not everything was lost. At this time PAVA intensified its

---

9   A. Wisła "Prawda pali" ["The Truth Hurts"] in: *Weteran [The Veteran]* Janaury 1927, pp. 5-6

10 PAVA NEB Archives, sign. A-XXVII/2, file: Dr. Teofil Starzyński, Correspondence 1921–1930; "Koncert I. J. Paderewskiego na rzecz Stowarzyszenia Weteranów A.P. w Ameryce" ["I. J. Paderewski's Concert on Behalf of the Polish Army Veterans Association of America"] in: *Weteran [The Veteran]* June 1926, p. 13

11 "Jak się przedstawia sprawa Funduszu Inwalidzkiego im. I. J. Paderewskiego" ["The state of the I. J. Paderewski Invalid Fund"] in: *Weteran [The Veteran]* June 1926, p. 14

fundraising activity for the Invalid Fund, which did bring some results. Despite the difficult times the Polish American community was generous. In 1930 the "income" side of the Invalid Fund account was almost $22,000, while expenses for relief and funerals were more than $8,000 and (what is worse) this phenomenon was showing an upward trend in the face of shrinking revenues. And the number of persons needing support kept growing.

Many veterans after losing their jobs had to look for new employment outside their place of residence. This phenomenon became so widespread that many PAVA posts were dissolved. Veterans in search of work often went to little known nooks and crannies of the United States and Canada. They sometimes discovered comrades-invalids there, to their great astonishment. Jan Rajchel of Lyndora, PA wrote about such a case in his letter of November 12, 1931 to the PAVA National Executive Board: "I the undersigned member of dissolved Post Nr. 41 in Pittsburgh, moved a couple of months ago to Lyndora, PA. And to my astonishment I found one of our colleagues here in a critical situation. This colleague, M. Kuczman, had been severely poisoned by gasses at the battle front. He had spent a long time in the municipal hospital in Butler, PA, but had been literally thrown out of there to fend for himself and currently he goes from house to house begging. So because this colleague does not know how to write, I am turning to the Board with a request on his behalf for any kind of one time grant, or a monthly one, so that this colleague of ours doesn't die of starvation. As evidence I enclose the note from the municipal physician in Butler, PA and his military documents."[12]

Now veterans in need, who had hitherto kept their distance from the organization, turned to PAVA for help; and this included many war invalids. Even though they were not members of the organization, they were not denied aid, but they had to listen to many bitter comments that they had remained outside the organization for so long.

The scale of relief granted to veterans by SWAP during the great economic crisis (1929–1932) is illustrated by a comparison of the sums paid out from the I. J. Paderewski Invalid Fund in those years:

Year	Invalid Relief	Funeral Grants	Total
1929	$4,281.24	$1,356.22	$5,637.46
1930	$7,032.40	$1,300.00	$8,332.40
1931	$8,389.41	$2,200.00	$10,589.41
1932	$8,832.93	$2,400.00	$11,232.93[13]

---

12 PAVA NEB Archives, sign. VII/27, File: Requests for Help
13 New Documents Archive (Warszawa), sign. 231, I. J. Paderewski Archives, p. 9; *Weteran [The Veteran]* April 1933, p. 13

The subsidies were very modest, and their sum, due to the small size of the Invalid Fund, remained unchanged for many years. Franciszek Truszkiewicz wrote about the real market value of this aid: "The lone veteran, in a shelter, receives $2.50 a month—just anough for cigarettes. The lone veteran living with a family gets $5 per month, and the married one, regardless of how many members there are in his family, gets $10 per month, that is, 33 cents per day. These figures show us clearly that a family, and even the solitary person, receiving 33 cents a day, even if they have clothes, a place to live, heat, light, etc., for free, in today's conditions must be near starvation."[14]

According to its capability the Auxiliary Corps also helped the veteran invalids with financial aid from funds that it had obtained through its own efforts. For instance District I of the A.C. in Chicago in 1929 spent $1,014.67 for this purpose. 43 invalids in hospitals received this money. There was both monetary and material help, such as underwear, shoes, socks, sweaters, etc.[15]

Aside from war invalids and sick veterans PAVA also took care of veterans' widows and orphans, and also of certain mothers of volunteers from America who had been killed in action. That was the case of a homeless senior citizen, Zofia Patelska, who in a letter to the PAVA National Executive Committee of July 26, 1930 wrote as follows: "In 1917 my son, Franciszek Patelski, volunteered for the Polish Army in France.

"I was informed by a letter from the Polish National Committee that my son Franciszek had died on the field of battle on July 15, 1918 in Champagne (France).

"My son was my sole support and would certainly have been that today, when I am 74 years old. I have no resources for living, and I maintain myself only thanks to the charitableness of merciful people, and currently I am not even able to go begging for bread, and find myself in the most extreme poverty."[16]

PAVA began supporting Zofia Patelska in December 1930, granting her a regular monthly stipend. The ladies of Auxiliary Corps Post Nr. 1 found her a modest place to live, where they visited her regularly, bringing her food, clothes and small sums of money. In a letter of April 6, 1931 to the PAVA National Executive Board, Maria Gniazdowska of the A.C. Post Nr. 1 wrote: " I enclose the receipt from Mrs. Patelska for the most recent stipend... You have no idea how happy this poor old lady is, when we take her a couple of dollars." Zofia Patelska died in March 1932.[17]

---

14 F. Truszkiewicz "W trosce o przyszłość inwalidów" [Out of Concern for the Future of the Invalids"] in: *Weteran [The Veteran]*
15 PAVA NEB Archives, sign. VII/27, File: Requests for Help. 1921–1939
16 PAVA NEB Archives, sign. VII/27, File: Requests for Help. 1921–1939
17 Ibid.

With the idea of gaining allies for a mutual effort to increase the financial means of the I. J. Paderewski Invalid Fund, the National Executive Board of the Polish Army Veterans Association of America established the Alliance of Friends of Polish Army Veterans in August of 1931. The purpose of this step was thus explained in *The Veteran*: "The members of the Alliance, our true friends, scattered all across America, will first of all help us in the promoting our cause to the Polish American community. They will be a great help to us in activities and fund drives which we are to organize on behalf of the invalids. They will give us their advice, they will be our patrons, and in their localities they will take care of those of our invalids who truly need immediate relief."[18]

Soon *The Veteran* had a regular column devoted to the AFPAV. Lists of new members were printed in it as well as photographs and thank you letters from known figures in the Polish American community (former activists from the recruitment period, leaders of Polish American organizations, priests, physicians, lawyers, entrepreneurs, journalists, etc.) for including them on the list of honorary members of the AFPAV. But a well planned action on a larger scale did not materialize, because the Great Depression had a negative impact on the economic situation of the entire Polish American community. The activity of the AFPAV slowly faded away. At the beginning of 1933 the page devoted to the Alliance in *The Veteran* disappeared.

Various social Welfare Committees for Polish Army Veterans that were formed under the PAVA umbrella had a similar aim. They were active in certain Polish American enclaves, for instance in Hamtramck near Detroit, in Camden, NJ, in Weirton, WVa. Their activity consisted of organizing collections and of gaining access to all organizations, companies and wealthier families with a request for donations on behalf of the war invalids. By this method the small Polish American community in Weirton, numbering about 250 families, gave $133.32 which in those times was a very good result.[19]

Unfortunately, the veterans were not successful in organizing such committees everywhere. For instance in Greenpoint, Brooklyn—a Polish community in that borough of New York City—that attempt ended in a fiasco. Piotr Pawlik, the secretary of the local Post Nr. 102, wrote bitterly about this to the PAVA National Executive Board: "A meeting of the members of the Invalid Welfare Committee was called for November 6, 1931 at the Polish National Home at 261 Driggs Avenue. I wrote 50 letters in this matter to outstanding Citizens of this neighborhood and also sent an appeal to the Polish press asking that all the Citizens come to this meeting. But

---

18 "Ile mamy prawdziwych przyjaciół?" ["How Many Real Friends Do We Have?"] in: *Weteran [The Veteran]* August 1931, p. 18

19 *The Veteran* February 1932, p. 13

not one Citizen came. We waited until 10:30 p.m. in the hope that maybe they will come later, but our vigil was in vain, nobody showed up. I thought to myself that 14 years ago, when the Fatherland had to be defended, these very same Citizens knew how to send us off to France to the field of battle. And today, when these invalids need help, having been wounded and currently are laid up inhospitals, these same Citizens don't want to know anything about them. Truly, I had tears in my eyes and was deeply grieved."[20]

Many patriotic priests hastened with financial help for the war invalids. They spoke to their parishioners' conscience from the pulpit and exhorted them to be generous, thanks to which they were always able to send small sums to the Invalid Fund. Father Lucjan Bójnowski of New Britain, CT was unfailing in this regard. He was a former recruitment officer in the years 1917–1919, who (systematically sending checks for the above-mentioned purpose) often had the habit of adding notes in a letter, that the veterans had the right to remind him, should he ever forget to send a check.[21]

Unfortunately, it did happen in those difficult times that certain groups of dishonest people, abusing the good hearts of the Polish priests, organized fund drives for the war invalids in front of the churches, but in fact kep the money for themselves. In order to stop the recurrence of such situations, local PAVA authorities wrote letters to the Polish clergy, informing them that all committees organizing fund drives on behalf of war invalids must have written authorization with a stamp of the local PAVA Post or District.

In difficult, critical times, the PAVA National Executive Board energetically pressed the biggest Polish American organizations for help for the war veterans. The PAVA president and other Board members were invited to the general assemblies of these organizations, where they presented the necessity of helping the most deprived Polish soldiers of the Blue Army. This gave positive results in the shape of resolutions by the conventions for sizeable donations to the Invalid Fund. Unfortunately, their execution did not go as smoothly. The Polish Falcons of America at its convention in Toledo, Ohio in 1930 approved $500 for the I. J. Paderewski Invalid Fund. But this sister organization of the PAVA was unable to make good on its promise. In 1931 the "Falcons" collected $287.27 for the disabled veterans. Two years after the General Assembly the leadership of the Polish Falcons in a letter of April 1, 1932 to the National Executive Board of PAVA thus justified this failure: "This obligation will be carried out as soon as funds and circumstances allow.

---

20   PAVA NEB Archives, sign. A-XVII/31, File: the Invalid Fund Drive. 1931
21   PAVA NEB Archives, sign. A-XVII/33, File: The I. J. Paderewski Invalid Fund. Donations 1931–1933

"In the meantime, however, due to the serious economic stagnation and the serious arrears of our nests, which must be considered to some extent, we are not in a position to immediately pay out the sum and for this reason we ask that you accept this explanation as justified."[22]

There was a similar situation with the resolution of the 26th Parliament of the Polish National Alliance in 1932 to transmit $5,000 to the I. J. Paderewski Invalid Fund. A couple of months after the parliament the leadership of the PNA in a letter of October 7, 1932 to the Board of PAVA informed, that they were not in a position to carry out the resolution: "one cannot ask the members today to pay their dues; since tens of thousands of them are in a very critical situation and themselves expect relief and help."[23]

Five months later the PNA Censor, F. X. Świetlik (leader of the largest Polish American organization in the United States) wrote as follows to W. Dorosiewicz, the secretary of PNA Group 559 in Buffalo: "Regarding the Parliament's resolution to pay out $5,000 on behalf of the Polish Army Veterans, I wish to inform you that just like all institutions of this sort, so also the Alliance currently has its serious financial problems and that is why there is a delay in carrying out this resolution…it will require some patience and understanding for the current abnormal economic and financial situation, which has brought on this delay in the paying out of the donation that was approved by the Parliament."[24]

Nonetheless the resolution was never carried out. At the next, 27th PNA Parliament in 1935 new resolutions were approved regarding help for the disabled veterans.

The second largest Polish American organization, the Polish Roman Catholic Union of America, despite its difficult situation, was able to raise the sum of $1,304.35 from its membership for the needs of the war invalids.[25]

The person after whom the Invalid Fund was named, I. J. Paderewski, did not forget about the victims of war even in the most difficult years of the economic crisis. He felt morally obligated to help the war invalids, because it was in response to his appeals in the years 1917–1919 that they had enlisted in the ranks of the Polish Army in France. Guided by his moral compass, Paderewski once again gave his financial support to the invalids, donating $5,000 in June 1932, and less than a year later another $2,000 to which he added yet another check for $850.33. This latter sum was the remainder of a closed account in North Western Trust and Savings Bank.[26] From

---

22 PAVA NEB Archives, sign. A-XX/3, File: Polish Falcons of America. 1924–1933
23 PAVA NEB Archives, sign. A-XX/2, File: Polish National Alliance
24 Ibid.
25 M. Haiman. *Zjednoczenie Polskie Rzymsko-Katolickie w Ameryce 1873–1948* [*The Polish Roman Catholic Union of America. 1873–1948*] Chicago 1948, p. 559
26 PAVA NEB Archives, sign. A-XXVII/3, File: Ignacy Jan Paderewski

the beginning of PAVA's existence up to 1933 I. J. Paderewski donated $23,350.33 for the needs of the war invalids! Three years later, with the thought of honoring its benefactor, PAVA had the jeweler Roman Dzikowski create a souvenir watch. It was made of gold and precious stones. Its cost ($5,000) was covered by PAVA thanks to a special fundraiser for this purpose. This watch, a masterpiece of the jeweler's art, was given to Paderewski by the PAVA veterans as a gift of the Polish American community. It is currently displayed at the Polish Museum in Chicago.[27]

When in the Fall of 1933 the reserves of the I. J. Paderewski Invalid Fund were dangerously low, PAVA President Franciszek Dziób decided to go to Poland to get some sort of help from the Polish government for the Polish war invalids living in the United States. Great was his disenchantment when instead of an offer of help he heard the reply: "You were in General Haller's Army, so let General Haller help you!"[28]

This was a clearly sarcastic remark, because the Polish authorities knew very well that General Haller's financial situation was difficult. Franciszek Dziób went to Gorzuchow in Pomerania to General Haller, to whom he personally presented the dramatic situation of Polish war veterans in America. Despite the approaching winter General Haller decided to make a trip to America to render personal support for another fund drive to augment the I. J. Paderewski Invalid Fund.

This was General Haller's second trip to America, but this one in contrast to the first (which he made it 1923) was hard work for him. From December 1933 to June 1934 J. Haller went on an exhausting tour to almost all the Polish parishes in America. The General would stop at one of the larger cities, then would be driven from there by car to the smaller localities (every day he was somewhere else!), where he passionately appealed for help for the war veterans. His person attracted enormous crowds—both Poles and Americans—beause, especially in the smaller towns, this was a great event. The grand tour of General Haller around the Polish parishes was crowned with great success, because more than $78,000 was collected for the war invalids, which in those times was a very significant sum of money. The most was collected in the following states: Illinois: $22,400; New York: $11,000; Pennsylvania: $11,000; Michigan: $7,000.

Thanks to this the existence of the Polish war invalids was secured and General Haller gained the eternal gratitude and universal respect of Polish veterans in America. When later on news reached America from Poland about the "Blue General's" financial difficulties, the veterans in America helped on several occasions.

No doubt, the improving economic condition of the country also influenced the

---

27 *The Veteran* March 1936, p. 6
28 J. Haller. *Pamiętniki [Memoirs]* London 1964, p. 417

fundraising camapign's success. Thanks to the reforms instituted by the new president, Franklin D. Roosevelt, the country began to emerge from the deep ecomonic crisis.

It also had a positive influence on the large Polish American organizations. The economic improvement influenced the improvement of the financial situation. Thanks to this the organizations were able to help the disabled veterans. The Polish National Alliance at its 27th Parliament in Baltimore decided to pay out subsidies to war invalids on its own according to specifications provided by the PAVA National Executive Board. There was a certain dose of distrust of the PAVA leadership in this decision, but thanks to this move the PAVA Board was unexpectedly relieved of the administrative work connected with the I. J. Paderewski Invalid Fund. From October 1935 to June 1939 the Polish National Alliance paid out $20,785 to war invalids.[29]

In the last few months prior to the outbreak of World War II (July-August 1939) the Polish National Alliance Invalid Fund paid out $2,375.50 to 168 war invalids and sick veterans according to lists provided by the PAVA NEB.[30] The Polish Women's Alliance of America, on the other hand, beginning in 1936, set aside $2,500 per year for the same purpose, which amounted to $10,000 up to 1939 (inclusive).[31] In that same period the Polish Roman Catholic Union offered $1,101 for the war invalids.[32]

The idea for fundraisers on behalf of the I. J. Paderewski Invalid Fund made its way all the way to the Pacific (California). For instance the Polish American Community in Los Angeles collected about $300 in just one day—on August 14, 1937. Among the sponsors of this action were, among others, Merian C. Cooper, the Vice President of Selznick International Pictures, Inc., a former pilot in the famous 7th Squadron, "The Kościuszko" during the Polish-Bolshevik War of 1920.[33]

Funds raised during the so-called Blue Cornflower Day were an important addition to the revenues of the I. J. Paderewski Invalid Fund. This was a custom borrowed from American veterans, who on Memorial Day, the last Sunday of May, had fundraisers for their war invalids, and gave each donor a silk red poppy.

Some PAVA posts began imitating this custom toward the end of the 1920s. In May 1935 the PAVA NEB officially introduced the Blue Cornflower Day to emphasize the connection to the veterans of the Polish Blue Army. From that time on donors

---

29 PAVA NEB Archives, sign. XX/2, Polish National Alliance
30 PAVA NEB Archives, Folder: P.N.A. Invalid Fund: List of grants to be paid out to invalid and sick veterans for July and August 1939
31 *Na marginesie Funduszu Inwalidzkiego i wypłat zapomóg* [*On the Margins of the Invalid Fund and the Pay-Out of Relief Money*] in: *Weteran [The Veteran]* April 1939, p. 3
32 M. Haiman. *Zjednoczenie Polskie Rzymsko-Katolickie w Ameryce* [*The Polish Roman Catholic Union of America*] Chicago 1948, p. 560
33 H. U. Drelenkiewicz-Rekwart "Polonia pamięta" ["The Polish American Community Remembers"] in: *Weteran [The Veteran]* September 1937, p. 10

received an artificial blue flower, which was a miniature of the blue Cornflower that grows near the Vistula River in Poland. This pleasant custom quickly took hold in the entire organization, and the Polish American community took a liking to it as well. It was a pleasing sight to behold when the prettiest ladies from the Auxiliary Corps, dressed in their organizational uniforms, pinned the tiny Polish flower on the lapels or dresses of the donors, in thanks for supporting the war invalids.

Nothing speaks better for the success of Blue Cornflower Day than the fact that while in 1935 $2,500 was collected on this occasion, by 1939 the figure had risen to $8,000.[34]

Independent of the fund raisers, during the Blue Cornflower Days the PAVA and Auxiliary Corps posts held all sorts of events (dances, pertinent celebrations, etc.) and part of the profit from these went to augment the I. J. Paderewski Invalid Fund. In 1938 the PAVA and Auxiliary Corps posts contributed about $3,000.[35]

Toward the end of the 1930s the PAVA National Executive Board renewed its efforts in Poland to obtain some kind of permanent help for Polish war invalids living in the United States. Those who went into action first of all were: Wojciech Albrycht, the Commander of PAVA Post 130 in Poland, and the national PAVA commander Lucjusz Kajko, who took this issue to the highest level of the government during his visit in Poland in 1938. Stefan Lenartowicz, the Director of the World Alliance of Poles Abroad, was helpful in these endeavors. The result of these efforts was a permanent $3,000 annual grant by the government of the Second Polish Republic for Polish war invalids living in the United States. The first and last time that such a sum was sent to the United States from Poland occurred in March 1939.[36]

In April 1939 Leopold Krzyżak, the PAVA Adjutant General, reported that the annual income of the I. J. Paderewski Invalid Fund totaled $24,000 from the following sources:

- $8,000 from the Blue Cornflower Day
- $6,500 annually from the Polish National Alliance
- $3,000 from the Polish Government
- $3,000 annually from PAVA and Auxiliary Corps posts
- $1,000 annually from various small donations[37]

It might appear that by the beginning of 1939 the situation with the revenue of the I. J. Paderewski Invalid Fund had stabilized to some degree. It could appear that

---

34 *The Veteran* April 1939, p. 3
35 Ibid.
36 L. Krzyżak, "Na marginesie Funduszu Inwalidzkiego i wypłat zapomóg" ["On the Margin of the Invalid Fund and the Pay-out of Relief Money"] in: *Weteran [The Veteran]* April 1939, pp. 2-3
37 Ibid.

way only to the casual observer. In reality the Invalid Fund was constantly in danger, because the number of veterans that PAVA was forced to help kept growing. The figures tell it best: 1928—49 invalids; 1931—58; 1937—150. In 1939 there were 210 invalids in the following categories:

- 75 wounded in battle and poisoned with battlefield gasses
- 35 sick with TB due to war time trials
- 8 blind
- 8 insane
- 9 without one or both legs
- 9 paralyzed
- 3 deaf
- 9 age 65 and over[38]

This growing phenomenon gave the PAVA Board no rest and forced it to make constant efforts to obtain funds for the Invalid Fund. It must be stated with the greatest respect that from the very beginning of its existence the PAVA organization was able to provide constant, though very modest, care for its disabled colleagues. Up to 1939 there never arose a situation where the help for this group of veterans was halted due to exhaustion of funds designated for this purpose. By the same token the Polish Army Veterans Association of America succeeded in attaining its main goal, which it had set for itself at the founding convention in Cleveland in 1921.

The Unemployed

The veterans of the Polish Army in America had to contend with the problem of unemployment from the very moment of their arrival in America after the war. This phenomenon in the years 1920–1939 was experienced by them in varying degrees. The years 1920–1923 were the most difficult of all, as was the period of the Great Depression of 1929–1933. In the first period problems with finding employment were caused by an economic recession in the first post-war years, when American industry was forced to shift from war-time production to peace-time production. The unemployment problem among Polish veterans was augmented by the fact that they were returning to America several years after the conclusion of the war in Western Europe. In the meantime the soldiers who had been discharged from the American army had had time to set themselves up. The tardy veterans of the Polish army had to make a lot of effort to find jobs. They often had to make long journeys all over the country to achieve that goal. For some the ending was tragic. Those who were less adroit, alone in a foreign environment, without money and without their own place to

---

38 Ibid.

live, bereft of any help from the Polish American community, dropped of starvation on city streets. The death of Blue Army veteran Piotr Malinowski in September 1922 was widely publicized. Wandering about in search of work and food, he dropped dead of exhaustion on a street in Kingston, Pennsylvania. His military ID and documents were found on his body. After performing an autopsy the doctors concluded that it was a typical case of death by starvation. The Polish language periodical *Górnik (The Miner)* published out of Wilkes Barre, PA, stated bitterly: "This is a horrible, incredible case, proving better than any appeal how the Polish emigration reacts to those of whom it is constantly proud, whom it persuaded to go into the line of fire, under whose feet it threw flowers as they departed...in order, after their return, not have have even a slice of bread for them!... Yes, in prosperous America, in a country flowing with milk and honey, in an area where 200,000 Polish Americans live and exist in well-to-do circumstances, the Polish soldier, the Polish veteran, the young Pole looking for honest work, dies of starvation along the way!

"There is no room for one like he among us. But the swindler and ne'er do well, the gangster and con man, the loafer and the hooligan with a knife near at hand, with a lock pick and long arms, always finds a place among us... Sorrow squeezes the throat. Bitterness coats one's lips, and a curse stirs the vocal chords..."[39]

Fortunately those were isolated cases at that time. Almost all the Polish veterans found some kind of work in the end. But some continued to be down on their luck. There were cases when, after many failures the former soldier decided to return to Poland. The enticing factor was the possibility of getting land as part of a military resettlement program. Those, however, who decided to remain in America, could count on some help from PAVA, which according to its modest means also functioned as something of an employment office at that time.

With the unemployed in mind, the PAVA National Executive Board published "The Hallerian's Calendar" in 1921 for the year 1922, which the veterans still without work were to sell. Individual PAVA posts bought the calendar, paying the PAVA headquarters between 30 and 40 cents per copy—depending on how many were ordered. The unemployed veterans sold it for 60 cents, giving them a 30 to 50 percent profit per copy.

Another form of work for the unemployed veterans was the selling of subscriptions to *The Veteran* and getting paid advertising for it. In this case the National Executive Board paid a flat 25 percent commission.[40]

At first the unemployed veterans could count on the financial support of their

---

39 "Hallerczyk umarł z głodu" ["A Hallerian Died of Hunger"] in: *Weteran [The Veteran]* October 1922, pp. 9-10
40 PAVA NEB Archives, sign. A-VI/I, Circulars and Dispositions 1921–1927

colleagues from the local PAVA post, if one existed there and they had been a member of it earlier. In exceptional cases the posts also lent a helping hand to veterans who were not members of the association.

A huge miners' strike erupted in 1927 in a mining town near Wheeling, WV where many Polish veterans worked. In the eleventh month of the strike the Polish veterans (gathered around PAVA Post Nr. 82) after having exhausted their savings, turned for financial help to their colleagues scattered across the United States and Canada. The appeal was backed by the PAVA National Executive Board, which in *The Veteran* printed an appeal to all the posts in the field. We read there: "Don't delay! 'He gives twice who gives fast.' So let us all give quickly, so that our help will signal our soldierly solidarity with our colleagues.

"Often several of us would smoke one cigarette together, or divide one piece of bread between us. In the name of that soldierly boom and bust of fortune let us share today with our colleagues the miners, fighting for their rights, a portion of our earnings in line with our slogan: 'One for all and all for one.'"[41]

Thanks to this appeal the Polish veteran miners received help from various PAVA posts and were thus able to survive the most difficult period of the strike.

When the Great Depression began in 1929, the number of unemployed veterans grew rapidly. The wanderings of people in search of work began. Unfortunately, very often these journeys came to a dead end. Some of the veterans, after having arrived at what were often very distant places, did not find employment there. Having spent the last of their money, they landed out on the proverbial sidewalk. They would use their last pennies to send letters to the PAVA headquarters, begging for help. In such cases one-time financial relief grants were made, which allowed the hapless person to return to his place of origin or to a city where there was a larger Polish American community. A telling example was the fate of Wacław Mościcki, a Blue Army veteran, who (being already on in years) made it all the way up to Winnipeg, Manitoba, in Canada, where he worked as a lumberjack. But even there work soon stopped due to lack of orders. In anticipation of new orders he spent seven months there sitting on his hands together with a hundred other laborers, mainly Ukrainians and Huculs, who gave him a very hard time because of his Polish nationality. When his modest savings began dwindling to nothing, W. Mościcki turned to the PAVA National Executive Board for advice on how to get out of "that Siberia," as he called it, and where he should go. On the advice of the secretary of the Board, Czesław Mrozowski, he joined PAVA, becoming a member of the flying Post Nr. 100. Later,

---

41 "O pomoc dla strajkujących górników, Naszych Kolegów" ["An Appeal for Help for the Striking Miners, Our Colleagues"] in: *Weteran [The Veteran]* March 1928, p. 30

thanks to further cues, he made it to Toronto where his money ran out for good. In another letter to the Board Mościcki wrote: "Dear and Respected Friends. I am currently in Toronto. There is a lot of poverty here. I made it here to Toronto, but I can't go any further, because I'm flat broke. Dear fellow countrymen, I beg you for help with all my heart, don't let me die of starvation. Please help me and I will repay you amply when I get a job somewhere."[42]

The PAVA Board reacted positively to this request It sent W. Mościcki a one-time grant and gave him the addresses of several local PAVA posts, as also the addresses of Polish priests in Toronto, so he would have some sort of support in a city he did not know. Thanks to these contacts the veteran was able to get odd jobs, which allowed him to eke out a living. In the ensuing years the PAVA National Executive Board helped him out on several occasions with needed financial shots in the arm when he had a serious accident while renovating a house.[43]

As the economic crisis continued the PAVA National Executive Board undertook various steps to help its unemployed members. In 1931 regional employment bureaus were set up at PAVA District Offices. They kept a register of unemployed veterans and made efforts to find them employment. District II was in the most difficult situation. Its area was the New York metropolitan region. New York, as a great port city, was a real Mecca at that time, to which unemployed veterans from all parts of America came, and also newly-arrived veterans from Poland. Most of them did not belong to the association. PAVA District II, having a large number of its own unemployed members, was unable to help the unaffiliated veterans. Nonetheless, due to a feeling of solidarity toward their colleagues in need, the District leadership could not just brush off the problem. For this reason a permanent Relief Fund was established and efforts were made to collect money for this purpose. Dr. Mieczysław Marchlewski, the Polish Consul General in New York, became a regular donor, designating $50 per year for the fund. The Council of Polish Democratic Clubs in New York also supported the Fund by organizing many fundraising events on its behalf. Appeals were made through the press to the Polish American community, and especially to businessmen, to employ Polish veterans. For instance in the May issue of *The Veteran* the following notice appeared: "We would like to remind our sympathizers once again, homeowners, industrialists and merchants, that the District's Employment Office has a list of unemployed Polish veterans which has reached 150. Many of them have been without work for several months, and they are often the breadwinners for several people. So if you have any sort of job, even

---

42 PAVA NEB Archives. Collection: PAVA Posts. Folder: Mobile Post Nr. 100.
43 Ibid.

a short-term one, please call or write to L. C. Kajko, the Office's director, 203 East 49th Street, New York. Tel. Eldorado 5-7490. Don't forget about our request, Dear Fellow Countrymen."[44]

These efforts were not enough to totally resolve the veteran unemployment issue, but at least they ameliorated the problem. Its scale can be gauged from a letter of November 5, 1932 that was sent by PAVA Post Nr. 7 in Detroit, which had the largest number of members in the entire Association, to former PAVA president Wacław Rżewski, who lived in Chicago: "Large-scale unemployment continues in Detroit, most of the members of Post Nr. 7 are without work. The revenues from our Club business are also meager. In the last few months we were barely able to meet our tax payment to the National Executive Board from our members' dues. None of our events are successful. If these "Hoover" times continue Post Nr. 7 will have to go bankrupt."[45]

In wanting to help their unemployed colleagues PAVA Post Nr. 7 started a permanent kitchen that gave the jobless veterans and their families free meals.[46]

The joblessness was accompanied by an increase in crime. Polish veterans also were victims. The *Pittsburczanin (The Pittsburghian)* ran a story about a shocking case that happened in Pittsburgh, and it was reprinted in *The Veteran* of October 1931: "An unconscious veteran of the Polish Army, PAVA Post Nr. 16 member Kazimierz Dobrowolski, 37 years old, was found on the tracks of the Pennsylvania Railroad at South 21st Street. At the time the unfortunate veteran was found he had both his legs crushed by the wheels of a freight train. He was immediately taken to St. Joseph's hospital, where the doctors had to amputate both legs.

"…After regaining consciousness, Dobrowolski, questioned by detectives about the specifics of the accident, revealed the horrible, blood-curdling truth. He was not the victim of an unfortunate accident, as was thought at first, but had been purposely placed on the railroad tracks by bestial scoundrels.

"That fatal evening Dobrowolski had been on business at a friend's house on the south side of town. After going out onto the street, he wanted to head home, but lost his sense of direction. He turned to three young men passing by and asked for directions to the nearest trolley car. They took him with them, but instead of toward the trolley, they took him to the Pennsylvania Railroad area. There they fell on him, robbed him of his watch and two dollars. Next, they beat and kicked him mercilessly until he lost consciousness. The perpetrators, in order to hide the traces of their

---

44 *The Veteran* May 1932, p. 8
45 Central Polish American Community Archives in Orchard Lake, MI; PAVA District VI Archives: Włodzimierz Żmurkiewicz Collection
46 *The Veteran* May 1932, p. 9

dastardly deed, dragged Dobrowolski's massacred body by his feet and laid it on the railroad tracks, after which they calmly walked away... As a result of Dobrowolski's deposition and the police's own investigation the police made arrests. As it turned out, the bestial bandits were... Poles—our own Polish young people!"[47]

For many veterans unemployment was the cause of their personal dramas and tragedies. After exhausting all their savings they had no way to feed their families and pay the rent. They would then get thrown out of their apartments to wander the streets. They could not count on the help of the American authorities, because the majority of them did not have American citizenship. It was lucky if somebody offered such a family a corner in a dark, damp basement. Not everyone was able to withstand such conditions. There were cases of a spouse abandoning his or her family. One of the veterans who found himself in such a situation wrote bitterly to the PAVA Board: "I was a platoon leader in the Army and was able to handle 100 men. And here I couldn't handle one snake of a woman....She ruined my life and money, my kids are wasting away, and I am sick and don't have a roof over my head!"[48]

PAVA helped such people with ad hoc financial relief grants.

Those who were the least resistant to the poverty that they had to contend with, made attempts on their own life. *The Veteran* of August 1931 reported two cases of veteran suicides. One took place in Detroit, the other in Chicago. The Auxiliary Corps President, Zofia Kosobucka, moved by these cases, noted bitterly: "The saddest thing about this case is that when a veteran dies, frequently an expensive coffin is purchased for him, beautiful flowers, an expensive funeral. For this somehow money can be gotten. But while he was alive, nobody could be found who would offer him even a tiny bit of help."[49] Unfortunately, it must be admitted, that the comments of the President of the Auxiliary Corps were very accurate.

During the height of the Depression the Polish American press reported many deaths by starvation, whose victims were Polish Army veterans. Marcin Tomaszewski died in December 1932. Here is what *The Veteran* wrote: "In Chicago Marcin Tomaszewski, a veteran of the Polish Army who was jobless and without any income for quite some time, abandoned by friends and acquaintances, died of hunger and exhaustion on Madison Street. ...the police found his remains on the sidewalk. His military documents were found in his pocket, and he had the Cross of Valor, given to him by Poland, pinned to his torn vest. ...The late Marcin Tomaszewski came from the Małopolska region of Poland, near Tarnów. He had no family here, so when he

---

47 *The Veteran* October 1931, p. 19
48 PAVA NEB Archives, sign. A-XVII/27. File: Requests for Help
49 *The Veteran* August 1931, p. 16

had a few pennies earned by the sweat of his brow in a factory, he would send them to his poor family back in Poland. Receipts to that effect were found on his person.

"The deceased had enlisted in the Polish Army in March 1918. He served in the 2nd Regiment of the Polish Riflemen, which later was the 44th Regiment of Borderland Riflemen. He served his Fatherland faithfully, he fought bravely for it, as his military documents and hero's cross amply show.

"...Chicago's Polish American community, as if prodded by pangs of conscience, attended his funeral in large numbers, and hastened en masse to the grave of this hero who had been forgotten by everyone and who died of hunger out on the street."[50]

The entire Polish American press commented on this case. The dominant opinion was that the major responsibility for this and similar tragedies fell on the Polish American community as a whole. The *Pittsburczanin* opposed this thesis, stating that the victims were first of all themselves responsible for these tragic accidents: "If memory has not failed us, one can read almost monthly in the papers that a former member of the Polish Army in France died of hunger. Recently another such case happened in Chicago. ... It should be noted openly that over 90 percent of these cases happen due to the fault of the veterans themselves. First of all the majority of soldiers who came from overseas did not want to join PAVA, though many of them had jobs and could have easily paid the membership dues. Nobody had power of attorney over them, so the posts, which at first had some sort of documentation, slowly began losing contact with the former colleagues.

"Next the economic situation began deteriorating, more and more people, and so also Veterans, were left jobless. The Association, wanting to help the cause, again appealed to the former soldiers to sign up to the posts, even if they did not pay their dues, so they could be helped on the basis of the numbers, to appeal to the community at large for help. The result was very meager. So who is to blame here? It has to be admitted, that often the Veterans themselves."[51]

The reported case of Marcin Tomaszewski's death by starvation greatly moved the Polish diplomats working in the Polish Embassy in Washington, D.C. They sent $50 of their own money to the PAVA headquarters in support of ad hoc help for Polish Army veterans.[52]

The last known case of a tragic Polish Army veteran's death occurred in Detroit in September 1938. Franciszek Pyzik committed suicide by jumping into a river. He

---

50 "W stolicy Polonii amerykańskiej bojownik o wolność Polski umarł z głodu" ["A Fighter for Poland's Freedom Died of Hunger in the Capital of the Polish American Community"] in: *Weteran [The Veteran]* January 1933, p. 16
51 Quoted from: *The Veteran* February 1933, p. 14
52 PAVA NEB Archives, sign. A-XVIII/1, File: Polish Embassy in Washington 1921–1933

was a jobless war invalid who hailed from the Lublin region of Poland, Janów county, Radziąc Parish.

That was the fifth case of suicide by a Polish veteran in Detroit since 1921.[53]

It is not possible to give an exact figure for the number of Polish veterans who, after returning from the war, died of hunger or committed suicide in the United States and Canada. Leopold Krzyżak, the PAVA Adjutant General, estimated in March 1939 the number at about 45 persons since 1921.[54]

Veteran Shelters

From the beginning of its existence the Polish Army Veterans Association tried to help first of all those war invalids and jobless colleagues who had no support, care, or roof over their heads. With them in mind, already by late fall 1921, PAVA opened its first shelter for veterans in Chicago, where the problem was the greatest. Here is what Professor Witold Bogucki remembered: "The general unemployment heightened by the oncoming freezing weather, hastened the organization of fast relief for the most needy colleagues, who sometimes wandered all over the city to which they were strangers, without a place to sleep or a spoon of warm food. And more and more of them came from the provinces, driven by the oncoming freezing weather and unemployment out on the farms, and by the hope that here, in the capital of the Polish Emigration, they will find care and relief from their wandering fate.

"Help had to be found, and fast. Money was needed for that, which the District did not have. To obtain the necessary funds meetings were held one after another in all the neighborhoods of Chicago, at which the speakers spoke to the hearts and feelings of the citizens, asking them for material help. The Polish press was appealed to, and it quickly responded with an appeal to the community. *Dziennik Związkowy (The Alliance Daily)* printed a donation list, which attracted over $700. PAVA Post Nr. 5, coming to the aid of the District, opened a temporary shelter at Milwaukee and Racine Avenues for homeless and sick colleagues, in which they received not only a warm place, free medical advice from Doctors A. Pietrzykowski and F. Lenart, but also three hot meals a day."[55]

The hastily organized shelter functioned until the Spring of 1922. Due to the homeless war invalids and the unemployed who were in the most difficult situation, permanent veterans' shelters had to be organized in the largest concentrations of Polish Americans.

---

53 *The Veteran* October 1938, p. 14
54 PAVA NEB Archives, sign. Box – 17/pl.130 PAVA, Letter of L. Krzyżak to PAVA Post Nr. 130 in Bydgoszcz of March 6, 1939
55 W. Bogucki. "Słów kilka o Okręgu 1 SWAP" ["A Few Words About PAVA District Nr. 1"] in: *Weteran [The Veteran]* December 1925, p. 29

That was the idea that Dr. Pietrzykowski, a former army doctor from the Blue Army, presented in 1922 at the 2nd PAVA General Assembly in Chicago. He received permission from the City authorities to organize and run such a center. Nonetheless the PAVA leadership concentrated its efforts on the idea of organizing and running a central shelter in Poland for war invalids from America. It was to be established on the farm purchased by PAVA at Kuligi in Pomerania. The difficulties encountered in the ensuing years in administering this shelter and the unwillingness of the war invalids to leave America, forced the shelter to close in 1929.

In the years of the Great Depression of 1929–1932 and the accompanying enormous unemployment, the creation of a shelter for veterans became a pressing need. In those difficult times the Auxiliary Corps came to the veterans' aid with invaluable help. At the initiative of Agnieszka Wisła, a temporary shelter was organized in Chicago in the Fall of 1931. She reminisced years later: "At that time we established a temporary shelter for unemployed veterans. We went with the late N. Chmielińska to the headquarters of the Polish National Alliance with a request that they give us the empty buildings on Emma Street for this purpose, which we outfitted with the most essential things, so they would have a roof over their heads, and with the help of good people we maintained 22 veterans there, though many of them slept on the floor, because there was a lack of those things too.

"For Christmas Eve we were able to get pigs, half a side of beef, chickens, bread, cakes, etc. Gift baskets were made up for homeless veterans in Mrs. Jaworski's basement. We were able to get clothes, shoes, etc. for many of them. We also got meal tickets to our colleague Lenard's restaurant, for which the Corps paid minimum prices, until the unemployed veterans found jobs.

"Unfortunately, as usual some individual veterans from PAVA District I started complaining around that the women were butting in too much, so we handed the maintenance of this shelter over to the Veterans District Committee on April 18, 1932, which after several weeks was dissolved, because there was no one to get the food, and it wouldn't come by itself."[56]

The temporary shelter, although only active for six months, allowed the Polish veterans to endure in the company of their compatriots several of the most difficult winter months without having to waste away in city shelters.

In that same period a social Civic Committee to Build a Shelter for the Polish Soldier was founded in Chicago. It gathered many representatives of Chicago's Polish American community. It was headed by Mrs. M. Milewska. In 1934 this committee forwarded the $2,500 it had raised to the account of the Polish Army Veterans Home

---

56   PAVA NEB Archives, File: Auxiliary Corps. Agnieszka Wisła

Construction Committee which was part of PAVA District I. This account also contained donations collected by PAVA District I during General Haller's tour. The funds were retained, and not forwarded to the PAVA National Executive Board for the I. J. Paderewski Invalid Fund. After PAVA President Franciszek Dziób's visit in Chicago it was explained that the money would be designated for organizing a permanent shelter for veterans.[57]

Thanks to these funds, in 1934 PAVA District I was able to purchase on credit a sizeable building at 1239 N. Wood Street in which one story was designated as a shelter for disabled and unemployed veterans. There was space for 30 homeless as well as a kitchen and dining room. The remaining floors held spacious multi-function halls for meetings, celebrations, balls, etc. and District offices. The building remained in this configuration together with the shelter in it until the outbreak of World War II.[58]

In the spring of 1932 the PAVA District VI in Detroit (at the initiative of PAVA President Franciszek Dziób) purchased a suburban ten acre farm in Wanda Park, which was quickly transformed into a shelter for veterans. Both in theory and practice, as became evident later, it was a permanent shelter for PAVA members—invalids as well as the unemployed. The official opening of this shelter took place on June 19, 1932. A large group of veterans participated in it, together with leaders of the Polish American community and representatives of the American authorities for the State of Michigan and the City of Detroit. Already then 40 veterans lodged in the shelter. After a couple of months there were 68 of them. By June 1933 that figure decreased to 44. At that time there were seven invalids and 37 unemployed in that group.

Although the shelter at Wanda Park was the property of PAVA, its maintenance became the responsibility of the Polish American community in Detroit, organized into a Civic Committee, which established a Committee for the Care of the Shelter. The first president of the committee was a local lawyer, Artur Kościński. At his suggestion the committee sent out many letters to Polish and American companies and grocery stores with a request for donations. Many of them replied in the affirmative and began supporting the shelter with their products. A list of the donors of that time shows 21 food companies and bakeries, and 18 grocery stores.

Individual organizations and private persons took care of furnishing and outfitting the shelter. Three local PAVA Auxiliary Corps posts purchased part of the

---

57 PAVA NEB Archives, *Księga Protokółowa Zarządu Głównego Korpusu Pomocniczego przy SWAP. 1934–1955, Protokół z nadzwyczajnego posiedzenia ZG SWAP dnia 7 grudnia 1934 roku* [*Minute Book of the PAVA Auxiliary Corps Main Governing Board. 1934–1955. Minutes of the Special Meeting of the PAVA NEB of December 7, 1934.*] p. 15

58 "Historia Okręgu I SWAP w streszczeniu" ["A Summary of the History of PAVA District I"] in: "Pamiętnik XII Walnego Zjazdu SWAP. 28–30 maja 1955 roku," Chicago 1955; ["Souvenir Journal of the PAVA 12th General Assembly. May 28–30 1955," Chicago 1955] *Weteran [The Veteran]* June 1934, p. 19

beds, blankets, bedding, towels and kitchen utensils. The veterans were supplied with clothes by charities, Polish clothes stores and private individuals. The local congressman, John Lesinski, also helped out, supplying wood to build the pantry, etc.

Among the larger cash donors the names of priests predominated. They passed on offerings given by the faithful during Mass.

The activity of the Committee for the Maintenance of the Shelter was not a one-time thing. It had the character of permanent supervision. It made every effort to ensure that the veterans in Wanda Park always had food, clothes, heat, guaranteed medical care and fair work. A farming business was organized for them, where they worked gladly, thus contributing to a partial coverage of the food needs of the shelter. The nearby Polish Seminary at Orchard Lake was of great help in outfitting the farm, providing farm machines and tools, seeds and seedlings and professional farming literature.

The Committee, with the strong support of the local clergy and the Felician Sisters, took care of the religious and spiritual life of the veterans, organizing religious services for them, communal Christmas Eves and Easter fesitivities. Especially the Christmas Eve suppers and Christmas midnight masses were deeply satisfying emotionally for the veterans, and gave them a sense of real belonging.[59]

The successful venture of Detroit's Polish American community showed that in the presence of a noble goal, strong will power and desire to act, backed by good organization, one could count on the support of one's fellow countrymen.

The veterans who found a roof over their heads and care in the Wanda Park shelter, knew how to appreciate it. When in December 1932 they found out through the newspapers about the death of their colleague Marcin Tomaszewski, who had died of hunger on a street in Chicago, they wrote a letter to *The Veteran*: "In the name of our colleagues and our own we want to thank the entire Polish American community in Detroit for the care that they surround us with, us former soldiers of the Polish Army from America, who found themselves, not of our own fault, abandoned and in poverty.

"...We ask the Editorial Board to correct our poor correspondence so that it really reflects what our hearts feel, that is: gratitude to the entire Polish American community for taking care of us and thanks to those persons who spare neither hardship nor work, and bring us, in these difficult times, clothes and food, so that we don't have to die of hunger out on the street, as happened to one of our colleagues in Chicago, which we read about in the newspapers.[60]

---

59 PAVA NEB Archives, sign. A-VIII/28, PAVA District VI, vol. 28
60 *The Veteran* February 1934, p. 10

An unforgettable event in the life of the shelter and the veterans living there was General Józef Haller's visit, who came to Wanda Park in 1934 during his tour of Polish American communities in America, to help the PAVA National Executive Board in fundraising on behalf of the I. J. Paderewski Invalid Fund.

In 1937 PAVA District VI, thanks to determined efforts, was able to get a tax exemption for the shelter. This made it possible, a year later, to build another home for over $4,500, because the earlier one was too small and in such bad shape that it was a threat to the veterans living there. This investment proved with what great care PAVA District VI treated its homeless disabled veterans.

In comparison to other shelters, the home at Wanda Park proved to be the most stable outpost of this type in the entire Association.

Detroit's example showed the way for other veteran groups. In the summer of 1932 in Milwaukee, the Veterans' Home owned by PAVA Post Nr. 3 organized, with the help of the local Polish American community, a shelter for homeless and unemployed veterans on its premises. The St. Vincent de Paul society, a Polish American charitable organization, furnished it. Through Dr. Paradowski, its Vice President, the organization donated beds, mattresses and blankets. Meanwhile PAVA Auxilary Corps Post Nr. 1, which was part of PAVA Post Nr. 3, furnished the kitchen and purchased the needed utensils, and some of the ladies offered bedding and pillows.

In September 1932 the shelter took in five unemployed veterans. Thanks to this the City of Milwaukee exempted PAVA Post Nr. 3 from real estate taxes on the veteran home that it owned. [61] In large part this was made possible thanks to Assemblyman Bronisław Spott (a delegate to the State Assembly) a former commander of PAVA Post Nr. 3.

The next veteran shelter was founded in New York in Manhattan. It was located at 75 Fifth Avenue, corner of 10th street. Stanisław Wilk, the commander of PAVA Distict II, made a great contribution to its founding. He was able to gain the support of many of the top figures in the local Polish American community. Half of the capital required to get the shelter operational was provided by PAVA Post Nr. 21. The opening of the shelter took place on February 11, 1933. General Józef Haller, who was in New York at the time, honored the celebration with his presence.[62]

The shelter was of a temporary nature. It functioned for about a year in Manhattan. The rising rent, which was a sign of a stronger economy, forced PAVA District II to find another, cheaper place for the needs of the shelter. The Polish American Civic Committee came to the veterans' aid, offered an unused property on

---

61 *The Veteran* September 1932, p. 13
62 PAVA NEB Archives, sign. A-VIII/10, *Souvenir Journal for the Polish Army Veteran Shelter*

Long Island for this purpose, which was to have been an orphanage. But this place was not well suited for a veteran shelter. In 1935 it was moved to new quarters in the Bronx, and in July 1936 to Passaic, NJ to the building of the local PAVA Post Nr. 36. There were four veterans in this shelter, maintained chiefly by the efforts of PAVA District II and the Auxiliary Corps. At this time an unexpected, significant donation came into the shelter's coffers. The donor of this pleasant surprise was the Polish steamship company Gdynia-Ameryka, which sent a check for $1,407 for the needs of the shelter. This money had been obtained during the first docking of the transatlantic steamer Batory in New York. It was income from entrance tickets sold to tour the boat during its stay at the port.[63]

The PAVA District II shelter had no luck in terms of a permanent location. In 1937 it was moved to Newark, NJ where a workshop was organized for the unemployed invalids. The ladies from the Auxiliary Corps took care of the sale of the products manufactured in that workshop.[64]

PAVA Efforts to Secure American Veteran Privileges

The Polish Army Veterans Association, desiring to render measurable aid to their colleagues as well as to the veterans outside the organization, tried to obtain from the American authorities privileges similar to those that veterans of the American Army had. They had no success on the federal level, so some of the more resourceful PAVA members made attempts at the state and municipal government levels. In two instances these endeavors were successful. The first was in New Britain, CT, where in 1931 the members of the local Post Nr. 111 (S. F. Wojtusik, W. Jabłoński and J. Zieliński) with the help of L. Maciora—a state assemblyman of Polish extraction from Hartford, CT, and the mayor of the city of New Britain, George A. Quigley, were able to obtain, from the State Legislature, the same privileges for Polish Army veterans that veterans of the American army had.[65]

The second instance was in Milwaukee, Wisconsin, where in 1932 Polish Army veterans of Post Nr. 3 received permanent financial aid and aid in kind from the local American Red Cross, similar to the sort that sick and unemployed veterans of the

---

63 PAVA NEB Archives, sign. A-VIII/10-13, File: Gdynia-America Line
64 "Krótki zarys historii Okręgu II SWAP" ["A Short Outline of the History of PAVA District II"] in: *Pamiętnik Placówki Nr. 39 w Passaic, NJ, wydany z okazji Zjazdu II Okręgu SWAP i Korpusów Pomocniczych w dniach 2 – 3 IX, 1939* [Souvenir Journal of Post Nr. 39 in Passaic, NJ published on the occasion of the General Assembly of PAVA District II and the Auxiliary Corps September 2–3, 1939] Passaic 1939.
65 "Zarys historii Placówki No 111 SWAP im. Generała Józefa Hallera w New Britain, CT" ["An Outline of the History of the General Józef Haller PAVA Post Nr. 111 in New Britain, CT"] in: *Pamiętnik IX Walnego Zjazdu SWAP w New Britain, CT 30–31 maja 1–2 czerwca 1946 roku* [Souvenir Journal of the 9th PAVA General Assembly in New Britain, CT May 30–31 and June 1–2, 1946]; J. Wójcik, M. Kierkło, *Z dziejów Żołnierza-Emigranta "Haller Post" w New Britain* [A History of the Soldier-Immigrant from the Haller Post in New Britain] New Britain, 1991, p. 15

American Army had. The aid was financed by the local Community Fund. This became possible thanks to the tireless efforts of Haller soldier Bronisław Spott, who was a delegate to the Wisconsin State Assembly at that time. He had excellent contacts there and was well versed in the procedure required to take care of those types of matters.[66]

PAVA Posts in Pennsylvania, Massachusetts and New Jersey tried to follow in the footsteps of the posts in New Britain and Milwaukee; unfortunately, without success. For years, the PAVA National Executive Board, and particularly Leopold Krzyżak, the association's adjutant general, made strenuous efforts in the states of New York and New Jersey. For this purpose an Equal Rights Committee was organized in the state of New York, composed of the best known representatives of New York's Polonia, who as American citizens already had a certain influence in the local American community. Frank Kosiński, the chairman of the committee, wrote in his report of May 1939 about the difficulties which had to be overcome: "Taking care of our issues in the state legislature is not as easy as we had at first imagined. It is not so easy for two men from our Equal Rights Committee to educate 150 assemblymen and 50 senators about the history of our veterans in the State of New York. Most of them have no idea who we are, and think that we are veterans from the Polish Army who have nothing to do with the veterans of the World War from the French front. It is all the more difficult to convince 13 million people in the State of New York, whose opinions the legislators must contend with since they are elected by them. It is also difficult to convince, and get the agreement and support of all the American Army veterans, of whom there are 400,000 in the State of New York."[67]

Unfortunately, the efforts made by the Equal Rights Committee in the State of New York were not successful. The lack of influence at the municipal and state government levels, the lack of a strong Polish lobby, proved to be insurmountable barriers.

Help in Obtaining U.S. Citizenship

In addition to their most important task, that is organizing help for war invalids and the unemployed, the Polish Army Veterans Association rendered aid to their members (and not to them alone) in many other matters, for instance in endeavors to obtain U.S. citizenship.

At the moment of PAVA's founding the idea was floated to take care of this issue for all veterans on the basis of a bill in the U.S. Congress. The person who came up with this idea was Bronisław Spott, the commandant of PAVA Post Nr. 3 in Milwaukee, Wisconsin, who with time became an assemblyman of the Wisconsin State Legislature. On his initiative PAVA organized a committee in 1921, which

---

66 *The Veteran* September 1932, p. 13
67 PAVA NEB Archives, sign. A-IV/17

appealed to U.S. senators to help in resolving this problem. After some time a reply came from Senator Medill McCormick that all Poles who served in the American Army, by decision of the United States Congress, were immediately receiving the right to obtain American citizenship, but the matter of the volunteers to the Polish Army in France was complicated and at the moment impossible to take care of. He further informed the PAVA Board that the problem was well known because Senator Lodge's motion of June 10, 1919 to grant Polish Army veterans the rights of U.S. citizenship was waiting for resolution for two years already. Unfortunately, that initiative was to remain unresolved in a positive manner for many years to come—with great injury to Polish veterans wanting to live permanently in this country. The lack of citizenship greatly complicated their lives, created many legal barriers, for instance in obtaining a well-paying job, hospital care or in efforts to receive unemployment compensation.

Polish veterans had trouble with the Immigration Bureau which was responsible for matters related to the naturalization of immigrants settling in the United States. For instance in August 1922 there were 170 Polish veterans with their families on Ellis Island in New York harbor, which was the gateway that all emigrants coming into the United States had to pass through. Immigration officials ordered the whole group to be deported to Poland. The Polish consular corps in New York was helpless. Fortunately their PAVA colleagues came to the aid of the detained veterans. Thanks to their efforts a representative of the Polish National Alliance in Washington, Mr. Wedda, presented the U.S. Department of Labor and the Immigration Bureau with a special PAVA declaration, in which the Association guaranteed with their own assets that if in the future any one of their detained colleagues were to become a burden for American society, then PAVA would send him back to Poland to its invalids' farm at its own expense. On the basis of this guarantee almost all the veterans and their families gained admission to the United States; three persons, however, were sent back because they were found to be incurably ill.

The statement of Dr. Sokołowski, the immigration attaché at the Polish Consulate General in New York, is evidence of the measurable significance of PAVA's intervention. He reported that thanks to the action undertaken by PAVA the Polish government saved about $60,000, which would otherwise have been spent to cover the expenses of maintaining this group of immigrants on Ellis Island and later of their deportation to Poland.[68]

The problem of the bill to grant citizenship to Polish Army veterans could not be resolved not only in the U.S. Congress, but also at successive PAVA General

---

68 The Veteran November 1922, p. 6

Assemblies. The veterans who tried to get citizenship had to do this individually, with the help of attorneys (some of whom proved unscrupulous) which was a very expensive and long-term procedure.

There were cases of unusually successful conclusions of this issue. One of them was widely publicized in PAVA and broadly commented throughout the Polish American community. A Polish veteran, Józef Kubala of Buffalo, NY, a member of local PAVA Post Nr. 1, already had U.S. citizenship, but lost his citizenship certificate in 1933. He tried to get a copy, but it became apparent that this had to be done by the federal authorities and, in addition, it cost $10. The unemployed Kubala couldn't afford it. So he turned to his local representative, Congressman Meade, for help in getting his documents for free. The congressman was unable to help. He then decided to write to President Roosevelt, although he wasn't sure whether he would be successful, because he had heard that F. D. R. was very well disposed toward veterans.

A few days later he was surprised to receive a letter informing him that the President had directed his request to the Department of Labor in order to ascertain the facts stated in the letter. After a week the following letter arrived: "At the express request of President Roosevelt we are sending you by return mail a copy of your lost citizenship papers, for which you do not have to pay, as per the order of the President."[69]

This isolated incident did not change the fact that thousands of Polish veterans in the USA were not citizens of this country. For nearly twenty years attempts to pass a bill in Congress to solve this problem, failed.

The greatest proponent of this issue in PAVA ranks, Bronisław Spott, did not give up the fight. He finally caught the attention of Wisconsin congressman R. Cannon on this issue, who introduced the draft of an appropriate bill on the floor of Congress in 1934. Simultaneously PAVA carried on correspondence with many senators and congressmen, to get their support. Czesław Mrozowski, the PAVA Secretary General, made a trip to Washington at his own expense. He spoke with many congressmen, among others with R. Cannon. At that time PAVA posts, instructed by the organization's headquarters, mailed their own resolutions on this subject to their congressmen and senators.[70] This worked, because the newly elected PAVA Adjutant General, Leopold Krzyżak, was summoned to Washington to testify before the Congressional Immigration Committee. He explained and argued the virtue of granting Polish Army veterans the right to obtain American citizenship on a par with the other veterans of allied armies from World War I.

---

69 *The Veteran* October 1933, p. 12

70 PAVA NEB Archives, sign. A-II/7, file: 6th PAVA General Assembly in Newark, NJ, 1934, Report of PAVA National Executive Board officials at the 6th PAVA General Assembly in the city of Newark, New Jersey for the period 1931 to 1934

After passing the House and Senate, the bill was signed into law by President Franklin Delano Roosevelt on July 3, 1935. It was to be in force until May 25, 1937.

On the basis of this bill veterans of allied armies who had legally arrived in the United States before August 1914 and had left this country to serve in allied military units between August 1914 and April 5, 1917 or (unable to be accepted to U.S. Army or Navy service) had left this country after April 5, 1917 to sign up and in fact serve prior to Armistice (November 11, 1918) in the armies of countries allied with the United States and participating in the World War, were guaranteed the right to apply for U.S. citizenship. The petitioning veteran also had to have an honorable discharge from military service.[71]

Unfortunately, the Immigration authorities (in putting this bill into play) excluded Polish veterans, claiming that in the time period designated by the bill the Polish State did not yet exist. Thus the applications of Polish veterans were being rejected, which made them very bitter. In this situation the PAVA National Executive Board was forced to intervene at the highest levels of government. The PAVA Adjutant General, Leopold Krzyżak, was delegated to Washington, where for several days he held discussions in the Department of Labor, the Department of State, the Department of Defense and in the French Embassy. In the end the federal government decided that since the U.S. Government recognized the Polish National Committee in Paris as the representative of the Polish nation, then by the same token it recognized the existence of the Polish State fighting alongside the allied nations.

On this basis the immigration authorities introduced appropriate amendments to the executive regulations of the bill of July 3, 1935, which finally enabled Polish veterans to take advantage of its possibilities, without the necessity of waiting out the required number of years to obtain the so-called second citizenship papers, and without having to pay the required fees.

Due to the time-consuming procedural requirements connected with obtaining appropriate attestations, for instance confirmations of military service from archives in Poland, very many veterans applying for citizenship papers were unable to deliver all legally required documents by May 25, 1937, that is, by the termination date of the bill. At that time John Lesinski, a congressman of Polish descent from Detroit, Michigan, came to the rescue. Thanks to

his efforts the effective term of the bill concerning the ability of Polish veterans to apply for U.S. citizenship was extended by a year, to May 25, 1938. A

---

[71] "Okólnik Nadzwyczajny Nr. 15 w sprawie uobywatelnienia(sic!)" ["Special Circular Nr. 15 on the Issue of Obtaining Citzenship"] in: *The Veteran* September 1935, p. 14

resolution to that effect, approved by both the House and the Senate, was signed into law by President Roosevelt on August 23, 1937.[72] Unfortunately, despite the extended deadline, once again many Polish veterans were unable to obtain the required documents in time, especially from Poland. The main reason was the fact that there were thousands of requests from the veterans, and the Polish military archives were unable to take care of all the requests in time because they were understaffed. On average one had to wait five to six months to get an attestation from the military archives.

There was a similar situation in the offices of the PAVA National Headquarters in New York, which was the intermediary in contacts with the archives in Poland, and also had the right to issue other needed documents, for instance proof of enlistment at a recruiting station in the United States or Canada for the Polish Army in France in the years 1917–1918. The avalanche of requests and applications was so huge that the PAVA National Executive Board, in the interest of its members, published an announcement directed mainly at Blue Army veterans who did not belong to PAVA: "The PAVA National Executive Board reserves the right not to issue any documents to colleagues who are not members of the organization. The National Executive Board renders its organizational services free of charge only to its own members.

"Since the signing into law of the right to obtain citizenship the National Executive Board has been receiving letters regarding application procedures from colleagues who never belonged to the Association, despite that fact that our organization has been in existence for fifteen years."[73]

This was the first instance when the PAVA leadership so categorically denied help to former war-time colleagues who, after returning to America, despite frequent encouragements, did not want to join the association. Now they had to pay a high price, because they were unable to take care of all necessary documents in time.

In this difficult situation Congressman Lesinski again came to the aid of the veterans. In May 1938 he presented another resolution in Congress (HR 10815) for a second extension of the bill allowing Polish veterans-volunteers from America for the Polish Army in France to apply for American citizenship. Unfortunately, this time the legislative branch of the federal government had no sympathy for the tardy (as the legislators saw it) Polish veterans and the resolution was not approved.[74]

During the life of the bill concerning American citizenship for Polish Army veterans, from June 1936 to May 1938, 2,000 Polish veterans—almost half of all

---

72 *The Veteran* September 1937, p. 12

73 "Komunikat urzędowy w sprawie papierów obywatelskich" ["Official Communiqué Regarding Citizenship Papers"] in: *The Veteran* January 1936, p. 11

74 *The Veteran* May 1938, p. 12

PAVA members—were able to apply.[75] From that time on they were able to access the same rights as those available to United States citizens.

Parallel to the efforts made to obtain citizens' rights the PAVA Board endeavored to have the U.S. Congress give Polish soldiers the same veterans' rights that U.S. Army soldiers had. Some of the PAVA posts and districts made similar efforts on the state level. With the exception of the State of Wisconsin, which was detailed before, these efforts ended in failure.[76]

Other Forms of Mutual Aid

Aside from the above described forms of mutual aid, the Polish Army Veterans Association of America also offered other services to members and non-members as well. The PAVA Board formed a special Information Bureau for this purpose in 1922 in Cleveland, Ohio. It offered the following services:

- help in finding employment, lodging, assistance in American agencies, etc.
- wire transfers of money to Poland
- searching for lost veterans at the request of their families in Poland
- sale of steamship tickets, so-called schifcards
- taking care of all matters connected with bringing the families of veterans to America from Poland.

This was quite tedious work, because everything had to be detailed in writing for the people living in Poland concerning the procedure for taking care of matters related to this issue, that is, getting a passport, obtaining an American visa, receipt of the steamship ticket sent from America and money for the trip, comments concerning the trip across the ocean itself, meeting with an agent of the Information Bureau in New York, etc. These comments were invaluable for persons planning to go to America who mainly came from rural areas. For these people even a trip to Poland's capital, Warszawa, was a traumatic and stressful experience, what to say of a trip to America without knowledge of the English language.

The PAVA Information Bureau was active from 1922 to 1925, up to the time when the PAVA headquarters was moved from Cleveland to Chicago. In the coming years it no longer did money transfers to Poland, nor sold steamship tickets, nor helped bring veteran families from Poland to America. This was done only in exceptional cases, and was outsourced to other specialized firms. Nonetheless the Bureau continued to help veterans, and to the extent possible also non-members of PAVA in solving

---

75 "Zasłużone uznanie (dla kongresmana Jana Lesińskiego)" ["Deserved Recognition (for Congressman John Lesinski)"] in: *Dziennik Dla Wszystkich [Everybody's Daily]* March 24, 1950, p. 4

76 PAVA NEB Archives, File: PAVA National Executive Board Plenary Sessions in 1963; Report on the Plenary Session of November 16, 1963

various problems, where knowledge of English, America or its regulations proved to be barriers difficult to surmount for immigrants from Poland. Without exception help was given to families searching for missing Blue Army soldiers (missing at the front or after returning to America). In such cases printing the details in *The Veteran* often gave good results.

The PAVA Information Bureau, which was active in the first years of the organization's existence, proved to be a very useful agency, helping its members with many small, but important issues.

2nd Brigade of the Polish Legions. He died suddenly in Detroit on October 1, 1925

Funerals of PAVA Members

The funeral rites of deceased Polish Army veterans played an important role in the integration of the Polish community in the United States. They often beame transformed into great patriotic manifestations. This was especially true when the deceased was the victim of a tragic accident or a universally respected citizen.

If the deceased was a PAVA member, his uniformed veteran colleagues participated in the funeral together with a color guard, with ladies from the Auxiliary Corps, representatives of various Polish American organizations, and also delegations of American Army veterans. When the funeral of a particularly distinguished person was held, representatives of local American authorities would also be present.

Some funerals created a great stir in the local Polish American community. That was, for instance, the case with veteran Walenty Orlik, who (while working on the construction of St. Thomas church in Detroit) was killed by a high voltage electric shock. As a Blue Army man he had fought in the Champagne region of France and in Poland where as a member of the 13th Division of Polish Riflemen he participated in the Bolshevik campaign, for which he received the Cross of Valor. The members of PAVA Post Nr. 7 (the largest post in the entire organization) to which the deceased had belonged, were almost all present in full uniform and with all their flags for their colleague's funeral.[77]

The funeral of Lieutenant Marian Kowalski was held in Cleveland, Ohio on May 15, 1934. He was a Chevalier of the Order of Virtuti Militari. It was a great and sad event, of the kind which had not been witnessed in the Polish American community for a long time: "The funeral procession was impressive. At the head rode the police on motorcycles, next came the flags: the American and the PAVA Post Nr. 6. Behind the flags marched the veterans in uniform, behind them many ladies of the PAVA

---

77 *The Veteran* November 1925, pp. 32-33

Post Nr. 6 Auxiliary Corps. Colleague Zaleśny walked in front of the coffin, carrying a small pillow with all of the deceased colleague's military decorations. There was an escort of twelve veterans-colleagues on either side of the coffin. Six carried their rifles with the muzzles pointing toward the earth. There was a long column of about 150 cars behind the coffin. The first was a car filled with flowers. The most noticeable was a wreath with a sash that had the following words on it: 'To the Chevalier of the Order of Virtuti Militari, from General Józef Haller.' ... The funeral procession stopped one more time in front of the home of PAVA Post Nr. 6. The coffin was taken out of the car and placed in front of the Post. Colleague W. Karolczak in short but heartfelt words bid farewell to the dear remains in the name of the Post. Colleague Jan M. Lewandowski bid farewell to the deceased in the name of Post 13 of the Polish Legion of American Veterans...The deceased was buried in his blue uniform. His cap, the pillow with his decorations and his crossed sword were placed on top of the coffin. At the moment of death the deceased was only 41 years old."[78]

But the greatest patriotic manifestations occurred when the few remaining veterans of the Jnaury 1863 Uprising were laid to their eternal rest. That happened on February 23, 1935 in Philadelphia, Pennsylvania, when the Polish American community bid farewell to former insurrectionist Hilary Skwierzyński. One of the participants in that funeral had this to say about the ceremony:

"The funeral of the late Skwierzyński was a beautiful manifestation of the Polish American community's patriotic gratitude for the efforts of the late Hilary Skwierzyński on the field of glory during the January Uprising.

"On Saturday February 23rd at 9 a.m. the funeral procession formed in front of the funeral home in the following order: the Polish Army veterans, the Auxiliary Corps, The Boy Scouts of the Polish National Alliance, St. Adalbert's Society, and numerous delegates of various other societies. The Polish Falcons: Nests 516 and 171, the Polish National Home and Polish National Alliance Groups.... The Reverend Pastor Wyborski assisted by two priests. ... Also participating in the funeral cortege were veterans from Trenton, NJ, Camden, NJ and Chester, PA. The procession was headed by PAVA Post Nr.12 Commander J. Zbytniewski. The funeral march was played by the ensemble of the Polish Musicians Association."[79]

The funeral of former January Uprising participant Wincenty Smołczyński was held with even greater splendor. He died on October 15, 1936 in Chicopee, Massachusetts. The deceased was a well known and respected Polish American

---

78 L. Z. Adamczak. "Zwłoki Ś.p. Mariana Kowalskiego, porucznika Armii Polskiej w rezerwie, złożono na wieczny spoczynek" ["The remains of the Late Marian Kowalski, Lieutenant of the Polish Army Reserves, Were Laid to Eternal Rest"] in: *The Veteran* June 1934, p. 6

79 *The Veteran* April 1935, p. 10

civic leader, who worked in several organizations (The Polish Falcons, The Polish National Alliance, the Polish Roman Catholic Union of America, PAVA). He was also a founding member and the first commander of PAVA Post Nr. 79 in Chicopee. His funeral attracted crowds of people. Marching in the funeral procession were the Polish Falcons, veterans of the Polish Army and the American Army, local and regional Polish American leaders, Anthony J. Stonina, the mayor of Chicopee, together with the city's administration officers. The retinue was headed by thirty priests who had come from neighboring states.[80]

The death of their organizational colleague Andrzej Panek shocked PAVA members. He died "on his watch" in 1938 during the 9th General Assembly of PAVA District VI which was held in Flint, Michigan. He died suddenly during a parade while carrying the American flag. All the posts of PAVA District VI participated in his funeral as well as thousands of Flint residents. There were over 280 cars in the funeral procession.[81]

The large participation of the Polish American community at the funerals of Polish Army veterans demonstrated the scale of the community's patriotism and the degree of respect for those who had fought for Poland's freedom.

Custody of the Graves

The PAVA National Executive Board, the individual posts in outlying areas, and especially the Auxiliary Corps, made special effort to maintain the graves of the deceased veterans. Memorial Day was helpful in this, because that is when Americas generally go to visit the graves of veterans and to decorate them with flowers, wreaths and national flags.

Polish veterans marked their deceased colleagues' graves with large metal plaques with the PAVA emblem and decorated them with small Polish and American flags. Earlier the ladies of the Auxiliary Corps would clean up the gravesites.

PAVA Veterans took great care in maintaining the cemetery at Niagara on the Lake in Canada, the resting place of their colleagues who had died in the local training camp in the years 1917–1918. In 1924 PAVA passed a resolution to establish a capital fund, whose income was to be used for this purpose.[82]

The PAVA National Executive Board appreciated the work of Elizabeth C.

---

80 "Wspaniały pogrzeb weterana Powstania z roku 1863 Wincentego Smołczyńskiego" ["The Magnificent Funeral of 1863 Uprising Veteran Wincenty Smołczyński"] in: *Weteran [The Veteran]* November 1936, p. 18; T. Lachowicz, "Cośmy zaczęli, wy dokończycie..." ["What We Began You Will Finish..."] in: *Przegląd Polski [Polish Review]* New York, January 21, 2000, pp. 1-2
81 "Tysiące ludzi wzięło udział w pogrzebie zmarłego na posterunku" ["Thousands of People Participated in the Funeral of the Deceased Who Died at his Post"] in: *Weteran [The Veteran]* September 1938, p. 15
82 PAVA NEB Archives, sign. XVIII/4, File: Polish Consulate in Buffalo, NY 1922–1931

Ascher, a Canadian who for many years had maintained the graves of the Polish soldiers in this little cemetery. PAVA asked the Polish government to bestow a decoration on her. She received the Polonia Restituta and the Cross of Merit of the Polish Republic. General Józef Haller personally pinned the latter decoration on her in 1934. Parenthetically speaking, General Haller decorated the Memorial Monument at this tiny cemetery with the Cross of Valor on November 27, 1923.[83]

A monument dedicated to Polish Army veterans was unveiled on July 4, 1932 at the local Polish cemetery of St. John Kanty thanks to the efforts of PAVA Post Nr. 42 in Omaha, Nebraska and its president Franciszek P. Kawa (a state inspector with the Nebraska Department of Agriculture). Participants in the ceremony included, in addition to the many members of the public at large, Polish and American veterans and a detachment of American soldiers from nearby Fort Crook, which fired off an honorary salute.[84]

In the years 1921–1939 PAVA supported various initiatives to maintain the graves of soldiers who had died for Poland's freedom.

Already in 1922 they had reacted positively to a letter from Colonel Cedric Fauntleroy, former leader of the Kościuszko Air Force Squadron from the time of the Polish-Bolshevik war, who turned to PAVA with a request to raise $1,000 to build memorial monuments in Warszawa and Lwów (now Lviv in the Ukraine) for Americans who had died there. The PAVA National Executive Board sent out a circular to all the posts, to designate half of the profits from the celebrations of the second anniversary of "Miracle on the Vistula" toward this goal.[85]

In 1927 the PAVA Board contributed financially to the construction of a memorial monument on the grave of 58 fallen insurrectionists of the January 1863 uprising in the village of Władyki, Wilejka County.[86]

When the Union of Hallerians in Poland organized a fund drive for a memorial monument to honor fallen Polish soldiers lying at the St. Hilaire cemetery in France, the PAVA Board enabled Lieutenant Stanisław Pałaszewski (President of the Pomeranian Chapter of that Union) to come to the United States with General Haller in 1933 and conduct a fund drive for that purpose.

The members of some PAVA posts, foreseeing that one day they too would come to bid farewell to this world, tried to have special sites set aside at local cemeteries,

---

83 *The Veteran* November 1930, pp. 3-4; June 1934, p. 7
84 "Odsłonięcie Pomnika Weteranów Armii Polskiej" ["'Unveiling of the Monument Dedicated to Polish Army Veterans"] in: *Weteran [The Veteran]* August 1932, p. 24
85 PAVA NEB Archives, sign. A-VII/1, PAVA Board Minute Book. 1921–1925; "Minutes of the Plenary Session of the PAVA Board held on July 6, 1922.
86 PAVA NEB Archives, sign. A-XVII/27, File: Requests for Help From Abroad

the so-called veteran plots. They were established, among others, at Polish cemeteries in Chicago, Detroit and New Britain. This was yet another symptom of the unusually strong collegial bond that characterized this social group—they were so strong that even after death they wanted to rest among their own kind. We also believe that the veterans' cemeteries will have a special significance in the process of patriotic education for the present and future generations of Polish émigrés in America.

Culture and Education in PAVA Organizational Life

This Association, in addition to its top priority of organizing mutual aid for members who were in the most difficult living conditions, was also engaged in other forms of activity. As a patriotic organization that concentrated some of the most valuable elements of the Polish emigration to the American continent, it laid great emphasis on upholding tradition among its members, and simultaneously tried to influence the entire Polish American community to do the same. The scope of this work and the effort made were considerable for the modest financial means which PAVA had at its disposal for this sort of enterprise. It is difficult to evaluate the effects of this work, as it has to do with activity whose goal was the propagation of the good name of Poland and the Poles in American society.

As far as cultural and educational activity is concerned, primary attention should be focused on publications which aside from an informational function, also played an educational role among PAVA members and other readers.

PAVA Publications

Weteran (The Veteran) is the press organ of the Polish Army Veterans Association of America. It was created on the basis of a resolution passed at the 1st General Assembly in Cleveland, Ohio. The first issue appeared without a day date in October 1921 in Chicago under the editorship of Czesław Żuławski. The next issue was published in Cleveland, where the PAVA Board was located, under the editorship of Stanisław Z. Stachowicz, the secretary general of this organization, an experienced journalist and co-editor of *The Monitor,* a local daily.

From October 1921 to February 1922 *The Veteran* was published as a monthly. In March and April 1922 it was issued as a weekly (Nr.'s 6-14). This was due to the need to intensify the amount of information connected with the fund drive on behalf of the resettlement and invalid fund. As of May 1922 it was again published as a monthly and continued in that vein.

From 1921 to1925 *The Veteran* was published in Cleveland. For reasons of economy (these were the very beginnings of PAVA) it only had sixteen pages and was printed on regular, cheap newsprint. Its run varied from 2,000 to 2,500 copies.[87] At that time it was a typical veteran periodical, limited almost exclusively to veteran issues.

In 1925 the headquarters of the organization and the periodical moved to Chicago. The publication now sported a new graphic design, was printed on higher quality paper, and the number of pages was increased to twenty-four. The monthly, thanks to its new editor, Józef Harasimczuk, also changed its character, taking on something of the persona of a popular magazine with a variety of subjects that were acceptable to almost every family. This new form became popular among the readership, and their number began to grow quickly. In 1925 *The Veteran* had a circulation of 2,000 while one year later it already had 3,000 readers![88]

The veterans of individual PAVA posts did a lot to make that success happen. There was a healthy rivalry between the posts over new subscriptions. Sometimes it was reminiscent of the so-called Polish carol—in Poland priests would go caroling to the houses of their parishioners after Christmas Day. The *Rekord Codzienny (The Daily Record)* published in Detroit wrote about this: "On November 19 members of PAVA Post Nr. 7 will visit all the Polish houses on Dubois Street in order to popularize in that neighborhood the illustrated monthly published by their Association. We believe that due to the great contributions that a periodical of this sort makes and can make toward the national cause, the veterans will find a cordial welcome, for which we warmly ask all the Polish citizens residing in that area."[89]

After yet another move of PAVA headquarters, this time to Detroit in 1928, Kazimierz Bałdyga became the new editor of *The Veteran*. He also was the PAVA president at that time. Thanks to him *The Veteran* was built up to 28 pages and (as of Nr. 89, August 1928) in a format twice the size of the old one. But this innovation was not well received and as of January 1929 (Nr. 94) the monthly returned to its original size. But the periodical now had a color cover and (taking its example from American publications) it was printed on glossy paper for the first time. As a result of these innovations *The Veteran* became quite effective. During that period it was the only Polish American magazine of its type.

Unfortunately, this lasted only one year. The deepening economic crisis forced the PAVA leadership to curtail expenses connected with the printing of the publication. At the beginning of 1930 *The Veteran* returned to two-color covers, though it kept the coated paper, which improved the quality of photographs. The periodical varied from 24 to 32 pages up to the outbreak of World War II.

---

87 PAVA NEB, sign. A-VII/1 "Report of the Secretary General for December 1922" in: *The Minute Book of the PAVA National Executive Board for the Period June 1921 to May 1925*

88 *Rekord Codzienny [The Daily Record]* Detroit, November 12, 1926

89 Ibid.

There were noteworthy exceptions in the history of *Weteran,* when special issues were published on important occasions. Thus in June 1929, on the occasion of the Universal Countrywide Exposition in Poznań, Poland, a special showpiece number (Nr. 99) was printed with a record press run of 35,000 copies, of which 25,000 were sent to Poland.[90] It was a real gem in the publication history of the periodical up to that time. The issue had many interesting stories about the Polish Falcons of America, about the Polish American community's military effort in World War I, about the seven year history of PAVA and the history of other Polish American organizations. Richly illustrated (96 pages!) it was a real calling card for the Polish Army Veterans Association of America at the largest trade show that illustrated the ten-year accomplishment of independent Poland.

The next special issue of *The Veteran* (Nr. 179) was printed in May 1936 for the fifteenth anniversary of PAVA's founding. It was almost entirely devoted to the accomplishments of the Association since 1921. It was a 92 page issue.

The last jubilee issue (up to 1939) of *The Veteran* (Nr. 196) was published in October 1937 to commemorate the twentieth anniversary of the commencement of recruiting efforts to the Polish Army in France in 1917. But it was significantly thinner than its two predecessors, because all told it only had 48 pages.

Its editors had the greatest influence on the shape of PAVA's press organ. The shape of the periodical edited by them depended on their knowledge, creative invention, temperament, knowledge of the editorial art, and also on how they read the social context. It was characteristic of all *The Veteran* editors in the years 1921–1939 that they had all been Polish soldiers at one time, most of them had fought in the Blue Army, although some also hailed from other formations, which was clear evidence that the organization was truly open to all former Polish soldiers, regardless of the military formation in which they fought on behalf of Poland's independence. The editors as a rule worked simultaneously for other Polish American publications, where they presented their own political views. But in editing *The Veteran* they tried to subjugate their political bias (with varying results) to the Association's general interests.

In the years 1921–1939 the office of *The Veteran's* editor was held by: Czesław Żuławski—a Polish Falcon from America (Polish Army in France—PAF); Stanisław Z. Stachowicz—sergeant, Polish Falcons member from America (PAF), and the PAVA secretary general; Lucjan Adamczak—captain, a Polish Falcon from America (PAF), PAVA vice president; Roman Hanasz—2nd Lieutenant, a Polish Falcon from America (PAF); Józef Harasimczuk—a former officer of the Russian Army who in 1917 made

---

90   PAVA NEB Archives, sign. A-VIII/1, File: PAVA District II, Newark, NJ 1928–1930; letter of Kazimierz Bałdyga to Adam Łyczak—President of PAVA District II, April 13, 1929

the trip to the Polish Army in France via Siberia—Vladivostok—Singapore—Suez; Mieczysław Sichrawa—1st Brigade of the Polish Legions (in America as of 1926); Kazimierz Bałdyga—a volunteer from America (PAF), PAVA president; Artur L. Waldo—sergeant, a Polish Falcon from America (PAF); Karol Burke—lieutenant, Polish Falcon from America (PAF); Franciszek Dziób—lieutenant, Polish Falcon from America (PAF); Wacław W. Sojda—sergeant, a volunteer from America (PAF); Tomasz Zieliński—sergeant, Polish Falcon from America (PAF); Józef Chojnacki—platoon leader, Polish Falcon from America (PAF); Leopold L Krzyżak—a volunteer from America (PAF); Stanisław Wilk—2nd lieutenant and a Polish Falcon from America (PAF).[91]

The editors of the monthly kept in constant touch with many other Polish American publications, from which they received copy on a mutual exchange basis, and most importantly, photographic material, which enhanced the attractiveness of the publication in a fundamental way.[92] It helped that former soldiers of the Polish Army in France also worked in some of those other publications, for instance the *Monitor Clevelandzki* which was published in Cleveland, Ohio advertised itself in 1928 as "a Polish daily edited by Hallerians, employing Polish Army and American Army veterans."[93]

The Veteran was an original periodical in those times. It carried few current news items that reflected the daily, often humdrum life of the Polish immigrant. Its pages contained much by way of reminiscences, light and gay soldierly literary fiction authored by young writers who were often just starting out on a writing career, for instance Franciszek Waluś. They wrote soldierly short-stories, tales and poems. There were many items published about Polish history and culture, and also about the accomplishments of newly independent Poland. In the 1930s Henry Archacki's cycle of drawings: "Did you know, that…" was very popular. This author in a terse cartoon format presented interesting events from Polish history and culture and showed the past and current accomplishments of Poles scattered around the world. Reading this cycle one could feel proud of being Polish. It was a real lesson in Polishness, so important for Poles and their children living in the United States. Notably, Henryk Archacki was an excellent draughtsman, and the author of many of *The Veteran*'s covers.

Thanks to such authors the monthly fulfilled a most important educational function for its readers, while staying away (in line with PAVA By-Laws) from the political battles being fought in Poland and throughout the émigré community.

---

91   PAVA NEB Archives, PAVA membership file; "Słowa uznania dla redaktorów *Weterana*" [Words of Praise for the Editors of *The Veteran* "] in: *Weteran [The Veteran]* October 1961, p. 4
92   PAVA NEB Archives, sign. A-XIII/1, File: Correspondence of *The Veteran* editorial staff 1921–1931
93   *The Veteran* January 1928, p. 27

This made *The Veteran* a truly unique periodical on the Polish American market. No wonder that its popularity kept growing systematically and together with it the number of its readers, who in 1937 were scattered over five continents. For instance, the Polish Home in Brisbane, Australia, subscribed to it. Poles serving in the French Foreign Legion in Morocco in Africa read it; in Yugoslavia Polish general-emeritus Aureli Serda-Teodorski was a constant reader—he frequently had his articles published in *The Veteran*.

Thanks to the growth in subscriptions, especially in the second half of the 1930s, *The Veteran* began turning a profit. In 1927 it had a $500 monthly deficit. In 1937 it had a profit of $4,700 on its account.[94] This was very visible proof of the success which the PAVA press organ had finally achieved, which (it should be noted) was not financed from the outside.

The *Kalendarz Hallerczyk (The Hallerian Calendar)* was published for commercial and promotional reasons by the PAVA National Executive Board in 1921 for the calendar year 1922. Unfortunately, the PAVA NEB archive does not have a single copy of it. All we know is that the publication contained many articles connected with the history of the Polish Army in France and the beginnings of PAVA. Tying in this type of subject matter to a typical calendar was meant to popularize these issues throughout the Polish American community.

The *Hallerian Calendar* was printed in an issue of 10,000 copies. Due to a lack of experience in the distribution and sales of this sort of product the income proved to be negligible in comparison to the amount of work that was involved. No wonder then that for 1923 only 3,000 copies were printed. This proved to be the last edition of a PAVA calendar.[95]

The History of the Polish Army in France. In 1922 the PAVA Board, carrying out a decision of the General Assembly, signed a contract with Wacław Gąsiorowski, who was working at the PNA College in Cambridge Springs, Pennsylvania, to write the history of the Polish Army in France.[96] At first the aim was to publish this work together with the Polish Falcons, but soon the Falcons, for financial reasons and due to objections toward Gąsiorowski, backed out of the deal. PAVA decided to undertake the great task without a co-publisher.

Aside from Gąsiorowski others were also involved in gathering materials for this monumental study, including PAVA Board members, the association's rank and file, and PAVA representatives in Poland, whose task it was to find and copy appropriate

---

94 PAVA NEB Archives; sign. A-XXVII/22, Letter of L. Krzyżak to A. L. Waldo of April 10, 1937
95 PAVA NEB Archives, sign. A-VII/1 Minutes of the Meeting of the PAVA NEB of July 22, 1923
96 PAVA NEB Archives, sign. A-XIV/1, File: Wacław Gąsiorowski. The History of the Polish Army in France. Correspondence 1922–1931

documents in the military archives there. The work on this publication became inordinately prolonged. The first volume of the *History of the Polish Army in France*, covering the years 1910–1925, did not appear in Warszawa until 1931, a year after W. Gąsiorowski returned to Poland. In addition this study appeared at the least favorable time, that is, during the great economic crisis, which did not help sales.

Volume II, covering the years 1915–1916, was printed in Łódź in the summer of 1939, just before the outbreak of World War II.

The Polish Army Veterans Association of America financed the publication of both volumes.

Wacław Gąsiorowski was in possession of the typescript of volume III (1917–1919), which was the period of greatest interest to Polish veterans in America. The PAVA National Executive Board sent the funds necessary for its publication to Poland in the spring of 1939. Unfortunately, the outbreak of war did not allow the project to go forward. Wacław Gąsiorowski died a few months after the September 1939 campaign, and his typescript was lost after the war in circumstances that were never fully clarified, supposedly while an attempt was being made to send it to America.

The publication by PAVA of the two volumes of *The Polish Army in France* without the financial help of the Polish government was a great achievement, clearly showing that the veterans, despite the political tendencies dominant in Poland, stood by their military traditions and wanted to safeguard them for future generations, so that they would know that the Polish American community during the First World War had made a significant contribution to the securing of Poland's independence.[97]

Movies

From the very first moments of the founding of their organization, the PAVA leadership was cognizant of the great role that movies could play, due to their great popularity, in cultural and educational work. After the 1st PAVA General Assembly the Board endeavored, through Polish military attaché Major Kazimierz Mach in Washington, D.C., to obtain films with a military theme from the Ministry of Defense in Warszawa. But there were no results. The PAVA Board decided to buy a Polish movie that was about to go into movie theatres in Poland. In January 1923 the PAVA Delegation in Warszawa purchased the movie *Faithful River* (based on the novel by Stefan Żeromski) for $2,000. It was immediately sent to America, where a five-member team of PAVA members toured the largest Polish American communities and the PAVA posts active there, with paid film showings. Unfortunately, the costs of the tour, hall rental and maintenance of the crew brought a financial deficit.

---

97 PAVA NEB Archives, sign. A-XIV/1, File: Wacław Gąsiorowski. The History of the Polish Army in France. Correspondence 1922–1931

One of the members of this team, Captain Stanisław Nastał, undeterred by this failure, started his own company, "Poland's Film Exchange," which did screenings of movies from Poland and also rented movie projectors. The company prospered for many years. From a surviving letter of April 1934 it is apparent that it had its own offices in Chicago and New York and had the following movies for rent: "Halka," "Trędowata," "Czerwony Błazen," "Wampiry Warszawy," "Parada Cierniowa," and "Pan Twardowski."[98]

The PAVA Board helped Captain Nastał and others by advertising in *The Veteran* the films that they were showing, so long as they had important patriotic and educational content. That was the case with the movies: "Odrodzona Polska," ("Poland Reborn"), "Pan Tadeusz" ("Mr. Thaddeus") and "Halka."

In 1927 a documentary film was made which was completely financed by PAVA. It was a movie documentary of the largest tour of France and Poland in the history of the Association. The movie was shown later in many PAVA posts. Thanks to it veterans and other viewers could recall or get acquainted with places that were formerly connected with the Polish Army in France in the years 1917–1919, see the modern port of Gdynia, admire the historical landmarks of Warszawa, Kraków, Lwów, and Wilno, view the Monastery of Jasna Góra, the beautiful landscapes of the Polish Tatra Mountains and visit Polish Army units that the volunteers from America had served in. The film was very popular, because it brought the viewers unforgettable, emotional moments. Nothing spoke to the imagination like a movie image.

It became evident that PAVA members were also working in the Hollywood film industry. Due to the character of their work and the lack of a local PAVA post, they belonged to the "flying post," Nr. 100. One of them was Richard Bolesławski, a lawyer by education (received his law degree in Odessa, Russia). As a Polish lancer he participated in the Polish-Bolshevik war as a member of General Haller's Volunteer Army in 1920. He sustained a serious wound in one of the skirmishes; its effects bothered him for the rest of his life. In the United States he directed stage plays on Broadway in New York, from where he left for Hollywood in 1929, where among others he directed the film "Rasputin." After losing his job in 1931 he described his war-time experiences in the book *The Way of the Lancer*. It was very popular in the United States in 1932 and allowed him to return to work in the film industry, where he directed many movies, including: "Operator Thirteen," "Clive of India," "Strange Woman," "Smart Sister," "Les Miserables," "Manhattan Madness." In January 1937, working on the film "The Last of Mrs. Cheney," for the Metro Goldwyn Mayer

---

98   PAVA NEB Archives, sign. A-XVII/52

motion picture studio, he died of a heart attack at the age of 47.[99] In addition to directing films in Hollywood, Bolesławski (whose real name was Bolesław Ryszard Szrednicki) co-founded the "Actor's Studio" in New York, teaching what became known as "Method" acting. It was the most influential modern acting academy in the United States.[100]

Colonel Merian C. Cooper, an American pilot, and member of PAVA Flying Post Nr. 100, was a vice president and director of production for the David O. Selznick International Pictures company. He had initiated and organized the 7th Air Squadron named after Tadeusz Kościuszko, composed mainly of American pilots, which participated in the Polish-Bolshevik War in the years 1919–1920. One of the most famous movies produced by this film studio was "King-Kong," the story of a monster gorilla that destroys New York City. Merian C. Cooper personally arranged the film scene which presents the battle of King-Kong with the airplanes attacking it at the top of the Empire State Building. This well known pilot and film producer joined PAVA in February 1937, just after the death of Ryszard Bolesławski.[101]

Radio Programs

In the 1920s and 30s the United States saw a rapid development of the radio, the new mass communications medium. Public and private radio stations started sprouting up all over the country, broadcasting programs that catered to millions of listeners. Ethnic programs also began to appear. One of the pioneers of Polish radio programs in the United States was Captain Stanisław Nastał, a Blue Army veteran who was full of energy and interesting ideas. In 1932, together with Frank Żołyński (also a former Polish soldier) they created the "Polish Program" which was broadcast by station WCBD out of Waukegan, Illinois. This program was enthusiastically accepted by Polish listeners from Chicago all the way up to Milwaukee, Wisconsin. In 1935 Stanisław Nastał became the director of administration and programming for the newly created radio station WEMP. He created his own program there, "Our Polish Hour," which because of its high entertainment value and good educational content (with information about Poland's history and culture) was very popular among the local Polish American community. This program was broadcast every day during World War II. It gave the latest information from the battle front and mobilized the Polish American community to appropriate effort on behalf of the needs of the war.[102]

---

99   S.J.W., "Sudden Death of Outstanding Film Director and Our Member" in: *The Veteran* February 1937, p. 7
100 www.jbactors.com/Master Acting Teacher Biographies.html
101 "A Tried and True Friend of Poland—New Member of Our Association: in: *TheVeteran*, February 1937, p.1
102 S. Nastał, Jr. "Captain Stanisław Nastal—Pioneer of Polish Radio" in: *The Veteran* September 1981, ppp. 26-27

Exhibitions

Occasional exhibitions played an important role in the work undertaken by the Polish Army Veterans Association of America. They were connected with the propagation of the Polish American community's contribution to Poland's independence during World War I, and with the promotion of the Association's activities. The first such exhibit at which PAVA made its presence known was the Universal Countrywide Exposition in Poznań, Poland in 1929. There, thanks to PAVA's efforts, for the first time thousands of Poles in Poland who came to view the exposition could acquaint themselves with the history of the Polish American community's war effort. A collection of recruitment posters from the years 1917–1919 was used for this purpose, as well as numerous documents and photographs from America, Canada and France, and publications, including the very popular special issue of *The Veteran* which had been published at PAVA's own expense for this occasion, with a record printing of 35,000 copies! The PAVA exhibit was located in the "Poles From Abroad" pavilion.

This pavilion also contained an exhibit from the former National Defense Committee. In contrast to the PAVA exhibit, where there was an attempt to represent the Polish American community's efforts to help regain Poland's independence, the NDC's display was an exposition of contemporary texts-lampoons attacking the most outstanding figures connected with the idea of creating a Polish Army in France. No wonder that this display was poorly attended.[103]

In May 1931 PAVA organized an exhibit in Pittsburgh, Pennsylvania, as an event accompanying the 5th General Assembly. Visitors could view, among others, a series of posters from the recruitment action of 1917–1919, uniforms of volunteers from America, many interesting photographs, diplomas, etc. An important place was reserved for the painting representing the commander of the Blue Army, General Józef Haller, by artist Tadeusz Styka. After the conclusion of the exhibition the artist donated his painting to PAVA.[104]

A second exhibition (with a similar theme) was organized in Detroit, Michigan from March 12 to 19, 1932 on the suggestion of Artur L. Waldo (commander of PAVA District VI). The exhibit was located in the headquarters of PAVA Post Nr. 7. With the help of local Polish and American veterans a huge amount of items was collected: French weapons, captured German weapons (including a machine gun!) uniforms of the Polish Falcons and of Polish Army units in Canada, France and Poland, a lot of military accessories, for instance helmets, canteens, belts, buckles,

---

[103] S. Sobolewski. "Mój pobyt na Wystawie," ["My trip to the Exposition"] in: *Weteran [The Veteran]* December 1929, p. 14

[104] PAVA NEB Archives, sign. A-II/5, Documents of the Pre-Assembly Committee in Pittsburgh, File: 5th General Assembly, Pittsburgh 1931

maps, and a large collection of medals and decorations. There was even a recreated battlefront trench surrounded by sandbags, gunner posts, rifles and telephones. The success of the exhibit exceeded all expectations. Its hours had to be extended to 11 p.m.! Veterans served as tour guides of the exhibit, and their number had to be increased every day due to the growing crowds of visitors.

Their opinions were very enthusiastic. One of the most interesting was voiced by Tomasz Siemiradzki, editor of *Wiadomości Codzienne (Daily News)* published in Cleveland, Ohio, who during World War I was the president of the National Defense Committee, the famous NDF which had fought the idea of a Polish Army in France. This is what T. Siemiradzki wrote about the PAVA exhibit in Detroit: "Everything here interests me so much that I don't feel like leaving. This hall has been transformed into a spiritual temple of the Polish American triumph. Here finally the Immigration's War Effort took on meaning, one can even touch it, not just see it. This exhibit is a real feat, a national contribution. I congratulate colleague Waldo, the veterans and the Polish Falcons. Of the entire Polish American community no one was able to mount such an exhibition of our own endeavor, yet those who yesterday fought for Poland with weapons in hand, even risking their lives, were able to do this now."[105]

The former head of the Polish Falcons, and president at that time of PAVA, Franciszek Dziób, maintained: "If I had $25,000 available, I would immediately try to buy this entire collection. All the items gathered here are national souvenirs that are just plain invaluable for the Polish American community and should be saved for later generations."[106]

The PAVA exhibit in Detroit was intended as the first concrete initiative toward creating a permanent museum of the Polish American community. The idea was to interest the largest Polish American organizations in this matter. Since they were substantially well off financially, they ought to have undertaken the realization of this extremely important idea for the immigration. Unfortunately, none of those organziations was willing to take over the exhibit organized by PAVA, and showed no interest in the collections. To create a Museum of the Polish American community on its own was beyond PAVA's modest means. All this was taking place during the Great Depression of 1929–1932 after all, when many veterans were expecting help from their organization. Nonetheless the idea of creating a Polish American Museum had taken root. Several years later the Polish Roman Catholic Union of America, with its headquarters in Chicago, decided to shoulder the task. The person directly

---

105 A. L. Waldo *Sokolstwo. Przednia straż narodu* [*The Polish Falcons of America. Vanguard of the Nation*] vol. V, Pittsburgh 1984, p. 345

106 Ibid.

responsible for bringing it to fruition was a well-known historian, a researcher of Polish American history—Mieczysław Haiman.

During the World's Fair in Chicago in 1933, PAVA together with the Polish Falcons, organized an exhibit depicting the activity of both sister organizations.[107] This was the last such intiative known to us undertaken by PAVA before 1939.

Book and Press Readership

From the beginning the PAVA Board laid a lot of emphasis on the development of Polish books and press readership as an indispensable condition for the maintenance of Polishness anong veterans living on American soil. Already in October 1921, when PAVA posts were just being organized, the governing board of the Association through its representative in Poland, Franciszek Małek, purchased $100 worth of books, and several annual subscriptions to military periodicals.[108]

After importing them to America the list was publicized in *The Veteran,* thanks to which veterans could obtain them by mail.

During the first years the books imported from Poland included many positions on the history of political science; there was also poetry and good literary fiction. Several years later the PAVA Board decided in favor of profit, at the expense of promoting good literature; for example the catalogue of books for sale published in January 1924 listed many valuable items, often by well known authors, on the other hand, of new books imported from Poland in 1928, out of 68 titles only 6 fulfilled that criterion, the remainder were romance novels.

With time certain PAVA posts, especially the wealthier ones, began putting together their own small libraries, which were very popular with the veterans. The book collections were modest on the whole, but quite interesting nonetheless. Books on historical subjects, especially on World War I and the battles for Polish national independence, were in the majority. Of course, publications whose subject was connected with the history of the Blue Army were the most popular. There is evidence of this in the loan register for readers of the small library at PAVA Post Nr. 6 in Cleveland, Ohio. The most sought after books were Józef Sierociński's *The Polish Army in France;* historical studies of individual regiments that were part of the Blue Army, *The History of the Polish Army in France,* Volume 1 by Wacław Gąsiorowski, *About Józef Haller* by Edward Ligocki, and others.[109]

A short note which appeared in *The Veteran* in 1924 shows the care that the PAVA

---

107 PAVA NEB Archives, sign. A-XX/3
108 PAVA NEB Archives, sign. A-XXVII/1, File: Dr. Teofil Starzyński. Correspondence 1921–1930
109 PAVA NEB Archives, Box, Archive of PAVA Post Nr. 6 in Cleveland, OH, 1934–1969; Loan Register from the PAVA Post Nr. 6 library

Board took in propagating education and learning among its members: "Winter. Long evenings. Where do you spend them, colleagues? And how do you spend them? Remember that there are relatively few long winter evenings. They should be used wisely. Study. In every town there is a library where you can get Polish books for free. For those who know the English language the rich American libraries stand wide open. Public schools stand wide open. Remember, that time wasted on playing cards, at social events, in bad company is time lost for ever."[110]

Aside from libraries certain PAVA posts also established periodical and newspaper reading rooms. The best one was organized by Post Nr. 42 in Omaha, Nebraska. Thanks to its efforts a "Reading Room of the Polish Newspaper in America" was organized in the local Polish Home, where one could read many Polish periodicals and newspapers from various corners of the United States. In the first months after its opening the following publications were available there: *Wiadomości Codzienne (Daily News)* from Cleveland, Ohio; *Nowiny Polskie (Polish News)* from Milwaukee, Wisconsin; *Dziennik dla Wszystkich (Everybody's Daily)* from Buffalo, NY; *Pittsburczanin (The Pittsburger)* from Pittsburgh, Pennsylvania; *Polak Amerykański (The American Pole)* from Perth Amboy, New Jersey; *Trybuna Polska (The Polish Tribune)* from Erie, Pennsylvania; *Jedność (Unity)* and *Gwiazda (The Star)* from Philadelphia, Pennsylvania; *Górnik (The Miner)* from Wilkes Barre, Pennsylvania; *Gwiazda Zachodu (Star of the West)* from Omaha, Nebraska, and *Pulaski Magazine* from Omaha, Nebraska.[111]

In 1938 Artur L. Waldo, the President of PAVA District VI, intiated the Year of the Polish Book under the sponsorship of the Polish American Council. At his suggestion the Polish Roman Catholic Union began publishing a Library of Writers of the Polish American Community, which published his work *An Outline of the History of Polish Literature in America* which was well received by scholarly circles in Poland.[112] That same year yet another book was published in Chicago, edited by Artur L. Waldo. It had the title *The War Effort In Soldierly Short Stories, Tales and Stories*. It contained short reminiscences from the years of the Polish Falcons of America activity in the United States, the recruitment operation for the Polish Army in France, training at the Niagara on the Lake camp, and military service in the Blue Army in France and Poland up to the Polish-Bolshevik war of 1919–1920. The following veterans were the authors of those narratives: Wojciech Albrycht, Władysław Borzęcki, Karol Burke, Stanisław Czuwara, Rev. Michał Godlewski, Józef Karaś, Stanisław Nastał,

---

110 *The Veteran* December 1924, p. 9
111 *The Veteran* November 1938, p. 20
112 T. Lachowicz, "Artur Leonard Waldo" (1896–1985) in: *The Veteran* October 1995, pp. 21-25

Janusz Ostrowski, Jan J. Przyprawa, Mieczysław Sichrawa, Stanisław Z. Stachowicz, Leonard Stefański, Rudolf Tarczyński, Franciszek Truszkiewicz, Artur L. Waldo, Franciszek J. Waluś and Marian Zawadzki.

Theater

It might be something of a surprise that amateur theatrical productions as well as plays which they staged by themselves, were very popular among PAVA veterans. The following data is evidence of the degree to which this form of entertainment was popular among former soldiers. In October 1921 the PAVA Board purchased various books in Poland—the largest position (50 percent) were scripts of stage plays. They were mostly light comedies by little known authors, but there were also some comedies by Moliere and dramas by Stanisław Wyspiański.[113]

Some of the PAVA posts prepared stage plays using their own resources. One of them was described in the January 1924 issue of *The Veteran*: "Post Nr. 6 in Cleveland, Ohio, which has been occupying its own premises for the last two years, is getting down to work. The Post's Dramatic Circle performed two plays twice in November. On the last Sunday of November the Post organized a celebration of the sixth anniversary of the founding of Independent Poland. It purchased a grand piano. It is organizing a singing circle. It is preparing to perform Żeromski's drama *Turoń* in January. The play is based on the massacre in Galicia."[114]

Artur L. Waldo, editor of *The Veteran* in the years 1931–1932, and also PAVA District VI president, was a great fan of the theater. In addition to his day job as a journalist he wrote plays for Polish American theater groups. From 1921–1932 he wrote more than thirty of them. Though not of highest quality, they nonetheless represent an interesting attempt to depict in dramatic form many of the actual problems that were part of Polish American community life.The best of them are: *Zamerykanizowani* (*The Americanized Ones*), *Felek Milioner* (*Felix the Millionaire*), *Król Ben* (*King Ben*), *Michalina w Ameryce* (*Michelle in America*), *Chicago w nocy* (*Chicago at Night*), *Mężobójczyni* (*The Husband-Killer Wife*), *Potępieniec* (*The Condemned Man*). A. L. Waldo's interest in the theater also bore fruit in the form of the book *Teatr Polski w Ameryce* (*Polish Theater in America*).[115]

His wife, Stefania Eminowicz, was a well known actress of the Polish American

---

113 PAVA NEB Archives, sign. A-XXVII/1 File: Dr. Teofil Starzyński. PAVA President. Correspondence 1921–1930, Letter of PAVA Secretary of October 10, 1921; *The Veteran* January 1924, pp. 14-15

114 *The Veteran* December 1924, p. 9

115 T. Lachowicz, "Artur Leonard Waldo (1896–1985). (Z dziejów dziennikarstwa polonijnego w Stanach Zjednoczonych)" ["Artur Leonard Waldo (1896–1985). (A History of Polish American Journalism in the United States)"] in: *Przegląd Polski [The Polish Review]* New York, October 12, 1995, pp. 10-11; *The Veteran* October 1995, pp. 21-25

stage. Thanks to her Waldo became well acquainted with the problems plaguing that environment, which during the Great Depression experienced especially difficult moments. In order for actors of the Polish stage in America to be eligible for financial aid from the Polish National Alliance, Artur L. Waldo wrote the By-Laws of the Tadeusz Eminowicz Polish Artists Society, which made it possible to register the actors as PNA Group 2689.[116]

Lectures

As part of ongoing educational activity, the PAVA Board recommended that its posts organize, to the extent of their capabilities, lectures by known persons. PAVA District VI with "Lwów" Post Nr. 7 in Detroit, Michigan in the lead, excelled in this.

Beginning in December 1927 Professor Józef Stemler, freshly arrived from Poland, gave a series of lectures at PAVA posts. He was the Director of the Polish Alma Mater. His lectures, illustrated with slides, pertained to the achievements of the Polish State and also to Polish history, geography, culture and art. In addition he conducted instructor courses for civic leaders, lecturers and educational speakers.[117]

The lectures of PAVA member Professor Rudolf Tarczyński were very popular. He was a former education officer in the Polish Army in France who after arriving in Poland was the editor of the *Dziennik Tczewski* (*The Tczew Daily*) in Tczew, and also the main organizer and vice-director of the Military Museum in Poznań.After returning to America he became a lecturer in the history of Polish Literature at the Orchard Lake Seminary in Orchard Lake, Michigan. He also taught Christian sociology and French language courses there. He lectured frequently in Chicago and Detroit on historical and literary themes. He also contributed articles to *Weteran* (*The Veteran*), *Przegląd Katolicki* (*The Catholic Review*), *Przegląd Muzyczny* (*The Musical Review*) and the monthly *Poland*.[118]

Veteran Orchestras and Schools of Polish Dance

Already by February 1921 former Blue Army soldiers had organized a thirty piece orchestra in Chicago. It was called the Haller Men Band. It was organized by B. Kulik, A. Dwojak, Jan and Józef Tomczyk, Stanisław Kopeć and Franciszek Jędryaszek. The conductors were: A. Dwojak, L. Hibner, Hebensroth and Prof. Wander Cook. Under their direction the Haller Men Band, which at first performed as part of PAVA Post Nr. 5, reached a good standard, thanks to which

---

116 PAVA NEB Archives, sign. Box-3/Pl.7 Collection: PAVA Posts; PAVA Post Nr. 7 in Detroit, MI, vol. 3
117 "Działalność oświatowa Kolegi prof. Rudolfa Tarczyńskiego w Detroit, MI" ["The Educational Activity of Colleague Professor Rudolf Tarczyński in Detroit, MI"] in: *Weteran [The Veteran]* October 1929, p. 27
118 "Działalność oświatowa Kolegi prof. Rudolfa Tarczyńskiego w Detroit, MI" ["The Educational Activity of Colleague Professor Rudolf Tarczyński in Detroit, MI"] in: *Weteran [The Veteran]* January 1929, p. 27

its performances began to attract a lot of interest. In the first, difficult years, when there was no money to pay a high class conductor, the orchestra members taxed themselves for this purpose. In recognition of its determination and progress it became the official orchestra of PAVA District I, and received permanent financial support from it. Under the auspices of PAVA District I the orchestra gave tens of public concerts, performing at special events and banquets, and also gracing many Polish American parades and manifestations.[119]

In Chicago the orchestra also accompanied the dancing couple of Janina Butkiewiczówna and C. Jankowski that was very well known at that time. They performed in almost all of the large cities in the United States and Mexico. It ought to be noted that C. Jankowski was a Blue Army veteran and in some of his dances he performed in a Blue Army uniform.[120]

With time American Army veterans also joined the Haller Men Band. Unfortunately, in 1931, due to misunderstandings inside PAVA District I, the orchestra left the District and joined the Alliance of American Army Veterans of Polish Descent Post Nr. 1, where it performed under a new name—World War Veterans Orchestra.[121]

PAVA Post Nr. 134 in Buffalo, NY also had its own orchestra made up of veterans. It was one of the first intitiatives of this post shortly after it was founded in 1933.[122]

Toward the end of the 1930s certain PAVA posts formed youth wind orchestras; their members were the children of veterans from the Sons and Daughters of Polish Army Veterans organization. They were active at Post Nr. 12 in Philadelphia, PA, Post Nr. 21 in New York, NY, and Post Nr. 111 in New Britain, CT. Their performances graced many a veteran event. Directed and financed by the veterans the youth orchestras were very popular among veteran children because of the effective costumes, the opportunity to participate in the most important Polish American and local events, and also the frequent visits to attractive localities.

With the young people in mind Czesław Sołczyk, member of PAVA Post Nr. 21 in New York, a professional dance and gymnastics instructor, formed the School of Polish Dance in September 1936. The program of his school included the teaching of classic dance, Polish folk dances, singing, Polish language instruction, the art of public speaking, and declamation of poetry. It was located on the premises of PAVA Post Nr. 21 at 73 Fourth Avenue in New York City.[123]

---

119 "Pięciolecie Orkiestry Hallerczyków przy 1-szym Okręgu SWAP w Ameryce" ["The Fifth Anniversary of the Haller Men Orchestra of PAVA Post Nr. 1"] in: *Weteran [The Veteran]* January 1926, p. 52
120 PAVA NEB Archives, sign. A-XVIII/2, File: Polish Consulate General in New York. 1921–1933
121 PAVA NEB Archives, sign. A-VIII/1, Collection: PAVA Districts, vol. 1
122 *The Veteran* October 1933, p. 21
123 *The Veteran* September 1936, p. 13

Celebrations and Patriotic Manifestations

Anniversary celebrations played an extremely important role in the cultural and educational activities of the Polish Army Veterans Association of America. They had patriotic and educational value, and had a positive influence on the preservation of Polishness and the internal integrity of the Polish American community. It ought to be emphasized, that in the area of patriotic education the veterans belonged to the most conscious group in the entire Polish American community. They were a living symbol of the greatest sacrifice for Poland, and for this reason, in general, they were surrounded with great respect. They themselves were perfectly aware of this and therefore shouldered the task of organizing and participating in all sorts of events of a patriotic character: commemorative meetings, parades, assemblies, etc. These were mainy organized on the occasion of important historical anniversaries, which filled up the annual events calendar in a specific manner:

- January Uprising (1863) anniversary
- May 3 Constitution parades
- Memorial Day
- August commemorations of the "Miracle on the Vistula"; October celebrations of the beginning of recruitment for the Polish Army in France
- November commemorations on the anniversary of Armistice on the Western Front in 1918, later combined with the commemoration of Polish Independence Day
- Anniversary of the outbreak of the November Uprising (1830)

These events were often organized together with American veteran organizations, especially the Polish Legion of American Veterans.

Aside from these events PAVA veterans participated in many other patriotic affairs—both Polish and American—whereby their presence reminded American society of the contribution of the Polish American community to the work of helping Poland to regain its independence, and of overcoming a common enemy, Germany and Austria-Hungary.

Here is a chronological listing of those events:

- November 1921—PAVA veterans in many cities participated in welcoming ceremonies for Ferdinand Foch, the Marshall of France. In Chicago the Polish veterans formed a battalion which paraded before the distinguished guest. They also kept an honor guard at the Lincoln Monument at the foot of which Marshall Foch laid a wreath. In Detroit more than 500 former soldiers of the Blue Army paraded before the Commander-in-Chief of the

French Armed Forces. The same happened in Pittsburgh and Philadelphia. In Cleveland Marshall Foch met with a PAVA delegation which included: S. Z. Stachowicz, S. Staniszewski, A. Wilkoń and J. Olkowski. He greeted them with the words: "A, soldats Polonais," ("Oh, Polish soldiers") and then he shook everybody's hand.[124]

- November 11, 1921—Polish Army Veterans Association of America participates in funeral ceremonies for the Unknown soldier of the American Army, which took place in Washington, D.C. and at Arlington National Cemetery. At the head of the PAVA delegation which consisted of veterans from Post Nr. 48 in Wilmington, DE and Post Nr. 12 in Philadelphia, PA stood Captain Stanisław Nastał, who laid a wreath from PAVA with the inscription: "Polish Army Veterans of America to our Brother in Arms the Unknown American Hero."[125]

- May 30, 1923—wreath laying ceremony at the Polish soldiers' cemetery in Niagara on the Lake, ONT, Canada. Polish Consul Straszewski of Montreal participated in this event along with veterans of local PAVA posts from the United States and Canada.[126] (The May meetings of veterans at the cemetery in Niagara on the Lake became an annual tradition).

- August 1923—A PAVA delegation including: W. Karolczak (PAVA Vice President), S. Nastał (in the uniform of a Lancer Captain), W. Grzywiński (in a Haller Army uniform) and a representative of the Association of Polish Invalids (who was visiting in the United States at that time) Lieutenant B. Frankowski, participated in the funeral of the suddenly deceased (August 2, 1923) U.S. President Warren G. Harding, who was buried in Marion, Ohio. The funeral organizing committee, surprised by the arrival of the Polish delegation in Army uniforms, very courteously assigned it a place in the parade marching order immediately following the representatives of the U.S. government and the U.S. Army. The Polish delegation placed a modest wreath with a red and white sash crossed by a black ribbon with the inscription: "Polish Army Veterans of America to our beloved President."[127]

---

124 PAVA NEB Archives, sign. A-XXVII/1, File: Dr. Teofil Starzyński. PAVA President. Correspondence 1921–1930; Letter of S. Z. Stachowicz to Dr. Starzyński of November 11, 1921; *The Veteran* Nr. 3, December 1921, p. 9

125 Ibid

126 PAVA NEB Archives, sign. A-XVIII/5, File:Polish Consulate in Montreal 1921–1933; Letter of PAVA NEB of June 1, 1923

127 "Delegacja SWAP na pogrzebie Prez. Hardinga w Marion, OH" ["PAVA Delegation at the Funeral of President Harding in Marion, OH"] in: *Weteran [The Veteran]* September 1923, p. 10

- November 11, 1925—Pittsburgh, PA. PAVA Posts Nr. 16, 41 and 61 participate in a great, 15,000 marchers-strong parade of World War I veterans. Dr. Teofil Starzyński, PAVA president, stood on the reviewing stand. After the parade PAVA District II was organized at a joint meeting of the above-named posts[128]

- July 4, 1926—trip of all the posts in PAVA District II to the Military Academy at West Point, NY where, beneath the statue of General Tadeusz Kościuszko, a great manifestation was held on the occasion of the 150th anniversary of the General's arrival in America.[129]

- September 5, 1926, Philadelphia, PA. Veterans of PAVA Posts Nr. 7, 12, 21, 25, 36, 51, 57, 77, 80, and 81 participated in "Polish Day" celebrations during a great exposition organized on the occasion of the 150th anniversary of U.S. Independence. PAVA Post 77 from Shenandoah, PA was there with all its members. The "Polish Day" celebration connected with the 150th anniversary of the arrival of Tadeusz Kościuszko in America gathered about 50,000 Polish Americans from local states. Polish Ambassador Jan Ciechanowski from Washington, D.C. also came. The culmination and most stirring moment was the hoisting of the Polish flag on the flag staff. Here is how Czesław Żuławski described this moment: "This was an unforgettable moment, when the army presented arms, the American Army orchestra played the Polish National Anthem, and our Polish flag sailed toward the sky and unfurled majestically at the top of the flag pole— the emblem of our nation's independence, for which our grandfathers and fathers fought and suffered, and which it has been given us to see. Truly we have been generously rewarded for our toil and sacrifice on behalf of regaining Poland's independence."[130]

- May 30, 1927—Chicago, IL—PAVA District I veterans march in a great parade of World War I veterans. Organized for Memorial Day this event had about 10,000 marchers. Of the non-American participants the Polish contingent was the most popular. They marched energetically in their blue uniforms to the tune of their own orchestra playing Polish military marches.[131]

---

128 The Veteran December 1925, p. 18
129 The Veteran July 1926, p. 11
130 Cz. Żuławski, "Niezapomniana chwila 'Dnia Polskiego' w Filadelfii" ["An Unforgettable Moment at 'Polish Day' in Philadelphia"] Weteran [The Veteran] October 1926, pp. 16-17
131 The Veteran June 1927, p. 53

- March 1929—visit of a PAVA delegation to Savannah, Georgia and to Washington, D.C. to discuss with American government officials the preparations for a joint commemoration in those two cities of the 150th anniversary of the death of General Kazimierz Pułaski. The PAVA delegation, headed by Dr. Teofil Starzyński (honorary PAVA president) and Kazimierz Bałdyga (PAVA president) had a forty minute audience with President Herbert Hoover at the White House. They discussed the project to construct a memorial mound honoring General Pułaski in Savannah, Georgia. President Hoover approved of the project, all the more so because the city of Savannah had secured the land on which the mound was to stand.[132] This plan, the brain child of the PAVA National Executive Board, did not come to fruition because the time (six months) which remained for the organizers to accomplish the task was too short, and there was lack of support from the largest Polish American organizations, such as the Polish National Alliance, the Polish Roman Catholic Union of America and the Polish Women's Alliance. Also, the funds needed for this purpose—about $150,000—were not forthcoming.[133]

- October 9–11, 1929—participation of PAVA veterans in the celebrations commemorating General Kazimierz Pułaski in Savannah and Washington. In Savannah, due to an unexpected flood, only the delegation from District I in Chicago took part, headed by commander Kostrubała. It was able to arrive by taking a circuitous route. On the other hand, after the ceremonies in Washington, D.C. President Herbert Hoover visited in front of the White House with a group of Polish veterans headed by Czesław Mrozowski (PAVA Secretary General) and with delegations from other Polish American organizations, thus giving yet another expression of his highly favorable view of the Poles, and especially of the former Polish soldiers. The following PAVA District and Post delegations participated in this meeting: District I (Chicago)—nine veterans, District III (Pennsylvania)—sixteen veterans, District VI (Michigan), Post Nr. 8 from St. Louis, Missouri—two veterans and Post Nr. 105 of Utica, NY—two veterans.[134]

- November 1930—PAVA posts commemorate the 100th anniversary of the November Uprising (1830). In the largest Polish American centers (Chicago,

---

132 PAVA NEB Archives, sign. A-XXXI/4, File: 150th Anniversary of the Death of K. Pułaski

133 K. Bałdyga, "Co zrobiono a czego nie zrobiono w sprawie uczczenia Kazimierza Pułaskiego" ["What Was Done and What Wasn't Done to Commemorate Kazimierz Pułaski"] in: *Weteran [The Veteran]* November 1929, pp 3-6, 16

134 *The Veteran* November 1929, p. 18

Detroit, New York, Buffalo, Pittsburgh) these celebrations were organized with the cooperation of Polish consulates.[135]

- October 11, 1931—PAVA posts participate in Pulaski Day celebrations, proclaimed once again by President Herbert Hoover, this time for the entire United States.[136] This commemoration became a permanent annual tradition.

- October 1932—celebrations of the fifteen anniversary of the commencement of recruitment for the Polish Army in France. These commemorations (lectures, parades, special religious services, etc.) were organized by PAVA together with the Polish Falcons of America. For this occasion PAVA created a new decoration: the Cross of Merit of the Polish Army from America.[137]

- August 1933—Celebrations of the 250th Anniversary of the Relief of Vienna combined with the consecutive anniversary of the "Miracle on the Vistula." On this occasion, for instance in Chicago, there was a huge manifestation of the local Polish American community with the participation of PAVA posts. An impressive parade of all Polish American organizations, which marched through the main streets of the city, ended with a gathering by the statue of Tadeusz Kościuszko in Humboldt Park, where a resolution was approved, in which the goal of the manifestation was clearly stated: "To remind the entire civilized world, constantly and for all time, of the two great historical events that affirm that Poland as a free nation twice saved Western culture and civilization from the horrific attack of untold hordes from the East."[138]

- June 6, 1935—participation in funeral commemorations honoring the deceased Marshall of Poland, Józef Piłsudski.[139]

- 1936—15th anniversary of PAVA celebrations. For this occasion the Association established the Medal of the Polish Army Veterans Association. It was bestowed on veterans who had been its active members for fifteen years without a break. The capping of the celebrations was the Great PAVA Jubilee Ball in New York on November 13, 1936 with the participation of the local diplomatic corps, representatives of city and state government, local Polish American community leaders and uniformed veterans of the American,

---

135 PAVA NEB Archives, sign. A-XVIII/3, File: Polish Consulate in Pittsburgh. 1921–1933
136 *The Veteran* October 1931, p. 8
137 PAVA NEB Archives, sign. A-XXXII/2, File: Celebrations of the 15th Anniversary of Recruitment for the Polish Army in France. 1932–1933
138 *The Veteran* August 1933, p. 24
139 *The Veteran* September 1935, p. 24

Canadian, French and Italian Armies. Fiorello La Guardia, the Mayor of New York City, was the honorary chairman of the ball, which testified to the recognition that Polish veterans enjoyed in the metropolitan New York region at that time.[140]

- August 1936—funeral commemorations honoring the tragically deceased General Orlicz-Dreszer.[141]

- January 31, 1937—Observance in New York on the occasion of the 59th anniversary of the death of General Włodzimierz Krzyżanowski—Polish war hero of the American Civil War of 1861–1865.

- October 10–11, 1937—PAVA representatives participated in the ceremony of the transfer of the remains of General W. Krzyżanowski from Brooklyn, NY to the National Cemetery at Arlington near Washington, D.C. Lucjusz Kajko, PAVA National Commander, was the Vice President of the Main Committee for the ceremony. Veterans of the Polish Army were part of the Honor Guard at Gen. Krzyżanowski's coffin. These PAVA members were all Chevaliers of the Order of Virtuti Militari: Józef Staszewski—PAVA Post Nr. 73 in Meriden, CT; Bogusław Przywarski—PAVA Post Nr. 57 in Elizabeth, NJ; Franciszek Kosiński—PAVA Post Nr. 18 in Schenectady, NY; Jan Wojtczuk—PAVA Post Nr. 85 in Bayonne, NJ; and Polish veterans of the American Army who had been decorated with the Distinguished Service Cross: Alojzy Kmotek of Brooklyn, NY; Wacław Soliński of Bayonne, NJ; Stanisław Kozikowski of Maspeth, NY; and Piotr Dachnowicz of the Bronx, NY.[142]

- October 1937–April 1938—celebrations of the 20th anniversary of the Polish American Community's War Effort under the aegis of the Polish Interorganizational Council and its Main Committee headed by Polish Falcons of America president and former PAVA president Dr. Teofil Starzyński. The PAVA National Executive Board sent out a special appeal to the Polish American community, which was published in virtually the entire Polish American press. PAVA purchased more than 20,000 commemorative lapel buttons, and printed several thousand copies of a souvenir edition of *The Veteran*. Thanks to the efforts of the committee to Celebrate the 20th Anniversary of the Polish American Community's War Effort, the Polish

---

140 *The Veteran* October 1936, p. 13

141 W. Łepski. "Z akademii żałobnej gen. Dreszera i obchodu sierpniowego w Passaic" [About the Funeral Commemoration of Gen. Dreszer and the August Observance in Passaic"] in: *Weteran [The Veteran]* September 1936, p. 21

142 *The Veteran* Spetmber 1937, p. 11

American community, with the active support of local PAVA posts, organized activities in the following cities:

September 12, 1937	Gary, Indiana
October 3, 1937	Bridgeport, Connecticut
October 17, 1937	West Lynn, Massachusetts; Jackson, Michigan; Syracuse, New York; Milwaukee, Wisconsin
October 31, 1937	Elyria and Lorain, Ohio; Johnson City, New York
November 7, 1937	Racine, Wisconsin; Hamtramck, Michigan
November 14, 1937	Bridgeport and New London, Connecticut; Passaic, New Jersey
November 21, 1937	Hammond, Indiana; Kensington, Illinois; Wyandotte, Michigan
November 25, 1937	Chicago, Illinois; New York, New York
November 28, 1927	Newark, New Jersey, St. Roman's Parish neighborhood in Chicago, Illinois
December 5, 1937	Town of Lake area in Chicago, Illinois; Detroit, Michigan; Scranton, Pennsylvania
December 12, 1937	Buffalo, New York; Cicero, Illinois; East Chicago, Indiana
April 10, 1938	Baltimore, Maryland[143]

Thanks to these celebrations and the events that accompanied them (commemorative meetings, banquets, etc.) significant funds were collected which augmented the bank accounts of local PAVA posts.

- 1937–1938—preparations and participation in ceremonies honoring the 330th anniversary of the arrival of the first Poles in America. Among former Blue Army soldiers the person who most distinguished himself in these celebrations was Artur L. Waldo, former editor of *The Veteran*, who by virtue of his promotional and information efforts gained acces to the White House, where he received the full approval of President Franklin D. Roosevelt. The latter in a personal letter of February 17, 1937 to the Polish journalist wrote: "Dear Mr. Waldo! I have found out with great interest that the first Poles

---

143 "Sprawozdanie Głównego Komitetu 20-lecia Czynu Zbrojnego Polonii Amerykańskiej" ["Report of the Main Committee for the 20th Anniversary of the Polish American Community's War Effort"] in: *Weteran [The Veteran]* May 1938, pp. 8-9

arrived in America in 1608. The research establishing the date of their arrival a year after the formation of the English colony at Jamestown by Captain John Smith, has great significance.

"From the first colonial days the Poles thus played an outstanding role in populating our country, in fighting for our freedom as a nation and in discovering new territories, which expanded our borders from the Atlantic all the way up to the Pacific Ocean.

"You will do a great service to our society by familiarizing it with the outstanding role that pioneers of Polish blood played in our history."

As this letter shows, the President of the United States first learned of the arrival of the first Poles in America already in 1608 and of their pioneering role, from a Polish veteran, who often later repeated: "…you cannot ever just rely on publications alone, even in English, until you have placed them almost by force in the proper hands with an appropriate letter and at the right moment."[144]

- May 14, 1938—a PAVA delegation participated in the unveiling and dedication of a monument on the grave site of Gen. W. Krzyżanowski at the National Cemetery in Arlington. This ceremony was honored by numerous delegations of American veteran societies: American Legion, Veterans of Foreign Wars of U.S., Disabled American Veterans of the World War, The GAR Loyal Legion of U.S. and representatives of the diplomatic corps. Poland was officially represented by: Polish Ambassador Count Jerzy Potocki, Consul General in New York Dr. Stanisław Gruszka and General Roman Górecki, President of FIDAC—the international federation of combatant societies. The ceremony was broadcast by radio all over the United States and also across the Atlantic to distant Poland![145]

- May 1, 1939—participation of the top PAVA Board officials in the Exposition Committee preparing the opening of the Polish pavilion at the New York World's Fair.[146]

From the listing of these events it is easy to notice how much weight they carried, and also that this activity was carried on and developed despite great difficulties. The

---

144 T. Lachowicz, "Artur Leonard Waldo (1896–1985)" in: *Weteran [The Veteran]* October 1995, pp. 21-25
145 *The Veteran* April 1938, p. 10
146 PAVA NEB Archives, sign. A-VII/1, File: PAVA NEB, Minutes of Meetings. 1939–1949. "Minutes of the Plenary Meeting of the PAVA National Executive Board of June 30, 1939

scope of these activities and their echo in the local communities contributed in a significant way to the shaping of a positive image of Poland and the Polish Army Veterans Association of America throughout the Polish American community and other ethnic groups in American society.

V.

PAVA Business Activity

How PAVA Posts Conducted Their Business

The Polish Army Veterans Association of America is a non profit, that is, a charitable organization. Thanks to this PAVA is exempt from federal taxes. The organization was allowed to carry on business, but the profit therefrom had to be designated for the needs of the Association. Moreover the activity had to be limited to its own members, for instance if a post opened up its own bar, it could only serve members. If the bar had a public character then taxes had to be paid: either local or state, depending on local laws.

The same was true of income-producing events, such as dances, movies, and theatrical productions.

Thanks to this form of activity the posts in some instances built up significant assets in the form of cash reserves as well as buildings and recreational areas. These assets could not be taken over by PAVA members and divided among them, beause that would have been against federal law, and carried painful penal consequences.

The ways in which the PAVA posts came by their at times significant assets were similar. It was always a long and very intense effort, stretched out over decades. It always began with the proverbial zero. As a rule the work was started by a small group of veterans, often inspired by a local Polish pastor. Their enthusiasm and determination mobilized others. Commemorative meetings were organized and dances, picnics and entertainment of various sorts, as also bazaars, trips and fundraisers for various causes, of which the most popular was the so-called blue cornflower.

In this work the veterans, on their own free time, step by step, contributed to the enlargement of their posts' bank accounts. The ladies from the Auxiliary Corps supported them in this work, helping to make many a veteran event a success by their support. For many PAVA posts the Auxiliary Corps became their mainstay.

In the course of work that was both tedious and of many years' duration, there was frequent friction, tussling, even serious conflicts and abuses, some of which ended in collegial arbitration and resulted in banishment from the organization. This happened for instance in 1931 at the General Assembly in Pittsburgh, Pennsylvania, where Kazmierz Bałdyga, the PAVA President, accused of poor financial management to the detriment of the organization, was banished from the ranks of the organization. This decision was preceded by several months of internal organizational investigation by the Investigations Committee, a judgement of the Honor Court which suspended his PAVA membership rights and a referendum conducted at the PAVA posts.[1]

But these were only sporadic happenings which proved that PAVA is an organization based on democratic principles, where no quarter is given to those who break the rules of the PAVA By-Laws, regardless of the office they may hold in the Association.

Jan Wójcik and Mieczysław Kierkło, in their work *A History of the Immigrant Soldier*, gave an excellent description of the asset-building process by individual PAVA posts, using the example of Post Nr. 111 in New Britain, Connecticut.[2] That post, active since 1920, did not join PAVA until 1930. What its asset-building process looked like in the years 1920–1939 is depicted by the annual listings below:

- 1922—the bank account of the Independent General J. Haller Post of Polish Veterans of the World War stood at $497.70. Post meetings were held at the local Falcons hall;

- 1923—The bank account stood at $929.91

- 1925—The account held $1,470.65

- 1927—the Post rented space for its club at 15 Broad Street. A canteen was started there with a loan from the Post's own bank account and from the veterans themselves. It was paid off several months later. In just the one month of December the canteen had a profit of $211.35;

- 1928—the Post rented new, more appropriate space, for which a clock was purchased and a telephone installed. A better system of managing the place's business activities and a buffet was introduced;

- 1929—the Post's bank account showed the sum of $3,938.69. Better, more comfortable premises were rented at 121 Broad Street, and supplied with appropriate furniture at an expense of $367. The monthly rent was $50. Thanks to these changes the Post now had at its disposal several smaller rooms and a large dance hall. The entrance fee for such a dance varied from 10 cents to 15 cents;

---

1   PAVA NEB Archives, sign. A-XXVII/5
2   J. Wójcik, M. Kierkło, *Z dziejów żołnierza-emigranta. Historia "Haller Post" in New Britain [A History of the Immigrant Soldier. The Story of the Haller Post in New Britain]* New Britain 1991

- 1930—the Post joined PAVA, and was registered as Nr. 111. On October 5 the local organizations and Polish American societies held a bazaar on its behalf. The profit from this event was the sizeable sum of $256.22;

- 1932—PAVA Post Nr. 111 had assets worth $7,936.73;

- 1933—the bank account shrank to $5,018.14. During this period financial subsidies were paid out to 28 unemployed and sick members of the Post;

- 1935—at the end of this year its assets in bank accounts, loans and cash on hand amounted to $5,188.79. Plus there was a Relief Fund in the amount of $2,586.45. Together that gave $7,775.24;

- 1936—a period of economic stability began for the Post, thanks to which the premises were renovated, a cash register was purchased for the canteen and the Post's office, and a new radio, a desk with armchair and eighteen chairs were acquired. By the end of the year the Post's assets were $12,458.80;

- 1938—at the beginning of the year the Post's assets were $14,876.99. Three quarters later they stood at $17,516.22;

- 1939—PAVA Post Nr. 111 in New Britain, CT noted in its account the sum of $4,781.97 thanks to which the over-all assets came in at $22,298.19.[3]

The Post wasn't just concentrating on generating funds to grow its assets. For almost twenty years it supported those members who were in the most difficult life circumstances and subsidized various social initiatives, mainly charitable ones. During the ten first, most difficult, years the Post paid out from its funds $2,151 in subsidies for the sick, $126 in one-time relief grants, $459 for humanitarian and social purposes. During this time $620 was spent on necessary furniture and equipment. The total was $3,356.[4] The proportion of money spent on the Post's needs in comparison to social needs shows clearly the charitable nature of PAVA Post Nr. 111 in New Britain, Connecticut.

Some PAVA posts during the period between the world wars, due to proper management, were able to purchase their own buildings. Most of them were obtained with mortgage loans at extraordinarily low interest rates during the Great Depression of 1929–1932. Part of them were immediately adapted for ad hoc shelters for unemployed veterans, for instance in Chicago and Milwaukee.

In the case of many PAVA posts their dynamic development would not have been

---

3   Ibid., pp. 8-22
4   Ibid., p. 13

possible without strong backing from the Polish American community, its generosity, understanding, and support of the veteran cause. It should be stated generally that the wealthiest and strongest PAVA posts existed in well organized Polish American communities. They were a visible symbol of the cooperation and solidarity of the local Polonia. They helped each other. The veterans were given access to premises for meetings, the I. J. Paderewski Invalid Fund was supported many times; the community participated in social events, at which all had a good time, at the same time helping build up funds. Help was also rendered in the maintenance of the shelters, and flags were purchased for some of the PAVA posts, for instance the publisher of *Kurier Narodowy* (*National Courier*) in New York, Emil S. Brykczyński, paid for the flags of several posts out of his own pocket, among others Post Nr. 24 in Bridgeport, CT, and Post Nr. 129 in Stamford, Ct.[5]

When a PAVA post got a mortgage loan to buy a building for its needs, then the local Polish American community attended events organized by the veterans to help them pay off their financial obligations. The day (usually celebrated with a banquet) when the last mortgage payment had been made and the mortgage document on the veteran's home was burned in front of all the gathered guests, was always a big event in the life of such a post and of the local Polish American community.

When the financial situation of PAVA posts stabilized, then the veterans helped others, participating in their events, rendering financial support and giving access to their premises for the needs of those organizations which did not have their own place yet.

The Independent Economic Activity of PAVA Members

Former Blue Army soldiers upon returning to the United States after the war, found work, often with great difficulty, in various sectors of the American economy. In the main they worked in factories, construction companies or on farms. It is not possible to cite concrete data because there is a total lack of any sort of statistics concerning the Polish ethnic group. This also concerns PAVA members, who in the best period of the organization's development constituted barely one third of all former soldiers of the Polish Army who had returned to America. Unfortunately, membership files did not require those who had just joined to give information about their place of employment. Thus we only have fragmentary data, which can be fished out of the pages of *The Veteran* and from inter-organizational correspondence. *The Veteran* has the most information: members of the organization who ran their own businesses advertised in it. In February 1922 information was published together with an ad for

---

5   *The Veteran* May 1936, p. 54; *The Veteran* July 1936, p. 10

the "Hallerczyk Cigar Co." in Chicago, Illinois, which was founded by several Blue Army veterans. Unfortunately, we don't know their names.

The company, as the ad states, produced "fine cigars made of good leaf, without any additives." It began its activity from a tiny space with three workers. It soon became known on the local, Polish American market, that their product was good and well priced, thanks to which they received many orders. Soon *The Veteran* could inform its readers that the company "Hallerczyk Cigar Co." "…has gained the full confidence and support of the local Polish American community, so that today, aside from its tiny factory they have opened a second larger one at 1121 Milwaukee Avenue in Chicago, Illinois, in a three story rear building. This happened only thanks to the quality of production and business savvy."[6] This company fortunately survived the Great Depression years (1929–1932) and in 1934 it changed its name to "Weteran A.P. Cigar Co." and advertised itself as the largest Polish cigar factory, producing cigars under the "Veteran" name. Now the quarters of the company were relocated to Nr. 24 141 Canton Street. This company's last ad in the PAVA press organ appeared in December 1935. Is it possible that the change of name hurt it?

Another example of a Polish American veteran who became a successful businessman was Henryk Godek, a volunteer from America who joined the Blue Army in France. He participated in battles in France in 1918 and in the Polish-Bolshevik war in 1920. After returning to America he settled in Chicopee, Massachusetts where after some time he opened his own restaurant. He employed mostly Polish veteran colleagues in it. The professionally run business developed well and with the passage of years H. Godek with his sons Theodore and Kazimierz opened a chain of restaurants in the Springfield—Chicopee area. A Polish veteran in need could always count on support from H. Godek. "During the Great Depression his generosity was without a par. He gave veteran-colleagues, who asked him for help in difficult times, weekly $5 meal tickets to his restaurant. When the depression ended many wanted to pay off the debt they had incurred. Colleague Godek called all of his "debtors" over to his restaurant, and told them that they owed him nothing and as proof of what he said he burnt the account book in which he had recorded the meal tickets. The total sum was quite large for those times." Thus wrote *The Veteran* (February 1975, p. 25). Henryk Godek was the co-founder of PAVA Post Nr. 158 in Chicopee and its commander for many years. He bought a building for the Post at the bargain price of $10,000. Thanks to his thriftiness that sum was paid off in just two years. For many years thereafter Godek was the manager of the building. Henry Godek also participated in other organizations. He was the president of the Polish American

---

6   *The Veteran* February 5, 1922, p. 16

Civic Club in Chicopee and of the Political Club for Hampden County. He was the founder and treasurer of the Polish American Club for the State of Massachusetts. On behalf of these organizations he helped to elect several Americans of Polish descent to offices in local and state government.

In 1929 he was elected to the Chicopee city council and became the council chairman. During the mayor's long illness he stood in for him. In 1938 he was instrumental, as a member of the selection committee, in the federal government's choice of the Chicopee area for the North-East Air Force Base. This had a serious impact on the economic development of the city and the growth of its residents' prosperity.

The "Auto Repair Shop" was located in Chicago. It was founded by Blue Army veteran E. M. Basowski—a member of PAVA Post Nr. 2 and Vice President of PAVA District I. In advertising this company *The Veteran* wrote: "Colleague Basowski completed a number of courses in this area of technical expertise before the war, and after returning from the war he finished a technical school, so we cordially commend his repair shop to all our automobile owning colleagues and sympathizers, because knowing him to be a good mechanic, we believe that by recommending him we are doing our sympathisers a favor."[7]

Another Hallerian, Jan Mruz of Detroit, Michigan advertised his "First Class Clothes Repair Shop."[8] His colleague from nearby Hamtramck, M. Domienik, informed *The Veteran's* readers: "...I have taken over a haberdashery, under the name Domienik & Bros. We always accept all tailoring work and dry cleaning.

"I am a veteran, a Hallerian and ask my comrades in arms for their support. Why go to somebody else when I, your Colleague, will give you the same service."[9]

Both the ads, for verification, had photographs of the owners, in which they are visible in army uniforms from their days in France.

Captain Stanisław Nastał's company "Poland's Film Exchange" was well known among the veterans and the wider Polish American community. It did movie distribution and screenings of movies imported from Poland.[10]

A product that was produced in 1935 with PAVA's permission was a bronze souvenir clock which was ideally suited for PAVA posts. On its façade were the figures of two armed soldiers of the Blue Army, and above them a sacred flame as a symbol of victory and the inscriptions: "Honor of the Moment," and "For Your Fatherland" with the dates 1917–1920. Above the clock face was the PAVA emblem: the Cross of Volunteers from America.

---

7   *The Veteran* June 1928, p. 27
8   *The Veteran* January 1929, p. 29
9   *The Veteran* February 1930, p. 20
10   PAVA NEB Archives, sign. A-XVII/52

Jan J. Uszyński of Newark, New Jersey, a former Blue Army soldier in France, was the creator of the idea and the producer of the clock. The designer was sculptor Jan Skiba. Part of the profits from the sale of these clocks ($3.50 per piece for the regular version and $4.50 for the gilded version) were designated by the producer for the I. J. Paderewski Invalid Fund.[11]

Agnieszka Wisła, the first president of the PAVA Auxiliary Corps also ran her own business. After returning to America from Poland in 1921 she opened a flag, banner, standard and badge workshop called "Wisła's Art Shop." Many PAVA posts and districts ordered their flags from her. The PAVA Board commissioned a PAVA standard from her workshop. It was dedicated in an official ceremony on November 18, 1923 in Cleveland, Ohio with the participation of General Józef Haller who was in the United States at that time.[12] It should be added here that Agnieszka Wisła's company had a very good reputation and was active without interruption up to her death in 1980.

The Veterans' Workshop

An interesting business initiative ventured by PAVA was the organization of workshops for veterans who were war invalids and unemployed. This idea was born in the years of the Depression, when unemployment dealt a painful hand to members of the Association. At that time PAVA district I in Chicago, District II in New York and District VI in Detroit were pondering how to make the idea work. Yet after several years the idea took root only in PAVA District II in New York, where at the suggestion of PAVA Post Nr. 25 commander Jan J. Uszyński (the above-mentioned watchmaker) a decision was made in 1937 to organize a veteran workshop at the temporary district shelter, which a few months earlier had been moved from Passaic, NJ to Newark. This workshop, functioning together with the shelter in a large rented building at 203 Morris Avenue, officially began its activity on April 1, 1938, specializing in small wood products. Under the experienced supervision of Bronisław Wodyński, a sculpture instructor from the famous Zakopane School of Sculpture, invalids and the unemployed in a short time learned how to craft small items out of wood, for instance trays, ash trays, picture frames, vases, Polish eagles on coats of arms, various kinds of boxes, etc., which PAVA posts and the Auxiliary Corps gladly purchased and used as rewards for various lotteries organized by them and also as holiday gifts. The products of this workshop were even sold in distant cities, as for instance Pittsburgh, PA, Detroit, MI, and Chicago, IL.[13]

---

11   *The Veteran* March 1935, p. 15
12   *The Veteran* May 1928; PAVA NEB Archives; AO: File: Agnieszka Wisła
13   *The Veteran* April 1938, p. 11

A surviving financial report of the workshop shows that, from September 11, 1938 to January 1, 1939 production costs totaled $254.42, while sales income on the products was $354.42. In other words there was a $100 profit.[14]

A steady job for nine invalids was an invaluable success. Despite their years they again believed that regardless of their handicaps they could earn their keep and not be a burden on the Polish American community.

The workshop's success brought it great renown in veterans' circles. The workshop was visited by activists from many PAVA districts. Encouraged by what they saw, they tried similar projects in their own districts. Unfortunately, the outbreak of World War II removed those plans to a distant future.

The Information Office

Yet another form of business activity engaged in by the Polish Army Veterans Association of America was the organization in 1922 of an Information Office at the PAVA Headquarters in Cleveland. It did money transfers to Poland, assisted in bringing Polish families to the USA, and sold steamship tickets. This office (described in greater detail in the subchapter "Other Forms of Mutual Aid") brought a profit in the years 1922–1925 of $2,263.54. This was a significant sum, which paid the rent for the PAVA National Executive Board offices and covered administrative and office expenses: office staff, the cost of telegrams, telephones, etc.[15]

PAVA Assets and Finances

In the period 1921–1939 the assets of the Polish Army Veterans Association of America, aside from membership dues, modest business activity and the sporadic donations of wealthy patrons, mainly consisted of sums collected during fundraisers in the Polish American community, for instance for the I. J. Paderewski Invalid Fund and the Settlement Fund. The PAVA National Executive Board was in charge of these sums.

The Association's assets were built systematically by the individual posts, districts, the PAVA Board and the auxiliary organizations, especially the Auxiliary Corps and the Alliance of Friends of Polish Army Veterans. The PAVA posts kept some of those funds for themselves, and gave the rest for the needs of the districts or directly to the central headquarters, that is the PAVA Board, known from 1934 on as the PAVA National Executive Board (NEB).

---

14 "Sprawozdanie finansowe Warsztatu Pracy i Schroniska II Okręgu SWAP w Newark NJ za okres 11 IX 1938-1 I 1939" ["Financial Report of the PAVA District II Workshop and Shelter in Newark, NJ for the period September 11, 1938 to January 1, 1939"] in: *Weteran [The Veteran]* March 1939, p. 22

15 PAVA NEB Archives, sign. A-XVII/29, Financial Report of Income and Expenses of the Information Office for the period November 1, 1922 to March 30, 1925.

In this manner, with the passage of time, the posts built up a separate asset base, as did the districts and the PAVA Board. For this reason it is difficult to describe the overall financial status of the organization. The reports submitted at all PAVA general assemblies divulged the over all financial status only in terms of assets managed directly by the PAVA Board without taking into consideration the financial status of the posts and districts, which was a substantial sum that consisted of buildings, land and cash in bank accounts.

The following PAVA districts and posts owned their own buildings prior to World War II:

- PAVA District I in Chicago, IL, a large two story building at 1239 N. Wood Street, purchased in 1934;

- PAVA Distict VI, a shelter purchased in 1932 in Wanda Park near Detroit, MI;

- PAVA Post Nr. 1 in Buffalo, NY, a building purchased in 1928;[16]

- PAVA Post Nr. 3 in Milwaukee, WI, a building purchased in 1931 at 1629 South 10th Street;[17]

- "Lwów" Post Nr. 7 in Detroit, MI, building purchased in 1923;[18]

- PAVA Post Nr. 12 in Philadelphia, PA, building purchased in 1929 at 2733 E. Clearfield Street;

- PAVA Post Nr. 78 in Detroit, MI, building purchased in 1934 at 4959 Martin Street.[19]

- PAVA Post Nr. 85 in Bayonne, NJ, a four-story building purchased in 1937 from the city together with an acre of land that adjoins it;[20]

- PAVA Post Nr. 113 in Hamtramck, MI, building purchased in 1938.[21]

---

16 PAVA NEB Archives, sign. A-VI/7; Organizational Circular Nr. 20, February 14, 1928
17 *The Veteran* May 1931, p. 25
18 *The Veteran* October 1947, p. 42
19 *Pamiętnik 55 Zjazdu Okręgu VI SWAP [PAVA District VI 55th General Assembly Souvenir Journal]* Detroit, September 1–2, 1984
20 *The Veteran* May 1951, pp. 47-50; *The Veteran* April 1961, p. 7
21 G. J. Hadrych. *History of the Stefan Starzyński Post Nr. 113 in Hamtramck, MI (typescript)*, p. 6 in: Central Polish American community Archive at Orchard Lake, MI, collection: PAVA District VI Archive, Collection of PAVA Post Nr. 113 in Hamtramck, MI.

These assets were neither taken into consideration in the annual reports of the PAVA National Executive Board, nor in reports presented at the general assemblies. From those reports it appears that the general financial status of PAVA in the particular years was as follows:

1922	$113,391.43
1924	$ 95,751.17
1926	$112,682.50
1928	$100,757.71
1929	$100,537.53
1934	$133,360.89
1937	$ 85,509.92
1940	$ 80,170.01[22]

The cited figures included bank accounts, stocks and bonds, loans made, and real estate (the farm at Kuligi in Pomerania, Poland, etc.). Cash was held in bank accounts, in accordance with the rule of diversification, that is, bank accounts were held in various banks. Thanks to this rule great losses were averted during the stock market crash of 1929. No more than $5,500 held in PAVA accounts was frozen in banks in Chicago and Detroit.[23]

PAVA had no luck with its investments in Poland. The farm in Kuligi, shares in the Military Settlement Cooperative in Warszawa and in the "OSKRES" Cooperative in Równe all had losses. The only successful investment seemed the Polish government bonds. In 1937 they were worth about 27,000 zlotys. Unfortunately, the outbreak of war in 1939 forced PAVA to write this investment off as a loss as well (more details on this subject in the subchapter "PAVA's Business Activity in Poland").

---

22   PAVA NEB Archive, sign. A-II/2-6; A-XI/2
23   PAVA NEB Archives, sign. A-II/8, *Report of the Officers of the PAVA National Executive Board for the 7th PAVA General Assembly in Rochester, NY for the period 1934 to 1937*, p. 37

VI.
PAVA's Cooperation with the Socio-Political Emigré Milieu

The Role of the Roman Catholic Church in PAVA Life
In the Polish émigré milieu in the United States and Canada the leading role was unquestionably played by the clergy of the Roman Catholic Church. For their parishioners they were the most important support in a foreign land. For them the Polish priest was an irreplaceable confidant in many matters, from the purely personal to problems arising from the language barrier, which the Polish émigrés were unable to overcome for a long time. In those situations the faithful came to their priest, who (being an educated man) also knew English, thanks to which he was able to help in many matters, for instance at American agencies and banks. For these reasons the Polish clergy enjoyed unquestioned authority among their parishioners.

The influence which the patriotically minded Polish clergy (from bishop down to vicar) had on the faithful was particularly evident during the recruitment drive for the Polish Army in France that was held across the United States and Canada in the years 1917–1919. In response to appeals from the pulpit men reported en masse to the recruiting stations. When in some instances these appeals were not sufficient, the clergy were able to apply rather original forms of pressure on those who balked. That is what Reverend Józef Kuta of Elyria, Ohio did, who "refused to perform the marriage ceremony for young men until they had enlisted in the Polish Army."[1]

Aside from making appeals for enlistment in the ranks of the Polish Army that was being organized in France, many Polish clergy also supported this action materially by organizing fundraisers.

---
1 D. Piątkowska. "Duchowieństwo polskie w Stanach Zjednoczonych Ameryki wobec rekrutacji ochotników do Armii Polskiej we Francji (1917–1919)" ["The Polish Clergy in the United States of America and the Recruitment of Volunteers to the Polish Army in France (1917–1919)"] in: *Niepodległość. Z historii polskiej myśli społecznej i politycznej [Independence. A History of Polish Social and Political Thought]* W. Piątkowska-Stepaniak and L. Rubisz, eds., Opole 1999, p. 137; PAVA NEB Archives, gr. XXX/vol. 5

The broad scope of engagement of some of the clergy in the recruitment drive is clearly visible in the fact that the recruitment officer in Center Nr. 41 in New Britain, CT was the Rev. Lucjan Bójnowski, a great civic leader in that region. Thanks to his great authority, which held sway everywhere, and to his personal engagement, New Britain was the leader in this action, supplying 965 volunteers, which was almost one third of all the men in that Parish.[2] Moroever nineteen priests decided to follow the faithful, also enlisting in the ranks of the Polish Army. After training in the camp at Niagara on the Lake they left with their detachments for France, where they fulfilled the duties of Catholic chaplains in the Polish Army in various divisions, regiments, camps and military hospitals. They accompanied the units during the military campaign in France and Poland. One of them, Rev. Jan Dekowski, was decorated with the Order of Virtuti Militari for his participation in a military campaign. After demobilization some of the priests remained in Poland, for instance Rev. Zygmunt Rydlewski. But most of them returned to their parishes in America, where they were held in high regard by the faithful. These clergymen, having directly experienced the war-time fate of the volunteers from America, actively engaged themselves in the life of the first veteran clubs that were being formed, on the basis of which the Polish Army Veterans Association of America was later created. In their religious posts they were initiators and organizers of veteran organizations. That was the case of Blue Army chaplains Rev. Colonel Jan Dekowski of Toronto, Ontario, Canada and Rev. Major Aleksander Kowalski of Utica, New York.[3]

They were assisted in this work by priests who had actively supported the recruitment effort of 1917–1919. Among the most active was Rev. Lucjan Bójnowski, thanks to whom the local Polish American community there was the only one in the entire United States that was properly prepared to receive its volunteers upon their return from the war. Also at his suggestion already in May 1920 a veteran association was formed in New Britain, called the "Polish Veterans of the World War." Reverend Bójnowski gave the first $300 for its purposes and paid the membership dues of the newly joined members for six months in advance.[4]

It should be added that the governing board of the Polish Army Veterans Association of America, founded in 1921, fully appreciated the great role that the

---

2   Ibid., p. 138; "Praca Polonii w New Britain, CT na rzecz niepodległości Polski w latach 1915–1920" ["The Work of the Polish American Community in New Britain, CT on Behalf of Polish Independence in the Years 1915–1920"] in: *Weteran [The Veteran]* August 1998, pp. 7-12

3   Z. Choromański. *Działalność duchowieństwa w Stowarzyszeniu Weteranów Armii Polskiej w Ameryce w latach 1921–1939.* [*Activity of the Clergy in the Polish Army Veterans Association of America in the years 1921–1939*] A Master's dissertation written under the supervision of Rev. Professor Dr. Zygmunt Zieliński of the Department of Theology of the Catholic University of Lublin 1988, pp. 26-27

4   J. Wójcik, "Haller Post 111. Diamond Jubilee" in:*75 Years of Post Nr. 111*, New Britain 1995, p. 7 (A Souvenir Journal)

Polish clergy played during the recruitment drive for the Polish Army in France in the years 1917–1919. Many of them were recommended for the "Haller Swords" decoration bestowed by the Union of Hallerians in Poland. On the list of persons designated to receive this decoration in the years 1924–1926 were the names of 227 priests from seventeen states in the United States. Most of them came from the state of Pennsylvania—55, next came Illinois with 33 and Michigan with 22.[5]

In the years 1920–1921 in many of the newly established veteran clubs and societies the Polish Catholic priest, at the request of the young veterans, took on the role of chaplain, for instance the Rev. Wawrzyniec Cyman was the chaplain of the Gen. Józef Haller Society of Polish Army Veterans founded in Chicopee, MA in August of 1920.[6]

At the PAVA founding meeting in Cleveland Ohio (May 28–30, 1921) there was a discussion about having a chaplain for the new organization. We read in the report from the convention: "It appears that the veterans, who had their own chaplains while on active duty, ought to have them in civilian life. During the election of the Board it was approved to appoint an honorary chaplain." The delegates to that convention chose Rev. Łukasik of Buffalo, NY.[7]

According to the PAVA By-Laws the PAVA Board had the right to appoint a head chaplain.[8] But his role was limited to an advisory voice at PAVA general assemblies or meetings of the PAVA Board. The presence of the chaplain at important organizational meetings had a calming effect on their course, restraining the hot-heads from violent outbursts, thanks to which it was possible to devote the time to quality discussion and the resolution of concrete problems in a calm atmosphere. The chaplain administered the oath of office to newly elected PAVA Post or District Boards.

In the years 1921–1939 the head PAVA chaplains (at that time they were called honorary chaplains) were the following priests: Rev. Karol Łukasik, Rev. Marian Godlewski and Rev. Antoni Wojcieszczuk.

The most visible symptom of the close ties between PAVA and the clergy was the activity of chaplains in PAVA organizational ranks. They participated vigorously in the life of their posts and districts. Flag and veteran home consecration ceremonies took place with their participation, as did commemorative meetings and holiday get togethers, such as the traditional blessing of the food (święconka) and breaking of

---

5   D. Piątkowska "The Polish Clergy..." op. cit., pp. 132-136
6   "Życiorys Tow. Weteranów Armii Polskiej im. Generała Józefa Hallera, Plac. 168, w Chicopee, Mass." ["A Biography of the General Józef Haller Polish Army Veterans Society, Post Nr. 168 in Chicopee, Mass."] in: *Weteran [The Veteran]* May 1941, p. 82
7   "Historyczny protokół" ["Historic Minutes"] in: *The Veteran* May 1951, pp. 22, 26
8   "Konstytucja i Regulaminy Stowarzyszenia Weteranów Armii Polskiej w Ameryce" ["The By-Laws and Regulations of the Polish Army Veterans Association of America"] Chicago 1925, p. 9

the Christmas Wafer (opłatek), and also the saddest ceremonies—funerals. None of these events could be imagined without the participation of a chaplain or other Roman Catholic priest.

The veterans did not accept the participation of clergy from the Polish National Catholic Church because they felt resentment to the "national" priests for their policy during the recruitment action for the Polish Army in France in the years 1917–1919. At that time the Polish National Catholic Church was against that action, and actively backed the National Defense Committee (Komitet Obrony Narodowej—KON).[9]

The nature of the role which chaplains played in PAVA's organizational life is best exemplified by the following fragment from a posthumous reminiscence about Rev. Józef Lempka, chaplain of PAVA District VI who died on August 12, 1932 in Detroit, MI: "You have left us. You have orphaned us. A huge void remains after your passing, as after a good, loving father. Only memories and your teachings—only the healthy seeds sown by your hand in our hearts have remained.

"And who will step into your place for us? Who will teach us God's justice and love of one's neighbor with such cordial words, who will encourage us to work, to sacrifice, to devote ourselves to Poland? Who will give us not only teachings and words, but also live action and a living example? What will all our celebrations, anniversaries and national observances look like without you?

"… It was your principle to marry Polish Army veterans free of charge, baptize the children of veterans free of charge, conduct veteran funerals free of charge—who will step into your shoes, most worthy Priest, in that selfless and heartfelt function?"[10]

Facts connected with the visit in the United States of Wilno Archbishop Rev. Jan Cieplak, who had been incarcerated earlier for several years in Bolshevik prisons, testify to the strong ties of the young veterans' organization that PAVA was, with the Roman Catholic Church. During his three month stay in America the Archbishop visited 375 Polish parishes and many PAVA posts, including those in New York City, Buffalo and Chicago, where he gave over 800 homilies and patriotic speeches in which he appealed to harmonious cooperation between countrymen living abroad and resistance to indifference to Poland's needs. The bishop's death due to illness and exhaustion on Febraury 17, 1926 at St. Mary's hospital in Passaic, NJ was a great shock for everyone, and especially for the veterans, to whom the deceased was particularly close due to his trials in Bolshevik Russia, that Russia with which they had fought in 1919–1920. The PAVA posts of Distict II, headed by President of the Board Stanisław J. Wilk, participated in the funeral ceremonies of Rev. Archbishop

---

9   D. Piątkowska "Duchowieństwo polskie…" op. cit., p. 140
10 K. Burke "Nad świętą mogiłą naszego Przyjaciela i Opiekuna" ["At the Holy Grave of Our Friend and Protector"] in: *Weteran [The Veteran]* August 1931, p. 7

Cieplak. Veterans in blue uniforms formed the honor guard at the coffin.[11]

The role of Catholic priests—spiritual guides for Polish veterans in America—was significant. Often the existence of the local PAVA post depended to a large extent on the personal attitude of the priests toward the veterans and on an understanding of their needs. Without the overt support and engagement of priests in the numerous activities undertaken by the veterans it was hard to count on success. Where the veterans had priests in their favor, there the posts blossomed and developed. Appeals to the community from the pulpit to support the veterans always worked. Where there was no support the results were the most meager, because it was only with the approval of the priests that fundraising could be done in front of the churches, where the largest sums were usually collected.

Unfortunately, Polish priests favorable to the veterans were not to be found in every parish. These facts were noted with bitterness already in 1922 during a great fund drive arranged by PAVA to create the Settlement and Invalid Fund. Lucjan Adamczak, who was in charge of that activity, spoke about this without beating around the bush during the deliberations at the 2nd PAVA General Assembly in Chicago in May 1922: "Of the clergy I place Rev. Bishop Rhode in first place. The clergy divided itself into two sections during our campaign. Some worked and even sent in donations, others wouldn't even think of rendering any sort of help. Not one priest helped us in Buffalo, with the exception of Rev. Chaplain Łukasik, who overextended himself on our behalf. Rev. Dr. Pitas in Black Rock also worked with us. The same in Philadelphia. There the following priests worked very hard: Stachowicz and Zbytniewski. In Detroit, Rev. Lempka. In Cleveland all the priests worked to help us and the indefatigable Rev. Pastor Orzechowski was outstanding."[12]

The same was true of other fundraisers organized by PAVA. The greatest difficulties occurred in Roman Catholic parishes that were headed by pastors of Irish descent. One of them, for instance, said of his Polish parishioners: "what do they need some kind of Poland for," it is enough that they support their own parish, and "after death they will reign in Heaven with the Lord Jesus and Our Lady." One of the Polish parishioners wrote about this to the PAVA Board on August 30, 1923. He reacted as follows to his pastor's statement: "I, however, as an unbeliever prefer to contribute something toward Poland's needs than toward the Roman Church or an Irish seminary. I enclose herewith a postal money order for $10 for the Polish invalid soldiers. Stanisław Gądek (Polish laborer)."[13]

---

11 *The Veteran* March 1926, p. 23; April 1926, p. 18
12 PAVA NEB Archives, sign. II/1 Minutes of the PAVA General Assembly of May 28, 1922 in Chicago.
13 PAVA NEB Archives, sign. A-XXI/2

But in particularly difficult times even the most recalcitrant Polish priests showed understanding of the veterans who were seeking financial support at Polish parishes for their colleagues who were war invalids. This became quite apparent during the years of the Great Depression. It is confirmed by the copious correspondence of Polish priests with the PAVA Board, which in most instances informs of the sums being transmitted on behalf of the I. J. Paderewski Invalid Fund. For instance Rev. K. Smogór, a pastor from Steubenville, Ohio, wrote on August 25, 1930: "Dear Brothers: I hereby enclose a check in the sum of $20.97 for the Polish Army invalids in the United States.

"I apologize that the people here did not give more on the occasion of the 10th anniversary of the Bolshevik defeat outside Warszawa. Due to unemployment these are poor times for a collection, job prospects for the nearest future are not favorable. It is unfortunate that those who did the recruiting in the United States for the Polish Army did not insure soldiers against disability, which I had strongly advised them to do. There is nothing left now but to collect several times a year for the fund for invalids of the Polish army living in the United States. Cordially, Rev. K. Smogór"[14]

Another Polish clergyman, Rev. Monsignor A. Zychowicz of Scranton, PA, sent a check for $346 on September 2, 1930 and informed the PAVA Board in Detroit that independently of this the Priests Association in the diocese of Scranton had collected the sum of $200 for Polish war invalids.[15]

The Polish clergy were no less involved in 1933–1934, when General Józef Haller, who had arrived from Poland at the request of the PAVA Board, toured dozens of Polish parishes, where with the permission of local priests he appealed from church pulpits for financial aid on behalf of the war invalids. As we know the drive was a great success (more than $78,000 was raised for this purpose). Without the help of Polish priests that success would not have been possible.[16]

The most active priests, who supported Polish veterans, were given the titles "Honorary PAVA Member" or "Honorary Member of the Alliance of Friends of Polish Army Veterans" by the Board and recommended for the "Hallerian Swords"decoration, and in the field they were requested to accept the function of chaplains of PAVA posts and districts, and were also given the title of honorary president. Their biographies were systematically printed in *The Veteran*, with the addition of very laudatory comments. Here are a few of them: "Rev. M. Lipiński in Trenton, NJ was elected an honorary member of Post Nr. 81 by a vote of the local PAVA Post Nr. 81 in

---

14   PAVA NEB Archives, sign. A-XXI/3
15   Ibid.
16   New Documents Archives (Warszawa) sign. 139, Polish Consulate General in New York, "Financial Report on the Tour of General J. Haller on Behalf of the I. J. Paderewski Invalid Fund of PAVA of America" p. 21

recognition of his work and support on behalf of Polish Army Veterans, especially his care of the invalids. The PAVA National Executive Board welcomes him into its ranks and extends its congratulations and the soldierly CZEŚĆ! (Hail!)" (*The Veteran*, June 1931, p. 21); "Rev. Monsignor Andrzej Zychowicz, honorary member and chaplain of PAVA Post Nr. 117 in Scranton, PA. A great friend of Polish Army veterans, patron of former volunteer soldiers who are invalids or need help." (*The Veteran* September 1931, p. 23); "Rev. Dr. Lucjan Bójnowski, of New Britain, CT, cordial and devoted friend of Polish Army veterans." (*The Veteran* March 1932, p. 9); "The Reverend Father Walenty Gierlacki, honorary president of PAVA Post Nr. 50 in Cohoes, NY. Greatly loved and respected pastor of St. Michael the Archangel Parish. One of the most sincere and generous workers on educational, national and veteran issues, supporting every endeavor with all his might and every penny. Chevalier of the Hallerian Swords medal and member of the Friends of Veterans." (*The Veteran* May 1932, p. 13)

PAVA also made *The Veteran's* pages available to priests. For instance the following priests printed their poems in it: PAVA chaplain Rev. Karol Łukasik and Rev. Jan Dekowski—chaplain of PAVA Post Nr. 114 in Toronto, Ontario, Canada.[17]

Another example illustrating the strong ties of PAVA with the Roman Catholic Church in the United States was the mutual organizing of financial aid for Gen. Józef Haller, who was facing foreclosure on his little land estate, a so-called remainder, for non-payment of debts. He had bought it in 1921 in Gorzuchów, in Pomerania (part of northern Poland on the Baltic coast). His wife, Aleskandra, appealed for help for the general. She wrote on this matter to PAVA president Dr. Teofil Starzyński. On his recommendation the PAVA Board turned to Rev. Bishop Paweł Rhode to conduct a fundraiser together for this purpose. Bishop Rhode expressed his full understanding and from his side included the Polish clergy in the enterprise. Due to the sensitivity of the issue the drive was not announced publicly. The collection among parishes, PAVA posts and known private persons lasted over one year. In consequence of it General Haller received a loan (not subject to repayment) for the sum of $4,000 in January 1926.

At the turn of 1927–1928 the PAVA Board together with the Polish clergy quietly undertook another collection for Gen. J. Haller, this time to rescue his seaside estate in Hallerów—Nowa Wieś. From November 1927 to March 1928 more than $1,300 was raised. On the list of silent donors there are twenty eight priests and twelve PAVA posts.[18]

---

17 Z. Choromański "Activity of the Clergy in the Polish Army Veterans Association in the Years 1921–1939." A Master's Thesis written under the supervision of Rev. Dr. Zygmunt Zieliński in the Department of Theology of the Catholic University of Lublin 1988, p. 50

18 PAVA NEB Archives, sign. XXVI/8 "Financial Report of the General J. Haller Fund"

Without a doubt the most important close cooperation of PAVA with the Polish clergy in America in the years 1921–1939 was to obtain funds on behalf of Polish war invalids. The PAVA Board was very well aware of the great role that Polish priests played in these efforts. When in October 1938 a Congress of Polish Clergy in America was being held, the PAVA National Executive Board sent a very telling letter to its participants, in which we read: "…we believe the Congress in Pittsburgh to be an opportunity where we can express our words of thanks to all the Polish Clergy in America for their cooperation in our efforts to help disabled veterans.

"We want to state that the Polish Clergy was the only body in our effort in this direction that stood loyally with us from the very beginning up until today, keeping the promises given to the volunteers from America who were departing for the battlefront."[19]

In reply the Congress of Polish Clergy in America unanimously approved the following resolution: "Taking into consideration that the so-called Blue Army, recruited in America with the prominent participation of the Polish Clergy, rendered extremely important service in the regaining of Polish Independence and fulfilled with great honor its patriotic duty, the Polish Clergy in America cordially supports and considers it its duty to render all manner of material as well as moral assistance in raising funds to help the invalids of this Army, who have found themselves in need in the Land of Washington."[20]

The above quoted fragments of two documents well reflect the essence of the successful cooperation in that period between the Polish Army Veterans Association of America and the Polish clergy in the United States and Canada.

PAVA and Other Polish American Organizations

The Polish Army Veterans Association, operating within the Polish American Community (Polonia), had to cooperate with other organizations created by that community. This was also true of the umbrella organizations that some of those institutions established. Among the central inter-organizational structures that PAVA had contact with, were: The Polish National Department in America, The Polish Social Welfare Council of America, The Polish Catholic Organization Clearing House of America, the Polish Inter-Organizational Council, and the American Relief for Poland.

Among them the Polish National Department, established during World War I, enjoyed the highest respect of all, because it had made enormous contributions to the mobilization of the Polish American community on behalf of regaining Poland's independence. When PAVA was organized in 1921 the activity of the Polish National Department was already on the wane. The PAVA veterans felt very bitter toward the

---

19 *The Veteran* November 1938, p. 12
20 Ibid.

Polish National Department, which had spent money raised in the Polish American community (which was to have been used to secure the welfare of Blue Army soldiers returning from the war to America) on other—equally important—goals, such as food for Poland. Nonetheless mutual contacts continued. PAVA representatives were invited to Parliaments of the Immigration organized by the Polish National Department. That was the case with the 4th Parliament in Detroit, MI in 1923 and again in 1925 which was in fact the end of the Polish National Department as an organization. The capabilities of the National Department in the last years of operation kept dwindling, so it had little to offer. In September 1924 the Department turned down the proposal of the PAVA National Executive Board to transform the PAVA branch office in Warszawa into a branch office of the Polish Immigration which would have been administered by the National Department, because that would have meant an expenditure of $150 to $170 per month.[21]

In 1925 many attempts were made to create some sort of umbrella for Polish American organizations. They kept ending in failure because none of them represented a majority of the unions and associations. The rivalry between the Polish National Alliance and the Polish Roman Catholic Union had a decisive influence on this state of affairs. It paralyzed all endeavors to form a supra-organizational body. For this reason the initiatives undertaken now and then all had short lives.

The PAVA Board was in favor of creating one strong umbrella for all Polish organizations. In 1925 it supported the idea of convoking a Congress of the Immigration, which took place in Detroit, Michigan. At the deliberations of the Congress, during which a Polish Social Welfare Council of America was founded, the Polish Army Veterans Association was represented by Wojciech Karolczak (Vice President) and Stanisław Z. Stachowicz (Secretary General).[22]

Unfortunately, the new body created at the Immigration Congress did not last, nor did the next one—the Polish Catholic Clearing House of America (Polska Centrala Katolicka w Ameryce), which was the brainchild of the Polish Roman Catholic Union of America. Attempts to establish a supra-organizational Polish American coordinating body were not helped by the fact that Polonia was divided into two warring camps, popularly called the Right and the Left. It was a political division, in existence since the World War, with supporters of the old Polish National Department in the United States (which in the years 1917–1919 had supported the Polish National Department in Paris which was identified with the figures of Roman

---

21 PAVA NEB Archives, sign. A-XX/4, Letter of the PAVA Board to the Polish National Department of September 24, 1924
22 PAVA NEB Archives, sign. A-XX/4, Letter of the PAVA Secretary General to the Polish National Department of January 31, 1925

Dmowski, Ignacy Jan Paderewski and General Józef Haller) on one side and the adherents of the old KON (National Defense Committee) in the United States and Józef Piłsudski in Poland on the other side. Although several years had passed since the conclusion of the war, these divisions in Polonia persisted, paralyzing effective joint activity. From the very beginning PAVA attempted to reconcile the opposing parties, which it often gave expression to in its press organ. Outside observers—arrivals from Poland—noted these efforts. Among them was Professor Roman Dyboski from Kraków, who (writing about PAVA) maintained that the organization "…is working very hard of late to ameliorate the old and deep-seated party squabbles among the émigrés…I recall with pleasure the fact that perhaps in no other Polish community in the States were the émigrés from all political factions gathered so convivially together at a lecture of mine as they were in Detroit's Polish Home under the auspices of the Veterans. I recall with equal warmth the speech Mr. Mrozowski, a representative of the Veterans (PAVA secretary—T. L.) in Detroit, gave at the foot of the monument to General Pułaski in Washington, D.C. on October 13, 1929, at a wreath-laying ceremony there attended by Polish delegations from all over the United States. That speech, with its appeal to cast aside all old quarrels at the foot of the memorial to the hero on the anniversary of his death, was a paragon of the spirit of conciliation, and of loyalty to the Polish State."[23]

The PAVA Board, in line with its apolitical principles, continued to voice hope for a political unification of Polonia. It expressed this view in *The Veteran* in a first-page article titled "The Polish Army Veterans Association of America an Agent of Conciliation in the Émigré Community," which stated:"…we believe in the "common sense" of the Polish émigré, in his instinct to do the right thing, we are certain that he will soon shake off the orientations that have been foisted upon him by his leaders, that he will drive away the demagogues who pay homage to damaging partisanship, and having offered the hand of concord—will begin working together fruitfully to raise himself up to a higher rung of American life. Because only by this means can the cause of the Polish immigration best be served, as well as the cause of our distant Fatherland."[24]

Unfortunately, the next attempt at an organizational consolidation of Polonia had to wait for a long time. Not until 1936, after long-lasting preparations, did the three largest Polish America organizations (The Polish National Alliance, The Polish Roman Catholic Union of America, and the Polish Women's Alliance of America) organize the Polish Inter-Organizational Council in the United States with headquarters in Chicago.

---

23 R. Dyboski, *Stany Zjednoczone Ameryki Północnej. Wrażenia i refleksje* [*The United States of North America. Impressions and Reflections*] Lwów – Warszawa 1930, p. 280

24 *The Veteran* June 1930, p. 2

This happened at the Inter-Organizational Convention in that city on May 2, 1936. This new body arrived at an understanding of the principles of cooperation between Polonian organizations, and of cooperation between the Polish American community and the World Union of Poles from Abroad (Światowy Związek Polaków z Zagranicy). The main goal of its activity was determined to be: coordination of joint actions to defend the Polish name and Poland; coordination of the Polish American community's activities with the World Union of Poles from Abroad in the fields of culture, education and business; coordination of activities aimed at elevating the significance of the Polish American community in American society.[25]

Francis Świetlik, the Censor of the Polish National Alliance, became the Chairman of the Board of Directors of the Inter-Organizational Council. The Vice Chairpersons were: Józef Kania (President of the Polish Roman Catholic Union of America) and Honorata Wołowska—the President of the Polish Women's Alliance.

The Polish Army Veterans Association of America also joined the Polish Inter-Organizational Council (PIOC), and paid annual membership dues of $50.

PAVA (taking the opportunity that the newly formed central body representing the entire Polish American community presented) turned to the PIOC in February 1937 with a request for publishing a special appeal to Polonia for help for war invalids—members of PAVA. In reply the PIOC commited itself to publish a special appeal in the press and to address all the organizations that were part of it to designate more significant sums from their organizational funds on behalf of the I. J. Paderewski Invalid Fund.[26]

At the next meeting, on March 22, 1937 the Board of Directors of the Council, on a motion by chairman Świetlik, decided to support the efforts of the Polish Army Veterans Association of America in its fund drive to transfer the ashes of General W. Krzyżanowski to Arlington National Cemetery near Washington, D.C. [27]

The PIOC was very favorably disposed to the Polish Army Veterans. This is confirmed by the fact that on June 9, 1937 a Veterans' Commission and a Committee to Honor the Immigration's War Effort were organized. The purpose of the Veterans' Commission was the propagation of veteran issues in the Polish American community and to mediate in the resolution of issues concerning veterans from America in Poland. The commission membership included: Lucjusz Kajko (National PAVA Commander—Honorary President); Jan Kostrubała (President of the Officers'

---

25 PAVA NEB Archives, sign. A-XX/22, Draft of the By-Laws of the Polish Inter-Organizational Council in the United States

26 PAVA NEB Archives, sign. A-XX/22, File: Polish Inter-Organizational Council in the United States, 1936–1938

27 Ibid.

Alliance and President of the Commission); O. Gustyniak (Vice President); Witold S. Bogucki (Secretary); members: Adam Trygar, Witold Trawiński, Gabriel Pawłowski, Józef Rekucki, Jan Drętkiewicz and Józef Wawrzyniak. The Commission was to present requests (after their prior clearing with the PAVA NEB) at meetings of the Council, and the latter was to pass them on in the form of motions to the World Alliance of Poles from Abroad in Poland whose director, Stefan Lenartowicz, was to present them to appropriate ministries in the Polish government. On July 21, 1937 the Veterans' Commission at its second meeting presented the PIOC, in the form of requests, the most important issues to be taken care of in the near future: a)the publication of "A History of the Polish American Community's War Effort," b) giving the 13th Infantry Division the name Division of the American Polonia, c) to have the Polish government establish a permanent subsidy grant for disabled Polish veterans in America, d) to have the Polish government resolve the complaints of veterans from America concerning promotions in rank and military decorations, e) organizing a representative trip of veterans from America to their native country on the occasion of the twentieth anniversary of Polish Independence.[28]

The PAVA National Executive Board applauded the creation of the commission, and admitted that it counted very heavily on the help of the PIOC in handling veteran affairs with the Polish government. PAVA's adjutant general, Leopold Krzyżak, wrote about this to the Veterans' Commission for its meeting of August 6, 1937: "We are extremely glad that your little group wanted to interest itself in issues which have been bothering our Board for the longest time and which, despite efforts, we have been unable to resolve. ... Nothing stands in the way except the ill will of various functionaries in the Polish government, which has been replying with silence to all our requests and interventions.

"... We know from reliable sources that the World Alliance of Poles from Abroad in Warszawa has a lot of influence in government spheres and that with their help much can be accomplished, nonetheless it is difficult for us to do anything directly because, as is apparent, we are on their black list. At any rate it is evident that they want to erase our effort from the pages of history if for no other than personal reasons."[29]

Independently of the Veterans' Commission, on June 9, 1937 the PIOC formed a Committee to Honor the Immigration's War Effort headed by Dr. Teofil Starzyński. Two other veterans were also on the committee: J. Kostrubała and A. Trygar.[30] The task of this committee was to coordinate in the United States the commemoration of

---

28 Ibid.
29 Ibid.
30 Ibid.

the twentieth anniversary of recruitment to the Polish Army in France, which was being organized by the major organizations of the Polish American community.

In the Spring of 1938 the Polish Inter-Organizational Council transformed itself into the American Relief for Poland (Rada Polonii Amerykańskiej). Surviving correspondence shows that the PAVA NEB did not maintain close contact with it and stopped using it to mediate in contacts with the Alliance of Poles Abroad, instead writing directly to the headquarters of this organization in Warszawa. When, however, the Polish government made a grant of $3,000 to help disabled Polish veterans in America, the sum was sent in installments through the Alliance of Poles Abroad to the account of the American Relief for Poland in Chicago, from where in March 1939 it made its way to the PAVA NEB in New York to the account of the I. J. Paderewski Invalid Fund. On March 16, 1939 Leopold Krzyżak, the PAVA Adjutant General, acknowledged receipt of this sum.[31]

From the above examples it is clear that the PAVA Board in the years 1921–1939 was engaged in some of the activities of successive Polish American umbrella institutions, but only to the extent that they were convergent with the organizational goals of the Association.

The Veterans and the Polish Falcons of America

The majority of PAVA members came from the Falcon ranks. So it was natural that the veterans maintained close contact with this organization. The cooperation mainly concerned the efforts of the young organization, which PAVA was at that time, to obtain financial contributions to help its members—the war invalids. The inter-organizational contacts were facilitated by the fact that many PAVA members were simultaneously members of the Polish Falcons, the Polish National Alliance or the Polish Roman Catholic Union of America, or else of all three of those organizations simultaneously—and there were such cases. The presence of PAVA members in those organizations was fully understandable, because they were also the largest fraternal insurance companies in the Polish American community.

Evidence of the close ties between PAVA and the Polish Falcons of America, popularly called "Sokolstwo" (the Falcons) is the fact that the first PAVA president for three consecutive terms in the years 1921–1928 was Dr. Teofil Starzyński, who simultaneously held the office of President of the Falcons. Later presidents and national commanders of PAVA also came from the Falcons. The same was true of most of the PAVA Board members and of individual posts and districts, thanks to which both organizations worked together well. It ought to be added that in the years

---

31 PAVA NEB Archives, sign. A-XX/23, File: American Relief for Poland

1921–1925 the offices of the PAVA National Executive Board were located at the Falcon House of Nest 141 in Cleveland, Ohio. The first PAVA General Assembly took place in that same building in May 1921.

As an expression of high regard for the Falcons Dr. Teofil Starzyński (as President of the Falcons) was invited to be the godfather of the PAVA organizational flag. On September 18, 1923 Dr. T. Starzyński made a special trip from Pittsburgh to Cleveland for that gala ceremony. General Józef Haller, who had come from Poland, also participated in it.[32]

From the beginning of PAVA's existence the Falcons, as a sister organization, supported fund drives on behalf of war invalids. Over $1,500 was collected for this purpose in 1923.[33] In later years the Falcons continued to support the I. J. Paderewski Fund of PAVA to the extent of their capabilities. The money for this purpose was obtained through social events organized by individual Falcon nests, such as dance parties, lotteries and official collections on behalf of the invalids.

Beginning with 1924, thanks to the efforts of the PAVA Board, many Falcons in America received the Hallerian Swords decoration from Poland for their work on behalf of the Polish Army in France in the years 1917–1919.

Sometimes unusual situations arose in the cooperation, for instance in 1925 the head of the Polish Falcons of America, W. Pawlak, while on a visit in Poland, at the request of PAVA president Dr. T. Starzyński, brought the Blue Army veteran and former Falcon Piotr Kaczyński back to the United States with him at his own expense. The expense of his trip to America, $178, was later refunded by the PAVA Board, which treated it as a loan to the new arrival, who made a commitment to repay it.[34]

In January 1926, at the request of the Executive Board of the Polish Falcons of America, the PAVA National Executive Board recommended its member, Karol Burke, for the post of editor-in-chief of *Sokół Polski* (*The Polish Falcon*), the press organ of the Falcons. PAVA secretary general Jan Szymański wrote in his recommendation: "If it were not for the fact that I am personally devoted to the Falcons, I would under no circumstance have recommended Burke, whom we had planned to appoint the editor of our *Veteran* in the near future. But we are also interested in the welfare of our mother organization, the Falcons, and are ready to give it our best men."[35] This fact best exemplifies the extraordinary ties that bound PAVA and the Falcons.

---

32 PAVA NEB Archives, sign. XX/3
33 PAVA NEB Archives, sign. XXVI/1
34 PAVA NEB Archives, sign. XIX/3
35 Ibid., Letter of Janaury 5, 1926 of PAVA Secretary General Jan Szymański to the National Executive Board of the Polish Falcons of America

There was also the permanent tradition of mutual invitations to each other's events, including PAVA and Falcons general assemblies. The cooperation was closer during commemorations of anniversaries of the recruitment drive for the Polish Army in France. Special editions of *The Veteran* were published then. Those issues devoted a lot of space to the Falcons, which by its many prior years of work had done so much for the success of recruitment in the years 1917–1919.

In June of 1933 PAVA District II and the Falcons District I organized a commemoration of the 15th anniversary of the founding of the Polish Army in France. The occasion was honored by the arrival from Poland of General Roman Górecki, who was at that time the president of FIDAC (The world combatant federation). Thanks to him the ceremonies were transformed into a huge combatant event, with a parade of Polish, American, Canadian, British, French, Belgian and Italian veterans.[36]

During the cermonies many PAVA veterans were decorated with Falcon medals bestowed on them by the National Executive Board of the Polish Falcons of America. PAVA president Franciszek Dziób was especially honored by the highest Falcon decoration, the Polish Falcons of America Legion of Honor. Dziób had been the Falcons' leader during World War I and commander of the first cadet school at Cambridge Springs, Pennsylvania.[37]

Another symptom of the cooperation between PAVA and the Falcons was the mounting of a joint exhibit at the Chicago World's Fair in 1933 which displayed the activities of both organizations.[38]

The Polish National Alliance on Behalf of the Veterans

The Polish National Alliance, the largest Polish American organization, was one of the most generous in supporting PAVA activities, which aimed at securing the welfare of war invalids. Shortly after the founding of PAVA in 1921 the Polish National Alliance, at its 23rd congress in Detroit, approved a contribution of $10,000 for this purpose. That was very serious assistance for the young veteran organization, enabling it to fulfill its most important statutory obligations.

Less than a year later, in the Spring of 1922, during a great fund drive initiated by PAVA on behalf of the Settlement and Invalid Fund, the PNA contributed $2,000 for that purpose.

In the Fall of 1923 during General Józef Haller's first tour of the United States and PAVA's fund drive to benefit the Home for War Invalids of the Republic of

---

36 "Piękna uroczystość Weteranów i Sokołów w N.Y." ["A Beautiful Veteran and Falcon Ceremony in N.Y."] in: *Weteran [The Veteran]* July 1933, p. 19

37 "Weterani Armii Polskiej odznaczeni przez Sokolstwo" ["Polish Army Veterans Decorated by the Falcons"] in: *Weteran [The Veteran]* August 1933, p. 19

38 PAVA NEB Archives, sign. A-XX/3, Polish Falcons of America

Poland in Radzyń near Warszawa, the PNA contributed $2,000.[39]

It ought to be added that the Polish National Alliance gave space to the veterans in its publications and invited PAVA representatives to its most important events, including PNA conventions, which became a tradition. PAVA returned the favor.

In the following years (1924 and 1925) the Polish National Alliance gave PAVA $1,000 per year from its central budget in support of war invalids. In 1925 an additional $585 was contributed for this purpose, collected by individual PNA lodges.

PAVA gratefully accepted this assistance, and returned the favor by requesting that the Polish National Alliance receive the Hallerian Swords decoration, which was bestowed on the organization in May 1925.[40]

In 1928, on the strength of a resolution of the PNA's 25th convention, PAVA received a consecutive serious contribution to the I. J. Paderewski Invalid Fund. This time the PNA gave $5,000.[41]

Up to that time the cooperation between PAVA and the PNA was harmonious. But in 1929 serious misunderstandings arose in connection with the idea of building a memorial mound to honor General Kazimierz Pułaski in Savannah, Georgia. The idea came from PAVA president Kazimierz Bałdyga, who wanted to maximize promotion of the approaching 150th anniversary of the death of the Polish patriot, by giving it wide exposure in American—Polish relations. In his efforts to bring his idea to fruition, Bałdyga was able to obtain the approval and support of the State of Georgia and of the federal government in Washington, including U.S. president Herbert Hoover, whose sympathies for Poland and the Poles were widely known. The problem was that the cost of building the monument was estimated at $130,000, which was to be contributed by the Polish American community. The Polish National Alliance decided the venture was unrealistic, especially since there was less than six months to get the money and build the mound.

Due to this essential divergence of opinions the project never happened. Nonetheless there were mutual recriminations in the Polish American press, on the one side for squandering a great moment to showcase the Polish American community in American society, on the other side accusations of megalomania, building castles in the air and immature attempts at abusing the generosity of the Polish American community.[42]

---

39 PAVA NEB Archives, sign. A-XX/1, Polish National Alliance
40 Ibid.
41 "Hojny dar Związku Narodowego Polskiego dla inwalidów Armii Polskiej" ["Generous Gift of the Polish National Alliance for Polish Army Invalids"] in: *Weteran [The Veteran]* September 1928, p.8
42 K. Bałdyga, "Co zrobiono a czego nie zrobiono w sprawie uczczenia Kazimierza Pułaskiego" ["What Was Done and What Wasn't Done to Honor Kazimierz Pułaski"] in: *Weteran [The Veteran]* November 1929, pp. 3-5

Mutual relations were only dampened for a short time by that misunderstanding. Several months later everbody was nervously watching the market crash on the New York Stock Exchange.

During the Great Depression years the PNA was forced to cut back its financial support of PAVA, because the universal depression had also undermined that wealthiest Polish American organization. For instance, due to pervasive unemployment it was unable to make good on the pledge it made at its 26th Convention (Scranton, Pennsylvania, 1931) to give PAVA $5,000 for war invalids.[43]

Only after the American economy had climbed out of the crisis was the Polish National Alliance able to once again come to the aid of PAVA veterans. Up to that time the help had been sporadic. At 27th PNA Convention in Baltimore in 1935 the decision was made to tax every PNA member ¼ of one cent per month to support the I. J. Paderewski Invalid Fund of PAVA. That was significant help, because at that time the PNA had 300,000 members. Veterans played a significant role in the adoption of this resolution at the PNA convention in Baltimore. They (also being PNA members) took the floor as ambassadors (about thirty strong) defending the interests of PAVA and their comrades the war invalids.[44]

Thanks to the decisions made in Baltimore the Polish National Alliance was able, over the next four years (to 1939), to designate over $20,000 for permanent subsidies for war invalids, with lists of the beneficiaries delivered to the PNA by the PAVA National Executive Board.[45]

Thus the PNA was the single largest donor to the Polish Army Veterans Association of America. The total financial aid which PAVA received from the PNA in the years 1921–1939 was more than $42,000.

Cooperation with the Polish Roman Catholic Union of America

The Polish Army Veterans Association of America also received significant help for war invalids from the second-largest Polish American organization, the Polish Roman Catholic Union of America (PRCUA), which had in the years 1919–1939 between 100,000 and 150,000 members. It contributed more than $14,000 to the veteran cause. (Please see addendum 12)

Comparison shows that after taking into consideration the number of members (of whom many also belonged to PAVA) the PRCUA was not lagging behind the PNA in this matter. It is worth noting that in the first three years of operations PAVA

---

43 PAVA NEB Archives, sign. A-XX/1, Polish National Alliance
44 "Związek Narodowy Polski uchwalił miesięczny podatek na Fundusz Inwalidzki" ["The Polish National Alliance Has Voted a Monthly Tax for the Invalid Fund"] in: *Weteran [The Veteran]* October 1935, p. 12
45 PAVA NEB Archives, sign. A-XX/2, Polish National Alliance

received more than $8,000 from the PRCUA.

No wonder that just as it had done for the PNA, PAVA requested that the PRCUA be decorated with the Hallerian Swords for its service on behalf of the Polish Army in France during World War I and for supporting veterans of that army after their return to America. The ceremony of decorating the flag of the PRCUA with the medal took place at the 38th Convention of the PRCUA in St. Louis, Missouri, in September 1925. The chronicler of the Polish Roman Catholic Union of America, Mieczysław Haiman, described that event: "A beautiful moment at the Convention was the decoration of the PRCUA's flag with the Hallerian Swords medal for services rendered to the Polish Army, by a delegation of the Polish Army Veterans Association, which included: Lt. Jan Kostrubała, Vice President; Lt. Jan Szymański, Secretary General; Captain Dr. Franciszek Lenart and Major Dr. Aleksander Pietrzykowski"[46]

The next distinction bestowed on the PRCUA by PAVA was the organizational decoration of the Cross of Merit. On April 8, 1934, at the request of the PAVA National Executive Board, the ceremonial decoration of the PRCUA flag was done personally in Chicago by General Józef Haller, who at that time was conducting his second tour around the United States.

The PAVA–PRCUA cooperation was conducted on many levels. There was very close cooperation during General Haller's successive visits in 1923 and in the years 1933–1934, when welcoming committees were organized, which included representatives of many Polish American organizations.

There were mutual invitations to various ceremonies and events: conventions, banquets, commemorative meetings, balls, solemn masses, anniversary celebrations, etc. There was also participation in joint trips, of which the most memorable were trips to Poland. For instance a large group of PRCUA members participated in the largest trip organized by PAVA to France and Poland in 1927. One of those members, Emil P. Banasiak, who directed the PRCUA sports program, died of a heart attack during the trip, which was a great shock to all the participants.[47]

The former president of the PRCUA during World War I, Piotr Rostenkowski, was a great friend of the PAVA veterans. At the suggestion of the PAVA National Executive Board he was decorated with the Hallerian Swords medal for his work in recruitment for the Polish Army in France and for his activity on behalf of the veterans of that army. When that distinguished civic leader died on June 17, 1936, the PAVA press organ devoted a lengthy article to him, which concluded with the words: "The late Piotr Rostenkowski made a great contribution to the national cause

---

46   Ibid., p. 365
47   Ibid., p. 404

during the battles for Poland's independence, he rendered moral and material support to the organizing Polish Army, and when the Motherland finally stood among free nations of the world, he as a member of the Friends of the Polish Army in America, opened his Polish heart to Her defenders, the Polish soldier-invalids.

Therefore we express our Respect and Recognition for the memory of this brave Pole for His great service for the national cause."[48]

The Polish Army Veterans Association of America (in returning the compliment to the PRCUA for supporting war invalids) actively supported some of the activities of the PRCUA. That was true of the PRCUA initiative in 1929 to establish a Polish Catholic Organizations Clearinghouse in America. The president of PAVA at that time, Kazimierz Bałdyga, fully backed the initiative, declaring in a letter of October 18, 1929 to PRCUA president Jan Olejniczak, that: "...I am ready to come at any time and to any city for a joint conference."[49]

The conference, convoked by the PRCUA, was held in Cleveland, Ohio on December 11 and 12, 1929, but did not bring any permanent results.

Another PRCUA initiative backed by PAVA, which did give a permanent result was the establishment of the Archive and Museum of the Polish Roman Catholic Union of America, which, under the direction of well known Polish American historian Mieczysław Haiman, became a central archival and museum institution for the entire Polish American community (Polonia). The official opening of this important post took place on January 12, 1937 in the building of the PRCUA. PAVA veterans supported this museum, donating many historical souvenirs from the time of their military service, thanks to which the department depicting the Polish American community's war effort during World War I became the most interesting part of the museum. The importance of this initiative was affirmed by the thousands of visitors who toured the museum's exhibits since its opening, and the dozens of researchers who made use of the rich collections in the archives for their scholarly studies.

At the request of the curator, Mieczysław Haiman, the PAVA National Executive Board sent copies of the PAVA By-Laws, the Regulations of the PAVA Auxiliary Corps and organizational decorations of the Association for inclusion in the museum's collections.[50]

This institution founded by the PRCUA fostered historical research about the Polish American community's past by establishing in 1937 the Polish Historical and Museum Society of America and by publishing the *Annals of the Polish R.C. Union*

---

48 *The Veteran* July 1936, p. 18
49 PAVA NEB Archives, sign. A-XX/5, Polish Roman Catholic Union of America, 1925–1939
50 PAVA NEB Archives, sign. A-XX/5, Polish Roman Catholic Union of America. 1925–1939, Letter of October 10, 1936 from M. Haiman to the PAVA NEB

Archives and Museum. The help rendered to historians in publishing their works proved to be very important. Among others Artur L. Waldo, the former president of PAVA District VI and the former editor of *The Veteran*, availed himself of that assistance. His articles and historical studies enjoyed great interest.[51]

The fruitful cooperation of PAVA and the Polish Roman Catholic Union of America lasted without interruption over the next many years.

Collaboration with the Polish Women's Alliance of America

In the twenty years between the two world wars the Polish Army Veterans Association of America collaborated closely with the largest Polish women's organization, the Polish Women's Alliance of America (PWA). It had also distinguished itself greatly in the recruitment action on behalf of the Polish Army in France. For this activity the PWA, on the initiative of PAVA, was honored with the Hallerian Swords decoration in 1925, and many of the most deserving members of this organization received thr distinction personally a year later.

From the very beginning of PAVA's existence the PWA kept in close contact with it, cooperating on civic committees during the largest actions undertaken by PAVA. That was the case during the great fund drive for the Settlement and Invalid Fund in 1922 and during the visits of General Haller in 1923 and again in 1933–1934.

The PWA also helped the much newer PAVA Board in 1925, when its headquarters was moved from Cleveland to Chicago. From June 1925 to November 1926 it occupied guest quarters in the Polish Women's Alliance building.[52]

The form of the invitation that PWA president Emilia Napieralska wrote in 1927 to PAVA president Dr. Teofil Starzyński on the occasion of the pending 15th PWA convention speaks eloquently of the relations between these organizations. President Napieralska wrote: "For several years, our Organization, the Polish Women's Alliance of America, has given proof of its good will toward fellow organizations, striving to firm up brotherly feelings by its sincere and noble behavior.

"Today, at the threshold to its 15th convention, we would like once more to give proof of our sincere sisterly feelings and therefore we invite you, Most Respected Mr. President, to our convention."[53]

The fact that the Polish Women's Alliance of America considered itself a sister organization of PAVA was fully justified, because very many of its members belonged to the PAVA Auxiliary Corps, which had made invaluable contributions on behalf of

---

51 M. Haiman, *Zjednoczenie Polskie Rzymsko-Katolickie w Ameryce 1873–1948* [*The Polish Roman Catholic Union of America 1873–1948*] Chicago 1948, p. 441

52 PAVA NEB Archives, sign. A-XX/7, Polish Women's Alliance of America

53 Ibid.

war invalids and homeless veterans. At almost all levels of the PWA everything was known about what was going on at PAVA and vice versa. The greater sensitivity of women's hearts was important: it did not allow them to pass by human tragedy with indifference. This fact was well documented by the help, in the sum of over $13,200, that the PWA contributed for the support of war invalids and homeless veterans from 1921 to September 1939, despite the fact that this was not a huge organization. In 1938 it had a membership of about 60,000 women.[54]

Such an outstanding result was possible because following the example of the Polish National Alliance the PWA at its 17th convention in 1935 pledged 5 cents annually from every membership dues toward the support of PAVA's I. J. Paderewski Invalid Fund.[55] That gave an annual average of $2,500. With each year those sums were regularly transmitted to PAVA for the Fund's account, for instance in June 1939 the Alliance transmitted the sum of $2,546.75 for this purpose.[56]

Taking into consideration the cited facts it must be stated that the help rendered war invalids and homeless veterans by the Polish Women's Alliance of America was proportionately the greatest of all the Polish American organizations.

PAVA Contacts with the Alliance of Poles in America and Other Organizations

One of the relatively small Polish American organizations with which PAVA had close contacts was the Alliance of Poles in America (APA), founded in 1895 and headquartered in Cleveland, Ohio. In 1938 that fraternal insurance organization counted over 20,000 members.

As we know, the Polish Army Veterans Association of America was founded in that same city in 1921 and the National Executive Board had its offices there from 1921 to 1925. That helped contacts between the two organizations, especially since many local PAVA members also belonged to the Alliance of Poles, for instance Lodge 145 of the APA was organized by members of PAVA Post Nr. 6 in Cleveland and took the name General Józef Haller Society. The meetings of this group, whose members were sympathizers and friends of the veterans and also veterans themselves, were held on the premises of PAVA Post Nr. 6.

---

54 "Udział Związku Polek w Ameryce w Czynie Zbrojnym Wychodźstwa" ["The Contribution of the Polish Women's Alliance of America to the Immigration War Effort"] in: *Jednodniówka na Zjazd b. Oficerów i Pracowników Rekrutacyjnych. 19 – 20 luty 1938 [Souvenir Journal of the Convention of former Officers and Recruitment Workers. February 19–20, 1938]* Cleveland 1938, p. 35

55 "Związek Polek opodatkował się na rzecz Funduszu Inwalidzkiego" ["The Polish Women's Alliance Has Taxed Itself on Behalf of the Invalid Fund"] in: *Weteran [The Veteran]* October 1935, p. 12

56 PAVA NEB Archives, sign. A-XX/7, Polish Women's Alliance of America. 1923–1939. Letter of June 7, 1939 from Polish Women's Alliance Secretary General to the PAVA NEB

In 1925 the PAVA National Executive Board had a hand in the decoration of many APA activists with the Hallerian Swords medal. These were men who had contributed to the recruitment drive for the Polish Army in France in the years 1917–1919.[57]

During PAVA's beginnings the APA gave $500 to help Polish veterans. In 1932 at its convention in Akron, Ohio this organization was the first in the United States to approve a resolution that designated October 6, as the anniversary marking the beginning of recruitment for the Polish Army in France, an official holiday of the Alliance of Poles in America. An appropriate note was also included in the By-Laws of the organization: "In order to uphold the ideology of the one and only War Effort of the Polish Immigration in the history of civilized peoples, October 6 shall be an official holiday of our organization, as the day on which in 1917 the recruitment of volunteers to the Polish Army in France began in America."[58]

In 1938 the leadership of the Alliance of Poles in America cooperated closely with PAVA Posts Nr. 6 and 152 in Cleveland and also with other local associations and societies during the organization of the Convention of Former Officers and Recruitment Workers and Presidents of Civic Committees, which was held on February 19 and 20, 1938.[59]

Other organizations of the Polish community that were active in the United States and Canada, with which PAVA had sporadic contacts in the years 1921–1939, were: The Polish Singers Alliance of America (headquarters in Chicago); the Polish Union in the United States of America (headquarters in Wilkes-Barre, PA); the Polish Youth Alliance (headquarters—Chicago); the Polish National Alliance of Brooklyn (headquarters—Brooklyn, NY); the Polish American National Union (headquarters—Scranton, PA); The Alliance of Poles in Canada (headquarters—Toronto, ONT, Canada); Polish Fellowship Society (headquarters—Coleman, Alberta Province, Canada).

Cooperation of PAVA with Veteran Organizations in the United States and Canada

The Polish Army Veterans Association of America was the largest Polish veteran organization in the United States and Canada, but not the only veteran institution. Aside from PAVA there were other veteran societies founded by Poles—former soldiers, who had served in the Polish Army, the American Army and in Canadian units of the British Army. PAVA maintained contact with almost all of these organizations.

---

57 PAVA NEB Archives, sign. A-XX/9 Alliance of Poles in America

58 "Związek Polaków w Ameryce" ["The Alliance of Poles in America"] in: *Jednodniówka na Zjazd b. Oficerów i Pracowników Rekrutacyjnych* [*Souvenir Journal of the Convention of former Officers and Recruitment Workers*] Cleveland 1938

59 Ibid.

Cooperation with Veteran Organizations of Polish Provenance

The only Polish veteran organization that was active in the United States besides PAVA in the years 1924–1932 was the Union of Polish Army Reserve Officers of America. It was founded in January 1923 in Chicago by Dr. Aleksander Pietrzykowski, a former Blue Army doctor, who was instrumental in organizing help for Polish Army veterans returning from the war to Chicago in the years 1920 and 1921.

The Union of Polish Army Reserve Officers of America was an apolitical, independent and autonomous organization. Most of its members were officers who were also PAVA members. The reason for its formation was, as Dr. Pietrzykowski maintained, "constant threats, harassment and provocations by rank and file colleagues."[60]

It was not a universal phenomenon, PAVA Secretary General Stanisław Z. Stachowicz tried to explain in his letters to Dr. Pietrzykowski. The Secretary General held it against Dr. Pietrzykowski that he had left the ranks of the PAVA and had formed a new organization instead of leaving the Post where he had had unpleasant experiences, and moving to another one. This is how Stachowicz explained the dislike of the regular soldier for officers that manifested itself here and there: "The rank and file soldier was often dealt with unjustly by the officer from America. I admit that those who did the soldiers wrong are not in America, and if they are, they won't want to work with you or us. But do believe me that this disrespectful treatment of you by the rank and file was not provoked by the soldier himself, nor the non-commissioned officer even, but by various aspirants to officer titles. They didn't get the promotions because either they hadn't been mature enough to get them, or like so many others, they had been wrongly passed over, thus the dislike of those who have the rank. I heard one of the course attendees at the school in Quentin speak—he had been an officer in Canada, and fortunately he didn't make rank in France and Poland (he's in Chicago these days in the rank of officer cadet and belongs neither to your organization nor to ours); here's what he said: 'Hell, in about a month I'll get my officer's stripe, then I'll show those jerks [the rank and file soldiers] who I am.' There were lots of those. And they are the ones who sowed prejudice against you. If one of those shows up in the ranks today, even if he had been nominated in Grupa [the military camp in Pomerania, Poland for demobilized volunteers from America] for 2nd Lieutenant, he will call you names."[61]

---

60 PAVA NEB Archives, sign. A-XXII/1, Letter of Dr. A Pietrzykowski to PAVA Secretary General S. Z. Stachowicz, dated August 15, 1924

61 PAVA NEB Archives, sign. A-XXII/1, Letter of S. Z. Stachowicz of August 16, 1924 to Dr. A. Pietrzykowski. This letter signals the class differences that were evident among the volunteers from America for the Polish Army in France.

As a result of the exchange of letters a thread of understanding formed between the officers' organization and PAVA. Dr. Pietrzykowski assured the PAVA NEB that:"The officers of the reserve want to work together with their colleagues regardless of their military rank, for the good of PAVA, for the good of the Fatherland and for the good of the colleagues."[62]

In reply the PAVA Board agreed to publish Dr. Pietrzykowski's appeal in *The Veteran*, directed to all Polish officers in the United States, to join the Union of Polish Army Reserve Officers of America. In addition the Union was extended the following good wishes: "May this organization truly include all the officers of the Polish Army living in America, so that it can be an example for us by reason of its seniority, in our national and social work."[63]

An appeal was also made to the rank and file soldiers who were PAVA members to treat their officer colleagues appropriately and not to create divisions inside the organization: "May the colleagues who snipe here and there at the establishment of an officers' organization, rather take this as a good sign for themselves. Let them not see the officers as people who, while working together with them in Posts of the Association, frequently gave them orders in times of need. Let them see the officers as 'caring, just patrons, and teachers and benevolent fellow citizens,' as examples of love of country and honor."[64]

Several months after these explanations and appeals appeared the problem of friction due to these reasons returned, when the Polish Army Reserve Officers Club was organized in Detroit in 1924. Its president was Captain Stanisław Nastał, an emerging activist in the PAVA ranks. Whereas the existing problem of friction between the soldiers and the officers had previously been mainly limited to the Polish American community in Chicago, now it made itself heard in Detroit, home to the largest post in the organization, PAVA Post Nr. 7. Wanting to forestall further serious disruptions due to this irritating issue, S. Z. Stachowicz, the PAVA Secretary General, published an eloquent article in *The Veteran* titled "Once Again the Officers." He wrote: "If the officers are with us, hand in hand, if they are members of our organization, which they are usually proud of, if they work sincerely for this organization with passionate devotion, if they have not anywhere nor at any time shown that they are against the organization as such, nor against the Posts or individual members, then why should we sulk at them, why should we distrust them, why let them feel, as sometimes happens, that we don't want them in our work? Is it

---

62 *The Veteran* August 1924, p. 6
63 Ibid.
64 Ibid.

because they usually give sound advice as to what ought to be done and how, how to proceed, how to seek counsel, how to work? Is that why we should move away from them or else push them away from us?

"Or maybe, if they complete some work for us that is most often successfully done, are we to show them dark ingratitude for it?

"Or are we maybe to hate them because in order to have closer contact with their colleagues in Poland, who are organized into a Union of Reserve Officers, in order to cooperate and work together with us more effectively, in order to help us with their advice, often with their experience, cooperation, they organize their own clubs or associations? Does that disturb us in our work?"[65]

As proof that these sorts of frictions were not common to all the posts, there is this letter, which was received by the PAVA Board in Cleveland, Ohio, sent by Corporal Kostrzewski, the secretary of Post Nr. 21 in New York, in which he wrote: "We are honored to inform you that we have been able to gain two new members for our Post, both officers, of whom we are very glad, because we believe that they will bring a new spirit to the Post and will bring it new life. These members are: Major of the Reserves Michał Fibich and Chaplain Rev. Leon Kaszyński, also an Officer of the Reserves."[66]

The businesslike clarifications and calm persuasion of PAVA Secretary General Stanisław Z. Stachowicz in his article to the PAVA soldiers helped bring about a gradual calming of flared tempers in the relationship between the officers and the regular soldiers. It was a lengthy process, which never ended, but the years 1923–1925 were definitely its climax. After 1925 this problem never again appeared in *The Veteran*. Instead, the monthly ran articles about the activities of the Union of Polish Army Reserve Officers of America.

The following ventures of the Union deserve mention; in most instances they were undertaken in cooperation with PAVA:

- participation in various anniversary celebrations;
- participation in welcoming committees for prominent individuals: General J. Haller, Marshall F. Foch, General Goureau, General Bella, Minister Skrzyński, I. J. Paderewski, Ambassador J. Ciechanowski, Archbishop Cieplak, and consuls and envoys from Poland;
- initiation of financial subscriptions to build the Chemical Research Institute in Warszawa;
- participation in fund drives on behalf of Upper Silesia;

---

65 *The Veteran* February 1925, pp. 4-5
66 Ibid.

- establishment in 1927 of the Polish Army Veterans Political League, to support talented Poles who were candidates for public office in America. The league was active only for a short time in Chicago. It played an important role in the election of Edward Jarecki for County Judge and Piotr Schwab for a judgeship as well;

- support of the building of a memorial mound to honor General Kazimierz Pułaski in Savannah, Georgia;

- organizing a trip to Poland in 1929 for, as it was advertised, the Polish American professional intelligentsia;[67]

- organizing a great parade in Chicago in September 1932 on the occasion of the fifteenth anniversary of the recruitment effort for the Polish Army in France.[68]

Unfortunately, it is not possible to give the number of members that belonged to the Union of Polish Army Reserve Officers of America, because neither the surviving correspondence with the PAVA Board nor the contents of *The Veteran* (discussing the activities of that Union) contain such data. As for the leadership of that organization it included the following persons in 1928: Dr. A. Pietrzykowski—president, Dr. F. Lenart—Vice President, W. S. Bogucki—secretary, J. Kawszewicz—treasurer, Rev. S. Godlewski—chaplain, J. Jurewicz—attorney.

The various committees included the following members: J. Kostrubała (PAVA Vice President), R. Hanasz (editor of *The Veteran*), Cz. Żuławski (former editor of *The Veteran)*, J. Kawszewicz, J. Kraus, W. Brudziński, W. Pytlowany, P. Świerczewski, M. Basowski, T. Kwaśniewski, E. Руциński, E. Jerheń, K. Bobrzecki, R. Gierlach, A. Kobylański, G. Pawłowski, G. Pieprzny, M. Kowalski, J. Łukomski, J. Matecki, J. Rozwadowski, W. Sobczyk, E. Oleksy, Dr. M. Lewiński, R. Kapturkiewicz, Jerzy Pientoski.

Interestingly enough, this list also includes Lt. Col. Pilot Cedric Fauntleroy, former commander of the famous 7th Air Force Squadron, the "Kościuszko," in which American pilots served during the Polish-Bolshevik war of 1920.[69]

We are unable to present the activity of the Union of Polish Army Reserve Officers of America after 1932, due to lack of source material.

PAVA also maintained close contact with American veteran organizations that included veterans of Polish descent who had served in the American Army

---

67 "W piątą rocznicę założenia Związku B. Oficerów Armii Polskiej w Chicago" ["On the Fifth Anniversary of the Founding of the Union of Polish Army Reserve Officers of America in Chicago"] in:*Weteran [The Veteran]* January 1928, p. 27

68 *The Veteran* June 1932, p. 12

69 PAVA NEB Archives, Individual Archive, File: Dr. Aleksander Pietrzykowski: Notes and Memoirs, 1917–1927

during World War I. The beginnings of these organizations go back to 1920. At that time the Polish-American Veterans Club for the State of Michigan was formed in Hamtramck, Michigan, and the Polish-American Veterans of the World War Club was founded in Cleveland, Ohio. The Union of Polish-American World War Veterans was established in Chicago.[70] That organization was founded on April 24, 1920 by Leon T. Walkowicz, a former soldier of the American Army in the years 1917–1919, a participant in battles at the French front in 1918. After returning from the war he worked as a journalist in the Polish American press in Chicago, in succession at *Dziennik Narodowy* (*The National Daily*), *Dziennik Związkowy* (*The Alliance Daily—organ of the PNA*) and *Dziennik Zjednoczenia* (*The Union Daily*—organ of the PRCUA). It was his initiative that brought about the coalition of the above organizations at the Chicago convention of 1925 into the Alliance of the American Veterans of Polish Extraction (Związek Weteranów Amerykańskich Polskiego Pochodzenia), though the joining organizations retained their autonomy. In this new central structure Leon T. Walkowicz first held the office of adjutant general and later of head commander. Under his guidance the Alliance of the American Veterans of Polish Extraction (AAVPE) supported many Polish causes, for instance publicizing the Polish independence loan, organizing a mass rally in the center of Chicago on behalf of the plebiscite in Silesia (the several hundred dollars collected at the rally was sent to the Plebiscite Committee in Silesia), organizing a protest against a bishop in Buffalo, New York who tried to remove the Polish language from the curriculum of the local Polish parish schools (the Board of the Alliance sent a resolution on this issue to the President of the United States, to the Secretary of State, to senators and congressmen). A similar protest was organized when the *Chicago Evening American* tried, in a tendencious way, to argue against granting of loans to Poland by American banks. Moroever Leon T. Walkowicz on his own organized the Związek Oświaty i Obrony Kresów Polskich (The Education and Defense Union of the Eastern Polish Borderlands) under the auspices of which over a thousand dollars was collected on behalf of impoverished children in Eastern Poland. The money was sent for the above purpose to the Zjednoczone Polskie Towarzystwa Oświatowe w Warszawie (The United Polish Educational Societies in Warszawa). For his activity on behalf of the Polish cause Leon T. Walkowicz was decorated with the Hallerian Swords medal, thanks to a petition by PAVA on his behalf.[71]

---

70 Letter of B. Skrzypczak (Vice President of the Pre-Parliamentary Committee of the 5th General Parliament of the Pplish Legion of American Veterans) to the Federation of Polish Societies of Defenders of the Fatherland, July 30, 1939; New Documents Archive [Warszawa, Poland], collection: F.P.Z.O.O., sign. 188, pp. 34-35

71 New Documents Archive (in Warszawa), sign. 86/5-6, Collection: Documents of Gen. Haller, Biographical Note of Leon T. Walkowicz

The close cooperation that existed between PAVA and the AAVPE is evident from the many events to which the organizations mutually invited each other, or else which were organized with joint effort, for instance commemorative anniversary celebrations, ceremonies related to Polish and American national holidays, joint participation in welcoming committees and in hosting prominent guests from Poland, such as Gen. Józef Haller, Ignacy Jan Paderewski, Aleksander Skrzyński and Polish parliamentarians. From time to time articles about AAVPE activities appeared in *The Veteran*. This helped to increase the number of subscribers to the periodical, because the Polish veterans from the American Army on the whole knew Polish.

It is apparent from the fragmentary surviving correspondence between the PAVA and the AAVPE leadership that the Polish American Veterans Club of Hamtramck, Michigan, which had retained its autonomy, kept in close touch with PAVA Posts Nr. 7 and 78 in Detroit, Michigan. This is confirmed by a letter of F. Pochmara, the Club's secretary, who wrote to PAVA secretary Jan Szymański on December 9, 1926: "...We live on very friendly terms with Posts 7 and 78 and always help each other."

In 1927 the work of the AAVPE was directed by an executive board which included: head commander Leon T. Walkowicz; vice commander Marian Pietrowicz; vice commander for the state of Ohio Stefan A. Krawczyk; vice commander for the state of Wisconsin Józef C. Górski; adjutant general Frank J. Kempa; treasurer Mikołaj Piotrzkowski; directors: Stefan Kozuch, Walter Wojciechowski, Frank Czernek, John Gall, Wincenty Wiśniewski, Stefan Zaremba; chief physician Dr. Edward Dombrowski; head chaplain Stefan Bubacz.

The honorary AAVPE members at that time were: General John J. Pershing, General Józef Haller, General Ferdinand Foch and Colonel pilot Cedric C. Fauntleroy.[72] The names of General Haller and Colonel Fauntleroy on this list very eloquently testify to the strong currents existing in this organization that united Polish and American military traditions.

The Ladies Legion, an auxiliary organization, was active alongside the AAVPE. Its president was Olimpia Makowska.[73]

The Polish Legion of the American Army operated outside the structures of the Alliance of the American Veterans of Polish Extraction (AAVPE). It was established in the Bronx in the City of New York in 1927. In 1929 that organization supported PAVA's efforts to build a memorial mound in honor of General Kazimierz Pułaski in Savannah, Georgia, by sending telegrams to all the congressmen in the state of New York asking for federal financial support of the initiative of the Polish PAVA

---

72 Ibid.
73 Ibid.

veterans. Benjamin Anuszkiewicz, the chief commander of the Polish Legion of the American Army (PLAA) at that time, was an enthusiastic supporter of the idea. But the Legion's efforts brought no results.

A letter of February 7, 1929, on a different subject, has survived. It was written by Frank Krakowski, the secretary of the PLAA Post Nr. 1 in the Bronx, N.Y., to the PAVA National Executive Board in Detroit, Michigan. He noted in it, as a passive observer, that he was bothered by a certain issue of a political nature, which was painfully felt at that time by PAVA members who were mainly Blue Army veterans. Frank Krakowski wrote: "Piłsudski's Legionnaires were not the only ones involved in fighting for Poland. With my own eyes I personally saw your great power in France, but here only the Legionnaires are given credit."[74]

At the urging of the Alliance of the American Veterans of Polish Extraction, a Consolidation Congress was held on September 6 and 7, 1931 in Cleveland, Ohio, for all organizations of veterans of Polish descent who had served in the American Army. At this congress the delegates established one joint organization called the Polish Legion of American Veterans (PLAV). At the moment of consolidation it had 31 posts. There were 17 posts in the states of Wisconsin, Illinois and Ohio, 11 in the state of New York, and 3 in the state of Michigan. The next conventions of the PLAV took place in Hamtramck, MI, Cicero, IL, Milwaukee, WI, and Cleveland, OH. The fifth PLAV convention was held in Maspeth, NY from September 2 to 4, 1939.[75]

The consolidation of organizations of Polish veterans from the American Army greatly facilitated their cooperation with PAVA. Its forms remained pretty much unchanged. The mutual invitatons to each other's conventions, balls and commemorative meetings continued, as did participation in each other's Polish and American celebrations of national holidays and important anniversaries, for instance during the commemoration of the 250th anniversary of the Relief of Vienna. At that time, during the grand parade in Chicago organized for that occasion, units of veterans representing the Polish Army Veterans Association of America marched alongside units of the Polish Legion of American Veterans, as well as of the American Legion.[76]

The most important collaboration of PAVA and the PLAV in 1937 was their joint participation in the Committee to Honor the Memory of General Włodzimierz Krzyżanowski, which had been organized to transfer the ashes of the Polish hero of the American Civil War from their resting place in Brooklyn, New York to the

---

74 PAVA NEB Archives, sign. A-XXII/2, File: Polish Legion of the American Army
75 Letter of B. Skrzypczak, op. cit.; "Koledzy z Armii Amerykańskiej złączyli się w jedną organizację" ["Colleagues from the American Army Have United Into One Organization"] in: *Weteran [The Veteran]*
76 "250-ta rocznica Odsieczy Wiedeńskiej" ["250th Anniversary of the Relief of Vienna"] in: *Weteran [The Veteran]* October 1933, p. 13

National Cemetery at Arlington near Washington, D.C. Thanks to the contacts of PLAV's Benjamin Anuszkiewicz this event was given a high ranking and involved the top echelons of the U.S. government.

Several months later at the suggestion of this committee, on May 14, 1938 a monument funded by the Polish American community was unveiled and consecrated on General Krzyżanowski's grave site. Thanks to the efforts of the Committee's president, Major B. T. Anuszkiewicz, this ceremony was again given a high ranking, which is evident from the list of its distinguished participants: Deputy Secretary of Defense Louis Johnson (representing the U.S. government and the Armed Forces); Ambassador of the Polish Republic Count Jerzy Potocki; FIDAC president (the international combatant organization) General Roman Górecki; the General Quartermaster of the American Army, Colonel J. C. Barzynski; Consul of the Republic of Poland in New York, Dr. Sylwester Gruszka; delegates from various veteran organizations; the army band from the military academy at Ft. Mayer, Virginia, and a squadron of the 3rd Regiment of the U.S. Cavalry.

The representatives of several nations accredited to the government of the United States were also present at the ceremony. The ceremony was broadcast live across the entire United States and also beyond the ocean, to distant Poland.[77]

Just before the outbreak of World War II the Polish Legion of American Veterans had 54 posts in eight states: Illinois—21; New York—10; Ohio—7; Michigan—7; Wisconsin—5; Connecticut—2; Indiana—1 and Pennsylvania—1.[78]

PAVA Collaboration with American Veterans

In the years 1921–1939 the Polish Army Veterans Association of America had closest ties with the largest of the American veteran organizations, the American Legion, which was founded in 1919. It members were former soldiers of the American Army who had participated in the battles in France in the years 1917–1918. This fact had a decisive impact on the establishment of contacts between the two veteran organizations.There were mutual invitations for events organized by the one and the other organization, mainly concerning American and Polish national holidays, such as May 3 (the commemoration of the ratification of the Polish national constitution on May 3, 1791), Memorial Day, July 4 and November 11 (simultaneously commemorating the day Armistice began on the Western Front, and Polish Independence Day).

---

77 "Odsłonięcie i poświęcenie pomnika na grobie Generała Włodzimierza B. Krzyżanowskiego na Cmentarzu Arlington w Waszyngtonie" ["The Unveiling and Consecration of the Monument on the Gravesite of General Włodzimierz B. Krzyżanowski at Arlington Cemetery in Washington"] in: *Weteran [The Veteran]* April 1938, p. 10

78 Letter of B. Skrzypczak of July 30, 1939, op. cit.

The closeness of collaboration was evident during effective parades and marches, when uniformed members of both organizations proudly marched under their own banners. It took place in large cities as well as in small towns (wherever posts of both the American Legion and the Polish Army Veterans Association of America were active side by side).

Some of the largest collaborations of PAVA and the American Legion occurred in 1923, when General Józef Haller was jointly welcomed in America. He had been invited as the keynote speaker to the American Legion convention in San Francisco which took place from October 15 to 19 of that year. As part of his tour of the United States, from October 6 to December 8, 1923, General J. Haller logged more than 11,000 miles just on his route from New York to San Francisco. It was a huge organizational success both for PAVA and for the American Legion. The following members of the two organizations participated in the preparations and the supervision of the tour; from PAVA they were: Colonel Dr. Teofil Starzyński, Captain Lucjan Adamczak, Wojciech Karolczak, Captain Stanisław Nastał, Lieutenant Roman Hanasz; from the American Legion they were: Alvin Owsley (national commander), Colonel Lemuel Bolles (adjutant general), C. King, Colonel Bowman Elder, Lieutenant Stanley H. Reaney.[79]

During this trip Gen. Haller also visited Washington, D.C. where on October 9, 1923 he was received at the White House by President Calvin Coolidge, and later by Secretary of State Charles E. Hughes, General John J. Pershing (the commander of the American Forces at the front in France during World War I) and by General Hines—the Chairman of the Joint Chiefs of Staff. That same day Gen. Józef Haller, as the President of the Polish Red Cross, visited the headquarters of the American Red Cross, where in a special ceremony he decorated the flag of that organization with the Polish order of "Polonia Restituta" (Poland Reborn) for distinguished servce to the reborn Polish State.[80]

At PAVA's suggestion special Welcoming Committees were organized all along the enormous route of General Haller's tour, under the patronage of local American authorities. Thanks to this General Haller's visit was widely publicized in the American press, which wrote extensively about the General, about Poland and also about PAVA. It was terrific free promotion thanks to which PAVA became known throughout the United States. This greatly enhanced the prestige of the young organization in the eyes of America and the Polish American community, and especially among the leaders of the largest Polish American organizations, which from that moment became more open and generous toward the veterans.

---

79   PAVA NEB Archives, sign. A-XXVI/1

80   "Generał Józef Haller w Ameryce" [General Józef Haller in America"] in: *Weteran [The Veteran]* Cleveland, Ohio, Nr. 33, November 1823, p. 11

At the request of the PAVA Board the leadership of the American Legion prepared a list of 22 Americans who had made the greatest contribution in preparing Gen. Haller's tour. These individuals, American veterans and civilians, were decorated for their work with the Hallerian Swords medal. Among them were: Brigadier General Asher Miner and the governors of California (W. D. Stephens) and Michigan (A. J. Grosbeck).[81]

Representatives of the Polish American community who had contributed to Gen. Haller's visit were rewarded with similar decorations. Among those who were decorated was also the famous Polish film actress Pola Negri, who hosted a great banquet at her own expense in the "Blue General's" honor in Beverly Hills. Many of the luminaries of the film world participated in it.[82]

At the beginning of 1924 the Board of the American Legion through PAVA requested the Polish government to bestow military and civilian decorations on American military leaders from the First World War. On March 21, 1924 the PAVA secretary general, Stanisław Z. Stachowicz, informed the leadership of the American Legion that according to information received by Lt. Jan Roskosz, the PAVA delegate in Warszawa, General Pershing had received the Order of Virtuti Militari IInd Class, and General Liggotti the Order of Virtuti Militari Vth class, and five other higher officers of the American Army had received Orders of Poland Reborn (Polonia Restituta) of various classes.[83]

Among the top executives of the American Legion, Colonel L. Bolles (who valued Poles very highly) deserves special mention. Making use of the strong influence that he had at high levels of the American government he helped mold a favorable opinion there of Poles and Poland. Moreover he engaged himself in the cause of the Kościuszko Foundation, which was established in 1925. Polish diplomatic circles in the United States noticed this and in September 1926 Colonel Lemuel Bolles received the Officer's Cross of the Order of Poland Reborn from Polish Consul Marynowski in New York, during a ceremonial banquet organized especially for that occasion at the Hotel Pennsylvania in New York City. Polish veterans living in New York gave Colonel Bolles honorary membership in PAVA Post Nr. 21.[84]

William Siple was also very favorably disposed to Poland and the Poles. He was one of the first organizers of the American Legion in Paris in 1919, and later the adjutant general of that organization in the state of Oklahoma. For his positive work on behalf of Poles he was decorated by the PAVA National Executive Board with the

---

81 PAVA NEB Archive, sign. A-XXII/6, File: American Legion 1924–1926
82 PAVA NEB Archives, sign. A-XXX/11, File: Hallerian Swords. 1925–1934
83 Ibid.
84 "Polska odznacza pułkownika Bolles" [Poland Decorates Colonel Bolles"] in: *Weteran [The Veteran]* September 1926, p. 30

Hallerian Swords medal in 1932.[85]

Another intensification of contacts between PAVA headquarters and the American Legion occurred in 1929, when the PAVA National Executive Board developed a plan to build a memorial mound in honor of General Kazimierz Pułaski in Savannah. The national commander of the American Legion at that time, Paul V. McNutt, agreed to accept honorary membership in the committee that had been organized specifically for that purpose. The idea did not bear fruit, but both Polish and American veterans participated in many events connected with that project.

The next venture in which both American and Polish veterans played an important role, was the transferal of General Włodzimierz Krzyanowski's ashes from a cemetery in Brooklyn to Arlington National Cemetery and the unveiling of a monument on his grave site several months later. A unit of specially uniformed American Legionnaires from the District of Columbia participated in this latter ceremony on May 14, 1938. Moreover delegations from other American veteran organizations were also present: the Veterans of Foreign Wars of the U.S. Disabled American Veterans of the World War, and the GAR Loyal Legion of the U.S.[86]

The ties that connected PAVA with the American Legion and their significance can be attested to by the fact that in July 1939 the PAVA Board received an invitation to participate in the 21st Convention of the New York district of the American Legion, which numbered over 16,000 members in 121 posts. PAVA national commander Lucjusz Kajko represented the Polish veterans at that convention.[87]

Collaboration with Canadian Veteran Organizations

After World War I, the veteran movement developed quite energetically in Canada, which at the time was a British dominion. In the first years after the conclusion of the war there were already more than a dozen independent veteran associations. The consolidation of this movement began in June 1925, and by November of that year one strong union had been formed: The Canadian Legion of the British Empire Service League.[88]

PAVA began working rather quickly with the Canadian Legion on the local level around the border region near Buffalo, NY where PAVA Post Nr. 1 was active. At its suggestion Polish, Canadian and American veterans held joint festivities in Canada to

---

85 "Legion Amerykański przesyła podziękowanie naszej organizacji" ["The American Legion Sends its Thanks to Our Organization"] in: *Weteran [TheVeteran]* January 1933, p. 3

86 "Odsłonięcie i poświęcenie pomnika na grobie gen. Włodzimierza Krzyżanowskiego na cmentarzu Arlington w Waszyngtonie" ["The Unveiling and Consecration of the Memorial Monument on the Gravesite of Gen. Włodzimierz Krzyżanowski at Arlington National Cemetery in Washington, D.C."] in: *Weteran [The Veteran]* April 1938, p. 10

87 PAVA NEB Archives, sign. A-XXII/7, File: American Legion. 1929–1931

88 Information from The Canadian Legion web page

commemorate Memorial Day at Niagara on the Lake. They began with the laying of wreaths at the grave sites of Polish volunteers to the Polish Army in France who had died at the local camp there in the years 1917–1918. Next, the veteran groups with their flags marched to the center of the town, where wreaths were laid at the memorial monument honoring fallen Canadian soldiers. The ceremony held in 1930 was particularly impressive. Polish diplomats from Canada and the United States participated, together with General Nelles, the Mayor of the City of Niagara on the Lake, Polish and Canadian veterans and the entire fully uniformed Adam Plewacki Post of the American Legion from Buffalo. The most inspiring moment came with the laying of wreaths on the memorial cross at the local cemetery by the veterans of the Canadian Legion. The American Legion veterans gave a three gun salute, and the trumpeter, standing among the Polish graves, played Taps in honor of the deceased Polish soldiers.[89]

From 1930 on Polish veterans from the Canadian territories also joined the various commemorative events. They had formed the Polish Veterans Mutual Aid Society of Ontario in nearby Toronto. The Society joined PAVA on June 23, 1930 and was registered as PAVA Post Nr. 114 in Toronto, ONT. This post received its flag on November 9 of that year. A delegation of the local Canadian Legion joined the ceremony, which was distinguished by the presence of PAVA president Lt. Wacław Rżewski.[90]

From that time on PAVA Post Nr. 114, as also the other PAVA posts in Canada that were formed at a later date, participated in cermonial events organized by the Canadian Legion. The Canadian Legion, on the other hand, returned the favor and participated in events organized by the Polish veterans.

A big event in the organizational life of the Polish and Canadian veterans was the presentation of a new flag to PAVA Post Nr. 114 in Toronto by General Dr. Roman Górecki, the president of FIDAC. This occurred on March 20, 1938 in the church of St. Stanislaus Kostka with the participation of Polish Consul General Jan Pawlica from Ottawa, Canada, Colonel Alley, the President of the Canadian legion, and representatives of many Polish Canadian organizations.[91]

The presence of the President of the Canadian Legion was distinct evidence of the good mutual relations between Polish and Canadian veterans.

Another Polish veteran organization formed in the country of the Maple leaf, was The Defenders of the Fatherland Association of Canada, which was organized

---

89 "U grobów żołnierzy polskich w Niagara on the Lake" ["At the graves of the Polish soldiers at Niagara on the Lake"] in: *Weteran [The Veteran]* July 1930, p. 19
90 PAVA NEB Archives, sign. Box-15, vol. 1, Files of PAVA Post Nr. 114 in Toronto. 1930–1946
91 "Z poświęcenia, rozwinięcia i wręczenia sztandaru Placówki 114 SWAP" ["On the Consecration, Unfurling and Presentation of the Flag to PAVA Post Nr. 114"] in: *Weteran [The Veteran]* May 1938, p. 16

in December 1933 in Winnipeg, Manitoba. In 1937 A. Nowak stood at the head of this association, which had 85 members.[92] This association had the support of the pro-Piłsudski Federation of Polish Associations of Defenders of the Fatherland (FPADF), which saw the Winnipeg organization as a beachhead for its activities to gain influence in individual PAVA posts in Canada. An expression of this policy was the offering in March 1938 by FPADF president Gen. Roman Górecki (at that time also the president of FIDAC) of the flag for the above-mentioned PAVA Post Nr. 114 in Toronto.[93]

A Polish post was also formed in Winnipeg alongside the local Canadian Legion. Its full name was Canadian Legion of the British Empire Service League, Polish Branch No. 34. In 1934 its executive board consisted of: T. R. Coslik—honorary president; B. Zeglinski—president; W. A. Drelenkiewicz—secretary and treasurer; members: B. Kanonowicz, T. Tylko and C. Bloom.[94]

The membership of the post also included Blue Army veterans, for instance the post's secretary, W. A. Drelenkiewicz, served as a sergeant in the 9th Regiment of Polish Riflemen (later called the 51st Regiment of Borderland Riflemen). He knew Lucjusz Kajko (who later became the PAVA national commander) from their army days. In a letter of August 30, 1935 to the PAVA National Executive Board he wrote: "Please extend my greetings to colleague Kajko, who took the instructor courses together with me at Niagara on the Lake and in Quentin, France, and also to other colleagues who remember my name from our time of service in the Polish Army."[95]

From sparse archival documentation it is apparent that this post had a hand in the financing of a memorial tablet dedicated to soldiers of the Polish army who had been members of the Polish Falcons Nest in Winnipeg. It was unveiled in the local Falcons hall in November 1934. On November 11, 1935 the post commemorated the anniversary of Armistice on the Western Front and the regaining of Polish independence. At that event the post's secretary, W. A. Drelenkiewicz, gave a lecture on the history of the Polish Army in France. Józef Sierociński's book *Armia Polska we Francji* (*The Polish Army in France*) proved to be a great help in preparing the lecture. The speaker had received it by mail from PAVA adjutant general Leopold Krzyżak.[96]

There was yet another, little known, organization in Canada, the Marshall Józef Piłsudski Veterans Union in Montreal. This organization no doubt had very close

---

92 M. Jabłonowski. *Polityczne aspekty ruchu byłych wojskowych w Polsce 1918–1939* [*Political Aspects of the Movement of Former Servicemen in Poland 1918–1939*] Warszawa 1989, p. 189
93 *The Veteran* May 1938, p. 16
94 PAVA NEB Archives, sign. A-XXII/vol. 10, File: Canadian Legion of the British Empire Service League, Polish Branch.
95 Ibid.
96 Ibid.

ties with the Polish government, since in February 1937 it received two crates of uniforms from Poland for its members.[97] This was eloquent evidence of the attitude of pro-Piłsudski authorities in Poland toward Polish veteran organizations active in other countries. Those that approved of the pro-Piłsudski government in Poland after 1926 could count on the help of the Polish government.

To be frank it should be added that PAVA had no contacts with the Veterans Union in Montreal.

From the above cited evidence it is apparent that the Polish veteran movement in Canada in the years 1921–1939 was rather weak. This was in some sense the effect of the poor results that were noted in that country during the recruitment activities for the Polish Army in France in the years 1917–1919 (barely 231 volunteers, or about 1 percent of the number of volunteers from the United States).[98] Subsequent veterans who arrived in Canada as part of the non-military post-war emigration came from various military formations and hence were very amenable to the influence of existing Polish veteran organizations, or ones that were in the process of organizing, that supported the pro-Piłsudski government in Poland. That was what the pro-Piłsudski Federation of Polish Societies of Defenders of the Fatherland was counting on. Its activities were aimed at gradually including all Polish veteran organizations in Canada in its organizational structure. Those efforts were crowned with success just before the outbreak of World War II.

---

97 New Documents Archive (Warszawa), sign. 113, World Federation of Poles Abroad: Letter of February 4, 1937 from the Polish Consulate in Montreal to the World Federation of Poles Abroad in Warszawa, p. 76

98 J. Walter. *Czyn zbrojny wychodźstwa polskiego w Ameryce* [*The War Effort of the Polish Immigration in America*] Warszawa 2001, p. 394

VII.
Fighting Anti-Polish Propaganda and Communist Infiltration

Former Blue Army soldiers, who after the conclusion of the war returned to the United States and Canada, were very interested in everything that had to do with Poland. The old country, for whose freedom they had fought with weapons in hand, was very close to their hearts. Although it was their lot to work and live on American soil, they felt permanently connected with Poland. That was certainly true of those who made up the ranks of the Polish Army Veterans Association of America. For good reason one of the most important goals written into the By-Laws of that organization is: "To improve the cult for the Fatherland, Its Government, authorities and the entire Polish name in the broadest sense of that word. To hold high the standard of national dignity. To repel all encroachments and attacks against the Polish state in peacetime, as we did on the field of battle, remembering that we owe total loyalty and devotion to our adopted Fatherland, the United States of America."[1]

Guided by these directives PAVA reacted energetically from the beginning of its existence (in line with its modest possibilities) to symptoms of anti-Polish acts in the United States and Canada.

Among the most frequently occurring anti-Polish happenings after World War I was propaganda from German, Jewish, Ukrainian and communist circles aimed at the reborn Polish state and its representatives. The common characteristic of this propaganda was denial of the existence of the Polish state itself, which was represented in the worst light possible, describing it as an imperialist, seasonal governmental creation with a hostile attitude toward all ethnic minorities.

Aside from hostile propaganda in the press there were also sporadic anti-Polish demonstrations in front of Polish diplomatic posts. One of them, organized by Ukrainians, took place on February 22, 1922 in front of the Polish consulate in New York. In their speeches the demonstration leaders accused Polish volunteers from

---

1 *By-Laws and Regulations of the Polish Army Veterans Association of America* Cleveland 1925, p. 4

America, who fought in the Blue Army, of murder, robbery and rape perpetrated against the Ukrainian civilian population in the years 1919–1920 in Eastern Galicia.

In reply to these accusations a front-page article in English appeared in the March issue of *The Veteran* titled"Ukrainian Blackhanders," authored by PAVA secretary Stanisław Z. Stachowicz, who (rejecting the Ukrainian imputations) cited examples of Ukrainian barbarity perpetrated on Polish civilians and Polish prisoners of war. Stachowicz also sent this text to American and Polish American newspapers. Consequently, a Polish voice was also able to reach broader American public opinion.[2]

Unfortunately, the Polish American press also came to the aid of circles in America that were hostile to Poland. It transferred the post-war political quarrels in Poland onto American soil. In the intense political warfare that took place on its pages there were no restraints in the attacks against any opponent who dared hold different political views. The casting of calumnies and insinuations against even the highest authorities and values, with the reborn Polish state included, was the order of the day. This testified to the very low level of the persons who were practicing journalism, and who had great influence through the press on broad public opinion. The PAVA veterans frequently warned of the disastrous effects of such behavior. One of them, Czesław Żuławski, the editor of *The Veteran*, wrote: "The effects of this behavior are lamentable. For despite the fact that this "warfare" is carried on in the Polish language, its echoes also filter through to American opinion, shaping the worst kind of opinion not only for the Polish immigration in America, but also for our native country....Did the publishers and journalists of the Polish press in America ever ask themselves that question? Has this kind of airing of internal Polish party strife before the public forum in America helped even in the tiniest way to normalize governance in Poland, to instill confidence throughout financial spheres in Poland's creditworthiness; has this kind of washing of dirty Polish political laundry in the wide market of American opinion helped to raise the prestige of the Polish State in American government spheres?"[3]

A reading of the Polish American press of those days (the first years of reborn Polish statehood) was wonderful fodder for the anti-Polish propaganda cultivated by the above-named spheres of American society. The PAVA leadership saw this, but unfortunately it was unable to neutralize it effectively.

In 1923 PAVA veterans (who were sensitive to every act of anti-Polish propaganda) noticed that it was being carried on not only in the ethnic press, but also in the American press, which was writing about Poland with increasing ill will.

---

2 *The Veteran* Nr, 10, March 27, 1922, pp. 1-2
3 C. Żuławski, "Walka o urojenia, czy wspólna praca dla przyszłości Polski?" ["Battle Over Delusions, or Joint Work on Behalf of Poland's Future?"] in: *Weteran [The Veteran]* June 1923, pp. 5-7

This was a big, unpleasant shock for the veterans, because after 1918 the American press was rather positively disposed toward the reborn Polish state. Nonetheless after several years this attitude began to change. Poland (battling against enormous problems that it inherited from the partitioning powers) was unable to resolve all the issues in a satisfactory way. Voices started appearing in the American press that questioned the rationale of having awarded Poland part of Upper Silesia and the Gdańsk region of Pomerania, as also Southeastern Poland, and even the entire Eastern Borderlands.

PAVA veterans explained this state by the susceptibility of American journalists to the influence of German, Ukrainian and Bolshevik propaganda due to a lack of appropriate Polish source material. In order to counteract this, in September 1923 the PAVA leadership proposed to create a joint press office in Washington, D.C. and its permanent representation in Poland, which would together, on a daily basis, submit to the American and Polish American press the most important information about current events in Poland. PAVA argued that there would be ample benefits for Poland and the Polish community in America if this project were to come to pass.[4] Unfortunately, this interesting initiative did not find any takers among other Polish American organizations. *The Veteran* returned to this question in its subsequent issue (October 1923), taking a stand regarding an anti-Polish article "Poland Threatens Peace" which appeared in the monthly *Current History*. The editor of *The Veteran* concluded his critical remarks with a question directed at the Polish American community: "What is the Polish American community doing to counteract this propaganda? Nothing. Absolutely nothing. We can at best refute this propaganda in our papers, but we have no access to American society, even though we are so tightly coupled with it. We have no influence. We have absolutely no writers in the English language. Our Polish journalists, who are so skilfull at cutting each other's throats, at hanging Piłsudski, Haller, Witos, Paderewski, Dmowski and others from the gallows, have no access to the American press, because nobody would pay them even a penny for their views."[5]

In the fall of 1923 anti-Polish circles in the United States used General Haller's first visit to carry out a massed propaganda attack directed at him personally and also at the Polish State. The Jewish and German press were especially good at it. *The Jewish Tribune,* which was published in New York City, printed an article by Herman Bernstein which accused Gen. Haller in these words: "General Haller, whose name is connected with the infamous days of liberated Poland, is identified with and in great

---

4   "Antypolska propaganda" ["Anti-Polish Propaganda"] in: *Weteran [The Veteran]* September 1923, pp. 1-2
5   *The Veteran* October 1923, pp. 45-46

measure responsible for anti-Jewish escapades, he only represents the dark forces of Poland ... Inviting General Haller to the convention of the American Legion is an affront ... it is also an insult to the American nation. This peculiar Polish general, whose record is sullied with the blood and tears of peaceful, helpless citizens of his own country, should not be honored by Americans."[6]

The German *New York Staatszeitung* came to the aid of the Jewish paper by printing various calumnies against General Haller: "The decision of the American Legion to bring the famed "Polakengeneral" Haller to America, to host him in New York and invite him to the convention in San Francisco, caused a reaction in the ranks of this organization. ... The entire Legion is branded in the sharpest words for daring to invite this notorious manslayer (*Menschenschlaechter*) who in Upper Silesia together with his volunteers committed horrific and just unbelievable cruelties, ordering the burning, robbery and murder of the civilian population. And for these reasons such a person should not be allowed to associate with American soldiers."[7]

In support of its thesis the newspaper cited a resolution that had been approved by the Sydney Resenberg Post of the American Legion in Brooklyn, in which the following accusations are enumerated against General J. Haller: "General Józef Haller of the Polish Army, who led a regiment of Polish soldiers in 1918, initiated and purposely perpetrated acts of cruelty against defenceless men, women and children, residents of his country, Poland. ... The Polish soldiers commanded by Józef Haller murdered hundreds of Jews in cold blood in Jewish settlements in Poland, Galicia and Lvov."[8]

Stanisław Z. Stachowicz, the PAVA secretary, answered these kinds of accusations against Gen. Haller. He asked the question in *The Veteran* if it were possible for Gen. Haller and his soldiers to commit pogroms against the Jewish population of Poland in 1918, when he was with his army in France at that time?"[9]

But the attacks against Gen. J. Haller continued. On October 29, 1923 Levy I. Kaufman wrote in the *New York Call*: "General Haller, whose hands are red with the blood of innocent Jews, was everywhere greeted and hosted here. The Army that General Haller commanded was the worst of all. Its soldiers not only robbed, but also killed men, women and children. As soon as his army entered our town [unfortunately, its name was not given—T. L.] in 1920, it began terrorizing us. First they cut off Jews' beards, then they began robbing, and finally murdering. They

---

[6] Quoted after: S. Z. Stachowicz, "Kto jest kto?" ["Who is Who?"] in: *Weteran [The Veteran]* March 1924, pp. 13-15
[7] Ibid.
[8] Ibid.
[9] Ibid.

exposed young girls to shame in front of their parents. They committed thousands of other outrages, which it is impossible to describe here."[10]

Unfortunately, part of the Polish American left-wing press mindlessly copied the accusations against Gen. J. Haller that appeared in the Jewish and German press. In their political passion they only saw a man of the right in the person of Gen. Haller, and did not want to notice that the General (in coming onto American soil) represented the Polish Armed Forces—the armed hand of the independent Polish State. They did not know how to respect this fact. PAVA members were forced to counteract the malevolent propaganda flowing not only from foreign spheres, but also coming from the Polish community in America. That policy was mainly enacted by the Polish socialists in their press and at the rallies organized by them. This was most strongly evident in October 1923 in Detroit. The *Dziennik Polski* (*The Polish Daily*) attacked the "Blue General," and agitators at the rallies echoed these attacks. The veterans of PAVA Post Nr. 7 reacted in a very decisive fashion. En masse, and one must remember that this was the second largest post in the entire PAVA, dressed in their blue uniforms, they went to the next rally organized by the socialists. When insults started flying against Gen. Haller, one of the veterans, Zygmunt Rowiński, tried to get on stage to publicly ask the speaker why he was dishonoring such a distinguished soldier. In reply he was hit with a chair. At that, the rally in the Dom Ludowy (People's Home) hall turned into a general melee, in which many of the participants were wounded and badly beaten up. The bats and other tools that, as it turned out, the socialists were armed with, were no match for the soldiers' fury and collegial solidarity. The veterans used their bare fists to teach respect for the Polish soldier and his commander. In the encounter Lt. Wacław Rżewski proved to be the best of all. He was a Chevalier of the Cross of Valor, and later the PAVA president. After the fight, in reply to attacks from the leftist press, the veterans of PAVA Post Nr. 7 gave their answer in *Rekord Codzienny* (*The Daily Record*): "We went as a group, to forestall the desecration of the uniform of the Polish soldier, which is a symbol not of the right, nor of the left, nor of any party, but of Polish armed might—the Polish Army. ... We proclaim and we swear, that as we previously defended the honor, dignity and entirety of the Polish name in the thick of enemy fire at the front, so we will defend it here against Bolshevik threats and a deceitful enemy."[11]

The events in Detroit were a drastic example of how strong the political divisions were in the Polish American community. They had begun in 1914 with the definition of two opposing camps: the National Department and the National

---

10 Ibid.
11 PAVA NEB, sign. Box -3/1, Collection: PAVA Posts, File: PAVA Post Nr. 7 in Detroit, MI.

Defense Committee. The visit of General Haller in the United States made that division fully visible.

The climax of hostile propaganda aimed at Gen. Haller occurred in Boston. There the attacks of the German, Jewish and crypto-communist press, together with the support of the Polish American leftist press headed by the *Dziennik dla Wszystkich* (*Universal Daily*) published in Buffalo, caused the Mayor of Boston to order a public hearing concerning the accusations being leveled by German and Jewish circles not only against Gen. Haller, but also against the Polish Army and the Polish State. Given the circumstances General Haller did not pay the Mayor the visit that had been announced earlier, and instead accepted an invitation from the Governor of the State of Massachusetts.[12]

The American press was of great help to the Polish side in refuting the hostile attacks against Gen. Haller. This was possible mainly because PAVA 2nd Lt. Roman Hanasz was active on the American military staff that was supervising the course of the general's visit. Hanasz prepared appropriate press releases for the American and Polish press. Lt. James Grant was of great help to him in this work. Working on the staff as a professional journalist he had access to every American newspaper. Thanks to this the American (national and local) press and partially the Polish American press received a steady, fresh stream of information about General Haller and Polish issues throughout the general's U.S. tour. This information differed from the news that the German, Jewish, Ukrainian and crypto-communist press used to try to smear the guest from Poland, the Polish armed forces, and the nation which he represented. What an outstanding job Lt. Hanasz did can be seen by the fact that the entire visit of Gen. Haller in the United States, thanks to a properly run campaign in the American press, was a great promotional success for the General himself, and for Poland.[13]

The attacks against Poland in the American press did not stop in the following years. The staff of *The Veteran* was particularly sensitive to them. In an article titled "We are Fighting for Poland's Good Reputation" Czesław Żuławski noted in 1925 the positive fact that representatives of the Polish government had frequently corrected erroneous information concerning Polish matters in the high-circulation American press. But he drew attention to the danger of anti-Polish propaganda that was being printed in the local press, to which the Poles were not reacting at all. He appealed passionately to PAVA members to react to such facts, and simultaneously advised on what to do in case of poor knowledge of the English language: "Colleagues! We have to watch the American press attentively and reply to every accusation that is

---

12 *The Veteran* March 1924, p. 2

13 R. Hanasz "Sprawozdanie z objazdu gen. Hallera: ["Report on Gen. Haller's Tour"] in: *Weteran [The Veteran]* February 1924, p. 10

unfair and damaging to Poland. But reply **immediately**. You can't delay that, just as you can't delay in parrying a punch. The answer must be as swift and decisive as a bayonet thrust, as clear and clean as the glint of steel, and as simple and honest as our soldierly hearts.

"It is true, many of our colleagues would write often to the American papers, but they don't have an adequate knowledge of English. Yet there is a remedy. Let everybody write the best they can, and then ask a student, doctor, pharmacist, in other words somebody who knows English, to correct the text, and that person will edit the contents appropriately. I don't think that anybody would reject rendering this kind of service.

"Acting in this way, Polish veterans can with time influence the editors of American papers to first check out the accuracy of their information before they print an article that is damaging to Poland."[14]

The Veteran's staff, wanting to give the non-English speaking PAVA members access to the American press, translated and printed extensive fragments and even entire articles of the hostile, anti-Polish propaganada. Their very titles were indicative, for instance: "Poland Threatens Peace," "Poland's Suicide," etc.[15] Some of these articles (written from the American point of view, and being objective analyses of the complex internal relations of the Polish State and its difficult external political situation) often contained very accurate observations, which were, unfortunately, unacceptable to Polish public opinion, which described them unequivocally as anti-Polish.

The PAVA veterans were also sensitive to all manner of communist propaganda and infiltration. During the battles on the Eastern front in Poland in the years 1919–1920 they often had the opportunity to experience communism in practice, and that is why their relationship to this ideology was unequivocally negative. Leopold Krzyżak, the PAVA adjutant general, said the following on this subject in 1937: "We do not see the communists as our comrades and we don't admit them to our organization, unless they keep their communist views to themselves and don't try to publicize them among their colleagues at their Post, because our organization is truly apolitical and we do not recognize any kind of politics."[16]

The phenomenon of infiltration by communist elements also affected veteran circles in Winnipeg, Canada. A patriotic Polish veteran organization, The Association of Polish Defenders of the Fatherland of Canada, was active in that town in 1937. Several of its members turned out to be communists, and were therefore removed

---

14 *The Veteran* September 1925, p. 16
15 *The Veteran* September 1923, pp. 45-46; April 1926, pp. 8-12
16 PAVA NEB Archives, sign. Box-19, Collection: PAVA Posts, Post 160. 1937–1938, letter of December 7, 1937 from L. Krzyżak to A. Szczurski

from the ranks. The rejected group got the idea to join PAVA. Unaware of this, the PAVA National Executive Board in New York City gladly agreed to form a new post in Canada, and registered it as Number "160" in August 1937. What a great surprise it was when in December a letter, written by a former Blue Army soldier, arrived from Winnipeg at the PAVA National Executive Board offices informing that in the PAVA Post Nr. 160: "… there is not a single former volunteer, but there are plenty of open friends of Moscow, active and leading members of the local Polish People's Communist Society. The first public appearance of the Post, at the celebration of the 14th of this month, was announced by the Bolshevik *The Voice of Work*, which is proof that the communists consider Post Nr. 160 to be their own. The announcement and the invitation to the celebration organized by Post Nr. 160 in a paper as hostile to Poland as *The Voice of Work* is an affront to your organization and to the local former Blue Army volunteers. … If it were possible to maintain a Post of your organization here, you would have had it long ago already. But because there are only four of us we therefore joined the Polish Branch of the Canadian Legion in 1921 and work within its structure. …The names of the former Blue Army volunteers currently living in Winnipeg are as follows: W. A. Drelenkiewicz, Karol Gidziński, Antoni Wiktor, A. Kawalec. Piotr Wojtanowicz died last summer. All told about twenty individuals from Winnipeg served in the Polish Army in France, but several stayed in Poland, two were killed in battle, and the rest dispersed over various cities of the United States and Canada.[17]

At the request of the PAVA NEB Dr. Juliusz Szygowski, the Polish Consul in Winnipeg, checked out the situation at PAVA Post Nr. 160. He informed as follows in a letter of December 29, 1937: "I unfortunately have to declare that Post Nr. 160 is controlled by communist individuals, who are even present on the Post's Executive Board. The Commander, A. Szczawurski, is playing a murky role. The Post's Vice Commander, K. Dębkowski, belongs to the communist party; A. Kowalski, the financial adjutant, also, and the same is true of P. Fedor, the treasurer. The remaining members are at least communist sympathizers, if not party members. …I want to note at this opportunity that there are at least 4 persons in Post Nr. 160 who participated in the fight for our independence, the others are, at best, post-war soldiers."[18]

After receiving this information the PAVA National Executive Board dissolved Post Nr. 160 in Winnipeg, Canada in January 1938.

After the beginning of World War II one veteran was dismissed from PAVA ranks for promulgating communist propaganda. This took place in Post Nr. 155 in

---

17 PAVA NEB Archives, sign. Box-19, Collection: PAVA Posts, Post Nr. 160 in Winnipeg, Manitoba, Canada 1937–1938
18 Ibid.

Flint, Michigan. The financial adjutant of that post, F. Pacyna, in a letter to the PAVA NEB dated October 3, 1939 wrote: "I want to also let you know that Post Nr. 155 member F. Nowak was removed from our organization for communist agitation in our Post and for morally reprehensible machinations within the ranks of our organization. The Post concluded that there is no place in our ranks for a nest of red Stalin's unjustified barbarians. We ask that the mailing of *The Veteran* to the former colleague—presently a Bolshevik—be immediately halted, and that he be listed in the registers as harmful to Poland."[19]

The PAVA NEB reacted instantly and by October 5, 1939 it informed Post Nr. 155 that F. Nowak had been stripped of PAVA membership.[20]

PAVA veterans were very sensitive to all types of anti-Polish propaganada, which they counteracted to the full extent of their modest capabilities. Their action often did not go far enough, because there was a lack of properly trained people who could write fluent English, and the financial means were not available to access the American press, radio and film. Nonetheless the PAVA leadership was highly effective in combating attempts at hostile propaganda within its own ranks.

---

19 PAVA NEB Archives, sign. Box-18/1, Collection: PAVA Posts; Post Nr. 155 in Flint.
20 Ibid.

VIII.
PAVA IN POLAND'S SOCIAL AND POLITICAL LIFE

In the years 1921–1939 the Polish Army Veterans Association of America maintained constant contact with Poland on various levels. These links had both a direct and indirect character. Regarding the latter, PAVA cooperated with Polish diplomatic posts in the United States and Canada, with the Polish legation in Washington, D.C.– which was later the Polish Embassy—and with the consulates in New York, Chicago, Detroit, Buffalo, Pittsburgh and Winnipeg, Canada. Moroever there was contact with Polish companies doing business in the United States, such as Bank Pekao, or the transportation firm Gdynia-America Line.

The veterans eagerly availed themselves of the services of the Polish outposts, because they could take care of all their matters there in Polish, and in addition they had the awareness that (in using those services) they were supporting Poland financially. Thus both sides were pleased with their cooperation.

Direct contacts with Poland were chiefly maintained through correspondence, official visits of emissaries, group tours and the maintenance of organizational structures in the old country, such as the PAVA Delegature in Warszawa (1922–1923) and PAVA Post Nr. 130 in Bydgoszcz (1933–1939).

Within the framework of cooperation with Poland contacts were maintained with the highest authorities, with the Polish Armed Forces and with social (mainly veteran) organizations and institutions. Attempts were made at business activity. The quality and intensity of these contacts was undoubtedly greatly influenced by the great distance that divided PAVA from Poland and by issues of a political nature. The latter were essential enough that they deserve more attention.

Let us recall that the war effort of the Polish immigration in America during World War I was politically connected with the National Defense Committee in Paris. The Polish Army in France under the command of General Józef Haller, in which 20,000 volunteers from America served, was generally seen in Poland as the military arm of the National Democratic Party whose leader was Roman Dmowski—

the political opponent of Józef Piłsudski. The latter symbolized the Polish leftist independent movement and simultaneously the Polish Legions that formed alongside the Central European states that during the war fought, among others, with France. For these reasons the soldiers of the Polish Army in France were popularly called Hallerians, ascribing to them ad hoc a national democratic provenance, while soldiers that served under the command of J. Piłsudski in the years 1914–1919 were called legionnaires—pow-iaks (adherents of the Polska Organizacja Wojskowa—the Polish Military Organization) or Pilsudski-ites. Those who sided with Piłsudski had a decidedly anti-national democratic attitude, and saw themselves as the main liberators of Poland and creators of the Polish Armed Forces. This simplistic political division had a serious impact on mutual relations between individual veteran circles in independent Poland in the years 1921–1939. These divisions became especially apparent after J. Piłsudski's May 1926 coup d'état.

All those political complexities were not always understood by the simple soldiers—the volunteers from America, who didn't see themselves as some sort of "-ites," but only as soldiers of the Polish army who had done their patriotic duty toward the old country. They stressed that they had been soldiers and fought for Poland's freedom, and not for the leaders and their political cliques. Unfortunately, in the political realities of post-war Poland, the views and attitudes of the volunteers from America were not noticed at all. Casual observers unequivaocally associated Blue Army veterans with the national democrats, without checking if this had anything to do with reality. The uniform color and the name of the military formation from the war period were often the only determinant used to make political classifications in veteran spheres. The divisions that were thus created proved to be quite permanent and continued throughout the entire inter-war period. Unfortunately, in the case of PAVA the results of these divisions were essential enough that they made their mark on relations with Poland, especially after 1926.

Up to the May 1926 coup the political element did not play a significant role in relations, especially since PAVA had always emphasized that it was an apolitical organization, agglomerating Polish soldiers of many military formations who had fought for Poland's freedom. Nonetheless the vast majority of members in the Association had come from the ranks of the Blue Army, which naturally attracted this organization to similar veteran spheres active in Poland, which unlike PAVA were deeply involved in national political intrigues, such as for instance the Union of Hallerians. The PAVA leadership tried to keep its distance, but in some instances it could not remain indifferent, especially when key events of life inside Poland were concerned, or when external threats were aimed at the security of the Polish State.

PAVA Business Activity in Poland

The Polish Army Veterans Association of America had strong ties with Poland, for whose freedom its members had fought. During the years of Poland's independence the veterans from America wanted to continue to help their old country. Some of them intended to return to it permanently, but only after having built up enough financial capital to give them a good start in Poland. An important factor that hastened the decision to return to Poland was the news that the Polish government was making land grants (in line with the parliamentary bill of December 17, 1920) to former volunteer soldiers from America. The average size of land granted was between 15 and 40 morgs (21 to 55 acres). This was bare land without buildings. Each settler could only count on help from the Polish government in the form of 80 cubic meters of wood to construct his farm buildings.[1]

PAVA's first Board (on noticing the great interest in this Bill among the veterans) decided to engage in the organizational preparation of a resettlement operation. For this purpose a Resettlement Committee of the PAVA Board was organized, whose members were: S. Z. Stachowicz, M. Kowalski, W. Karolczak. By August 1921, after an exchange of correspondence with the Military Affairs Ministry in Warszawa, the Committee drafted a Resettlement Plan which projected the raising of about $200,000 for resettlement needs. This money was to be used to buy a large farm in Poland, which would serve as a shelter for disabled veterans—PAVA members. The plan also included financial aid for veterans from America who were settling on the Eastern Borderlands (Polish territory east of the Curzon Line). The plan also projected the establishment of a settler construction company, which was to erect residential and farm buildings for the settlers from America, and also act as a broker in the purchase of argicultural equipment, seeds and livestock and in the sale of their products without the use of Jewish middlemen who dominated across the Eastern Borderlands. The PAVA Delegature in Poland was created specifically to direct the activities of the veterans from America.[2]

Agribusiness and the Veteran Shelter in Kuligi

The attempt was made to put the plan in operation. In the spring of 1922 PAVA organized a fund drive for the Settlement and Invalid Fund, which brought in $107,000. The next step was to send a PAVA delegation to Poland, which included: Captain Lucjan Adamczak, Captain Stanisław Nastał, and Lieutenant Jan Roskosz.[3]

---

1 PAVA NEB Archives, sign. A-XV/1, Text of the Bill of December 17, 1920 "On the Taking For Government Property of Lands in Certain Counties of the Polish Republic"
2 PAVA NEB Archives, sign. A-XV/1, Resettlement Plan
3 *The Veteran* April 1924, p. 5

This group purchased the land estate Kuligi near Brodnica in Pomerania for almost $15,000. It was to serve as a shelter for war invalids and also as a transit point for veteran settlers arriving from America. After taking agricultural courses on this estate the settlers were to be directed further—to the Eastern Borderlands—in order to take possession of their own plots of granted land.

In the winter of 1922/1923 renovations were conducted in the largest two-story building, the so-called palace, which was to serve as a shelter for fifteen war invalids. Jan Paśniewski, a disabled veteran from Cleveland, Ohio, was the manager of the farm and the shelter. His farm assistant was Stanisław Żebracki, a former soldier of the 5th Siberian Division.

The first group of fiteen Polish war invalids arrived from America at PAVA expense on March 21, 1923.

The ceremonial opening and dedication of the shelter did not take place until September 2, 1923. It took place with the participation of General Józef Haller, General Zieliński, representatives of the Ministry of Military Affairs, Ministry of Agricultural Reforms, Ministry of Labor and Social Welfare, and representatives of religious and veteran organizations. Secretary General Stanisław Z Stachowicz represented PAVA. He was in Poland in connection with the military resettlement operation. At that time there were already nineteen invalids in the shelter. For some of them the stay in Kuligi was only a temporary episode, because after having received land grants on the Eastern Borderlands they moved to take possession of their plots. This concerned: Mieczysław Dzwonkowski, Roman Dzikowski, Feliks Rakoczy and Sentkowski.

By November 1923 two more disabled veterans had left the shelter: Józef Rygielski (he died after being transferred to the sanatorium in Rajcza) and Mikołaj Kulesza, who returned to America at his own expense.[4]

Other disabled veterans from America sporadically came to the shelter in Kuligi over the next several years. These were just individual cases of sick and single veterans, whom PAVA sent at their own request and its expense to Poland and placed in Kuligi. In the case of a veteran's death the association covered the funeral costs. That happened with Jan Szczepanek, who had tuberculosis. Shortly after arriving from America in 1925 he was transferred from the shelter to the hospital in Brodnica, where he died.[5]

The shelter at Kuligi, although well thought out, did not function as foreseen by the planners of this venture. As it became evident, the idea of a collective farm business was not realistic. Most of the veterans worked, it is true, but they did so

---

4 *The Veteran* November 1923, p.5
5 PAVA NEB Archives, sign. A-XVIII/7, Polish Consulate in Detroit. 1921–1932

unwillingly. Their dream was to work on their own farms. Several simply refused to do any work at all, while taking advantage of free room and board, which had a very demoralizing effect on the others. In addition they would send letters to the Polish American press back in the States, complaining that they were living like slaves, that they were being starved, etc. This caused a big stir in the Polish American community, and forced PAVA to organize a committee to investigate the matter. The inquiry showed that the authors of the letters had committed libel. The committee's report set the false story straight, but unfortunately the rumor had made its rounds and proved to be a very effective argument that restrained the invalids in America from resettling to Poland. The matter was even further complicated by the fact that Kuligi did not turn a profit and there was lack of direct supervision of the farm business by PAVA due to the distance separating Poland and America. The constant deficits at Kuligi (about $2,000 in 1928)[6] had to be covered by PAVA with money from the Invalid Fund, which placed the entire venture under a cloud.

The shelter at Kuligi was disbanded in 1929 and the farm itself was leased out. The inmates of the shelter were given a financial subsidy of $500 each to buy a small farm which remained the property of PAVA but on which the veteran could live to the end of his life without any financial obligations toward the Association. When they accepted the offer the veteran invalids also signed a declaration that they were renouncing the right to any complaints or claims against PAVA.[7]

The farm business at Kuligi proved to be a bottomless pit for PAVA. Subsequent lease holders cared more for their own interests than for the veterans' estate. No wonder then, that year after year the indebtedness on the estate kept growing, until finally in 1939 it was on the verge of bankruptcy, despite the $30,000 that PAVA had poured into it. Kuligi proved to be the biggest financial and business failure in PAVA history up to that time.

The Failure of the Resettlement Operation

The resettlement operation in Poland, prepared with such great exertion, did not succeed either. Despite special efforts the number of veterans from America arriving in Poland was negligible. The facts speak for themselves: in the summer of 1921, according to PAVA Board estimates, there were about 4,000 veterans willing to accept land grants in Poland. But of the first 400 plots of land in the counties of Włodzimierz, Równe, Dubno and Krzemieniec, granted by the Ministry of Military Affairs to Polish veterans from beyond the ocean, barely 65 were claimed by

---

6 PAVA NEB Archives, sign. A-XVI/4, Report of the Management Committee of the Kuligi Estate, May 9, 1928
7 PAVA NEB Archives, sign. A-XVI/7 Report of the Dissolution and Audit Committee for Matters Related to the Kuligi Estate. January 30, 1919

volunteers from America. In this situation in February 1923 the PAVA Delegature in Warszawa was forced to return 335 of the granted plots to the Ministry of Military Affairs and to conclude its activity, which occurred in January 1925.[8]

The PAVA Board spent $27,500 of the funds that it had, for the resettlement operation on the Eastern Borderlands, of which $20,000 was spent on helping the settlers get started, $5,000 on the development of military cooperatives for the settlers (OSKRES at Równe in Volhynia Province and the Miltiary Settlers Cooperative in Warszawa) and $2,500 for the construction of a church and school for the peasants in the military colony at Horyńgród, in Równe County.

The individual loans for military settlers dispensed by PAVA, mainly went to settlers from America. These were usually sums of $75 to $100. In many cases loans were also given to settlers who did not come from America but who were former Blue Army soldiers. In such instances the loans were mostly $50 each. For example on December 5, 1932 the PAVA Resettlement Committee granted loans to 28 settlers from America (Please see addendum 13) of $100 each for a total of $2,800, while 54 other settlers received loans of $50 each for the sum total of $2,700.[9]

The loans given by PAVA to the military settlers on the Eastern Borderlands (more than $8,000) were never repaid by them, because for many years (when they were on the make) they were unable to repay them, and when they were finally in a position to start doing so World War II began and destroyed all that they had accomplished.[10]

The largest investment was made in the Military Settlers Cooperative in Warszawa ($4,000 as the founding capital) which was to be an umbrella for the cooperatives operating on the Eastern Borderlands. Warehouses and stores were activated in the capital and stocked with products supplied by local borderlands cooperatives. Honey, smoked meat products, cheeses, fruit, mushrooms, and other goods were sold there.

In 1925 the Cooperative of Borderlands Settlers in Warszawa had a capital of 120,000 Polish zlotys and supplied the settlers and other farmers in the Eastern Borderlands with products that they needed for agricultural production: machines and farm tools, synthetic fertilizers, building materials, hard coal, iron, and even typewriters and fireproof safes.[11]

---

8 PAVA NEB Archives, sign. A-XV/1, Letter of June 14, 1923 from PAVA Secretary General S. Z. Stachowicz to K. Szymczak

9 PAVA NEB Archives, sign. A-XV/1

10 J. Stobniak-Smogorzewska, "Osada Krechowiecka: ["The Krechowiec Colony"] in: *Zeszyty Historyczne* [*Historical Papers*] Literary Institute, Paris 1981, pp. 175-188

11 J. Bonkowicz Sittauer "Udział Stowarzyszenia Weteranów Armii Polskiej w Akcji Osadnictwa Wojskowego w Polsce" ["The Contribution of the Polish Army Veterans Association of America to the Military Settlement Operation in Poland"] in: *Pamiętnik Placówki Nr. 7 SWAP [Souvenir Journal of PAVA Post Nr. 7]* Detroit, 1925

Aside from the cooperative in Warszawa PAVA also owned shares ($500) in the settlement cooperative OSKRES at Równe in the province of Volhynia.

Life did not turn out the same for all of the former soldiers from America who took up farming. Most stuck to their farming and stubbornly tried to make a go of it on the plots of land that they had been given. Some leased their plots out to others and went into government service, or worked as businessmen or craftsmen.

In 1938 at the Hallerowo settlement, Tuczyn hamlet, Równe County there were over a dozen settlers from America farming, among them were: Stanisław Rybakowski and Antoni Wiącek. Stanisław Sielawa, who came from the same village, was a businessman. Meanwhile Józef Biernacki due to financial difficulties leased his plot out without letting the authorities know, and was forced to hand it over to the State Treasury.

At the same time the following settler-soldiers from America were farming in other settlements:

- Bajonówka, Tuczyn hamlet, Równe County: Franciszek Klusek, Lucjan Rzewuski, Aleksander Świerski (a volunteer from Brazil), Piotrowski, Bolesław Wiśniewski;

- Hiosków, Tuczyn hamlet, Równe County: Kowalski, Stanisław Lentas, Wincenty Miecznikowski, Wawrzyniec Rękawik;

- Jarłowce: Żebrowski;

- Zdołbica, Zdołbunów County: Grajewski, Puławski;

- Stołpin, Międzyrzecz-Korca hamlet: Franciszek Wójcik;

- Sielawka, Hoszczań hamlet, Równe County: Stanisław Łączkowski.

Aside from the above, the following volunteers from America who remained in active military service also had plots of land: Major Władysław Pawłowski, Ułanowiec hamlet (his sister did the farming on the plot that he was granted); Jan Sejler, whoseplot was in the area of Luck; Wacław Ciecierski, in the area of Radziwiłłów; Michał Lewandowski, in the Mirocz area.[12]

By 1938 three military settlers from America had died: Bolesław Kowalewski (in 1923 in Hallerowo hamlet); Kazimierz Dąbrowski (died in the Równe area, buried alive while digging a well); Stanisław Chmiel (the chief of Hallerowo hamlet, died in 1936).

---

12 S. Sielawa. "Życie ochotników z Ameryki w Polsce na roli" ["The Life of Volunteers from America Who Were Farming in Poland "] in: *Weteran [The Veteran]* August 1938, pp. 4-5

Stanisław Chmiel was an example of a great community leader working for the welfare of all the settlers, for which he was universally respected. In addition to being the chief of Hallerowo hamlet he also fulfilled many other functions: he was the president of the Board of Directors of Sołczyk's Savings Bank in Równe, a member of the County Executive Board of the Union of Military Settlers, a council member of Tuczyn hamlet and its chief in the final years of his life. His funeral became transformed into a great public demonstration of the local population, which thus honored his work on behalf of the Polish nation: "In Równe the deceased was bid farewell by the entire County Department, the County Union of Settlers with President Smocztanin, The County Union of Reservists, all the village heads of the local hamlets and the mayors of the magistrate districts, delegates of all the organizations, a squadron of Krakovians with cavalry captain Obrzeński of the hamlet of Jazłowiec in the lead, the military orchestra of the 13th Infantry Division and despite the bitter cold a crowd several thousand strong of all nationalities, including Poles, Ruthenians and Jews. Everybody knew him and everybody wanted to pay their last respects even at the peril of their own health due to the cold—because of which many later suffered illness. That is how he was taken leave of in Równe.

"The squadron of Krakovians led him from Równe to the hamlet, followed by the settler's orchestra and a countless number of carriages and settler wagons filled to the brim with relatives, friends, settlers and their families. His final tour ended at the chapel in Horyńgród, where a huge crowd of the populace gathered, school children from all the nearby hamlets, the local authorities with the assistant subprefect and the inspector of the local municipality in the lead, the staff of the community administration, the village heads and delegations, in a word, the entire population regardless of nationality or political affiliation."[13]

In 1936 in Równe County the village chiefs in three of the nine hamlets were former volunteers from America. Aside from the deceased Stanisław Chmiel, there were also: Łączkowski in Korzec and Budzyński in Dziatkiewicze. In addition almost all the settlers—the former soldiers from America—were councilmen in their communities or in nearby towns. They also held various offices in social organizations. Some of them received proposals to take up posts in the local government administration, but they refused because they did not want to part with their place of work, that is, their own farms.[14]

It is clear from the above that the former volunteer soldiers from America, thanks to having been out in the world, had proven themselves not just in battle

---

13 Ibid., p. 5
14 Ibid.

but also during the times of tedious work in free Poland, where their social skills and experience in hard, honest labor not only for themselves but for the general population came in handy.

Within the resettlement venture PAVA also participated in settlement on the Western Borderlands, where in accordance with the "Journal of Laws of the Polish Republic" Nr. 112 of December 20, 1922 it was possible to purchase a post-German farm with all the out buildings. The candidate had to have one thousand dollars.

This decidedly limited the number of persons willing to acquire those farms, because there were few veterans from America who could afford it. The PAVA Delegature in Warszawa served as the broker in the purchase transaction of the post-German farms. Two of its members, Stanisław Z. Stachowicz and Stanisław Nastał, at a meeting with Polish Prime Minister Wincenty Witos on September 7, 1923, asked that the Liquidation Agency in Poznań issue a confirmation for post-German plots for fifteen candidates who were settlers from America. Among the veterans who were candidates willing to purchase post-German farms were: Frank Cichowski, Antoni Dutkowski, Frank Jakubowski, Ludwik Jakubowski, Jan Kuroś, Jan Paśniewski, Stan Ruciński, Franciszek Tatarski, J. Wróblewski, Michał Ziemianek and Ignacy Zapytowski.[15]

Unfortunately, a lack of precise data makes it impossible to known which of the candidates actually settled and where.

Generally speaking the resettlement operation on Polish lands by former Polish volunteers from America, which had been prepared by the PAVA Board with an investment of great energy and money, ended in failure. The main reason, despite the good organizational preparation by the PAVA Board, was the very difficult living conditions which awaited the settlers on the pieces of raw land that had been given to them. They had to set themselves up with minimum government help on a piece of empty, run-down land, far from human settlements that were inhabited by a populace of foreign ethnic background. They had to have some capital, and above all a very resilient spirit and strong willpower to make it through the first, most difficult years, while living mostly in sod houses or in some small space at somebody else's house. The severe conditions frightened off many a candidate for resettlement who had already become used to many creature comforts. The purchase of post-German farms in Pomerania and Great Poland (Wielkopolska) in this situation would have probably been the best solution, but those plans were not realistic because the former soldiers just did not have the sizeable capital required to purchase the farms.

---

15 PAVA NEB Archives, sign. A-XVI/4, Letter of September 8, 1923 from S. Z. Stachowicz to the PAVA National Executive Board

A factor that also frightened people away was the publication of correspondence and reports in the Polish American press depicting the dark sides of life in the old country, and private letters from relatives and friends living in Poland and from those who had returned to America. These letters spoke of the unstable political situation in Poland, about the constantly changing governments, about the business problems, of which the inflation of the Polish mark was the most painful for the settlers, because it wiped out savings that they had scraped together with such great difficulty in America. The descriptions of the difficulty of the trip, the plague of robberies, lost baggage, etc. also frightened people away.[16]

Another, equally important reason for the failure of the settlement operation supervised by the PAVA Board was the improving economic situation in the United States. The Polish veterans were now able to find jobs and postponed their departure for Poland, which they justified with the need to save up adequate capital. But once they had it (its accumulation often lasted many years) they "melted" into the new environment, started families, and in the end decided to stay in America for good.

Up to 1935 the PAVA secretaries general in their reports indicated the sums that had been invested in Poland, for instance the farm business in Kuligi (value estimated at $15,000 to $35,000), shares in the Central Military Settlers' Cooperative in Warszawa ($4,000), shares in the settlers' cooperative OSKRES in Równe ($500), loans to military settlers ($8,000).

As of 1937 these sums were no longer reported on, because the debts which burdened the Kuligi farm were greater than its worth. The military settler cooperatives had gone bankrupt and the settlers, living under very difficult financial conditions, were unable to pay off the loans they had received. PAVA was forced to write all these investment off at a loss. The Kuligi matter was especially painful. PAVA held onto it until 1939, after having invested $30,000 in it.

After 1939 PAVA also had to write off the investments it had made in Polish government obligations and in shares of Bank Polski. Their combined value in 1937 was $25,750![17]

The over-all losses that PAVA sustained in the years 1922–1939 by investing in Poland amounted to almost $70,000. The veterans were not amused by this turn of events, but they told themselves that although PAVA had lost on these investments, in the end Poland had gained by them.

16　R. Mazurkiewicz. *Polskie wychodźstwo i osadnictwo w Kanadzie* [*The Polish Emigration and Settlement in Canada*] Warszawa 1928, pp. 103-104; A. Waloszek, "reemigracja ze Stanów Zjednoczonych do Polski po I wojnie światowej 1919–1924" *Zeszyty Naukowe UJ, [Jagiellonian University Scholarly Papers*], Prace polonijne, z. 7 [Polonian Studies, issue # 7] Warszawa-Kraków 1983

17　Ibid.

The money that PAVA districts and posts had raised and sent to Poland for various purposes was significant support for that country. It is difficult to estimate the total value of that help, because it was not detailed by PAVA's central authorities. The scope of generosity of the individual PAVA posts on behalf of Poland is exemplified by the statement of sums raised for Poland by one of PAVA's biggest posts, Post Nr. 7 in Detroit, MI:

- $150 for the Polish Red Cross
- $550 for the Kościuszko Fund
- $1,930 for the construction of a Falcons House in Warszawa's Praga neighborhood (a fund drive done together with the Polish Falcons of America in Detroit)
- $100 for construction of a Student Dormitory in Warszawa
- $522 for the construction of a People's Home in Jarycz Nowy in the Eastern Borderlands (a collection taken up together with the Polish Falcons of America Nest # 86)
- $200 for a library in that same Borderlands town
- $6,500 for Polish flood victims in 1934
- $500 for the Polish National Defense fund (from the post's account) and $1,150 offered by the post's members.[18]

In total, $11,600. After taking into consideration the fact that the dollar was worth about ten times more then than it is today, then it is clear that the value of the help rendered Poland in the inter-war years by PAVA Post Nr. 7 in Detroit can be estimated by today's valuation at about $116,000.

Individual PAVA members sent large sums to Poland mainly, but not only, to support their families. Thus the help given by the Polish veterans from America in the years 1921–1939 was quite significant.

This takes on a still different dimension when we realize that the money was given by mostly simple, uneducated people who worked hard and did not earn much (by American standards). Moved by authentic patriotism that is how they expressed their great love for the old country.

---

18 J. Strzałkowski "Historia Placówki 7 imienia miasta "Lwów" ["The History of Post 7 named after the city of Lwów"] in: *Weteran [The Veteran]* October 1947

Contacts with the Highest Authorities in Poland

The Polish veterans in America (in addition to private contacts with their families in Poland) also maintained official contacts (through PAVA) at the highest levels of the Polish government. PAVA had the highest respect for its representatives, especially in the first years of independence. For example, it was highly significant that the veterans gathered at the Founding Convention in May 1921 in Cleveland, Ohio made the head of the Polish State, Józef Piłsudski, the honorary president of the Polish Army Veterans Association of America. The veterans bestowed the same title on General Józef Haller.[19]

It later became a tradition that both of those eminent men received name day greetings from the entire organization in March of every year.

At the beginning of 1923 the PAVA Board contacted General Władysław Sikorski, who was then the Prime Minister of the Polish Republic. As a memento he sent his photograph with a dedication to the veterans in America. It read: "To the Polish veterans in America with a soldierly greeting—Władysław Sikorski, General."

That same year, after the change of government in Poland, PAVA Secretary General Stanisław Z. Stachowicz, who was in Poland on a visit, and the director of the PAVA Delegature in Warszawa, Stanisław Roskosz had a meeting with Wincenty Witos, the new President of the Council of Ministers. They presented him with three petitions: to allow General Haller to go to America in an official capacity to attend the American Legion convention in San Francisco; to send a recommendation to the Liquidation Agency in Poznań to approve fifteen candidates from America for settlement on post-German land; to obtain the administration's or parliament's approval of a special resolution acknowledging the contributions of the Polish American community to the regaining of independence by Poland. The Prime Minister was well disposed to all three petitions and invited his guests to Lwów for a Convention of Settlers from the Eastern Małopolska (Little Poland) region. Prior to the fifth anniversary of the conclusion of the world war Prime Minister Witos (making good on the promise he made to the PAVA representatives) personally wrote a little known address, dated September 22, 1923, to the Polish emigration to America. (Please see addendum 14).

Prime Minister Witos made it possible for Gen. J. Haller to pay an official visit to America. Polish President Stanisław Wojciechowski and many leftist politicians and military circles were against this. The PAVA-financed tour of Gen. Haller across America (which took place in the fall of 1923) was a great promotional success. General Haller covered the entire American continent. He was greeted with high

---
19   PAVA NEB Archives, sign. A-II/1

honors everywhere he went, and the American press devoted a lot of attention to him and Poland. During his tour the General, in the name of the President of Poland, decorated the official PAVA flag with the Order of Poland Reborn (Polonia Restituta) at a ceremony in Cleveland. Thanks to earlier PAVA efforts General J. Haller (in the name of the President of Poland) also decorated the flags of the American Red Cross and the American Legion with the same Order, which was very well received by American public opinion.

In 1924 some of the persons at the highest levels of power in Poland became members of the Committee for the Restoration of the Invalid Home in Radzyń near Warszawa. The Committee turned to PAVA with a request for financial support of this venture. The following signatures were visible on the special document that was sent to the PAVA Board: Cardinal Aleksander Kakowski, The Marshal of the Senate Wojciech Trąmpczyński, Prime Minister Władysław Grabski, Minister of Defense General Władysław Sikorski, Inspector General of Artillery General Józef Haller, and also the signatures of the presidents of the individual parliamentarian clubs, the rectors of universities in Warszawa and Poznań and the presidents of Poland's most important banks.[20] The PAVA Board backed this initiative by organizing a separate fund drive for this purpose in its ranks.

In July 1925 the PAVA Board and District I hosted Poland's Minister of Foreign Affairs, Count Aleksander Skrzyński, in Chicago.[21] Three months later, also in Chicago, PAVA co-hosted a delegation of ten Polish parliamentarians headed by Professor Bronisław Dembiński.[22]

In September 1926 a PAVA Board delegation headed by Vice President Jan Kostrubała visited Poland. Its purpose was to prepare the political foundations for a great tour of Poland that was being organized by PAVA. The delegation had an audience with Polish president Ignacy Mościcki. During the hour-long meeting the President expressed interest in PAVA's work in America and asked about the details of the planned grand tour of Poland, an idea very much to his liking, which he confirmed in a personal letter to the PAVA Board of October 4, 1926: "During their meeting with me the delegates of the Polish Army Veterans Association informed me of their project to organize their tour of Poland.

"I told the delegates of my satisfaction at their undertaking, which will allow the members of your Association to make still more intimate the ties that bind the Polish emigration in America with Its Motherland."[23]

---

20 PAVA NEB Archives, sign. A-VIP/3
21 *The Veteran* September 1925, pp. 7, 20
22 *The Veteran* November 1925, p. 9
23 PAVA NEB Archives, sign. A-VIP/5

This attitude of the President toward PAVA's plans opened the doors to many other offices for the delegates of the Association, for example the Ministry of Foreign Affairs exempted the participants of the planned tour from passport visa fees, which saved every participant ten dollars. Moreover a Main Committee to Host the PAVA Tour was organized in Warszawa, whose membership included the presidents of all organizations representing former servicemen. The hand and experience of PAVA President Dr. Teofil Starzyński is clearly visible in those preparations. As the president of the Polish Falcons of America he had organized a successful Falcons tour of Poland in 1925.

This favorable attitude of the Polish authorities to the event being organized by PAVA also had its political sub-text. After the May 1926 coup d'état the pro-Piłsudski government wanted to improve its image in the eyes of the Polish American community, which found it hard to swallow the installation of an authoritarian regime in Poland. The PAVA grand tour was a terrific opportunity for the new Polish government to present itself in the best light to a large group from the émigré community. And indeed, when the group arrived in Poland in August 1927 it was given tremendous promotional play. In Warszawa the tour members (several hundred strong) were hosted in the building of the Polish Parliament. A PAVA delegation

that included: PAVA president Colonel Dr. Teofil Starzyński, lieutenants: Stanisław Wilk, Witold Trawiński, Henryk Zając, Czesław Żuławski, Reverend Dean Michalski and Agnieszka Wisła paid its respects to Marshal of the Parliament Maciej Rataj, who made a speech to the guests from America as they sat in the seats of the delegates to the Parliament. In addressing the PAVA veterans Rataj said: "We understand and remember that when the war that was to decide Polish independence broke out, you made the highest sacrifice of your own blood on the altar of the Fatherland. I would like to note, however, that although the war is over your duty as soldiers is not completed. The soldier's duty continues to stand before you. You must continue to be soldiers of the Polish Republic, its ambassadors in the United States. I know that you are fulfilling that obligation to the fullest."[24]

Several days later, on August 14, 1927 a group of tour members with PAVA president Dr. Teofil Starzyński, went to Belvedere Palace for a meeting with the Polish head of state, Marshal Józef Piłsudski. The Lwów-based *Wiek Nowy* (*The New Age*) wrote about the meeting as follows: "The Marshal, accompanied by Colonel Prystor, appeared on the second floor balcony from the park side and talked with the arrivals. Next he asked the children who were born in America to step forward.

---

24 "A.B.C.," Warszawa, August 3, 1927

'How's this?!' the Marshal called out when the children had lined up in a row. 'Just young ladies? You don't have any boys?'

'There are, they came with us to Warszawa, but they are getting ready for a soccer match.'

The Marshal then asked:

'Do all the ladies speak Polish?'

They replied in a chorus:

'We do! We do!'

Finally Colonel Starzyński, the tour leader, asked the Marshal to come downstairs and sit for a photograph with the tour. The approaching head of government was greeted with a thrice-repeated shout: "Live Long!" which was repeated again at the end of the meeting."[25]

The meeting was immortalized on a photograph in which the Marshal is visible sitting in a wicker armchair, surrounded by children and uniformed PAVA veterans.

A PAVA delegation that included Colonel Dr. Teofil Starzyński, Witold Trawiński and Czesław Żuławski paid a visit to Minister of Internal Affairs General Felicjan Sławoj Składkowski, who received the veterans from America "…with a truly soldierly and sincere cordiality."[26] PAVA president Col. Dr. Teofil Starzyński remembered well the atmosphere of that meeting. Prior to his departure from Poland he wrote the minister a letter thanking him for the kindness shown the entire tour by himself personally and by his ministry.

Several weeks later, after he returned to America, Dr. Starzyński received a personal letter from General Składkowski, in which the minister wrote: "I was pleased to receive your letter with your expression of cordial feelings for myself as one of the ministers of the current Polish government.

"I am greatly heartened to know that the participants of the tour that you organized to the homeland are filled with belief and conviction that things are getting constantly better and that our country is becoming stronger from day to day as a nation state.

"I am sure that the frictions that still occur in our society will soon be totally removed under the influence of the work that continues to grow for the good of the nation. Mr. President please accept my expression of deepest respect and sincere good will."[27]

It is worth noting at this point that the tour by PAVA (which was perceived by the Polish American community as the so-called "right") coincided with a competing

---

25 "Weterani amerykańscy u marszałka Piłsudskiego" ["Polish American Veterans Visit with Marshal Piłsudski"] in: *Wiek Nowy* [*The New Age*] Lwów, August 7, 1927

26 *The Veteran* November 1927, p. 5

27 Ibid.

trip by the "left," that is, of American "Piłsudskists." That much smaller tour, in terms of number of participants, arrived in Poland under the leadership of Professor Siemiradzki. The Krakovian *Ilustrowany Kurier Codzienny (Illustrated Daily Courier)* in reporting on the reception of both tours in Lwów, wrote sarcastically: "America in Lwów! We had it here at the end of July in the form of two tours from the Polish American community, the first, "leftist," group was composed of members of the Józef Piłsudski Society, which brought the Marshal a golden saber, and the other was a "rightist" group composed of Hallerian war veterans, which didn't bring anybody anything. The reception of both tours in Lwów was as identical as two drops of water. ... Big politics was eliminated from the reception program."[28]

After the unusually successful trip to Poland the contacts of PAVA with the highest authorities in Poland became livelier. This became particularly visible in the spring of 1928 when in conjunction with the approaching 4th PAVA General Assembly Polish president Ignacy Mościcki sent special geetings well ahead of time to the entire Association (see Addendum 15).

The President of the Council of Ministers at that time, Marshal Józef Piłsudski, sent the 4th PAVA General Assembly courtesy geetings worded as follows: " I wish the Polish Army Veterans Association of America continued fruitful work on behalf of the Polish cause."[29]

The head of Poland's Catholic Church, Cardinal August Hlond, also sent the PAVA veterans his best wishes and blessings.[30]

Kazimierz Bałdyga, PAVA's new president, who wanted to make PAVA the main link between the Polish American community and Poland, went to Poland in July 1928. One of the most important reasons for this visit was the invitation of Marshal Piłsudski to America for the ceremonies connected with the 150th anniversary of the death of General Kazimierz Pułaski.

After many attempts in Warszawa president Bałdyga was finally able to secure an appointment with Marshal Józef Piłsudski and also with Polish president Ignacy Mościcki. Here is what the PAVA president wrote about his visit with the Marshal on August 3, 1928, without mentioning anything about the failure of his main mission: "After I had paid him respect and homage on behalf of his former subordinates and after having communicated other matters to him, the Marshal thanked me with a cordial squeeze of the hand for remembering him and asked me to convey his joy that we want to serve the Fatherland beyond the sea. At the same time I received an

---

28 H. Zbierzchowski. "Ameryka we Lwowie" ["America in Lwów"] in: *Ilustrowany Kurjer Codzienny* [*Illustrated Daily Courier*] August 3, 1927
29 *The Veteran* July 1928
30 PAVA NEB Archives, sign. A-VIP/8

invitation to the Convention of Legionnaires in Wilno, where I also received two honorary invitations to participate in the ceremonies. Prior to that, however, in the name of our Association I sent a congratulatory telegram to our comrades in arms, the brave Legionnaires."[31]

During his meeting with President Mościcki the PAVA president heard a telling assurance from his lips: "Please let the veterans in America know that Poland will never forget their service, blood and sacrifice."[32] During his talks at the Ministry of Military Affairs and the Ministry of Foreign Affairs president Bałdyga raised the issue of transferring the remains of Lieutenant Lucjan Chwałkowski from France to America. The PAVA president met with a large dose of mistrust in those talks. He had to convince his hosts long and hard that PAVA does not want to be a political party organization, and the veterans in America want to be known as Veterans of the Polish Army and not veterans of some political clique. In the end both Ministries promised to help in talks with the French side on this matter. Moreover the Ministry of Foreign Affairs committed itself to send PAVA at the nearest opportunity a promotional movie on the achievements of the Polish State up to that time.[33]

With the advent of the great American economic crisis in 1929 mutual relations between PAVA and the Polish government became dominated by the question of organizing aid for war invalids and sick Polish veterans who were living in America. Unfortunately, the efforts made by the PAVA Board, and specifically by Association president Franciszek Dziób to obtain some kind of help from the Polish authorities, ended in failure. Even his personal visit to Poland in 1933 and numerous talks in individual Ministries did not give any positive results. The Polish government did not get seriously interested in this painful problem until February 1936, when the Ministry of Foreign Affairs in Warszawa directed the Polish Consulate General in New York to check the matter out thoroughly. After doing so the Consulate recommended to the Ministry of Foreign Affairs in Warszawa that the Polish government needed to lend its financial support to Polish war invalids in America. The PAVA Board had appealed for support of exactly that kind of solution to, among others: Polish President Ignacy Mościcki and to well known, influential persons at the highest levels of the administration, for instance Marshal Edward Rydz-Śmigły, generals: Roman Górecki (the Minister of Trade and Commerce), Tadeusz Kasprzycki (the Minister of Military Affairs), Bolesław Wieniawa-Długoszowski and Gustaw Orlicz-Dreszer. Stefan Lenartowicz, the director of the World Union

---

31 *The Veteran* October 1928, p. 1
32 *The Veteran* February 1930, p. 18
33 Ibid.

of Poles Abroad, became interested in this problem. In a letter of March 5, 1938 which was sent to the most important government offices, including the Ministry of Military Affairs, he drew attention to the political consequences of indifference by Polish government policy-makers to the problems that were frustrating Polish veterans in America: "The complaints of Polish veterans which have not yet been addressed are the factor that is creating a serious foundation for the dissatisfaction of the Polish American community, for the general belief that the American Polonia is being treated carelessly by Poland and that Polonia's war effort doesn't mean anything in Poland. In a word, these issues have created a point of contention in relations between Poland and its émigrés in America, a point all the more dangerous because it continuously gives ammunition to the opposition, which has no other reason to systematically attack Poland and the Polish government except the injury being done to the veterans."[34]

S. Lenartowicz felt that the most urgent issues needing resolution were:

a) to prepare and publish a history of the Polish American community's war effort

b) to grant permanent financial aid to invalids and unemployable veterans of the Polish Army in America

c) to grant permanent pensions to Chevaliers of the Order of Virtuti Militari who were living in the United States and Canada and to hire them first for supporting positions in Polsh diplomatic posts and state-owned Polish enterprises such as PKO, Orbis and the Gdynia-America Line

d) to have the appropriate Polish government agencies make appropriate efforts toward the American government to obtain social assistance for Polish veterans in America, first of all free medical care

e) to take care of outstanding issues regarding military decorations for the volunteers from America.

In his letter S. Lenartowicz stressed that these postulates had been worked out by the Polish Inter-Organizational Council in Chicago, which represented all Polish organizations in the United States.[35]

Lenartowicz's argumentation gave the desired result. W. T. Drymer, the director of the consular department of the Ministry of Foreign Affairs, sent a letter on June 21, 1938 to the Polish Consul General in Chicago, Dr. Wacław Gawroński,

---

34 New Documents Archives (Warszawa), sign. 188, Federation of Polish Societies in Defense of the Fatherland, pp. 16-18

35 Ibid.

informing him that the Ministry of Labor and Social Welfare had granted Polish veterans in America a subsidy of $3,000 for invalids and the unemployable. The Consul in Chicago was directed to take diplomatic steps to ensure medical treatment in American hospitals and sanatoriums for Polish veterans, noting that veterans of other nationalities (the French and the Belgians) already had similar rights in the United States. Drymer also wrote that he would support the issue of a historical study of the Polish American war effort, by assigning a historian-specialist to the Military Historical Office. He also assured the Consul that he would send an appropriate letter to the head offices of Polish companies with branches in the United States, that they should, to the extent possible, first of all employ Polish veterans. He also directed the Polish consul to influence Polish institutions in the USA regarding pensions for the 22 Chevaliers of the Order of Virtuti Militari who were American citizens. Drymer wrote that this matter required an amendment to the appropriate bill by the Polish Parliament.[36]

Stefan Lenartowicz's stubborn determination resulted in the ratification by Parliament, in January of 1939, of a permanent financial subsidy to PAVA on behalf of the war invalids. The allocation was to be paid out annually from the budget of the Ministry of Social Welfare.

The long awaited and extremely important decision of the Polish Parliament showed that relations between the Polish emigration to America and the mother country had entered a new phase. In consequence of the new government policy PAVA was decorated with the Golden Cross of Merit of the Polish Republic. The pinning of the Cross onto PAVA's flag on May 18, 1939 was done by Minister of Commerce Antoni Roman at the Polish Consulate General in New York during the Polish government delegation's stay to attend the opening of the World's Fair. In addition seven PAVA members received Polish state decorations for their accomplishments as civic leaders. The PAVA national commander, Lucjusz Kajko, received the Knight's Cross of the Order of Poland Reborn; Golden Crosses of Merit were bestowed on: L. Krzyżak, Dr. J. Michalski and S. Wilk, and Silver Crosses of Merit were received by J. Kostrubała, W. Bogucki and J. Głowacki.[37]

Some of the PAVA posts developed lower-level contacts with the Polish government; for instance in March 1939, thanks to the efforts of Wincenty Kalinowski of PAVA Post Nr. 7 in Detroit, Michigan the City of Lwów became the post's patron and agreed to have the post use the name and coat of arms of the city of Lwów. This decision was in homage for the volunteers from Detroit who, as members of the 13th

---

36 New Documents Archives (Warszawa), sign. 1018/60, The Polish Embassy in Washington
37 *The Veteran* June 1939, p. 11

Infantry (the "Steel") Division in 1920 had defended the city from the Bolshevik hordes of Syemyon Budyonny. Many of them had been killed in that conflict.

The City of Lwów also gave a flag to Post Nr. 7 in Detroit. It had been made by girl scouts from Lwów. This valuable, touching gift was sent to America through the Ministry of Foreign Affairs in Warszawa and presented to the post in Detroit by Count Jerzy Potocki, the Polish Ambassador to the United States. This event was of historical significance for the post. From that time on PAVA Post Nr. 7 in Detroit proudly bears the moniker "Lwów."[38]

The outbreak of war on September 1, 1939 interrupted the contacts between the Polish Army Veterans Association of America and the pro-Piłsudski government in Poland. Many projects of great importantance to the veterans that had been begun and had dragged on for years, now could no longer be finalized.

PAVA in the Face of Political Events in Poland

The Polish veterans in America, when they were organizing the Polish Army Veterans Assocation of America at their convention in Cleveland, Ohio in May of 1921, wrote the principle of their organization's apolitical nature into their By-Laws, and also its openness to all former Polish Army soldiers, regardless of the military formation in which they had served. PAVA has tried to remain committed to these principles throughout its entire history. Special emphasis was laid on keeping away from the political squabbles that were rampant in Poland and also in the Polish American community. Attention was frequently given to this extremely important fact in editorials printed in *The Veteran* and in intra-organizational correspondence. This is what the fourth issue of *The Veteran* (January 1922) stated: "As soldiers, Hallerians cannot share the views of any party, because that is not the soldier's concern. ... Today this party, tomorrow another party will be directing the ship of state and therefore the soldier must steer clear of politics, so he doesn't look like a weathervane. ... A veteran may or may not morally tolerate a given political persuasion, but he cannot actively participate in any of them.

"Community work, and the cultural development of the community of which the veteran is a part, should lie within the citizen veteran's scope of activity. As a citizen, as a Hallerian, he should be a patriot, and not a politician."[39]

Adhering to these principles the PAVA Board maintained contact with every democratically elected Polish government regardless of its political make-up. This

---

38 "Placówka 7 'Lwów' w Detroit" ["'Lwów' Post Nr. 7 in Detroit"] in: *Weteran [The Veteran]* June 1981, p. 37. The flag is currently on exhibit in the PAVA District VI Museum which is part of the Polish American Archives at Orchard Lake, Michigan.

39 L. A. Wnęk-Stefański "Weteran polski a polityka" ["The Polish Veteran and Politics"] in: *Weteran [The Veteran]* January 1922, p. 2

behavior caused PAVA to be accused of flirting with the political opposition by both leftists and rightists during times of change in the relationship between Poland's power structures (depending on which parties at the given moment were in opposition to the government).

During the first years after their return to the United States from the war, Polish veterans in America continued to maintain interest in Poland's political life. But with time that interest gradually diminished. That was the result of the inevitable assimilation of the former Polish soldiers into American actuality, as a consequence of which events in Poland appeared ever more distant, incomprehensible and foreign. PAVA reacted only to events of a truly significant nature. The people back in Poland were unable to comprehend this attitude. For instance the Union of Hallerians made fruitless attempts to engage their colleagues from America in the whirlpool of political strife in Poland.

Respect for the legality of the governing bodies in Poland was a prime principle to which the PAVA leadership endeavored to be faithful, especially whenever news came from Poland about serious political tensions. That happened in December 1922 after the assassination of the Polish Republic's first president, Gabriel Narutowicz. According to the first reports that arrived in America this tragic fact was being linked indirectly with the person of General J. Haller, who was accused of stirring up National Democratic youth against the president prior to the assassination. The PAVA Board took a clear and decisive stance in the face of these reports, declaring itself on the side of the law and the principles that govern the functioning of a democratic state. Simultaneously it explained that PAVA is not Gen. J. Haller's political support team in the United States. In the Janury 1923 issue of *The Veteran* PAVA secretary Stanisław Z. Stachowicz wrote: "The political murder in Poland was preceded by demonstrations organized by the right which was unhappy with the election of President Gabriel Narutowicz. And the demonstrations supposedly occurred after an address delivered on the street by Józef Haller, the former four-star general who is presently a delegate to Parliament. In connection with this Blue Ar,y officers were to have been arrested.

"We do not want to presage events since we do not have specific data in hand. Nonetheless the veterans who live in America, members of the Polish Army Veterans Association, should always and everywhere remember one thing, namely, as Mr. Wacław Gąsiorowski pointed out to us in his letter sent for the 1st General Assembly in Cleveland, WE NEVER WERE THE SOLDIERS OF ANY PARTICULAR GENERAL, because that would have meant that we were mercenaries—WE WERE MERELY THE SOLDIERS OF A POLAND RISING FROM HER GRAVE.

"...let it be declared that all Polish Army veterans living in the United States condemn whoever is responsible for the murder perpetrated on the person of the First President of the Polish Republic, just as they always condemned all party strife, which never amounted to anything and won't."[40]

The national Union of Hallerians in Poland reacted sharply to this position. In a letter of January 29, 1923 to the PAVA Board in America it defended Gen. J. Haller, simultaneously presenting its political views on the situation in Poland: "The election of the late President Narutowicz with Jewish votes was seen as an insult to the Polish Nation and to every honest Pole, and all the more so every former soldier who had secured it with his own blood and toil had to protest against this. The slogan "Poland for the Poles" is heard more and more loudly and is taking on significance. You should understand that perfectly well, since you know what the slogan "America for Americans" stands for in your country.

"Our country is going through a serious crisis right now and only because we understand perfectly well the need for the unity and harmony of all Poles, do we claim the right to make demands of you, in line with the ideas and slogans with which we went into battle together...

/signed/ Gen. Edward Castellaz   Captain Józef Sierociński"[41]

In reply to its colleagues in Poland the PAVA Board wrote a letter on April 7, 1923: "Our views on the crime that was committed on December 16, 1922, which were expressed in Nr. 23 of *The Veteran,* do not coincide with your views. In the article "After the Crime" the crime was condemned as such and we cannot change our position. And from your letter and the words "The election of the late President Narutowicz with Jewish votes was seen as an insult to the Polish Nation and every honest Pole, and all the more so every former soldier who had secured it with his own blood and toil, had to protest against this" it would appear that you approve the crime. And that is why, not wishing to embarrass anyone, not wanting to put weapons into the hands of your enemies and ours, we will neither publish your letter nor ours."[42]

News accusing Gen. J. Haller of collaboration in the assassination of President Gabriel Narutowicz were publicized and long upheld in the Polish American community by the KONers, also called Piłsudskists, socialists or left-wingers. The secretary of Post Nr. 29 in Lowell, Mass., wrote about this to the PAVA Board in a letter of May 14, 1923: "There are too few of us veterans to be able to host a

---

40 S. Z. Stachowicz "Po Zbrodni" ["After the Crime"] in: *Weteran [The Veteran]* January 1923, pp. 1-2
41 PAVA NEB Archives, sign. A-XXIII/3
42 Ibid.

reception for our General, and the Poles here in Lowell are so vehement in their party views that we cannot even dream of a reception with the participation of the local Polonia…So it is not difficult to foresee what kind of reception will Gen. Haller get here in New England, given the provocative stance of various left-wingers regarding Haller, whom they consider jointly guilty of murdering the first president of Poland, the late Garbiel Narutowicz. We veterans are too weak to counteract that kind of nonsense coming from the "tovarishches" and their friends and for a while we will have to go stand between the devil and the deep blue sea, because there are many veterans (who don't belong to our Post) who side with these "heroes" from under the red star, who were saving Poland with their big talk. The poet said the pure truth: Neither Siberia nor the lash, but the poisoned spirit of the Nation is the pain of all pains. Our souls have been poisoned.

/illegible signature/"[43]

When the news came from Poland in June 1923 that Józef Piłsudski had removed himself from political life, the veterans from America took the correct view of this fact, worthy of a true Polish soldier, who keeps his distance from on-going political warfare. *The Veteran* in July 1923 wrote: "We always felt respect and esteem for the creator of the Polish Legions, the first armed force at the time of Poland's rising from the grave of slavery…Regardless of how and what his enemies say and write about him, the fact will remain that Piłsudski will pass on into history, from which future generations will be drawing their source of knowledge, as a great and distinguished person. … We former soldiers, as we have noted already, respected the soldier and leader in Piłsudski. After all he was our commander-in-chief since September 1, 1919."[44]

When in November 1924 at the Convention of the Union of Polish Legionnaires in Lwów a resolution was approved demanding the "immediate recall of Commander Józef Piłsudski back to the army," *The Veteran* reacted unusually sharply to that pronouncement. An editorial "The Bolsheviks Are Following Their Example" stated: "the ridiculousness of that demand aside—for nonbody had ever forced Piłsudski out of the army, he left of his own accord; disregarding the Bolshevik pronouncement against Minister of Defense Gen. Sikorski; setting aside the babble that Poland cannot make it without Piłsudski; disregarding the appeal to the Legionnaires that they should return the Marshal back to the army by force—the resolution approved in Lwów only leads to bolshevism.

"Because it is not just the Legionnaires who see their deity in the person of Piłsudski; the Hallerians have one in Haller, the Dowborites in Muśnicki, the

---

43 PAVA NEB Archives, sign. Box-7, Pl. 29/vol. 1
44 *The Veteran* July 1923, p. 2

national democrats in Dmowski, Paderewski and Korfanty. And if each of these groups begins to follow the Legionnaires' example and demand special treatment for its leader, what will come of it? Pure bolshevism, anarchy."[45]

In May 1926 Marshal Piłsudski together with his adherents carried out a coup d'état in Poland. *The Veteran* did not print a short editorial until the July issue, expressing the official position of PAVA regarding the situation in Poland: "In reply to many questions as to what position the Polish Army Veterans Association of America will take with regard to the newly created situation in Poland and what the aim of the Association is, we reply that our organization is an apolitical association, and *The Veteran* is the periodical of this organization… We are not getting mixed up in the party politics in Poland, because the Polish Army Veterans Association has taken a higher goal as its task, and that is to consolidate Polish strength in America to uphold Polishness here, that is, our blood ties."[46]

In that same number of *The Veteran* in an article titled "Revolt or Victory of Justice?" various opinions were quoted on the subject of the coup d'état that had been published in the Polish press in Poland and in America. To balance the explanations of *Polska Zbrojna* (*Armed Poland*) which was in favor of the coup, the editorial quoted a fragment of the *Kurier Poznański* (*Poznań Courier*) which printed the text of the oath that soldiers and officers of the Polish Army took, committing themselves, among others, to "stand guard over the Constitution and the honor of the Polish soldier, and to be subject to the Law and the President of the Republic of Poland…"[47]

In the article "Where Does the Road Lead?" the 1919 decree of Head of State Józef Piłsudski was quoted, which had been originally published in the "Journal of Laws" Nr. 7, position 107 about the penalty of heavy, life imprisonment for "those guilty of a coup against the Polish government and those guilty of an attempt on the life, health or freedom of a person holding the highest State office."[48]

In citing the text fragments from the Polish press, the PAVA press organ clearly defined its sympathies with regard to the parties to the conflict in Poland. Not all the readers of *The Veteran* liked the "apolitical" stance that it had declared at the very outset. One of them, Jan Kamiński of PAVA Post Nr. 25 in Newark, NJ sharply protested against this practice in a letter of July 9, 1926 to the PAVA Board. He wrote: "The local Polish American community stops us on the street and demands explanations of the hostile position that *The Veteran* has taken with regard to [political] parties."

---

45 *The Veteran* January 1925, p. 7
46 *The Veteran* July 1926, p.2
47 Ibid.
48 Ibid., p. 5

The PAVA secretary, Jan Szymański, replied to the accusations: "...this has nothing to do with holding with the right or the left. A government that has been elected legally cannot be abolished by coups, because regardless of who carries those coups out, of who is against the established law, which may even be bad law, the correction of evil can take place by constitutional means ... we are neihter the right nor the left, we just care about Poland's good name, which has been debased by the May action, which you can see for yourself by reading the American press...Our Board is far from a party mentality and tries to put this into practice in this monthly. ...Every honest Pole must admit that the lamentable relations in Poland cannot be corrected by coups and revolutions."[49]

When in the ensuing years news came from Poland about various anti-democratic actions of the pro-Piłsudski authorities, the PAVA Board did not go into the details of these problems, but instead concentrated on those elements which in some way could help to consolidate the ranks of the organization.

In 1928 the new PAVA president, Kazimierz Bałdyga, in the article titled "Our Credo" published in *The Veteran,* clearly presented the political principles that were to guide PAVA in the nearest future: "I want to mention that the color of our uniforms, that our name and our nickname—that is a matter of the historical fate of our historic campaign and not a matter of choice, because we were not permitted to choose: we were soldiers and not politickers.

"That is why we will defend our past and the historical past, and we won't allow anyone to cross it off.

"We all have equal respect and veneration for the great and meritorious Men of Reborn Poland, regardless if those great men are Józef Piłsudski, Maestro Paderewski or activists of this or that party, because the measure of our respect and veneration are the deeds inscribed on the page of history."[50]

A visible sign of this stance was the consistence of the Association's apolitical views throughout successive Boards. For example, Wacław Rżewski, the new PAVA president, while on a visit to Poland in 1930, in giving an interview for the press agency "Iskra" which was directed by people from the pro-government camp, when asked if PAVA was politically active, said: "We are the most apolitical association that you could imagine. It is even unjust to call us Hallerians. Not only soldiers of Haller's army that was organized in France belong to our Association, but every Pole who can document that in the years 1914–1920 he had served in the Polish Army regardless of the formation. We took 1914 as the time boundary so we could add

---
49 PAVA NEB Archives, sign. A-XIII/3
50 *The Veteran* August 1928, p. 1

soldiers from Piłsudski's Legions to our membership rolls."[51]

In this period the PAVA leadership tried to reconcile the warring political parties both in Polonia and in Poland. These attempts were doomed to failure because the Association was too small an organization to effectively influence change in those divisions. Nonetheless such endeavors were made persistently. This was clearly reflected in *The Veteran*. The covers of the periodical eloquently bear witness to this, in presenting the most outstanding figures of the Polish political scene: both those who were in power and those who were in the opposition: Polish president Professor Ignacy Mościcki (February 1930), Marshal Józef Piłsudski (March 1930), Gen. Józef Haller (April 1930), Ignacy Paderewski (July 1930), Gen. Władysław Sikorski (October 1930).

Not all PAVA members liked that attitude, especially when the news from Poland informed of the arrests of "Left-Center" opposition leaders and their imprisonment in the Brześć fortress. The situation in the ranks of the organization became unsettled enough that the PAVA Board decided to place an article on page one of *The Veteran*'s January 1931 issue defending the organization's apolitical principles: "We were soldiers of one mother—Poland.We stood up in defense of the entire Polish nation, not of this or that political party, this or that orientation from "the left" or "the right."

"As volunteer soldiers we did not recognize any orientations or parties in Poland. The soldier's duty is faithful service to the homeland, to the entire nation, regardless of the existence of any parties in the nation and the orientations they pay homage to.

"It is, therefore, not only not fitting and not proper for us, as former servicemen to introduce the embers of political strife into our veteran ranks, but we are simply not permitted to. ...As non-party people we consider it our duty and obligation to build, not to destroy and divide; we wish not to fester but to conciliate and unite, because our strength, significance and far-reaching influence depend on harmony and unity alone."[52]

In line with this principle, every year on St. Joseph's Day in March, the PAVA National Executive Board sent telegrams with name day greetings to Marshal Piłsudski and Gen. J. Haller. For example in 1931 J. Piłsudski, vacationing on the Portuguese island of Madera, received the following greetings: "Your former subordinates, Marshal, on your name day, send you their expressions of homage and wishes of many long years yet of work for Poland." Gen. Haller, who was in Poland at that time, received the following greetings: "Your former volunteer soldiers from America extend, General, cordial greetings on your name day."[53]

---

51 *The Veteran* August 1932, p. 22

52 "Byliśmy, jesteśmy i pozostaniemy wierni ideologii żołnierza polskiego" ["We Were, Are and Will Remain Faithful to the Ideology of the Polish Soldier"] in: *Weteran [The Veteran]* January 1931, p. 1

53 *The Veteran* April 1931, p. 16

The position of this veteran's organization in America with regard to the on-going battles between political camps in Poland was also reflected in the outside covers of the PAVA's press organ. For instance, the cover of the August 1932 issue of *The Veteran* was composed of three photographs: J. Piłsudski, J. Haller and I. J. Paderewski with the caption: "Hail to the Building of Our Fatherland's Indpendence on the Day Celebrating Victorious Polish Arms." But the most evocative cover of *The Veteran* came with the September 1932 issue. Head of State Józef Piłsudski is visible on it shaking hands with Gen. J. Haller during a meeting in Warszawa in April 1919. Under the photograph there is the telling caption: "Under the slogan of harmony." There was no press organ of any veteran organization in contemporary Poland that could allow itself that sort of gesture because the political friction between them was too great.

Unfortunately, despite the most evident external symptoms of PAVA's apolitical position, this organization was constantly perceived by the pro-Piłsudski power circles both in Poland and throughout the Polish American community as part and parcel of the Polish political opposition. No doubt the fact that the Association's leadership maintained close ties with the anti-Piłsudski Union of Hallerians and their main figure Gen. Józef Haller influenced the fact of that misleading categorization. The participation of a PAVA Board delegation headed by President Franciszek Dziób during a visit in Poland in 1932 in an event organized in Bydgoszcz by the Union of Hallerians and by native Fascists of the Great Poland Party, on the fifteenth anniversary of the beginning of recruitment to the Polish Army in France, gave Polish authorities much to ponder. By its participation in this ceremony the PAVA delegation wanted to honor the Polish American community's war effort during World War I. But they did not foresee that the organizers of the event had still other aims in mind. Stanisław Sobolewski, a member of the PAVA delegation who participated in that event, wrote about it in a letter of June 7, 1932 to PAVA Post Nr. 7 in Detroit: "I found myself at a commemorative event organized by the Hallerians and the Great Poland Party (Fascists) on the occasion of the fifteenth anniversary of the formation of the Polish Army in France. The ceremony took place in Bydgoszcz. The speakers were: Gen. Haller, our colleague the President, colleague Pałaszewski and an editor. The best speeches were by our colleague the President and colleague Pałaszewski who gave a terrific lecture on the subject of the Emigration's war effort. The remaining speakers made a so-so political revival meeting out of this commemorative event (we always have such patrons)."[54]

The participation of PAVA Board members in patriotic commemorative events in Poland, which transformed themselves without their desire into political, anti-

---

54 PAVA NEB Archives, sign. Box-3/vol. 3

government rallies, had an essential influence on the relationship of the Polish authorities to the Polish Army Veterans Association of America, which was perceived as part and parcel of the political opposition. The PAVA leadership approached this question differently. They tried to consistently keep away from political battles inside Poland. News from Poland of a political character was rarely included on the pages of *The Veteran*, and when it was printed, it carried no commentary from the organization.

In June 1933 the PAVA press organ, in a big page one article, honored the twenty fifth anniversary of the parliamentary work of Wincenty Witos, quoting a description of the great ceremony that took place in honor of the celebrant in Wierzchosławice: "Hundred of telegrams and letters arrived for this jubilee. On this list we see the following names: Gen. Józef Haller, Gen. Władysław Sikorski, Wojciech Korfanty, Rector Marchlewski of the Jagiellonian University and many others. All of peasant and nationalist Poland was there.

"Witos's home town of Wierzchosławice had an enormous parade organized by the peasant party "Piast," with the participation of thousands of people from all around the country. Many outstanding parliamentary delegates and distinguished citizens spoke. 125 flags were carried in that ceremonial parade."[55]

The article did not mention the persecution that Witos had suffered at the hands of the pro-Piłsudski government, his arrest, imprisonment and the Brześć trial.

The same happened with the information about the administrative decree of the pro-Piłsudski government in 1933 prohibiting the activity of certain posts of the Union of Hallerians of the Kraków District.[56]

Despite the PAVA Board's attempts at well considered, apolitical balancing between the adherents and opponents of the post – May 1926 governments in Poland, these actions were viewed critically in Warszawa. Reports sent to the Ministry of Foreign Affairs headquarters by the heads of Polish diplomatic posts in the United States greatly contributed to this. For instance, in his classified telegram of May 4, 1934 the Polish consul in Pittsburgh, J. Matusiński, wrote: "in the heart of the PAVA Board, currently represented by president Lt. Dziób, tendencies are taking hold that are rather against the Government and the camp in favor of working with the Government in Poland." It should be noted that the Polish Consul General in New York, Dr. Mieczysław Marchlewski, before the PAVA General Assembly in Newark, NJ, made cloakroom maneuvers to change the PAVA leadership and to transfer its Board from Detroit to New York. In a classified letter of May 17, 1934 to the

---

55 "Chłopu polskiemu – cześć" ["All Honor to the Polish Peasant"] in: *Weteran [The Veteran]* June 1933, p. 1
56 *The Veteran* May 1933, p. 13

Ministry of Foreign Affairs in Warszawa he wrote: "This transfer would mean not only a geographic change, linked with the removal of the current Board in Detroit, MI with Mr. Dziób at its head, but also placing the headquarters under the influence of the East Coast which, as I have notified several times already, has a correct and favorable attitude toward the Government."[57]

Consul Marchclewski's endeavors ended in his favor. By decision of the General Assembly in Newark the new PAVA Board was moved from Detroit to New York. This Board quickly showed that contrary to its predecessor it was more favorably inclined toward the authorities in Poland.

At the end of 1934 and the beginning of 1935 there was much ado in the PAVA ranks about the non-publication in *The Veteran* of Gen. J. Haller's address of October 1934, directed to his subordinates in America and the Polish American community on the sixteenth anniversary of Armistice at the front in France. The fact that several Polish American papers had published that address but PAVA's organ had not, upset some of the veterans. PAVA District IX, which grouped the posts in Cleveland and the surrounding area, reacted with particular vehemence. At a special meeting on January 20, 1935 the Board of District IX passed a resolution on this subject, in which it accused the PAVA leadership of slighting the person of Gen. J. Haller: "… we hereby express public censure in the name of the posts that we represent and in our own name, and we lodge a protest against the PAVA Board's behavior which is demeaning to Polish Army veterans."

The PAVA Board, in a letter of February 15, 1935 to the Board of District IX, replied that the address of Gen. J. Haller had not been published in *The Veteran* because that document had the title: "Internal Bulletin – to be read at meetings of Union of Hallerians posts and districts." That explanation did not satisfy the Board of District IX, which in its next letter accused the PAVA Board of: "…walking in the pro-Piłsudski retinue." In reply to this accusation PAVA secretary Leopold Krzyżak wrote in his letter of February 26, 1935 that: "…the current National Executive Board is not being directed by any pro-Piłsudskists, leftists or some other political faction… I myself care the least about politics because I was raised and educated here, and I am interested in Polish politics only from the international point of view. I do not get involved in internal politics and I do not belong to any camp, which is also true of almost all the officers of the National Executive Board."[58]

When news came from Poland of the death of Marshal Piłsudski, an editorial appeared in the May 1935 issue of *The Veteran* which stated: "The dismal news

---

[57] T. Lachowicz. "SWAP w tajnej korespondencji polskiej dyplomacji (1933–1939)" ["PAVA in Classified Polish Diplomatic Correspondence (1933–1939)"] in: *Weteran [The Veteran]* July 1997, p. 10

[58] PAVA NEB Archives, sign. A-VIII/32, PAVA District IX

which arrived from Poland on May 12 of the death of the Commander of the Nation Marshal Józef Piłsudski, brought universal sadness and regret throughout the Polish immigration in America.

"It caused an especially deep reaction in the hearts of those who had rushed to the battlefields at the first call of the Fatherland, in order to purchase Poland's freedom with their blood and wounds. ... Today on the day of Marshal Piłsudski's funeral, we pledge that we will always and faithfully stand guard in defense of the honor and interests of the Motherland, remembering that service to one's Country only ends at the moment of death of each one of us.

"Hail to the Memory of a Great hero and our Commander-in-Chief!"[59]

In the next issue of *The Veteran* there was a lengthy report from the funeral ceremonies for Marshal Piłsudski which were held in Kraków.

In August of the same year, on the fifteenth anniversary of the "Miracle on the Vistula," an occasional article appeared in *The Veteran* with photographs of Marshal J. Piłsudski, as the Commander-in-Chief, and generals: J. Haller and W. Sikorski. Such a juxtaposition would have been hard to find in contemporary government publications in Poland, because the mentioned generals were in opposition to the pro-Piłsudski government. It also showed that the PAVA Board, while favorably disposed toward the Polish government, continued its attempts to maintain an apolitical position for the organization guided by it, without sacrificing its former moral guides and military leaders, who at the given moment found themselves in opposition to those in power in Waeszawa. For example, the November 1935 issue of *The Veteran* was entirely devoted to Ignacy Jan Paderewski—the great philanthropist who had financially helped Polish Army invalids living in America—a passionate proponent of democracy, who opposed the post-May 1926 government in Poland.

The new PAVA National Executive Board which had been elected at the General Assembly in Newark, NJ in 1934 also avoided any official pronouncements on the political warfare going on in Poland, even though it concerned many figures toward which PAVA had traditionally shown its good will, for example I. J. Paderewski, Gen. J. Haller, W. Witos, Gen. W. Sikorski, W. Korfanty, R. Dmowski. The PAVA members could find out practically nothing from *The Veteran* about the actual, internal political situation in Poland, about the interrelationship of political powers, about political forecasts, etc. Only the truly major events were commented on.

The change of policy of the PAVA Board toward the Polish government can be seen in the fact that when in the autumn of 1936 General Edward Rydz-Śmigły,

---

59 *The Veteran* May 1935, p. 12

after a series of promotions, received the Marshal's baton, this event was reported at length on the first page of *The Veteran's* November issue. The behavior of *The Veteran*'s editors in January 1939 regarding the death of Roman Dmowski—the president of the Polish National Committee in Paris in the years 1917–1919, the standard-bearer of the Polish right-wingers, was an eloquent statement. The PAVA National Executive Board did not publish any resolution, instead a short, practically one sentence mention was placed on page 12 of *The Veteran*: "Two great men of Poland died within a short time of each other in our distant fatherland, who during their own lifetimes had found a place in the history of the nation's rebirth ... One of them is Cardinal Aleksander Kakowski, the Archbishop of Warszawa and a former member of the Regency Council during the war, a distinguished prince of the Church and a True Pole.

"The other is Roman Dmowski, a great thinker and a great Pole, the former president of the Polish National Committee in Paris, connected with the activity of the Polish Army in France."[60]

Here was a real contrast between the behavior on the death of R. Dmowski and the March 1939 issue of *The Veteran* where on the name day of Marshal Rydz-Śmigły the cover of the monthly had a large photograph of the General together with name day greetings. For the sake of balance the first page of text had a photograph of Gen. J. Haller, also with name day greetings.

In view of the deteriorating external political situation of Poland *The Veteran* printed in its February 1939 issue a commentary on the declaration of the Head Council of the Polish Peasant Party, which remained in opposition to the pro-Piłsudski government. This declaration expressed the readiness of the party to work and to rise above political divisions, when the interest of the State, and especially its security, demands it.

With regard to this resolution *The Veteran* permitted itself the following political commentary: "The peasant party members are the opposition, but a thinking opposition, which gives first place to care for the State and its defense. Other opposition parties that are being invited by the government to cooperate should find an example of behavior in the patriotism of the Polish peasant."[61]

In the June 1939 issue of *The Veteran* there was a report on the return of Wincenty Witos to Poland from his emigration abroad and the quote of the most eloquent fragment of the address he delivered at the convention of Peasant Party delegates in Tarnów: "We know how to value freedom, as we remember slavery. Due

---

60 "Podzwonne nad grobami Wielkich w Narodzie" ["Afterthoughts Over the Graves of the Great Ones of the Nation"] in: *Weteran [The Veteran]* January 1939, p. 12

61 *The Veteran* February 1939, p. 9

to patriotic concerns I want to stress clearly and openly, that the entire Polish nation will defend every clod of earth, not for payment, not for decorations, but out of duty. And should it happen that a hateful enemy should attack us—he will meet with a determined defense, which will end in victory! Every home will become a fortress, so help us God!"[62]

In the July 1939 issue of *The Veteran* there was a tardy report of a convention of Hallerians, which had taken place on May 21 in Bydgoszcz on the twentieth anniversary of the arrival of the Blue Army in Poland. In the face of the looming German threat the convention was transformed into a great demonstration of the union of all the forces of the Polish nation regardless of the political divisions that had heretofore existed. The report stated that representatives of the Polish Army, of the government and many politicians from many opposing parties had participated in the convention. The words of I. J. Paderewski which he had sent by telegram to the participants of the convention and especially his last words, were quoted: "We will not measure the offering of our blood nor of our possessions according to party guidelines."[63] Simultaneously the article reported that the Polish Army Veterans Assocation of America had actively engaged itself in the national fund raising activity on behalf of the National Defense Fund. By July 15, 1939 PAVA had collected $16,118.15 for this purpose.[64] By the end of August this sum had already grown to $18,000.[65] PAVA members once again gave proof of their great generosity on behalf of the old country in moments that threatened its security.

PAVA's Relationship to Polish Foreign Policy

Polish foreign policy was formed outside the sphere of influence of the Polish Army Veterans Association of America. Nonetheless the relationship of PAVA to certain issues connected with this question is worth noting.

In the years 1921–1939 the Association supported the general direction of Polish foreign policy, which aimed at defending the country that came into existence after 123 years of enslavement of the Polish State. This support in essence came down to fighting anti-Polish propaganda that was being disseminated in the United States and Canada by inimical ethnic circles and crypto-communist spheres.[66]

In the middle of the 1930s PAVA also began noticing the Czech problem, and concretely the situation of the Polish population in Teschen Silesia. In February 1936

---

62 *The Veteran* June 1939, p. 8
63 *The Veteran* July 1939, p. 5
64 Ibid., pp. 12-13
65 PAVA NEB Archives, Minutes of a Plenary Meeting of the PAVA NEB of August 27, 1939, p. 32
66 See: Section II, chapter 3

the National Executive Board passed a resolution on the issue of the persecution of Poles by the Czech authorities. The resolution was sent to the Czech Embassy in Washington, D.C. Its contents were also published in *The Veteran*. The PAVA veterans recalled the years of joint struggle for independence on French soil and in far off Siberia, reminded of the rights of the Czech population living in Poland, and made categorical demands in their resolution: "...we demand the cessation of persecution of our native countrymen who live inside the Czech borders, and the punishment of the offenders."[67]

In September 1938, as the political crisis around Czechoslovakia was coming to a head, and the Polish side started a big promotional campaign demanding the return of trans-Olza River Silesia, the veterans of the American Legion wrote a telegram to Polish President Ignacy Mościcki, calling for "Poland not to stand at the head of the "gang of Europe" that wants the partition of Czechoslovakia." When the contents of this telegram were published in the Chicago press, the Polish veterans of PAVA District I reacted immediately, printing on September 28 an "Open Letter to the American Legion and the Veterans of the Allied Armies," in which they reminded of the circumstances in which Teschen Silesia (the trans-Olza River territories) had found itself in Czech hands in 1920: "In 1920, when Poland was bleeding in the fight against the Bolshevik attack, defending Europe and civilization from the barbarian flood, the whole world passively watched the heroic fight of the Polish Nation, without giving it any help.

"At that time not only did the Czechs not allow the passage of weapons and ammunition into Poland, but taking advantage of the situation, they deceitfully encroached onto the Polish soil of Silesian Teschen and took it by force at the moment when the Polish armed forces were in the East ... The civilian population of Teschen Silesia put up a solitary, heroic defense against the attack of the Czech army.

"At that time nobody called Czechoslovakia a "jackal," nobody protested against that ignominious injury! But it was then that Czechoslovakia played the role of a jackal, plunging a knife into Poland's back! The Polish nation has never reconciled itself to that wrong. For 18 years it continually demanded justice and protested against the oppression of its brothers and sisters by the Czech authorities. ... Czechoslovakia has no moral right to take the position of the wronged party with regard to Poland from which it deceitfuly took Teschen Silesia."[68]

When the news reached America that the Polish Army had occupied Teschen Silesia at the moment when Hitler's army on the basis of the Munich Agreement was

---

67 *The Veteran* February 1936, p. 11
68 PAVA NEB Archives, sign. A-VIII/6

occupying the Czech Sudeten region, the PAVA National Executive Board let itself get carried away by propagandist euphoria and sent a congratulatory telegram to Polish president Ignacy Mościcki: "In the name of the coalition of former volunteers for the Polish Army living in North America, we ask you, Mr. President, to accept our words of esteem for taking a clear and determined stance in the question of Teschen Silesia in the face of the entire world in this most critical historical moment. We also ask that you accept our homage for the entire Polish Army and its Marshal Rydz-Śmigły for the demonstrated readiness to fight for the just demands of the Polish Government."[69]

The propaganda from Poland about the supposedly growing might of the Polish State also affected the Polish veterans in America. The January 1939 issue of *The Veteran* included a laudatory article written by Wojciech Albrycht, the commander of PAVA Post Nr. 130 in Bydgoszcz, about Poland's accomplishments in the twenty year period of independence that was just ending. He wrote as follows about Polish foreign policy: "Our foreign policy is full of dignity and power. What other European nation has relations as well regulated with its neighbors as Poland does? We had warned the Czechs for many years that their chauvinistic policy had to end catastrophically. And that is what happened. Currently there is no obstacle to good relations between Poland and Czechoslovakia. Poland has long proposed resolutions to amend the statutes of the League of Nations. But nobody listened. Currently the League has lost its dignity and rationale for existence. After we had signed a non-aggression pact with Russia others followed suit. After we signed a non-aggression pact with Germany, now the greatest powers of Europe are trying to get do the same. Poland's foreign policy stands out because it is well planned and far sighted. We don't want what doesn't belong to us, and won't give up what is ours. Only Poles can decide about Poland. These are the guidelines that we all agree to."[70]

Unfortunately, the coming period revised those words. A couple of months later, in March 1939, Adolf Hitler, the Chancellor of Germany, openly demanded a highway and a railroad line on Polish soil to run through the so-called Gdańsk Corridor and the inclusion of the City of Gdańsk in the Reich. When this news became known in America, the PAVA National Executive Board (convened at a special meeting) on April 3 approved a resolution which stated: "In consideration of the current danger to Poland's wholeness and inviolability, of the inborn aggressiveness of Germany and the behavior of their leader which gives no guarantee of the inviolability of Poland's

---

69 *The Veteran* October 1938, p. 12

70 W. Albrycht, "20-letni dorobek Polski" ["Poland's 20 Years of Accomplishment"] in: *Weteran [The Veteran]* January 1939, pp. 2-3

borders... and of the fact that the Polish Government has expressed the readiness to fight Germany in defense of its name and Poland's boundaries,

"We therefore approve the sum of $1,000 (one thousand dollars) for the National Defense Fund, which sum we are immediately sending to the Federation of Polish Societies of Defenders of the Fatherland, at the same time we appeal to all Districts, Posts, Auxiliary Corps and Circles of Friends of Veterans to approve specific sums to the extent of their ability.

"...At one time we had declared the readiness to sacrifice our lives, so what value does money have in relationship to our earlier sacrifice. The need is now—we have to give today—not put it off until tomorrow!

"Long live a Free, Independent and Inviolable Poland!"[71]

The ordered fund drive met with a dynamic response among the individual PAVA posts. The generosity of the veterans was extraordinary. For instance Post Nr. 7 in Detroit, on the first day of its fundraiser gave from its own account and collected among its members $525! The neighboring Post Nr. 113 in Hamtramck, MI, also on the first day, collected $350 for this purpose.[72]

When the German demands were rejected, Hitler in April 1939 unilaterally renounced the non-aggression pact with Poland. This found its reflection in the PAVA press organ. The April, Easter issue of *The Veteran* referred to these events on its first page: "After twenty years we have found ourselves in a new, important situation. The eternal enemy of the Polish nation in the person of Hitler is threatening the security of the Polish State.

"But just as before we believed in our own strength and that of the nation, so today we believe in the might of Poland and our heirs."[73]

The Veteran's May issue carried a programmatic article titled "We have to Stand Watch!" which contained clear directives for PAVA members on how to behave with regard to the growing threat against Poland: "Like a bolt out of the blue the news of the threats and appetites of our eternal enemies has tugged at our hearts and minds and has expressed itself in one single-minded question: what is going to happen?

"...And we, Polish veterans, participants in battles for independence, were the first to understand the demands of the moment.

"Deeply concerned for the existence and integrity of the Motherland and mindful of our duty we have stepped up to action and have been leading our countrymen

---

71 *The Veteran* April 1939, p. 12
72 Ibid.
73 *The Veteran* April 1939, p. 1

in many instances. In other words, we "took up our watch" as befits former Polish soldiers. And we will continue to stand guard until the danger passes. The "honor of the Pole" requires this of us.

"Let the conviction of duty well performed be the greatest encouragement for you. And remember that this is just the beginning of this great contest, which may yet require enormous sacrifice of possessions and blood, and from which Poland must emerge victorious...

"As former soldiers you know best that endurance is the surest guarantee of victory. So remain tenaciously at your posts and by personal example and generosity awaken the consciences of the torpid and the reluctant. For now Poland does not demand the sacrifice of blood from us, it isn't even demanding material help, but we ourselves, compelled by the feeling of national duty, and with an understanding of the interests of the emigration, should give as much as we can and even more! And we will do this."[74]

That same issue of *The Veteran* reported that Poland had achieved a direct border with Hungary. Glossing over the tragedy of Czechoslovakia's partition, the readers were informed that: "As a result of territorial changes in the former Czech State, Poland has gained a common border with Hungary which, basing itself on a one thousand year old tradition, occupied near-Carpathian Ruthenia. The contact of Poland's southern border with the Hungarian state must delight the heart of every Pole.

"In its new neighborhood Poland is gaining sincere and devoted friends who have never let her down, and always came to her aid in the most crucial moments, if not with action then with bracing words. ... Today when once again Hungary and Poland as free nations share a common border, they can more calmly look into the future, knowing that Poland will not be disappointed by Hungary, just as Hungary will not be let down by Poland's friendship."[75]

As the accelerated development of the political situation in Europe kept dramatically weakening Poland's strategic situation, the editor of *The Veteran*, unfortunately, was unable to come up with a critical analysis of the existing political realities, but instead just copied the arguments of the Polish government's official propaganda.

Against the background of the above articles (written with anxiety over Poland's systematically deteriorating international situation and the growing threat from Germany) the text that appeared in the May issue of *The Veteran* is nothing short of curious. It had the title "Why is Poland Demanding Colonies?" and it was prefaced by

---

74 *The Veteran* May 1939, p. 1

75 Ibid. p. 10

an editorial commentary: "...the obtaining of colonies and access to raw resources is an absolute necessity for Poland. The most essential considerations of the economy and the population require it, as also the normal development of the Nation's and State's power."[76]

Already after the famous speech of Minister Józef Beck in the Polish Parliament, the June issue of *The Veteran* carried the following headline on its front cover: "Polish Army Veterans Have Contributed $15,000 to the National Defense Fund." And below there was a reproduction of the scene that took place in 1410 before the Battle of Grunwald, when envoys from the Teutonic Knights offered King Jagiełło and his brother Witold two naked swords. Under the drawing there was a telling inscription: "At one time the Teutonic Knights had offered two swords for use on their own hides to the King of Poland, Władysław Jagiełło and his brother Witold, and today with the same aim in mind of cutting the Prussian arrogance down to size the Polish Army Veterans have presented their contribution to the Polish government."

Many articles with an anti-German bias appeared in *The Veteran* just before the outbreak of the war, to give moral support to the veteran brotherhood in America. Some titles spoke for themselves: "Poland's Mighty Airforce; The Prussian Whirlwind has fallen to Dust and Ashes; On the 750th Annniversary of the Founding of the Order of Teutonic Knights; 6 Prussian Homages, etc. For the August issue of *The Veteran* the front cover carried a scene depicting "The Attack of the Hussars at Vienna in Defense of Christianity," which echoed the title, adding the rhetorical conjecture: "Maybe history will soon repeat itself, but this time first of all in the interest of Poland."

Unfortunately, the nearest tragic years showed how illusory the opinions were concerning the might of the Polish nation and the hopes nurtured with regard to the western allies.

PAVA Contacts with the Polish Army

This was one of the most important contacts and in fact dated from the first moments of the Association's existence. Attaché Major Kazmierz Mach, the official representative of the Polish Army in the United States, participated in the Founding Convention in Cleveland in May of 1921. He had come specifically for that event from Washington, D.C. On his motion PAVA became an organization that was open to all former soldiers of the Polish Army regardless of the formation they had served in.

Throughout the first years of PAVA's activity contacts with the Polish Army wre dominated by the problem of the return to America of the last group of former

---

76 *The Veteran* May 1939, p. 9

volunteer soldiers from America, who for various reasons had not left Poland in the years 1920–1921. The Polish authorities had placed all of them, together with their families, in the Grupa camp near Grudziądz, where they were to await the financing of their trip to America. The general situation in this camp was bad. The inactivity, the difficult living conditions and the lack of military discipline had a negative effect on the former soldiers gathered there. Conflicts multiplied, laws were broken including robberies committed on the neighboring population and the stealing of government property. The PAVA headquarters in Cleveland, Ohio received many letters from the camp with requests for help in organizing transport to America and for financial support. The latter request was organized the quickest and $420 was sent to Poland for that purpose. At the request of the PAVA Board the distribution of this aid for the former soldiers and their families at Grupa was to be supervised by Wojciech Albrycht, a former acitivist with the Polish Falcons of America, one of the former instructors at the Officer Cadet School in Cambridge Springs, Pennsylvania. J. S. Małek, a special PAVA emissary, confirmed the difficult situation in Grupa. He spent two days on an inspection there in December 1921.[77]

The financial aid that PAVA had sent for the needs of its colleagues in the camp proved ineffective because of the galloping inflation in Poland, all the more so as it was paid out in Polish Marks. Lt. Franciszek Truszkiewicz who lived in the camp wrote about this to the PAVA Board: "The first time everybody received 1,013 Polish Marks …now again everybody received 900 Polish Marks (enough for two pairs of socks) …one shirt costs 5,000 Polish Marks here and a pair of shoes 10,000. … It would be better to knock on the door of the American government there, or of the Polish Government, to hasten our departure."[78]

The PAVA Board had been making such efforts for many months. Stanisław Stachowicz, the PAVA secretary, wrote about the results in a letter of April 19, 1922 to the Ministry of Military Affairs in Warszawa. He reported that the Department of Labor in Washington had replied that the soldiers of allied armies could come to the United States two years after the date of the signing of the peace agreement in Europe. After that date that right was only good for permanent citizens of the USA, while the others could come on the basis of immigration quotas that existed for every nation. Fortunately the efforts to finance the transport of the former volunteers from America who were living in Grupa, were successful. The Polish authorities, in recognition of their military service, committed themselves by a resolution of the Council of Ministers of April 3, 1922 to cover the cost

---

77 PAVA NEB Archives, sign. A-I/1, Letter of December 6, 1921 from J. S. Małek to the PAVA Board
78 PAVA NEB Archives, A-I/1, Letter of March 6, 1922 from F. Truszkiewicz to the PAVA Board

of transportation to the United States. The Minister of Military Affairs issued a directive that that right pertained to anyone who at the time of demobilization had not signed a declaration renouncing all claims to free passage to America.[79] Such declarations had been signed by those who had decided to remain in Poland permanently. But in many instances the Polish government showed understanding for those who, disillusioned with life in Poland, wanted to return to America as fast as possible. Thanks to these efforts, by the end of September 1922, 1,067 veterans and their wives and children left Poland for America.[80]

The Board of PAVA of America worked closely with Polish military authorities on the matter of military settlement on the Eastern Borderlands. In order to better coordinate this work a permanent representational office was opened in Warszawa in June 1922, at 1 Miodowa Street, with the name Agency of the Polish Army Veterans Association of America. As of 1924 its subsequent quarters were located in the offices of the Union of Hallerians at 6 Senatorska Street. Due to the difficult working conditions there, the head of the PAVA Agency in Warszawa, Lt. Jan Roskosz, turned for help in getting an office to the Minister of Military Affairs, General Władysław Sikorski. The request was approved, and Lt. Roskosz wrote about it in his letter of June 5, 1924 to the PAVA Board in Cleveland: "Due to the inability to work in the occupied premises belonging to the Union of Hallerians, I was forced to turn to the Minister of Military Affairs to assign me an office, because it is impossible to rent anything in Warszawa today. The Minister gave me an office at the "Pod Blachą" Palace (The "Tin Roof" Palace) in the Office of the Minister of Military Affairs. Please note the above and direct all correspondence to the following address: Agency of the Pol. Army Vet. of America. Offices of the Minister Department of Military Settlement. The Tin Roof Palace. Warszawa."[81]

At this time the PAVA Agency, frequently also called the Delegature, thanks to its contacts at the Ministry of Military Affairs, began making efforts to commence research for a study of the history of those military units that Polish volunteers from America had served in. This was in addition to work connected with military settlement, preparation of General Haller's visit to the United States in 1923, and resolution of the problem of Polish war invalids from America who wanted to settle in Poland. Generals Marian Kukiel and Władysław Sikorski reacted favorably to the research plan. Sikorski, as the Minister of Military Affairs, agreed to have copies made of appropriate documents that were located at the General Staff. Lt. J. Roskosz

---

79 J. Praga, *To dla Ciebie Polsko [Poland This Is For You]* Warszawa 1998, p. 180
80 PAVA NEB Archives, sign. A-!/1 List of names of the last transport from Poland. 1922
81 PAVA NEB Archives, sign. A-XV/40, PAVA Agency

wrote about this in the above-cited letter: "It is prohibited to carry documents off the premises of the General Staff, and copies can only be made from 10 a.m. to 2:30 p.m. Mr. Szostakowski is making them and we will start sending the results over. So far the regiments, despite several requests and the approval of the Minister, have not sent us their histories, I have therefore asked the Minister for intervention, in the meantime General Kukiel wrote me back that he had given an order to the regiments under his command to present those studies to him. ... As I am finding out he is one of the decent and clear thinking generals.

"With regard to Gen. J. Haller's attitude toward the dissolution of the Army that arrived from France and its inclusion in the Home Army, General Kukiel declared that in order for this document to have historical weight, that is, what he would write or say about it, the historian who is writing the study, that is Wacław Gąsiorowski, must write to him directly, listing his essential questions point by point. Then the General's reply will be a document that is valid for the history being treated. ... I have made several requests to Gen. Haller...The General is constantly out on inspections of the armed forces, and is working so hard that it is difficult to get a word in edgewise with him."[82]

The letter quoted at length here is evidence of the excellent cooperation that existed between PAVA and the military authorities in Poland in the first post-war period, particularly in the years 1924–1925, when the office of the PAVA Delegature in Warszawa adjoined the office of the Minister of Military Affairs! That exceptional situation lasted until June 1925, when the activity of the PAVA Delegature was termintated due to the failure of the military settlement operation on the Eastern Borderlands.

In that particularly favorable period many issues connected with military decorations for the volunteers from America were resolved successfully. In this instance the PAVA Board helped obtain the data and addresses of former Polish soldiers living in the United States who, on approval of the military authorities in Poland, were to receive the highest Polish military decorations, the Order of Virtuti Militari and the Cross of Valor. After completing legal and documentary formalities in Poland the volunteers from America were decorated during Polish American holidays by the Polish attaché from Washington or by local Polish consuls. Some veterans lived too far away from Polish diplomatic posts. In such instances the decorations that had been granted to them together with the diplomas were mailed to their address.

The first on the list of those who had been decorated were veterans of the January Uprising. One of them was 2nd Lt. Adolf Kirchner who lived in Syracuse, New York.

---

82 Ibid.

By order of the Minister of Military Affairs of March 23, 1923 he received the Cross of Valor Nr. 1980.[83]

In April 1923 the Ministry of Military Affairs granted a group of 100 Crosses of Valor to volunteers from America who were members of the Polish Army Veterans Association of America.[84]

The cooperation of the Ministry of Military Affairs with the Polish Army Veterans Association of America was developing well. But sometimes unpleasant situations arose, when the staff of the ministry badly treated former volunteers from America who had remained in Poland after the war and who were not members of PAVA. One of them was Paweł Hereta, who did not return to America because he had to take care of his gravely ill mother. After her death in the fall of 1923 he made fruitless efforts in various offices to be allowed to depart. This is how he remembered those moments years later: "After my mother's death I started petitioning for departure to America. I wrote and pleaded with various institutions for help in departure, but my requests were met with silence. I decided to go to Warszawa personally to the Ministry of Military Affairs. I was sure that I would be admitted there and listened to, but that turned out to be a big mistake and I will not forget the conversation with that colonel til the day I die.

"Here is what happened. When I was led in to a particular office in the Ministry I found a colonel there (I don't remember his name) and six officers of various ranks. The colonel asked me what I wanted. I described my problem to him in detail and asked that I be sent off to America at the Polish government's expense, and if that were impossible, that I get a job suitable to my qualifications. Here is what the colonel replied to me:

" 'I am not an employment agent and I can't send you to America. Nobody asked you to come to Poland. A whole bunch of you unwanted guests came here and now the Polish government has nothing but trouble with you.'

"At those words the other officers started laughing. I was deeply grief stricken and left."[85]

This sort of behavior of employees at the Ministry of Military Affairs toward that soldier sheds some light on other, unofficial opinions concerning volunteers from America that circulated among the highest military circles.

In October 1924, nine PAVA members who were chevaliers of the Order of Virtuti Militari, took the opportunity, by right of their decoration, to petition the Polish

---

83 PAVA NEB Archives, sign. A-XVIII/1 Letter of July 5, 1923 of Military attaché Kazimierz Mach at the Polish Embassy in Washington to the PAVA Board
84 *The Veteran* July 1923, p. 5
85 PAVA NEB Archives, sign. Box-52/vol. 1, Letter of P. Hereta of September 24, 1952

authorities for payment of an appropriate pension, as foreseen by law. They were as follows: Lt. Lucjan Zbigniew Adamczak, Lt. Marian Kowalski, Lt. Zygmunt Feliks Nowak, Lt. Józef Perzan, 2nd Lt. Bogusław Henryk Przywarski, Platoon Leader Jan Sadowski, Lt. Stanisław Solon, Lt. Zygmunt F. Więckus, 2nd Lt. Fryderyk Woźniak. One PAVA member, Jan Pikielniak, residing in Trenton, NJ, also decorated with the Order of Virtuti Militari, did not submit a petition. Volunteers from America who were U.S. citizens could not receive such a pension. That was the case of Lt. Jan Pela, who was born in America, but had nonetheless enlisted in the Polish Army in France, and fought in its ranks for Polish independence. He had never seen Poland with his own eyes, and knew it only from the stories his parents and immigrant colleagues had told him.[86] Unfortunately, that law created a sense of discrimination toward the volunteer group, which was keenly felt during the period of the Great Depression, when they were often without means of subsistence. That law was most painful for the families of those who had died on the field of battle. By their soldierly death they had given the best possible testimonial to their parents who had been able to raise them on foreign American soil as honorable sons of Poland. Unfortunately, free Poland was unable to appreciate this effort and the great patriotism that these families showed. Much bitterness and unalterable moral damage was done by this heartless, thoughtless regulation.

In the spring of 1926 the Polish government, due to its difficult financial situation, decided to temporarily abolish the post of military attaché at the Polish Embassy in Washington, D.C. The departing attaché, Lt. Col. Bohdan Hulewicz, wrote to PAVA president Dr. T. Starzyński in a letter of March 26: "I want to express to you, colleagues, my total appreciation for the selfless work which you conduct for the good of Veterans and the entire Polish community.

"In observing your noble actions I have formed the deep conviction that you are on the best road to fulfill our common postulates. Harmonious work, distant from political party frictions, your efforts to uphold noble Polish traditions, and first of all the continual arousal of the spirit of charity among the members of the Association, which has already once given of itself in the greatest sacrifice for the Fatherland, gifting it with entire hosts of young and brave hearts, of which quite a few bled for freedom on the fields of battle—that is the luminous page of your history."[87]

In reply the May issue of *The Veteran* carried an appropriate story and words of farewell for Lt. Col. Hulewicz. The note said: "With the Lt. Col.'s departure we are losing closer contact with one of the most cordial friends of our organization,

---

86 PAVA NEB Archives, sign. A-XVIII/1. Letter of October 31, 1924 of the PAVA Secretary to the Polish Embassy in Washington

87 *The Veteran* May 1926, p. 19

because rarely has a Polish representative abroad backed us so strongly and acted with such a thorough understanding of the vital needs of our Association."[88]

After the May 1926 coup, which brought with it changes at the highest levels of the government administration and in the military, changes also occurred in the power structure of veteran circles, where organizations that derived from military formations that were mainly tied to Józef Piłsudski's efforts on behalf of independence, i.e., the Polish Legions (and the First Brigade in particular) and the Polish Military Organization, became the most influential. On the other hand veteran circles that derived from Polish military formations that fought on the side of the nations of the Entente during the war, were pushed into the background in the post-coup political reality. This mainly concerned veterans of the Blue Army. The new tendency also, unfortunately, affected the volunteers from America regardless if they were members of some veteran organization, for instance the Union of Hallerians, or not. It was enough that they had been connected with the Blue Army.

Despite this difficult situation, PAVA did not boycott the new powers in Poland. Formal contacts were established. On two occasions there were meetings of PAVA representatives with Marshal Józef Piłsudski. The first time was his meeting with the PAVA tour in 1927, and a year later the conference with PAVA president Kazimierz Bałdyga.

Representatives of Polish military authorities were also encountered in the Welcoming Committees for PAVA tours, and among the individuals who personally greeted Polish veterans arriving from America. That was the case in 1927 in many Polish cities visited by members of the veterans' tour. In Gdynia the veterans were greeted to the sounds of the Navy Orchestra by General Mariusz Zaruski and retired general Józef Haller. In Katowice General Dr. Józef Zając, commander of the 23rd Infantry Division, was in theWelcoming Committee for the veterans from America. On the other hand at Równe in Volhynia the veterans were greeted by garrison commander Colonel Władysław Anders.[89]

Several months after they returned from their tour of Poland the veterans had the opportunity to host Gen. Dr. Stanisław Rouppert and Colonel B. Zakliński in America. They had come to New York in October for a medical convention. Their arrival added splendor to the celebrations commemorating the tenth anniversary of the beginning of recruitment for the Polish Army in France. General Stanisław Rouppert and Colonel Zakliński were invited to Buffalo for the grand anniversary ceremonies organized there by PAVA Post Nr. 1. The celebrations began on October

---

88 Ibid.
89 PAVA NEB, sign. A-XXV/2, The Welcoming Program in all of Poland of the Polish Army Veterans Assocation of America from July 8 to August 18, 1927

9, 1927 with an enormous field Mass with the participation of local Polish consuls Dr. S. Rosicki and Dr. Bujnowski, representatives of the city administration headed by Mayor Schwab, American veteran organizations and several thousand members of the local Polish American community. PAVA was represented by its president, Dr. Teofil Starzyński. Mayor Schwab gave keys to the city to the guests from Poland. In the evening at a ceremonial banquet Gen. Rouppert gave PAVA Post Nr. 1 portraits of Polish President Professor I. Mościcki, and of Marshal J. Piłsudski, with their personal signatures.[90] The next day the guests from Poland drove to the cemetery at Niagara on the Lake, where, in the name of the Polish Armed Forces, they laid wreaths on the graves of volunteers for the Polish Army in France in the years 1917–1918, who had died there.[91]

The next PAVA tour to Poland, which took place in 1930 (and was much more modest due to the continuing economic crisis in America) was greeted in Warszawa by, among others, Vice Minister of Labor and Social Welfare Gen. Dr. Stefan Hubicki, and the commandant of the garrison of the City of Warszawa, Colonel Bolesław Wieniawa-Długoszowski.[92]

A year later the veterans in America hosted General Gustaw Orlicz-Dreszer, the President of the Sea and Colonial League, who was also on the staff of the Armed Forces Inspector General, a former officer of J. Piłsudski's Polish Legions. During his stay in Detroit he was a guest of the PAVA Board and local Post Nr. 7, where he also met with Wincenty Smołczyński, the elderly veteran of the January Uprising who was very popular with the PAVA rank and file, and who had come from distant Chicopee, Massachusetts for that occasion.[93]

At that meeting General Orlicz-Dreszer addressed the assembled veterans with the following words: " 'I will report back about you, about your life in America, dear colleagues, to the one who has the right to be the First Soldier of Reborn Poland; I will relate your activities to him in the greatest detail possible, to him who always has the biggest heart for every Polish soldier—Marshal Józef Piłsudski.' There was thunderous applause, everyone rose from their seats. 'In all your affairs, in all your needs turn to me with full confidence. Have confidence in me as strong as one has in the courier between army units, on whose report you can always rely. Let me end with a shout: Long Live the Veterans of the Polish Army in America!' "[94]

---

90   These portraits are still hanging in the headquarters of PAVA Post Nr. 1 in Buffalo
91   *The Veteran* November 1927, p. 10
92   *Polska Zbrojna [Armed Poland]* June 21, 1930, Nr. 197
93   *The Veteran* October 1931, p. 13
94   *The Veteran* November 1931, pp. 7-8

During his second visit to the United States in March 1932 General Orlicz-Dreszer gifted the PAVA District II in New York with an officer's saber with the engraved inscription: "To Comrades in Arms Veterans of the Polish Army in America District—II. General Orlicz-Dreszer. Warszawa March 17, 1932."[95] Upon his return to Poland the general sent the veterans another gift, which he mentioned in his letter of April 4: "Having returned to Poland from the United States, I would like to express my cordial and deep gratitude for the unusually warm reception which I experienced from your Association of former soldiers of the Polish Army, those representatives of our emigration who at the deciding moment did not hesitate to lay down their lives in defense of the distant Fatherland. At the same time I am sending you my modest gift, in the form of books for the library of the Association.

"Being a soldier myself, the more pleasant was my impression from the direct contact I had with you, gentlemen, and I want to state that it allows me to nurture fruitful hope and belief in your work to bring closer together the emigration and the Old Country. Please accept my sincere soldierly handshake."[96]

In the years 1933–1934 PAVA hosted the following Polish generals: Roman Górecki and Józef Haller. Although at that time they were no longer on active service, they still embodied the Polish Armed Forces for the veterans and the American Polonia. At that time General Górecki had the important function of president of the world combatant federation, FIDAC. While in the United States in 1933 at the invitation of the American Legion, he visited the following cities: New York, Pittsburgh, Indianapolis, Chicago, Detroit, Cleveland, Buffalo, Washington, Richmond, Wilmington, New Haven, where he also met with Polish veterans and the local Polish American community.[97]

Retired General J. Haller who was on his second American tour from December 1933 to May 1934 at the invitation of PAVA, visited almost every Polish parish, appealing for generosity on behalf of the I. J. Paderewski Fund.

In the spring of 1935 PAVA hosted another soldier from Poland. This time it was Colonel Stefan Iwanowski, an emissary of the Sea and Colonial League, who during his stay in major Polish American centers was instrumental in the formation of new League chapters, in the organization of a central executive board and creation of a New York District. During his stay in America the guest from Poland visited many PAVA posts, including Post Nr. 7 in Detroit and Post Nr. 12 in Philadelphia. These meetings were very popular among the veterans, because during the war Col.

---

95 This saber is currently part of the collection of the New York Museum of the Tradition of Polish Arms in America
96 *The Veteran* May 1932, p. 14
97 *The Veteran* June 1933, p. 20

Iwanowski had been the deputy chief of staff of the Polish Army in France.[98]

Three Polish generals arrived in New York in September 1935: Gustaw Orlicz-Dreszer, Bolesław Wieniawa-Długoszowski and Aleksander Osiński. They were part of the official state delegation that was headed for Washington and a meeting with President F. D. Roosevelt. Vice Minister of the Treasury Colonel Adam Koc headed the delegation. During the meeting with the PAVA National Executive Board in New York generals Orlicz-Dreszer and Wieniawa-Długoszowski promised their help in obtaining a permanent financial subsidy for Polish war veterans living in the United States.[99]

In July 1936 the veterans were shocked by the news of the tragic airplane accident that claimed the life of General Gustaw Orlicz-Dreszer. His wife (an American) after some time offered various memorabilia that belonged to her husband to the PAVA museum collections, including the general's insignia from the collar of his uniform.[100]

PAVA tried to maintain constant contact with military units that originated in the Blue Army and in particular with those in which the most volunteers from America had served during the war. The 43rd Infantry Regiment of the Bayonne Legion, which derived from the 1st Regiment of Polish Riflemen in France, was one such unit. In peacetime the regiment was stationed at Dubno in Volhynia. In 1928 the commander of the regiment, Lt. Col. Benedykt Chłusewicz, began to correspond with the PAVA Board in connection with the plan to publish the regiment's history and to strike a special regimental emblem, as well as to purchase a new regimental flag. The PAVA Board enthusiastically supported the project and tried to help as best it could, especially in gathering historical materials, for instance written narratives, photographs, etc.

In the spring of 1929 thirteen PAVA members—former officers of the 43rd Infantry Regiment, received personal invitations from Lt. Col. Chłusewicz to attend the presentation of the new regimental flag offered by the city of Paris. In the ceremony, which took place on July 25, 1929, PAVA was represented by Kazimierz Bałdyga, Stanisław Sobolewski (PAVA treasurer), Dr. Teofil Starzyński (honorary PAVA president) and veteran Stanicki. The only person to come directly from America for the event was Gustaw Pieprzny (head of the Polish Falcons of America), Chevalier of the Order of Virtuti Militari and four-time recipient of the Cross of Valor. It was an unusually exalted ceremony, because the regimental flag was decorated with the Order of Virtuti Militari. Moreover, by decision of the French authorities the flag was

---

98 *The Veteran* July 1935, pp. 11-12, 20
99 *The New York Sun* September 26, 1935, p. 25
100 *The Veteran* August 1936, p. 15 These memorabilia are today a part of the Museum of the Tradition of Polish Arms in New York

decorated with the Legion of Honor and the Grand Croix de Guerre. The latter was only bestowed in wartime for extraordinary service on the field of battle. The French Parliament by a special resolution renewed this decoration only and exclusively so that the former 1st Regiment of Polish Riflemen of the Polish Army could receive it. At the regimental holiday in Dubno the veterans from America received the new regimental emblem and a souvenir from the entire organization—a hand painted diploma with the signatures of all the officers of the 43rd Infantry Regiment.[101]

In the ensuing years PAVA members, former soldiers of the 43rd Infantry Regiment, also received insignia of their regiment, but by mail.

In the summer of 1930 the 43rd Infantry Regiment in Dubno was visited by a PAVA tour headed by PAVA president Wacław Rżewski. The veterans from America, as always royally entertained in their own regiment, invited its commander to pay a visit to America. But Lt. Col. Chłusewicz didn't come until 1937 as a delegate of the Ministry of Military Affairs. He was a special guest at the 7th PAVA General Assembly in Rochester, NY. In the final years before World War II Col. Chłusewicz supported the veterans from America in their efforts to obtain the Cross of Independence.

With the Convention of Colleagues of the Circle of Polish Army Volunteers of America to take place in Gdynia on August 8, 1937, the Minister of Military Affairs, Lt. General Tadeusz Kasprzycki, gave soldiers on active duty and employees of military institutions who were former volunteers from America, two days off so they could participate in the convention. This order was accepted with gratitude, because it gave a real opportunity to meet with colleagues they had not seen in a long time.[102]

The next PAVA tour to Poland was organized in the summer of 1938. The veterans were invited to participate in the celebration of the 13th Division of Borderlands Riflemen in Równe. During the sixty member tour's stay in Kraków a PAVA delegation led by commander Lucjusz Kajko laid wreaths in the name of the organization at the Grunwald monument and on the coffin of Marshal J. Piłsudski in the crypt beneath the Tower of the Silver Bells on the Royal Hill of Wawel.

The welcome the veterans from America got in Równe was extraordinary: "On July 30 in the morning, an honor guard holding historic flags lined up at the train station in Równe. The Division Commander, the Regimental Commanders, the President of the City, the Deputy County Executive all came. A full military band was playing. The tour went to the military barracks where they were given free meals and lodging. On that day commander Kajko also paid a visit to the military and civilian authorities. ... In the afternoon great crowds of the public, the honor guard,

---

101 The souvenir is on display at the Museum of the Tradition of Polish Arms in New York
102 Central Military Archive, sign. 302,4.97, Inspectorate General of the Armed Forces

and officials of the federal and local governments gathered on the beautiful square, which after a speech by the president of the city and by Commander Lucjusz Kajko, was named The American Polonia Square. Commander Kajko unveiled the plaque. After the ceremony was concluded everyone went to the Krzemieniec manor house where we were entertained by the City of Równe. Those were pleasant moments. ... In the evening, in the barracks yard of the 45th Infantry Regiment, there was a roll call of those killed in battle. It was a moving moment for us, as the names of the dead that were being read were well known to us.

"July 31 began with a review of the entire Division. It was a beautiful sight. We experienced a feeling of power seeing such a compact mass of men and arms grouped together on one site. ... Next the Division Commander Colonel Józef Ćwiertniak greeted the veterans in front of the Division, after which he gave them regimental insignia, and Commander Kajko gave the Division and the Regiments diplomas and souvenir PAVA gold crosses. After filing past the veterans took their places on the reviewing stand to watch the parade of the Division. ... After the parade the soldiers' dinner was held in the regiments, and then we went by car to the military settlements in Hallerowo and Bajonówka. The settlers greeted us with the traditional Polish bread and salt, after which they entertained us cordially. ... The divisional celebrations bound the veterans even more strongly with the current rank and file. At every step the young soldiers honored us by saluting, with the desire to be of assistance, with expressions of courtesy."[103]

In Dubno, where the 43rd Infantry Regiment was garrisoned, one of the streets was renamed Lucjan Chwałkowski Boulevard, in honor of the first officer from America, a soldier of the Blue Army, to be killed at the front in France in July 1918.

At the conclusion of the tour a PAVA delegation (L. C. Kajko, J. Tyrka, J. Szwiec, J. Czuba, W. Albrycht), accompanied by "Światpol" (World Association of Poles Living Abroad) director Stefan Lenartowicz, met with Marshal Rydz-Śmigły, who was presented with the problems that were frustrating Polish veterans in America and their colleagues living in Poland, especially the issue of obtaining financial aid for Polish war invalids in America. Marshal Rydz-Śmigły promised the veterans from America that he would help them to resolve the problems they had presented to him which, to the astonishment of the PAVA delegates, he was very well versed in. During this meeting the Marshal was presented with the PAVA Golden Cross of Merit.[104]

---

103 "Polacy Zagranicą" ["Poles Abroad"] Organ of the World Union of Poles Abroad, Nr. 1, September 1938, p. 4; The Veteran October 1938, p. 4

104 The Veteran September 1938, p. 10

The PAVA leadership, by developing personal contacts with the most influential figures in the Polish Army, laboriously moved toward the creation of a military lobby which would be able to effectively back the efforts of veterans from America to obtain government financial aid on behalf of their war invalid colleagues. The pressure of the lobby, headed by Marshal Rydz-Śmigły, had a real influence on the ultimately successful resolution of that issue at the beginning of 1939, when the Polish Parliament in January of that year approved a permanent subsidy of $3,000 per year to augment the I. J. Paderewski Invalid Fund of PAVA and a permanent pension for chevaliers of the Order of Virtuti Militari, whether they were American citizens or not. And things started moving with regard to the issue of military decorations for the volunteers from America. On June 1, 1939 the army and air force attaché at the Polish Embassy in Washington, Lt. Col. A. Chramiec, sent the PAVA national commander Lucjusz Kajko a list of names of 2,210 volunteers from America, former members of the 44th Regiment of Borderlands Riflemen, who had been selected to receive the Medal for the War of 1918–1921, and a list of 1,363 soldiers from the regiment (also volunteers from America) who had the right to wear that medal.[105]

Lt. Colonel Chramiec had a conference with PAVA national commander Lucjusz Kajko and the PAVA adjutant general Leopold Krzyżak, on the sensitive matter of passing over volunteers from America when the Cross of Independence was being conferred. Of the 35,258 veterans who had received this high decoration there were only ... 57 volunteers from America! It should be remembered that there were over 20,000 of these volunteers and they formed the core of the Polish Army in France. To make matters worse not one of them had received the Cross of Independence with Swords. In Poland 1,816 persons had received that decoration. The above cited figures are evidence of the discrimination that took place against the volunteers from America.[106]

During the meeting with Lt. Col. Chramiec it was decided that the Independence Cross ought to be received by all volunteers from America who had enlisted in the ranks of the Polish Army in France from October 1917 to May 1918. Those who had enlisted later would receive the Independence Medal. But taking care of this matter in Poland hit a serious legal roadblock, because the Chapter in charge of these decorations was already closed. As a result of the efforts of the indefatigable Stefan Lenartowicz, the director of Światpol, who was able to interest Aleksandra Piłsudska, the Marshal's widow, in this matter, assurance was received from government authorities that the issue would be presented at the fall 1939 session of Parliament.

---

105 PAVA NEB Archives, sign. A-XXX/13

106 Z. Wesołowski. *Polish Orders, Medals, Badges and Insignia and Civilian Decorations 1705–1985* Miami, Florida 1986, pp. 21-22; PAVA NEB Archives, sign. Box-17, PAVA Post 130 in Bydgoszcz

The initial plan was to open up the Chapter of the Independence Cross and Medal only for the purpose of honoring the volunteers from America.[107]

The PAVA National Executive Board in cooperation with the military and civilian authorities in Równe planned to begin preliminary work in the fall of 1939 to erect a monument in that town in memory of the Polish American community's war effort during World War I. PAVA leaders wanted the monument to stand in the local American Polonia Square. It was to depict a Blue Army soldier on the attack, holding a rifle with a bayonet fixed to it. Unfortunately, the outbreak of war in 1939 thwarted that plan.[108]

PAVA Post Nr. 130 in Bydgoszcz

Of the more than 20,000 volunteers from America who served in the Polish Army in France, several thousand decided to stay in free Poland after the conclusion of the war. It is impossible to ascertain their exact number, because no one had collected that type of information. Those who remained dispersed all over Poland, mostly to their native regions. After the beginning of the resettlement operation on the Eastern Borderlands some of them took possession of the land that had been granted them. The colonists in Volhynia decided to form a PAVA post in order to maintain contact with their colleagues in America. A post was organized in the fall of 1923 in Równe. The PAVA Board at its meeting of Augsut 8, 1924 decided to accept it into the organization on the same basis on which posts in America had been accepted.[109] Unfortunately, the PAVA post in Równe did not prove to be a lasting structure. The main reason was the financial problems of the new settlers and by the same token their inability to pay membership dues.

The volunteers from America, scattered all over Poland, sporadically joined other veteran organizations, mainly the Union of Hallerians, which mostly had former Blue Army soldiers in its ranks. Those who did not want to join the Union of Hallerians, because they did not agree with its political activities, and who had many years of membership in the ranks of the Polish Falcons behind them, constantly thought of creating their own organizational structure.

Here is what Wojciech Albrycht wrote about the former volunteers from America who had remained in Poland: "We worked peacefully, delighting in reborn Poland, glad at the growing army, seeing a brother in every former serviceman.

---

107 Ibid.
108 Ibid.
109 PAVA NEB Archives, sign. A-VII/1, Minutes of the August 8, 1924 meeting of the Board of the Polish Army Veterans Association of America

"But voices started circling over our heads expressing in our name our supposed attitude to serious political issues. The volunteers from America, scattered all over Poland, unorganized, unable to give a collective reply—remained silent. Without our participation we were ranked with the so-called opposition and only because we at one time had been called "Hallerians," and because the main figures on the Board of the Union of Hallerians belong to the opposition, therefore the volunteers from American were also devilishly included. In the end, the unemployed former volunteers were being denied jobs in Poland. The jobless Stanisław Kunior of Busko in Kielce Voiyevodship wrote to us about this, asking bitterly:

'Are we thanks to our toil and ill-treatment unworthy of eating Polish bread, are we to always look for it abroad?'"[110]

The unorganized former volunteers from America were unable to publicize the problems with which they were struggling in free Poland. In order to change that, in the fall of 1932 during a visit of the PAVA delegation in Poland headed by President Franciszek Dziób, a post was organized in Bydgoszcz, with commander Wojciech Albrycht at the helm. He was a well known Falcons activist from America, a former instructor in the Cadet School in Cambridge Springs, Pennsylvania and the former chief of training at the Niagara on the Lake camp in Canada in 1917. The Bydgoszcz PAVA post was organized under truly veteran circumstances, which Stanisław Sobolewski recalled in his letter of November 17, 1932 to PAVA Post Nr. 7 in Detroit: "In Bydgoszcz several of us met at Colleague Albrycht's home and there we began a royal feast, of course our host was constantly busy supplying us with bottles of cognac (four star); you have no idea what a spree that was! ... The order was exemplary, because our colleague the President was present at this ceremony, so there was great respect for "the boss."

"The result of this feast is a new Post of our Veteran Family on the Eastern Borderlands headed by colleague Albrycht."[111]

Aside from Wojciech Albrycht the other organizers of the PAVA post in Bydgoszcz were: Stanisław Pałaszewski, Jan Paśniewski, Polikarp Dzierżgowski, Idzi Czachla, Adam Linkowski, Henryk Klimczewski and Stanisław Sobolewski. By a decision of the PAVA Board the new PAVA post in Poland received the number 130.[112] But the Polish government did not agree to register it because PAVA's controlling authorities were outside the Polish State. So the Bydgoszcz post was officially registered as the Circle of Volunteers of the Polish Army in America, whose main purposes were: a)

---

110 W. Albrycht, "Jakim był i jest duch żołnierza ochotnika z Ameryki" ["What Was and Is the Spirit of the Soldier Volunteer from America"] in: *Weteran [The Veteran]* September 1934, p. 6

111 PAVA NEB Archives, sign. Box – 3/ vol. 3

112 *The Veteran* December 1932, p. 15

to honor the memory of colleagues who had died for Poland's freedom; b)to transmit to the younger generations the ideals and traditions of the volunteer soldier from America; c) to cooperate with state authorities and social organizations along the guidelines mapped out by government policy-makers; d) to cultivate the memory of the war effort of the Polish emigration to America.[113]

On January 15, 1933, at Wojciech Albrycht's suggestion, a convention of colleagues of former volunteers from America who stayed in Poland after the war was held in Toruń. Only 22 volunteers showed up. It was mostly those who could afford the trip, because those were times of deep economic crisis in Poland. During that convention a magnificent ceremony was held in the Old Town Square. In the presence of 3,800 uniformed Polish Falcons, 96 color guards and thousands of members of the public, the volunteers from America (Albrycht, Sierociński, Seiler) received the decoration of the Falcons' Legion of Honor from Count Adam Zamoyski—the President of the Falcons in Poland.[114]

From a report sent by A. Albrycht to the PAVA Board in Detroit it appears that many of the former volunteers, who had been making their mark as members of the Polish Falcons of America, had managed to set themselves up quite well in Poland. Those who were in active military service in Poland were: Captain Henryk Sieradzki—the 11th Infantry Regiment in the Tarnów Mountains; Captain Jan Seiler—59th Infantry Regiment in Inowrocław; Major Stanisław Sosień—55th Infantry Regiment in Leszno—commander of the cadet school there; Captain Władysław Pawłowski—61st Infantry Regiment in Bydgoszcz; Captain Franciszek Górecki—43rd Infantry Regiment in Dubno; Captain Baskiewicz in Tczew; Captain Stępniewski in Skierniewice; Captain Jan Drągłowski—instructor at the cadet school in Nisko; Marcin Gąsior—45th Infantry Regiment. Zarzecki, a former volunteer from America, worked for the Government Police in Poznań with the rank of commissioner.

The following were doing well in civilian life: Wojciech Albrycht—teacher of physical education and military preparedness at the Gimnazjum in Bydgoszcz; Stanisław Pałaszewski—a journalist in Bydgoszcz; Jan Guba—owner of a printing press and bindery in Bydgoszcz; Polikarp Dzierżgowski—Commissioner of the Treasury in Wąbrzeźno; Henryk Klimczewski—owner of a tobacco warehouse in Toruń; Kuźmicki—employee of the National Health Service in Inowrocław; Linkowski—city official in Toruń; Józef Sierociński—landowner near Warszawa; Józef Szwiec—owner of a movie theater in Toruń; Antoni Wiącek—owner of a store

---
113 *The Veteran* September 1934, p. 6
114 PAVA NEB Archives, Box-17, PAVA Post Nr. 130, Bulletein Nr. 1/33 of the Circle of Volunteers from America

in Korzec in Volhynia; Czesław Żuławski, former editor of *The Veteran*, owner of a farm in Bochnia near Kraków; Myjak—a village schoolteacher near Grudziądz; Jan Paśniewski—landowner near Bydgoszcz; Figler—a Border Patrol inspector in Kościerzyna; Alfred Krzyżanowski—retired in Toruń.

According to W. Albrycht, the "veterans are doing quite well, some very well and several terrifically well."[115]

At the convention in Toruń Wojciech Albrycht, the president of the Circle of Volunteers for the Polish Army from America, addressed an important declaration to the highest authorities in Poland: "We honor the majesty of the Republic in the person of its president Ignacy Mościcki, we recognize and respect the great contributions to Poland of Marshal Józef Piłsudski and if the need should arise, at their call, we will again gladly rush to arms."[116]

At the convention new leadership was elected for the Circle of Volunteers for the Polish Army from America as follows: Wojciech Albrycht—president; Józef Czuba—secretary; Józef Sierociński—deputy for the City of Warszawa; Henryk Klimczewski—deputy for the City of Toruń; Franciszek Wójcik—Deputy for Volhynia.

The election of Józef Sierociński, the former president of the Union of Hallerians, to a leadership position in the Circle was not a smart move, because his person was unequivocally linked in the minds of the government authorities with the political opposition. But in 1933 Sierociński resigned from the Circle of Volunteers for the Polish Army from America, because the Union of Hallerians demanded from those of its members who were former volunteers from America that they declare themselves to which of the two organizations they want to belong, or else they would be removed from the Union's rolls.[117]

Those volunteers who were scattered all across Poland were of necessity correspondence members of the Circle, which had its headquarters in Bydgoszcz (in Wojciech Albrycht's private apartment). In April 1934 the Circle had 203 former volunteers on its rolls, of whom 163 were active members.[118]

The next Convention of former volunteers from America was held from June 26 to June 30, 1934 at Równe in Volhynia, where the headquarters of the 13th Infantry Division was located. This event was connected with festivities of the 13th Infantry Division's commemoration the fifteen anniversary of the arrival of

---

115 W. Albrycht, "Miłe wiadomości o naszych kolegach w Polsce" ["Pleasant News About Our Colleagues in Poland"] in: *Weteran [The Veteran]* March 1933, p. 4

116 *The Veteran* October 1933, p. 22

117 PAVA NEB Archives, sign. Box-17, PAVA Post Nr.130 in Bydgoszcz, Letter of W. Albrycht of November 11, 1934

118 PAVA NEB Archives, sign. A-XXIII/3 Letter of April 5, 1934 from W. Albrycht to the PAVA Board

the Blue Army in Poland. The convention in Równe was attended by 115 former volunteers from America who came from all over Poland, which was a great success, all the more so as the government refused to give the convention participants any special railroad discounts.

At the convention's forum Wojciech Albrycht gave a speech in which he referred to the current issues of a political nature: "It almost always happens, that when we first inform somebody about the organization of the Circle, their first question is:

" 'And what is your relationship to General Józef Haller, and what is it to Marshal Piłsudski?'

"Well, we are a proud, sincere and brave element. What we feel we express. When in the pre-war years we were organizing the war effort, we knew neither Haller nor Piłsudski. Later, from telegrams and newspapers we got to know the deeds of both of them. Our leader at that time was the manly Polish heart.

"We were going to France, not to General Haller's army, because he wasn't even there yet, and we were going to join the Polish Army. Before and during the war we wanted to help win independence for Poland. After the war, as our strength permits, we are working to make independence permanent. Whoever moves along this same path, we consider useful

"We have the respect for General Józef Haller that ought to characterize the relationship of a subordinate former soldier to his commander. The denigration of our former leader would be degrading to our knightly dignity.

"We revere Marshal Piłsudski as the Father of the Polish Army. We see in him the actual organizer and spiritual leader of reborn Poland. The Marshal is a paragon of endurance for us and by his deeds and contributions he is equal to the historic figure of George Washington, called the Father of the United States."[119]

The declaration of organizational affiliation bore fruit in the form of an invitation for the Circle of Volunteers for the Polish Army from America to the August Convention of the Union of Polish Legionnaires in Kraków on the occasion of the twentieth anniversary of the 1st Cadre Company's marching off to war in 1914.[120]

That summer the Circle of Volunteers from America for the Polish Army had 107 members. In the group of 77 veterans who had sent in their applications, were: 1 Lt. Colonel, 2 majors, 8 captains, 15 lieutenants, 2 2nd lieutenants, 3 adjutants (?), 8 sergeants, 1 platoon leader, 12 corporals and 20 privates. Of this number, the following had been decorated: Virtuti Militari—13; Independence Cross—16; Cross of Valor—48; Independence Medal—10; Polonia Restituta—1; Cross of Merit—7.

---

[119] *The Veteran* September 1934, p. 7
[120] PAVA NEB Archives, sign. Box-17, PAVA Post Nr. 130, Letter of May 3, 1934 from W. Albrycht to the PAVA Board

These veterans lived in the following voievodships: Kielce—19; Poznań—18; Volhynia—12; Pomerania, Kraków and Tarnopol—6 each; Śląsk—3; Białystok, Lwów, Łódź—2 each; Warszawa—1.[121]

In the fall of 1934 Wojciech Albrycht, the president of the Circle of Volunteers from America for the Polish Army made a proposal to the leadership of Światpol (World Association of Poles Living Abroad) to organize in Poland a Museum of the War Effort of Poles from America. The plan was declared useful, but the suggestion was made that since Światpol was to organize the museum, the PAVA should also participate actively, optimally by joining the organization. The PAVA leadership decided that such a move would have political overtones and it did not accept the proposal.

Parenthetically it is worthwhile to cite a written description by W. Albrycht as to what the display dedicated to the Polish American war effort during World War I looked like at the Museum of the Polish Armed Forces in Warszawa: "The Polish American community's war effort is represented in a manner that jeers at reality. There are two uniforms there. One belonging to some church orchestra and the other is some kind of (church-related) uniform of the Polish Army from America. We were told that the one is the uniform of the Polish Army from America and the other is a sport uniform. A mockery!"[122]

In the summer of 1935 the Circle of Volunteers from America for the Polish Army held its annual convention in Lwów. One of its aims was to commemorate the fifteenth anniversary of the formation of the 7th "Kościuszko" Air Force Squadron which was part of the Polish Air Force and was manned by a group of American pilots. The meeting took place on July 4, 1935 (American Independence Day) and was coupled with a visit to the Lwów Eaglets Cemetery, where the convention participants paid homage to three American pilots from the 7th Squadron who had died in battle.[123]

In the spring of 1935 the Circle of Volunteers from America for the Polish Army received information that a chapter of the National Defense Committee of America (the famed KON) and a Circle of Legionnaires of America, that is those who in the years 1914–1915 had left America to join Piłsudski's Legions, existed in Warszawa. Those two groups expressed interest to join with the Circle of Volunteers from Bydgoszcz and form one organization. The Board in Bydgoszcz received a letter to this effect from the office of Marshal Rydz-Śmigły which expressed the wish that such a union come to pass. After lengthy preparations a joint meeting of

---

121 The National Ossoliński Foundation Library in Wrocław, sign. 15286/II, MS of W. Gąsiorowski, pp. 205-213
122 Ibid., Letter of November 11, 1934 from W. Albrycht to the PAVA Board
123 Ibid. Letter of November 11, 1934 from W. Albrycht to the PAVA Board

the three organizations took place on January 15, 1936 in Warszawa. After a long and heated debate a joint organization was formed—the Association of Volunteers and Independents from America. Unfortunately, shortly after the election of the leadership of the new organization, the KON members, who had not been elected, quit the just-formed organization.So only the Hallerians and the Piłsudskists remained, among whom friction arose at the very beginning when they were preparing the association's By-Laws.

Lieutenant of the Reserves Feliks Chociszewski became the president of the organization. He was a former member of Polish Falcons of America Nest # 7 in New York. He was unable to agree on anything with secretary Sienieński and as a result for the entire year of 1936 the organization accomplished nothing. The impatient former members of the Circle of Volunteers from American turned to Wojciech Albrycht with demands that the Circle be reactivated. Under these circumstances on November 8, 1936 in Bydgoszcz, with the participation of PAVA national commander Lucjusz Kajko who was in Poland at that time, the PAVA post was formed a second time with the following Board: Post commander Wojciech Albrycht; vice commander Henryk Klimczewski; secretary Józef Czuba; treasurer Jan Paśniewski.

L. Kajko, the PAVA commander-in-chief, after administering the oath of office to the Post's Board, asked everybody, in line with the PAVA By-Laws, to eliminate politics from the life of the Association, leaving everyone free rein in their private life, or in another organization. This requirement was essential, because from that moment on the Post in Bydgoszcz was to pilot PAVA's most important matters in Poland.[124]

After reactivating PAVA Post Nr. 130 in Bydgoszcz its first order of business was to get it registered. After two years of strenuous efforts that seemingly simple matter could not be taken care of. The organization went back to its old name of Circle of Volunteers from America for the Polish Army, although at the PAVA National Executive Board in New York it had functioned the whole time as Post Nr. 130.

The pro-Piłsudski authorities did not give their approval for the registration of Post Nr. 130 in Bydgoszcz. They explained that PAVA is an organization active outside the Polish borders and in addition did not belong to the Federation of Polish Societies of Defenders of the Fatherland—a pro-Piłsudski structure of veteran associations. The authorities also suggested that the members of the Circle in Bydgoszcz abandon their own separate structure and join the pro-Piłsudski Association of Polish Army Veterans in France. The Circle in Bydgoszcz balked at the suggestion. In the end the authorities levied an import duty on the monthly *The Veteran* which was imported

---

[124] PAVA NEB Archives, sign. Box-17/Post Nr. 130, Minutes of the members' meeting of the volunteers from America and the Formation of the all-Poland Post of the Polish Army Veterans Association of America, held on November 8, 1936 in Bydgoszcz

to Bydgoszcz from America. Frequent petitions to remove it proved fruitless. Even the discussion of this issue at a personal meeting of Wojciech Albrycht with Prime Minister Felicjan Sławoj Składkowski on December 14, 1937, did not help.[125] Despite the promises of the Prime Minister himself this matter was not taken care of by the end of 1938. No wonder then that PAVA members living in Poland wrote in *The Veteran* as follows: "Imposing an import duty on a periodical of Polish veterans irritates our feelings, because we were not taxed when we came to Poland from France with weapons in hand, and those were rifles and feelings that had also been developed outside Polish borders. Sure, let them tax German, Jewish or other periodicals being shipped to Poland, but not a periodical of the veterans, who fought for and won the current customs borders."[126]

Another matter which they were unable to take care of was the problem of identical occasional railroad discounts for all veterans, regardless of their military formation. The legionnaires received a 75 percent discount for their conventions, whereas the volunteers from America at first got nothing at all. That was the situation in 1934 during the convention at Równe for the 13th Infantry Division celebrations.[127] Nonetheless thanks to W. Albrycht's continued efforts the former volunteers from America received a 50 percent railroad discount for their subsequent conventions. But that resolution of the matter by the authorities was still discriminatory. No wonder that the volunteers from America felt wronged. In one of their letters to the Ministry of Communication they wrote: "We start with the basic idea that the life of the soldier fighting for Poland, regardless of where he fought, had equal value; so the ones should not be favored over the others."[128]

Unfortunately, many letters of that sort remained without a reply, which confirmed the volunteers from America in the belief that in free Poland the authorities were dividing the veterans into better and worse.

The most important and most painful issue was the matter of decorations. This particularly concerned the Independence Medal and Cross, because their recipients had significant privileges, for instance railroad discounts, priority in getting employment, a pension of 90 zlotys per month if they were not employable, a 20 percent addition for a spouse, and a 10 percent addition for each child, etc.[129]

---

125 PAVA NEB Archives, sign. Box-17/ PAVA Post Nr. 130, Letter of December 21, 1938 of Circle of Volunteers from America for the Polish Army Commander W. Albrycht to PAVA NEB in New York

126 *The Veteran* December 1938, p. 8

127 PAVA NEB Archives, sign. Box-17/PAVA Post Nr. 130, Communiqué Nr. 21 of the Circle of Volunteers from America for the Polish Army

128 *The Veteran* December 1938, p. 8

129 Legislation Journal of the Polish Republic Nr. 59, August 6, 1937, position 464

In reply to their petitions to the Chapter in charge of these decorations the former volunteers from America were told that their petitions had to be confirmed by the verification committee of the Polish Army Veterans Association in France—a small pro-Piłsudski veteran organization (created in 1929) which worked within the structures of the Federation of Polish Associations of Defenders of the Fatherland (FPADF).

The former volunteers from America rejected the idea of being subjected to this procedure. According to them the above-mentioned organization was incompetent, because it mostly included former Blue Army soldiers who had come from Austrian prisoner of war camps in Italy, thanks to which they could not have known the realities of the Polish pro-independence activities in America.

Proof of the above commission's verification incompetence was the fact that to April 1938, of the 20,000 volunteers from America who were former Blue Army soldiers, only 57 received the Independence Cross or Independence Medal. Not one of them received the Independence Medal with Swords.[130]

How small that number was can best be seen by the following comparison: in February 1938 the *Soldier of the Legions and the Polish Military Organization* gave a report on the activity of the Circle of the 1st Infantry Regiment of the Legions, with a detailing of the Mutual Aid section for the period March 1, 1993 to December 30, 1936, wherein we read:

"Decorated with the Independence Cross—2,610;

Decorated with the Independence Medal—191;

Candidates for decoration with the Independence Cross—1,404;

Candidates for decoration with the Independence Medal—569"[131]

That is just the data from one regimental circle of former legionnaires, and there were plenty more.

In that same report we also read:

"610 members received permanent or temporary employment;

Higher pensions and promotions—339 members;

Agencies and concessions—36 members;

11,464.13 złotys was spent on grants-in-aid;

Loans—2,896.334 złotys;

One-time subsidies—1,213 złotys."

The former volunteers from America who lived in Poland and the United States could only dream of such effective help from the Polish government. No wonder

---

130 PAVA NEB Archives, sign. Box-17/PAVA Post Nr. 130, Communiqué Nr, 21 of the Circle of Volunteers from America for the Polish Army

131 *Żołnierz Legionów i P.O.W.* [*The Soldier of the Legions and the Polish Military Organization*] Nr. 1, Warszawa, February 1938, p. 62

that on reading reports of that sort they were very bitter about the open favoritism of veterans from one military formation alone, the Polish Legions.

The limited possibilities available to the Circle of Volunteers from America for the Polish Army with its headquarters in Bydgoszcz are best seen in the report it submitted in its "Communiqué" Nr. 21 on April 23, 1938: "The Circle presently has 349 members. …some of the members have asked the circle for short-term financial aid. The Board of the Circle has no funds. Only several of the better educated and well off members support the Circle's administrative expenses. Without them our Circle would not exist. All the membership dues that you members send in barely cover the cost of printing, postage and 20 złotys per month for the typist. We get no money from anywhere, aside from the members of the Circle, for the Circle's activities. … Orphans and widows of deceased volunteers from America are turning to us for help."[132]

The meeting with Dr. Teofil Starzyński, the President of the Polish Falcons of America, was a very emotional experience for the veterans from the Circle of Volunteers from America for the Polish Army, most of whom were former Falcons. It took place at the Bydgoszcz Falcons building on February 2, 1938. The local Falcons were represented by Nest Nr. 1 president Kazimierz Sokołowski and District Nr. 5 president Malczewski. President Starzyński was greeted in the name of the veterans by Wojciech Albrycht who thus recalled those moments: "I had not yet concluded thespeech on the page before me, when speaking of the beginnings of the formation of the Falcon Field Squads, of their development, of the formation of the Polish Army, the magnificent results of all that work on behalf of Polish independence, and when I looked at that modest President, fighting all those problems for the last 25 years, when I thought of his great contribution to Poland, when I still wanted to mention those whose contributions are marked by crosses from Niagara on the Lake to France, and all the way to Kiev, I recalled their faces that stood next to me in the ranks at one time… and the emotion robbed me of my voice…Others spoke beautifully, gave the President decorations, souvenirs, finally the vagabonds sang: "How quickly pass the moments" and the Bydgoszcz Falcons in return sang the Falcons hymn, with which they bid farewell to the President as he was leaving the building."[133]

In the spring of 1938 the Board of the Circle of Volunteers from America for the Polish Army in Bydgoszcz (aware of the fruitlessness of its efforts) decided to join the Federation of Associations of Defenders of the Fatherland as a separate veteran group. But the leadership of the FADF did not want to agree to this, because they wanted to merge this group with the Association of the Veterans of the Former Polish

---

132 PAVA NEB Archives, sign. Box-17/PAVA Post Nr. 130, Communiqué Nr. 21 of the Circle of Volunteers from America for the Polish Army

133 *The Veteran* April 1938, p. 4

Army in France. The veterans from America would not give in, and pursued the formal recognition of their group within the structure of the Federation. The matter kept being delayed, but finally one could see a clear change in the attitude of the authorities toward the volunteers from America, because in April 1938 the head of the Department of the Infantry in the Ministry of Military Affairs, Col. Bronisław Prugar-Ketling, asked the leadership of the circle in Bydgoszcz to write an article about the war effort of the Polish American community for the publication *Book of The Infantry's Glory* which was being prepared by the Ministry. Wojciech Albrycht wrote it and his text was included in that monograph. It was concise, but very concrete information about the Polish American community's war effort during World War I. Thus the false information and plain lies were finally straightened out, that had been published in the otherwise serious publication, the *Illustrated Encyclopedia*, published by Trzaska, Evert and Michalski, where the greatest contributions to the formation of the Polish Armed Forces from America were attributed to...Wincenty Skarżyński. In fact it was primarily Dr. Teofil Starzyński who deserved the credit for it, who was never adequately honored for his enormous work on behalf of Polish independence by the government of the Second Polish Republic. Anyhow, he never made any effort to obtain those honors.[134]

After this small minor victory came others. At the request of the Circle of Volunteers from America for the Polish Army one of the town squares in Równe in Volhynia received the name "American Polonia Square." And in Dubno one of the streets was named Lucjan Chwałkowski Boulevard. He was the first officer from America in the Blue Army who died at the front in France in 1918.

Thanks to the efforts made by the volunteers from America who lived in Poland they received assurance from the government that their period of service in the Polish Falcons of America Field Squads would count toward their pensions. In addition they received the right to vacation days for the duration of their collegial conventions.

Stefan Lenartowicz, the director of Światpol (World Association of Poles Living Abroad) was of enormous help to the former volunteers from America in taking care of these matters. He also helped them find a solution for the tremendous headache which was the supervision in the name of the PAVA NEB of the unprofitable and deeply indebted farm estate in Kuligi. In fact it was only thanks to his personal efforts that PAVA was able to save the estate from being auctioned off for nonpayment of income taxes.[135]

---

[134] PAVA NEB Archives, sign. Box-17/ PAVA Post Nr. 130, Letter of April 20, 1938 from W. Albrycht to the PAVA NEB

[135] W. Albrycht, "Współpraca Placówki Nr. 130 w Bydgoszczy ze Stowarzyszeniem Weteranów Armii Polskiej w Ameryce" ["The Cooperation of Post Nr. 130 in Bydgoszcz with the Polish Army Veterans Association of America"] in: *The Veteran* December 1938, p. 7

In October 1938 the PAVA leadership in New York decided to join the Federation of Polish Associations of Defenders of the Fatherland. But the admission of PAVA to the Federation did not occur until February 1939. At that time the Ministry of the Interior registered Post Nr. 130 in Bydgoszcz as a legally active organizational unit on Polish territory of The Polish Army Veterans Association of America whose National Executive Board was located in New York.[136] After six long years of tedious effort the volunteers from America had finally succeeded.

The nearly seven year activity of Post Nr. 130 in Bydgoszcz proved to be the least expensive, and the most effective organizational formation which the Polish Army Veterans Association of America had in Poland in the inter-war period.

Cooperation with Veteran Organizations in Poland

Contacts with veteran organizations played a very important role in PAVA's relations with Poland. The common war time experiences in the battles for Poland's freedom created strong bonds between the former soldiers, who found themselves living in countries far from each other after the conclusion of the war. It was natural to aim at maintaining those ties by the creation of community-based organizations and by contacting organized colleagues, wherever they might be. Of the veteran organizations that were founded in Poland after the regaining of independence, PAVA made contact most quickly with a sister organization: the Union of Hallerians.

Contact with the Union of Hallerians

That organization was formed at the Convention of Hallerians in Katowice (October 21–22, 1922). The union wanted to aggregate former soldiers who had served in various former military formations that had been commanded by General J. Haller, beginning with the 2nd Brigade of the Polish Legions and ending with the Volunteer Army of 1920. The veterans in America studied with interest all information about the newly organized Union of Hallerians, which had all the marks of a sister organization. No wonder that contact was established with it very quickly. It was very helpful that Józef Sierociński, the former commander of the Falcons' Cadet School in Cambridge Springs, Pennsylvania, had been elected to the leadership group of the Union of Hallerians. An exchange of publicatons helped to get mutually acquainted. The Union of Hallerians sent *Straż nad Wisłą* (*Sentry on the Vistula*) and PAVA returned the favor by sending *The Veteran* and the *Hallerian Calendar*. In January 1923 there was a crisis in relations because of the way both sides evaluated the murder of Polish President Gabriel Narutowicz. PAVA condemned that murder unequivocally and

---

136 PAVA NEB Archives, sign. Box-17/PAVA Post Nr. 130, Letter of March 13, 1939 from W. Albrycht to the PAVA NEB

did not agree with the position of the Union of Hallerians, which tried to justify this act by political considerations. The polemics on this issue were not publicly aired. Thanks to this the tension dissipated, which served further cooperation well; for instance the Union of Hallerians gave space to the PAVA Delegature in its offices in Warszawa.

Close cooperation between PAVA and the Union of Hallerians occurred in the summer and fall of 1923 during preparations for the first voyage of Gen. J. Haller to America. The importance of those mutual contacts is underscored by the fact that Gen. Haller's adjutant on that trip was Union of Hallerians Vice President Józef Sierociński, and the person accompanying him was the director of the PAVA Delegature in Poland, Jan Roskosz. During General Haller's tour of the United States there was talk of joining PAVA, the Union of Hallerians and other veteran associations into one federation. Decisive talks were held at a joint conference in Cleveland, Ohio in November 19, 1923, with the participation of Gen. J. Haller, PAVA president Dr. Teofil Starzyński, and Captain Józef Sierociński.[137] A special PAVA committee that was organized after that conference at a meeting of December 5, 1923 declared itself in favor of creating such a federation, and it postulated that PAVA (as an organization active on neutral American soil) should convoke in Warszawa an assembly of delegates from the governing boards of all veteran organizations active in Poland in order to discuss the operational principles and foundation of a federation of veteran associations. "In proposing the above, we are not doing so to put our Association above others. We are doing it solely for the good of the common cause and for its success," the above-mentioned PAVA Committee wrote in its report.[138] The proposal was sent to Poland where Union of Hallerians Vice President J. Sierociński tried to interest other veteran associations in it. At first the interest was quite large, even the Association of Legionnaires took a friendly stance toward the proposal. The possibility of creating a Union of Associations of Former Servicemen was debated. Later, for various reasons, mainly having to do with ambition and politics, the issue started to get complicated. In April 1924 *The Veteran* reported bitterly: "And so it has happened that our military associations, instead of uniting exclusively with each other in the name of broader ideals, which had always and everywhere led all the members to serve under various, but always Polish flags, are looking for friends and allies among all sorts of political organizations. ...The military associations that exist in Poland have not succeeded in embracing even five percent of the former participants in the World War and Polish War. ... The dry skeleton of a monopolized

---

137 PAVA NEB Archives, sign. A-XXIII/3
138 Ibid.

Fatherland, of dashed hopes, non-recognition of contributions made like a dark shadow wends its way through the life of the existing associations, and ideologies have been nailed to the standard-bearing names of the patrons. ... Not a sectarian, not a party-spirited military association, but one created under the patronage of the Most Serene Republic will unite hearts, minds and hands of all: the legionnaires, the hallerians, the adherents of Dowbór, the Upper –Silesian insurrectionists and the Kaniovites, for work on behalf of the FAtherland, as at one time it united them for the common fight for Fatherland's freedom."[139]

The issue that influenced the breakup of the feeble structure of the just-formed Union of Associations of Former Servicemen was the departure of a Polish delegation to the FIDAC (Federation Interallee des Anciens Combattants) in London, which was to be held from September 14 to 21, 1924. Poland could send ten delegates. Since invitations came to the Association of Great Poland Fighters and Insurrectionists (Związek Wojaków i Powstańców

Wielkopolskich) and to the Union of Hallerians, these two organizations were not too willing to share those invitations with other associations. Two organizations that had not received invitations (The Association of Legionnaires and the Association of Kaniovites) left the toddling Union of Associations of Former Servicemen. In the end, after much hemming and hawing the following delegates left for the congress in London: Dr. Śliwiński, Kęszycki, Głowacki—representing the Association of Great Poland Fighters and Insurrectionists; J. Sierociński and T. Starzyński—the Union of Hallerians; Kossowski and Smogorzewski—The Association of Combatants in France; P. Kantor—the Association of Invalids; Dr. Szurley—The Association of Reserve Officers and J. Roskosz the Polish Army Veterans Association of America. That was the only time when PAVA had its representative at a FIDAC congress. Jan Roskosz, the PAVA representative, participated in the work of the Pension and Invalid Issues Committee. During the election of a new slate of FIDAC officers Col. Miller of the United States was elected president, and nine vice presidents were elected representing each of the individual nine nations. Mr. Śliwiński of the Association of Great Poland Fighters and Insurrectionists became Poland's representative in FIDAC—he was the Mayor of Bydgoszcz at that time. It was also approved that the next FIDAC congress would take place in Rome in 1925, and in Warszawa in 1926.[140]

Here is how *The Veteran* commented on the choice of Warszawa as the site for the subsequent FIDAC congress: "The convention in Warszawa will have great significance for Poland and for its former soldiers. The only thing that has to be done

---

139 *The Veteran* April 1924, p. 2
140 *The Veteran* November 1924, p. 5

is that the Polish veterans, who continue to be divided into various "ists" should finally undertstand what their obligations to their country and their colleagues are, they should understand that they did not serve Leaders but Poland, they should finally eliminate from their leadership those people who only see their own interests—and then both in Rome and in two years in Warszawa, they can accomplish great things.

"In the face of the sluggishness with which the creation of a unified organization of former servicemen is moving forward in Poland, since certain individuals are constantly putting their own ambitions first, the Polish Army Veterans Association of America, which ventured both the idea and the initiative to create such an organization, will proabably have to remove itself not only from fostering the initiative, but even from further cooperation. Maybe when the Assocation has removed itself our colleagues in Poland will realize, that in coming forward with the initiative we only had in mind the sincere intention of serving Poland, nothing more."[141]

PAVA removed itself from any firther work on behalf of uniting veteran organizations in Poland. The short-sighted policy of the Union of Hallerians and the Association of Great Poland Fighters and Insurrectionists, especially toward the Legionnaires Association which had a lot of influence, hardened the existing divisions among veterans and narrowed the unifiying action solely to include veteran organizations of a rightist provenance.

The May 1926 coup was the final blow that buried the idea of unification which had been initiated by PAVA in 1923. The Legion of the Republic of Poland, created under the auspices of the Union of Hallerians limited itself to the following veteran organizations: The Association of Dovborites (followers of General Józef Dowbór-Muśnicki, commander of the Greater Poland Front in WWI and opponent of Marshal Piłsudski), the Association of War Invalids of the Polish Republic, the Association of the Defenders of Lwów from November 1918, the Association of Officers of the Reserve of the Polish Republic, the Association of Societies of Insurrectionists and Fighters of the VII Corps District.[142]

The PAVA Board, while removing itself from work on uniting veteran organizations in Poland, did not limit its contacts with the Union of Hallerians. Information was mutually exchanged on the activities of both organizations and the general living conditions in both countries. To the extent possible they came to each other's aid in the matter of supervising the farm business in Kuligi that belonged to PAVA or in distributing *The Hallerian* in the United States, which was an attempt to save the periodical from bankruptcy. The editor of *The Hallerian*, Stanisław

---

141 Ibid., p. 6
142 *The Veteran* February 1928, p. 26

Pałaszewski, tried to export the periodical to America and to distribute it through individual Falcon Nests and PAVA posts. He wrote in a letter of September 1, 1925 to the PAVA Board: "Brothers. By subscribing to our organ *The Hallerian* you will help it a lot to overcome the unpleasant financial conditions in which it currently finds itself. Poland is currently going through an economic crisis. There is tremendous stagnation. About 75 percent of the members of our Union are without a job at present, and not only are they unable to pay the subscription, but themselves need help for bread for their children. To halt the mailing of our periodical to them means to stop publishing the periodical, because they constitute 90 percent of our readers and *The Hallerian* is for many of them the only periodical which they read, and to stop sending it to them means to deprive them of the living word from time to time, which as it were holds this scattered group of former soldiers together in one whole. If they can't get *The Hallerian* then the communists and other revolutionaries will come in, and will give them their reading matter which is laced with anti-government venom and they will introduce disease into the healthy group. That is why we must not do it."[143]

Unfortunately, there wasn't much interest in the individual PAVA posts to buy permanent subscriptions to this periodical. The attempt to distribute the periodical in the United States was not successful and the periodical went bankrupt soon thereafter.

In the fall of 1926 there was a serious conflict between PAVA and the Union of Hallerians over the firing of Jan Paśniewski (a member of the Union of Hallerians) from the position of administrator of the farm at Kuligi by PAVA Vice President Jan Kostrubała. The President of the Union of Hallerians, Dr. E. Loth, in a letter of January 26, 1927 found this act to be "illegal" and demanded that the PAVA officials restore J. Paśniewski to his job, and threatened to boycott the PAVA tour which was to arrive in Poland in the summer of that year. We read in the reply of PAVA General Secretary Jan Szymański, which is addressed to the National Executive Board of the Union of Hallerians as follows: "… one gets the impression that our Association is an organization subordinated to the Union of Hallerians and that the decisions of our Board require the approval of that Union. … Our Association sees no reason, nor does it plan to give any satisfaction to anyone with regard to the administration of our estate."[144]

The letter proved effective. In July 1927 the great PAVA tour was hosted in many cities by the local branches of the Union of Hallerians, and the Great Poland District arranged a "Blue Ball" for its colleagues from America. It took place in Poznań on

---

143 PAVA NEB Archives, sign. A-XXIII/3
144 PAVA NEB Archives, sign. A-XXIII/4

July 14, in the ballroom of the Hotel Belvedere on Głogowska Street. The Lwów District of the Union of Hallerians invited the PAVA tour to the ceremony of pounding in nails into the staff of the new flag. Despite the expressions of friendliness by the outposts of the Union of Hallerians toward their American colleagues, the National Executive Board of that organization did not participate in welcoming the PAVA in Warszawa.[145]

From 1928 on (after changes in the top leadership of the Union of Hallerians) the relationship between the two organizations became more cordial. For instance, the National Executive Board of the Union of Hallerians sent an invitation to the PAVA leadership for its Special Convention which was to take place in Poznań from July 2 to 4, 1929. The following persons represented PAVA at this convention: President Kazimierz Bałdyga, Treasurer Stanisław Sobolewski and veteran Stanicki. During the convention the PAVA standard was decorated with the Hallerian Swords medal, which General Józef Haller presented to president Bałdyga.[146] In a letter of July 30, 1929 a witness to these events, Stanisław Sobolewski, wrote to PAVA Secretary General Czesław Mrozowski: "After arriving in Poznań for the Union of Hallerians Convention we went with Prez. Bałdyga and Dr. Starzyński to a meeting with Gen. Haller.

"One could tell the party bias among the colleagues from the Union of Hallerians. I even had a run-in with some of them. I was constantly being fed politics, until I finally had to tell them that I do not care for political parties.

"The entire ceremony was quite modest thanks to the carelessness of the Poznań District (i.e. the Great Poland District). Our President did a great job with his speech at the commemoration ceremony. Then we gave an Honorary President of the PAVA of America diploma to Gen. Haller. I have to note that this was the most beautiful moment in the entire ceremony. One could hear the ovations in honor of our Association."[147]

A year later the individual districts of the Union of Hallerians were greeting the next PAVA tour, which was headed by the new president, Wacław Rżewski. It went to Gdynia.

In July, 1931 a statue of U.S. President Woodrow Wilson, funded by I. J. Paderewski, was unveiled in Poznań. On July 5 General J. Haller, surrounded by a large delegation from the Union of Hallerians and PAVA representatives, laid a joint wreath at the foot of the memorial to the American president. The inscription on

---

145 *The Veteran* February 1928
146 *The Veteran* October 1929, p. 17
147 PAVA NEB, sign. A-XXVII/11

the sash of the wreath read: "Polish Army Veterans Association of America." Rev. Lucjan Bójnowski of New Britain, CT, and Dr. Franciszek Fronczak of Buffalo laid the wreath in PAVA's name.[148]

In the fall of 1932, a PAVA delegation headed by President Franciszek Dziób was in Poland on the occasion of the fifteenth anniversary of the beginning of recruitment in America for the Polish Army in France. The delegation participated in the main ceremony, which took place on October 16 in Bydgoszcz with Gen. Haller present. The organizer was the local Union of Hallerians District.

A year later (1933) PAVA president F. Dziób, during his next visit in Poland, was preparing Gen. Haller's visit to America in close cooperation with the Union of Hallerians. The aim of the trip was to have Gen. Haller help in the great fund drive on behalf of PAVA's I. J. Paderewski Invalid Fund. President Dziób accompanied the General from the very beginning of that trip. Lt. Stanisław Pałaszewski was the General's adjutant. He was the president of the Pomeranian District of the Union of Hallerians. He was conducting a fund drive in the United States for a memorial to and the maintenance of the cemetery in France dedicated to Hallerians who had died in battle. As we already know, Gen. Haller's second tour of America was a great success.

A new period in mutual relations began after the 6th PAVA General Assembly in Newark, NJ in 1934 and after the PAVA's National Executive Board had been moved from Detroit to New York City. The new PAVA Board proved to be more amenable to cooperation with the Polish government. It did not share the oppositionist activities of the Union of Hallerians, from which it gradually began to distance itself. PAVA also stopped using the Union as a go-between in taking care of various problems in Poland. That role was ceded to PAVA Post Nr. 130 in Bydgoszcz. In effect contacts with the Union of Hallerians became limited to correspondence concerning the Hallerian Swords, whose Chapter was run by the Union of Hallerians. Although the National Executive Board of the Union of Hallerians kept sending the PAVA Board in New York its *Information Bulletin*, its contents (mainly of a political nature) found no response from the PAVA leadership. The activities of the Union in open opposition to the pro-Piłsudski government in Poland was irreconcilable with the apolitical position of PAVA and caused the parting of ways of the two sister organizations. Wojciech Albrycht, commander of the unofficial PAVA Post Nr. 130 in Bydgoszcz, wrote about this in a letter of December 21, 1937 to the PAVA Board: "General Haller has involved himself in purely political work, taking the helm of the Labor Party, which the Union of Hallerians also joined. Because the Union of Hallerians membership is mostly composed of National Democrats, and currently the National

---

148 *The Veteran* August 1931, p. 13

Democrats are hurling thunderbolts against the Labor Party and General Haller, therefore fights and friction have broken out in the Union of Hallerians, threatening the organization with a break up. We are standing aside and keeping quiet. We will not get involved in those matters."[149]

PAVA Post Nr. 130 in Bydgoszcz remained true to that principle until the end of the Second Polish Republic.

Controversies Concerning the Association of Veterans of the Former Polish Army in France

In March 1929 the Association of Veterans of the Former Polish Army in France was formed in Warsaw. It was meant to serve as a counter-weight to the Union of Hallerians which opposed the pro-Piłsudski authorities. The founders of that Association were: Captain Zygmunt Piątkowski, Lt. Nikodem Polak, Stefan Fijałkowski and Nikodem Wentkowski.[150]

This Association quickly established contact with the Polish Army Veterans Association of America. Its first letter, dated April 18, to the PAVA Board, stated: "The Association of Polish Army Veterans in France wants to unite in its ranks all those who in the period 1914–1919 belonged to Polish formations that were organized in France, and who presently live in Poland or one of the other nations of Europe. We believe that the founding of such an organization is the only way to properly represent the Polish Army in France among other organizations of former servicemen."[151]

The PAVA National Executive Board replied with a letter on June 21, in which it gladly welcomed the creation of the new organization: "We cordially welcome your organized ranks, the ranks of comrades in arms from the same Army as us, and we pledge that depending on the need, we will cooperate with you and will make efforts together with you to ensure that the deeds, blood and battle for the ideals for which we jointly fought, do not die away in the struggle of daily life and in daily strife."[152]

The PAVA leadership thought that this was a Polish veteran organization active in France. This mistaken notion was caused by the organization's misleading name.

On July 25, 1929, during a PAVA delegation's visit to Poland for ceremonies of the 43rd Infantry Regiment in Dubno, a meeting was arranged with leaders of the Association of Polish Army Veterans in France who were also present there. The PAVA delegation was astonished to learn that this organization was active in

---

149 PAVA NEB Archives, sign. Box-17, PAVA Post Nr. 130 in Bydgoszcz. Letter of W. Albrycht of December 21, 1937
150 PAVA NEB Archives, sign. A-XXIII/6, An Outline of the Founding and Activity of the Association of Veterans of the Polish Army in France
151 PAVA NEB Archives, sign. A-XXIII/6
152 Ibid.

Poland and that its vice president was Wincenty Skarzyński, a former volunteer from America, nicknamed "the Cannon" in Polish Falcons circles there. W. Skarzyński did not have a good reputation in PAVA, nor in the Polish Falcons of America. The main reason was that in the book *The Polish Army in France According to the Facts* he had assigned to himself the main role for its formation.

Here is what PAVA president Kazimierz Bałdyga wrote in *The Veteran* about his reaction to that meeting: "After a soldierly dinner a "convention" was arranged, to which I was also invited and had reluctantly agreed to after I found out what those gentlemen wanted. They wanted then and want now to break the Union of Hallerians apart, and to create a new and similar organization. Although I do not agree with some of the Union of Hallerians' moves and often cannot side with its politics, I cannot lend a hand to the disintegration of this organization.

"It so happened that Col. Skarzyński (honorary PAVA president), whom various persons present started to tease, was the first to give edifying instruction to these gentlemen and did not give his moral sanction for this sort of work. Others, asked to speak, one after another said the same thing, and a Bayonne veteran, whose name I do not recall, told Mr. Skarzyński in a soldierly and sincere way what he thought of him. ... After the conclusion of that unfortunate "convention" a split occurred between me and Mr. Skarzyński. I told him that if he is a Hallerian and a veteran [W. Skarzyński had earlier been a member of the Union of Hallerians, which he left—T. L.] and if he doesn't like the organization's policies, then he should fight it with generally accepted methods, in the press, at meetings and conventions, but nobody has the right to form a state within a state, an organization inside an organization. That is what the communists do."[153]

The effect of that split was the publication of *Scabby Greatness* in the Polish press by the Association of Polish Army Veterans in France. It was a brutal attack against PAVA president Kazimierz Bałdyga. Here is a fragment of that article: "Taking advantage of the presence in Poland of several old colleagues from the Polish Army Veterans Association of America, we learned some incredible things. K. S. Bałdyga became their president.... illegally. K. S. Bałdyga is a shady figure, K. S. Bałdyga is a..."deserter"(!)

"From this very moment, for obvious reasons, we stopped being interested in the person of the president of the Polish Army Veterans Association of America, to whose members, as our senior colleagues, we hereby send our expressions of sincere astonishment due to their having gifted the "deserter (!) with an office which he maybe deserves, but only in an association of deserters."

---

153 *The Veteran* January 1930, p. 5

This article was also sent to the PAVA Board in Detroit with a letter which demanded "far reaching consequences" against K. Bałdyga.[154] The PAVA Board did not reply to that letter, and broke off all contacts with the Association of Polish Army Veterans in France, which in the meantime was accepted into the ranks of the pro-Piłsudski Federation of Polish Associations of Defenders of the Fatherland.

In the April 1930 issue of *The Veteran*, the PAVA Board unequivocally wrote of its attitude toward the Association of Polish Army Veterans in France, which was active in Poland: "We openly admit that this new "blue organization" is not favorably viewed by us for the following reasons: 1) it shows evident hatred toward and lack of respect for our distinguished Honorary President, our former commander, Gen. Józef Haller; 2) it has set as its goal and action guideline the destruction of its sister organization, the Union of Hallerians; 3) it admits into its ranks people who are total civilians, which is against our understanding of the principles and aims of a soldier's organization."[155]

Despite these unequivocal statements, contacts between the two bickering organizations were renewed. It happened in July 1930, when Lt. Wacław Rżewski, the new PAVA president, was in Poland with a veteran tour. He accepted an invitation to participate in the General Assembly of the Association of Veterans of the Former Army in France, which was held on July 13 in Warszawa. In speaking at the convention forum, he expressed joy at the opportunity to meet with many comrades from the former 13th Infantry "Steel"Division, and he wished those gathered there successful deliberations and continued development of the organization.[156]

It is noteworthy that after a wave of criticism the new organization of "blue veterans" modified its name, indicating with the word "former," that it derived from the former Polish Army in France.

One of the results of the convention was the exchange of courteous telegrams between the new organization of "blue veterans" in Poland and PAVA in America. It seemed that a normalization of mutual relations would now ensue. But that did not happen, because in October of 1930 the Association of Veterans of the Former Polish Army in France sent a communiqué to the PAVA Board and certain Posts as well as to the Polish American press, appealing to Polish veterans in America to apply for decorations connected with the drive for independence, i.e., the Independence Cross or Independence Medal. Those applications were to be sent to the office of

---

154 PAVA NEB, sign. A-XXIII/6

155 "Jeszcze jedni 'Błękitni'i o ich celach i zamiarach" ["One more 'Blue' Organization, and About its Aims and Intentions"] in: *Weteran [The Veteran]* April 1930, p. 17

156 PAVA NEB Archives, sign. A-XXIII/6, Minutes of the General Assembly of the Associations of Veterans of the former Polish Army in France, held on July 13, 1930 in Warszawa

the Association in Warsaw, from where after approval they were to be sent on to the Chapter in charge of those decorations.

That brought a sharp reaction from PAVA of America's Board, which sent a circular to all its posts and districts: "A Warning to all Former Soldiers of the Polish Army in France." In this document the action of the "blue veterans" from Poland was treated as a pretext to break up PAVA's organizational ranks: "The newly organized Association of Veterans of the Former Polish Army in France, which hasn't done anything thus far, is starting to demand decorations from the Polish government for those who were supposedly "passed over" and "wronged," which must not and cannot be the primary goal of any veteran organization. Because no just-minded soldier will ever DEMAND a decoration for his service to his country, and all the more so a volunteer soldier—a volunteer from America, who understands that he did his sacred duty for his country.

"Therefore we call upon all our colleagues, volunteers for the Polish Army in France, to reply with silence to this "appeal" of the Association from Warsaw. ... Let us not lend a hand to the attempts to break us apart. Let us not lend a hand to the attempts to drag our organization into the whirlpool of political or party maneuvers in Poland."[157]

That position of the PAVA Board gained the full approval of the association's members. The vote of confidence for the Board that Post Nr. 6 in Cleveland sent was very significant. The lengthy letter stated that: "Poland has its agents in America, who, since they were able to dig up the "contributions" of people who spit on the deeds of the volunteer soldier from America [this refers to decorations of National Defense Fund activists—T. L.] all the more can and should dig up the contributions of that Polish soldier from America who through his blood, health and ill-treatment at least earned the right to be remembered by intermediaries of such ilk as the just-organized Association of Veterans of the Former Polish Army in France, which instead of uniting our efforts ... only acts to demolish them."[158]

Such a stance by the PAVA leadership caused the reduction of contacts by both organizations to a minimum for several years, although *The Veteran* did publish short notes on the activities of the Association of Veterans of the Former Polish Army in France. That organization, under the leadership of Lt. Col. Markus, tried to subordinate to itself the Circle of Volunteers from America in Bydgoszcz, which was the informal PAVA Post Nr.130 in Poland. When that failed, the Board of the Association demanded in November 1934 that those few of its members who

---

157 PAVA NEB Archives, sign. A-XXIII/6, Circular Nr. 35 of October 30, 1930
158 *The Veteran* January 1931, p. 10

simultaneously belonged to the Circle of Volunteers from America should declare unequivocally which organization they want to belong to. Since the volunteers from America declared themselves in favor of membership in the Circle in Bydgoszcz, they were stricken from the rolls of the AVFPA in France. In his letter of November 11, 1934 to the PAVA Board, Wojciech Albrycht (the president of the Circle of Volunteers from America) thus defined his opinion about that association: "Markus's Association is not a serious organization. It is packed with screaming people, career seekers who pose as big Piłsudskists. When they asked me once:

'Is the Circle working for Piłsudski?' I answered: "No! The Circle is working on behalf of the same cause that Piłsudski is working for.'

'Rightly so," they replied."[159]

In June 1936 the AVFPA in France informed PAVA of America that they had succeeded in pushing through the right to receive the French Combatant Cross for former soldiers of the Blue Army. Its recipients receive a pension of 500 francs a year after reaching the age of 55, and after reaching the age of 60 they get 1,500 Francs per year. Nonetheless, due to lack of budgetary international agreements, Polish veterans living outside the French borders could not count on such pensions. But they did have the right to receive the decoration. The Association of Veterans of the Former Polish Army in France offered its assistance for a fee to get the decoration. The PAVA leadership did not accept the offer.[160]

A couple of months later, in November 1936, the AVFPA in France tried another approach to increase contacts with PAVA of America. Michał Kwapiszewski, a member of the Association who was leaving for America received power of attorney to represent the organization in talks with the PAVA authorities. In order to "break the ice" Kwapiszewski took with him to New York a special gift in the form of earth from the grave of Lt. Lucjan Chwałkowski—the first officer from America who as a soldier of the Blue Army was killed in action in France in 1918. Kwapiszewski presented the PAVA National Executive Board with a special letter from the Association of Veterans of the former Polish Army in France. In this letter PAVA was invited to participate in the planned ceremonies on the twentieth anniversary of the formation of the Blue Army. The letter stated: "It is unthinkable that you, colleagues, would not organize a large scale tour of your members to Poland, or at least you should send the color guards of your Posts and Districts in America."[161] Once again the proposal was made to the PAVA leadership to mediate in attempts

---

159 PAVA NEB Archives, Box-17, PAVA Post Nr. 130 in Bydgoszcz, 1934–1939
160 PAVA NEB Archives, sign A-XXIII/6
161 Letter of November 14, 1936 from the Association of Veterans of the Former Polish Army in France to the PAVA NEB

to obtain independence decorations for PAVA members: the Independence Cross and the Independence Medal. In connection with the bestowing of the Marshal's baton on Marshal Rydz-Śmigły it was suggested that PAVA prepare a decorative book containing resolutions of homage in his honor, to be signed by all the members of the posts and districts. Moreover PAVA was informed of work being undertaken to prepare a study of the history of the Blue Army and PAVA was requested to form a Historical Committee which would gather all documentation on this subject in the United States and Canada.

The PAVA leadership accepted the touching gift in the form of the little case with earth from Lt. Chwałkowski's grave.[162] In replying to the letter after a long delay, PAVA took a negative psoiton with regard to the propositions contained in it, justifying them as unrealistic due to the costs involved (the trip of all the color guards to Poland), and because PAVA had already sent its congratulations to Marshal Rydz-Śmigły. The work to be done on the history of the Blue Army was fully approved, however, and PAVA announced the commencement of activities in this regard on its part. At the same time the AVFPA in France was asked about the following matter: "It would be our desire that you communicate with colleague Wojciech Albrycht, commander of PAVA Post Nr.130 in Bydgoszcz, who is obliged not to get involved in national politics due to the character of our organization. We expect that you will have no trouble in developing relations with them, and in maintaining closer ties with them we will be able to crown with success our future joint cooperation."[163]

It was clear from the letter that the PAVA NEB did not want to see the AVFPA in France as its plenipotentiary in Poland. In the end the leadership of the AVFPA in France accepted this and no longer made similar proposals, but felt offended by the veterans from America. This became evident when the Circle of Volunteers from America in Bydgoszcz tried to obtain the Independence Cross or Medal for its members. This was connected with essential, real privileges for veterans living in Poland. But an insurmountable obstacle appeared. It was the already mentioned Col. Stanisław Markus, who as a leader of the AVFPA in France had strong contacts in the pro-Piłsudski Federation of Polish Associations of Defenders of the Fatherland. He chaired the Community Committee of former soldiers of the Blue Army, which reviewed petitions for the Independence Cross and Independence Medal decorations. Under his guidance that committee rejected most of the petitions of the volunteers from America. It was a very important fact that Col. Markus was not a volunteer from America, because he had made his way to the Blue Army in France directly from a

---

162 This souvenir is on display at the Museum of the Tradition of Polish Arms in New York
163 PAVA NEB Archives, sign. A-XXIII/6, Letter of April 8, 1937 from the PAVA NEB to the AVFPA in France

prisoner of war camp in Italy. Wojciech Alobrycht in a letter of February 1938 wrote about his bias to the PAVA NEB: "The Alpha and Omega, the dictator, is the chair of the Committee for the Polish Army in France …Col. Stanisław Markus, director of the State Lottery, a man who … is of the opinion that we should not exist, and that we should join the Association of Veterans of the Former Polish Army in France.

"We want volunteers from Americe to be appointed to that Committee, who know our past. … Markus has strong backing and broad connections. Colleague Szwiec visited him together with Dr. Starzyński, the President of the Polish Falcons of America. Markus declared that the veterans from America do not deserve a single Cross with Swords, and only those who served in the 1st Regiment deserve the Cross. Others get a medal or nothing. Markus treats the entire sacrifice of the Polish American community as something small and squint-eyed."[164]

PAVA expressed its unfavorable attitude toward the AVFPA in France once again in *The Veteran* of March 1938 in connection with the list of members of AVFPA who had received high decorations from the Polish and French governments on the occasion of the twentieth anniversary of the decree that allowed the formation of the Polish Army in France. The list was published in *The Blue Veteran* (the press organ of the AVFPA in France). PAVA wrote: "We are searching the list for names of veterans from America. There they are! On one whole page of printed names there are two: Feliks Kędziorek and Władysław Sulewski. They received the Silver Cross of Merit. None of the American Poles (except for Aleksander Znaniecki) deserved the Golden Cross of Merit or the Legion of Honor. This is a mockery, and a comical mockery, because the list includes "deserving individuals" who arrived in France in 1919, so they were not present at the birth of the Army, nor did they take part in the battles, and found themselves in France long after Armistice, just before the Polish Army departed for Poland. They were the ones receiving the decorations 'on the occasion of the decree about the formation of the Polish Army in France'. These are merry contributions—one might say—dressing up in the feathers of other people's contributions. … The list of persons of merit in *The Blue Veteran* can rather be called the list of pesons who have distinguished themselves in work for the Association of Veterans of the Former Army in France. We would not question their contributions there."[165]

These critical remarks were a summary of the activities of the Association of Veterans of the Former Polish Army in France up to that point and of its contacts with PAVA of America, which never took on the shape of permanent cooperation.

---

164 PAVA NEB, sign. Box-17, Letter of February 2, 1938 from W. Albrycht

165 H. Lubatowski, "Stara piosenka. Strojenie się w cudze piórka" ["An Old Song. Dressing Up in Other People's Feathers"] in: *Weteran [The Veteran]* March 1938, p. 4

PAVA and the Federation of Polish Associations of Defenders of the Fatherland

After the May 1926 coup the pro-Piłsudski team began operations to widen its political base in Polish society. The sphere that according to those in power was the most fertile ground for this, were veteran organizations. In line with the aim of including them in the pro-government political orbit the Federation of Polish Associations of Defenders of the Fatherland (FPADF) was founded in Warszawa in February 9, 1928. Its president was Gen. Roman Górecki. It undertook ambitious efforts to concentrate within its organizational structures as many associations and societies of former servicemen as possible for the tenth anniversary of Polish independence.[166] Talks in that vein were held, among others, with the Legion of the Republic, which was a coalition of right-wing veteran organizationsled by the Union of Hallerians. But the talks were not successful.

In May 1928 PAVA received a proposal to join the FPADF. But due to the federation's political bias the proposition was not accepted.[167]

Two years later a rather sly attempt was made to force PAVA to join the FPADF. This happened during the FIDAC congress in Washington, D.C. on September 22–24, 1930, which was attended by PAVA secretary general Czesław Mrozowski. He had the PAVA Board's authorization and presented the chair of FIDAC's Polish section, Major Ludyga-Laskowski, an official, written application of the Association to join FIDAC. Here is what Mrozowski wrote about the results of his efforts in a letter of September 26, 1930: "The Polish delegation declared that our joining FIDAC is only possible through the Federation, to which I could not agree. I told them that I did not have the authorization from the Board to join the Federation and second of all in order to join the Federation the Board must have the approval of a plenary session, just as is required for joining FIDAC. Our colleagues from Poland were very unhappy about this and they told me that if we do not want to belong to the Federation then we cannot belong to FIDAC. At the last minute one of the delegates, envoy Pająk, took me aside and told me that our organization does not have to be a member of the Federation in order to join FIDAC. He also told me that his fellow delegates just want to use the opportunity to force us to join the Federation. ... I therefore told the chair of the Polish delegation and secretary general of the Federation that if they did not want to take care of our issue and if FIDAC wouldn't be accepting us through the Polish section, then we would be forced to do so through the American Legion and then we would see who would suffer the most morally

---

166 M. Jabłonowski. *Polityczne aspekty ruchu byłych wojskowych w Polsce 1918–1939* [*Political Aspects of the Movement of Former Servicemen in Poland 1918–1939*] Warszawa 1989, p. 96

167 PAVA NEB Archives, sign. A-XXIII/11

for it. Major Ludyga-Laskowski, after thinking about it, and conferring with the other delegates, declared that the issue of our joining would be taken care of by the Polish section at the next meeting of the FIDAC Board in Paris and that we would be members of FIDAC in two months. ...The promise to decorate the graves of our colleagues at Niagara on the Lake with "Polonia Restituta" came to nothing and we did not get "Polonia Restituta." ... When the FIDAC delegation was in Detroit last Wednesday, the secretary general of the Federation declared that he had brought the Silver Cross of Merit for the graves at Niagara on the Lake. Colleague W. Rżewski, the PAVA president, told him straight out that he should take that Cross back with him to Poland."[168]

The fact that PAVA did not join the Federation of Polish Associations of Defenders of the Fatherland provoked critical comments in the Polish American press. Here is how the PAVA Board responded to that criticism in *The Veteran*: "In Poland there are two veteran groupings, the so-called Polish Legion [should be: Legion of the Republic—T. L.] and the Federation of Polish Associations of Defenders of the Fatherland. Our association thus far belongs neither to the one group nor the other. ... We therefore declare that we will not petition for access to any group for the simple reason that we know very well that both the Legion and the Federation are forced to meddle in national politics, which, it is natural and understandable, breeds numerous misunderstandings, bitterness and battles that block the normal course of activity of these organizations. We are very well aware that the Federation adheres to a totally different political line than the Legion does and although generally speaking it is being publicized that it is just a matter of federating all those who fought for the freedom and rebirth of the Fatherland, in fact it has to do with a sort of political supremacy. ... Our joining either the one or the other camp would be a shove into a black political hole for us who are organized in America, and we want to avoid that at all cost."[169]

Despite the promises made in Washington, D.C. PAVA was not admitted into the Polish Section of FIDAC. Because each organization that belonged to FIDAC had to pay membership dues, and because the great depression in the United States continued, the PAVA Board halted further efforts to join that international veteran organization.

---

168 PAVA NEB Archives, sign. A-XXVII/11/ The members of the Polish section for the FIDAC congress in Washington, D.C. were: Major Ludyga-Laskowski (head), Adam Augustynowicz (editor of *The Federation*), Captain Dr. Jerzy Wroncki, W. Wyrzykowski (FPADF secretary general), Dr. Tadeusz Garbusiński, envoy Antoni Pająk (Union of War Invalids), Lt. Józef Szwiec (Association of Officers of the Reserve), Dr. Adam Kocur (Mayor of the City of Katowice), Lt. Kazimierz Smogorzewski, Wanda Pełczyńska, Dr. Maria Zalewska, Julia Mazaraki (vice president of the Polish section of women in FIDAC)

169 "W odpowiedzi na pytania i zabiegi" ["In reply to questions and maneuvers'] in: *Weteran [The Veteran]* October 1930, p. 17

For the next several years there were practically no official contacts between PAVA and the FPADF. Finally in May 1933 when Gen. Roman Górecki was visiting the United States—he was at that time the president of the FPADF and also the president of FIDAC—he met several times with PAVA veterans. In New York Gen. Górecki visited the PAVA shelter, where he met with about 100 veterans. This was reported in *The Veteran*: "The general spoke for about 45 minutes. He emphasized the need to forget all the party-related misunderstandings in the Polish American community. He depicted the current relationship in Poland, noting strongly that Poland today stands on a firm foundation thanks to the strong hand of the National Leader Marshal Piłsudski and has better relations than most of the nations of Europe.

"After his speech Gen. Górecki presented a portrait of himself as a souvenir and signed the memorial book and donated $100 to the shelter."[170]

The direct contacts with Gen. Górecki did not influence PAVA's position with regard to the question of joining the Federation of Polish Associations of Defenders of the Fatherland which he headed.

But the FPADF ideas found a certain resonance among Polish veterans living in Canada. This resulted in the founding of the Association of Polish Defenders of the Fatherland in Winnipeg, Canada in December 1933. In 1937 A. Nowak was the head of this association of 85 members.[171] The FPADF leadership saw the organization in Winnipeg as a beachhead for further activity aiming to subordinate to itself individual PAVA posts in Canada. The presentation of a flag to PAVA Post Nr. 114 in Toronto by the FPADF president in March 1938 was an expression of that policy.[172]

But PAVA's attitude toward joining FPADF had to change, because in the course of endeavors to get financial help for its members—the war invalids—from the Polish government, it became apparent that nothing could be done without joining the FPADF. The PAVA leadership knew that the passage of time was not to the veterans' advantage. Their ranks began to thin out, but the number of those needing help continued to grow. Under those circumstances it was decided to accede to the demands of the Polish government and join the FPADF. Numerous talks were held on this subject in the years 1937–1938. Wojciech Albrycht (the commander of the unofficial PAVA Post Nr. 130 in Bydgoszcz) conducted them in the name of PAVA, and PAVA commander-in-chief Lucjusz Kajko was also involved in them during his visit in Poland in the summer

---

170 *The Veteran* June 1933, p. 20
171 M. Jabłonowski. *Polityczne aspekty ruchu byłych wojskowych w Polsce 1918–1939* [Political Aspects of the Former Servicemen in Poland Movement 1918–1939] Warszawa 1989, p. 189
172 *The Veteran* May 1938, p. 16

of 1938. At first the FPADF leadership did not want to recognize PAVA as a separate combatant organization within the ranks of the FPADF. They were inclined to see the Association as part of the Association of Veterans of the Former Polish Army in France. Col. S. Markus was decidedly in favor of that solution. But the FPADF, (having met with stiff PAVA resistance) backed off of that idea. The Polish Army Veterans Association of America was finally admitted to the Federation of Polish Associations of Defenders of the Fatherland on February 16, 1939. At PAVA's request Wojciech Albrycht, the President of the Circle of Volunteers from America in Bydgoszcz, became a member of the Supreme Council of the FPADF.

Due to the new situation the National Executive Board committed itself, in its letter of March 16, 1939, to introduce an amendment to the PAVA By-Laws at its next general assembly, which was to take place in Philadelphia in May 1940.

PAVA's membership in FPADF intensified in an unusual way, and with positive results, most of the veteran issues that had been languishing on the back burner with the Polish authorities. That was the case with the question of permanent financial aid for Polish war invalids, and also with the problem of independence decorations. In his last letter to the PAVA NEB (one week before the beginning of World War II) Wojciech Albrycht, referring to the FPADF matters, stated: "We are working well with the Federation."[173] Unfortunately, the outbreak of war put an end to the work that had just begun.

PAVA Contacts with Other Veteran Organizations in Poland

Among other veteran organizations in the interwar period that PAVA maintained contact with, the Association of War Invalids of the Polish Republic is worthy of mention. The first trace of these contacts is a letter of September 6, 1922 from the County Circle of the Association of War Invalids of the Polish Republic (AWIPR) in Sosnowiec to the PAVA Board, with a request for financial support for the construction of a building that was to house work shops for war invalids. The PAVA Board reacted favorably to this request and sent several small amounts for this purpose (which amounted in sum to two million Polish Marks) which were raised in the Polish American community. Part of this amount ($34.70) was collected by the Stanislaus Kostka Society of Lowell, Massachusetts.[174]

The positive reaction of the PAVA Board to the request of the local circle of the AWIPR encouraged the leadership of the organization to get into closer touch with PAVA. In the summer of 1923 an official delegate of the AWIPR, Bronisław Frankowski, came to the United States. On July 20 in Cleveland he signed an

---

173 PAVA NEB, sign. Box-17. PAVA Post Nr. 130 in Bydgoszcz. Letter of August 24, 1939 from W. Albrycht to the PAVA NEB
174 PAVA NEB Archives, sign. A-XVII/27

agreement with the PAVA Board to conduct a fund drive for the construction of a shelter for war invalids. In fact it was to be a renovation of the ruined palace complex in Radzyń outside of Warszawa which was to be used for a home for war invalids. PAVA committed itself to conduct a fund drive in the Polish American community in the name of the Association of War Invalids of the Republic of Poland.

It ought to be remembered that in August 1923 the delegate of the AWIPR, Bronisław Frankowski, together with the PAVA delegation, participated in the funeral of U.S. President Warren G. Harding, who was buried in Marion, Ohio.

The fund drive on behalf of the home for war invalids was conducted during Gen. Haller's first visit in the United States in the fall of 1923. At that time about $5,000 was collected. The cost of renovations was estimated at $30,000.[175]

Another effort on behalf of the war invalids home was made in 1926, when Dr. Tadeusz Dymowski, a delegate to the Polish Parliament, in the name of the AWIPR, brought 50,000 one-dollar "bricks" to America for the construction of the Home for Invalids in Warszawa. He gave the PAVA Board most of those bricks (over 37,000) and requested that a fund drive be conducted.[176] By June 1926 $1,033 had been collected. PAVA Secretary General Jan Szymański wrote in his letter of June 12, 1926 to the AWIPR National Executive Board as follows: "This isn't much, but we can do nothing about it, because our Post, after the incidents in Poland [J. Piłsudski's May coup—T. L.] are writing to us that they have halted the fund drive until things come to order in Poland.

"... The recent events have saddened our émigré community, and even the newspapers are writing that no money should be given for the various purposes in Poland, to just send funds to family and relatives. They are justifying this by saying that if they are capable of committing murder on their own kind, then let them also take care of their own social needs."[177]

From that time cooperation between the two organizations practically ceased, though it bears mentioning that PAVA helped some of the AWIPR members, taking them into their shelter for war invalids in Kuligi near Brodnica in Pomerania.[178]

In the years 1921–1939 PAVA maintained sporadic contact with the following associations and societies:

- Union of Defenders of Lwów
- The "To the Glory of the Fatherland" Association of Dovborites

---

175 PAVA NEB Archives, sign. A-XXIII/8 Letter of March 28, 1924 from PAVA secretary general to E. S. Brykczyński
176 *The Veteran* February 1926, pp. 6-7
177 PAVA NEB Archives, sign. A-XXIII/8
178 *The Veteran* August 1924, p. 12

- Union of Puławy Legionnaires
- Union of Officers of the Reserve
- General Union of Non-Commissioned Officers of the Reserves of the Polish Republic
- Dissolution Committee for the Polish Legion in Finland
- Union of Participants in the Great Poland Insurection of 1918–1919
- Union of Societies of Insurrectionists and Fighters
- Union of Former Upper Silesian Insurrectionists of the Polish Republic
- Legion of Invalids of the Polish Armed Forces
- Marine Department of the Union of Former Volunteers for the Polish Army
- 1st Polish Corps of Military Veterans in Podgórze outside Kraków
- Polish Society of Military Veterans in Kraków.

This group also included veterans from the group of Gen. Stanisław Bułak-Bałachowicz.

The Veteran wrote about this in June 1930: "A soldier young in age, but old in service, Lt. Bolesław Olechnowicz-Gradziecki (representative of the Polish tourist agency "Polekspress") visited the PAVA Board in Detroit, Michigan and also the offices of *The Veteran*. He conveyed greetings from his colleagues back home, and especially from the famous guerilla warrior Gen. Bułak-Bałachowicz, which our 13th Division had frequent contact with in operations against Budyonny's cavalry army near Zamość. Our guest who was (and is!) Gen. Bałachowicz's adjutant, brought crosses of valor of his volunteer army for our honorary president Col. T. A. Starzyński; for the former lieutenant of his army and our colleague J. Beczkowski and for colleague Cz. Mrozowski, the secretary general of our organization."[179]

The Polish Army Veterans Association did not maintain official conact with the Union of Polish Legionnaires, which was the most influential veteran organization in Poland in the years 1926–1939. This state of affairs wasn't even changed by the fact that when PAVA president Kazimierz Bałdyga was in Poland in August 1928, he was personally invited by Marshal Piłsudski to participate in the Convention of Polish Legionnaires in Wilno.[180] Historical events of 1914–1918 had an essential influence on this state of affairs, when the work of the Legions was equated on

---
179 *The Veteran* June 1930, p. 22
180 *The Veteran* October 1928, p. 1

American soil with actions of the National Defense Fund, which tried by all means possible to fight the idea of the Polish Army in France. No wonder that the veterans of that army were cool to the former legionnaires in Poland, even though a few legionnaires belonged to PAVA of America. One of them, Mieczysław Sichrawa, was editor of *The Veteran* for some time. He published his reminiscences of the legions, as well as that of other legionnaires, in *The Veteran*, for instance the memoirs of Jan M. Chodorowicz.[181]

---

181 J. M. Chodorowicz "Ze wspomnień legionisty" ["Reminiscences of a Legionnaire"] in: *Weteran [The Veteran]* November 1930, pp. 15, 24

Conclusion

The Poles coming to the United States from the very first years of its existence were a special kind of emigrant group. It was first of all a political immigration—both voluntary and forced. In speaking of voluntary emigration we have in mind those participants of Polish wars for national independence who (not wanting to live in an enslaved country or else who were escaping from repression by Poland's occupiers) emigrated to countries of Western Europe, from where of their own free will they traveled across the ocean. These included those who (guided by higher considerations) wanted to fight on American soil "For Your Freedom and Ours," for instance T. Kościuszko and K. Pułaski. These two Polish generals, thanks to their contribution to the success of the American Revolutionary War, became a permanent part of the history of the United States, and remain still today the best known symbols of friendship and cooperation between America and Poland.

But the largest groups of Polish veterans came to the American continent under duress. We are thinking here of the Polish prisoners of war—participants in the Napoleonic Wars who were British prisoners, and who were incorporated into British detachments and sent to fight on the Canadian-American border; as well as the more than 500 former November insurrectionists who were deported by the Austrians to America. After arriving on American soil they at first meet with the great sympathy of American society. No other group of veterans (both earlier and later) had such a cordial welcome.

The group of November insurrectionists was distinct from other Polish veteran groups that came to the United States first of all in that it tried to create the first community organization called The Polish Committee in New York, which was later changed to The Society of Polish Exiles. The veterans in this group were the founders of subsequent Polish organizations in America, such as the Society of Poles in America and the Democratic Society of Polish Exiles. These organizations (which also had political aims, for instance support of all activity to weaken the occupiers of Poland—Russia in particular) clearly showed that the veterans, although they had to live far away from their country, did not accept defeat, were attached to their national culture and continued the fight for the freedom of their homeland., although by the use of different methods. This end was to be served by Paweł Sobolewski's publication of the first Polish newspaper in English in the United States, called *Poland*, as also the publication of the first Polish books.

The Polish veterans who came to the Land of Washington, first of all looked for a place for permanent settlement and for the opportunity for unfettered political and socio-cultural activity. The United States offered that, but guaranteed nothing. Things did not always go smoothly with the building of a new life in a foreign land and in a totally different environment. Not everyone knew how to find their place in the new reality and to subscribe to its requirements. For many veterans it was a painful fact that their former social position and the titles and privileges that pertained to it had no meaning on American soil. The awareness of this fact combined with nostalgia for the homeland and families left behind frequently led to tragedy, including suicide. Those who were the most durable and enterprising, after overcoming numerous difficulties, were able to rise above the gray mediocrity of émigré life. It was fortunate that the veterans of the November Uprising were relatively young and well educated, which given the large demand on the American market for professionals, especially in technical and engineering areas, created great opportunities for a professional career, which was coupled with material and social advancement. Some veterans were able to develop a truly America-style career, such as Kazimierz Gzowski and Henryk Kałussowski.

Of all the waves of the Polish politico-military emigration to the United States in the 19th century, the veterans of the November Uprising made the most noticeable contribution to the development of this country.

The large group of November insurrectionists was unable, despite their attempts, to create permanent organizations. Their successors, the veterans of subsequent Polish uprisings on behalf of national independence—such as the Spring of Nations and the January 1863 Uprising—also were unable to do so. The latter however made a large contribution to the founding of many Polish organizations which aggregated the large masses of emigrants who arrived in America from Polish territories at the turn of the 19th century. Erazm Jerzmanowski decidedly stood out in the group of January Uprising veterans. An industrialist and philanthropist, he was probably the first Polish millionaire in the United States.

For the decided majority of Polish veterans who came to America in the 19th century this country was to become their final place of residence. Only a few made the decision to return to Europe, mainly to France, and later (when that became possible) to Polish lands, especially to Galicia. Only a few individuals were able to return to their native regions in order to take part in the next uprising for national independence. Some veterans of the January Uprising who lived in the United States had the good fortune to be able to see the day when Poland regained her independence, and they were able to visit their ancestral regions after many years of life in the emigration. That was the case of Wincenty Smolczyński of Chicopee, Massachussets.

The veterans of the January Uprising who lived in America made an essential contribution to the education of the younger patriotic émigré generation of Poles. The influence of this education was especially visible in the ranks of the Polish Falcons of America, which during World War I supplied the most volunteers for the Polish Army in France. The almost 15,000 Polish veterans who returned to America after the conclusion of war in Europe derived from them.

They were the largest group of Polish veterans on American soil up to 1939. By virtue of their numerical force they opened a great new chapter in the history of the Polish military emigration in America. The veterans of the Blue Army differed from their predecessors in the 18th and 19th centuries not only by their numerical superiority, but also by other characteristics that had capital significance. First of all, they already knew the country and its social environment, to which they were returning. After all they had lived and worked in the United States and Canada before they joined the Polish Army. For many of them the United States and Canada were their native countries, because they were born and brought up here. A significant part of the veterans, unlike their predecessors in the 19th century, had their immediate families here, where they could always find shelter and help in the most difficult of life's moments. They also knew how to speak English, which was the basic condition of normal functioning in the USA and Canada.

No less essential was the fact that the Blue Army veterans returned to a country where quite a few Poles were already present, where there were Polish parishes, churches, schools, libraries, where many Polish newspapers were being published and where various Polish organizations were active, with which the veterans were very closely connected before they had left for war, for instance the Falcons.

It was also psychologically important that they were returning from war victorious, that they had contributed by their armed effort to the restoration of Poland's independence after 123 years of slavery, and by doing so they had fulfilled their dreams and the dreams of their ancestors. They were truly proud of this fact and nothing could undermine that pride. They were victors, not defeated wretches as their predecessors in the 19th century had been. Moreover (upon leaving Poland) they knew that they could always return, whenever they wanted to. Their predecessors had no such opportunity. Thus, the 15,000 man group of Blue Army veterans already at the moment they landed in the United States had a decidedly better situation than the one their predecessors, the Polish veterans of the 19th century, had found themselves in. The knowledge of life in America and organizational experience gained in the Falcons helped them create an effective veteran organization which though it wasn't large in numbers, quickly gained a significant position among the most important Polish American organizations. Cooperation with those organizations had substantive meaning for the Polish Army Veterans Association of America, because those organizations supported the I. J. Paderewski Invalid Fund of PAVA.

The basic task that the Polish Army Veterans Association of America has set for itself in 1921—the care of war invalids—was consistently realized. Thanks to strong organizational effort, sizeable donations from I. J. Paderewski and the generosity of the Polish American community, this group of veterans had modest but permanent aid secured. In the years 1929–1932, thanks to the existence of PAVA and its auxiliary organization, the Auxiliary Corps, many jobless Polish veterans could make it through the dramatic period of the Great Depression.

By 1939 PAVA had been able to accumulate sizeable property, which was evidence of the industriousness and thrift of its members. The real estate that belonged to the Association, for instance buildings and recreational grounds, also served the Polish American community as such, which was very effective in helping the process of integration into local communities.

The PAVA leadership laid much emphasis on cultural and educational work on behalf of its members and the entire Polish American community. The aim of these activities was to preserve Polishness on foreign soil and to nurture patriotism. These goals were greatly furthered by tours to Poland organized by PAVA. The cultural and educational work carried on by the Polish veterans in America gave positive results with regard to the older generation of immigrants. Despite efforts made it was not possible to prevent the process of Americanization of the younger generation—which identified itself with the United States and Canada as their homeland. Its apolitical position was an extremely important element in the effective functioning of PAVA. It was not an easy task to maintain this principle in the life of the organization, nonetheless, (despite numerous attempts by various spheres in America and also in Poland) PAVA did not allow itself to be dragged into the strife of party politics. The PAVA leadership did not give in to Polish pressure until 1939 when it joined the pro-Piłsudski Federation of Polish Associations of Defenders of the Fatherland, because that was a necessary condition that had to be met in order to obtain permanent financial help from the Polish government for those members of PAVA who were war invalids.

The Association tried to maintain its apolitical character in the midst of party strife in Poland and in the Polish American community. But that principle did not hold in the case of hostile, foreign acts that were aimed against the interests of the Polish State. This especially concerned anti-Polish propaganda practiced in the United States by inimical ethnic spheres. PAVA ruthlessly fought this propaganda to the full extent of its modest means.

The work which the PAVA members did on behalf of Poland was evidence of their great patriotism and attachments to their old country. Some members of the Association returned to Poland and (like the Roman veterans of old) they settled on the outskirts of the country near their former military units, contributing to the polonization of the Polish Republic's Eastern Borderlands. They paid an enormous price for their effort and sacrifice after the outbreak of war in 1939.

The war effort of the Polish emigration in America, as also the multi-faceted generosity of PAVA members on behalf of Poland, were not appropriately appreciated in Poland, and after the May 1926 coup d'état they became even less appreciated due to political reasons. This brought negative feelings among the Polish American community toward the pro-Piłsudski government in Poland. The means to change this situation could only be found by having those authorities meet the expectations of the Polish American community, which gave first place to the care of the Polish veterans living in America who were war invalids. Thanks to the efforts of Stefan Lenartowicz, the director of Światpol (The World Association of Poles from Abroad) this matter was brought to a successful conclusion, although at the price of political concessions by PAVA. The outbreak of war in 1939 obliterated all the agreements that had been worked out with such difficulty, and Poland's tragedy created new assignments for the Polish veterans in America.

The Polish veterans in America in the years 1921–1939 did not make as obvious a mark on the development of the United States as the November insurrectionists had made. In contrast to that aristocratic and educated generation, the Blue Army veterans came in greater measure from the peasant emigration. Their educational level was on the whole very low, which caused them to have to take the meanest jobs in factories, mines, construction, on farms, in the lumber industry, etc., where they became anonymous co-creators of the economic might of the United States and Canada.

The organization that they created, the Polish Army Veterans Association of America, although not large, nonetheless, thanks to it dynamic and multi-faceted activity, proved that it deserved the title of the most patriotic element of the Polish emigration in America.

After returning to America: Camp Dix, NJ, 1920

The Founding Convention of the Polish Army Veterans
Association of America. Inc., Cleveland, OH, May 28–30, 1921

II PAVA National Convention in Chicago, IL, May 28–30, 1922

V PAVA National Convention in Pittsburgh, PA, May 29-31, 1931

1st Annual Meeting of PAVA District VI in Detroit, MI, 1931

PAVA Post # 5 in Chicago, IL, 1928

PAVA Post # 28 in Kensington, IL, 1928

PAVA Post # 36 in Passaic, NJ, 1928

PAVA Post # 57 in Elizabeth, NJ, 1928

PAVA Post # 78 in Detroit, MI

Conclusion

The Logo of the Polish Army Veterans Association of America, Inc.

Dr. Teofil Starzyński, PAVA President, 1921–1928

Kazimierz Bałdyga, PAVA President and Editor of "The Veteran" during the years 1928–1930

Wacław Rżewski, PAVA President,
1930–1931

Franciszek Dziób, PAVA President,
1931–1936

Lucjusz Kajko, PAVA National
Commander, 1936–1946

Dr. Franciszek Lenart, PAVA's National Physician up to 1930

Michał Stypuła, PAVA District III Commander in organizational uniform

Dr. Aleksander Pietrzykowski, President of the Association of Polish Army Officers' Reserve in America (1924–1932)

| Organ Stowarzyszenia Weteranów Armji Polskiej w Ameryce. | **WETERAN** | Organ of the Polish Army Veterans Ass'n of America. |

NR. 1.   347   CHICAGO, ILL. PAŹDZIERNIK.   ROK I

Nasze gospodarstwo rolne w Polsce

Jakie znaczenie będzie mieć nasze osadnictwo na Kresach Wschodnich dla poprawy stosunków ekonomicznych i kulturalnych w Polsce.

Jak już wiemy wszyscy, Sejm Ustawodawczy w Warszawie przeprowadził ustawę, nadającą wysłużonym żołnierzom armji polskiej ziemię na Kresach Wschodnich, zaś Oddział Wojskowych Osad Rolnych Ministerstwa Spr. nom, którzy z niej korzystać będą bezpośrednio, ale i całemu krajowi. Oto w krótkim zarysie korzyści naszej pracy dla ogółu:

Zdjęcie ciężaru z bark ogółu.

Korzyść najpierwsza, to zdję- nia Inwalidów Armji Polskiej i korzystać z niego będą tylko i jedynie wysłużeni żołnierze Rzeczypospolitej Polskiej. A po wymarciu wszystkich byłych ochotników z Ameryki, istnieć będzie nadal jako dowód rozumnego poj-

The title page of the first issue of the periodical "The Veteran," October, 1921

Czesław Żuławski, the first editor of "The Veteran"

Lieutenant Jan Roskosz, head of the PAVA Delegation in Warsaw
In the years 1922–1925

Julian Krasnodębski, participant in the first PAVA National Convention In 1921, Commander of PAVA Post #123 in Maspeth, NY

Opening of the shelter for Polish war invalids from America in Kuligi (Poland), September 2, 1923

General Józef Haller, speaking as the main guest at the American Legion convention in San Francisco, California, October 15, 1923

General Józef Haller with Polish-born film star Pola Negri in a film studio in Hollywood, Califormia

Conclusion

Official greeting of General Haller in Chicago, IL, November 8, 1923

Count Aleksander Skrzyński, Polish Minister of Foreign Affairs, among Polish veterans in Chicago, IL, July 1925

PAVA tour in Gnezno—Poland's first capital, July 11, 1927

PAVA tour participants visiting with Marshall Józef Piłsudski, Warsaw, August 4, 1927

Conclusion 387

U.S. President Herbert Hoover with Polish veterans in Washington, D.C., October 1929. Second from left Jan Kostrubała of Chicago, Commander of PAVA District I.

Ignace Jan Paderewski, world-famous Polish pianist, great philanthropist on behalf of Polish war invalids in America.

Agnieszka Wisła, organizer and first president of the Ladies Auxiliary of the Polish Army Veterans Association of America

The Ladies Auxiliary Corps of PAVA Post 36 in Passaic, NJ

Conclusion

The shelter for Polish war invalids in Wanda Park near Detroit, MI

Bronisław Spott, the Commander of
PAVA Post 3 in Milwaukee, WI, delegate
to the Wisconsin State Assembly

Film director Ryszard Bolesławski

General Józef Haller during his second visit to the USA. A meeting with the Falcons in Pittsburgh, PA, 1934. Dr. Teofil Starzyński is standing next to the General.

Stanisław and Helena Nastał

Franciszek Waluś, a former soldier of the "Blue Army," a Polish American journalist

Captain Franciszek Górecki, former volunteer from America, a professional Polish Army officer, murdered by the Soviet NKVD at the Katyn Massacre in 1940.

Minister Antoni Roman decorates the PAVA colors with the Golden Cross of Merit of the Polish Republic, New York, May 18, 1939.

ADDENDA

Addendum 1

A List of Polish Emigrants (Participants in the November 1830 Uprising) Who Remained in the USA[1]

1. Abramowicz, Dominik
2. Bernacki, Karol
3. Bogusławski, Aleksander
4. Bieliński, Aleksander
5. Boczkiewicz, Feliks
6. Bystrzonowski, Ferdynand
7. Bono de Mara, Edward
8. Brzeziński, Franc. Józef
9. Białogłowski, Roman
10. Benich, Karol
11. Berens, Karol
12. Barszcz, Stefan
13. Bańczakiewicz, Ludwik
14. Barszczewski, Henryk
15. Beter, Teofil
16. Benit, Roman
17. Bienias, Jan
18. Bełżecki, Feliks
19. Batowski, Michał
20. Białkowski, Michał
21. Borkowski, Wojciech
22. Browiński, Mikołaj
23. Borzek, Ksawery
24. Bartkowski, Aleksander
25. Cwierdziński, Wiktor
26. Czerwiński, Józef
27. Chłopicki, Ludwik
28. Ciechanowski, Józef
29. Czernicki, Józef
30. Czechowski, Ignacy
31. Czechowski, Tytus
32. Dembicki, Napoleon
33. Dymowski, Jan
34. Dłuski, Tomasz
35. Dąbrowski, Jan
36. Dobiecki, Władysław
37. Dobiecki, Fortunat
38. Dobiecki, Józef
39. Dąbski, Teodor
40. Dziwanowski, Klemens
41. Dryniewicz, Józef
42. Eysmont, Lucjan
43. Filipowski, Kacper
44. Faliński, Kazimierz
45. Gwinczewski, Feliks
46. Gajkowski, Antoni
47. Górski, Michał
48. Głuszewski, Konstanty
49. Gutowski, Rudolf
50. Gliński, Stanisław
51. Głowacki, Ignacy
52. Gąsiorowski, Stefan
53. Gzowski, Kazimierz
54. Grylski, Jan
55. Grabowski, Sylwester
56. Gura, Zenon
57. Górski, Antoni
58. Garbaczuk, Mikołaj
59. Grabowski, Adolf
60. Henrykowski, Ludwik
61. Holowiński, Józef
62. Hyż, Jan
63. Horodyski, Ludwik
64. Jaszowski, Maksymilian

---

1 Copy of: Library of the Czartoryski Muzeum, Kraków, MS 5313, Lists of persons 1815–1854, pp. 335-338

65. Janowski, Walery
66. Jakubowski, August
67. Jakubowski, Franciszek
68. Jabloński, Józef
69. Jaworski, Tomasz
70. Jaworski, Mikołaj
71. Jełtuchowski, Mikołaj
72. Juźwikiewicz, Julian
73. Jański, Antoni
74. Jaroszewski, Ignacy
75. Jagiełło, Hieronim
76. Iliński, Ksawery
77. Iwanowski, Aleksander
78. Jerzykiewicz, Ludwik
79. Jakutowicz, Antoni
80. Jasiński, Kazimierz
81. Jasiński, Jan
82. Kuryłowicz, Franciszek
83. Kosyłowski, Napoleon
84. Kowalski, Konstanty
85. Komorowski, Władysław
86. Komar, Karol
87. Kossowski, Józef
88. Kunicki, Alfons
89. Krawczyński, Mateusz
90. Kułasiewicz, Jan
91. Kotowski, Franciszek
92. Kisielewski, Paweł
93. Kotowicz (left America)
94. Kwiatkowski, Józef
95. Kimel, Salomon
96. Kwiatkowski, Józef
97. Korczyński, Franciszek
98. Kręgliński, Jan
99. Kwieciński, Franciszek
100. Kadmus, Jan
101. Kamiński, Jan
102. Konarzewski, Wojciech
103. Kwiatkowski, Jan
104. Kwiatkowski, Karol
105. Kwiatkowski, Andrzej
106. Kwiatkowska, Marcela (married couple)
107. Kuczmiński, Mateusz
108. Krzyżanowski, Piotr
109. Krajewski, Roman
110. Krysiński, Tomasz
111. Łepkowski, Numa
112. Liskowacki, Florian
113. Lebedowicz, Antoni
114. Ludwikowski, Daniel
115. Lemański, Stanisław
116. Lange, Władysław
117. Lepin, Jan
118. Lewkowicz, Marian
119. Łuszczyński, Paweł
120. Molisan, Mikołaj
121. Markiewicz, Fabian
122. Mniszek, Stanisław
123. Młodzianowski, Edward
124. Mostowski, Wiktor
125. Marski, Dyonizy
126. Miliński Edward
127. Morawski, Sebastian
128. Maszewski
129. Mierzwiński, Cyprian
130. Materski, Franciszek
131. Morozowski, Józef
132. Niedźwiezki, Karol
133. Nowakowski, Michał
134. Nowomiejski, Michał
135. Nietupski, Feliks
136. Naruszewicz, Hipolit
137. Oladowski, Hipolit
138. Ostapowski, Julian
139. Olszański, Honory
140. Olszewski, Teodor
141. Pieńkowski, Tadeusz
142. Plinta, Karol
143. Polkowski, Edward

144. Paustecki, Józef
145. Plewiński, Karol
146. Puchalski, Eugeniusz
147. Pawliński, Stanisław
148. Porczyński, Eugeniusz
149. Piechowski, Aleksander
150. Podosowski, Grzegorz
151. Petranowski, Franciszek
152. Praniewski, Aleksander
153. Pędziński, Jan
154. Piotrowski, Ksawery
155. Poniatowski, Antoni
156. Pietrowicz, Teodor
157. Pawlowski Dominik
158. Piekarski, Aleksander
159. Rostkowski, Wojciech
160. Rutkowski, Teofil
161. Romani, Joachim
162. Romer, Kacper
163. Rząźewski, Ludwik
164. Roiecki, Tomasz
165. Rychlicki, Jan
166. Rosienkiewicz Marcin
167. Rodziewicz, Werner
168. Rosenfeld, Ludwik
169. Rutkowski, Józef
170. Rudzimiński von Lust, Karol
171. Rosnowski, Kazimierz
172. Szablicki, Antoni
173. Sobolewski, Paweł
174. Sumowski, Antoni
175. Szymański, Antoni
176. Sienicki, Franciszek
177. Szemetyło, Teodor
178. Szczurowski, Bonawentura
179. Sokalski, Władysław
180. Snitowski, Adolf
181. Stachurski, Daniel
182. Stachowski, Aleksander
183. Sikorski, Apolinary
184. Skrzyński, Aleksander
185. Stefański, Michał
186. Swierdziński, Teofil
187. Szeleszczyński, Andrzej
188. Sułkowski, Jan
189. Sularzycki, Jan
190. Sanicki, Józef
191. Sosiński, Antoni
192. Sadowski, Michał
193. Sadowski, Aleksander
194. Skibiński, Józef
195. Sulmirski, Wincenty
196. Skorupski, Jan
197. Stasiewicz, Grzegorz
198. Strzelecki, Konstanty
199. Słoma, Jan
200. Samiec, Mikołaj
201. Swak, Józef
202. Szumlański, Jan
203. Sawicki, Albert
204. Turowski, Ludwik
205. Turzański, Karol
206. Teliga, Ignacy
207. Trzaskowski, Bolesław
208. Tołoczka, Karol
209. Wierzbicki, Szczęsny
210. Wyszyński, Karol
211. Wyszyński, Eustachy
212. Wesołowski, Ludwik
213. Wierzbicki, Aleksander
214. Wardzyński, Andrzej
215. Wojciechowski, Antoni
216. Włodecki, Franciszek
217. Wyszomirski, Paweł
218. Wolnicki, Tomasz
219. Wodzyński, Józef
220. Wnorowski, Józef
221. Wierciński, Bertold
222. Węgierski, August
223. Żukowski, Tomasz

224. Żółkiewski, Józef
225. Zygadło, Józef
226. Zajączkowski, Wincenty
227. Żelazowski, Józef
228. Zaręba, Franciszek
229. Żywicki, Mikołaj
230. Zacharzewski, Mikołaj
231. Zakusiło, Jan
232. Zalewski, Tomasz
233. Zalewski, Jan
234. Zakrzewski, Mikołaj

Paris 16 January 1835.

Found in America:

1. Pral, Jan
2. Krajcer, Karol
3. Szymański
4. Mycielski
5. Izdebski
6. Kotowski left for Gibraltar
7. Wierciński to London
8. Nyko to London

On April 30 the following left Trieste, and on July 30 they arrived in New York on the corvette "Lipsia":

1. Bohuszewicz
2. Czarnecki
3. Dolanowski
4. Gorecki
5. Jaroszyński
6. Kopecki
7. Kruszewski
8. Kocowski
9. Lewandowski
10. Magnuski
11. Nyko
12. Putrament
13. Straszewski
14. Skarżyński
15. Sadowski
16. Targowski

Document quoted after: F. Stasik, *Przyczynek do dziejów polskiej emigracji politycznej w Stanach Zjednoczonych A.P. po powstaniu listopa-dowym (1831–1836)*, [in:] *Problemy Polonii Zagranicznej*, vol.V, Warszawa 1964-1966, pp. 29-45.

Addendum 2

Farewell Address of General Bolesław Roja to Soldiers Returning to America. April 29, 1920

Soldiers!

The time has come for your return to America; your service in the ranks of the fighting Motherland is coming to an end. You crossed the ocean voluntarily several years ago to fight for Her freedom. You have honorably and honestly fulfilled your holy duty toward Mother Poland.

On various fronts in the alliance with the free peoples of the West—you did your share to safeguard the world from Prussian physical aggression.

And so you have received the highest reward for a Polish soldier; today you are looking with your own eyes at the fulfillment of our dearest hopes, a Poland free and full of glory.

Today you are leaving your native land in old and worn-out uniforms. This Poland that loves you dearly, plundered by its aggressors, depleted by a drawn-out war, cannot equip its children as it would wish to with all its heart, and as you so rightly deserve.

Soldiers, this threadbare uniform, which you are taking back with you, is today, thanks to the valor of the Polish soldier, the uniform of glory—these rags speak loudly of your splendid martial deeds.

Let the heads of your fellow Polish Americans bow before their returning sons, who have won nothing for themselves except these rags. But they have ornamented Poland with the purple robe of Freedom.

You have become the tie that powerfully binds our American emigration to its old Fatherland. I know that in America you will spread love and attachment to Poland and that always, whenever the need arises, you will stand strong in the defense of Mother Poland.

Our heartfelt feelings will accompany us on all the further paths of life, and the memory that you had a hand in the rebuilding of a free Republic of Poland, will be for you and your families for ever a source of deserved pride and may it accompany you throughout all the days of your life.

Rest assured of your Motherland's eternal gratitude! And just as we have done until now in the ranks, so also in the future, though divided by an ocean, we shall gather under Her flag and communicate with one shout:

Long Live Free Poland!
Roja, General and Commander.

Source: Order Nr. 17. General Headquarters Pomorze District. Grudziądz, 29 April 1920; *The War Effort of the Polish Emigration in America* New York-Chicago 1957, p. 778.

Addendum 3

The Members of PAVA National Executive Boards, 1921–1940

1921–1923: President Dr. Teofil Starzyński, I Vice President Lucjan Adamczak, II Vice President Czesław Żuławski, Secretary General Stanisław Z. Stachowicz, Recording Secretary J. Kruszyński, Treasurer W. Karolczak; Directors J. Matecki, M. Kowalski, J. A. Żebrowski, W. F. Gruszka, A. Joniec, W. Kulczycki, Stanisław Nastał;

1923–1925: President Dr. Teofil Starzyński, I Vice President M. Kowalski, II Vice President W. Karolczak, Secretary General Stanisław Z. Stachowicz; Directors: J. A. Żebrowski, Franciszek Bubacz, F. B. Woźniak, Zygmunt Rowiński, W. Świeciaszek, L. Bobiński, A. Krakowiak;

1925–1928: President Dr. Teofil Starzyński, I Vice President J. Kostrubała, II Vice President J. Wróblewski, Secretary General Jan Szymański; Directors: J. Chojnacki, J. Poźniak, Stanisław Grykowski, Franciszek Jendryaszek, H. Sobieski, K. Kołodziejczyk, Stanisław Wilk, J. Karaś, B. S. Spott;

1928–1931: President Kazimierz Bałdyga, I V.P. Wacław Rżewski, II V.P. M. Paluch, Secretary General Czesław Mrozowski; Directors: M. Rudnicki, L. Gruchacz, S. Cichowski, J. Wiśniewski, S. Szymański, K. Brykalski, L. Budziak, Michał Stypuła, S. Ryszkowski;

1931–1934: National Commander Franciszek Dziób, I Vice Commander K. Brykalski, II Vice Commander Jan Pela, Adjutant General Czesław Mrozowski, Treasurer S. Sobolewski, Chief Physician Dr. Józef Michalski; Directors: T. Duda, S. Baliński, Ig. Zapytowski, J. Wiśniewski, Aleksander Żakiewicz;

1934–1937: National Commander Franciszk Dziób, I Vice Commander Lucjusz Kajko, II Vice Commander Adam B. Łyczak, .Adjutant General Leopold Krzyżak, Treasuer Aleksander Żakiewicz; Directors: S. Wojtusik, Stanisław Wilk, Jan Dec, Franciszek Kosiński, J. Piekielniak, S. Szczygieł, H. Kolakowski, J. Cichowski, P. Pastula; Chief Physician: Dr. J. Michalski, Chief Chaplain Rev. A. Wojcieszczuk.

1937–1940: National Commander Lucjusz C. Kajko, I Vice Commender Jan Dec, II Vice Commander S. F. Wojtusik, Adjutant General Leopold Krzyżak, Treasurer Aleksander Żakiewicz; Directors: J. Kiela, Stanisław Wilk, M. Drzyzga, Fr. Kosiński, Józef Klimek, A. Czarnota, J. Zieliński, Stanisław Szczygieł, Stanisław Węglarski; Chief Physician Dr. J. Michalski, Chief Chaplain Rev. A. Wojcieszczuk.

Source: *The Veteran* Jubilee edition, June 1971, p. 87

Addendum 4

PAVA Districts 1921–1939

PAVA District I (founded in Chicago in 1921). It included the following posts:

PAVA Post 2, Chicago, IL
PAVA Post 3, Milwaukee, WI,
PAVA Post 5, Chicago, IL,
PAVA Post 8, St. Louis, MO,
PAVA Post 9, Chicago, IL,
PAVA Post 10, Cicero, IL,
PAVA Post 14, Chicago, IL,
PAVA Post 15, Gary, IN,
PAVA Post 20, Chicago, IL,
PAVA Post 28, Kensington, IL,
PAVA Post 39, Chicago, IL,
PAVA Post 42, Omaha, NE,
PAVA Post 45, Steubenville, OH,
PAVA Post 56, Chicago, IL,
PAVA Post 75, St. Paul, MN,
PAVA Post 68, Chicago, IL,
PAVA Post 90, Chicago, IL,
PAVA Post 94, Milwaukee, WI.

The Presidents and Commanders of PAVA District I in the years 1921–1939 were, successively: Dr. Aleksander Pietrzykowski (to July 1921), Roman Hanasz (1921–1922), Lt. Witold Bogucki (1922–1925), Stanisław Krygowski (1925–1927), J. S. Ćwik (1927–1928), Jan Kostrubała (1929–1930), H. Sobieski (1930), K. Kołodziejczyk (1931–1932), Stanisław Krygowski (1932–1935), A. Trygar (1935–1938), K. Frenzel (1938–1939).

PAVA District II was founded on August 16,1925 at the headquarters of Post Nr. 36 in Passaic, NJ during a meeting of delegates from several posts on the occasion of the dedication of the Post Nr. 36 flag. The following posts formed PAVA District II: Post 21 from New York, NY; Post 25 from Newark, NJ; Post 36 from Passaic, NJ; Post 51 from Jersey City, NJ, and post 57 from Elizabeth, NJ.

At first Newark, NJ was the headquarters of District II; later New York, NY. In the years 1925–1939 the following posts belonged to District II:

PAVA Post 21, New York, NY,
PAVA Post 25, Newark, NJ,
PAVA Post 36, Passaic, NJ,

PAVA Post 51, Jersey City, NJ,
PAVA Post 57, Elizabeth, NJ,
PAVA Post 79, Glen Cove, L.I., NY,
PAVA Post 81, Trenton, NJ (from 1934 in PAVA District X),
PAVA Post 84, Yonkers, NY,
PAVA Post 85, Bayonne, NJ,
PAVA Post 99, Harrison, NJ,
PAVA Post 101, South Brooklyn, NY,
PAVA Post 102, Brooklyn, NY,
PAVA Post 106, Ozone Park, NY,
PAVA Post 116, Wallington, NJ,
PAVA Post 118, Bay Way, NJ,
PAVA Post 123, Maspeth, NY,
PAVA Post 140, Southampton, NY,
PAVA Post 148, Port Washington, NY,
PAVA Post 154, Paterson, NJ.

The Presidents and Commanders of PAVA District II in the years 1925–1939 were: pilot J. M. Matecki, Dr J. Michalski, Adam B. Łyczak, Józef Cichowski.

PAVA District III was organized on November 11, 1925 at a founding meeting at PAVA Post Nr. 16 in Pittsburgh. At that time District III included three posts: Post 16 in Pittsburgh, PA; Post 41 in Pittsburgh, PA, and Post 61 in Braddock-Wilmerding, PA. Pittsburgh was the location of District III headquarters.

In the years 1925–1939 PAVA District III included the following posts:

PAVA Post 16, Pittsburgh, PA,
PAVA Post 17, Erie, PA,
PAVA Post 19, Monessen, PA,
PAVA Post 30, Johnstown, PA,
PAVA Post 41, Pittsburgh, PA,
PAVA Post 44, Freeland, PA,
PAVA Post 47, Washington, PA,
PAVA Post 60, Ambridge, PA,
PAVA Post 61, Braddock, PA,
PAVA Post 69, New Kensington, PA,
PAVA Post 72, McKees Rocks, PA,
PAVA Post 77, Shenandoah, PA,
PAVA Post 82, Lansing, OH,
PAVA Post 83, Natrona, PA,

PAVA Post 86, Barnesboro, PA (formerly the post in Scranton, PA was number 86),
PAVA Post 88, Wilkes-Barre, PA,
PAVA Post 104, Chester, PA,
PAVA Post 108, New Castle, PA,
PAVA Post 109, McKeesport, PA,
PAVA Post 117, Scranton, PA.

The Presidents, and later the Commanders of PAVA District III in the years 1925–1939 were, successively: Michał Stypuła, W. A. Pawlak, J. A. Ryżowicz, Piotr Kempisty, J. A. Ryżowicz, Michał Stypuła.

During the entire period PAVA District III had its headquarters in Pittsburgh, PA.

PAVA District IV was organized on 8 October 1926 and included the posts that were active in Philadelphia and the surrounding areas. J. Wolski was elected President. But shortly thereafter this District folded.

It took another three years before District IV was permanently organized. That happened on June 10, 1929, when the PAVA National Executive Board registered it. It was activated by the following posts: Nr. 24 in Bridgeport, CT, Nr. 98 in New Haven, CT, and Nr. 103 in Wallingford, CT. By 1939 the following posts joined the district for the duration of their existence:

PAVA Post 24, Bridgeport, CT,
PAVA Post 73, Meriden, CT,
PAVA Post 93, Southington, CT,
PAVA Post 98, New Haven, CT,
PAVA Post 103, Wallingford, CT,
PAVA Post 107, Terryville, CT,
PAVA Post 110, Torrington, CT,
PAVA Post 111, New Britain, CT,
PAVA Post 119, Hartford, CT,
PAVA Post 120, Union City, CT,
PAVA Post 129, Stamford, CT,
PAVA Post 132, Norwich, CT,
PAVA Post 145, Derby, CT,
PAVA Post 150, New London, CT,
PAVA Post 156, Bristol, CT.

The President and Commanders of District IV in the years 1929–1939 were: H. Augustyn, Stanisław Wojtusik, Dębiczak, Józef Staszewski, S. J. Robak. The headquarters of District IV was successively located in: Meriden, CT; New Britain, CT; Hartford, CT.

PAVA District V was organized in November 1930 by Post 18 in Schenectady, NY, Post 105 in Utica, NY, and Post 50 in Cohoes, NY. It was officially registered by the National Executive Board on December 8, 1930. In the years 1930–1939 the following posts were part of it during the period of their existence:

PAVA Post 18, Schenectady, NY,
PAVA Post 23, Adams, MA,
PAVA Post 35, Amsterdam, NY,
PAVA Post 46, Binghamton, NY,
PAVA Post 50, Cohoes, NY,
PAVA Post 105, Utica, NY,
PAVA Post 124, Syracuse, NY,
PAVA Post 131, Auburn, NY.

In that period the Presidents and Commanders of District V were: J. Ziemba, S. Potaczała, F. Kosiński. The District V headquarters was, successively, located in: Schenectady, NY; Utica, NY, and Syracuse, NY.

PAVA DISTRICT VI was organized on February 22, 1931 at a founding meeting held at PAVA Post Nr. 7 in Detroit, MI. District VI was created by the following posts: Post 7 in Detroit, MI; Post. 74 in Toledo, OH; Post 78 in Detroit, MI; Post 97 in Grand Rapids, MI; and Post 113 in Hamtramck, MI. In the years 1931–1939 the following posts were part of PAVA District VI:

PAVA Post 7, Detroit, MI,
PAVA Post 22, Toledo, OH,
PAVA Post 74, Toledo, OH,
PAVA Post 78, Detroit, MI,
PAVA Post 89, Jackson, Mi,
PAVA Post 95, Wayandotte, MI,
PAVA Post 97, Grand Rapids, MI,
PAVA Post 113, Hamtramck, MI,
PAVA Post126, Windsor, ONT, Canada,
PAVA Post 146, Muskegon, MI,
PAVA Post 155, Flint, MI,
PAVA Post 165, Saginaw, MI.

The Presidents and Commanders of PAVA District VI in the years 1931–1939 were, successively: Kazimierz Brykalski, Artur L. Waldo, Franciszek Cichowski, Czesław Mrozowski, Andrzej Szczygielski, Wacław Bagiński, Leon Budziak. The headquarters of District VI was located in Detroit, Michigan.

PAVA District VII was formed in September 1939 by PAVA posts active in

Canada: Post 114 in Toronto, ONT; Post 133 in West Toronto, ONT; Post 135 in North Toronto, ONT; and Post 136 in Oshawa, ONT. This district was registered by the National Executive Board in October 1933.

The following posts belonged to District VII in the years 1933–1939:

>   PAVA Post 114, Toronto, ONT,
>   PAVA Post 133, W. Toronto, ONT,
>   PAVA Post 135, N. Toronto, ONT,
>   PAVA Post 136, Oshawa, ONT,
>   PAVA Post 162, Kirkland Lake, ONT,
>   PAVA Post 163, Hamilton, ONT.

PAVA Post Nr. 126 in Windsor, ONT, although it was located in Canada, did not belong to District VII, but to District VI because the city of Windsor is located very close to Detroit, Michigan, which facilitated mutual contacts and thus it was understandable that this PAVA Post would belong to District VI.

In the years 1933–1939 the President and Commanders of PAVA District VII in Canada were: Kazimierz Klimek, Stanisław Czajkowski, Aleksander Granat, Andrzej Rzepka.The headquarters of District VII was located in Toronto.

PAVA DISTRICT VIII was formed on March 23, 1934 at the initiative of Post Nr. 37 in Boston, MA. The founding posts were: the above-mentioned Post 37, Post 29 in Lowell, MA, and Post 11 in East Hampton, MA.

In the years 1934–1939 the following posts were included in PAVA District VIII:

>   PAVA Post 11, East Hampton, MA,
>   PAVA Post 23, Adams, MA,
>   PAVA Post 29, Lowell, MA,
>   PAVA Post 37, Boston, MA,
>   PAVA Post 52, Worcester, MA,
>   PAVA Post 53, West Lynn, MA,
>   PAVA Post 76, Haverhill, MA,
>   PAVA Post 91, Turners Falls, MA,
>   PAVA Post 122, Manchester, NH,
>   PAVA Post 138, Holyoke, MA,
>   PAVA Post 168, Chicopee, MA,
>   PAVA Post 180, Pittsfield, MA.

The Presidents and Commanders of District VIII were: Jan Drabiński and A. Czarnota. The headquarters of District VIII was located in Boston.

PAVA DISTRICT IX was created at the behest of PAVA Post Nr. 6 in Cleveland, OH, on May 13,1934. The following posts formed the District: Post 4 in Youngstown,

OH, Post 6 in Cleveland, OH, Post 17 in Erie, PA, and Post 92 in Elyria, OH.

The following posts belonged to PAVA District IX in the years 1934–1939:

PAVA Post 4, Youngstown, OH,
PAVA Post 6, Cleveland, OH,
PAVA Post 17, Erie, PA,
PAVA Post 82, Lansing, OH,
PAVA Post 92, Elyria, OH,
PAVA Post 152, Cleveland, OH.

The Commanders of PAVA District IX in the years 1934–1939 were: Franciszek J. Waluś, Wojciech Karolczak and again F. J. Waluś. Cleveland, Ohio was the site of the District's headquarters.

PAVA DISTRICT X was founded on May 20, 1934 at PAVA Post Nr. 12 in Philadelphia, PA. The founding posts were: Post 12 Philadelphia, PA; Post 81 Trenton, NJ; Post 112 Baltimore, MD; and Post 121 Camden, NJ.

In the years 1934–1939 PAVA District X included the following posts:

PAVA Post 12, Philadelphia, PA,
PAVA Post 48, Wilmington, DE,
PAVA Post 55, Reading, PA,
PAVA Post 81, Trenton, NJ,
PAVA Post 104, Chester, PA,
PAVA Post 112, Baltimore, MD,
PAVA Post 121, Camden, NJ.

The Presidents and Commanders of PAVA District X in the years 1934–1939 were: Władysław Szczygieł and Edward Pendrak.

The PAVA District X headquarters were located in Philadelphia, PA.

PAVA DISTRICT XI was created on July 8, 1935 in Scranton, PA at the behest of the local PAVA Post Nr. 117. The following posts were represented at the founding meeting: Post 117 S. Scranton, PA; Post 86 W. Scranton, PA; Post 143 Mayfield, PA; Post 44 Hazleton, PA; Post 139 Dickson City, PA; Post 77 Shenandoah, PA.

In the years 1935–1939 PAVA District XI included the following posts:

PAVA Post 77, Shenandoah, PA
PAVA Post 86, Scranton, PA,
PAVA Post 88, Wilkes Barre, PA,
PAVA Post 117, Scranton, PA,
PAVA Post 139, Dickson City, PA,
PAVA Post 143, Mayfield, PA,
PAVA Post 147, Wilkes-Barre, PA,

PAVA Post 161, Dupont, PA,
PAVA Post 164, Greenwood, PA.

Franciszek Lipiński was the Commander of District XI in this period. The headquarters of the District were located in Shenandoah, Pennsylvania.

PAVA District XII was created on 19 March 1939 in Buffalo, NY, at the suggestion of local PAVA Post Nr. 1. The District included the following founding posts: PAVA Post 1, Buffalo, NY, PAVA Post 134, Buffalo, NY, PAVA Post 169, N. Tonawanda, NY.

The Commander of District XII was Józef Kubala. The District offices were located in Buffalo, NY.

Source: T. Lachowicz, on the basis of PAVA NEB Archives.

Addendum 5

PAVA Posts in the Years 1921–1939

Post Number	Location	Number of Members (May 1, 1940)
1.	Buffalo, NY	53
2.	Chicago, IL	155
3.	Milwaukee, WI	120
4.	Youngstown, OH	11
5.	Chicago, IL	205
6.	Cleveland, OH	87
7.	Detroit, MI	160
8.	St. Louis, MO	37
9.	Chicago, IL	29
10.	Cicero, IL	28
11.	Easthampton, MA	6
12.	Philadelphia, PA	97
13.	South Bend, IN	Deleted
14.	Chicago, IL	30
15.	Gary, IN	21
16.	Pittsburgh, PA	59
17.	Erie, PA	52
18.	Schenectady, NY	40
19.	Monessen, PA	12
20.	Chicago, IL	42
21.	New York, NY	67
22.	Toledo, OH	15
23.	Adams, MA	12
24.	Bridgeport, CT	29
25.	Newark, NJ	52
26.	East St. Louis, IL	Deleted
27.	Rochester, NY	30
28.	Kensington, IL	20
29.	Lowell, MA	20
30.	Johnstown, PA	25
31.	Nanticoke, PA	Deleted
32.	Wilkes-Barre, PA	Deleted
33.	St. Joseph, MO	Deleted
34.	Ironwood, MI	Deleted

35.	Amsterdam, NY	22
36.	Passaic, NJ	53
37.	Boston, MA	43
38.	New Castle, PA	Deleted
39.	Chicago, IL	52
40.	Hammond, IN	33
41.	Pittsburgh, PA	44
42.	Omaha, NE	24
43.	Port Chester, NY	Deleted
44.	Freeland, PA	12
45.	Steubenville, OH	Deleted
46.	Binghamton, NY	8
47.	Washington, PA	8
48.	Wilmington, DA	11
49.	Minneapolis, MN	29
50.	Cohoes, NY	6
51.	Jersey City, NJ	42
52.	Worcester, MA	28
53.	West Lynn, MA	11
54.	Salem, MA	Deleted
55.	Reading, PA	7
56.	Chicago, IL	32
57.	Elizabeth, NJ	25
58.	Hamilton, ONT, Canada	
59.	Herkimer, N	Deleted
60.	Ambridge, PA	14
61.	Braddock, PA	35
62.	Indian Orchard, MA	Deleted
63.	Mocanaqua, PA	Deleted
64.	New Bedford, MA	Deleted
65,	Manayunk, PA	Deleted
66.	Barnesboro, PA	Deleted
67.	Carnegie, PA	Deleted
68.	Chicago, IL	39
69.	New Kensington, PA	16
70.	Gardner, MA	Deleted
71.	Askam, PA	Deleted
72.	McKess Rocks, PA	11
73.	Meriden, CT	30
74.	Toledo, OH	50

75.	St. Paul, MN	8
76.	Haverhill, MA	9
77.	Shenandoah, PA	27
78.	Detroit, MI	130
79.	Glen Cove, NY	Deleted
80.	Philadelphia, PA	Deleted
81.	Trenton, NJ	70
82.	Lansing, OH	8
83.	Natrona, PA	29
84.	Yonkers, NY	26
85.	Bayonne, NJ	43
86.	Scranton, PA	22
87.	Throop, PA	Deleted
88.	Wilkes-Barre, PA	22
89.	Jackson, MI,	16
90.	Chicago, IL	91
91.	Turners Falls, MA	14
92.	Elyria, OH	6
93.	Southington, CT	10
94.	Milwaukee, WI	39
95.	Wyandotte, MI	36
96.	Niagara Falls, NY	Deleted
97.	Grand Rapids, MI	41
98.	New Haven, CT	27
99.	Harrison, NJ	13
100.	FLYING POST	64
101.	Brooklyn, NY	18
102.	Brooklyn, NY	39
103.	Wallingford, CT	13
104.	Chester, PA	13
105.	Utica, NY	56
106.	Ozone Park, NY	13
107.	Terryville, CT	9
108.	New Castle, PA	20
109.	McKeesport, PA	15
110.	Torrington, CT	11
111.	New Britain, CT	67
112.	Baltimore, MD	38
113.	Hamtramck, MI	146
114.	Toronto, ONT, Canada	35

115.	Weirton, WV	8
116.	Wallington, NJ	10
117.	Scranton, PA	12
118.	Elizabeth, NJ	Deleted
119.	Hartford, CT	41
120.	Union City, CT	19
121.	Camden, NJ	11
122.	Manchester, NH	7
123.	Maspeth, NY	16
124.	Syracuse, NY	37
125.	South Bend, IN	38
126.	Windsor, ONT, Canada	30
127.	Winnipeg, MAN, Canada	Deleted
128.	Williamsburg, NY	Deleted
129.	Stamford, CT	Deleted
130.	Bydgoszcz, Poland	
131.	Auburn, NY	6
132.	Norwich, CT	21
133.	West Toronto, ONT, Canada	24
134.	Buffalo, NY	24
135.	New Toronto, ONT, Canada	Deleted
136.	Oshawa, ONT, Canada	Deleted
137.	Michigan, MI, IN	12
138.	Holyoke, MA	18
139.	Dickson City, PA	27
140.	Southampton, NY	19
141.	Chicago, IL	40
142.	East Chicago, IN	36
143.	Mayfield, PA	8
144.	Kansas City, KS	17
145.	Derby, CT	27
146.	Muskegon, MI	5
147.	Wilkes-Barre, PA	28
148.	Port Washington, NY	9
149.	Racine, WI	11
150.	New London, CT	23
151.	New York, NY	Deleted
152.	Cleveland, OH	26
153.	Waterbury, CT	Deleted
154.	Paterson, NJ	15

155.	Flint, MI	18
156.	Bristol, CT	17
157.	Oil City, PA	Deleted
158.	Pittsfield, MA	6
159.	Northampton, MA	8
160.	Winnipeg, MAN, Canada	Deleted
161.	Dupont, PA	10
162.	Kirkland Lake, ONT, Canada	16
163.	Hamilton, ONT, Canada	55
164.	Scranton, PA	10
165.	Saginaw, MI	13
166.	Central Falls, RI	7
167.	Bay City, MI	Deleted
168.	Chicopee, MA	38
169.	North Tonawanda, NY	22
170.	Lorain, OH	9
171.	Thompsonville, CT	20
172.	Kitchener, ONT, Canada	26
173.	Los Angeles, CA	8

Source: PAVA NEB Archives, sign. Gr.II/ vol.9, Report of the Officers of the PAVA and A.C. Boards for the 8th General Assembly of the Polish Army Veterans Association of America in the City of Philadelphia, PA, for the period 1937–1940.

Addendum 6

A Listing of the Number of PAVA Posts in Individual States in the USA and Canada in 1939

Pennsylvania	37
New York	24
Connecticut	18
Massachusetts	16
Illinois	13
New Jersey	11
Michigan	11
Ohio	9
Ontario (Canada)	9
Indiana	6
Wisconsin	3
Manitoba (Canada)	2
Minnesota	2
Missouri	2
California	1
Delaware	1
Kansas	1
Maryland	1
Nebraska	1
New Hampshire	1
Rhode Island	1
West Virginia	1

Source: T. Lachowicz, based on PAVA NEB Archives collections

Addendum 7

Development of Auxiliary Corps Posts Alongside PAVA in the Years 1928–1940

Year	Number of A.C. Posts	Number of Members
1928	15	536
1931	34	1765
1934	73	3126
1937	100	4207
1940	113	4252

Source: T. Lachowicz, based on PAVA NEB Archives collection

Addendum 8

PAVA Auxiliary Corps Posts in the Years 1925–1940

Post Number	Location	Number of Members (May 1, 1940)
1.	Milwaukee, WI	46
2.	Chicago, IL	47
3.	Newark, NJ	27
4.	Jersey City, NJ	36
5.	Detroit, MI	Deleted
6.	Bayonne, NJ	56
7.	Erie, PA	34
8.	Passaic, NJ	36
9.	Yonkers, NY	44
10.	Braddock, PA	Deleted
11.	Buffalo, NY	25
12.	Monessen, PA	27
13.	Niagara Falls, NY	Deleted
14.	Chicago, IL	190
15.	Cicero, IL	57
16.	Cleveland, OH	38
17.	Detroit, MI	Deleted
18.	Scranton, PA	23
19.	Pittsburgh, PA	15
20.	Chicago, IL	38
21.	Chicago, IL	40
22.	Philadelphia, PA	78
23.	Bridgeport, CT	46
24.	Schenectady, NY	132
25.	Natrona, PA	21
26.	Grand Rapids, MI	54
27.	Wilmerding, PA	30
28.	South Brooklyn, NY	Deleted
29.	Brooklyn, NY	26
30.	South Milwaukee, WI	Deleted
31.	Hamtramck, MI	82
32.	Southington, CT	22
33.	Chicago, IL	10
34.	Pittsburgh, PA	63

35.	Chicago, IL	46
36.	Chicago, IL	16
37.	McKeesport, PA	11
38.	Toronto, ONT	Deleted
39.	New York, NY	30
40.	New Britain, CT	48
41.	Chicago, IL	35
42.	Weirton, WV	22
43.	Utica, NY	75
44.	Cohoes, NY	Deleted
45.	Milwaukee, WI	23
46.	Toledo, OH	47
47.	Meriden, CT	28
48.	Terryville, CT	30
49.	Chicago, IL	70
50.	Scranton, PA	29
51.	South Bend, IN	50
52.	Watervliet, NY	Deleted
53.	Elizabeth, NJ	Deleted
54.	Omaha, NE	25
55.	St. Louis, MO	28
56.	Jackson, MI	73
57.	Baltimore, MD	45
58.	New Haven, CT	36
59.	Ambridge, PA	39
60.	Amsterdam, NY	70
61.	Johnstown, PA	31
62.	Hartford, CT	54
63.	Stamford, CT	Deleted
64.	New Kensington, PA	25
65.	Elizabeth, NJ	23
66.	Syracuse, NY	36
67.	Boston, MA	25
68.	Camden, NJ	37
69.	Union City, CT	40
70.	Chester, PA	33
71.	Buffalo, NY	Deleted
72.	Torrington, CT	46
73.	Norwich, CT	24
74.	Rochester, NY	24

75.	Toronto, ONT, Canada	Deleted
76.	Windsor, ONT, Canada	Deleted
77.	Brooklyn, NY	36
78.	Ozone Park, NY	30
79.	Wyandotte, MI	39
80.	Youngstown, OH	15
81.	Wallingford, CT	14
82.	Maspeth, NY	22
83.	Gary, IN	66
84.	Jermyn, PA	Deleted
85.	Chicago, IL	19
86.	Chicago, IL	9
87.	Lowell, MA	13
88.	Kansas City, KS	14
89.	East Chicago, IN	64
90.	Chicago, IL	31
91.	Bristol, CT	20
92.	New London, CT	45
93.	Trenton, NJ	63
94.	Reading, PA	63
95.	Cleveland, OH	35
96.	Racine, WI	23
97.	Williston Park, NY	Deleted
98.	Turners Falls, MA	13
99.	Wilmington, DE	17
100.	Flint, MI	46
101.	Southampton, NY	56
102.	Worcester, MA	20
103.	Wallington, NJ	20
104.	New Castle, PA	Deleted
105.	Easthampton, MA	22
106.	Oil City, PA	Deleted
107.	Binghamton, NY	15
108.	Adams, MA	27
109.	Detroit, MI	96
110.	Shenandoah, PA	24
111.	Detroit, MI	230
112.	Wilkes-Barre, PA	14
114.	Northampton, MA	10
115.	Paterson, NJ	58

116.	Calumet City, IL	45
117.	Toledo, OH	30
118.	West Lynn, MA	9
119.	Manchester, NH	22
120.	Dickson City, PA	17
121.	Saginaw, MI	26
122.	Scranton, PA	13
123.	Bay City, MI	9
124.	Minneapolis, MN	25
125.	Harrison, NJ	23
126.	Derby, ONT	30
127.	Hamilton, ONT, Canada	22
128.	North Tonawanda, NY	14
129.	Dupont, PA	10
130.	Wilkes-Barre, PA	12
131.	Kitchener, ONT, Canada	14
132.	Chicopee, MA	21
133.	Thompsonville, CT	13

Source: Report of the Officers of the PAVA and A.C. National Executive Boards for the 9th General Assembly of the Polish Army Veterans Association of America in the City of New Britain, CT, for the period from 1940 to 1946, pp. 16-17

Addendum 9

PAVA Auxiliary Corps Governing Boards in the Years 1928–1940

1928–1931: Agnieszka Wisła (President), J. Rzewska (Secretary).

1931–1934: Zofia E. Kosobucka (National President), Wanda Hintz—Snarska (I Vice President), Maria Pietrusińska (II Vice President), Anna Perzanowska (II Vice President), A. Zapytowska (Secretary General), S. Gruchacz (Treasurer); Directors: Ludwika Wilczyńska, Leokadia Śmiecińska, Julia Pela, Ewa Kurzeja, Anna Mleczko, Maria Brzozowska, Bronisława Brudzińska, Maria Dombska, Leokadia Raczyńska, Estera Przygócka, Zofia Mabillot.

1934–1937: Izabela Machalska (National President), Zofia Mabillot (Vice President), Stanisława Gruchacz (Secretary General); Directors: Lucyna Wilk, H. Piotrowska.

1937–1940: Agnieszka Wisła (Honorary President), Izabela Michalska (National President), Teresa Rak (Vice President), S. Gruchacz (Secretary General); Directors: L. Wilk, M. Brzozowska.

Source: *The Veteran,* Jubilee Edition, June 1971, p. 88.

Addendum 10

A Register of Membership in the Friends of the Polish Army Veterans Alliance Circles at PAVA Posts (May 1940)

Post Number	Location	Number of Members in the Circle of Friends
Nr. 7	Detroit, MI	23
Nr. 12	Philadelphia, PA	43
Nr. 15	Gary, IN	3
Nr. 16	Pittsburgh, PA	3
Nr. 21	New York, NY	15
Nr. 24	Bridgeport, CT	70
Nr. 27	Rochester, NY	40
Nr. 44	Freeland, PA	3
Nr. 74	Toledo, OH	40
Nr. 89	Jackson, MI	20
Nr. 97	Grand Rapids, MI	45
Nr. 112	Baltimore, MD	24
Nr. 119	Hartford, CT	27
Nr. 121	Camden, NJ	12
Nr. 125	South Bend, IN	36
Nr. 144	Kansas City, KS	16
Nr. 149	Racine, WI	20
Nr. 154	Patterson, NJ	5
Nr. 156	Bristol, CT	12
Nr. 159	Northampton, MA	7
Total:		484

Source: PAVA NEB Archives, sign. A-II/9, p. 20. Report of the Officers of the PAVA and A.C. National Executive Boards for the 8th PAVA General Assembly in the City of Philadelphia, PA, for the period 1937–1940.

Addendum 11

Excerpts from the PAVA "Uniform Regulation" of 1934

"Color of the uniform – Light Blue (Fr. Army)
Cut—officer's style—collar open at the shirt, long pants, four-cornered hat with black visor and trim, shoes (black if possible). Seam—external on the pants, with green edging.

Insignia—of service rank—the same as pertained during active duty.

Decorations and medals [what follows is a detailed description of the order in which they should be worn—T. L.]

...Officers' belts with diagonal belt, only staff sergeants (former adjutants) and officers have the right to wear them.

No other additions are allowed to be worn, such as: braided rope, whistles, stirrups.

Insignia for Officials

Officials (of Posts, Districts and the National Executive Board) wear the initials of their office on the right shoulder, outside, in the center between the elbow and the shoulder.

On pieces of cloth in the form of a shield 2" x 4", initials of the office, the number of the Post {District – star(s)} and the emblem (National Executive Board) embroidered in silver thread.

Color of Cloth Shield

National Executive Board—amaranth
District Board—green
Post Board—dark blue

Stars

National Executive Board—3
District Board—2
Post Board—1

Initials

(In English)

National Executive Board

National Commander—N.C.
1st Vice Commander—V.C. I
2nd Vice Commander—V.C. II
Adjutant General—A.G.
Purse Officer (Treasurer)—P.G.
Directors—G.S.
Chief Medical Officer—M.O.

District Board

Commander—D.C.
1st Vice Commander—D.V.C. I
2nd Vice Commander—D.V.C. II
Adjutant—D.A.
Purse Officer (Treasurer)—D.P.

Post Board

Commander—P.C.
1st Vice Commander—P.V.C. I
2nd Vice Commander—P.V.C. II
Adjutan—P.A.
Purse Officer (Treasurer)—P.P. ..."

Source: By-Laws and Regulations of the Polish Army Veterans Association of America New York 1934, pp. 44-46

Addendum 12

Financial Aid of the Polish Roman Catholic Union of America for Polish Army Veterans 1921–1937

Year	Purpose of Aid	Amount
1921	for aid to Polish Army Veterans	$ 3,564.15
1922	for the PAVA Settlement and Invalid fund	$ 3,161.25
1923	for PAVA on behalf of war invalids; to hand of	$ 1,000.00
	Gen. Haller for the War Invalid Home in Poland	$ 500.00
1927	for Polish Army veterans;	$ 500.00
	aid for Gen. J. Haller	$ 50.00
1929	aid for Gen. J. Haller	$ 500.00
1930	for the PAVA Invalid Fund	$ 2,500.00
1932	for the funeral of an indigent Hallerian	$ 25.00
1933	for the PAVA Invalid Fund	$ 1,304.00
1936	for the PAVA District I Veteran Home	$ 101.00
1937	for the PAVA Invalid Fund	$ 1,000.00
	Total	**$14,205.75**

Source: M. Haiman, *The Polish Roman Catholic Union of America 1973–1948* Chicago 1948, pp. 556-560

Addendum 13

Military Settlers—Volunteers from America on the Eastern Borderlands in 1932

Last Name, First Name	Name of Military Settlement
1. Biernacki, Józef	Hallerowo
2. Bojko, Julian	Hallerowo
3. Chmiel, Stanisław	Hallerowo
4. Dobrzeński,	Hallerowo
5. Kargol, Wojciech	Hallerowo
6. Kłusek, Franciszek	Hallerowo
7. Marszewski,	Hallerowo
8. Palewski,	Hallerowo
9. Rybakowski, Stanisław	Hallerowo
10. Rzewuski, Lucjan	Hallerowo
11. Świrski, Aleksander	Hallerowo
12. Taborek, Jan	Hallerowo
13. Wiśniewski, Andrzej	Hallerowo
14. Wojewódzki,	Hallerowo
15. Dąbrowski,	Basowy Kąt
16. Sosień, Stanisław	Basowy Kąt
17. Lentas, Stanisław	Horbów
18. Żebrowski, Stefan	Jazłowce
19. Rasnowski, Stanisław	Konstantynów
20. Zawadzki, Stanisław	Podzamcze
21. Hodorek, Piotr	SRtyrczeerlcske ie
22. Podhorski,	Szubków
23. Grajewski,	Zdołbica
24. Kuraszkiewicz,	Zdołbica
25. Pułaski, Stanisław	Zdołbica
26. Szepański, Wacław	Zdołbica
27. Wojciechowski, Piotr	Zdołbica
28. Nowaczyński, Janusz	Żytyń Wielki

Source: PAVA NEB Archives, sign. A-XV/1.

Addendum 14

Address of Prime Minister Wincenty Witos to the Polish Emigration in America, September 22, 1923

To the Polish Emigration!

Poland has always thought of you as close family. Your work and generosity for the homeland, your remembrance of those you left behind there, supported in us the hope, during the long night of slavery and oppression, that when the hour to fight for Poland's freedom strikes, you will hurry to the aid of the White Eagle and the ranks of those fighting under the slogan of independence. The reality was greater than our expectations. Living in a great nation, which developed, on that side of the ocean, before an astonished world, the resources of its indomitable energy, honest work and magnificent independence, with your eyes fixed on one hand on the great figures of Washington and Lincoln, on the other hand on Kościuszko and Pułaski, you were generous, offering your blood and possessions when the great war shook the old powers of Europe and when the magnificent President Wilson made his memorable proclamations. They were harbingers of Poland's rebirth and threw onto the scales of war the might of the United States of America, which then tipped to the side of justice and saved the liberty of nations.

Your enthusiasm was instrumental to a high degree in the formation of a Polish army, which stood alongside the great coalition, and simultaneously your hearts and generosity helped tormented and starving Poland to endure the long years of enormous bloody strife and to protect from imminent annihilation the multitude of Polish children, who are the hope and future of our nation. In a great historical moment you attained to an achievement which your hearts, your conscience and your feelings for humanity demanded.

It is five years since the end of the World War. In that time Poland has strengthened, developed, firmed itself up in its borders and progressed in its internal organization. Its fields, empty in time of war, have covered over with new, fertile seed; the industrious chimneys of our factories are steaming again; our children are acquiring knowledge and truth in their own schools; the entire national life of Poland is pulsing with life and strength.

On this fifth anniversary of the conclusion of the great war you are celebrating, together with all the citizens of the United States, the lofty holiday in honor of the disciplined and brave soldier. One of those who led you in the fight for freedom and independence—General Józef Haller—is coming to you for that holiday. He is bringing you the heartfelt greetings of the Old Country; he will submit together with you to remembrance of the great events in which you participated, and he will explain to you many happenings that it is not always possible to comprehend and judge correctly from afar.

On this day of your civic and martial holiday the Polish nation wants to thank you once again from the bottom of its heart, and at the same time to express the certainty that you will not forget about your native land. You will find the reward for your remembrance and for having rendered your support in the conviction that Poland is trying with all its might to be worthy of the great gift that Providence has bestowed on it, in returning its freedom.

Be sure that the ideals of your native country are in full harmony with the ideals of the magnificent American society. Those ideas, bequeathed to us by our national bards and the heroes in the wars for freedom, declare that the fulfillment of his duty is the prime virtue of every citizen, the common good is his constant concern, the sovereignty and independence of the nation his greatest happiness, and the welfare of humanity his ultimate goal.

Long live the United States of America! Long live Poland!

Chairman of the Council of Ministers
Wincenty Witos

Source: PAVA NEB, sign. A-VIP/2

Addendum 15

Greetings of the President of the Polish Republic Ignacy Mościcki for PAVA

To the Polish Army Veterans Association of America

I send cordial greetings in the name of your distant homeland to the Polish servicemen affiliated with the Polish Army Veterans Association of America.

The Polish Army has always been a paragon of virtue and sacrifice, educating whole generations of brave citizens, who whether serving in the Army or working in some other profession, always were a credit to their country.

It was from its ranks that almost all the national heroes emerged: the names of Commander-in-Chief Kościuszko, Prince Józef Poniatowski, and the victorious commander of Poland reborn, Marshal Józef Piłsudski, will always shine amid future generations as symbols of the steadfast heroism and sacrifice of the great ideal of the Motherland.

Taking example from their luminous figures, you, former Polish soldiers, scattered across the vastness of distant America, do not ever forget about your meritorious service in the ranks of distant America, do not ever forget about your distinguished service in the ranks of your native land, about your distant country – with hope for a better tomorrow work steadfastly, multiplying your prosperity and deserving of the name of good citizens of the United States – your second Fatherland!

President of the Polish Republic
Ignacy Mościcki
Warszawa – The Royal Castle, March 30, 1928

Source: PAVA NEB Archives, sign. A-VIP/5

Bibliography

I. Archival Sources

Archives in Poland

New Records Archives in Warszawa:
- Files of Gen. Józef Haller;
- Archives of Ignacy Jana Paderewski;
- Polish Embassy in Washington;
- Polish Consulate General in New York;
- World Association of Poles from Abroad;
- Document Collection of the Federation of Polish Associations of Defenders of the Fatherland.

Mechanical Documentation Archives in Warszawa:
- Polish Army Veterans Association of America;
- Union of Hallerians.

The Library of the National Ossoliński Foundation in Wrocław, Manuscript Collection:
- Kazimierz Oldziejewski;
- Wacław Gąsiorowski.

Central Military Archives in Rembertów:
- Chief Armed Forces Inspectorate.

Archives in the United States of North America

Archives of the Polish Army Veterans Association of America, New York:
- Records of the Ladies' Auxiliary Corps;
- Personal files;
- Demobilization and repatriation of the Hallerians
- Polish clergy in the United States and Poland;
- PAVA finances;

- Gen. Józef Haller;
- PAVA Membership Rolls;
- Contacts with American authorities;
- Contacts with the Polish Armed Forces;
- Kuligi—PAVA farm business in Poland;
- Commemorations and Ceremonies;
- Decorations;
- PAVA Districts. 1921–1940
- Circulars, directives, proclamations of the PAVA NEB. 1921–1940;
- Polish community organizations in the United States, Canada and Cuba;
- Veteran and charitable organizations in the United States and Canada; Veteran organizations in Poland 1922–1939;
- Special Personal Files;
- PAVA Posts. Correspondence 1922–1939;
- PAVA Posts. Special materials;
- Polish diplomatic posts in the United States and Canada;
- PAVA National Executive Board meetings;
- Studies on the history of the Polish Army in France;
- Veterans' mutual aid;
- Special file: VIP 1923–1999;
- PAVA participation in the military settlements in Poland;
- PAVA offices;
- PAVA General Assemblies;
- *The Veteran*—the press organ of the PAVA National Executive Board;
- PAVA tours to Poland;
- PAVA Post Boards. 1922–1938;
- PAVA National Executive Board. General Correspondence 1921–1940.

Central Polonia Archive at Orchard Lake, MI
- Artur L. Waldo Archive
- PAVA District VI Archive
- Collection of PAVA Post 113 in Hamtramck, MI;
- Włodzimierz Żmurkiewicz Collection.

Hoover Institution, Stanford, CA:
- Izydor Modelski Papers.

Piłsudski Institute of America:
- Personnel Archive: Aleksander Dubiński.

II. Printed Sources

Czyn zbrojny wychodźstwa polskiego w Ameryce. Zbiór dokumentów i materiałów historycznych, New York–Chicago 1957.

"Dziennik Ustaw RP" nr 59, Warszawa 1937.

"Jednodniówka na Zjazd Byłych Oficerów i Pracowników Rekrutacyjnych," Cleveland, OH, 19-20 February 1938.

"Jednodniówka Weteranów Armii Polskiej," Chicago, May 1920.

"Jednodniówka wydana nakładem Kolonii Hallerczyków im. Józefa Piłsudskiego w Detroit," MI, 19 III 1922.

75 Jubileusz Placówki 40-tej SWAP, Hammond, IN 1996.

Konstytucja i Regulaminy Stowarzyszenia Weteranów Armii Polskiej w Ameryce, 1925.

Konstytucja i Regulaminy Stowarzyszenia Weteranów Armii Polskiej w Ameryce, 1934.

Pamiętnik Gniazda 79-go S.P. w Ameryce i Legionu Weteranów Armii Polskiej z okazji odsłonięcia tablicy pamiątkowej dla uczczenia poległych członków Gniazda 79-go, 12 maja 1935 w Detroit, MI.

Pamiętnik Placówki Nr 7 SWAP, Detroit 1925.

Pamiętnik Placówki Nr 39 w Passaic, wydany z okazji Zjazdu II Okręgu SWAP i Korpusów Pomocniczych w dniach 2-31 X 1939, Passaic 1939.

Pamiętnik 55 Zjazdu Okręgu VI SWAP, Detroit, MI, 1-2 IX 1984.

Pamiętnik IX Walnego Zjazdu SWAP w New Britain, 30-31 May 1-2 June 1946.

Pamiętnik XII Walnego Zjazdu SWAP. 28-30 maja 1955, Chicago 1955.

Pamiętnik VIII Walnego Zjazdu SWAP i KP, 30 V-2 VI 1940, Philadelphia.

Pamiętnik XI Walnego Zjazdu SWAP w Utica, 30,31 May -1 June 1952.

Pamiętnik Walnego Zjazdu SWAP, 28-30 V 1955 r., Chicago 1955.

Pamiętnik Zjazdu Dwudziestego i Zlotu Szesnastego Sokolstwa Polskiego w Ameryce w dniach 7-12 July 1933 r., Chicago 1933.

Placówka Macierzysta Nr 5 SWAP w Ameryce. 70-lecie, 1920-1990, Chicago 1990 (okolicznościowy pamiętnik).

Address of the President of the United States to the Senate, 22 January 1917, 64 Congress, 2 Session. Document Nr 685. Washington D.C. Congressional Records, 1917.

Regulamin Korpusu Pomocniczego Stowarzyszenia Weteranów Armii Polskiej w Ameryce, 1925.

Sprawozdanie z kampanii prowadzonej przez Stowarzyszenie Weteranów Armii Polskiej w Ameryce za zebraniem funduszu na osadnictwo na Kresach wschodnich i na zabezpieczenie bytu inwalidom, Cleveland 1922.

Szczegółowy wykaz ofiar zebranych przez Wydział Narodowy Polski oraz Sprawozdanie z Kampanii prowadzonej przez Stowarzyszenie Weteranów Armii Polskiej w Ameryce za zebraniem funduszu na osadnictwo na Kresach wschodnich i na zabezpieczenie bytu inwalidom, *Cleveland 1922.*

Sprawozdanie finansowe Skarbnika Wydziału Narodowego Polskiego za czas od 1-go grudnia 1919 do 31-go grudnia 1920, Chicago 1921.

Sprawozdanie urzędnikow Zarządu SWAP i K.P. na 7-my Walny Zjazd SWAP w mieście Rochester, NY, za czas 1934 r. do 1937 r.

Sprawozdanie urzędników Zarządu S.W.A.P. i K.P. na 8-my Walny Zjazd Stowarzyszenia Weteranów Armii Polskiej w mieście Philadelphia, PA, za czas od 1937 r. do 1940 r.

Sprawozdanie urzędników Zarządu SWAP i K.P. na IX Walny Zjazd SWAP w mieście New Britain, CT, za czas od 1940 r. do 1946 r.

75 lat Placówki nr 111, New Britain, CT, 1995, s. 7 (okolicznościowy pamiętnik).

60-ta rocznica istnienia Stow. Weteranów Armii Polskiej. Placówka Nr 105, (okolicznościowy pamiętnik), Utica 1971.

XIX Walny Zjazd SWAP w Ameryce. 29-31 V 1976, Buffalo (okolicznościowy pamiętnik).

III. Memoirs and Reminiscences

Ameryka w pamiętnikach Polaków. Antologia, wybór i komentarze Bogdan Grzeloński, Warszawa 1975.

Amerykański dziennik mjra Horodyńskiego, oprac. Jerzy Lerski, Paryż 1955.

Juźwikiewicz Julian, *Polacy w Ameryce, czyli pamiętnik 15-to miesięcznego pobytu*, Paryż 1836, [w:] M. Haiman, *Ślady polskie w Ameryce*, Chicago 1938.

Haller Józef, *Pamiętniki*, Londyn 1964.

Oldziejewski Kazimierz, *Samotne wzloty i upadki. Wspomnienia podlasianina*, maszynopis w zbiorach rękopisów Ossolineum we Wrocławiu.

Trawiński Witold, *Odyseja Polskiej Armii Błękitnej*, Wrocław 1989.

IV. Press

"Blekitny Weteran," Warszawa;
"Dziennik Chicagowski," Chicago, IL;
"Dziennik Dla Wszystkich," Buffalo, NY;
"Dziennik Związkowy," Chicago, IL;
"Hallerczyk," Bydgoszcz;
"Ilustrowany Kurjer Codzienny," Kraków;
"Kurier Narodowy," New York, NY;
"Nowy Świat," New York, NY;
"Nowy Dziennik-Przegląd Polski," New York, NY;
"Naród Polski," Chicago, IL;
"Polacy Zagranicą," Warszawa;
"Polska Zbrojna," Warszawa;
"Rekord Codzienny," Detroit, MI;
"Straż nad Wisłą," Dowództwo Frontu Pomorskiego, Bydgoszcz-Toruń;

"Weteran," Cleveland, OH, Chicago, IL, Detroit, MI, New York, NY;
"Żołnierz Legionów i P.O.W.," Warszawa.

V. Studies

Bogucki, Andrzej, *Towarzystwo Gimnastyczne "Sokół" na Pomorzu 1893-1939*, Bydgoszcz 1997.

Bójnowski, Lucjan, *Historia parafii polskich w diecezji hartwordskiej w stanie Connecticut*, New Britain, CT, 1939.

Brożek, Andrzej, *Polonia amerykańska 1854-1939*, Warszawa 1977.

Choromański, Zbigniew, *Działalność duchowieństwa w Stowarzyszeniu Weteranów Armii Polskiej w Ameryce w latach 1921-1939*; Praca magisterska pisana pod kierunkiem ks. prof. dr. Zygmunta Zielińskiego na Wydziale Teologicznym KUL, Lublin 1988.

Drozdowski, Marian M., *Z dziejów stosunków polsko-amerykańskich, 1776-1944*, Warszawa 1982.

Grzeloński, Bogdan, Rusinowa Izabella, *Polacy w wojnach amerykańskich 1775-1783, 1861-1865*, Warszawa 1973.

Grzeloński, Bogdan, *Ameryka w pamiętnikach Polaków. Antologia*, Warszawa 1975.

Grzeloński, Bogdan, *Polacy w Stanach Zjednoczonych Ameryki 1776-1865*, Warszawa 1976.

Grzeloński, Bogdan, *Do New Yorku, Chicago i San Francisco. Szkice do biografii polsko-amerykańskich*, Warszawa 1983.

Dunlop, William, *Recollections of the American War 1812-1814*, Toronto 1906.

Dyboski, Roman., *Stany Zjednoczone Ameryki Północnej. Wrażenia i refleksje*, Lwów-Warszawa 1930.

Haiman, Mieczysław, *Polacy w walce o niepodległość Ameryki. Szkice historyczne* Chicago 1931.

Haiman, Mieczysław, *Z przeszłości polskiej w Ameryce*, Buffalo, New York 1927.

Haiman, Mieczysław, *Historia udziału Polaków w amerykańskiej wojnie domowej*, Chicago 1928.

Haiman, Mieczysław, *Ślady polskie w Ameryce*, Chicago 1938.

Haiman, Mieczysław, *Polish past in America 1608-1865*, Chicago 1939.

Haiman, Mieczysław, *Zjednoczenie Polskie Rzymsko-Katolickie w Ameryce. 1873-1948*, Chicago, Illinois 1948.

Hapak, Joseph T., *Recruiting a Polish Army in the United States 1917-1919*, Diss. University of Kansas 1985.

Jabłonowski, Marek, *Polityczne aspekty ruchu byłych wojskowych w Polsce 1918-1939*, Warszawa 1989.

Kos-Rabcewicz-Zubkowski, Ludwik; Greesing, William Edward, *Sir Casimir Gzowski*, Toronto 1959.

Kos-Rabcewicz-Zubkowski, Ludwik; Greesing William Edward, *Sir Gzowski*, przełożył Józef Radzicki, Warszawa 1984.

Kruszka, Wacław, *Historia polska w Ameryce*, t. I, Milwaukee, WI; t. II, Pittsburgh, PA, 1978.

Krzywobłocka, Bożena, *Chadecja 1919-1937*, Warszawa 1974.

Lerski, Jerzy Jan, *A Polish Chapter in Jacksonian America. The United States and the Polish Exiles of 1831*, Madison, WI, 1958.

Ławroński, Andrzej, *Polacy w dziejach Stanów Zjednoczonych*, Warszawa 1977.

Mazurkiewicz, R., *Polskie wychodźstwo i osadnictwo w Kanadzie*, Warszawa 1928.

Michałowski, Witold, *Najemnicy wolności*, Białystok 1991.

Murzynowska, Krystyna, *Henryk Korwin-Kałussowski (1806-1894)*, [w:] "Problemy Polonii Zagranicznej," vol. IV, Warszawa 1964-1965.

Opowieści historyczne, Lwów 1894.

Pachoński, Jan, *Polacy na Antylach i Morzu Karaibskim*, Kraków 1979.

Parafianowicz Halina, *Polska w europejskiej polityce Stanów Zjednoczonych w okresie prezydentury Herberta C. Hoovera, 1928-1933*, Białystok 1991.

Piątkowska Danuta, *Duchowieństwo polskie w Stanach Zjednoczonych Ameryki wobec rekrutacji ochotników do Armii Polskiej we Francji 1917-1919*, [w:] *"Niepodległość. Z historii polskiej myśli społecznej i politycznej,"* Opole 1999.

Pienkos, Donald E., *PNA: a Centennial History of the Polish National Alliance of the United States of North America*, New York, 1984.

Pienkos, Donald E., *One Hundred Years Young: a History of the Polish Falcons of America 1887-1987*, New York 1987.

Pilch, Andrzej, *Emigracja z ziem polskich do Stanów Zjednoczonych od lat pięćdziesiątych XIX w. do r. 1918*, [w:] *Polonia amerykańska. Przeszłość i współczesność*, Wrocław-Warszawa-Kraków-Gdańsk-Łódź 1988.

Pliszka, Stanley R., *The Polish-American Army 1917-1921*, [in:] *"The Polish Review."*

A Quarterly published by the Polish Institute of Arts and Sciences in America, New York, vol. X, No. 3/1965.

Podhorski Bronisław, *Osady wojskowe na terenie Szubkowa na Wołyniu oraz przyległe cywilne*, Warszawa 1931.

Polski Słownik Biograficzny, Kraków-Warszawa-Wrocław 1964-1965.

Rocznik Towarzystwa Historyczno-Literackiego w Paryżu, Paryż, 1867.

Sierociński, Józef, *Armia Polska we Francji*, Warszawa 1929.

Stasik, Florian, *Polska emigracja polityczna w Stanach Zjednoczonych Ameryki 1831-1864*, Warszawa 1973.

Stasik, Florian, *Przyczynek do dziejów polskiej emigracji politycznej w Stanach*

Zjednoczonych A.P. po powstaniu listopadowym (1831-1836), [w:] "Problemy Polonii Zagranicznej,"vol. V, Warszawa 1966-1964

Stobniak-Smogorzewska, J., *Osada Krechowiecka*, [w:] "Zeszyty Historyczne" (Instytut Literacki), Paryż 1981, z. 57.

Storozynski, Alex, *The Peasant Prince: Thaddeus Kosciuszko and the Age of Revolution*, New York: 2009

Szygowski, Juliusz, *Powstanie polskie w r. 1863 i Stany Zjednoczone*, Paryż 1962 Turek, Victor, *Sir Casimir S. Gzowski. A bigraphical Sketch*, Toronto 1957.

Valasek, Paul S. *Haller's Polish Army in France.[np] 2006*

Wahtl, Karol, *Polonia w Ameryce*, Philadelphia 1944.

Wałaszek, Adam, *Reemigracja ze Stanów Zjednoczonych do Polski po I wojnie światowej 1919-1924*, [in:] "Zeszyty naukowe UJ, Prace polonijne," z. 7, Warszawa-Kraków 1983

Waldo, Artur L., *Sokolstwo. Przednia straż narodu*, vol. I, Pittsburgh 1956, vol. III, Pittsburgh 1972, vol. IV, Pittsburgh 1974, vol. V, Pittsburgh 1984.

Waldo, Artur L., *Czyn zbrojny Polonii Stanów Zjednoczonych w nowelkach, gawędach i opowiadaniach wojskowych*, Chicago 1938.

Wandycz, S. Piotr, *The United States and Poland*, Harvard University Press Cambridge, Massachusetts-London 1980.

Wesołowski Zdzisław, *Polish Orders, Medals, Badges and Insignia Military and Civilian Decorations 1705-1985*, Miami 1986.

Wedrowski, Jacek Ryszard, *Stany Zjednoczone o odrodzenie Polski: polityka Stanów Zjednoczonych wobec sprawy polskiej i Polski w latach 1916-1919*, Wrocław 1980.

Wielecki, Henryk, *Pod znakiem srebrnego i złotego orła. Polsko-amerykańskie tradycje wojskowe od XVIII do XX wieku*, Warszawa 1998.

Wołodkowicz, Andrzej, *Polish Contribution to Art and Sciences in Canada*, Montreal 1969.

Winid, Bogusław, *W cieniu Kapitolu: dyplomacja polska wobec Stanów Zjednoczonych Ameryki 1919-1939*, Warszawa 1991.

Wójcik, Jan; Kierkło, Mieczysław, *Z dziejów żołnierza-emigranta. Historia "Haller Post" w New Britain*, New Britain, CT, 1991.

INDEX

Note: Page numbers in bold indicate illustrations.

A

Abłamowicz, Anna M., 32
Abłamowicz, Dominik, 395
abolition. *See* slavery
About Józef Haller, 216
Abramajtis, 78
"Actor's Studio," 213
Adamczak, Lucjan
    certificate for his Virtuti Militari medal, **110**
    editor of *The Veteran,* 208
    Haller's tour of the U.S., 271
    PAVA districts, planning and visits, 138–139, 142
    PAVA founding convention, 129
    PAVA officer and board member, 130, 400
    petitioned Polish authorities for pension, 328ff
    Polish officers' school in Canada, 80
    Settlement and Invalid Fund, 143, 172–173, 245, 289–290
Agency of the Polish Army Veterans Association of America. *See under* Polish Army Veterans Association (PAVA)
agribusiness, 289–293

Albrycht, Wojciech
    Assoc. of Veterans of the Former Polish Army in France, 358–360
    Book of the Infantry's Glory, 346
    cadet school in Pennsylvania, 80
    and the Circle of Volunteers, 342, 345
    convention of former volunteers from America, 340
    Falcon's Legion of Honor recipient, 338
    Federation of Polish Assoc. of Defenders of the Fatherland, 363–364
    historical narrative for book, 217
    import duty on *The Veteran,* 343
    Museum of the War Effort of Poles from America, 341
    officers' school in Canada, 80
    Poland's foreign policy, 320
    Polish government help for invalids in U.S., 182
    on the split between PAVA and the Union of Hallerians, 353–354
    teacher of physical education and military preparedness, 338
    volunteer soldiers returning to U.S., 324
    volunteers who remained in Poland, 336–339

Alliance of American Army Veterans of
  Polish Descent, 220, 267–269
Alliance of Friends of Polish Army
  Veterans (AFPAV), 157–158, 167, 177
Alliance of Poles Abroad, 253
Alliance of Poles in America (APA),
  261–262
Alliance of Poles in Canada, 262
Alliance of Polish Youth, 76
American Army
  mobilization of Poles, 81–82
  Poles join due to poverty, 19
  returning soldiers invited to join, 117
American Civil War
  Confederate soldiers, 45–47
  and the January Uprising in Poland,
    48–50
  Union soldiers, 39–45
American Legion, 270–273, 319
American Polonia Square, 334, 336, 346
American Red Cross, 94, 116–117, 195–196
American Relief Administration, 94
American Relief for Poland, 253
American Revolutionary War, 3–4, 369
Americanization, 30, 296, 372
amnesty for insurrectionists, 10–11
Anders, Władysław, 329
anti-German bias, 323
anti-Polish propaganda. *See* propaganda,
  anti-Polish
"Antigone" (ship), 115–116
Anuszkiewicz, Benjamin, 269, 270
"The Aquila," **61**
Archacki, Henry, 209
archives, 57, 259–260
artists, 31
Artwiński, Stanisław, 51
Ascher, Elizabeth, **106,** 204–205
assimilation, 30, 296, 372
Association of Combatants in France, 349
Association of Dovborites, 350
Association of Great Poland Fighters
  and Insurrectionists, 349–350

Association of Hallerians, 165
Association of Invalids, 349
Association of Kaniovites, 349
Association of Legionnaires, 348, 349
Association of Officers of the Reserve
  of the Polish Republic, 350
Association of Polish Army Veterans
  in France, 342
Association of Polish Defenders of the
  Fatherland of Canada, 283–284
Association of Reserve Officers, 349
Association of Societies of Insurrectionists
  and Fighters of the VII Corps District,
  350
Association of the Defenders of Lwów,
  350
Association of Veterans of Gen. Haller's
  Polish Armies, 121
Association of Veterans of the Former
  Polish Army in France (AVFPA),
  345–346, 354–360
Association of Volunteers and
  Independents from America, 342
Association of War Invalids of the
  Polish Republic (AWIPR), 350,
  364, 365
Augustyn, H., 403
Augustynowicz, Stefan, 19
Austrian government, 10–11
Auxiliary Corps of the Polish Army
  Veterans Association
  aid to abandoned veterans, 173–174
  described, 153–156
  emblem, insignia and uniform, 166
  established, 133
  General Assemblies, 135
  governing boards, 419
  helped abandoned former soldiers,
    173–174
  posts, 155–156, 414, 415–418
  predecessors, 170
  shelter in Chicago, 191, 192–195
award for Polish science, 59

B

Baca, M., 140
Bogacki, 26
Bagiński, Wacław, 404
Bakanowski, Adolf, 53–54, 54
Bałdyga, Kazimierz
    Assoc. of Veterans of the Former Polish Army in France, 355
    Convention of Polish Legionnaires in Wilno, 366
    editor of *The Veteran*, 207, 209
    memorial mound in Savannah for Gen. Pułaski, 256
    150th anniversary of Gen. Pułaski's death, 224, 302
    PAVA National Executive Board member, 400
    Piłsudski meeting, 329
    Polish Catholic Organizations Clearinghouse in America, 259
    political principals guiding PAVA, 311
    portrait of, **379**
    presentation of the new regimental flag to PAVA, 332
    Special Convention in Poznań, 352
Baliński, S., 150, 400
Banasiak, Emil P., 258
Bańczakiewicz, Ludwik, 11–14, 27, 395
Bank Pekao, 287
Bank Polski, 296
Bar Confederacy, 3–4
Baranowski, 78
Barszcz, Stefan, 395
Barszczewski, Henryk, 395
Bartkowski, Aleksander, 395
Bartmański, Jan, 93, **98**
Barzynski, J.C., 270
Barzyński, Wincenty, 53, 55–56, **69**
Baskiewicz, Captain, 338
Basowski, M., 266
Batowski, Michał, 395
Battle of Aldie, 44
Battle of Antietam, 40
Battle of Barnett's Ford, 43
Battle of Brandy Station, 43
Battle of Fredericksburg, 41
Beck, Józef, 323
Beczkowski, J., 366
Bednawski, Aleksander, 23–24
Bełżecki, Feliks, 395
Benda, Tadeusz, 164
Benich, Karol, 395
Beniowski, Maurycy, 3
Benit, Roman, 395
Berens, Karol, 395
Bernacki, Karol, 395
Bernstein, Herman, 279–280
Beter, Teofil, 395
Białkowski, Michał, 395
Białogłowski, Roman, 395
Biały, S., 142
Bielawski, Aleksander, 40
Bielawski, Kazmierz, 23–24
Bieliński, Aleksander, 395
Bienias, Jan, 395
Biernacki, Józef, 293, 424
Bilski, F., 140
Błędowski, Konstanty, 36, 39–40
Bloom, C., 275
Blue Army in France. *See* Polish Army in France
"Blue Ball," 351–352
Blue Cornflower Days, 181–182
"Blue Veterans," 354–360
Bobiński, L., 400
Bobrzecki, K., 266
Bochenek, 78
Boczkiewicz, Feliks, 395
Bodzenta-Chłapowski, K., 27
Bodzioch, Jan, 150
Bogacki, Dr., 78
Bogucka, H., 153
Bogucki, Witold
    PAVA District I President, 401
    shelters, 190

Silver Cross of Merit recipient, 305
Union of Polish Army Reserve
   Officers of America secretary, 266
Veterans' Commission member, 252
Bogusławski, Aleksander, 395
Bogusławski, F.J., 6
Bohuszewicz, Edward B., 32–35, **61**, 398
Bojko, Julian, 424
Bójnowski, Lucjan
   invalids, relief for, 178
   photo of last volunteers from
      New Britain, **102**
   Polish Veterans of the World War
      initiated, 121–122
   recognition of support for Polish
      veterans, 247
   recruitment of soldiers, 84, 242
   Woodrow Wilson, laid wreath at
      statue, 353
Bolesławski, Ryszard, 212–213, **389**
Bolles, Lemuel, 271, 272
Bolshevik army, 92–94, 122
Bonk, 140
Bono de Mara, Edward, 395
Book of the Infantry's Glory, 346
books and press readership, 17, 216–218.
   See also The Veteran
Borkowski, Wojciech, 395
Borzęcki, Władysław, 217
Borzek, Ksawery, 395
Boston settlement, 16
Bradowski, F., 141
Brotherhood of St. Stanislaus Kostka, 36
Brotherhood of the Holy Rosary, 36
Browiński, Mikołaj, 395
Brudzińska, Bronisława, 419
Brudziński, W., 266
Brykalski, K., 400, 404
Bryl, Kazimierz, 19
Brzeziński, Franc. Józef, 395
Brzozowska, Maria, 419
Bubacz, F., 158, 400
Bubacz, Stefan, 268

Buczyński, Bronisław, 149–150
Budyonny, Semyon, 92, 94
Budziak, Leon, 400, 404
Budzyński, 294
Buffalo, NY settlement, 14–15
Bujnowski, Dr., 330
Bułak-Bałachowicz, Stanisław, 366
Burant, Feliks, 158
Burdzicki, Andrzej, 19
Burke, Karol, 209, 217, 254
business owners in Poland, 338
Butkiewiczówna, Janina, 220
Bydgoszcz, PAVA Post Nr. 130, 287,
   336–347, 353–354, 357–358
Bystrzonowski, Ferdynand, 395

C

calendars, 170
California as it is, and as it may be; or a
   Guide to the Gold Region, 22
Cambridge, MA veterans, 125
Camp Dix, 116–117, **374**
Canada
   first hard-surface roads built
      by K. Gzowski, 28
   Poles fought British, 19
   Polish settlers, 8
Canadian Legion, 284
Canadian Legion of the British Empire
   Service League, 273–275
Canadian Society of Engineers, 29
Cannon, R., 198
Castellaz, Edward, 308
Catholic. *See* Polish National Catholic
   Church; Roman Catholic Church
celebrations, 73–74, 181–182, 221–229,
   274
cemeteries, 204–206
Central Military Settlers' Cooperative,
   292, 296
Central Polish Aid Committee, 75
Chaperone Committee, 158–159
chaplains, 53, 86–87, **109**, 242–244

Chicago, IL veterans, 121, 123–127, 191–192, 219–225
Chicago Daily, 56
Chicago Evening American, 267
Chicago World's Fair, 255
Chicopee, MA veterans, 123
Chłopicki, Ludwik, 13, 16, 395
Chłusewicz, Benedykt, 332–333, 333
Chlewski, 53
Chmiel, Stanisław, 293–294, 424
Chmielińska, N., 191
Chociszewski, Feliks, 342
Chodorowicz, Jan, 367
Chodźko, **102**
Chojnacki, Józef, 119, 209, 400
Chopin, Frederic, 33–34
Chramiec, A., 335
Chwałkowski, Lucjan
    first American casualty, 87
    gift of earth from his grave given to PAVA in New York, 358–359
    officers' school in Canada, 80
    portrait of, **106**
    remains transferred to America, 303
    street named in honor of, 334
Cichowski, 78
Cichowski, Franciszek, 295, 404
Cichowski, Józef, 400, 402
Cichowski, S., 400
Ciechanowski, Jan, 223
Ciechanowski, Józef, 395
Ciecierski, Wacław, 293
Cieplak, Jan, 244
Cieplikowie, Antoni i August, 126
Cieszewski, Stefan, 51, 59
Cikorski, 78
Cincinnati settlement, 16
Circle of Legionnaires of America, 341–342
Circle of Polish Army Volunteers of America, 333, 337–343, 342, 344–345
Circle of Volunteers from America in Bydgoszcz. *See* Bydgoszcz, PAVA Post Nr. 130

citizenship, 196–201
Civic Committee to Build a Shelter for the Polish Soldier, 191–192
Civil War. *See* American Civil War
Cleveland, OH veterans, 125–131, 209
Club of General Haller's Veterans, 122
College of St. Stanislaus Kostka, 55
Committee for the Maintenance of the Shelter, 193
Committee for the Restoration of the Invalid Home in Radzyń, 299
Committee of Polish Exiles, 14, 19
Committee to Help Veterans, 153
Committee to Honor the Immigration's War Effort, 251–252
Committee to Honor the Memory of General Włodzimierz Krzyżanowski, 269–270
communist infiltration, 277–285
Community Fund, 196
composers, 32–35
Confederates of Bar, 3–4
Congers Farm, 76
Congregation of the Resurrection, 53
Consolidated Congress, 269
Convention of Colleagues of the Circle of Polish Army Volunteers of America, 333, 339–340
Convention of Polish Legionnaires in Wilno, 366–367
Conversations for Facilitating the Study of the English Language, 17
Cook, Wander, 219
Cooper, James Fenimore, 27
Cooper, Merian C., 181, 213
Cooperative of Borderlands Settlers, 292
Coslik, T.R., 275
Council of Polish Democratic Clubs, 186
coup d'état of May 1926, 288, 310, 350
crime, 187–188
Cross of Independence, 335–336
Cross of Merit of the Polish Army from America, 164, 225, 258

Cross of Polish Soldiers from America, 166
Cross of Valor, 326–327
culture, 56, 158, 160, 220
Cwierdziński, Wiktor, 395
Ćwiertniak, Józef, 334
Ćwik, J., 140, 401
Cyman, Wawrzyniec, 123, 243
Czachla, Idzi, 337
Czachowski, 129
Czaja, S., 141
Czajkowski, Stanisław, 405
Czarnecki, 398
Czarnota, A., 141, 400, 405
Czechoslovakia problem, 318–320, 322
Czechowski, Ignacy, 395
Czechowski, Tytus, 395
Czekajski, S., 6
Czernek, Frank, 268
Czernicki, Józef, 395
Czerwiński, Józef, 395
Czerwonka, W., 141
Czuba, Józef, 339, 342
Czubakowski, Wacław, 123
Czupajło, Wacław, 88
Czuwara, Stanisław, 217

D

Dąbek, K., 158
Dąbrowski, 424
Dąbrowski, Jakub, 90
Dąbrowski, Jan, 395
Dąbrowski, Józef, 54–55, **68**
Dąbrowski, Kazimierz, 293
Dąbski, Teodor, 395
Dachnowicz, Piotr, 226
Dalcour, Calle, 33
dance, teaching folk dance to veterans' children, 158, 220
Danielkowicz, J., 7
David O. Selznick International Pictures Company, 213
de Botzen, 4
De Watteville Regiment, 7

Dec, Jan, 400
Dębicki, Napoleon, 25
Dębiczak, 403
Dębrowski, K., 284
Dębski, Aleksander, 78
decorations, See *names of specific decorations*
Defenders of the Fatherland Association of Canada, 274–275
Dekowski, Jan J., **109**, 242, 247
Delegature in Warszawa, 295
Dembicki, Napoleon, 395
Dembiński, Bronisław, 299
demobilized soldiers
    American Army invited to join, 117
    awards from General Haller, 119
    farewell in Skierniewice, 90–92
    Polish National Dept. help, 116–118
    transport ships, 115–116, 118
Democratic Society of Polish Exiles (DSPE), 26–32, 369
demonstrations, anti-Polish, 277–278
deportation of insurrectionists, 10–11, 18
Detroit veterans
    Club of Gen. Haller's Veterans formed, 122
    exhibit, 214–215
    fundraising, 321
    Haller Club 2 established, 128
    Józef Piłsudski Hallerian colony, 149
    Lwów patron of PAVA post, 305–306
    Polish American Community, 36
    Polish Home, 250
    propaganda rallies, 281
    Wanda Park shelter, 192–194
disabled veterans. See invalids
discrimination against American soldiers by Polish government, 327–328, 335
discrimination against Poles. See prejudice against Poles in U.S.
Dissolution Committee for the Polish Legion in Finland, 366
Division of the American Polonia, 252

Dłuski, Tomasz, 395
Dmochowski, Henryk, 31, **64, 66**
Dmowski, Roman, 87, 88, 287–288, 317
Dobiecki, Fortunat, 395
Dobiecki, Józef, 395
Dobiecki, Władysław, 395
Dobrowolski, 78
Dobrowolski, Kazimierz, 187–188
Dobrzeński, 424
documentary film, 212
Dodatko, 78
Dołęga-Lewandowski, Henryk, 51
Dolanowski, 398
Dombal, A., 150
Dombrowski, A., 126
Dombrowski, Edward, 268
Dombska, Maria, 419
Dorosiewicz, W., 179
Drabicki, A., 128
Drabiński, Jan, 405
Drągłowski, Jan, 338
Drętkiewicz, J., 121, 129, 252
Drelenkiewicz, W.A., 275, 284
"Druzhina Opolcheniya," 79
Drymer, W.T., 304–305
Dryniewicz, Józef, 395
Drzewnicki, 78
Drzyzga, M., 400
Dubiński, Aleksander, 78
Duda, T., 400
Durda, A., 128
Dutkowski, Antoni, 295
Dwojak, A., 219
Dyboski, Roman, 250
Dybowski, J., 130
Dymidas, 78
Dymowski, Jan, 395
Dymowski, Tadeusz, 365
Dzielak, Stanisław J., 126
Dzierżgowski, Polikarp, 337, 338
Dziewanowska-Walbridge, Maria, 30
Dziewanowski, Wincenty, 15–16
Dzikowski, Roman, 180, 290

Dziób, Franciszek
   cadet school director, 80
   editor of *The Veteran,* 209
   exhibit artifacts, 215
   Fascists and Union of Hallerians, 313
   15th anniversary of the recruitment
      for the Polish Army in France, 353
   PAVA National Executive Board
      member, 400
   PAVA organizational structures, 167
   PAVA post in Bydgoszcz, 337
   Polish Falcons of America Legion of
      Honor, 255
   Polish government aid for invalids,
      180, 303
   politics in Poland, 314–315
   portrait of, **380**
   recruitment for Polish Army, 82
   shelter in Chicago, 192
Dziwanowski, Klemens, 395
Dzwonkowski, Mieczysław, 290

E

Eastern Borderlands
   Agency of the Polish Army Vets
      Association of America, 325
   Education and Defense Union of the
      Eastern Polish Borderlands, 267
   land grants, 290
   military settlers listed by name, 424
   PAVA funds resettlement, 292
   PAVA post formed, 337
   polonization of, 373
Echo from Poland, 49, 50, **68**
education, 54–55, 206, 217, 219, 267
Education and Defense Union of the
   Eastern Polish Borderlands, 267
Elder, Bowman, 271
Elizabeth, NJ veterans, 126
Emerych, K., 6
emigrants who remained in the U.S.,
   395–398
Eminowicz, Stefania, 218–219

employment, See also *specific occupations*
in early settlements, 16–17
veterans have difficulty finding, 145-146, 183–190
work shops for war invalids, 364
workshop in Newark, 195
engineering, 28–29, 46, 58
Equal Rights Committee, 196
Eve, Paul F., 10
exhibitions, 214–216, 228, 255, 341
Eysmont, Lucjan, 395

F

Faithful River, 211
Fakutowski, 16
Falcons Alliance, 74–77
Falcon's Legion of Honor, 338
Faliński, Kazimierz, 395
Fannin, James W., 25
farm for veterans in Poland. See Kuligi
farm in Wanda Park, 192–194
Fascists, 313
Fauntleroy, Cedric
    Alliance of American Veterans of Polish Extraction honorary member, 268
    Bolshevik war, 92
    memorial monuments in Warszawa and Lwów, 205
    PAVA honorary member, 131
    Union of Polish Army Reserve Officers of America member, 266
Federation of Polish Associations of Defenders of the Fatherland (FPADF), 275, 321, 342, 344–347, 361
Fedor, P., 284
Felician Sisters, 55, 193
Feruś, P., 141, 150
Fibich, Michał, 265
FIDAC (Federation Interalliee des Anciens Combattants), 349–350, 361–363
field kitchens, 95
Figler, 78, 339

Fijałkowski, Stefan, 354
Filipowski, Jakub, 19
Filipowski, Kacper, 395
films, 211–213
Firlej, J., 130
Firley, H., 126, 127, 129
1st Polish Corps of Military Veterans in Podgórze outside Kraków, 366
1st Regiment of Polish Fusilliers in France, **102**
1st Regiment of Polish Riflemen, 86–87
Florkowski, A., 141
flu epidemics, 84
Foch, Ferdinand, 221–222, 268
folk emigration, 73
Fontana, Julian, 32, 33–34, **62**
Fort Goliad, 25, **63**
Fort Niagara, 83
43rd Infantry Regiment, 332–333
Frankowski, Bronisław, 222, 364–365
Fraternal Aid for Those Arriving from the Field of Battle, 50
fraternal insurance organizations, 261
The Free Voice, 49–51
French Combatant Cross, 358
French expeditionary corps, 4
Frenzel, K., 401
Friends of the Polish Army Veterans Alliance Circles, 420
Fronczak, Franciszek, 353
funds for the Polish uprising, 48–49
funerals for veterans, 172, See also *specific names*

G

Gądek, Stanisław, 245
Gąsior, Marcin, 338
Gąsiorowski, Stefan, 395
Gąsiorowski, Wacław
    assassination of Narutowicz, 307–308
    history of military units from America, 326

The History of the Polish Army in France, 210–211, 216
   recruited for Polish Army in France, 82
Gaczorowa, Helena, 94
Gadowski, S., 140
Gajkowski, Antoni, 395
Gałuszka, Wincenty, 128, 139
Gall, John, 268
Gallatin, Albert, 12, 14
Garbaczuk, Mikołaj, 395
Gardocki, K., 140
Garibaldi, Giuseppe, 36
Gas Light Company, 58
Gaszyński, T., 32
Gawroński, Wacław, 304–305
Gdańsk, 115–116, 117, 320–322
Gdynia-America Line, 287
Gębicki, Wawrzyniec (Lawrence), 8
General Józef Haller Polish Army Veterans Society, 123, 128, 151, 243
General Union of Non-Commissioned Officers of the Reserves of the Polish Republic, 366
Gepert, Citizen, 76
Gerard, Antoni, 17
Gerard, Mrs. Antoni, 17
Gesek, A., 141
Gidziński, Karol, 284
Giełgud, Ignacy, 9
Gierlach, R., 266
Gierlacki, Walenty, 247
Gierson, General, 44
Giller, Agaton, *56*
Głoskowski, Józef, 40–41
Głowacki, 349
Głowacki, Henryk, 27, 90
Głowacki, Ignacy, 395
Głowacki, Jan, 126, 305
Głuchowski, 78
Głuszewski, Konstanty, 395
Gliński, Stanisław, 395
Gniazdowska, Maria, 176

Godlewski, Marian, 243
Godlewski, Michał, 217
Godlewski, S., 266
Godziszewski, Konstanty, 89
Gołembiewski, S., 158
Gold Rush, 22
Golden Cross of Merit, 164, 305, 334, 360, **391**
Gomuła, J., 126
Gorczyński, Witold, 79
Gordon, Jakub, 36–37
Górecki, 398
Górecki, Franciszek, **391**
Górecki, Roman
   active military service after the war, 338
   Federation of Polish Associations of Defenders of the Fatherland, 361
   15th anniversary of the Polish Army in France, 255
   monument for Gen. Krzyżanowski, 228, 270
   PAVA Post 114 new flag, 274–275
   Polish government aid to invalids in the U.S., 303
   visit to U.S., 331, 363
Górski, Antoni, 395
Górski, Józef C., 268
Górski, Michał, 395
Gorzelnik, 139
Grabowski, Adolf, 395
Grabowski, Michał, 4, 129
Grabowski, Sylwester, 395
Grabski, Władysław, 299
Grajewski, 424
Granat, Aleksander, 405
Grand Croix de Guerre, 333
Grand Trunk Railway, 28
Grant, James, 282
Gray Samaritans, 84, 94–96, **105**
The Great Depression, 145–146, 257. *See also* employment; Ignacy Jan Paderewski Invalids Fund; shelters

Great Poland Party, 313
Grocholski, Antoni, 52
Grochowski, J., 128
Grosbeck, A.J., 272
Gruchacz, L., 400
Gruchacz, Stanisława, 419
Gruenbaum, 26
Grupa camp, 115, 118–119, 324
Gruszka, F.W., 125, 127, 129, 130, 400
Gruszka, Stanisław, 228
Gruszka, Sylwester, 270
Gruszka, W.J., 126
Grykowski, Stanisław, 400
Grylski, Jan, 395
Grzeloński, Bogdan, 39
Grzywiński, W., 222
Guba, Jan, 338
Gura, Zenon, 395
Gurowski, Adam, 31–32, 44–45
Gustyniak, O., 252
Gutowski, Rudolf, 395
Gwinczewski, Feliks, 11, 14, 395
Gydnia-Ameryka, 195, 304
Gzowski, Kazimierz, 28–29, **64,** 370, 395

H

Haiman, Mieczysław
   American Civil War, 39
   Poles incorporated into British ranks, 7
   Polish American Museum, 216
   Polish Roman Catholic Union of America, 258, 259
   Seminole War, 18–19
   war with Mexico, 52
Haller, Aleksandra, 247
Haller, Józef
   Alliance of American Veterans of Polish Extraction honorary member, 268
   assassination of Narutowicz accusations, 307–309
   biography, 216
   commander of the Polish Army in France, 87–88, 93
   Cross of Merit for Elizabeth Ascher, 205
   demobilization address and awards, **110,** 118–119
   federation combining veterans groups, 348
   15th anniversary of the Polish Army in France, 313
   foreclosure on his estates, 247
   funeral of Marian Kowalski, 203
   Hallerian Swords medal presented to Bałdyga, 352
   history of military units from America research, 326
   I.J. Paderewski Invalid Fund drive, 180, 353
   Invalid Home in Radzyń support, 299
   Kuligi shelter opening, 290
   marriage of Poland with the sea, 90
   name day greetings, 127, 312
   PAVA honorary president, 131, 298
   PAVA organizational flag ceremony, 254
   photos in *The Veteran,* 312, 313, 316
   photos of, **384–385, 390**
   Polish Army in France, taking oath as commander, **107**
   Polish Roman Catholic Union Flag, 258
   portrait painted by Styka, 214
   propaganda attacks on, 279–282
   16th anniversary of Armistice address, 315
   subordinated himself to Head of State in Poland, 89
   tour of Poland by American veterans, 329
   tours of Polish American communities, 194, 246, 255–256, 271–272, 298–299, 331

25th anniversary of Witos'
  parliamentary work, 314
The Veteran cover, 312, 313
Woodrow Wilson statue in Poznań,
  352–353
Haller Club, 128
Haller Men Band, 219–220
Haller Society, 126
The Hallerian, 350–351
"The Hallerian Calendar," 170, 184, 210, 347
Hallerian Swords
  Alliance of Poles in America, 262
  clergy received, 243
  Falcons in America, 254
  PAVA, 352
  PAVA members prized, 165
  Polish National Alliance, 256
  Polish Roman Catholic Union's flag, 258
Hallerians, 288
Hallerians Club Nr. 2 in Detroit, MI, 149
Hallerowo settlement, 293, 294
Hammond, IN veterans, 128
Hamtramck, MI veterans, 321
Hanasz, Roman
  editor of *The Veteran,* 208
  Haller's tour of the U.S., 271
  PAVA District I President, 401
  PAVA president of Dist. 1, 140
  Polish National Dept. finances reviewed, 130
  refutes attack against Gen. Haller, 282
  Union of Polish Army Reserve Officers of America member, 266
Harasimczuk, Józef, 207–209
Harding, Warren G., 222, 365
Hawrylewicz, 129
Hebensroth, 219
Heliński, Tadeusz, 82
Heliński, Teodor, 130
Henrykowski, Ludwik, 395
Hereta, Paweł, 327
heritage, teaching to children, 158–160, 220

Hibner, L., 219
Hintz-Snarska, Wanda, 419
"A History of the Polish American Community's War Effort," 252
The History of the Polish Army in France, 210–211, 216
History of the Polish Revolution and the Events of the Campaign, 9
Hitler, Adolf, 320
Hiż, Jan, 11, 14
Hlond, August, 302
Hodorek, Piotr, 424
Hofman, Mr. and Mrs., **106**
holidays, 73–74, 262, 270–271, 274.
  See also name day greetings
Hollywood, 212
Holowiński, Józef, 395
Home for War Invalids of the Republic of Poland, 255–256, 365
Hooker, General, 41
Hoover, Herbert
  director of American Relief Administration, 94
  150th anniversary of Gen Pułaski's death, 224
  photo of, **387**
  Pulaski Day, 225
  supported Poland, 256
Hordyński, Józef, 9–10
Horodyski, Ludwik, 395
Horoschak, Harvey J., 90
hospitals, 44, 94, 96, 123, 170–178.
  See also medical care
Howe, Samuel Gordon, 10
Hubicki, Stefan, 330
Hulak, 129
Hulewicz, Bohdan, 328–329
Hyż, Jan, 395

I

Ignacy Jan Paderewski Invalids Fund
  Alliance of Friends of Polish Army Veterans, 157

fund drives and donations, 174–183
Polish government support, 253, 335
Polish National Alliance, 256
shelter for veterans, 192
Igras, L, 150
Iliński, Ksawery, 396
Illinois, land grants, 13, 16
Illustrated Encyclopedia, 346
Imilkowski, Florian, 122
Immigration Congress, 249–250
Independence Cross, 343–344, 356–357, 356–360, 359
Independence Medal, 335–336, 343–344, 356–357, 356–360, 359
Independent District I of the Polish Army Veterans Association, 151
Independent Polish World War Veterans Gen. J. Haller Post, 149
Independent Post of Polish Veterans of the World War, 149
Indians, 14, 18–19
insurance, 261
insurrectionists. *See* November Uprising
International Bridge, 28
Invalid Home in Radzyń, 299
  invalids, See also *specific topics.*
    See also Ignacy Jan Paderewski Invalids Fund
  difficulties of, 169, 171–172, 173
  Kuligi shelter, 289–291
  Polish government help for invalids in U.S., 172, 173, 182
  St. Hedwig's Fund for Polish Invalids, 121
  Settlement and Invalid Fund, 245, 143–144
Irish clergy conflicts, 55, 245
"Iron Brigade," 92–93
Irzyk, Jan, 150
Iwanowski, Aleksander, 396
Iwanowski, Stefan, 331–332
Iwaszkiewicz, I., 6
Izdebski, 398

J

Jabłoński, Józef, 396
Jabłoński, W., 195
Jackowicz, Marian, 122
Jackson, Andrew, 18
Jackulak, L., 122
Jacquard, 30
Jagiełło, Hieronim, 396
Jakubowski, August, 396
Jakubowski, Frank, 295, 396
Jakubowski, Ludwik, 295
Jakutowicz, Antoni, 396
Janiewicz, Feliks, 32
Jankowski, C., 220
Jankowski, H., 141
Jankowski, Konstanty, 125
Janowski, Edward, 32
Janowski, Walery, 396
Jański, 53
Jański, Antoni, 396
Janta-Połczynski, Aleksander, 32
January Uprising
  Poles in the U.S. support, 48–50
  veterans of
    arriving in U.S. via Mexico, 52–53
    Catholic clergy, 53–55
    contributions to U.S., 370–371
    immigrating to U.S., 51
    Polish American organizations, 55–60
Jarecki, Edward, 266
Jarosz, S., 128
Jaroszewski, Ignacy, 396
Jaroszyński, 398
Jasiński, Jan, 396
Jasiński, Kazimierz, 396
Jastrzębski, A., 140
Jaszowski, Maksymilian, 395
Jaworowski, Roman J., 49
Jaworska, Z., 153
Jaworski, Mikołaj, 396
Jaworski, Mrs., 191
Jaworski, Tomasz, 396

Jędryaszek, Franciszek, 219, 400
Jełtuchowski, Mikołaj, 396
Jendrejaszek, Fr., 140
Jenkner, J., 140
Jerheń. E., 266
Jersey City, NJ veterans, 126
Jerzmanowski, Erazm J., 51, 57–59, **69**, 370
Jerzykiewicz, Ludwik, 396
Jeziorański, Citizen, 76
Jeżykowicz, Ludwik, 11
Johnson, Louis, 270
Joniec, A., 129, 130, 141, 400
Joniec, Władysław, 122
journalism
    American press depicts dark side of life in Poland, 296
    American press refutes attack against Gen. Haller, 282–283
    as career in Poland, 338
    father of Polish American press, 27
    first Polish newspaper in U.S., 49
    Jakub Gordon published newspapers, 37
    Jewish and German propaganda, 279–282
    post-war political quarrels of Poland in American press, 278–282
Józef Piłsudski Hallerian Colony, 149
Józiakiewicz, Andrzej, 35
Jóźwiak, J., 140
Juarez, Benito, 52
Jubilee Ball, 225–226
Jung, Władysław, 92
Jurewicz, J., 266
Jurkiewicz, J.R., 6
Juświkiewicz, Julian, 396
Juszczak, J., 140
Juszkiewicz, Józef, 54
Juźwikiewicz, Julian, 11, 13, 17

K

Kaba, Michal, 90
Kaczmarz, A., 140
Kaczyński, Piotr, 254
Kadmus, Jan, 396
Kajko, Lucjusz
    Circle of Volunteers, 342
    Drelenkiewicz friend, 275
    Federation of Polish Assoc. of Defenders of the Fatherland, 363–364
    Knight's Cross of the Order of Poland Reborn recipient, 305
    PAVA delegation in Poland, 333–335
    PAVA National Executive Board member, 400
    Polish government aid appeal, 182
    portrait of, **380**
    remains of Gen. Krzyżanowski transfered to Arlington National Cemetery, 226
    unemployment help for soldiers, 187
    Veterans' Commission member, 251
Kajsiewicz, Hieronim, 53
Kakowski, Aleksander, 299, 317
Kałussowski, Henryk
    American-style career, 370
    contributions to the Polish American community, 56–57
    Democratic Society of Polish Exiles, 26
    January Uprising, 49–50
    November Uprising anniversary, 20
    official representative of National Government in the U.S., 48
    portrait of, **66**
    Society of Poles in America founder, 19–20
    Spring of Nations, 35
Kalapiński, J., 141
Kalinowski, Jan, 128, 139, 141
Kalinowski, Wincenty, 305
Kamieński, E., 141
Kamiński, Jan, 310, 396
Kania, 129
Kania, Józef, 251

Kaniasty, Bronisław, 120
Kanonowicz, B., 275
Kański, Edward, 32
Kantor, P., 349
Kapela, Michał, 122
Kapturkiewicz, R., 266
Karaś, Józef, 129, 217, 400
Karczewski, Z., 26
Karge, Józef, 35, 39, 43–44, **67**
Kargol, Wojciech, 424
Karolczak, Walenty
    conference of local organizations under PAVA, 127, 128
    delegate to PAVA, 129
    Marian Kowalski funeral, 203
    PAVA district regulations, 139
    PAVA National Executive Board member, 400
    Polish Army Veterans Club member, 126
    President Harding's funeral, 222
    Resettlement Committee, 289
Karolczak, Wojciech, 249, 271, 406
Karpiński, I., 6
Karwacki, 126
Kasicki, 78
Kasperek, L., 153
Kasprzycki, Tadeusz, 303, 333
Kaszyński, Leon, 265
Kaufman, Levy I., 280
Kawa, Franciszek P., 205
Kawalec, A., 284
Kawecki, Stanisław, 90
Kawszewicz, J., 266
Kazanowski, Józef, 129
Kędziorek, Feliks, 360
Kępiński, F.K., 26
Kęszycki, 349
Kempa, Frank J., 268
Kempisty, Piotr, 403
Kiczek, 139
Kiczman, F., 26
Kiela, J., 400

Kiev campaign, 92
Kimel, Salomon, 396
King, C., 271
"King-Kong," 213
Kirchner, Adolf, 326–327
Kisielewski, Paweł, 396
kitchen for jobless veterans, 187
Kłos, Michał, 90
Kłusek, Franciszek, 424
Klara, H., 158
Kleczka, Jan C., 115, 116
Klimczewski, Henryk, 337, 338, 339, 342
Klimek, Józef, 400
Klimek, Kazimierz, 405
Kloc, B., 140
Klonowski, Teofil Tomasz, 32
Kmotek, Alojzy, 226
Knight's Cross of the Order of Poland Reborn, 305
Knights of Columbus, 117
Kobylański, A., 266
Koc, Adam, 332
Kocoń, Józef, 150
Kocowski, 398
Koczara, P., 150
Kołodziej, Jan, 123
Kołodziejczyk, K., 400, 401
Kolakowski, H., 400
Komar, Karol, 16, 396
Komorowski, Corporal, **108**
Komorowski, Władysław, 396
KON (Komitet Obrony Narodowej)
    assassination of Narutowicz, 308
    Association of Volunteers and Independents from America, 341–342
    division within Polonia, 250, 281–282
    military camp maintained, 76
    organization and purpose, 75
    Polish army, obstruction of, 84–85
    Polish National Catholic Church, 244

political attacks by, 79
Universal Countrywide Exposition, 214
Konary, 76
Konarzewski, Wojciech, 11, 396
Kondracik, J., 141
Konists. *See* KON (Komitet Obrony Narodowej)
Kopeć, Stanisław, 78, 219
Kopecki, 398
Korczyński, Franciszek, 396
Korfanty, Wojciech, 131, 314
Kornicki, Jan, 25
Korzeniowski, Błażej, 51
Kościałkowski, Napoleon, 25
Kościński, Artur, 192
Kościołowski, Władysław, 121
Kościuszko, Tadeusz
    American Revolution, 3–4, 369
    bust in Capitol, 31
    insurrection, 5–6
    monument unveiling, 74
Kościuszko Foundation, 272
The Kosciuszko Guards Society, 73
Kościuszko Insurrection, 5–6
Kosieniak, F., 140
Kosiński, Franciszek, 226, 400, 404
Kosiński, Frank, 196
Kosiński, W., 51
Kosobucka, Zofia, 188, 419
Kossowski, 349
Kossowski, Józef, 11, 32, 396
Kostrubała, Jan
    Committee to Honor the Immigration's War Effort, 252
    delegation to Poland, 299
    Hallerian Sword for Polish Roman Catholic Union, 258
    150th anniversary of Gen. Pułaski's death, 224
    Paśniewski fired as farm administrator, 351
    PAVA District I President, 401
    PAVA National Executive Board member, 400
    photo of, **387**
    Silver Cross of Merit recipient, 305
    Union of Polish Army Reserve Officers of America member, 266
    Veterans' Commission member, 251–252
Kostrzewski, Corporal, 265
Kosyłowski, Napoleon, 396
Kotkowski, Captain, 3
Kotowicz, 396
Kotowski, Franciszek, 396, 398
Kowacz, Michael, 4
Kowalewski, 158
Kowalewski, Bolesław, 293
Kowalski, Aleksander, 242, 284
Kowalski, J., 142
Kowalski, Konstanty, 396
Kowalski, Marian
    funeral of, 202–203
    journey to U.S., 6
    PAVA delegate, 129
    PAVA National Executive Board member, 130, 400
    Polish authorities petitioned for pension, 328
    Resettlement Committee, 289
    Union of Polish Army Reserve Officers of America member, 266
Kowalski, Władysław, 120
Kozikowski, Stanisław, 226
Kozuch, Stefan, 268
Kraitzir, Charles, 12–13, 14
Krajcer, Karol, 398
Krajewski, Roman, 396
Krakowiak, A., 141, 400
Krakowski, Frank, 269
Krasnodębski, Julian, **383**
Kraszewski, Józef Ignacy, 4, 49
Kraus, J., 266
Krawczewski, W., 124
Krawczyk, Stefan A., 268

Krawczyński, Mateusz, 396
Kręgliński, Jan, 396
Król, Ignacy, 93–94
"Królewiaks," 78
Kruszewski, 398
Kruszka, Wacław, 30, 53
Kruszyński, J., 130, 400
Krygowski, Stanisław, 154, 401
Krysiński, Tomasz, 396
Krzemieniecki, Józef, 51
Krzesłowski, 26
Krzyżak, Leopold
    accusations of PAVA being
      pro-Piłsudski, 315
    American veterans' privileges
      for Poles, 196
    citizenship for veterans, 198, 199
    communist propaganda fighting, 283
    Cross of Independence, Americans
      passed over, 335–336
    editor of *The Veteran,* 209
    Golden Cross of Merit recipient, 305
    I.J. Paderewski Invalid Fund, 182
    PAVA National Executive Board
      member, 400
    The Polish Army in France, 275
    Polish government grant to invalids
      received, 253
    Veterans' Commission, 252
    veterans who died of hunger
      or suicide, 190
Krzyżanowski, Alfred, 339
Krzyżanowski, Piotr, 396
Krzyżanowski, Włodzimierz
    Arlington National Cemetery, 226,
      228, 251, 269–270, 273
    59th anniversary of his death, 226
    portrait of, **66**
    Union Army general, 39, 41
Kubala, 129
Kubala, Józef, 198, 407
Kuc, 78
Kuczman, M., 175
Kuczmiński, Mateusz, 396
Kujawa, Franciszek, 60
Kukiel, Marian, 39, 325–326, 326
Kułasiewicz, Jan, 396
Kulczycki, W., 125, 127, 129, 130, 400
Kulesza, Mikołaj, 290
Kuligi
    agribusiness, 289–291
    in debt, 346
    finances, 296
    land grant, 172
    purchase of, 173
    shelter, 191, 290–291
    shelter opening, **383**
    supervision of, 350, 351
Kulik, B., 219
Kuliński, Paweł, 90
Kulkowski, Makary, 90
Kunicki, Alfons, 396
Kunior, Stanisław, 337
Kuraszkiewicz, 424
Kurek, Adam, 32, 33, 34, 39, 40
Kuroś, Jan, 295
Kuroski, John, 82
Kuryłowicz, Franciszek, 396
Kurzeja, Ewa, 419
Kuszewski, 129
Kuta, Józef, 241
Kuźmicki, 338
Kwapiszewski, Michał, 358
Kwaśniewski, T., 266
Kwiatkowski, Andrzej, 396
Kwiatkowski, J., 150
Kwiatkowski, Jan, 396
Kwiatkowski, Józef, 396
Kwiatkowski, Karol, 396
Kwiatkowski, Marcela, 396
Kwiatkowski, Marcin, 51
Kwieciński, Franciszek, 396

L

Ładniak, S., 140
Łepkowski, Numa, 396

Łukasik, Karol, 129, 130, 243, 245, 247
Łukomski, J., 266
Łuszczyński, Paweł, 396
Łyczak, Adam, 400, 402
La Guardia, Fiorello, 226
Lączkowski, 294
Ladies Legion, 268
land grants from Polish government, 172, 289–292
land grants in Canada, 8
land grants in the United States, 12–16
Lange, Władysław, 396
Langiewicz, Marian, 52, 53, 57
language, removing Polish from parish schools, 267
language, teaching Polish to veterans' children, 158
language, thoughts on, 30
Laski, Tomasz, 60
Lauzun Legion, 4
Le Pan, A.D., 83
League of Nations, 320
Lebedowicz, Antoni, 396
Lędzian, Józef, 90
Lech, 121
Legieć, A., 124
Legion of Honor, 333, 360
Legion of Invalids of the Polish Armed Forces, 366
Legion of Polish Army Veterans in Detroit, MI, 150
Legion of the Republic of Poland, 350, 361, 362
legionnaires, 288
Lelewel, Joachim, 10, 20
Lemański, Stanisław, 396
Lempka, Józef, 244, 245
Lenart, Franciszek
    Auxiliary Corps of PAVA, 154
    Hallerian Sword for Polish Roman Catholic Union, 258
    medical advice for veterans, 190
    PAVA formed, 123
    portrait of, **381**
    Union of Polish Army Reserve Officers of America vice president, 266
Lenart, Jan, 90
Lenartowicz, Stefan
    aid to veterans from Polish government, 182, 303–305, 346
    financial aid for war invalids in America, 334
    and military decorations, 335
    negative feelings toward pro-Piłsudski government, 373
    World Alliance of Poles from Abroad in Poland director, 252
Lentas, Stanisław, 424
Lepin, Jan, 396
Lepowski, Nuna J., 32
Lesicki, Franciszek, 121
Lesinski, John, 193, 199, 200
Leśniewski, B., 141
Lessen, Captain, 36
Leszczyński, Antoni, 36, 122
Leszczyński, Piotr, 36, 51
Lewandowski, 398
Lewandowski, Jan M., 203
Lewandowski, Michał, 293
Lewandowski, Mieczysław, 122
Lewiński, M., 266
Lewkowicz, Marian, 396
Library of Writers of the Polish American Community, 217
Liggotti, General, 272
Lignowski, B.R., 32
Ligocki, Edward, 216
Lincoln, Abraham, 41
Linkowski, Adam, 337, 338
Lipiński, Franciszek, 407
Lipiński, Julian, 51
Lipiński, M., 246–247
Liquidation Agency in Poznań, 298
Lisiecki, 121
Liskowacki, Florian, 396

Liszko, 78
Litomski, Karol, 4
loans to Poland by American banks, 267
Lodge, Senator, 197
Lopez de Santa Anna, Antonio, 24–25
Los Angeles veterans, 181
Loth, E., 351
Louisville settlement, 16
Lowell settlement, 16
Lubomirski, Kazimierz, 116
Lucjan Chwałkowski Boulevard, 334, 346
Ludwikowski, Daniel, 396
Ludyga-Laskowski, 361–362
Lutnicki, Wincenty, 23
Lwów, 93, 305–306

M

Mabillot, Zofia, 419
Mach, Kazimierz, 129, 211, 323
Machalska, Izabela, 419
Machinkowski, Leon, 90
Maciejewski, Feliks, 60, 139
Maciejewski, Jan, 126
Maciora, L., 195
Mackiewicz, Maksymilian, 32
Mackiewicz, Mieczysław, Dr., 51
Madejewski, Roman, 121
Magnuski, 398
Maguder, J., 150
Majcher, 78
Majtyka, S., 150
Makowska, Olimpia, 268
Makuszewski, 53
Małachowski, Kazimierz, 6
Małek, 129
Małek, Franciszek, 216
Małek, J.S., 324
Małkowski, Andrzej, 80
Małochleb, 78
Małuski, A., 26
Malczewski, 345
Malecki, 139
Malinowski, Piotr, 184

Marchlewski, Mieczysław, 186, 314–315
Marciszewski, S., 122
Marczak, Stanisław, 122
Marine Department of the Union of Former Volunteers for the Polish Army, 366
Markiewicz, Fabian, 396
Markowski, 32
Markus, Stanisław, 354–360
Marnik, Józef, 150
Marshall Józef Piłsidski Veterans Union, 275–276
Marski, Dyonizy, 396
Marszewski, 424
Maszewski, 396
Matecki, J., 129, 130, 266, 400, 402
Materski, Franciszek, 396
Matusiński, J., 314
Maźnicki, Władysław, 78
Mazur, J., 141
Mazurek, J., 141
McCormick, Medill, 197
McLernand, John A., 40
McNutt, Paul V., 273
Meade, Congressman, 198
Medal for the War of 1918-1921, 335
Medal of the Polish Army Veterans Association, 225
medical care, 44, 123, 172, 190, 305. *See also* hospitals
Medical Society in San Francisco, 22
Memorial Day celebration, 223, 274
Mexican Legion, 52
Mexico, 24–26, 52–53
Michalska, Izabela, 419
Michalski, Dean, 300
Michalski, Józef, Dr., 305, 400, 402
Michalski, Mikołaj, 51
Michniewicz, Józef, 93
Mickiewicz, Adam, 33
Międlar, Sebastian, 128
Mierzwiński, Cyprian, 396
Mieszkowski, Jerzy Kwiryn, 4
Milewska, M., 191

Milewski, 49
Miliński, Edward, 396
military camps, 83
military decorations, See *names of specific decorations*
military schools, 80–81
military settlers. *See* resettlement of veterans in Poland
Military Settlers Cooperative, 292, 296
Miller, Colonel, 349
Milwaukee, WI veterans, 122, 194, 195–196
Miner, Asher, 272
miners' strike, 185
Ministry of Military Affairs, 324–327
"Miracle on the Vistula," 225
Misiak, 129
mission churches, 53–55
Mitochor, 78
Młodzianowski, Edward, 396
Młotkowski, Stanisław, 35, 40
Młynarski, 78
Mleczko, Anna, 419
Mniszek, Stanisław, 396
Modrzejewska, Helena, 23–24, 27
Mogilski, Major, 14
Molisan, Mikołaj, 396
Monitor Clevelandzki, 209
Morawski, 16
Morawski, Ryszard, **66–67**
Morawski, Sebastian, 396
Morozowicz, J., 51
Morozowski, Józef, 396
Mościcki, Ignacy
    Czech problem, 319, 320
    4th PAVA General Assembly greetings, 302
    Golden Cross of Merit recipient, 164
    PAVA delegation to Poland, 299
    PAVA president meeting, 302–303
    President of the Polish Republic for PAVA greetings, 427
    10th anniversary of the recruitment for the Polish Army in France, 330

The Veteran cover, 312
Mościcki, Wacław, 185–186
Mostowski, Wiktor, 396
movies, 211–213
Mroczkowski, Kajetan, 60
Mrozowski, Czesław
    citizenship for veterans, 198
    cross of valor recipient, 366
    Detroit speech, 250
    FIDAC, 361–362
    150th anniversary of Gen. Pułaski's death, 224
    PAVA District VI President, 404
    PAVA National Executive Board member, 400
    Special Convention in Poznań, 352
    W. Mościcki encouraged to join PAVA, 185
Museum of the War Effort of Poles from America, 341
museums, 58, 259–260
musicians, 32–35, 219–220
mutual aid associations, 122–123, 150, 169. *See also* citizenship; employment; invalids; Polish Army Veterans Association (PAVA); shelters for veterans
Mycielski, 398
Myjak, 339
Myszak, 126

N

name day greetings, 127, 312, 317
Napieralska, Emilia, 260
Napoleonic wars, 6–8, 369
Naruszewicz, Hipolit, 396
Narutowicz, Gabriel, 170, 184, 210, 307–309, 347–348
Narwoyn, K.J., 6
Nastał, Helena, **390**
Nastał, Stanisław
    conflict between officers and rank and file soldiers, 264
    Haller's tour of the U.S., 271

history book narrative, 217
PAVA National Executive Board member, 400
"Poland's Film Exchange" started, 212
post-German farms, 295
President Harding's funeral, 222
radio program pioneer, 213
Settlement and Invalid Fund drive, 289–290
Tomb of the Unknown Soldier, wreath laid, 222
wedding portrait, **390**
National Committee of Poles in the United States of North America, 14
National Daily, 124
National Defense Committee. *See* KON (Komitet Obrony Narodowej)
National Defense Fund, 318, 321, 323, 357
National Democratic Party, 287–288
National Department, 88, 96, 171, 281–282
National Department of the Central Polish Aid Committee, 75
National Department of the Polish Central Relief Committee, 82
National Foundation of Erazm and Anna Jerzmanowski, 59
National Polish Department, 96
Native Americans, 14, 18–19
Negri, Pola, 272, **384**
Nelles, General, 274
New Britain, CT veterans, 121–122, 195
New Poland, 46
New York City veterans, 50, 126, 194–195, 225–226, 226
Newark, NJ veterans, 128, 195
newspaper, Polish, 49, 370
Niagara Falls, 28
Niagara-on-the-Lake training camp
baseball game, **103**
cemetery, **104, 106,** 204, 222
farewell to volunteers, **100**
Memorial Day celebration, 274
men qualified for training, 84
Polish American youth used tricks to get in, 83
10th anniversary of the recruitment for the Polish Army in France, 330
training photo, **103**
volunteers depart for France, 85, **104**
Niebylski, J. M., 141
Niebylski, Józef, 128
Niedźwiezki, Karol, 396
Niemcewicz, Julian Ursyn, 5–6
Niemiec, Paweł, 93, 139
Nietupski, Feliks, 396
Nieużytek, Stefan, 128
Nitecki brothers, 78
Nogacki, Józef, 122
November Uprising
in Lithuania, 19–20
national holiday in America, 20
veterans of
in California, 20–24
in the Musical Life of America, 32–35
Polish exiles, 9–11, 18
remained in the U.S., 395–398
Nowa Polska (New Poland), 46
Nowaczyński, Janusz, 424
Nowak, A., 275, 363
Nowak, F., 285
Nowak, J., 141
Nowak, Zygmunt Feliks, 328
Nowakowski, Marian, 158
Nowakowski, Michał, 396
Nowakowski, W., 141
Nowomiejski, Michał, 396
nurses, 84, 94–96, 105, 122. *See also* Auxiliary Corps of the Polish Army Veterans Association
Nyko, 398

O

Obarska, M., 153
Obrzeński, 294
Obrzut, Szczepan, 123

Odrowąż, Edward, 57
officers' conflict with rank and file soldiers, 264–265
Official Report of the Activities and Expenses of the Polish National Department in America on the Occasion of the Return and Demobilization of the Polish Army in France for the Period of April to August 1920, 115, 116
Oladowski, Hipolit, 39, 47, 396
Olechnowicz-Gradziecki, Bolesław, 366
Olejniczak, Jan, 259
Oleksy, E., 266
Olkowski, J., 222
Olkowski, P., 125, 126
Olszański, 16
Olszański, Honory, 396
Olszewski, Teodor, 396
Omaha, NE veterans, 217
150th anniversary of Kościuszko's arrival in America, 223
orchestras for veterans' children, 158, 220
orchestras of Polish soldiers, 219–220
Order of Virtuti Militari, 272, 326–327, 335
Order of Poland Reborn, 272
Orlicz-Dreszer, Gustaw, 226, 303, 330–332
Orlik, Walenty, 202
orphanages for village children in Poland after WWI, 95–96
Orpikowska, Z., 158
Orzechowski, Rev. Pastor, 245
Osiecki, 125
Osielski, A.P., 141
Osiński, Aleksander, 332
OSKRES at Równe, 292, 293
Ostapowski, Julian, 396
Ostrowski, 78
Ostrowski, Janusz, 218
"Our Polish Hour," 213
An Outline of the History of Polish Literature in America, 217
Owsley, Alvin, 271
Oyrzanowski, M., 6

P

Pągowski, Stanisław, 20–21
Pacyna, F., 285
Paderewska, Helena, 84, 94
Paderewski, Ignacy J.
  Golden Cross of Merit recipient, 164
  invalids, relief for, 170–171, 174
    (*See also* Ignacy Jan Paderewski Invalids Fund)
  Kościuszko Army, 84
  Polish Army in France, 82
  Polish Kościuszko Army, 80
  Polish science award recipient, 59
  portrait of, **387**
  20th anniversary of Blue Army's arrival in Poland, 318
  The Veteran cover, 312, 313
  The Veteran issue devoted to, 316
  watch gift for fundraising, 180
Pająk, 361
Pałaszewski, Stanisław
  editor of *The Hallerian,* 350–351
  15th anniversary of the formation of the Polish Army in France, 313
  journalist in Bydgoszcz, 338
  PAVA post in Bydgoszcz, 337
  St. Hilaire cemetery fund drive, 205, 353
Palewski, 424
Paluch, M., 400
Paluch, W., 128
Paluszek, L., 153
panSlavism, 32, 44–45
parades, 73–74. *See also* celebrations
Paradowski, Dr., 194
Paradzińska, Mrs., 76
Paris Peace Conference in 1919, 90
Partyka, Klemens, 123
Paskevich, Ivan, 10
Paśniewski, Jan
  Circle of Volunteers, 342
  farm and shelter manager, 290, 351
  landowner, 339

PAVA post in Bydgoszcz, 337
   post-German farm purchase, 295
Passaic, NJ veterans, 122, 195
Pastula, P., 400
Patelska, Zofia, 176
Patelski, Franciszek, 176
Paustecki, Józef, 397
Pawłowicz, Czesław, 93
Pawłowski, Gabriel, 79, 252, 266
Pawłowski, Władysław, 293, 338
Pawlak, A., 140
Pawlak, W., 254, 403
Pawlica, Jan, 274
Pawlik, Piotr, 177
Pawlik, Stanisław, 90
Pawliński, Stanisław, 397
Pawlowski, Dominik, 397
Pędziński, Jan, 397
Pela, Jan, **109**, 328, 400
Pela, Julia, 419
Peltz, L., 150
Pendrak, Edward, 406
pensions, 305, 328, 335, 346, 358
periodicals, 27, **65, 68,** 216–218
Pershing, John J., 268, 272
Perzan, Józef, 328
Perzanowska, Anna, 419
Perzga, M., 140
Petecki, Wawrzyniec, 121
Petranowski, Franciszek, 397
Petrowicz, Wincenty, 51
Petrussewicz, Adolf, 25
Petrussewicz, Franciszek H., 25, **63**
Philadelphia veterans, 128, 222, 223
Piątkowski, Zygmunt, 354
Piechowski, Aleksander, 397
Piecuch, B., 158
Piekarski, Aleksander, 397
Piekielniak, J., 400
Pieńkowski, Tadeusz, 396
Pientoski, Jerzy, 266
Pieprzny, Gustaw, **109**, 266, 332
Pietrowicz, Marian, 268
Pietrowicz, Teodor, 397
Pietrusińska, Maria, 419
Pietrzykowski, Aleksander
   became tourist in France to enlist
      in Polish Army, 86
   conflict between officers and rank
      and file soldiers, 263–264
   Hallerian Sword for Polish Roman
      Catholic Union, 258
   medical advice given, 190
   PAVA District I President, 401
   PAVA founded, 123, 124
   portrait of, **381**
   shelters, 191
   Union of Polish Army Reserve
      Officers of America president,
      266
Pikielniak, Jan, 328
Pikor, J., 128
Piłsudska, Aleksandra, 335
Piłsudski, Józef
   commander in Galicia, 75
   commander in Warszawa, 94
   Convention of Polish Legionnaires
      in Wilno, 366
   death of, 315–316
   Falcons greeted, 77
   farewell to soldiers leaving for
      America, 90–91, 116, 120
   4th PAVA General Assembly
      greetings, 302
   funeral commemorations, 225
   Head of State in Poland, 89
   honorary President of PAVA, 298
   May 1926 coup d'état, 288, 310
   Mościcki's greetings to PAVA, 427
   name day greetings, 127, 312
   PAVA honorary president, 131
   PAVA tour members meeting,
      300–301, 329
   photo of, **386**
   removed himself from political life,
      309

10th anniversary of the recruitment for the Polish Army in France, 330
The Veteran cover, 312, 313
The Veteran photos, 316
Volunteers from America Cross, **111**
Piłsudski Institute, 126
Piłsudski-ites, 288
Piłsudskists. *See* KON (Komitet Obrony Narodowej)
Pingielski, A., 129, 140
Piotrowska, H., 419
Piotrowski, Korwin, 23
Piotrowski, Ksawery, 397
Piotrzkowski, Mikołaj, 268
Pitas, Rev. Dr., 245
Pittsburgh, PA veterans, 223
Płachecki, Edward, 52
Plewiński, Karol, 397
Plinta, Karol, 28, 396
Pniewski, Józef, 60
Pochmara, F., 268
Pochrzyn, Józef, 60
Podhorski, 424
Podosowski, Grzegorz, 397
Poincaré, Raymond, 82
Polak, Nikodem, 354
Poland, 370
Poland—Historical, Literary, Monumental and Picturesque, 27
"Poland's Film Exchange," 212
Polish American Civic Committee, 194–195
Polish American community, *See also specific names of cities*
    apolitical nature of PAVA, 306
    assassination of Narutowicz, 308–309
    authoritarian regime in Poland, 300
    Book of the Infantry's Glory, 346
    books and press readership, 216–218 (*See also The Veteran*)
    donations to Poland after WWI, 96
    exhibits, 214–216
    Haller's visit, 194 (*See also* Haller, Józef)
    intensified military efforts during WWI, 80
    invalids, relief for, 173 (*See also* invalids)
    monument in Równe, 336
    negative feelings toward pro-Piłsudski government, 373
    PAVA helped integration into local communities, 372
    Poland's careless treatment of American soldiers, 304
    polarization of during WWI, 75
    political divisions within, 281–282
    20th anniversary of the war effort, 226
    tours of Poland, 302
    World Union of Poles from Abroad, 251
Polish American Council, 217
Polish-American demonstration in 1910, 74
Polish American Museum, 215–216
Polish American National Union, 262
Polish American organizations, 73–74, 75, See also *names of specific groups*
Polish-American Veterans Club for the State of Michigan, 267, 268
Polish-American Veterans of the World War Club, 267
Polish American World War Veterans Association, 123
Polish Armed Forces, 287–288
Polish Army in France
    administration of oath to volunteers, **100**
    anniversary of recruitment, 262
    battle over the borders, 89–90
    Blue Army 1918-1919, 85–89
    campaign against Bolsheviks, 92–94
    chaplain, **109**
    demobilization of volunteers, 90–92, **101**
    15th anniversary, 255, 313

National Democratic Party, 288
1918-1919, 85–89
organization of former soldiers, 119–120, 121–123, 125–126 (*See also* Polish Army Veterans Association (PAVA)
peasant emigrants, 373
recruitment, generally, 82–85, 163
recruitment by Alliance of Poles in America, 262
recruitment by clergy, 241–243
recruitment by Polish Women's Alliance, 260
recruitment center in Chicago, **99**
searching for missing soldiers, 202
summary of experience, 371–372
10th anniversary of recruitment, 163, 329–330
20th anniversary, 318, 358
volunteers returning to U.S., 115–119, 323–325
The Polish Army in France, 216, 275
The Polish Army in France According to the Facts, 355
Polish Army Reserve Officers Club, 264
Polish Army Veterans Association (PAVA)
agency, 325
agribusiness, 289–291
Alliance of Friends of Polish Army Veterans, 157–158, 167
Alliance of Poles in America, 261–262
American veteran privileges, 195–196
American Veterans, collaboration with, 270–273
apolitical nature of, 306–318, 372–373
assassination of Narutowicz, 347–348
Association of Veterans of the Former Polish Army in France controversies, 354–360
Auxiliary Corps (*See* Auxiliary Corps of the Polish Army Veterans Association)

books and press readership, 216–218
business activity in Poland, 289
Canadian post, 284
Canadian veteran organizations, collaboration with, 273–276
celebrations, 221–229
Chaperone Committee, 158–159
citizenship, 196–201
conference of all local organizations, 127–128
constitution (By-Laws), 129, 131–135, 277, 306, 364
culture, 206
delegates of founding convention, 129
Delegature in Warszawa, 287, 289, 292
districts, 138–145, 142–143, 143–145, **376,** 401–407
emblem, 163
employment help, 184–186
exhibitions, 214–216
Federation of Polish Associations of Defenders of the Fatherland, 361–364
FIDAC, 349, 361–362
15th anniversary of recruitment for Polish Army in France, 225
financial aid for Grupa camp, 324
Floating Post, 147
founded, 122–123, 123–125, 128–131, **374**
in France, 344
fundraisers by clergy, 245–248
fundraisers for Poland, 297
fundraisers for shelter for war invalids, 364–365
funerals, 202–204
General Assemblies, 135–136
Golden Cross of Merit, 164, 305, 334, 360, **391**
graves, maintenance of, 204–206
"Hallerian Swords," 165
Historical Committee, 359

The History of the Polish Army in France, 210–211
Information Bureau, 201–202
invalids, relief for, 169–183, 245–248, 299, 372 (*See also* Ignacy Jan Paderewski Invalids Fund)
investments in Poland, 296
kitchen for free meals, 187
lectures, 219
loans to military settlers, 292
logo, **379**
medal commemorating 15th anniversary, 164, 225
membership rules, 136–137
memorial monuments, 205
"Miracle on the Vistula," 225
Mother Post in Chicago, 134
movies, 211–213
name day greetings, 127, 312
National Convention in Chicago, **375**
National Convention in Pittsburgh, **375**
National Defense Fund, 318, 321
National Executive Board, 137, 316–317, 400
nonmembers, 200
official contacts in Poland, 298–306
150th anniversary of Gen. Pułaski's death, 224
100th anniversary of the November Uprising, 224–225
organizational decorations of, 163–165
Peer Court, 133
Polish army contacts, 323–336
Polish Falcons of America, 253–255
Polish foreign policy, 318–323
The Polish National Alliance, 253–255
Polish Roman Catholic Union of America, 257–260
Polish Women's Alliance, 260–261
Post 5 in Chicago, **376**

Post 28 in Kensington, IL, **377**
Post 36 in Passaic, NJ, **377, 388**
Post 57 in Elizabeth, NJ, **378**
Post 78 in Detroit, **378**
Post 130 in Bydgoszcz, 336–347, 347, 353–354
posts, generally, 124–125, 140–142, 145–151, 408–413
predecessors, 121
propaganda fighting, 277–285
property of, 372
publications, 206–211 (*See also The Veteran*)
relief grants, 185–186
Resettlement Committee, 289
Roman Catholic Church's role, 241–248
serial numbers of posts, 146–147
Settlement and Invalid Fund, 143–144, 245, 255, 260, 289–291
shelters, 190–195
Sons and Daughters of Polish Army Veterans, 158–161, 166
theater, 218–219
tours of Poland, 300–302, 329–334, 351–352, **386**
20th anniversary of the war effort, 226–227
250th anniversary of the Relief of Vienna, 225
umbrella organization initiated, 249–250
uniforms of members, 165–166, 421–422
Union of Hallerians, 347–354
veteran organizations of Polish provenance, 263–270
Welfare Committees, 177–178
women as members, 133, 136–137
Polish Army Veterans Club, 126, 150
Polish Army Veterans Home Construction Committee, 191–192
Polish Army Veterans Union, 123

Polish Catholic Organizations Clearing House in America, 259
Polish Catholic Clearing House of America, 249
Polish Central Relief Committee, 82, 96
Polish Committee in New York, 11–18, 369
"Polish Day," 223
Polish Democratic Society in Paris, 10, 57
Polish Embassy, 287
Polish Emigration Weekly, 15
Polish Falcon, 77, 254
Polish Falcons of America
    Chicago World's Fair, 255
    conference of local organizations under PAVA, 127
    in Detroit, 150
    education, influence of, 371
    Field Squads, 346
    15th anniversary of recruitment for Polish Army in France, 225
    first president, **97**
    1st Officers' Course in Canada, **99**
    founding of, 59–60
    instructor, **98**
    invalids, relief for, 178
    Legion of Honor, 255
    military schooling and mobilization, 80–81
    organizer of fighter units, **98**
    and PAVA, 253–255
    Polish independence, 73
    tour of Poland, 300–302
Polish Fellowship Society, 262
Polish government
    discrimination against American soldiers, 327–328
    foreign policy, 318–323
    invalids, relief for, 172, 173, 182, 253, 303–306
    land grants, 172, 289–292
Polish Historical and Museum Society of America, 259–260
Polish Home, 36

Polish identity, 30–31
Polish Inter-Organizational Council (PIOC), 226, 250–253, 252–253, 304
The Polish League, 56
Polish legation in Washington, D.C., 287
Polish Legion. *See* Legion of the Republic of Poland
Polish Legion of American Veterans (PLAV), 221, 269
Polish Legion of the American Army (PLAA), 269
Polish Legions, 75–78, 329, 345
Polish Military Organization (PMO), 78, 329
Polish Military School, 76
Polish Military Society, **97**
Polish National Alliance. *See also* Falcons Alliance
    financial aid for the arts, 219
    founded, 55, 56
    Haller Society, 126
    invalids, relief for, 171, 174, 179, 181
    library and archives, 57
    and PAVA, 255–257
    Polish independence, 73
    and Polish Inter-Organizational Council in the U.S., 250
    and Polish Roman Catholic Union, 249
    shelter in Chicago, 191
Polish National Alliance of Brooklyn, 262
Polish National Catholic Church, 244
Polish National Committee in Paris, 87
Polish National Department, 116–118, 248–250
Polish National Museum, 58
Polish Patriotic Organization under the Protection of the Queen of the Polish Crown, 56
Polish Peasant Party, 317
Polish People's Group, 18
"Polish Program," 213
Polish Red Cross, 122

Polish Roman Catholic Union of America (PRCUA). *See also* Roman Catholic Church
    financial aid, 423
    founded, 55
    invalids, relief for, 173, 179, 181
    Library of Writers of the Polish American Community, 217
    organizational consolidation, 249, 250
    and the Polish American Museum, 215–216
    and the Polish Army Veterans Association, 257–260
    and Polish independence, 73
    purpose, 56
Polish science award, 59
Polish Seminary at Orchard Lake, 193
Polish Singers Alliance of America, 262
Polish Social Welfare Council of America, 249
Polish Society in California, 23
Polish Society of Military Veterans in Kraków, 366
Polish Union in the United States of America, 262
Polish Veterans Club, 125, 126, 149
Polish Veterans From the World War, 149
Polish Veterans Mutual Aid Society of Ontario, 274
Polish Veterans of the World War, 121, 242
Polish White Cross, 84, 94, **105**
Polish Women's Alliance (PWA), 73, 96, 171, 181, 250, 260–261
Polish Youth Alliance of America, 76, 262
political orientations in WWI, 75
Polkowski, Edward, 396
Polonia. *See* Polish American Community
Poniatowski, Antoni, 397
Poniatowski, Józef, 427
Poniatowski, Stanisław, 82
Porczyński, Eugeniusz, 397
post-German farms, 295–296

Potaczała, S., 404
Potocki, Jerzy, 228, 270, 306
poverty, 18–19. *See also* employment; Ignacy Jan Paderewski Invalids Fund; shelters for veterans
pow-iaks, 288
Poźniak, J., 129, 400
Pral, Jan, 398
Praniewski, Aleksander, 397
Prechal, Jan, 13
prejudice against Poles in U.S., 16–17, 54, 55, 245
priests. *See* Roman Catholic Church
printing press in Belgium, 20
prisoners of war, 6–7, 78
propaganda, anti-Polish, 150, 277–285, 373
propaganda, communist, 283–285
propaganda about the might of the Polish State, 320
Prostka, Antoni, 122
Prugar-Ketling, Bronisław, 346
Prystor, Colonel, 300
Pryszmont, Wiktor, 125
Przygócka, Estera, 419
Przyprawa, Jan, 122, 218
Przywarski, Bogusław, 226, 328
Puchalski, Eugeniusz, 397
Pułaski, Kazimierz
    American Revolutionary soldier, 3, 4, 369
    bust commissioned by U.S. Congress, 31, **66**
    memorial mound in Savannah, 224, 256, 266, 268–269, 273
    monument unveiling, 74
    150th anniversary of his death, 302
Pułaski, Stanisław, 424
Puławski Legion, 79
Pulaski Day, 225
Pulaski's Volunteers, 73
Purowski, 16
Puścizna, L., 140
Putrament, 398

Pyszara, Jakub, 60
Pytlowany, W., 266
Pyzik, Franciszek, 189–190

Q

quarantine centers, 95
Quigley, George A., 195

R

Raczkowski, Antoni, 122
Raczyńska, Leokadia, 419
radio programs, 213
Radzimiński, Karol, 25
railroad discounts, 343
Rajchel, Jan, 175
Rak, Teresa, 419
Rakoczy, Feliks, 290
Rarz, Adolf, 26
Rasnowski, Stanisław, 424
Rataj, Maciej, 300
Rawicz-Gawroński, Leon, 32
Rawski, 78
reading for information and pleasure, 216–218
Reaney, Stanley H., 271
Regulation of the Alliance of Polish Army Veterans of America, 157
Rekucki, Józef, 252
relief committees in U.S., 48
Relief of Vienna, 27, 225
Rembieliński, Leon, 32
resettlement of veterans in Poland, 172–173, 291–297, 424
Resurrectionists, 53
Rey, Mikołaj, 27
Rhode, Bishop Paweł, 83–84, 245, 247
Riflemen's Association, 29
road construction, 28
Robak, S.J., 403
Rodziewicz, Werner, 397
Rogowski, Maciej, 3
Roiecki, Tomasz, 397
Roja, Bolesław, 116, 399

Rokosz, F.P., 141
Roman, Antoni, 305, **391**
Roman Catholic Church. *See also* Polish Roman Catholic Union
  chaplains, 53, 86–87, **109,** 242–244
  clergy as insurrectionists, 53–55
  Felician Sisters, 55, 193
  Knights of Columbus, 117
  Polish Catholic Organizations Clearinghouse in America, 259
  recruitment of soldiers for Polish Army, 242–243
  role in PAVA life, 241–248
  seminary at Orchard Lake, 193
Romani, Joachim, 397
Romanowski, Franciszek, 126, 139, 141
Romer, Kacper, 397
Roosevelt, Franklin Delano, 198–200, 227–228
Rosenfeld, Ludwik, 397
Rosicki, S., 330
Rosienkiewicz, Marcin, 11–14, 17, 32, 397
Roskosz, Jan
  federation combining veterans groups, 348
  FIDAC congress, 349
  Gen. Pershing received Order of Virtuti Militari, 272
  history of military units from America research, 325–326
  PAVA office in Warszawa, 325
  portrait of, **382**
  Settlement and Invalid Fund drive, 289–290
Roskosz, Stanisław, 298
Rosnowski, Kazimierz, 397
Rostenkowski, Piotr, 258–259
Rostkowski, Wojciech, 15, 397
Rouppert, Stanisław, 329–330
Rowiński, Zygmunt, 281, 400
Różańska, Z., 153
Rozenkranc, 41
Rozmus, J., 123

Rozwadowski, J., 266
Ruciński, E., 266
Ruciński, Stan., 295
Rudnicki, Michał, 123, 129, 400
Rudzimiński von Lust, Karol, 397
Rup, J., 128
Rupiński, Antoni, 78, 22
Rusiłowski, Wincenty, 93
Ruszel, S., 128
Rutkowski, Józef, 397
Rutkowski, Teofil, 397
Rybakowski, Stanisław, 293, 424
Rychlicki, Jan, 11, 16, 51, 141, 397
Rydlewski, Zygmunt, 242
Rydz-Śmigły, Edward
    Circle of Volunteers, 341–342
    financial aid for war invalids in
        America, 334–335
    Marshal's baton received, 359
    PAVA and the Polish government,
        303–304, 316–317
Rygielski, Franciszek, 90
Rygielski, Józef, 290
Rylski, Witold S., 75–78, **98**
Rymszewicz, S., 150
Ryszkowski, S., 400
Ryżowicz, J.A., 403
Rzążewski, Ludwik, 397
Rzepka, Andrzej, 405
Rzeszutek, A., 122
Rzewska, Józefa, 155, 419
Rżewski, Wacław
    Assoc. of Veterans of the Former
        Polish Army in France, 355
    FIDAC, 362
    PAVA National Executive Board
        member, 400
    PAVA tour to Gdynia, 352
    PAVA's apolitical stance, 311
    Polish Veterans Mutual Aid Society
        of Ontario, 274
    portrait of, **380**
    propaganda, fighting, 281
    unemployment among veterans, 187
    visited 43rd Infantry Regiment, 333
Rzewuski, Lucjan, 424
Rzucidło, S., 128

S

Sadłowski, Grzegorz, 14
Sadowski, 398
Sadowski, Aleksander, 397
Sadowski, B., 125, 129
Sadowski, Jan, 328
Sadowski, Michał, 397
St. Anthony of Padua, 58
St. Hedwig's Fund for Polish Invalids, 121
St. Hilaire cemetery, 205
St. Joseph's Day, 127, 312
St. Louis settlement, 16
St. Stanislaw Kostka Parish (Chicago),
    54, 55
St. Vincent de Paul Society, 194
Sajkiewicz, A., 141
Samborski, 129
Samiec, Mikołaj, 397
Samodziewicz, S., 125
San Jacinto, battle of, 25
sanatorium for veterans in Poland, 172
Sanicki, Józef, 397
Savannah, GA veterans, 224
Sawicki, Albert, 397
Scabby Greatness, 355
Schnuer-Pepłowski, Stanisław, 7
Schoepf, Albin Franciszek, 35, 39, 40, 42
schools for Polish children, 54, 55, 267
schools for village children in Poland after
    WWI, 95–96
Schwab, Piotr, 266, 330
science award, 59
scouting in Poland, 80
sculptor, 31
Sędzimir, Józef, 29–30
Seiler, Jan, 338
Sejler, Jan, 293
Semenenko, Piotr, 53

seminary for Polish priests, 55
Seminole Indians, 18–19
Sentkowski, 290
Sentry on the Vistula, 347
Serda-Teodorski, Aureli, 210
Settlement and Invalid Fund, 143–144, 245, 255, 260, 289–291
7th Kosciuszko Squadron, 88
shelters for veterans, 190–195, 255–256, 365, **383, 389**
Sichrawa, Mieczysław, 209, 218, 367
Sidor, Szczepan, 122
Sielawa, Stanisław, 293
Siemiradzki, Tomasz, 215, 302
Sienicki, Franciszek, 397
Sienieński, 342
Sienkiewicz, Henryk, 23, 59
Sieradzki, Henryk, 338
Sierociński, Józef
    assassination of Narutowicz, 308
    cadet school in Pennsylvania, 80
    deputy for the City of Warszawa, 339
    Falcon's Legion of Honor recipient, 338
    federation combining veterans groups, 348
    FIDAC congress, 349
    landowner near Warszawa, 338
    officers' school in Canada, 80
    The Polish Army in France, 216, 275
    recruitment of Poles to American army, 81
    Union of Hallerians leader, 347
Sierpiński, 53
Sikorski, Apolinary, 397
Sikorski, Władysław
    history of military units from America research, 325–326
    Invalid Home in Radzyń support, 299
    PAVA office in Warszawa, 325
    photos in *The Veteran,* 316
    sent photo and greetings to PAVA, 298

    25th anniversary of Witos' parliamentary work, 314
    The Veteran cover, 312
Silver Cross of Merit, 305, 360
Siple, William, 272–273
Sitek, 78
Sitko, W., 125
Sivori, Camillo, 33
Siwiński, K., 140
Skalski, J.S., 141
Skarżyński, 398
Skarzyński, Wincenty, 346, 355
Skibiński, Józef, 397
Skierniewice, 90–92, 115–116, 119–120
Składkowski, Felicjan Sławoj, 301, 343
Skorupski, Jan, 397
Skowroński, Jan, 60
Skrzyński, Aleksander, 299, **385,** 397
Skulski, Ludwik, 90
Skwierzyński, Hilary, 51, 57, 203
Słoma, Jan, 397
slavery. *See also* American Civil War
    in Poland, 317, 318
    in the U.S., 32, 39, 43, 45
    and war with Mexico, 24
Śliwiński, 349
Ślubowski, Józef, 128
Śmiecińska, Leokadia, 419
Śmietanka, Franciszek, 51
Śmigły-Rydz, Edward, 164
Smocztanin, President, 294
Smogór, K., 246
Smogorzewski, 349
Smolczyński, Wincenty
    activist in the Polish American community, 59
    ancestral regions visit, 371
    funeral of, 203–204
    General Józef Haller Society of Polish Army Veterans board member, 123
    January Uprising veteran who came to America, 51

Orlicz-Dreszer meeting, 330–331
Polish Falcons' 8th convention
   speech, 59–60
portrait of, **69**
Smoliński, Józef, 42
Smulski, Jan F., 116
Snitowski, Adolf, 397
Sobczak, J., 140
Sobczyk, W., 266
Sobieski, H., 400, 401
Sobieski, Jan, 52
Sobolewski, Edward, 32
Sobolewski, Paweł
   father of Polish American
      journalism, 27
   first Polish newspaper in English
      in U.S., 370
   magazine cover, **65**
   portrait of, **64**
   remained in U.S., 397
Sobolewski, Stanisław
   15 anniversary of the Polish Army
      in France, 313
   PAVA National Executive Board
      member, 400
   PAVA post in Bydgoszcz, 337
   presentation of the new regimental
      flag to PAVA, 332
   Special Convention in Poznań, 352
Sobótka, 129
Sochacki, 78
Society of Free Falcons, 74
Society of Free Polish Cracovians, 73
Society of Poles in America, 19–20, 369
Society of Polish and American Veterans
   of the World War, 149–150
Society of Polish Exiles, 369
Society of Polish Knights Under
   the Protection of St. Michael the
   Archangel, 73
Sojda, Wacław W., 209
Sokalski, Władysław, 397
Sokołowski, Kazimierz, 345

Sokołski, Dr., 197
"Sokolstwo." *See* Polish Falcons of America
Sołczyk, Czesław, 158, 220
*Soldier of the Legions and the Polish
   Military Organization,* 344
Soliński, Wacław, 226
Solon, Stanisław, 328
Soloski, K., 32
Sons and Daughters of Polish Army
   Veterans, 158–161, 166
Sorokosz, 53
Sosień, Stanisław, 338, 424
Sosiński, Antoni, 397
Sowiński, A., 32
Spaczek, Ludwik, 26
Special Convention in Poznań, 352
Spott, Bronisław
   citizenship, 196–198, 198
   founded PAVA post in Milwaukee,
      122
   Milwaukee shelter, 194
   PAVA National Executive Board
      member, 400
   permanent financial aid for veterans,
      196
   portrait of, **389**
Spring of Nations, 35–37
Stachowicz, Stanisław Z.
   anti-Polish propaganda fighting, 278
   audited the books of the Polish
      National Dept., 130–131
   conference of local organizations
      under PAVA, 127, 128
   conflict between officers and
      rank and file soldiers, 263–264,
      264–265
   defended Gen. Haller against
      propaganda, 280
   editor of *The Veteran,* 206, 208
   Ferdinand Foch welcoming
      ceremony, 222
   financing the transport of soldiers
      back to the U.S., 324

Kuligi shelter opening, 290
military decorations for WWI
  leaders, 272
narrative to book about Polish
  soldiers, 218
PAVA delegate, 129
PAVA districts, 138, 139, 142
PAVA National Executive Board
  member, 400
PAVA officer, 123, 124, 130
petitioned the Council of Ministers,
  298
Polish Social Welfare Council of
  America founder, 249
post-German farms, 295
Resettlement Committee, 289
supported soldiers in Philadelphia, 245
Stachowski, Aleksander, 397
Stachurski, Daniel, 397
Stanicki, W., 126, 332, 352
Stanislaus Kostka Society of Lowell, MA,
  364
Staniszewski, J.M., 126, 129
Staniszewski, S., 125, 141, 222
Stanton, E.M., 44
starvation, 184, 188–189, 190
Starzyński, Teofil
  on the abolishment of military
    attaché post, 328
  Circle of Volunteers, 345
  Committee to Honor the
    Immigration's War Effort leader,
    252
  cross of valor recipient, 366
  deserved credit for formation of Polish
    Armed Forces from America, 346
  Falcons delegation at the White
    House, 77
  federation combining veterans
    groups, 348
  FIDAC congress, 349
  15th Polish Women's Alliance
    convention, 260

  fundraiser for Gen. Haller, 247
  godfather of PAVA organizational
    flag, 254
  Golden Cross of Merit recipient, 164
  Haller's tour of the U.S., 271
  military decorations, 360
  150th anniversary of Gen. Pułaski's
    death, 224
  parade of WWI veterans, 223
  PAVA delegate, 129
  PAVA National Executive Board
    member, 400
  PAVA organizational structures, 167
  PAVA president, 130, 253
  PAVA regimental flag presentation,
    332
  PAVA telegram to Korfanty, 131
  photos of, **390**
  Polish Falcons of America president,
    74
  Polish Falcons president, 253
  portrait of, **97, 379**
  recruitment for Polish Army, 82
  10th anniversary of the recruitment
    for the Polish Army in France, 330
  tour of Poland, 300–302
  20th anniversary of the war effort, 226
Stasiewicz, Grzegorz, 397
Stasik, Florian, 18
Staszewski, Józef, 226, 403
Stec, Wincenty, 123
Stępniewski, Captain, 338
Stefanowicz, S., 125
Stefański, 129
Stefański, Leonard, 218
Stefański, Michał, 397
Stemler, Józef, 219
Stephens, W.D., 272
Stonina, Anthony J., 204
Straszewski, 398
Straszewski, Polish Consul, 222
Strawiński, Feliks Tadeusz, 32
Strawiński, Tadeusz A., 45

Strentzel, Jan, 23
Strzelecki, Konstanty, 397
Styka, Tadeusz, 214
Stypuła, Michał, **381,** 400, 403
Sudol, J., 141
suicide, 15, 30, 188, 189–190
Sułkowski, Jan, 397
Sułkowski, Leon, 79
Sulakowski, Walerian, 39, 46, **67**
Sularzycki, Jan, 397
Sulewski, Władysław, 360
Sulmirski, Wincenty, 397
Sumara, J., 128
Sumowski, Antoni, 397
Swak, Józef, 397
Światpol. *See* World Association of Poles Living Abroad
Świeciaszek, W., 400
Świerczewski, P., 266
Swierdziński, Teofil, 397
Świerszcz, J., 128, 140
Świetlik, Francis, 179, 251
Świrski, Aleksander, 424
Szablicki, Antoni, 397
Szaniawski, 78
Szara, A., 140
Szczawurski, A., 284
Szczepanek, Jan, 290
Szczepański, W., 150
Szczurowski, Bonawentura, 397
Szczygieł, S., 400
Szczygieł, Władysław, 406
Szczygielski, Andrzej, 404
Szeleszczyński, Andrzej, 397
Szembarski, Sebastian, 93
Szemetyło, Teodor, 397
Szepański, Wacław, 424
Szorynos, 78
Szostakowski, Mr., 326
Szreder, 23
Szrednicki, Bolesław Ryszard. *See* Bolesławski, Ryszard
Szulc, Gustaw, 19

Szumlański, Jan, 397
Szumowski, Ignacy, 25
Szurley, 349
Szwiec, Józef, 338, 360
Szygowski, Juliusz, 284
Szymański, Antoni, 397, 398
Szymański, Ignacy, 39, 47
Szymański, Jan
   Alliance of the American Veterans of Polish Extraction, 268
   and the coup in Poland, 311
   Hallerian Sword for Polish Roman Catholic Union, 258
   K. Burke recommended as editor of *The Polish Falcon,* 254
   Paśniewski fired as farm administrator, 351
   PAVA National Executive Board member, 400
   shelter for war invalids fund, 365
Szymański, S., 400
Szymczyk, K., 141

T

Taborek, Jan, 424
Tadeusz Eminowicz Polish Artists Society, 219
Tarczyński, Rudolf, 218, 219
Targowski, 129, 398
Tatarski, Franciszek, 295
Tax for National Sacrifice, 48
teachers, 338
Tefft, Thomas A., 34
Teliga, Ignacy, 397
Tenerowicz, W.A., 141
Terkowski, 53
Terlecki, 4
Teschen Silesia, 318–320
Texas Independence, 24–26
theater, 218–219
"The Third of May," **62**
13th Division of Borderland Riflemen, 89–90

13th Infantry Division, 92–93
330th anniversary of the arrival of Poles
 in America, 227–228
"Tin Roof" Palace, 325
"To the Glory of the Fatherland"
 Association of Dovborites, 365
Tochman, Kasper, 39, 45–46
Tołoczka, Karol, 397
Tomaszewski, 78
Tomaszewski, Marcin, 188–189, 193
Tomczyk, Jan, 219
Tomczyk, Józef, 219
Topolnicki, Norbert, 53
Trąmpczyński, Wojciech, 299
trans-Olza River territories, 318–319
transport ships, 115–116, 118
Trawiński, Witold, 93, 252, 300–301
Truskolaski, F., 6
Truskolaski, Józef, 27
Truszkiewicz, Franciszek, 176, 218, 324
Trygar, Adam, 79, 158, 252, 401
Trzaskowski, Bolesław, 397
Turczyn, A., 140
Turowski, Ludwik, 397
Turzański, Karol, 397
Tusiak, M., 158
Tuwalski, F., 140
Tylko, T., 275
Tyssot, J., 6
Tyssowski, Jan, 35

U

Union of Associations of Former
 Servicemen, 348–349
Union of Defenders of Lwów, 365
Union of Former Upper Silesian
 Insurrectionists of the Polish Republic,
 366
Union of Hallerians in Poland
   Agency of PAVA of America, 325
   assassination of Narutowicz, 347–348
   Circle of Volunteers for the Polish
    Army from America, 339
   Legion of the Republic, 361
   PAVA post in Bydgoszcz, 336
   and politics, 288, 307, 308, 313
   St. Hilaire cemetery fund drive, 205
Union of Officers of the Reserve, 366
Union of Participants in the Great Poland
 Insurrection of 1918-1919, 366
Union of Polish-American World War
 Veterans, 267
Union of Polish Army Reserve Officers
 of America, 263–266
Union of Polish Legionnaires, 309–310,
 340, 366–367
Union of Puławy Legionnaires, 366
Union of Societies of Insurrectionists
 and Fighters, 366
United Polish Educational Societies
 in Warszawa, 267
Universal Countrywide Exposition, 208,
 214
Urban, L., 93
Urbaniak, Jan, 93
Urbanski, John M., 90
Urbański, T., 6
Utica, NY veterans, 126
Uzdowski, Jerzy, 4

V

vacation days, 346
The Veteran
   anti-German bias, 323
   apolitical nature of PAVA, 314–318
   Assoc. of Veterans of the Former
    Polish Army in France, 357
   Auxiliary Corps official organ, 155
   column devoted to AFPAV, 177
   covers of, 312, 313
   creation of, 206–210
   editors, 208–209
   Gen Haller's address on the 16th
    anniversary of Armistice not
    published, 315
   import duty, 342–343

masthead, 163
Piłsudki's recall to army, 309, 310
propaganda, response to, 278, 282–283
title page of the first issue, **382**
Union of Hallerians received, 347
veterans employed to sell, 170, 184
Veterans Club in Bayonne, NJ, 150
Veterans' Commission, 251–252
Veterans District Committee, 191
veterans groups, 126–128, 148–151,
   See also *specific names of groups*
Veterans of the Allied Armies, 319
Virtuti Militari, 19, **109, 110,** 135, 335
The Voice of Work, 284
Volunteers from America Cross, **111**

W

Wachtl, Karol, 81–82
Wadsworth, James Wolcott, 115
Wajda, Franciszek, 123
Walaszczyk, Walenty, 93
Walczak, 121
Waldo, Artur
   editor of *The Veteran,* 209
   exhibit in Detroit, 214–215
   at grave of fallen comrade, **107**
   historical studies by, 260
   history book narrative about Polish
      soldiers, 218
   PAVA District VI President, 404
   theater supporter, 218–219
   330th anniversary of the arrival of
      Poles in America, 227–228
   Year of the Polish Book, 217–218
Walenciak, Jan, 122, 141
Walkowicz, Leon T., 267, 268
Waluś, Franciszek, J., 150, 209, 218, **391,
   406**
Wanda Park, 192–194, **389**
*The War Effort in Soldierly Short Stories,
   Tales and Stories,* 217–218
War of 1812, 7
War of Secession. *See* American Civil War

Wardzyński, Andrzej, 397
Warszawski, J., 125
Washington, George, 5
Wasowicz, 78
Wata, J., 125
Wawrzyniak, Józef, 252
The Way of the Lancer, 212
Węgierski, Antoni, 14
Węgierski, August, 397
Węglarski, Stanisław, 126, 400
Węglarstwo, 20
Wendziński, Ignacy, 57
Wentkowski, Nikodem, 354
Werwiński, Ignacy, 81
Wesołowski, Ludwik, 397
West Point Military Academy, 223
West Troy settlement, 16
Western Borderlands settlement, 295
Wiącek, Antoni, 293, 338–339
Więckowski, Jan, 165
Więckus, Zygmunt F., 328
Wieczorek, Szymon, 53
Wieniawa-Długoszowski, Bolesław, 303,
   330, 331
Wierciński, Bertold, 18, 397, 398
Wierzbicki, Aleksander, 397
Wierzbicki, Feliks, 21–22, 34, **61, 62**
Wierzbicki, Szczęsny, 397
Wiktor, Antoni, 284
Wilczyńska, Ludwika, 419
Wilk, Lucyna, 419
Wilk, Stanisław
   editor of *The Veteran,* 209
   Golden Cross of Merit recipient, 305
   PAVA National Executive Board
      member, 400
   PAVA tour of Poland, 300
   Rev. Archbishop Cieplak funeral,
      244–245
   shelter in New York, 194
Wilkoń, A., 222
Wilkoszewski, Edward, 51
Wilkowski, Jan, 90

Wilmington, DE veterans, 222
Wilson, Woodrow, 77, 80, 352–353
Winnipeg, Canada veterans, 283–284
Wisconsin land grants, 13
Wisła, Agnieszka
    Auxiliary Corps of PAVA, 153–154, 419
    Committee for Aid to Veterans, 170
    invalids, relief for, 173–174
    PAVA tour of Poland, 300
    portrait of, **388**
    shelter for veterans, 191
    supplied medical stations at the front, 94
Wiśniewski, 53
Wiśniewski, Andrzej, 424
Wiśniewski, J., 400
Wiśniewski, Wincenty, 268
Witos, Wincenty
    address to the Polish Emigration in America, 425–426
    PAVA petitions, 298
    Polish Peasant Party, 317–318
    post-German farms, 295
    25th anniversary of his parliamentary work, 314
Włodecki, Franciszek, 397
Wnorowski, Józef, 397
Wodzicki, Piotr, 51
Wodzyński, Józef, 397
Wojciechowski, Antoni, 397
Wojciechowski, Franciszek, 23, 129
Wojciechowski, Piotr, 424
Wojciechowski, Stanisław, 140, 298
Wojciechowski, Walter, 268
Wojcieszczuk, Antoni, 243, 400
Wójcik, Franciszek, 78, 339
Wójcikiewicz, J., 6
Wojewódzki, 424
Wojtalewicz, P., 81–82
Wojtanowicz, Piotr, 284
Wojtczuk, Jan, 226
Wojtusik, Stanisław, 195, 400, 403

Wołek, A., 140
Wołkowski, Jan, 53
Wołowska, Honorata, 251
Wolanin, Adam, 123, 129
Woldański, Zygmunt, 122
Wolf, J., 153
Wolnicki, Tomasz, 397
Wolski, J., 403
women volunteers, 84, 94–96
Women's Committee of Chicago, 76
work shops for war invalids, 364
World Alliance of Poles from Abroad in Poland, 252
World Association of Poles Living Abroad, 334, 341
World Union of Poles from Abroad, 251
World War I, 75
World War II, 306
World War Veterans Orchestra, 220
World's Fair in Chicago, 216, 228
Woroniec, J., 126
Woronowski, Stanisław, 89
Woźniak, F.B., 400
Woźniak, Franciszek, 123
Woźniak, Fryderyk, 328
Woźniak, Z., 158
Wróblewski, Dr., 149
Wróblewski, J., 295, 400
Wutkowski, Jan, 121
Wyborski, Pastor, 203
Wyspiański, Stanisław, 218
Wyszomirski, Paweł, 397
Wyszyński, Eustachy, 27, 397
Wyszyński, Karol, 397

Y

Year of the Polish Book, 217
Y.M.C.A., 117
Youngstown, OH veterans, 123

Z

Ząbek, S., 142
Ząbkowski, T., 125

Zacharzewski, Mikołaj, 398
Zaczek, Franciszek, 122
Zając, Henryk, 122, 300
Zając, Józef, 329
Zajączkowski, Wincenty, 398
Żakiewicz, Aleksander, 400
Zakliński, B., 329–330
Zakrzewski, Aleksander, 21
Zakrzewski, Mikołaj, 398
Zakusiło, Jan, 398
Zaleśny, Colleague, 203
Zalewski, Jan, 398
Zalewski, Tomasz, 398
Zaliwski, Józef, 9, 31
Zaliwski expedition, 20
Zamość, 93, 94
Zamoyski, Adam, 338
Zapytowska, A., 419
Zapytowski, Ignacy, 295, 400
Zaręba, Antoni, 51
Zaręba, Franciszek, 398
Zaremba, Stefan, 268
Zaruski, Mariusz, 329
Zarzecki, 338
Zawada, 129
Zawadzki, Marian, 218
Zawadzki, Stanisław, 424
Zawistowski, 32
Żbikowski, Jan, 122
Zbrzeźniak, Aleksander, 90
Zbrzeżny, J., 140
Zbytniewski, J., 203, 245
Żebracki, Stanisław, 290
Żebrowski, Jan A.
   conference of local organizations under PAVA, 127–128
   demobilization of soldiers, 116, 119–120
   PAVA board member, 130
   PAVA delegate, 129
   PAVA National Executive Board member, 400
   PAVA officer, 142
   Union of Polish Army Veterans founded, 121
Żebrowski, Stefan, 424
Zeglinski, B., 275
Żelazowski, Józef, 398
Żeligowski, Lucjan, 79
Żeromski, Stefan, 211
Zgoda, 57
Zieliński, August, 52–53, 290
Zieliński, Jan, 3, 4, 195, 400
Zieliński, Tomasz, 209
Ziemba, J., 404
Ziemiak, Rev., 158
Ziemianek, Michał, 295
Znamięcki, Aleksander, 82
Znaniecki, Aleksander, 360
Żółkiewski, Józef, 398
Żołyński, Frank, 213
Zuboff, Maksymilian, 32
Żukowski, Tomasz, 397
Żuławski, Czesław
   anti-Polish propaganda fighting, 278
   editor of *The Veteran*, 206, 208
   farm owner, 339
   PAVA books reviewed, 130
   PAVA founding convention, 129
   PAVA National Executive Board member, 400
   PAVA officer, 130
   PAVA tour of Poland, 300–301
   Polish Day celebration, 223
   portrait of, **382**
   propaganda attacks, refuting, 282–283
   Union of Polish Army Reserve Officers of America member, 266
Źwiardowski, Feliks, 53
Żychliński, Ludwik, 36, 41, 48–49, **67**
Zychowicz, Andrzej, 246, 247
Zygadło, Józef, 398
Zymirski, F., 6
Żytkowski, M., 141
Żywicki, Mikołaj, 398